Winning with Stories

Using the Narrative to Persuade in Trials, Speeches & Lectures

BY JIM M. PERDUE

I Remember Atticus: Inspiring Stories Every Trial Lawyer Should Know (2004)

Who Speaks for Justice? (editor) (1999)

Who Will Speak for the Victim? A Practical Treatise on Plaintiff's Jury Argument (1989)

The Medical Malpractice Handbook (1988)

The Law of Texas Medical Malpractice (1975 & 2d ed. 1985)

The Law of Strict Tort Liability in Texas (with James B. Sales) (1977)

Jim M. Perdue

Winning with Stories

Using the Narrative to Persuade in Trials, Speeches & Lectures

Austin 2006

The State Bar of Texas, through its TexasBarBooks Department, publishes practice books prepared and edited by knowledgeable authors to give practicing lawyers as much assistance as possible. The competence of the authors ensures outstanding professional products, but, of course, neither the State Bar of Texas, the editors, nor the authors make either express or implied warranties in regard to their use. Each lawyer must depend on his or her own knowledge of the law and expertise in the use or modification of these materials.

International Standard Book Number (10-digit): 1-892542-22-6
International Standard Book Number (13-digit): 978-1-892542-22-9
Library of Congress Control Number: 2006921014

Printed in the United States of America

To the legal secretaries
whose efforts in the search for justice
go unheralded and often unrewarded.

I miss you Mom.

I love you Nonie.

Contents

STATE BAR OF TEXAS

EDUARDO ROBERTO RODRIGUEZ
PRESIDENT

Mailing address:
P.O. BOX 2155
BROWNSVILLE, TX 78522

1201 E. VAN BUREN ST.
BROWNSVILLE, TX 78520
TEL: (956) 542-7441
FAX: (956) 541-2170
e-mail: er.rodriguez@rcclaw.com

The State Bar of Texas proudly presents *Winning with Stories: Using the Narrative to Persuade in Trials, Speeches & Lectures*, a landmark treatise that ably demonstrates the power of the story to persuade a jury.

Author Jim M. Perdue taps a deep well of experience in collecting and telling stories to move audiences. He gives generously of his more than forty years before the bar to show novice and seasoned trial lawyers alike how to make use of the narrative in practical advocacy.

The State Bar of Texas is committed to a continuing legal education program that includes publications designed to improve professional competence. We are grateful to Mr. Perdue for this generous gift of his time and expertise in the furtherance of that commitment.

Eduardo Roberto Rodriguez
President, State Bar of Texas

Preface

For more than forty years, I have been telling stories in speeches, continuing legal education presentations, and law school lectures. Still, for years I "argued" cases in court. In 1989 the State Bar of Texas published my book *Who Will Speak For the Victim? A Practical Treatise on Plaintiff's Jury Argument.* In the years and trials that followed, I began to learn that the best opening statements aren't arguments; they are stories. The most persuasive closing arguments flow from a narrative story presentation rather than the traditional topical debate.

My interest in stories and telling good ones led to *I Remember Atticus: Inspiring Stories Every Trial Lawyer Should Know* (State Bar of Texas, 2004). Writing that book taught me even more about the persuasiveness of combining fundamental truths found in fact with the mystical form of the fable. So it is in the courtroom, which is why for many years now my opening statements and closing arguments in trial are narratives, not arguments.

A persuasive courtroom narrative depends on the power brought by four components:

The Story

Lawyers construct the trial narrative from facts presented through clients, witnesses, and documents. The trial story may also include legal concepts and incorporate principles of business, science, physics, engineering, and medicine. Clients bring us part of the story; the rest is the result of the lawyer's hard work during the discovery phase in deposing witnesses and experts and requesting, obtaining, and reviewing relevant documents and records.

The Emotional Content

The strongest stories carry a visceral appeal, a compelling moral. This is what I call the "soul" of the story.

The Telling

How a narrative is sequenced, structured, and presented is a critical consideration. Gifted courtroom narrators employ rhetorical devices to drive salient points home, encouraging the listener to focus on the important rather than the trivial and accept the plaintiff's version over the competing ones offered by the defense.

The Speaker

The more dynamic and charismatic the narrator is, the more apt she is to be accepted as a credible and inspiring source.

Although we do not strictly follow the foregoing organizational format in this book, all these components will be explored in detail.

There is an axiom that says if you want to do something well, study it, do it, and think about it.

Many disciplines and materials are helpful in the study of persuasion. Over the years I have read books and articles in the fields of communication, psychology, creative writing, directing, screenwriting, propaganda, and acting and the catalog of writings by lawyers and jury consultants directed toward courtroom strategy. I include references to some of these materials in this book. Another old adage says that if you steal one person's idea it is plagiarism; if you steal two people's ideas it is research; but if you steal the ideas of three or more you are called a scholar. By that definition I must be a scholar, because over the years I've borrowed a lot from others in an effort to improve my speeches, lectures, and courtroom narratives.

The italicized portions of the beginnings of the following chapters are from speeches, opening statements, closing arguments, and articles I've written over the years. The final five chapters are opening statements and closing arguments from actual trials: doing it.

Finally, proficiency requires you to think a lot about what you're doing. The experienced advocate who is trying cases the same way she did five or ten years ago isn't realizing her full potential. Whether you are a novice or a veteran, the exciting thing about being a trial lawyer is that you can never stop thinking of ways to get better. Nothing makes you think more about the art of storytelling than to put pen to hand and express the things you have learned from study, the things you did, and why they work or fail.

I have tried to set out principles to guide those communicating through a narrative, whether it be in court, the lecture hall, or the classroom. None of the opinions I express in this book are those of the State Bar of Texas. I do, however, wish to express my appreciation to the State Bar and its Continuing Legal Education Committee for allowing me to share some of my ideas, values, and opinions.

—JIM M. PERDUE

Acknowledgments

PEOPLE HAVE ASKED, "How long did it take you to write this book?" My answer is, over forty years. It is not an exaggeration. The ideas, concepts, and anecdotes come from materials I have assiduously accumulated since becoming a lawyer in 1963. Some of the ideas are original; many are variations of thoughts etched in my brain by the great trial lawyers I have heard in courtrooms or at CLE programs.

Still, all I had was ideas and reams of material, some of which the editorial staff at the State Bar of Texas found was not accurate. This work now represents that which is not only hopefully interesting and informative but also documented as accurate.

Indira Gandhi said, "My grandfather once told me that there are two kinds of people: those who do the work and those who take the credit." I would not want be one of those who stood high on the efforts of others and failed to acknowledge them.

And so I recognize and applaud the efforts of Michael Ambrose of the editorial staff of TexasBarBooks. He served more as a coauthor than editor. His service to the Bar not only on this extensive effort but also on numerous practice manuals and legal treatises reflects the dedication of a committed and rare talent. We are lucky to have him.

I also acknowledge the work of Irene Aldrich, whose tireless efforts caught many factual errors and insured the accuracy of the quotations, stories, and anecdotes.

My secretary, Susie Parsons, has now worked with me on two books and hundreds of CLE papers. She deserves special recognition not only for typing, retyping, and redrafting but also for her thoughtful commentaries.

Finally, a salute to trial lawyers everywhere, who understand that we must never stop learning and improving our trial skills and must never waiver in our determination to preserve our jury system.

The author and the State Bar of Texas are grateful to the following publishers and authors for permission to reprint text selections in this work:

The story of "Little Louis Epstine," chapter 2:
Reprinted from *Verdicts Out of Court* by Clarence Darrow, edited by Arthur and Lila Weinberg, © 1963 by Arthur and Lila Weinberg, by permission of Ivan R. Dee, Publisher.

Abraham Lincoln stories, chapters 2 and 25:
Reprinted and adapted from *Abe Lincoln Laughing: Humorous Anecdotes from Original Sources by and about Abraham Lincoln,* edited by P. M. Zall. © 1995 by the University of Tennessee Press. Used by permission.

Rules for constructing and refining a story, chapter 2, part 2 introduction, and chapter 5:
Adapted from "Tell It to the Jury: The Role of Story Telling in Litigation" by Rodney Jew, from *News from the Mental Edge* 9, no. 1 (Spring 2003): 4–23, © 2003 Rodney Jew. Used by permission of the author.

Excerpt from "The Gambler" by Donald Alan Schlitz, Jr., chapter 3:
Copyright 1977 Sony/ATV Tunes LLC. All rights administered by Sony/ATV Music Publishing, 8 Music Square West, Nashville, TN 37203. All rights reserved. Used by permission.

Opening statement examples in chapter 3, page 34:
Reprinted from "The Difference Between 'Good Enough' and 'Safe Enough'" by Jim M. Perdue, from *Trial* 32, no. 3 (Mar. 1996): 45, by permission of the editor of *Trial.* © 1996 ATLA.

Excerpt from The Complete Guide to Writing Fiction, *chapter 5:*
Reprinted from *The Complete Guide to Writing Fiction* by Barnaby Conrad, © 1990 by Barnaby Conrad. Used by permission of Larsen-Pomada Literary Agency.

Excerpt from Successful Scriptwriting, *chapter 7:*
Reprinted from *Successful Scriptwriting* © 1988, 1991 by Jurgen Wolff & Kerry Cox. Used with permission of Writer's Digest Books, a division of F+W Publications, Inc., Cincinnati, Ohio. All rights reserved.

Jurors' deliberations, chapter 8, pages 89–90:
Reprinted from "Trial Themes: Winning Jurors' Minds and Hearts" by Jim M. Perdue, Sr., and Jim M. Perdue, Jr., from *Trial* 34, no. 4 (Apr. 1998): 34–42, by permission of the editor of *Trial.* © 1998 ATLA.

Discussion of visual aids, chapter 14:
Adapted from "The Art of Demonstrative Evidence" by Jim M. Perdue, Jr., from *Trial* 41, no. 5 (May 2005): 46–51, by permission of the editor of *Trial.* © 2005 ATLA.

Discussion of cross-examination objectives, chapter 15:
Adapted from "The Five-Question Rule: Cross-Examination Simplified" by Jim M. Perdue, *Trial* 29, no. 10 (Oct. 1993): 40–43, by permission of the editor of *Trial.* © 1993 ATLA.

Abraham Lincoln's cross-examination, chapter 15:
Excerpt from *Young Mr. Lincoln* © 1939 Courtesy of Twentieth Century Fox. Written by Lamar Trotti. All rights reserved.

The story of Bushell's Case, chapter 16:
Adapted from *The Ordeal of Edward Bushell* by Godfrey D. Lehman, © 1988 Lexicon Publishing, Sacramento. Used by permission of the publisher.

Excerpts from the writings of Rev. Martin Luther King, Jr., chapters 20 and 25:
Excerpt from "I Have a Dream" copyright 1963 Martin Luther King Jr., copyright renewed 1991 Coretta Scott King. Excerpt from "Why Jesus Called a Man a Fool" copyright 1967 Martin Luther King Jr., copyright renewed 1995 Coretta Scott King. Reprinted by arrangement with the Estate of Martin Luther King Jr., c/o Writers House as agent for the proprietor New York, NY.

Poems by Edgar A. Guest, chapter 24:
"Good Enough," "It Couldn't Be Done," and "The Broken Wheel" from *Collected Verse of Edgar A. Guest,* © 1934 Contemporary Books, © 1984 The McGraw-Hill Companies. Reprinted by permission of The McGraw-Hill Companies. All rights reserved.

Poem by Emily Dickinson, chapter 24:
"Surgeons must be very careful" [J108/F156]. Reprinted by permission of the publishers and the Trustees of Amherst College from *The Poems of Emily Dickinson,* Thomas H. Johnson, ed., Cambridge, Mass.: The Belknap Press of Harvard University Press, Copyright © 1951, 1955, 1979, 1983 by the President and Fellows of Harvard College.

Poem by Will Allen Dromgoole, chapter 24:
"The Bridge Builder" by Will Allen Dromgoole, copyright © 2001 The University of Tennessee Libraries. All Rights Reserved. Permission to use, copy, modify, and distribute these materials for educational, research, and not-for-profit purposes, without fee and without a signed licensing agreement, is hereby granted, provided that the above copyright notice and this paragraph appear in all copies, modifications, and distributions.

Poem by Ruth Gillis, chapter 24:
"The Wreck on Highway 109" by Ruth Gillis, © 1999 Ruth Gillis. All rights reserved. Reprinted by permission of the author.

The story of Butch and Eddie O'Hare, "From Chicago," chapter 25:
Reprinted from the Truth or Fiction Web site, http://www.truthorfiction.com, by permission of Rich Buhler. © 1998–2005 TruthOrFiction.com. All rights reserved.

The story of "A Brave Texas Lawyer," chapter 25:
Adapted from "The Rule of Law vs. Mr. Colt" by Robert Lewis Dabney, Jr., from *The Houston Lawyer* 36, no. 4 (Jan.–Feb. 1999): 10–15, by permission of the author and the editor of *The Houston Lawyer*. © 1999 The Houston Bar Association.

The story of "Big Wally's Big Heart," chapter 25:
"Trouble at the Inn" by Dina Donohue is reprinted with permission from *Guideposts* magazine. Copyright © 1966 by Guideposts, Carmel, New York 10512. All rights reserved.

Winning with Stories

Using the Narrative to Persuade in Trials, Speeches & Lectures

PART 1

THE STORY CONCEPT

ONCE UPON A TIME . . .

1

The Power of the Story

A FEW OF THEIR NUMBER had been here before. Most hadn't. Sitting behind the jury rail, they listened intently as the gray-haired woman in the black robe introduced them to this unfamiliar world of litigants, procedures, and formalities. Most of the dozen were surprised that they had been chosen to help the parties in their search for truth. The judge's instructions sounded heavy, legalistic, demanding:

"Do not mingle with nor talk to the lawyers . . ."

"Do not accept from, nor give to, any of those persons any favors . . ."

"Do not discuss anything about this case, or even mention it to anyone whomsoever . . ."

The judge, having completed her instructions to the jury, called on plaintiff's counsel for his opening statement. The jury expected him to sound like a lawyer. He would use a lot of words they would have trouble understanding. He would talk about evidence, procedures, and legal concepts. The lawyer would probably go down the list of witnesses that were to testify and summarize what they would say. He'd break the case down into issues and state the pros and cons.

The jury was surprised when none of this followed. Instead, they heard a story.

I am a story junkie. Growing up in a family that loved to tell stories hooked me at an early age. We also had the master narrator—a mahogany-colored plastic bread box with big ivory knobs and the letters "GE" on the tuning face. As a youngster I learned to use the most minor ailments as a way to avoid the dull tedium of math and English and enjoy the vividness of true-life drama. Staying home from school meant that I could listen to *Ma Perkins, Lorenzo Jones, Pepper Young's Family,* and *Stella Dallas* while my grandmother, a seamstress, worked at her big black Singer sewing machine. Later in the afternoon we got what for kids growing up in postwar America was our kind of stories—*Superman, Jack Armstrong, Terry and the Pirates,* and *The Green Hornet.* In the evenings, our minds were numbed by the mystery and suspense of *The*

Shadow, Inner Sanctum, and *Gangbusters.*

We story addicts who grew up with radio used our minds to make the pictures that entertained and freed us from the mundane and the troubles of the day. The radio also introduced us to the ways that other people lived, loved, and thought (mostly through inaccurate stereotypes such as *Amos 'N' Andy* and *Life with Luigi*). As a kid growing up poor in east Dallas, *One Man's Family* stretched my imagination to picture the domestic grandeur of life in a mansion overlooking San Francisco Bay.

Saturdays were movie days. It cost nothing to support our habit during the week, but Saturday kid shows cost a quarter. We would scrape up the two bits by whatever means—collecting bottles for deposit, mowing lawns, saving from allowances for lunch. The movies were a psychedelic mix of cartoons, serials, and double features. Our parents found comfort in the belief that our obsession didn't do any real harm. Keeping a child's mind entertained keeps him out of trouble even if he isn't learning anything. The truth is we learned a lot from movies. The lesson was a simple, straightforward one that stayed with us long after we had digested the popcorn, Holloway bar, and Coca-Cola: good triumphs over evil, virtue is always rewarded, the lie cannot live forever, people who work hard and follow the rules will be rewarded—simple truths from stories told with definable characters, motives, and morals.

My fundamentalist mother and grandmother believed that people should deny themselves the pleasure of entertainment at least one day a week. Sundays were the day you went cold turkey and suffered through lectures of religious rules and platitudes, all rife with threats of damnation preached in the name of morality. But even the preachers would lighten up now and then when they digressed into a novel and interesting narrative. The slumbering audience would perk up at the cue. The pastor was about to give us the dessert that follows the meal. As the preacher launched from the pulpit his narration of a historical event or personal experience, we munched down like chocaholics and readily accepted the kick—the lesson—the moral. Listening to the radio and going to movies, I had discovered the wonder of the story. In church I learned its power.

You can teach science, business, or law by describing the principles, defining the rules. You can preach morality, religion, and ethics by reciting the dry, sterile precepts. But if you want someone to learn, remember, or be inspired—use a story.

THE HISTORY OF STORYTELLING

The story is the most efficient vehicle for delivering facts and conveying information. An old allegory teaches that when Truth is born and goes among Mankind, the people turn their backs on him. Rejected and humiliated, Truth goes into the hills to live alone in a cave. One night, sitting alone by his fire, Story comes to him. She asks, "Why are you out here, alone and depressed?" Truth replies, "I am Truth, but when I went among Mankind, they would have nothing to do with me." Story observes that it is no wonder. "Look at you, you're naked!" She then says, "I am Story, I have many cloaks and robes. They come in all sizes and colors. Wear one of these and go among the people." Truth, clothed in one of Story's garments, returns to the people and is immediately accepted. It is said that since that day no matter how harsh, hard, or cruel Truth may be, when he comes clothed in a story, he is accepted.[1]

Storytelling is an ageless art. We speak of progress in science, but there is no progress in art. Beauty is beauty, even if the painting, sculpture, or musical composition is ancient. And the truth—the moral—of stories thousands of years old still holds today. While scholars are left to sift through volumes of now-defunct scientific theories, speakers continue to tell stories that were composed centuries ago. Those ancient storytellers' lives and physical circumstances may have been completely unlike our own, but the truth of their lessons still endures.

This is the difference between science and art. The physical sciences are constantly revising their assumptions, but the story—with its form, moral, and suggestion of a truth that adhered to past generations—is still as valid today as it was to our ancestors. Stories reaffirm our belief that our institutions exist as solutions to problems. Stories deny the proposition that life can only admit to hopelessness and uncertainty. Stories affirm that government works for everyone and that there is at least the appearance of fairness in education, medicine, and business. Since the beginning of time, narratives have carried the truths of hope and justice.

The power of the story can be traced back to prehistoric times, when early man sat in caves and told his stories with sign language. If prostitution is the oldest profession, storytelling is by far the oldest art form. Men and women were telling stories long before they began painting pictures and composing music. Even as mankind refined those art forms, their purpose remained that of telling the story. The prehistoric cave drawings in Lascaux, France, tell stories of the hunt. The stories have distinctly identifiable parts: a beginning, a middle, and an end. They are cathartic in their portrayal of tense conflict followed by resolution, defeat finally giving way to victory.

The Iliad and *The Odyssey* were classical products of the birthplace of Western civilization. And while these epics are still studied today, it is the simple stories of a Greek slave, Aesop, told as fables that are best remembered. The Old Testament is filled with stories—narratives depicting the range of human emotion. Stories of treachery, ambition, and heroism. One of the common themes found in the stories of the Old Testament is that of revenge—"an eye for an eye, a tooth for a tooth." But it is the lessons of brotherly love that the Great Teacher of the New Testament taught in the form of parables—stories—that are most quoted.

Alex Haley's *Roots* chronicles the pervasive oral tradition that has been preserved by generations of African cultures. The shaman or medicine man of the Native American tribes held his tribal position because he had a talent for storytelling. In the eighth century, minstrels and storytellers among the Anglo-Saxons and Goths sang of Beowulf's conquest of Grendel.

STORIES HAVE CHANGED HISTORY

Down through the centuries men and women have used stories to teach, persuade, motivate, and inspire. One of the lessons of history is that a persuasive story is the most effective way to communicate and change others' opinions. Perhaps nowhere was this phenomenon more readily demonstrated than in the tense and divisive political and social climate of the mid-1800s. No social or political issue so divided this country as did the discourse over slavery. The Lincoln-Douglas debates defined the issue on the political stump. The contentious and irreconcilable views of Northern abolitionists and Southern slave owners led to impassioned debates in Congress and the passage of legislation, including the Fugitive Slave Act and the Compromise of 1850. But it took a fictional story to raise the issue in the public conscience.

Harriet Beecher was the daughter of a liberal Presbyterian minister, Lyman Beecher, who became one of the most eloquent preachers of his day. He taught at Lane Seminary in Cincinnati, Ohio. Harriet Beecher married one of her father's students, Calvin Ellis Stowe, who was also an ardent abolitionist. One of Harriet's brothers, Henry Ward Beecher, was the pastor of the Plymouth Church of the Pilgrims in Brooklyn and known as one of the most accomplished and compelling orators of his day. An outspoken abolitionist, he attracted huge crowds to services and revival meetings.

While living in Ohio, Harriet Beecher Stowe began writing children's stories and textbooks. One of these, *Primary Geography for Children*, earned her a considerable royalty. Her husband obtained a teaching position at Bowdoin College in Maine. While living in Maine, Mrs. Stowe began writing articles condemning slavery. These ran in the *National Era* beginning in 1851.[2] Ultimately she turned her stories, which had been published in serial form, into a book: *Uncle Tom's Cabin, or Life Among the Lowly*. Published in 1852, the book enjoyed immediate and overwhelming success. Three hundred thousand copies were sold in the first year. Within five years, half a million copies of the book were sold in the United States. It was eventually translated into twenty languages.

Uncle Tom's Cabin had an immediate impact on the slavery debate. The story of the noble and virtuous Uncle Tom removed the slavery issue from dry political debate and inanimate sociological and theological discussion into the compelling arena of characters, plot, and motivation. The story of a pious slave torn from his family in Kentucky and sold into the deep South under the brutal domination of the sadistic overseer Simon Legree moved the public. The central character, Uncle Tom, is a man of great moral strength and nobility. Tom's noble qualities are personified through his care of Eva, an angelic little girl who has fallen ill. Meanwhile, Eliza, a slave mother, attempts to reach freedom while clutching her baby by crossing the icy Ohio River separating slave state Kentucky from free Ohio. It was a classic tale of a protagonist struggling against the oppressive will of an antagonist. The story reached the hearts of people in a way that the sanitized arguments of the abolitionists had not been able to do.

In our times, the public debate on such issues as anti-Semitism, nuclear power, and AIDS has been advanced through compelling stories. Technological innovation has moved the medium from books into movies and television. Two books, one a biography, the other a novel (both later made into movies), heightened the public awareness of the cruelty of anti-Semitism in Germany and its prolific existence even in postwar America. *The Diary of Anne Frank* was published in 1947 after intense negotiations with Anne's father, the sole survivor of the Frank family. The stage dramatization won a Pulitzer Prize. The story depicted the plight of the Franks, who spent two years hiding from the Gestapo in a tiny Amsterdam attic.

Earlier, Moss Hart adapted a novel by Laura Z. Hobson into a movie. *Gentleman's Agreement*, starring Gregory Peck, won the Academy Award for Best Picture in 1947. The story recounted the experiences of Phil Green, a journalist who posed as a Jew to write a series of hard-hitting articles on the scourge of anti-Semitism. Green exposed the subtle forms of bigotry and racism existing in America following World War II. One of the more poignant scenes is a vignette in which Phil Green's friend Dave Goldman, played by John Garfield, is denied a room in a posh resort hotel by a smarmy desk clerk who refuses to admit that his establishment has a no-Jews policy.

The potential dangers of nuclear power spawned vigorous debate in the late 1970s and early 1980s. Scientists disagreed on the extent of the hazards, but the movie *The China Syndrome* (1979) brought home the fact that significant dangers were associated with the operation of nuclear power plants. A TV reporter, Kimberly Wells (Jane Fonda), is visiting a nuclear power plant at the time the reactor is close to meltdown. The plant manager, Jack Godell (Jack Lemmon), becomes convinced that something is wrong at the plant and that his superiors are trying to cover it up. Out of frustration, he breaks into the reactor's main control room and threatens to kill his coworkers unless the public is warned and the reactor shut down. Administration at the reactor tries to portray Godell as crazy. The story's tension rises as it becomes clear that the reactor core is indeed very close to melting (the "China Syndrome") and could go at any moment. The film turned out to be chillingly prophetic. A short time after its release, the nearly catastrophic nuclear reactor accident at Three Mile Island occurred, followed later by the Chernobyl disaster in Russia.

A few years ago director Jonathan Demme brought the subject of AIDS into the mainstream with the story of Andrew Beckett, whose fast-track legal career ends when his employers discover that he is HIV-positive. When Beckett decides to sue his former employers, the only lawyer willing to take on the case is a homophobe played by Denzel Washington. The movie paints a compelling picture of the devastation of AIDS and the social and professional prejudice that exists against its sufferers. Tom Hanks won an Academy Award for Best Actor in 1993 for his portrayal of Beckett in *Philadelphia*.

Thus, stories told in books and movies have altered and shaped public opinion on issues ranging from slavery in the nineteenth century to contemporary issues like AIDS.

ADVERTISERS USE STORIES

Modern-day advertisers have learned the power of the story as a means of maximizing commercial campaigns. Some years ago Taster's Choice Coffee ran an advertising campaign that told the story of a young man coming on to his good-looking female neighbor. These one-minute vignettes progressed from his meeting his neighbor, to his sharing a cup of coffee with her, to his meeting another man in her house and being disappointed, and later learning that it was her brother. The message to young Generation Xers was straightforward: drink Taster's Choice and you can get the girl or guy of your dreams.

In the Bud Light Ladies' Night commercials, a group of guys dress up as women to try to win ladies' pool and bowling tournaments. The message was simple: if you want to have fun, drink Bud Light.

In the late nineties, Nike was uniquely successful in using the power of the story to promote its products. One of its ads presented a young man putting on his Nikes and going out for a run. He looks over his shoulder and sees a famous marathon runner behind him. Other runners start chasing him. Michael Johnson, the 400-meter champion, gets out of a cab and joins the crowd running behind the young fellow. The man speeds up, finally makes it back to his apartment, crashes through the door, and takes off his Nike shoes. The message on the screen asked, "What are you training for?" Another Nike ad showed football star John Randle entering a fabric store for some green and gold cloth. In the next scene, he is sewing together a small jersey with the name "Brett Favre" embroidered on the back. Next, Randle chases a chicken sporting the Favre jersey, reminiscent of the scene from *Rocky II*. The last shot of this sixty-second story shows Randle barbecuing the chicken. Again the message, "What are you training for?" The ads were targeted at active men and women who work out, play tennis or basketball—any sport. The subliminal lesson was that if you wear Nike you can be as good as Michael Johnson or John Randle.

USE A STORY—CHANGE AN ATTITUDE

People don't read newspapers and news magazines to get facts, figures, statistics, and dates. They read them for stories. The next time you watch the evening national or local television news programs, look for the way they present the day's events. Newscasters and producers use every opportunity to put their news pieces in story format.

For one to really become involved in a social, economic, or political issue, there must be a face on it. Welfare is a good example. Public attitudes toward welfare were changed in the Reagan era by stories depicting welfare mothers driving Cadillacs. Or consider the O. J. Simpson trial. The average person was bored by the scientific DNA evidence but fascinated with details of the story. What did O. J. have in the golf bag? How did he get the cut on his hand? The sensational sexual adventures of Nicole Brown Simpson. How the "race card" played out in trial.

If we learn only one thing from the history of the story, it is that one vivid anecdote can overcome a page of facts and statistics. Trial lawyers should best know the lesson. In the 1980s, insurance companies sponsored a number of ads in newspapers and magazines and planted stories on the AP wire. One anecdote recalled the story of an Ironman competitor who injured his back and sued the manufacturer of the refrigerator that was strapped to his back as part of the contest. Other widely publicized cases included a burglar suing the owners of a building when he fell through its skylight; a man injured while using his lawnmower as a hedger; the woman who sued her doctor for malpractice, claiming she had lost her psychic powers. The public attitude was turned against personal injury claimants and victims and their lawyers not by logic or factual analysis but rather by the power of the stories, most of which were untrue or inaccurately presented.

The lesson is clear. A narrative with characters, action, and events that leads to a moral is a powerful recipe. For sixty-five years I've been listening to radio and watching movies and television. For fifty years I've studied political campaigns and speeches. The last forty years of my life have been spent in courtrooms, engaged in or observing trials where cases were won or lost depending on how lawyers and witnesses told the story. During all these years my story addiction worsened. I went from simply enjoying stories to studying them and their tellers. You can find tips and techniques on storytelling in the works of many disciplines. Psychologists consider concepts such as schema and the essentials of the story in subliminal or subconscious persuasion. Directors and screenwriters write about structuring the story to give it dramatic impact. Texts on communication tell of the experiences of political consultants and advertisers in using the story format to persuade a mass audience. In this book I've tried to reference and incorporate those techniques of various disciplines that can be used by the courtroom storyteller or classroom lecturer.

In addition to studying storytelling technique, I've accumulated over the years a catalog of stories that make or illustrate a point. These are stories I have heard preachers, politicians, motivational speakers, teachers, doctors, and lawyers use to teach or persuade. In short, this book is the product of a lifetime of addiction to the most effective way that people have found to communicate with each other—the story.

2

Why a Story?

DURING THE EARLY PART of the twentieth century, a man spoke out against social and economic injustice, in courtrooms and lecture halls around the country. He preached against intolerance, bigotry, the abuses of wealth and privilege, and the plight of the poor. Often he used a story to make his point. This is one of them.

> *This story is about Little Louis Epstine, aged nine years. As might be guessed, Louis was a Jew. But there are different kinds of Jews. There are Jews who live on Grand Boulevard, and Jews who live on Maxwell Street. For the most part, the Jews on Grand Boulevard own wholesale clothing stores, and for the most part, the Jews on Maxwell Street work in the stores. Louis Epstine lived on Maxwell Street.*
>
> *When this tale began, he had only one hand. How he lost the other is a matter quite outside of this story. It seems he was run over by a beer wagon when he was a baby. Louis was not the only child in the family. His mother had five more besides him, and they all lived together in two large rooms back of a bakery. They had lived a whole year without moving. The rent was five dollars a month.*
>
> *When Louis was nine years old, he helped the family by selling papers. He got up at five o'clock in the morning and went over to Newspaper Alley and bought his papers, and then stood on the corner until about eleven o'clock, and sold them; then he went to school in the afternoon. In this way he managed to make three or four dollars a week, sometimes even five.*
>
> *Louis got along fairly well up to his ninth year. Nothing serious happened to him, barring the loss of his hand, and this never bothered him a great deal; in fact, he never thought anything about it. If boys had three hands, they would doubtless use them, but one is really quite enough. Louis could do almost anything that the other boys could do. Of course, he could run as fast, he could play all sorts of games, he could throw stones at cats, he never had any trouble to eat everything his mother gave him, and even his stub of a left arm was quite useful; he could hold papers under it and fix his*

hat on his head and use his stub in connection with his right hand to do almost anything he wished to do. He really felt quite lucky to think that only his hand was gone. He knew a boy who had lost his whole arm, and it was his right one, too.

One day, Louis' mother had been better to him than usual. She had bought him a nice warm cap that pulled down over his ears, and cost twenty-five cents at the department store. He felt very tenderly toward her. It was really more pity than love. And then he remembered a string of great red glass beads that he had seen hanging in the department store on the corner where he sold his papers, and which were marked forty-eight cents, and he thought how happy his mother would be if he could buy this string of beads. So in his foolish, boyish mind he conceived the thought of saving enough money to buy the beads and giving them to his mother at Christmas time. He kept out a penny or two each day and carefully hid it away until he had thirty-five cents that no one but himself knew anything about. Every morning when he took his stand before the great store he looked in through the polished window to see that the beads were still hanging in their place.

The eighteenth of December came around. The day can easily be remembered, because it was so very cold. This morning was far the coldest of the winter, and all through the night Louis had kept waking up because there were not enough quilts on the bed. In the morning he was ready to get up and go after his papers before the usual time. His mother urged him not to go, telling him it was too cold, but Louis would not hear to this; it was only a week till Christmas time, and, besides, if it was cold he could sell more papers, for some of the other boys would stay away.

Well, on this morning, after breakfast, Louis' mother bundled him up the best she could. His shoes were not very good. His pants had most likely been made from gray cloth, and certainly for someone else. These, too, were quite large, and had a number of patches scattered around in various places like sores. The cloth did not seem to hold the thread very well, and anyhow Louis expected a new pair—or, rather, another pair—this winter. He could have had them long ago only for the beads.

His coat was really a prize affair. This coat had been given to him two years before by a charity society. The lining, of course, was torn, and when Louis put his hand into the sleeve he had to grasp hold of the wristband of his shirt, and hold it until his hand came out at the bottom of the sleeve, but this was partly because the buttonhole of the shirt was broken out.

When Louis went to get his papers, he was in the habit of going down Van Buren Street and then along Franklin Street. The buildings on these streets were so big that they kept the wind away. When he would go down on the cold mornings, he would meet men and boys with great stacks of overcoats on their heads and in their arms. He looked in through the great square windows and saw endless heaps of overcoats, and other nice new coats and pants, too, piled up in great high heaps and long rows as far as he could see. Louis used to think that there were more coats than all the boys he ever heard of could possibly use; and then in his foolish way he wondered why these were locked up all the cold winter when none of the little boys had coats; but Louis was not a statesman or a political economist, he was only a poor little Jew boy, nine years old.

He went on down to Franklin Street, and turned north past the great clothing stores. The coats and pants and vests seemed to be piled up higher than ever. He looked at them and said, "Gee, I wish I had one o' dem." He got his bundle of papers, thrust them under his stub arm and started off. Besides the cold, there was a cutting wind, and as he came north it was all he could do to walk, but when he turned south with his papers it was easier, though the drifting snow bothered him quite a bit.

Finally, he got down to the department store and took his stand just in front of the great red beads and began to call off something that they had told him was in the papers, something about some grand affair, a charity ball, or an inaugural, or something of the sort.

Louis did not stand there very long until he began to get cold, so he commenced walking up and down the block and calling his papers whenever anyone passed. There were not many people out on the street that morning and they all hurried pretty fast, most of them not stopping long enough to buy a paper. Along toward eight o'clock, his hand had begun to get very cold. He couldn't put it in his pocket and use the other one. He was obliged to make all the change with this one, and could only use his stub to hold the papers. Two or three times he stepped into the outside doorway of the store for a minute, but he could not sell papers there, and then the last time the floorwalker drove him out.

Two or three times in the morning Louis thought he would give it up and go home, but then there were the glass beads, and besides he had the papers and could not afford to get "stuck" with them on his hands; so he stayed at his post and sold out his papers and went back home about the usual time. Soon after he got into the house his hand commenced to feel queer—it was all prickly and numb, and seemed to burn. He told his mother, and she had him put it in cold water; still it ached so bad that she finally sent over to the corner for a doctor. He looked the hand over carefully, and then shook his head. The doctor finally said that the hand was badly frozen.

In a few hours he came back. The hand did not pain as much as before, but it felt numb and queer. The doctor took off the bandage and shook his head again. It was red and purple clear up to the wrist. The doctor told Louis and his mother that he must go to the hospital, and he was afraid they must cut off the hand, but they would ask the doctor at the hospital first.

They found the big doctor, and he looked at Louis' hand and said it must be amputated at once. It had all come so suddenly that neither of them fully realized what it meant, and then poor people never do object to anything that the rich say must be done. They took him into a great long bedroom, where there were dozens of little white cots all the same size, and most of them with a child lying on top. They told him that they would give him something which would put him to sleep, but that he would wake up all right, and it would be all over without his knowing it.

Louis went to sleep, and the next thing he knew he was lying in one of the little cots, and his mother, the doctor and a girl with a striped blue and white dress were standing by the bed. His hand was tied up in a cloth and was aching pretty bad. It took him some time to remember where he was, and then he asked them about his hand, why it was hurting so much. Then his mother told him all about it, although it was almost as hard for her as for Louis. But the little fellow was rather dazed at first, and did not seem to think much about his hand.

Finally, he turned away from his mother, and pretty soon they heard a sob. The poor woman went around to the other side of the cot, and stroked Louis' face and hair gently, and asked him not to cry. She told him that he would be well again before long, and that she and his brothers and sisters would always be good to him and take care of him as long as he lived. Louis told her that he knew this, but it was so near Christmas and he couldn't get the rest of the money. She asked him what he meant, and then between his sobs he told her about the beads.[1]

All good speeches begin with a story. Think about it. Do you remember any speeches, sermons, or lectures that you enjoyed—that were truly memorable—that didn't begin with a story? Stories have magic. Humorous stories loosen up the audience. Personal anecdotes connect speakers with their audience by sharing values, challenges, or experiences. Biblical stories convey principles of morality, ethics, and courage. Historical vignettes may illustrate almost any human virtue or failing imaginable. Good speakers know there is magic in a story. It is a format that everyone can understand, that is apt to get attention, that makes what is said interesting and understandable.

It's hard to keep an audience's attention without using stories. It takes only 15 percent of the human mind to understand spoken language. This means that 85 percent of the brain is left to wander in any direction during an oral presentation. Stories keep the mind engaged, the listeners listening. Daydreams have difficulty intruding when the theater of the mind is filled with pictures it is creating from words spoken by an engaging speaker.

Good speeches, inspiring sermons, the best opening and closing arguments—all are built around a story. The story is the framework for the speech. The technical points, the science, the details, the facts, are all tied into the spine like ligament and muscle are attached to bone. Other anecdotes may be told along the way to make a point, but the essential framework remains the same—the speech's story.

There are many reasons why using a story to persuade works.

Psychologists teach that the concept of vividness works at a subliminal level. Because stories appeal to the visual senses, they are more persuasive. A vivid message trumps an inert one. In *Age of Propaganda,* Anthony Pratkanis and Elliot Aronson give the example of a person who reads in *Consumer Reports* that a Toyota is the car with the best repair record. On the basis of the facts and statistics set out in the reports, the person decides to buy one. It is a decision based on logic. But the night before he is to buy the car, he attends a dinner party and tells his friends about his decision. One of his friends is incredulous. "You can't be serious," he says, "my cousin bought a Toyota last year and has had nothing but trouble ever since. First the fuel injection system broke down; then the transmission fell out; then strange undiagnosable noises started to come from the engine; finally, oil started to drip from some unknown place. My poor cousin is literally afraid to drive the car for fear of what will happen next."

If we suppose that the ranking made by the consumer reports was based on a sample of 1,000 Toyota owners, the friend's cousin's experience has increased the size of the sample to 1,001. It has added one negative case to the statistical bank. Logically, this addition should not affect the buying decision. But research has demonstrated that a single experience, because of its vividness, assumes far more importance than its statistical status would imply. The narrated event is frequently decisive. All other things being equal, most people are more deeply influenced by one clear, vivid, personal experience than by a host of statistical data. Anecdotal evidence may overcome statistical proof.[2]

Stories work because they involve the listener. The basic premises of persuasion are—

> *Tell* me and I will *forget.*
>
> *Show* me and I will *remember.*
>
> *Involve* me and I will *understand* and *act.*

Abraham Lincoln was an accomplished storyteller. He understood the power of the story to disarm his antagonists and cajole others into agreement. Most of his stories were short, spiced with a bit of humor and a dose of psychology, all of which led to an anecdote illustrating the point.

A team of high-powered Eastern lawyers were representing the railroad in a case brought against a barge owner whose Mississippi River barge had rammed the abutment of the company's newly built railroad bridge. The barge owner hired Abraham Lincoln as his trial counsel. When Lincoln's turn to argue the case came, he rose, strode to the jury box, smiled, and made a single statement: "My learned opponents," he said, "have presented an impressive case. There is no question they have their facts absolutely right. But they have drawn completely wrong conclusions."

The jurors broke out laughing. Later, after the jury returned its verdict in favor of Lincoln's client, the railroad lawyers asked him how he could get away with such a simple argument and use that to sway the jury in his favor. Lincoln replied that during the lunch recess that day, he had dropped into the saloon where the jurors were eating and told them a little story. The story was about a farmer who was working in his barnyard one day when his ten-year-old boy came rushing up to him, all excited. "Paw," said the boy, "come quick. The hired hand and Sis are up in the haymow and he's pulling down his pants and she's lifting up her skirt. Paw, they're getting ready to pee all over our hay." The farmer said, "Son, you've got your facts absolutely right, but you've drawn a completely wrong conclusion."[3]

In telling that story to the jury during a lunch break, Lincoln was not violating any ethical standards of the day. But it certainly made the point that he needed them to carry into their deliberations. Lincoln involved his jury with his argument by using a story.

Audiences become involved when speakers use a story format that incorporates a consistent point of view. The storyteller's viewpoint is the audience's. Just as most writers and their readers prefer the third person, so do audiences hearing a story. The speaker puts the audience into the story by employing the active voice and present tense. Storytelling works to involve the audience when they live the story as it is happening. A good storyteller describes not only the events but the innermost thoughts of the person, second by second, as the scene unfolds. The involved listeners are asking themselves, "What happens next?" Curiosity is quickened by a suspenseful narrative.

Stories work to educate and persuade because the story format is most consistent with the way people organize and store information. Psychologists use the term "schema." Like a computer, the human brain has its own unique filing mechanism. When we are learning, we take the facts and data and by association store, catalog, and relate them. Many people have a hard time storing much material under individualized topics, which is the way most speakers present it. Using a story format for the presentation makes it easier for people to recall and use facts, dates, events—even principles of science and medicine. The story is everyone's most usable filing cabinet.

Trial lawyers appreciate the role of the schema concept in persuasion. People use schemas to assign meaning to incoming information by providing a preexisting frame of reference within which to interpret it. As a result, the audience filters out what it perceives to be irrelevant information and focuses on that which is useful or important to support the schema. When jurors deliberate, they explain the events and the conflicts in the testimony within the context of the schema they have accepted.

Whether in the courtroom, church, or lecture hall, many people are uncomfortable about the prospect of learning. Some members of the audience may not have done well in school and may feel threatened or intimidated by the prospect of learning and remembering. Stories alleviate that fear. The person who is insecure in his ability to retain, analyze, and relate to scientific, mathematical, or technical data has no apprehension about his or her ability to understand a series of events. "Who did what when" is easy to discuss, even when others disagree with us and we do not fully grasp relevant scientific or mathematical data.

Stories work because listeners make their own meaningful pictures. Psychologists use storytelling as a therapeutic technique. Stories allow people to distance themselves from problems, yet remain involved enough to deal with them. People can deal with mind pictures that are familiar and comfortable images.

Noted jury consultant Rodney Jew suggests that a story holds attention by appealing to curiosity and holding a promise of reward.[4] The reward can take many forms—amusement, satisfaction, even a thrill. Whatever the payoff, some degree of emotion is involved. By interlacing facts with emotions, the narrative helps the audience absorb information, make sense of experience, and reinforce what is already known. The feelings evoked by a story are essential to the jurors' understanding of the information contained in the story. Feelings make that information more memorable for jurors. Jurors come "preloaded" for stories about real emotions and real people. Logic, legal instructions, and "stacks of facts" are secondary for them. Thus jurors are much more adept at using stories to make sense of what they see, hear, and feel in the courtroom. And this is why mastery of storytelling is so critical for building and presenting a case to jurors.

Stories appeal to powers of imagination, which are not logical, methodical, or scientific. But stories are actually vehicles that satisfy jurors' demands for information.

Storytelling empowers the speaker. The narrator gets into the skin of her characters and lives the actions. A speaker seeing and living a story has no time to be looking at herself. The person telling a story is not conscious of movement, gestures, or inflections. Everything comes naturally as the narrator "lives" the story. A powerful story makes the audience forget the speaker even as she has forgotten herself.

The story format of presentation is easier on the speaker. Stories give speakers power, because once they are learned we can tell them without reference to notes or text. Any speaker who knows her subject will know her story. She has already visualized the people, the places, the events. The motion picture of the mind flashes the images, which are then conveyed by words to the audience. Characters are created, events occur, persons react, all leading to a conclusion—a moral lesson.

Stories are fun. Using a story format for a lecture, speech, or closing argument enlivens the speaker and engages the audience. We love stories because that is the way we learned as children. Our parents gave us our values through stories. Our pastors inspired our religious principles with narratives thousands of years old. All our lives we have been entertained by stories.

Finally, studies have demonstrated that the effective storyteller induces a form of hypnosis in his audience. I know this sounds farfetched, but it is true. A good story creates a kind of trance. People tighten up and feel defensive when they hear what seems to be an argument or a lecture. But once they realize the speaker is telling a story, rather than giving directives attempting to change their minds, they relax. The effective storyteller relaxes his audience with a calm, pleasant voice, giving enough details to the story to distract the audience from whatever is making them tense. Curiosity then pulls the listeners into a relaxed state that allows the storyteller's words to paint images on the canvas of their minds.

So—why a story? Because stories persuade at the subliminal level by using the concept of vividness. They involve the audience. The story uses the schema format for storing and organizing information. The story empowers the speaker by making the presentation easier and enlivens the audience by making facts fun. Do you want your audience to learn? Use a story. Do you want to inspire? It's done best by a narrative example. Is your goal to motivate and empower? Can that be done without a compelling narrative? Have you ever seen a speaker motivate a group of people, empower them to do what is right, without using a story? I haven't.

PART 2

CRAFTING A STORY

A BALDING GRAY HEAD, *deeply wrinkled jowls, and bags under the eyes paint the portrait of a man older than his forty-one years. His attractive wife with her fluffy, curled, bleached-blond hair and overdone makeup shares her husband's rage, but he is the spokesman for it.*

"Laura is only fifteen. She will carry this scar for the rest of her life."

Their adolescent daughter and a friend had gone to a shopping center on the north side of Houston. As they walked by the dimly lit side of the store, a man approached them from behind and put a gun to their backs. He took them behind the store to a dark, partly fenced trash cubicle and forced them to disrobe and perform sexual acts on him. The daughter has been under psychiatric care since then. The parents want to sue the owner of the shopping center.

"You can't believe how dark it is back there," are the words from the tightened jaw.

These are proud and angry parents. They have a story to tell. They know only part of it. Their lawyer will have to get photographs of the premises, run a criminal screen on the shopping center and neighborhood, interview and depose the investigating police officers. Later he will interrogate under oath the officials and employees of the shopping center's anchor tenant, a large grocery chain, and of the shopping center's management.

Trial lawyers get their stories in bits and pieces over time. But the rules of construction are the same as for other writers of fact and fiction. First we have to get a feel for the story we want to tell. It has to be based on a simple idea or proposition that grabs our minds and infects our hearts. A good courtroom story won't work unless you can write the idea in one or two sentences. Here the idea might be: "Poorly lit premises invite sexual predator to abuse young girls."

A courtroom story has to support a high-stakes issue and present compelling values. Character motivation is as important in the courtroom as it is on the page or the screen. The conflict is a wronged plaintiff seeking to hold responsible a defendant who denies any accountability. A trial narrative has to have a logical appeal. Facts come together to present a conflict the audience must resolve. What identifiable acts are "wrong" and intuitively connect to the plaintiff's injuries and harm? Is the plaintiff deserving? Can the verdict make a difference?

During the months of developing this premises case, the lawyer begins to expand his story and fill in the details. Constructing the trial narrative starts with an outline. There will be a beginning, middle, and end. Finally, the resolution, a final chapter only a jury can write. Only after the lawyer has developed all the facts will he begin constructing the trial story that he will tell in opening statement. As he puts it together, he will focus on the mechanics of the narrative: exposition, dialogue, scene-setting, supporting documents and exhibits, legal principles. They are all a part of crafting the trial narrative. But it won't end there. The lawyer will then tell the trial story to colleagues and friends. He will consider their advice. He may even present the story to a focus group, a representative sampling of citizens drawn from the community, for their reaction and input. Like the novelist, he uses all possible resources for editing and improving the story.

Whether you are a novelist or a historian, the principles for constructing a story are the same. Lecturers, teachers, and preachers are free to act as novelists. They can fictionalize the setting, characters, and events needed to illustrate a principle. For instance, a lawyer speaking to management on sexual harassment in the workplace can construct a mythical version of an interaction between a supervisor and an employee to illustrate a case of sexual harassment. The lawyer can take the fictional setting and change a few facts to demonstrate the legal principles involved—what is and isn't sexual harassment. Or consider how the dry world of Accounting 101 is enlivened by the professor's story of an accountant who lost a big account as a result of not being up to date on a recent provision in the Internal Revenue Code. Each of these professionals is essentially a novelist creating a story. A short narrative of people and events serves as the spine of a presentation designed to teach.

CONSTRUCTING THE STORY

When putting the story together, have in mind these basic rules:[1]

- Establish the mood, time and place, and the point of view in the first minute.
- Within the first three minutes, introduce the main character and the character's main objective.
- Concentrate only on the most relevant details.
- Simplify facts, events, and language.

- Identify the beginning, middle, and end.
- Summarize the story in twenty-five words or less.

Refining the Story

- *Step One:* Identify the facts that will make your story come alive.

Start by considering the individual you have chosen as the point-of-view person. To tell a story from her viewpoint, be sure to describe her clothes, mannerisms, appearance, things in her hands, and other details as well as where she was, what she was doing, and why she was there. Connect the character to the audience by describing what she was thinking. Explore the mood. Describe the setting: the weather, physical surroundings, what other people were doing. Such details anchor your story and make the point-of-view person more real and memorable.

- *Step Two:* Decide where to start and end the story.

The central conflict of a good story is made clear in the first three minutes. The start of your story should involve such a conflict—a change, decision, or dispute. The ending of the story should resolve the conflict and answer the question raised for jurors in the opening scene.

- *Step Three:* Outline the scenes and structure of your story.

The further removed jurors are from the lawyer's frame of reference (for example, social standing, income level, education), the more likely they are to "hear" a different story from the one the lawyer believes is being told. Successful storytelling across cultural, social, and interpersonal boundaries requires a mutually familiar frame of reference. Otherwise the story will seem disconnected from teller, listener, or both, and credibility will be weakened or lost.

Trial lawyers are historians. Even the slightest exaggeration or misstatement spells peril. The evidence must fully support what the courtroom advocate says. Dealing with fact does not lessen the creative challenge. While real people with real problems may present a story no more compelling than "bad things happen to good people," the advocate must take historical events and craft them into a forceful story that will drive a just verdict. This is accomplished by following the courtroom storyteller's basic formula:

- Start strong.

- Set the scene.
- Develop strong characters.
- Present a compelling plot.
- Let the audience live the action.
- Tie it all together with a theme.
- Inoculate against the negatives.
- Complete the circle with a strong ending.

All storytellers need not follow this exact recipe. However, in the courtroom, the trial lawyer should give thoughtful consideration to each element, omitting only those that time or tactic does not support.

3

The Strong Beginning

SHE WAS FRIGHTENED. In her eight short years of healthy, active, happy life, Jill Newsome had never known fear. The male nurse anesthetist comforted her in a soft, calm tone.

"Don't fret, little girl, I'm going to give you something that will make you a little drowsy."

Jill knew she could trust Dr. Johnson and his nurse anesthetist. After all, he had performed plastic surgery on her mother. And this was such a minor procedure—removing a small birthmark on her calf. Her mother was waiting in the doctor's reception area to take her home as soon as the operation was over.

"Don't worry, sweetheart, everything will be fine. Are you beginning to feel a little drowsy?"

Her anxiety was lessening. With the anesthetic drugs flowing into her veins came the mist that clouds consciousness.

"Jill, can you count backwards for me, beginning with the number ten?"

She started to count. "Ten, nine, eight, seven . . ."

Then she was unconscious, asleep.

Four years later, Jill is still asleep. She is not in Dr. Johnson's office; she is in a nursing home. Her body is not that of an active, robust twelve-year-old. It is a wretched corpse of muscles shriveled from lack of use, a body distorted from four years of being fed intravenously and being incontinent of bladder and bowel.

The last words Jill heard were the reassuring ones of Dr. Johnson's nurse anesthetist telling her that she was in good hands and would be all right.

In the coming days you will learn how anesthesia misadventure robbed these parents of their most precious treasure and left them with a child who requires constant medical care and attention at an annual cost that will stagger your mind. In the coming days you will hear how these defendants attempted to cover up their medical mistakes by rewriting the anesthesia chart not once, but twice. After you have heard all the evidence, we will ask you to hold these defendants responsible not only for what these parents have lost but for the mountain of medical expenses they will have to shell out for the rest of Jill's life. Some weeks from now, we will call on you to hold them to the words they spoke to Jill: "Don't worry, we'll take care of you."[1]

Stories are constructed by appreciating the purpose of each part of the story. The beginning, or introduction, of the story should—

- get the listeners' attention;
- arouse curiosity;
- let the listeners know where the speaker is going; and
- tell the listeners what will be expected of them at the end.

The middle, or body, of the story develops the characters, lays out the action, events, and motivations, and defines the conflict. The end, or conclusion, of the story delivers the lesson or moral. The moral is taught through the resolution of the conflict and the suggestion of what the audience should do with the lesson. Because a powerful conclusion ties back with the introduction and completes the circle, crafting the introduction forecasts how the storyteller intends to wrap up the narrative.

EXAMPLES OF STRONG BEGINNINGS

Great stories are remembered for their powerful beginnings.[2] Strong introductions mark memorable political documents, speeches, novels, movies, and songs. The most significant political document in American history is the Declaration of Independence.

> When in the Course of human events, it becomes necessary for one people to dissolve the political bands which have connected them with another, and to assume among the powers of the earth, the separate and equal station to which the Laws of Nature and of Nature's God entitle them, a decent respect to the opinions of mankind requires that they should declare the causes which impel them to the separation.[3]

The most time-honored of American speeches and one that we all committed to memory in high school begins:

> Four score and seven years ago our fathers brought forth, upon this continent, a new nation, conceived in Liberty, and dedicated to the proposition that all men are created equal.[4]

America's best-known orator liked to start strong. On March 7, 1850, Daniel Webster rose to speak in what is now the Old Senate Chamber. The debate was over the extension of slavery to the territories, and he entitled his speech "The Constitution and the Union." Webster's first words were—

> I wish to speak today, not as a Massachusetts man, nor as a Northern man, but as an American, and a member of the Senate of the United States. . . . I speak today for the preservation of the Union. "Hear me for my cause."[5]

In school, we read authors like Charles Dickens, Edgar Allan Poe, and Robert Louis Stevenson. *A Tale of Two Cities* begins:

> It was the best of times, it was the worst of times, it was the age of wisdom, it was the age of foolishness, it was the epoch of belief, it was the epoch of incredulity, it was the season of Light, it was the season of Darkness, it was the spring of hope, it was the winter of despair, we had everything before us, we had nothing before us. . . .[6]

Poe's *The Raven* has this memorable beginning:

> Once upon a midnight dreary, while I pondered, weak and weary,
> Over many a quaint and curious volume of forgotten lore—
> While I nodded, nearly napping, suddenly there came a tapping,
> As of some one gently rapping, rapping at my chamber door.[7]

Remember Robert Louis Stevenson's *Treasure Island* that we all read in school? It begins:

> Squire Trelawney, Dr. Livesey, and the rest of these gentlemen having asked me to write down the whole particulars about Treasure Island, from the beginning to the end, keeping nothing back but the bearings of the island, and that only because there is still treasure not yet lifted . . .[8]

What a beginning for a book children read! There is still treasure there! Young readers can't wait to get into the story in hopes that maybe they will be able to locate Long John Silver's treasure chest.

O. Henry's "Gift of the Magi" begins with a great problem to be solved:

> One dollar and eighty-seven cents. That was all. And sixty cents of it was in pennies. Pennies saved one and two at a time by bulldozing the grocer and the vegetable man and the butcher until one's cheeks burned with the silent imputation of parsimony that such close dealing implied. Three times Della counted it. One dollar and eighty-seven cents. And the next day would be Christmas.[9]

Memorable characters inform the opening of James Joyce's "The Boarding House":

> Mrs. Mooney was a butcher's daughter. She was a woman who was quite able to keep things to herself: a determined woman. She had married her father's foreman and opened a butcher's shop near Spring Gardens. But as soon as his father-in-law was dead Mr. Mooney began to go to the devil. He drank, plundered the till, ran headlong into debt. It was no use making him take the pledge: he was sure to break out again a few days after. By fighting his wife in the presence of customers and by buying bad meat he ruined his business. One night he went for his wife with the cleaver and she had to sleep in a neighbor's house.[10]

Many movies have memorable beginnings. One that most people would recognize as being an American classic begins:

> There was a land of Cavaliers and Cotton Fields called the Old South . . . Here in this pretty world Gallantry took its last bow . . . Here was the last ever to be seen of Knights and their Ladies Fair, of Master and of Slave . . . Look for it only in books, for it is no more than a dream remembered. A Civilization gone with the wind . . .[11]

That, of course, is the beginning of the movie *Gone with the Wind*.

Finally, even songs, particularly when they tell a story, have a beginning that arouses the listener's curiosity, gets his attention, and gives some idea of where the story will go. Remember—

> On a warm summer's evenin', on a train bound for nowhere,
> I met up with the Gambler. We were both too tired to sleep,
> So we took turns a-starin' out the window at the darkness
> 'Till boredom overtook us and he began to speak.
> He said, "Son, I've made a life out of readin' people's faces,
> And knowin' what their cards were by the way they held their eyes.
> So if you don't mind my sayin', I can see you're out of aces.
> For a taste of your whiskey, I'll give you some advice."[12]

We all know the beginning of Kenny Rogers's recording of "The Gambler."

THE ATTENTION GETTER

Audiences give speakers a narrow window of opportunity. The ordinary person forms impressions about a speaker—whether she is an interesting person with something interesting to say—within a few minutes. An attention-getting formula that works every time is: hook, headline, and question. The hook gets the listeners' attention and arouses their curiosity. The headline tells them where the speaker is going. The question alerts the listeners to what will be expected of them at the end.

More than a century ago, the psychologist William James suggested that getting the listener's attention was the first step in the act of persuasion. Storytellers know that people need help to remember a concept. A touch of drama adds color and emphasis. The hook accomplishes that goal by introducing the basic concept at issue in the case.

Here are some hooks I have used for opening statement or closing argument:

- It was supposed to be such a routine surgery.
- A courtroom is a magical place. I can prove it to you.
- A man lost an eye because a company wanted to save a dollar on their high-pressure gauges.
- They were the saddest words Lisa Lee ever heard—"Mrs. Lee, your child is brain damaged."
- Mr. Alexander, my name is Dr. Crowder. I will be giving you your anesthesia.
- Lois, you have cancer. We need to operate right away.
- Nothing is more inviting to the criminal mind than a dark place. The defendants knew this when they designed the lighting for their shopping center.

The hook leads into the headline. A storyteller's headline serves the same function that it does for a newspaper writer. It is the brief capsule of the story that will follow. Samuel Goldwyn is supposed to have said that if the screenwriter could not put his idea for a movie on the back of a napkin, he didn't have a story. Speakers work in an abbreviated-attention-span environment that is the product of remote-control television. If the program is not interesting, the listener will simply switch channels.

A good storyteller formulates a precise but accurate headline. For example, in an obstetrical case the headline might be—

> Obstetrician botches delivery and changes records.

Obviously, that is not the way the storyteller delivers it. But it helps frame the first paragraph as a lead-in to the core issue—the challenge to the audience to take action at the end of the case.

The attention-getting introduction that flows from the headline might be—

> Julia and Juan entrusted with the defendant the most precious vessel in their guardianship—the life and health of their yet-unborn daughter. That trust was violated with an inexcusable blunder and miscalculation. The defendant cuts Angelita from her mother's womb twelve weeks too early. August's blessed event is turned into May's bloody nightmare. The only serious debate that arises out of this legal wrong of shameful proportions is over how many entries in the medical records the defendant and his staff change after discovering their mistake.

The hook for this story might be, "Your baby is overdue. We need to take her by C-section." The headlines that follow are like the trailer for a movie—abbreviated scenes of what will follow in more detail. The audience knows where the story is going and remains curious about how it will get there.

Nothing is expected of an audience when the goal of the storyteller is to entertain. But in the courtroom the audience must act at the conclusion of the story. It must render a verdict. The courtroom narrator should alert the audience early on about what will be expected of it. The speaker should define the question in the broadest of terms.

For readers and viewers to be involved in the adventure, to care about the hero, they have to know at an early stage exactly what's at stake. In other words, what does the hero stand to gain or lose in the adventure? Make sure the stakes are high—life and death, big money, or the hero's very soul.

> After you hear Juan and Julia's story, after you hear the defendants' excuses, you will ask, "Is it fair that these parents be saddled with a lifetime of constant care and medical expense?"

Or—

> Some weeks from now, at the end of the evidence, you will wonder: "Could we ever let these parents continue to serve as coolies to the burden of these defendants' medical misadventure?"

Most audiences generously grant attention to the narrator at the beginning. The speaker shows appreciation for the gift by supplying the wonder of curiosity. After gaining the listeners' attention, the speaker tells them where the story is going and what will be expected of them.

CURIOSITY

A strong beginning arouses the listeners' curiosity. Another psychological principle is that a curious audience is an attentive one. Curious listeners will attend to the speaker because they want to know what comes next.

Many techniques can be used to arouse curiosity. For example, the lecturer might say, "You will learn today that a simple but successful method to . . . is to . . . " Or, "Later, I will share with you one of the closely guarded secrets of . . . " Audiences are attracted to novel and unknown ideas that help them personally or professionally.

In the courtroom, an early preview of critical evidence can draw in the audience.

> The answer to what caused Ed Hudson's brain damage will be found in the drug manufacturer's own records in an obscure notation about reported side effects during early testing on animals.

Another example might be—

> The mystery of why the Welstone truck brakes failed will be solved when you see the maintenance records.

Later—much later—in these stories, the narrator will explain how the experimental animal tests should have alerted the drug company of bleeding problems or how the maintenance log identified a potential problem with the brake shoes.

When the television announcer during a commercial break says, "Police foil daring holdup of downtown bank. Details at ten," the news people are using the power of curiosity to keep listeners tuned in to their channel. The news hook always works because it is about real events happening in the audience's community. People are particularly drawn to discovering behind-the-scenes facts that may affect them personally.

The same things that arouse curiosity in the nightly news programs work in the courtroom. An approach of, "You will be taken behind the scenes of how a major pharmaceutical firm works and learn how drugs are conceived, developed, and tested" is designed to pique the listeners' curiosity.

Visual props or artifacts create suspense and curiosity. The narrator draws the audience's attention to a thing by referencing it or showing it but keeps the audience in the dark as to its significance. For example, the Maltese Falcon was mentioned early but seen only later in the Humphrey Bogart film classic of the same name. In *Raiders of the Lost Ark,* the mystery of the Ark of the Covenant was not solved until the conclusion of the film.

One of the best illustrations of the phenomenon of curiosity as a storytelling technique comes from Bill English, who was the debate coach at the University of Houston and is now director of the Division of Speech Communication at Baylor. The story of a college freshman giving his speech for his final grade may be apocryphal, but it graphically makes the point.

> The young man in the freshman speech class stood behind the podium and said to his fellow students: "My name is Jimmy Jackson. I am one of your classmates. The topic of my speech today is 'Magic is

fun—magic is entertaining—the hand is quicker than the eye.'" With that statement he pulled out of his shirt pocket a fountain pen. Black ink gushed from the pen onto the blouse of one of the young female students sitting on the first row.

"Don't worry, it's all part of the act," the freshman speaker said. "That is disappearing ink that I made up last night in my laboratory at home. Before your very eyes that ink will disappear from your blouse."

Well, the ink, instead of disappearing, got darker and darker. Finally, in desperation he said, "I'm sorry, I don't know what could have gone wrong. If you will see me after class I will see that the blouse is cleaned or I will buy you a brand-new one."

Jimmy then continued, "The topic of my speech today is 'Magic is fun—magic is entertaining—the hand is quicker than the eye.'" And with that he pulled from his shirt pocket a cigarette. "I'm sure most of you have seen this one before." He asked the audience if anyone had a handkerchief. One was produced by a male student sitting in the front row.

"What a fine handkerchief, brand new," Jimmy said. He then lit the cigarette, took a few puffs, dropped it into the middle of the handkerchief, and folded it. "I'm sure many of you have seen this one before and wondered how it was done." Then, grabbing the handkerchief by its corner, he let it fully unfold with the cigarette dropping onto the floor. There was a dark black hole in the middle of the handkerchief where the cigarette had burned through.

"I don't know what could have happened. That trick has always worked before."

Exhibiting a little exasperation, he walked over to a table in the front of the classroom that had been set up with a tablecloth with a china and crystal place setting on it.

"Like I said, the topic of my speech today is 'Magic is fun—magic is entertaining—the hand is quicker than the eye.' I know you believe it can't be done, but I will pull on this tablecloth and remove it from the table without disturbing the china and crystal that you see on it."

He gave the tablecloth a yank and, of course, the china and crystal went crashing onto the floor.

"I don't know what could be wrong. These tricks have always worked before."

At this point, Jimmy walked back to the lectern, reached under it, and brought out an old, crumpled, brown paper bag. He set it on top of the lectern. Out of it he removed a very crude, obviously homemade guillotine. It had a heavy, rusty, but evidently very sharp blade.

"The topic of my speech today is 'Magic is fun—magic is entertaining—the hand is quicker than the eye.' This is a trick no one will

> believe when they see it."
>
> With that he raised the blade on the guillotine by use of the crude chain and crank on the side. He snapped the lever into place, holding the blade. He pulled from his coat pocket a round wooden dowel half an inch thick. He stuck the dowel in the hole at the base of the guillotine. Then he flipped the lever. The blade came crashing down. The dowel was cut in half. Then, slowly, agonizingly, he raised the blade again and locked it into place. This time he stuck his finger in the hole. The room was silent. Everyone held their breath. He flipped the lever and the blade came crashing down again. His finger was not cut off. The trick worked.
>
> Jimmy stood back from the lectern and said to his class, "I told you that the topic of my speech today was 'Magic is fun—magic is entertaining—the hand is quicker than the eye.' Well, it was not. The topic of my speech, and the persuasive technique that I wanted to illustrate, was that if you can arouse an audience's curiosity they will listen to and watch almost anything.
>
> "If the day before I was to give my speech I had posted on the bulletin board outside this classroom that Jimmy Jackson would amputate himself as part of his freshman speech—no one would have come. You would have been offended. Yet you have all just watched something where you thought, while it happened, and as sure as night turns into day, that my finger was going to be cut off. But you weren't sure. You watched what would otherwise be offensive to you for the simple reason that I aroused your curiosity."[13]

An audience, whether it is there to learn, be entertained, or act, gives a speaker the benefit of the doubt at the beginning. Listeners presume the speaker represents a large, filled vessel of information that will be interesting and serve their purpose. Weak beginnings punch a hole in the barrel. If curiosity is not aroused and the speaker seems directionless, the keg may appear empty before the audience begins to fill its cup. Thus opening statements and closing arguments are best given in the framework of a compelling story. But many trial advocates open impotently with something like the following:

> This is the state of trial proceedings that is called the opening statement. It is the lawyer's opportunity to give you a road map of where we are going to go in this case. Some people liken it to a movie preview that you see in the papers or a book preview that you find on the inside jacket of a book that you may buy at the bookstore. But this is a summary or preview of the evidence that we think will be offered. What we say is not evidence. The evidence can only come from the witness stand.

Such a beginning cannot possibly capture the jury's attention. Where is the curiosity? Why listen?

WHERE THE STORY IS GOING

Accomplished storytellers hook the listener, set the tone of the story, suggest where it's going, and get across a mass of information without slowing the pace. They understand that the beginning is a delicate time. A time to tie listeners to characters, a time to share life's stages. The opening scenes should create an identification between audience and hero, a sense that they are equals in some ways. How to achieve this? The storyteller creates identification by giving heroes universal goals, drives, desires, or needs.[14]

Mentors of creative writers teach that the first paragraph of a story or a novel should preview the conflict. The audience needs to know right off not only that the protagonist has problems but that the problems will be interesting. Of course, conflict is inherent in the story the trial lawyer tells. If there were none, why would we be here? Even so, I have heard many courtroom advocates begin a story so leisurely that by the time the conflict comes, the audience has lost interest or begun to wonder whether it is worth continuing to listen.

A hook without a headline is a fishing pole lying on the bank. The fish may bite but will probably slip off the hook. Consider the following courtroom story involving the parents of a young medical student suing the hospital where he fell to his death.

> At 6:15 on the morning of April 23, 1991, Rich Larson pulls into the parking garage at the Smithson Medical School in Houston, Texas. He is a third-year medical student. He goes by the medical school and puts some belongings in his locker.[15]

The narrator could then tell about Rich or how much he wanted to be a doctor. She might tell a little about Rich growing up, or perhaps describe the hospital—how it is configured—what is dangerous about the premises. But what is missing is direction. The listeners are not sure of their destination. I know Oscar Wilde said, "The suspense is terrible. I hope it will last." But too much uncertainty can kill a story.

What if the storyteller were to follow the introductory paragraph with—

> Rich leaves the school and goes over to the Allen Pavilion at St. David's Hospital. He cannot know that in less than one hour he will be lying at the bottom of a concealed shaft with his skull crushed and his brain bleeding—injuries that will claim his life one week later, his death caused by decisions the hospital made. The decisions it made, the hospital says, were "good enough." You will ask, "Were they safe enough?"[16]

This introduction includes hook, headline, and core issue question. It tells the audience where it will be going on the magic carpet of the story. The Wolof of Senegal have a saying: "We go quickly where we are sent when we take interest in the journey."[17] The storyteller may not be concerned with how fast his listeners reach their destination, but he sure wants them with him when he gets there.

What Is Expected of the Audience

Effective speakers tell their listeners early on what will be expected of them at the end of the presentation. In Speech 101, college professors admonish to "tell the audience what you're going to tell them, tell them, and then tell them at the end again what you told them." Many speakers follow this axiom when they present material with a topical outline. Storytellers can also use the technique. They can use the narrative format to bring persuasive purchase to their lesson but structure it so that the audience knows where it is going, enjoys the trip, and is reminded at the end that the narrator described the destination at the beginning. In the courtroom, the listener must act—render a verdict—once the telling of the story is complete. A strong beginning is the first light of the torch that will be used to fire the verdict.

A trial story is presented in a unique form. It is three stories about the same thing. The first narrative is the opening statement. The story is then told again through the witnesses' testimony. The story is told a third time in closing argument. The goals for each presentation are different.

The law imposes dissimilar restrictions on opening statement and closing argument. What is said in opening statement is limited to what the evidence will show. The lawyer is confined to stating facts that the testimony of witnesses and documents offered in evidence will prove. In closing argument, counsel is permitted to draw inferences from those facts. Inferences from the evidence are improper when offered during opening statement.

The goal of the trial advocate in opening statement is for the jury to learn something. The listeners need to understand what happened to whom—when—where—why. What is expected of jurors after the opening statement is that they will hear the testimony and understand the evidence in the context of the opening narrative. All this is done with the understanding that, sometime down the line, they will decide the facts—choose between two competing stories.

On the other hand, the closing argument calls for immediate action. As soon as the lawyers finish, the audience deliberates and decides. The listeners render a verdict. That verdict can be inspired from the facts. Jurors use the witnesses' testimony and exhibits received in evidence in their determination of the action they will take. But they are not limited to the facts alone; they can make inferences from them. They can use their common sense. They can empower their decision with the concepts of justice, fairness, and courage. A good closing argument tells the jury not only that they can do this, but that they should. It is expected because it is right.

Experienced advocates know that it is the power of the story that moves the jury. Begin with a hook that grabs the listeners' minds, holds them captive, and keeps them on the edge of their seats with curiosity. Follow with a short thumbnail sketch of the story you will tell. Give a brief preview of what will come at the end. It is a simple formula but one that experience teaches is designed to lead to the construction of a strong beginning.

Novelists and authors of the stage and screen follow the axiom that if you have a strong beginning and a strong ending, the middle will take care of itself. Courtroom advocates who concentrate on the body of their story and ignore or neglect the beginning imperil their course. A strong start is essential to trial persuasion.

4

Setting the Scene

THE BRONZE-TINTED floor-to-ceiling windows on the thirty-second floor refract a rose-yellow cast into the cavernous room. Drapes of dull orange stretch across the thick, plush brown carpet that spreads from wall to wall. A vast granite-topped aircraft carrier of a conference table is moored in the middle of this sea of thick woolen pile. The dark-paneled walls reveal ancient hardwoods that once stood tall in nature's oasis but, failing to protest, were sacrificed in the name of ambience. Dark-toned classical oil paintings mounted in ornate frames stretch around the perimeter as further evidence of the wealth and power held by those privileged to be here.

A cadre of suits surrounds the table. Quiet, somber men speaking in soft voices. The shirts are white, starched, and pressed. The burnt-orange glow from the sun setting on the horizon draws an expensive sheen from the suit fabric here and there. The heads protruding from the collars are white, some balding, some gray. But each face has a serious countenance—a brooding, stern expression.

In this quiet room high above the teeming masses who struggle through life five hundred feet below, the silence is broken every now and then by the shuffling of papers or the turning of pages in a notebook. In some ways these subtle sounds seem more prominent than the voices. Quiet voices, precise articulation, soft tones, scarcely more than a whisper—words that carry no rancor, no disagreement, no emotion—form muffled sounds that carry a short distance off the aircraft carrier, then plunge into the sea like an unfueled plane sent aloft.

The suits are making decisions. Cold, hard, calculating business decisions expressed without inflection and in monotone. Decisions that affect thousands of men, women, and children. Decisions about the kind of medical care people thousands of miles away and hundreds of feet below will be able to obtain in the coming years.[1]

Storytellers are part novelists, screenwriters, directors, and actors. Being a bit of all of these means that some of the rules and techniques of each discipline work and should be followed, while others may fall flat. The novelist or screenwriter may paint a scene in great detail before the characters come to life and spring into action. But the storyteller subordinates the setting to the characters and plot. Speakers using narratives to teach or persuade need just enough setting to put the audience into the characters' situation. For example, if the story's central scene is a hospital emergency room, the listener needs to see the bustle of activity: children crying, pained moans from patients on gurneys, sterile voices over the intercom, the smell of alcohol and disinfectant, the sense of urgency. Industrial injuries occur in workplaces that may be grimy and dirty. The air may smell of gasoline or chemicals and be filled with the sounds of heavy machinery. An auto accident can occur on a clear, bright day on a sparsely traveled road or when the sky is dark, the rain is falling, the streets are slick, and the freeway is strangling with traffic. The proper setting of a scene allows the storyteller to use the concept of verisimilitude—portraying a sense of truth. Scene setting does not have to be done in detail. Good storytellers provide just enough to permit listeners to fill in the details with their own mental images.

CREATING A MOOD

The object of scene setting for the storyteller is the creation of a mood. Tragedy has more impact when it storms out from a serene, quiet setting. But it can be born from the dark premises in a security case or the party atmosphere of a bar. The critical scene may be a quiet office or a bustling department store. The way the narrator sets the stage can elicit the whole range of human emotion, from peaceful to electric, secure to threatened.

Communicators understand the psychological phenomena associated with setting. During Ronald Reagan's second term, members of the media became concerned that the president was not addressing the country's problems. He was attending a lot of patriotic and political events—flag factories, fund-raisers, and banquets hosted by business interests. Commentator Leslie Stahl decided to do a critical report on Reagan's lack of a meaningful agenda for the country on the *CBS Evening News*. The event used to capture the president was one with a lot of red, white, and blue balloons and American flags. The day after Stahl's critical piece aired, the deputy chief of the White House staff, Michael Deaver, called Stahl to congratulate her. He was very complimentary of her televised segment. After she reviewed the show, Stahl realized that while her words were critical, the setting of balloons, flags, and patriotism had portrayed the president in a favorable light. The images had overpowered the words.

Scene setting is the storyteller's first opportunity to use some of the concepts of neurolinguistic programming (NLP). NLP teaches that seeing, hearing, and feeling are the primary sensory ways people understand the world, process information, and evaluate communication. Every person has a preferred "representational system." Visual people make pictures in their minds—they need to see to believe. Auditory people talk to themselves—they are influenced by words and sounds. Kinesthetic people think in terms of feelings—they are attuned to movement and emotions. The gifted storyteller engages all three systems during the narrative to reach every member of the audience. This is particularly critical when the narrator describes the place where the events will unfold.[2]

Storytellers use setting to create mood and give the audience a sense of direction. The setting is a way to "signpost" where the story is headed. Successful writers know they must carefully set the scene. Good storytellers take a little time to develop a setting for the action. Set the mood and the signpost, and then move on.

Use of Color

Because one of the storyteller's goals is to set a mood, some of the precepts of the visual artist may apply. The speaker is creating in the mind's eye a portrait of a time and place—a setting for the cast to act out the play. Some literary theorists postulate that the storyteller's use of color should follow the principles of the impressionist painters. Choose colors with regard to the emotional reactions associated with them. Almost two hundred years ago, Johann Wolfgang von Goethe proposed the idea that emotional reactions to colors were caused by physiological changes in the eye that brought about psychological changes in the mind.[3] Goethe believed that the color red produced a high state of energy and excitement in the viewer. Red was associated with disturbing emotions and violence. Yellow, by contrast, produced a warm and agreeable sensation unless it was contaminated by other colors, which would then provoke negative feelings of revulsion and impending calamity. Blue and green conveyed more peaceful moods. Modern researchers have extended and expanded Goethe's analysis and found that the psychology of color is a complex topic. Color preferences and emotional responses change with the variation of an individual's age, gender, and cultural background. Tints and hues of primary colors may change their meanings. A "color wheel" of psychological responses based on modern research is contained in the notes to this chapter.

One American writer particularly gifted at setting a scene was Stephen Crane. In the beginning paragraph of *The Red Badge of Courage,* he references colors five times.

> The cold passed reluctantly from the earth, and the retiring fogs revealed an army stretched out on the hills, resting. As the landscape changed from brown to green, the army awakened, and began to tremble with eagerness at the noise of rumors. It cast its eyes upon the roads, which were growing from long troughs of liquid mud to proper thoroughfares. A river, amber-tinted in the shadow of its banks, purled at the army's feet; and at night, when the stream had become of a sorrowful blackness, one could see across it the red, eye-like gleam of hostile campfires set in the low brows of distant hills.[4]

Scene setting needn't take a lot of time. Consider the opening paragraph of "An Occurrence at Owl Creek Bridge," by Ambrose Bierce:

> A man stood upon a railroad bridge in northern Alabama, looking down into the swift water twenty feet below. The man's hands were behind his back, the wrists bound with a cord. A rope closely encircled his neck. It was attached to a stout cross-timber above his head and the slack fell to the level of his knees. Some loose boards laid upon the ties supporting the rails of the railway supplied a footing for him and his executioners—two private soldiers of the Federal army, directed by a sergeant who in civil life may have been a deputy sheriff. At a short remove upon the same temporary platform was an officer in the uniform of his rank, armed. He was a captain. A sentinel at each end of the bridge stood with his rifle in the position known as "support," that is to say, vertical in front of the left shoulder, the hammer resting on the forearm thrown straight across the chest—a formal and unnatural position, enforcing an erect carriage of the body. It did not appear to be the duty of these two men to know what was occurring at the center of the bridge; they merely blockaded the two ends of the foot planking that traversed it.[5]

Courtroom storytellers often neglect to set a scene that conjures up the proper emotional backdrop for the action. Lawyers are dialogue-proficient. We tell our stories in good part by witnesses' answers to questions asked. Lawyers know to concentrate on "who did what when" but sometimes neglect the "where." Gifted storytellers begin with the "where." They set the scene and create the mood before introducing the characters and the action.

Setting Reflects on Characters and Events

Good narrators use the place—the setting—as a way to introduce characters before we meet them. Stephen King suggests that locale and texture are far more important to an audience's sense of "living" the story than any physical description of the characters.[6] A good description consists of a few details that stand for everything else. Because people look for and crave consistency, they will impute qualities to characters from the settings in which they are found. In "The Man That Corrupted Hadleyberg," Mark Twain paints an idealized portrait of a town and its inhabitants that seems too good to be true. Yet we are drawn in by the satirical description and want to know who this man who corrupts the "incorruptible town" will be:

> It was many years ago. Hadleyburg was the most honest and upright town in all the region round about. It had kept that reputation unsmirched during three generations, and was prouder of it than of any other of its possessions. It was so proud of it, and so anxious to insure its perpetuation, that it began to teach the principles of honest dealing to its babies in the cradle, and made the like teachings the staple of their culture thenceforward through all the years devoted to their education. Also, throughout the formative years temptations were

> kept out of the way of the young people, so that their honesty could have every chance to harden and solidify, and become a part of their very bone. The neighbouring towns were jealous of this honourable supremacy, and affected to sneer at Hadleyburg's pride in it and call it vanity; but all the same they were obliged to acknowledge that Hadleyburg was in reality an incorruptible town; and if pressed they would also acknowledge that the mere fact that a young man hailed from Hadleyburg was all the recommendation he needed when he went forth from his natal town to seek for responsible employment.[7]

A scene can introduce place through people. James Joyce, in the opening paragraph of "The Dead," shows how the tight, confined circumstances of the interior shapes the limited lives of the characters:

> Lily, the caretaker's daughter, was literally run off her feet. Hardly had she brought one gentleman into the little pantry behind the office on the ground floor and helped him off with his overcoat than the wheezy hall-door bell clanged again and she had to scamper along the bare hallway to let in another guest. It was well for her she had not to attend to the ladies also. But Miss Kate and Miss Julia had thought of that and had converted the bathroom upstairs into a ladies' dressing-room. Miss Kate and Miss Julia were there, gossiping and laughing and fussing, walking after each other to the head of the stairs, peering down over the banisters and calling down to Lily to ask her who had come.[8]

Or consider another Joyce passage, from *Ulysses*:

> A sterling good daughter was Gerty just like a second mother in the house, a ministering angel too with a little heart worth its weight in gold. . . . Everyone thought the world of her for her gentle ways. It was Gerty who turned off the gas at the main every night and it was Gerty who tacked up on the wall . . . the grocer's christmas almanac the picture of halcyon days where a young gentleman in the costume they used to wear then with a threecornered hat was offering a bunch of flowers to his ladylove with oldtime chivalry through her lattice window. . . . She often looked at them dreamily . . . and felt her own arms that were white and soft just like hers with the sleeves back.[9]

The storyteller needs to visualize the scene and its relation to the story. What is the essential visual component? The narrator can quickly draw the parameters of place, time, and people. How can we use the setting as a signpost? Will the setting tell the audience what is coming and why it is important? These are all important considerations for the narrator creating a word-picture setting for the action that follows.

The dichotomy of courtroom storytelling explains why setting a scene is an integral part of the opening narrative but is often omitted altogether during closing argument. The opening statement tells the story that will be told again by witnesses. The closing argument summarizes the evidence and introduces the affective theme. The goal of the courtroom storyteller in opening statement is markedly different from the goal in closing argument. Later chapters will consider how the courtroom storyteller furthers the cognitive goal of opening statement with characters, action, and theme. The affective theme or moral is a product of bringing soul to the story.

THE CRITICAL SCENE

The opening statement dramatizes one critical or pivotal scene. In a commercial case it may be the boardroom where the parties conducted negotiations that led to the agreement. The pivotal scene in a case brought as a result of a plant explosion might be the explosion itself, or it might be a meeting in the plant offices that identified a potential safety hazard some months before the explosion occurred. The advocate representing a patient in a malpractice case may determine that the critical scene is the operating room, or it may be in the hospital hallway weeks later when the patient is being rushed to a second surgery to correct the complications flowing from the first. The critical scene should be the one that gives listeners a framework they can use to predict character, action, and motive. Thus in civil cases involving personal injury damages, the pivotal scene may not necessarily be the occasion of the plaintiff's injuries.

The effective storyteller uses the subliminal technique of tweaking the listener's subconscious by referencing the essential senses—sounds, images, textures, tastes. Psychologists believe that the sense of smell is most tightly tied to the subconscious.[10] Referencing a sensation of the olfactory nerve affects attitudes, values, and judgments. The courtroom story can use this psychological principle. Consider the following business litigation case.

> Paul Arnold, the head of ClickTek's software development section, resigned from the company. He was the key employee developing the new manufacturing business software package that would replace "Data on Time." One month later, Computer Geniuses Corporation appointed Mr. Arnold Senior Vice-President of Software. The company provided him with a number of stock options that would be valuable if the company's stock substantially increased in price. Computer Geniuses Corporation took the industry by surprise three months later when it released a software package that represented a significant technological advance over both ClikTek's program and the preexisting Computer Geniuses Corporation software. The product took the market by storm, and almost overnight Mr. Arnold's stock options were worth several million dollars. ClickTek purchased a copy of the "Instant Inventory" prototype, be-

> gan analyzing the software codes, and determined that they were eerily similar to those of the prototype Mr. Arnold had been designing for their company.
>
> In April 2000, the president of ClickTek ran into a former top software engineer at Computer Geniuses Corporation who, after a couple of drinks, told him that when Arnold showed up at their company, it was many months away from developing any type of upgrade. The company was stunned at how much progress they made, especially since Arnold insisted on doing most of the work himself and would often do it after hours and on weekends.

What would be the critical scene for the courtroom storyteller? How could smell be referenced in a way that ties in with Arnold's deceitful conduct? Consider the following as part of the opening statement:

> The building in the business park on the west side of Austin is one of a smattering of modern buildings. The gleaming towers are dark this night. The sky is moonless, the clouds slowly float overhead in the evening breeze. The only light comes from the halogens mounted atop the poles along the ground-level parking area. Standing at street level, we see the custodian carrying out the black plastic bags filled with the day's refuse. The air has the sour-sweet smell of decaying sandwiches and donuts—leftovers of a hectic day. A rat scampers out of the dumpster as the custodian tosses in the big black bundles.
>
> We can look up and see that the offices of Computer Geniuses Corporation are dark. Everyone has gone home. But if we look carefully, we see a figure in one of the offices. The parking lot lights through the window cast his shadow against the wall. Software designer Paul Arnold works over his computer. Maybe he is thinking about the green Computer Geniuses Corporation paycheck in his pocket that is twice what he made before at Computer Geniuses Corporation's rival, ClickTek. Maybe he is thinking of stock options that could make him a millionaire many times over when his software program is sold by the company.
>
> If we look over on Mr. Arnold's desk we see, off to the side, issues of *Field & Stream* and *Ammo* magazines. The people who work at the company say that this is what he does during normal work hours—read these magazines. Mr. Arnold doesn't work during the day. Too many witnesses—too many questions.
>
> But now that is not a problem. The offices are silent, deserted. Everyone else has gone home. But not Paul Arnold. This is when his real work begins. The work he can do without any witnesses. The work he can do after he unlocks his safe and pulls out his worksheets on a business software called "Instant Inventory." A software that he

> started and nearly finished when he was working for ClickTek. A software he took with him when he quit ClickTek to double his salary at Computer Geniuses Corporation. A software that could make Paul Arnold a multimillionaire from stock options he will be granted from the people he now works for—Computer Geniuses.

Testimonial Scene Setting

The opening-statement canvas, limited by time and attention, does not allow counsel to paint all scenes relevant to the trial story. Testimony is the panorama that allows witnesses to expand on the places critical to their role in the story.

An anxious husband sits in a small lounge adjacent to the intensive care unit. Family friends and relatives are waiting with him to hear from the neurologist called to evaluate the wife who arrested following routine back surgery. The news won't be good. How does the trial lawyer best enable the witness to bring the audience into the place, understand the fear and uncertainty, feel the punch in the gut when the doctor says, "Your wife is brain damaged. It is probably irreversible"?

Creating a vivid and graphic scene is critical to courtroom storytelling by witnesses. Plaintiffs and lay witnesses may testify about the place an accident occurred, a doctor's visit in the hospital, or an experience with the decedent or injured person. The plaintiff is suing her employer for sexual harassment. One of the relevant incidents occurred at an after-hours company function at one of the corporate executive's homes. Amidst the casual social event, people laughing, glasses tinkling, music playing, the plaintiff's supervisor pulls her off to the side and makes offensive, inappropriate, ribald remarks that conclude with sexual propositioning. The full impact of the incident will be felt by the audience only if the plaintiff, the storyteller, vividly describes the venue—the luxurious mansion, the shop talk, the atmosphere of socializing under the umbrella of corporate sponsorship. The witness creates a setting consistent with the vulnerability she felt in the presence of her superiors. How does the trial lawyer enable the witness to revisit this painful experience?

The courtroom storyteller can use the concepts of psychodrama developed by Jacob Moreno in the early 1900s.[11] At its most basic, psychodrama is role playing. This psychological technique has been used by therapists to treat patients, by actors to prepare for movie roles, and by lawyers to succeed in trial. The use of psychodrama emphasizes the following precepts of courtroom storytelling:

- The average trial lawyer focuses on the facts that reveal *what happened.*

- The better trial lawyer includes additional facts that describe *why it happened.*

- The exceptional trial lawyer develops *how it was experienced* by the characters.

Psychodrama techniques can be used in direct examination, cross-examination, opening statement, and closing argument. Chapter 26 illustrates the use of psychodrama in an opening statement by placing jurors in the cab of an eighteen-wheeler. Chapters 28 and 29 show the technique of role playing by suggesting that jurors stand beside a nurse attending a laboring mother and beside a pathologist interpreting a biopsy.

Psychodrama is a particularly effective technique to bring to the direct examination of an injured plaintiff or grieving survivor in a wrongful death case. An excellent example of this comes from a trial in Wyoming in June 2001 that resulted in a multi-million-dollar verdict against the manufacturers of the antidepressant drug Paxil. The plaintiffs claimed that the drug was the proximate cause of four tragic deaths. The decedent had taken the drug for two days before he shot and killed his wife, his daughter, and granddaughter, and then turned the gun on himself. Penny Durant was the grandmother of Alyssa, the nine-month-old granddaughter. Her testimony went like this:

A: Well, for the both of them I think, this being a first child, they were both—they had specific ideas about how she was going to be raised and what they were going to do and how she was going to eat and how things were going to be cleaned and, you know, it is the first child and you do that. You want to be particularly careful. Tim would spend a lot of time with Alyssa. When we were there it was, I guess, one of my proudest moments of my son seeing him relate to his daughter this way. He loved her very much. Their house was multi-level. You walked in the front door and went upstairs to the living room and kitchen and downstairs to the family room and garage area.

Q: Let me take you there. Can we do that?

A: Yes, I'm sorry.

Q: Because I would like to hear some detail about this. You describe that you go to this house and there's kind of—is it bi-level?

A: Yes.

Q: So you can go upstairs into the living area or downstairs?

A: Yes.

Q: And you've been there yourself?

A: Yes.

Q: So take us there. Take us to the top of the stairs, if you would, because where we're going to go here is something that you've already told me that we're going to relate to the Court and the jury about something that you saw, an interaction between Tim and Alyssa, correct?

A: Yes.

Q: So you're there at the house, you're at the top of the stairs. What do you see?

A: Well, Tim was downstairs.

Q: I know, but—

A: And I'm going downstairs.

Q: What are you seeing?

A: I'm seeing my son sitting in a green rocking chair.

Q: All right. The green rocking chair is in a room down in this basement?

A: It is in the den or family room.

Q: And is that a room you have to open the door to go into?

A: No, there was no door.

Q: There's a landing—

A: You walk downstairs and turn to the right and you're in the room.

Q: So we see—you see Tim, we see Tim there in the chair. He's in this green chair, right?

A: Yes.

Q: What's the texture of that chair?

A: The chair was a green plush velour, kind of alternating green and a green pattern. Very soft chair. And it was a rocking chair.

Q: How was this room lit?

A: It has windows along the one side that look out on the front yard and so there's a lot of soft light that comes into that room. It has not got a lot of direct light. It is very soft lighting, more ambient lighting, very warm in that room.

Q: Is this chair a rocking chair?

A: Yes, it is.

Q: Who do you see in the chair?

A: Tim and Alyssa.

Q: And what do you see? Is she on his lap? What is it?

A: Well, he's holding her. He's rocking her to sleep. She's had a fitful time. And he's rocking her to sleep. And she's just very quietly laying against his shoulder and he's holding her.

Q: Is he patting her?

A: No, he's just holding her. She's started to fall asleep so he's just rocking her and holding her very quietly.

Q: Do you see love there?

A: I would say the purest kind of love you will ever see between a parent and a child.

Q: And this is the child that we see [in photograph] 48?

A: Yes.

Q: You know, I think we've got the picture.[12]

Only by reliving, going back in time and place can a witness bring a scene to life.

The lawyer is the facilitator who assists (and insists) that the witness "see" the place again and describe it as though she were there. This is accomplished by introductory phrases like—

> Can you see [the place]?
>
> Is there any one color you can associate with the place?
>
> What is the first thing you see? [Describe its shape, color, feel.]
>
> Who else is there? [Describe how they are dressed, their demeanor, actions and interactions, mood, and so forth.]
>
> What is the weather like, or the lighting of the conference room, office, or residence?
>
> Can you smell anything?
>
> What is the first sound you hear?
>
> What are you feeling?

After the witness fully sets the scene, the action or dialogue can follow. The use of psychodrama allows the witness to create a vivid portrait of a place in which she will sketch the details of what was said, done, and felt. Through this technique the witness becomes a powerful and persuasive narrator of her part of the trial story.

Set the scene in a way that appeals to the listener's primary sensory system. Visual components are important, but not all of the audience will be primarily visual. Reference the sounds of the setting to engage the auditory sense. Appeal to the olfactory sense by describing things in the setting with which the listener will associate a scent, fragrance, or odor. Appeal to the kinesthetic with a scene that creates mood. In short, don't neglect to set the table before serving the meal.

5

Developing Strong Characters

THEY SAY A PICTURE IS worth a thousand words. Maybe so. But when it comes to people, the axiom can be a canard, a misconception, a fiction.

A photograph of Prim Gupta would tell us he was a dark-skinned, middle-aged man with coal-black hair and a short, slight stature. His round face flashed a broad, friendly smile. Those who knew him tell us Prim was born with that smile. The faculty members at the Houston Community College where Prim taught mathematics must have wondered what he had discovered that produced his perpetual happiness. A photograph wouldn't tell us that his gentle and friendly demeanor made him a favorite of his students. Professor Gupta's office door was always open. That's the way type B personalities work. He was always available. His students knew this; that is why an afternoon passerby would find Prim hunched behind his desk working out a mathematical problem on his calculator or tutoring one of his students. No, a snapshot wouldn't tell us how revered this humble man from India was by his disciples, graduates who had gone on to successful careers in science and business, or by his academic colleagues, who knew he would always accept the most difficult committee assignments, or by his students, whose questions were always met with understanding and patience.

A photograph of the Gupta family home in the modest suburb on the west side of Houston would not begin to tell how close Prim was to his wife and three children. And while Prim's wife persisted in the Hindu traditions of the sari and the bindi, Prim's appearance was white-collar American—dark suit, white shirt, conservative tie. He would have it no other way. He was an American, and while his children were schooled in some of the Hindu traditions, they were raised to be a part of the mix of the American melting pot.

Three decades ago Prim came to the United States in search of the American dream. He was like your grandfather or great-grandfather or my great-great-great-grandfather. They came here in search of a better life. They committed themselves to a unique proposition, one that is not accepted in other parts of the world, particularly India: play by the rules, work hard, be responsible to your family and community—be a good citizen—and there is no limit to what you can do. Others will be fair and judge you on your merits. Here, there are no artificial castes, no invisible barriers.

No photograph could tell us these things. We would find more clues about this gentle *man if we looked in the wallet he carried in the back pocket of his trousers. Faded photographs of his wife and three children, a crumpled and yellowed certificate of U.S. citizenship, a Texas voter registration card, a Texas driver's license, two credit cards, and probably no more than $40 in cash. The evidence we would find inside the worn and beaten brown leather would tell us things we can't see in a photograph. They would say, "I'm proud to be an American."*

When Prim traveled those thousands of miles in the 1960s to his new homeland, when he studied the long hours to master the idioms of American English, when he wrote out his check to pay his taxes, while he studiously obeyed our laws to the point that he never got so much as a parking ticket, Prim could never know that his American dream would be bludgeoned, battered, and strangled by men speaking in soft voices thousands of miles away.[1]

I used Prim Gupta's story in a number of speeches during the debate that raged in 1996 and 1997 that led to the Texas legislature's being the first to enact a law permitting patients of managed-care corporations to sue when they had been denied needed medical benefits. Advocates of the legislation could quote facts, opponents used a lot of statistics, but I found that Prim's story was more persuasive in arguing for managed-care accountability than all the facts, statistics, and scientific data that others brought to the debate.

THE CONSISTENT PERSONALITY

A good story has strong characters. Character and story are interdependent. One drives the other. In the hero's journey, the hero and the journey are one.[2] Storytellers create memorable characters by creating in the listener's mind not only a picture of the way the person appears but also a personality that will be motivated and act the way similar persons behave. Audiences crave consistency. When producers and directors cast movies and plays, they look for someone whose physical characteristics support the character's persona. Storytellers understand that the listener judges and predicts actions from personality. If the narrator intends to create empathy for a protagonist, she must engraft on the character subtleties in scene and physical appearance from which the listener can infer laudable qualities of personality and behavior. The protagonist in Herman Melville's classic novel *Moby-Dick* introduces himself in the very first sentence. Notice how Melville creates a thoroughly consistent character in just one paragraph.

> Call me Ishmael. Some years ago—never mind how long precisely—having little or no money in my purse, and nothing particular to interest me on shore, I thought I would sail about a little and see the

> watery part of the world. It is a way I have of driving off the spleen and regulating the circulation. Whenever I find myself growing grim about the mouth; whenever it is a damp, drizzly November in my soul; whenever I find myself involuntarily pausing before coffin warehouses, and bringing up the rear of every funeral I meet; and especially whenever my hypos get such an upper hand of me, that it requires a strong moral principle to prevent me from deliberately stepping into the street, and methodically knocking people's hats off—then, I account it high time to get to sea as soon as I can.[3]

Charles Dickens's *Hard Times* may be the archetypal Dickens novel. Its protagonist, Thomas Gradgrind, lives with his family in the imaginary industrial city of Coketown. He is obsessed with misguided "Utilitarian" values. The author causes the reader to project qualities onto Gradgrind: no-nonsense, practical, trusting more in dry facts and statistics than in intuition and emotion. Gradgrind forces this same unnatural way of life on his own family, to the detriment of his children's lives, though he eventually comes to see the errors of a life lived without imagination.

> Thomas Gradgrind, sir. A man of realities. A man of facts and calculations. A man who proceeds upon the principle that two and two are four, and nothing over, and who is not to be talked into allowing for anything over. Thomas Gradgrind, sir—peremptorily Thomas —Thomas Gradgrind. With a rule and a pair of scales, and the multiplication table always in his pocket, sir, ready to weigh and measure any parcel of human nature, and tell you exactly what it comes to. It is a mere question of figures, a case of simple arithmetic. You might hope to get some other nonsensical belief into the head of George Gradgrind, or Augustus Gradgrind, or John Gradgrind, or Joseph Gradgrind (all supposititious, non-existent persons), but into the head of Thomas Gradgrind—no, sir![4]

The storyteller uses the same principle in creating in the audience's mind the role of the antagonist. While the following example is an oversimplified exaggeration, consider how John Grisham pens a character with whom no reader could identify.

> The shoes were shark, and the vanilla silks ran all the way to the kneecaps where they finally stopped and caressed the rather hairy calves of Barry Muldanno. . . . The dark green suit had a shine to it and appeared at first glance to be lizard or iguana or some other slimy reptile, but upon closer look it was not animal at all but polyester. Double-breasted with buttons all over the front. It hung handsomely on his well-built frame. And it rippled nicely as he strutted to the pay phone in the rear of the restaurant. The suit was not gaudy, just flashy. He could pass for a well-dressed drug importer or perhaps a

> hot Vegas bookie, and that was fine because he was The Blade and he expected people to notice, and when they looked at him they were supposed to see success. They were supposed to gawk in fear and get out of his way.
>
> The hair was black and full, colored to hide a bit of gray, slicked down, laden with gel, pulled back fiercely and gathered into a perfect little ponytail that arched downward and touched precisely at the top of the dark green polyester jacket. Hours were spent on the hair. The obligatory diamond earring sparkled from the proper left lobe. A tasteful gold bracelet clung to the left wrist just below the diamond Rolex, and on his right wrist another tasteful gold chain rattled softly as he strutted.[5]

Grisham's Barry Muldanno in *The Client* hasn't done anything, hasn't hurt anyone. But after this description the audience will presume the worst. Here is a man capable of any evil that the storyteller calls on us to imagine. The reader predicts future conduct and probable action from the character's physical appearance and surroundings.

Sometimes character development is not essential to the story. If the story is an anecdote to illustrate a point, any in-depth character development will bog down the story so that it loses its impact. What happened—the action—is the essence of short stories, vignettes, and anecdotes that speakers, lecturers, and pastors use to make a point. The characters may be relatively insignificant to the lesson.

THE IMPORTANCE OF CHARACTER

In the courtroom, character may be king. If a lawsuit is a competition of stories, it is even more so a competition of characters. Trial lawyers don't need to give a physical description of their characters. The jury will see them. But the narrative needs to tell what the person is—the kind of human being that is before them. Studies demonstrate that the way the jury views the plaintiff may be pivotal to its verdict. People help those they admire and respect. There is little compunction in closing the door of justice in the face of someone viewed as unworthy, unreliable, or dishonest.

For the litigator, the lesson is to make sure the story is about people, not facts. Writer Orson Scott Card has identified several likeable character types.[6] Here are a few.

- *Characters who experience unavoidable misfortune through no fault of their own*

Compelling stories come from protagonists who are decent, compassionate human beings but who are victimized and brought down by the actions of others. In the movie *The Verdict,* Frank Galvin's legal career goes on the skids when he is a victim of wrongdoing by one of the senior partners in his firm. Classic literature gives us Jean

Valjean in *Les Misérables,* a man whose strength and ability to change save him from his misfortune and relentless malicious persecution. History is filled with such stories. Legendary filmmaker Steven Spielberg selected one of the most memorable for *Amistad.* Plaintiffs in personal injury actions inherently represent men and women suffering and surviving through tragedy and misfortune occasioned by the acts of others.

- *Characters who attempt to save other characters*

Audiences can admire saviors for their sense of responsibility for others, even if the rescue fails. Ethan Edwards, John Wayne's character in *The Searchers,* is a brooding Confederate veteran who presents few redeeming qualities, but his relentless pursuit of his niece's kidnappers draws the audience to him.

- *Characters who make sacrifices, doing the right thing at the expense of personal gain*

Whistleblowers like Jeffrey Wigand in the movie *The Insider* exemplify stories of people driven by laudable motives going up against a ruthless adversary. Even lawyers can be protagonists who lose something when they do the right or noble thing. Attorney Fred Gailey in *Miracle on 34th Street* gives up his career at a law firm to represent Kris Kringle and help restore people's belief in the spirit of Christmas.

- *Characters who are dependable*

They keep their word; they do not let others down. These are men described as "the one I would want to have with me in a foxhole" or a woman exemplified in the country-and-western song, "Stand by Your Man." The classic 1986 coming-of-age movie *Stand by Me* illustrates that the quality of dependability carries with it a component of courage. In 2003, the American Film Institute named the fifty top heroes and fifty top villains of American movies. The number one, the greatest of heroes in the tens of thousands of movies, was none other than Atticus Finch of *To Kill a Mockingbird.* We all have our own reasons for admiring this Southern lawyer who fought bigotry and prejudice while trying to save an innocent black man. We must note, however, that Atticus represents all the admirable character types: an unfortunate (widowed and raising two small children) savior who sacrifices by being dependable and courageous.

As for what makes a character unlikeable, obviously someone who causes others pain, a sadist or bully, will not win much audience sympathy. But as Orson Scott Card observes, there are some less obvious characteristics that also have a negative effect.

- *Characters who are self-serving or self-important*

People who have inflated and unrealistic views of themselves, are self-indulgent and obsessed with their own welfare, not only are not admirable, they are offensive. The Joan Crawford character in *Mommie Dearest* and Mrs. John Iselin in *The Manchurian Candidate* are two fictional examples. In the courtroom, this quality is sometimes found in medical and scientific experts. Counsel must caution those who possess these traits against projecting them from the witness stand.

- *Characters who gain wealth and position at the expense of others*

The classic example all of us remember is Mr. Potter in *It's a Wonderful Life*. Potter's greed almost destroys George Bailey, an extraordinarily decent, self-sacrificing man.

- *Characters who betray a trust or fail to keep promises*

Sometimes these are people who follow the Machiavellian principle that "a prince never lacks legitimate reasons to break his promise." Goneril, King Lear's selfish, ruthless daughter, professes her love for him to gain part of the kingdom. Once Lear trusts her, she shirks her obligations. Oftentimes the breech of a trust or failure to keep a promise is at the heart of a civil lawsuit. It has been said that lawyers would have a hard time making a living if people behaved themselves and kept their promises.

- *Characters who are intelligent, educated, and condescending*

Book learning is distrusted as out of touch with common sense or knowledge gained through hands-on experience, especially when coupled with a DIA (Doctorate in Arrogance).

- *Characters who blame others, whine and complain, or take all the credit*

We recognize these instantly as characters who are childish, self-centered, and not to be trusted.

CARING ABOUT THE CHARACTER

Dramatists recognize the importance of character development. Barnaby Conrad, in *The Complete Guide to Writing Fiction*, uses a story to illustrate that even in a dramatic setting action may not be the most critical aspect of the story. The noted film director Budd Boetticher had invited a famous producer to view the first version of a new film. On the screen appeared a speeding car at the top of a steep hill. The automobile careened around one curve after another and finally went screaming off the edge of a cliff to crash and explode on the rocks a hundred feet below.

The lights in the room came on. One of the audience commented: "Isn't that the greatest opening of a film ever?" The producer puffed on a cigar for a moment and then asked: "Who's in the car?"[7]

A good story makes the listener care for the characters. Writers of fiction avoid boring characters. Boring characters are people who whine and complain too much. Boring characters feel sorry for themselves. Boring characters are passive; they just let things happen to them. An interesting character doesn't have to be well-educated but must think interesting thoughts. Interesting characters are resourceful. They fight back against difficult situations. Santiago, in Hemingway's *The Old Man and The Sea,* didn't prevail against the sharks, but he fought back. Robin Hood was arrested by the sheriff, but he escaped. Regardless of the consequences and against great odds, Tom Hanks's Captain John Miller in *Saving Private Ryan* carried out his orders. Persuasive narrators know that a good story begins with interesting characters.

People commonly think of heroes as strong or brave, but these qualities are secondary to sacrifice—the true mark of a hero. Sacrifice is the hero's willingness to give up something of value, perhaps even her own life, on behalf of an ideal or a group. Heroes accept the responsibility of sacrifice. The most effective heroes are those who experience sacrifice. They may give up a loved one or friend along the way.[8]

Interesting flaws humanize a character. We can recognize bits of ourselves in a hero who is challenged to overcome inner doubts, errors in thinking, guilt or trauma from the past, or fear of the future. Heroes are often honorable men who have withdrawn from society's corruption, perhaps ex-cops or soldiers who became disillusioned and now operate in the shadow of the law as private eyes, smugglers, gamblers, or soldiers of fortune. We love these characters because they are rebels, thumbing their noses at society as we would all like to do.[9]

Developing Character in the Courtroom

Many differences separate the courtroom storyteller from the teaching, preaching, or entertaining narrator. The most notable are in the area of character development. Courtroom storytellers deal with real people whom the audience will meet when they testify. When the characters are first introduced during jury selection or opening statement, jurors begin to form impressions and expectations. The characters have to "live out" on the witness stand the picture portrayed of them in the story.

During pretrial development, experienced trial lawyers learn as much as they can about witnesses. People infer character from actions. A witness may have done things that epitomize a noble, respected quality. The affective appeal of the trial story may come from the virtues presented by one or more witnesses. The working mother who continued to concern herself with and sacrifice for her children despite her disability is an exemplar of commitment and dedication. Courage is the essence presented by the engineer willing to finger a bad product design by the corporation he worked for or the doctor willing to identify bad practices being followed by local colleagues in his specialty. A witness who tells how another was always helpful to the elderly and children, treated service people kindly, stopped on the side of the road to help stranded motorists, picked up and took wounded animals to clinics for care, paints that person as compassionate and caring. Character can be developed in the courtroom through what the witnesses tell us about themselves or what others describe. We want virtue and admirable qualities associated with our witnesses: courage, chivalry, fortitude, grace, compassion, kindness, honesty, integrity, and morality.

To the extent we can within our ethical limits, we hope to depict those who oppose us as less than admirable. The corporate executives who chose not to make a relatively inexpensive change in their product despite receiving complaints that consumers were being injured paints a vivid portrait of greed. The plant employee who in an effort to hold his job won't own up to dangerous practices, will be seen as cowardly. The professional witness who routinely testifies for the defense may be cast into the character of the unethical.

A historical example illustrates how critical in the courtroom character development can be. The trial of *Theodore Tilton v. Henry Ward Beecher,* also known as the Brooklyn Scandal, is an example of how character can drive jury determination of issues. Henry Ward Beecher was a pastor at the Plymouth Church in Brooklyn, New York, in the mid-1860s. Theodore Tilton was a young parishioner who worked for one of Beecher's newspapers, *The Independent.* Tilton accused Beecher of having an affair with his wife and filed a civil suit for alienation of affection. Tilton claimed that Beecher had violated his role as a spiritual father and seduced Elizabeth Tilton. The plaintiff's narrative attempted to cast Beecher into the traditional masculine role—that is, that Beecher took the initiative in the relationship and was responsible for the seduction. The plaintiff presented Mrs. Tilton as the epitome of innocent womanhood betrayed. The defense had a different gender role for Beecher. As a minister, Beecher embodied the characteristics that were typically associated with femininity, that he was incapable of seducing a woman. From this portrayal of character, the defense was able to construct a "plot" that Theodore Tilton and his friend, Robert Moulton, had conspired to ruin Beecher. Elizabeth Tilton had simply aided the conspiracy by signing a confession in which she admitted to an adulterous affair. The defense constructed the character of an obedient, subservient female trying to hold onto her husband by confessing to an imaginary affair. Beecher's evidence at trial included proof establishing not only his pious character but also his physical afflictions.

The trial resulted in a hung jury. While the plaintiff's case had all the elements necessary for a jury to condemn Beecher, persuasion theorists suggest that the plaintiff was deprived of a victory by the defense's reinterpreting Beecher's character and drawing another narrative from essentially the same facts relied on by the plaintiff.[10]

The Beecher story illustrates how trial lawyers have a generous opportunity to develop character and the greatest obligation to do so. How the jury views the parties determines the outcome. Trial advocates achieve the greatest success by approaching a trial as if they were directing a play. The client is the protagonist. The audience must be able to identify what the protagonist wants and what opposes him in his quest. Counsel presents the client as a real person with admirable virtues and understandable faults.

Beware of the common mistake of assuming that liking someone is the same as identifying with him. Many literary protagonists are not necessarily people that we would like to sit and have a drink with. The Macbeths, for example, were hardly Ozzie and Harriet, but most people can see a little of themselves in these Shakespearean characters. The best protagonist is someone we like and someone whom we would like to be. The goal of the trial lawyer is to develop a protagonist that the audience will be able to identify with on some level.

Courtroom storytellers introduce the characters during jury selection and in opening statement. The way the lawyer describes the characters forms impressions and expectations. If the expectations are not met, disastrous consequences may follow.

Character Flaws

In *Effective Opening Statements: The Attorney's Master Key to Courtroom Victory*, Fredric G. Levin suggests a hypothetical introduction of "Bob Jones." Before the meeting, a good friend of the stranger tells him that while Jones is loud and obnoxious on the outside, underneath Jones is one of the most kind and sincere people he will ever meet. When the stranger meets Jones he will have a totally different impression than if his friend had told him Jones is loud and obnoxious and a crook who ought to be avoided. Contrast this situation with an introduction to "Jim Smith." The friend says that Smith comes across as one of the kindest and sincerest people he will ever meet but that everyone knows him as the world's number-one con man. With an introduction like that, few people would trust Jim Smith when they met him.[11]

It's hard to predict exactly how someone will be perceived on the witness stand. Courtrooms are an unfamiliar environment for most people. Other than professional witnesses, few are comfortable at the dock. The witness stand magnifies nervous tics, unnatural mannerisms, speech idiosyncracies, and intellectual weaknesses. For this reason, character development in the courtroom includes laying out the witnesses' faults, warts, handicaps, and shortcomings. Preparation helps, but few lawyers ever have the opportunity to confirm the characters we would like to paint in our stories with flawless testimony.

Fortunately, most people can accept someone's flaws if they are presented with a reasonable explanation. Consider a worst case. The plaintiff has contradicted himself in the medical records and sworn deposition. He has a hard time looking anyone in the eye while talking to them. Despite the lawyer's best efforts, the plaintiff cannot be made to appear neat and organized. Deal with it by creating empathy and understanding. Describe the problems the plaintiff had with his social life growing up. Girls wouldn't go out with him and others broke dates, causing him to lose any confidence with the opposite sex. Tell about the problems he has had getting a job because he isn't too bright. Develop a character kicked around and abused so much that he is frightened and intimidated by everyone. Use character development to short-circuit character defects that will become apparent when the witness testifies.

THE WORTHY PROTAGONIST

Part of the way a lawyer develops his protagonist as an identifiable character is by having the witness testify about the obstacles he has overcome. The best trial story has the greatest obstacle as justice at the hands of the jury. All of us admire a winner, but we reserve a special place in our hearts for the underdog who prevails against the odds. Theirs are the stories that inspire and excite us to consider some people as heroes. Sometimes these heroic figures show such consistent ability to overcome adversity, such confidence in their ability to succeed when lesser men and women would fail, that they become legends.

I have been a faithful supporter and follower of my alma mater's football team for more than forty years. During that time, I have witnessed many victories authored by the University of Houston Cougars, but it is one of our defeats that sticks in my mind to illustrate this principle of character. On January 1, 1979, the University of Houston met Notre Dame in the Cotton Bowl, the annual postseason game held in Dallas. It is one of the coldest days to ever grip the metroplex. The windchill factor is below zero. Joe Montana is the quarterback for the Irish. Suffering from the flu, he develops hypothermia at halftime and sits out the first two offensive series of the second half. My beloved Cougars hold a commanding 34–12 lead with 7:37 remaining in the fourth quarter. We feel so assured of victory we are substituting our backups into the game. Notre Dame blocks a Cougar punt and runs it back for a touchdown. Montana connects on a two-point conversion. On their next possession, the Irish drive sixty-one yards to score, followed by another two-point conversion. With 4:15 remaining, the score is 34–28. The Irish get the ball for a final chance and drive down the field. Montana connects on an eight-yard TD pass as time runs out on the clock. The walk-on kicker makes the extra point. Notre Dame wins 35–34. The Irish victory is considered by sports experts to be one of the top ten greatest bowl games. Even Cougar fans admired Montana's heroic performance that day. Fighting illness and down by twenty-two points, he would not give up. He later became a professional football legend with similar heroic come-from-behind performances.

Books and movies celebrate those who continue to fight and win even when they seem to be down and out. The book and movie *Seabiscuit* (2003) tells the story of a racehorse no one wanted, a down-and-out jockey, and a reclusive trainer. Even though Seabiscuit lost races, he continued to compete until he beat the legendary War Admiral in a historic match race. The movie was a critical success and was followed two years later by another story of a sports hero who rose from the ashes to become a winner. *Cinderella Man* celebrates the life of James J. Braddock, who became heavyweight champion of the world during the Depression. Braddock lost a lot of fights, had to give up his children because he could not support them, but continued to compete in the world of prizefighting until he climbed to the top of the ladder.

At the height of the Cold War, the young U.S. ice hockey team faced the Soviets in the 1980 Winter Olympics. The Russian team was made up of wily veterans and was considered invincible. The American victory became known as the "miracle on ice." The next year, a TV movie dramatizing the victory aired on ABC to enthusiastic audiences.

We take into our hearts those who refuse to quit or accept failure. These are the characters that in our everyday dramas inspire us to pull for them. So it is in the courtroom.

A trial lawyer accomplishes good character development with questions that allow his client to give an abbreviated but insightful vision of her life. The witness describes her childhood in terms of her relationship to her parents, siblings, and other key people in her youth. She tells how she grew up—how she lived—how she was educated. She talks about her hobbies and interests. She tells of her current relationships to her parents, siblings, and other people in her life. The lawyer asks questions that provoke responses about the client's romantic life. Is she now married? Has she been in the past? The lawyer asks not only about the character's children but also her relationship with them. What have they done together and enjoyed?

Work adds dimension. The client describes what kinds of jobs she's held and what the work was like. She tells about her relationship to her boss and coworkers. The plaintiff talks of her feelings about her work. Eliciting testimony about the witness's philosophy of life adds yet more dimension. Does she believe "Good deeds are sometimes punished"; "Work is its own reward"; "Always tell the truth"? The witness testifies about actions she has taken that demonstrate that she does indeed follow these principles.

Toward the end of the examination, the lawyer may encourage the witness to share something about what she is proud of and what she is ashamed of. What aspect of her personality makes her vulnerable and at the same time admirable? By the end of the trial, the jurors have in their minds a three-dimensional person. They know the virtues, vulnerabilities, and circumstances of a person's life that have put her there. They identify with the struggles and challenges the client has faced in life and faces now in the courtroom. In the best of worlds, the citizens chosen to serve view the client as a deserving protagonist, someone they like and can identify with, someone they want to win.

When I speak to law students, I am often asked, "What kind of formula do you use to argue damages?" When I ask them what they mean by that question, they say it is their impression that the monetary award in a civil case is the product of some precise arithmetic calculation. What a poor way to view justice. If that were true, "fair and reasonable" would be the same for the shiftless, dishonest, and immoral as it is for the hardworking, committed, and law-abiding. There are no formulas for putting a price on the loss of a loved one or the suffering of an innocent human being. There is, however, a relationship between the way the jury views the defendant, the defendant's culpability, and the character of the plaintiff. Justice becomes clear when the contrast is sharp.

MOTIVE

Novelists know that in a good story the protagonist must have an identifiable goal. This is especially true in the trial arena. But the plaintiff's goal cannot be simply money. The plaintiff's quest may be represented by the money the plaintiff seeks, but that goal should certainly not be limited to the dollars themselves. Courtroom protagonists may be seeking security in the form of future medical care for their brain-damaged infant, financial security to provide for their family while they are disabled, or college education for their children. They may see compensation as a form of apology for wrongdoing. Money damages may be presented as society's way of insisting on civil responsibility. Whatever form money damages take, it must be seen as a worthy and desirable goal. The courtroom storyteller realizes that she is bound by the same axiom that compels the novelist or screenwriter: create a character with a worthy goal opposed by an antagonist. The conflict makes the story. In the end, the protagonist prevails and achieves his goal, to the delight of the audience.

In the world of fiction, gung-ho heroes are rare. Most heroes must be prodded, cajoled, wheedled, tempted, or shanghaied into adventure. Most heroes put up a good fight and entertain us by their efforts to escape what noted screenwriter Christopher Vogler labeled "the Call to Adventure."[12] So it is with plaintiffs. They do not want to be in court. They were reluctant to sue. If there were any way to solve their problem, restore their lives, other than by resorting to the legal system, they would have taken it. The best plaintiffs are indeed reluctant heroes.

> Sarah Walker doesn't want to be here. Thirty months ago when she left her home to go to work at Compaq, she never dreamed she'd be here in a courtroom placing her fate in the hands of twelve neighbors. That morning in July, she thought she'd put in her usual workday, get home at six, and start making dinner for her two teenage daughters. After dinner was over, she would sit down with them and help with their studies.
>
> Sarah couldn't imagine that a Dydrill truck would blow the red light and broadside her going forty miles an hour, putting her in the hospital for four weeks. A broken pelvis kept her in home traction for another six months. Still, Sarah never thought she would be here. Like most good people, she sees herself in everyone else. They will be fair with me and own up to what they did. They won't weasel out with alibis and lame excuses.
>
> Single working mothers know you work whether you feel like it or not. There are no excuses. That's why she never thought she would be sitting in this courtroom listening to the defendant's driver trying to excuse what happened with "I was in a hurry and just didn't see the light." The Sarahs of the world never shirk responsibility. Sometimes they take it when it isn't even theirs. When Melanie Lawson fouled up the project assigned her, Sarah took the blame. Mela-

nie had just started at Compaq and Sarah would not jeopardize her job. Sarah doesn't belong here listening to this defendant try to blame her and deprive her of the repayment she deserves.

An old Hebrew saying is that God made mothers because he couldn't be everywhere at the same time. It's amazing how many places mothers can be. Sarah was the leader of her daughter's Girl Scout troop. She was the parent with the least time but who gave the most. She took the girls camping, on field trips, attended all the meetings. Every Sunday, Sarah and the girls were in church. Some years she taught Sunday school. Her faith was no hypocritical exercise to her. She lived the charity of its teachings when she served every year on Compaq's United Way Fund.

Sarah doesn't want to be here. She'd rather be out taking those long hikes with the Girl Scout troop. But she can't, and it's doubtful she ever will again. She'd rather be doing the family dinners at home when she gets in from work instead of ordering out as they have to do most nights now. Sarah would rather be that good employee that never missed a day from work rather than the one that has to miss days to see her doctor or go to physical therapy.

There are a thousand places Sarah would rather be. She doesn't want to be here listening to this defendant admit it hired a driver who had four moving violations in the three years before he crashed its truck into the side of her Mercury Cougar. Sarah didn't want to be in the ambulance going to the hospital. She didn't want to be in the OR for four hours. She didn't want to be in the hospital or in therapy for all those months. All because this defendant didn't take the time to train and caution its driver.

Even when times were tough, Sarah couldn't bring herself to ask for anything from anybody else. She never asked for charity even though there were times she could have used it. Times when the girls needed clothes for a dance and she couldn't afford them. Times when they couldn't take a vacation because Sarah was trying to put away a few pennies for their college education.

The fact that Sarah doesn't want to be here doesn't mean she doesn't deserve to be here. It's the only place for her. It is the only place for her to come and say, "I am innocent, I followed our laws, paid the taxes, played by the rules, now all I ask is that you make these folks do the same. Make them pay me back for all that I have lost and will lose. Do justice, not out of sympathy, but because it is right."

Interesting characters make for a good story. We pull for good people and want them to prevail. We like to see those who lie, cheat, cut corners, or are callous get their comeuppance. We call it a tragedy when the noble and heroic fail. Unfortunately, some of the greatest tragedies are sometimes written with a jury's verdict. Successful trial lawyers develop the plaintiff's character in such a way that the jury finds it hard to close the door of justice in her face. We show a plaintiff who deserves to win the respect of the jury and their verdict. Someone whom they want to carry off the field on their shoulders, proudly raising the trophy of justice.

6

Presenting a Compelling Plot

SOME OF THE GREATEST *authors of the day were among the small group sitting around the fireplace at the Villa Diodati on the shores of Lake Leman in Switzerland in 1816. The ominous gloom, torrential rains, and foreboding lightning storms that had rushed in on the evening inspired the host to issue a challenge. The group had been reading aloud a collection of German ghost stories when the Englishman challenged his guests to tell a ghost story. Surely the young woman was intimidated. After all, she was in the presence of such great writers as her husband, Percy Shelley, and Lord Byron. Using her imagination, eighteen-year-old Mary wove a story in the traditional formula incorporating character, plot, and moral. She told the story in the first person, from the point of view of the protagonist, a man of science. He hopes the protégé he has created will be the source of a new species. Ironically, the creature evolves into a self-acknowledged Satan who swears eternal revenge and war upon his creator and all the human race. The audience in that great villa near where Rousseau and Voltaire had resided were completely absorbed by the story and emotionally spent at the end. Mary Shelley's* Frankenstein *went on to be considered the greatest Gothic Romantic novel and is today generally thought of as the first science fiction novel.*

A little less than two centuries later, a diminutive man, barely five feet tall, told a story to his professional peers. My presence on this occasion was far from the only difference between this man's story and the one told almost two hundred years earlier in a distant land. Unlike young Mary, who told her story to an audience much older than she, the narrator who addressed us that day was by far the oldest in the group, having lived almost a full century. This New Yorker, speaking to a group of fellow trial lawyers in Florida, constructed his story along the same traditional lines Mary used. His quiet voice recounted the tale of a disturbed protagonist—a man who had been charged with murder.

On a September evening in 1974, seventy-one-year-old Irving Pasternak and his wife were stabbed to death in their Waterbury, Connecticut, home. Their former son-in-law, Murray Gold, was soon indicted. Mr. Gold had no motive, and only the most tenuous circumstantial evidence linked him to the crime. At trial, the defense showed that another man, Bruce Sanford, was the most likely suspect. Sanford was an avowed Satanist with a long criminal record. Witnesses confirmed that he was covered with blood on the night of the mur-

ders. He confessed his guilt to his friends. Still, the police charged Gold and tried him for the crime. At the first trial, the jury deadlocked. Sanford then killed himself. In the second trial, the judge dismissed as "hearsay" the evidence against Sanford. Murray Gold stood convicted.

At this point Louis Nizer entered the case. Standing before this audience on a warm, sunny day in Florida, wearing his distinctive bow tie, he mesmerized his listeners with a story into which he wove details of scientific evidence, time lines, and psychological profiles. The audience was spellbound as the character of Murray Gold was developed. A sad and solitary man, racked with guilt from surviving the Holocaust, Gold seemed determined to seek his own delayed punishment by refusing to help his earlier lawyers with his defense. The climax of the story came when Nizer secured the right to a new trial through the mechanism of habeas corpus in 1991. The writ was based on psychiatric reports demonstrating that Murray Gold suffered from paranoia and schizophrenia and was not competent to assist his previous lawyers in his defense. After ten years of incarceration for a crime he probably did not commit, Murray Gold was finally freed from prison.

The storytellers in both examples took hostage their audience's attention and kept their listeners confined within the walls of their story for an hour or more. But there the similarity ends. Mary Shelley's Frankenstein *was her first effort at storytelling, while Nizer's* Catspaw *was his last. Mary captured the attention of some of the greatest writers of fiction and poetry of her day. Louis Nizer held spellbound an audience of trial lawyers. But the biggest difference is an obvious one: the story Mary Shelley told on that stormy night of June 16, 1816, was fiction—the product of her imagination—while the story Louis Nizer told on May 27, 1993, in that banquet hall in Amilia Island, Florida, was true.*[1]

The essence of any narrative, fictional or real, involves events. *Who* did *what, where, when,* and *why?* The speaker telling a story that illustrates a point usually presents a short narrative concentrating on events. The story doesn't have to be true if it makes the point. Storytelling in the courtroom is different. That is why I believe trial lawyers are the greatest storytellers. The successful trial advocate must accomplish things the Hemingways, Dickenses, and Shakespeares never attempted. We must present a story that not only is interesting, that makes sense, but that also inspires cognitive and affective judgments by our listeners. No other storyteller faces the challenges that confront the courtroom advocate.

Stories for the stage and screen can succeed when they do little more than develop and explain characters. Interesting characters can carry a story that entertains. *On Golden Pond* and *My Dinner with André* were character-driven stories. On the other hand, the movies of Arnold Schwarzenegger and Sylvester Stallone don't normally involve much character development. The strong plot with lots of action and intrigue is what captures the audience and makes the story interesting.

Plot Formula

Novelists and screenwriters use plot to convey the events of the story and theme to bring meaning to those events. Aristotle maintained that a plot must have unity—that is, each action should initiate the next rather than stand alone without connection to what comes before or after. The traditional formula initially places characters in conflict or entanglement, builds suspense through rising action, crisis, and climax, and finally winds toward resolution through falling action. Writers of fiction devise plots designed to manipulate, entertain, move, and surprise the audience. Screenwriters have great license to do this in almost any imaginable manner. They might run the hero up a tree, throw rocks at him, make him fall, and then bring him back at the end. They enjoy the liberty of fiction in creating characters, events, and outcomes. Screenwriters live by the apothegm that drama is life with the dull parts taken out and have the freedom to create the drama by whatever means they choose.

Courtroom storytellers have no fictional liberty. They must tell the story their clients bring them. Mark Twain, who worked as a newspaper reporter under his real name, Samuel Clemens, was once asked whether it was harder to write true stories or fiction. He replied that it was harder to tell a true story persuasively, because "fiction is obliged to stick to possibilities. Truth isn't."[2]

Sometimes, real people with real problems present their advocates with a story no more compelling than "bad things happen to good people." The challenge is to put the facts together into a story that will move the audience and inspire justice. The additional burden is to bring the evidence together in a way that supports an identifiable legal theory. Trial advocates must take facts that are already written by the time they hear them, put them in the context of legal concepts, and then bring drama to the story. The courtroom narrative can create strong characters with a compelling plot and yet fail in its goal of instructing and motivating the listeners in their final judgments. Trial plots not only must involve action; they must also carry a message.

Many trial lawyers approach storytelling, particularly in the opening statement, in one of two ways. Some advocates adopt anticipated legal concepts even to the point of using a PowerPoint display of presumed legal instructions to structure their narrative. There are several problems with this approach. First, it inherently takes the narrator out of the story concept that paints pictures of places, characters, events, and theme. More importantly, it presumes that jurors think inductively, like lawyers. The ordinary citizen is not familiar with and may be uncomfortable reasoning from general propositions to specifics. Most people cannot accept a new proposition unless it is a natural extension of one they already hold. This approach to courtroom storytelling, while it may fit with the way the lawyer learned in law school, is not apt to begin the persuasive process by creating a compelling image of what the case is about.

Some lawyers use a different approach. They adopt the essential story framework and present a narrative that is basically "Nice guy, this is how he got hurt, this is why the defendant is liable, these are the damages." The problem with this approach is that it does not use all the persuasive elements of storytelling. A persuasive story has some of all the critical elements—strong beginning, scene setting, character development, plot, theme, and moral.

A trial involves competing scripts or stories. During deliberations, jurors arrive at a schematic consensus, ultimately deciding which story is believable. The story leads to a result. The script writes the verdict.

A good trial story telegraphs critical events. It leaves the listeners with no doubt that the defendant's actions caused the plaintiff's injuries. The talented courthouse scriptwriter crafts a story with characters, actions, and motives leading up to the plaintiff's injuries. It is at this point in the narrative that counsel can say, "Do I have to tell you what happened next?" She doesn't need to, because the audience already knows. Even though the audience knows what is going to follow, the plot is strengthened by the phrase, "Do I have to tell you what happened next?" because it tells the listeners that the results, the tragedy, will be as bad as they are now imagining. Counsel constructs the story in a way that the jury foresees a tragic ending just as the defendants should have foreseen the risks of their conduct.

Advocates know sequence is significant in telling the story through narration and testimony. The most logical way to structure a story is to narrate in chronological order using the same point of view, detailing the events as they occurred. This method, however, may not be the most effective way to construct a trial plot. Simply recounting the facts in chronological order may rob the story of some of its power and suspense. This lack of suspense, or failure to keep the jury's attention, may lull the audience into a sense of indifference. One way to solve the problem is to flip back and forth like a movie director.

The plaintiff's supervisor at work repeatedly subjects her to sexual harassment. In frustration, she finally quits her job and files suit. The trial story would include the plaintiff's personal and employment history before she went to work at the company, the hiring by the defendant, her work on the job, the incidents of lascivious and overbearing behavior, her complaints to the company supervisors, their failure to act, the psychological problems the employee experienced, quitting the job, and the problems the plaintiff now experiences. These are the essential facts and milestones in chronological order. But the narrator enlivens the story by using flashbacks or fast-forwards. She might begin by sketching out the company's adopting inadequate policies to control the work environment, how these led to ignoring complaints from other employees about vexing actions and remarks by the supervisor. Then the narrator would flash back to the plaintiff's moral and religious upbringing and how she had worked hard at other companies with no problem. When the defendant hired her, she was excited about her new job. When she started work, she had no problems, was a good employee, was always prompt and dependable. Counsel would then contrast how troubled the victim is today, then flash back to the incidents of harassment. Deviating from the strict chronological order of events brings energy and curiosity to the story.

Rearranging the chronology is only one way to vary sequence. Another is to change the point of view.

An abdominal aneurysm is diagnosed in a middle-aged man. As a result of surgical mistakes, he bleeds to death on the operating table. The story could be told from the same point of view, outlining the events of surgery. But power is brought to the story by flipping back and forth at intervals, describing on one hand what is happening at surgery and, on the other, the man's wife and daughter anxiously sitting in the waiting room down the hall.

Introduce the Antagonist First

One of the most important decisions the trial narrator makes is where to begin the story. Studies show that a trial's outcome is influenced by the way counsel tells the story and presents the proof. [3] Sometimes the strongest plaintiff's story develops the antagonist's character and unjust motive before the jury hears anything about the protagonist at all.

In a products liability case, the plaintiff must prove how the dangerous product was conceived, how tests or literature warned of the potential for danger. The evidence must show how the manufacturer decided to market the product despite known dangers and how the company knew that the product was injuring consumers but continued to keep it on the market. It is only in the second act that the storyteller introduces the protagonist, who buys and uses the product. The jury foresees the devastating injury before the plaintiff's story is told. The more tragic the consequences, the more likely will a jury perceive the defendant as negligent.

One of my favorite John Wayne movies is *Big Jake*. The story presents the antagonists first and introduces them one by one to the audience. They raid the McCandles ranch, shoot the men and women who work there, kidnap a boy, make a ransom demand, and are off to Mexico before the audience sees (let alone gets to know) the character of Big Jake. By the time they do, everyone is pulling for Jacob McCandles to rescue his grandson and get the bad guys—to prevail.

Courtroom storytellers should consider leading off with the antagonist, depicting its actions and motives first. If this is done well, the audience will sense the way the story is going even though they see the antagonist's part first. Lawyers representing the injured must not forget that it is the defendant that is on trial. The issue is the defendant's actions. The defendant's responsibility.

Subplots

Cognitive Subplotting

In the world of fiction, authors use subplots to connect minor characters and tangential events to the main story. The novelist's subplot may be used to explain motivation or define character. Every trial has subplots, but these are defined much differently than in the world of fiction. Trial subplots are the judgments that juries are called on to make about the story. A brief reference to the field of psychology serves to explain the role of a cognitive subplot in the courtroom narrative. Because the goal is to have the listener make judgments of culpability and monetary recovery, the presentation takes into account that decision making depends on the personalities of those sitting in judgment. Psychological profiling is a complex task, but most people can be identified as either cognitive or affective personalities. The cognitive person makes decisions primarily on the basis of reason, whereas the affective person's decisions are usually dominated by feelings. Cognitive thinkers are very orderly in their daily lives, processing information by tending to detailed facts and reasoning inductively. In contrast, the affective personality might be considered impulsive. Affective thinkers base decisions on selective perception of the information presented, which they reformulate and shape to fit their previously held views of how they feel about something. They are often influenced by religious or moral principles and their sense of what is right, fair, and just.

The trial lawyer's audience—the jury—makes both cognitive and affective judgments. Cognitive judgments are logical conclusions drawn from specific facts. Affective judgments inspire the result. Questions of negligence, proximate cause, fraud, and damages make up the cognitive subplot in a personal injury case. The jury may see the characters as the plaintiff wants them seen, believe the events occurred as he says they did, and yet fail to find legal culpability. Trial advocates use the concept of subplot to support the desired cognitive judgment.

While driving in a heavy rainstorm, a truck driver loses control of his eighteen-wheeler and crashes into a passenger car coming in the opposite direction. The man and his wife in the car are killed. Was the driver of the truck at fault, or was this "an accident" that could happen to the best of us? A young child complains of headaches and poor vision. An ophthalmologist sees him several times and prescribes glasses. The child ends up blind because a tumor on the optic nerve is not timely diagnosed and treated. Do we blame the ophthalmologist? The parents? Is this just a medical complication that could not have been prevented by ordinary care? The cognitive subplot resolves these issues in favor of the desired culpability.

The number of judgmental subplots expands exponentially in cases involving multiple defendants. Different evidence and reasons support the liability of each defendant. But neglect the subplots, and no matter how well the advocate tells the story he cannot drive the audience to the cognitive determinations necessary for a favorable verdict.

Logical analysis produces cognitive courtroom subplots. Often they come from basic propositions to which any fair person must agree. It was once said of Daniel Webster that you should be careful when you agree to his first (usually innocuous) proposition, for once you did, he had won the argument. From that principle he would logically build others that made you accept the proposition he was advocating.

A high-pressure gauge used in oil-field operations explodes. The glass fragments from the face of the gauge seriously injure the plaintiff. He sues the manufacturer of the gauge because it failed to use safety glass on the gauge.

The cognitive subplot for the manufacturer might be—

- the designer of an industrial appliance should take into account the environment where it will be used;

- it should take into account how it will be used;
- Benton Corporation designs a gauge intended to be used in the oil field with high pressures;
- some drilling operations may result in pressures greater than the gauge's capacity;
- if this occurs, the gauge could blow out the face;
- the use of safety glass in the face could significantly reduce the risk of harm to users;
- safety glass was available and would have added little to the cost;
- Benton Corporation decided to save the cost of using safety glass;
- high pressures caused the gauge to explode;
- the shattering face propelled glass into the plaintiff's eye, causing him to lose it.

Plaintiff's counsel develops the cognitive subplot during the direct and cross-examination of witnesses. Some witnesses may not be knowledgeable or qualified to testify on some of the propositions. For example, the plaintiff's coworkers might affirm the fourth through sixth and ninth and tenth propositions. Counsel might qualify the manufacturer's representatives and plaintiff's experts on all ten.

Trial advocates consider the propositions they can suggest with which any reasonable witness must agree. They use those propositions in their opening statement and examination of each expert. They place themselves in a position where they can put those propositions up at the end of trial during closing argument. Basic premises naturally flow from one proposition to the next and lead to the cognitive conclusion that the plaintiff needs to support culpability.

Commission vs. Omission

While negligence may consist of omission or commission, the more compelling case is based on commission—the defendant did something wrong. The defendant didn't *fail* to do something. It *did* something, and it was wrong. The defendant made choices, took risks, and decided on a course of conduct. In constructing a trial plot, the courtroom storyteller focuses on conscious decisions and actions taken by the defendant.

Choice Subplots

Juries decide questions that are in part scientific debates. But they must not only resolve the conflict presented by complex testimony; they must also apply the scientific proof to the facts of the case. The issue in a negligence case is whether the actions met the legal standard of "ordinary care." Defendants emphasize the "ordinary." Plaintiffs stress the "care." One way of putting the issues in perspective uses the subplot of "choice."

Mark is a healthy, forty-year-old man who develops pain in his right shoulder. He consults an orthopedist, who recommends an outpatient arthroscopic procedure. The surgeon advises that the procedure be carried out in a small outpatient facility—a hospital specializing in day surgery. On the day of surgery, Mark meets the M.D. anesthesiologist, who introduces herself as "the person who will be giving you anesthesia." After Mark is intubated, the anesthesiologist leaves the anesthesia administration to one of the nurse anesthetists who works part-time at the hospital. She has problems ventilating the patient and does not document the problems that develop. The patient arrests, and the M.D. anesthesiologist is called back to the operating room. Mark is resuscitated but never regains consciousness and dies two weeks later. A subplot based on choice could be presented showing the multiple choices made by the defendants (which anesthesia drugs to use, how to intubate, who would do the intubation, how to supervise, how to monitor, what equipment to be used, and so forth) as opposed to the plaintiff (who chose his surgeon). This approach to subplot reinforces the idea that because the patient made few choices and was in fact denied some and the defendants made many wrong ones, the defendants are culpable.

Risk Subplots

Another subplot structure involves an analysis of risk. The story is presented in terms of what the risks were and who knew them. But the narrator must be careful in structuring this approach. The advocate who raises too much anxiety in the listener can be flirting with disaster. Placing too much emphasis on the negative, dangerous aspects of an industrial environment, product use, or medical care can produce the psychological effect of disassociation. The average citizen does not want to believe that where people work or get medical care is fraught with peril. A good subplot emphasizes that the defense's conduct clearly violated the norm. Most people drive safely. Most product manufacturers make safe products. Most medical professionals practice good, safe medicine. If the defendant had done what he should have done, this never would have happened—we wouldn't be here.

Jurors are problem solvers. They want to be a part of the solution. If they sense that their verdict will have a negative effect on the parties or society, they will resist all calls for a plaintiff's verdict. Many years ago, I had a case against a wealthy West Texas family who operated several ranches. One of the ranch foremen had put his young son on a horse named "Crowbar." The colt was wild, unbroken, and the young boy was thrown. He landed on his head and was in a coma for the rest of his life. One of the problems in trying the case was the attitude that, "If we find against the cattle company, young boys won't have anybody willing to hire them and train them to be cowboys." We dealt with the problem using a "risk versus reward" subplot.

- People who work as cowboys on large ranches are exposed to some risk of injury;
- a large, successful cattle operation can bring large rewards;
- the financial rewards of cattle raising are never shared with working cowboys;
- the cowboys take all the risks;
- the ranch owner realizes all the rewards.

The idea that the defendant gets all the benefits of the plaintiff's hazardous undertaking rings unfair in the ears of many. It can trump the antagonism that sometimes sponsors defense verdicts.

The plaintiff's subplots must also carry the message that damages sought will truly benefit the victim. The defendant's mischief not only disrupted a life that was on the right track; it produced consequences that can be repaired only with a substantial monetary award. This is particularly significant in wrongful death cases, where the average person needs a persuasive argument to support the conclusion that damages are the price the defendant pays when its carelessness visits tragedy on the innocent.

Incorporating Legal Elements

The essential elements of any negligent tort action are duty, negligence, legal causation, and damages. In lay terms, the plaintiff must prove that the defendant owed a duty to the plaintiff to act or perform; that the defendant breached or violated that duty; that the defendant's omission or commission was the actual and foreseeable cause of the plaintiff's injuries; and the resulting damages. Because in most jurisdictions duty is a legal question, it is not submitted to the jury. But the lack of jury submission does not prevent counsel from incorporating the concept of duty in their stories. Many malpractice cases incorporate the concept of the defendant's promises or the plaintiff's trust. Premises owners encourage invitees with assurances of safety and security. Product manufacturers promote their wares as being "safe."

The plot must also include the legal element of proximate cause. The advocate constructs a story of a defendant who knew of danger and, cognizant of the risk, made unwise choices. The events are put together in a way that clearly links a defendant's actions with the resulting harm. The fact that the case must meet legal criteria shouldn't prevent the narrator from structuring a story that is interesting and compelling while supporting the legal requirements. For example, a patient attempting to recover on an abandonment theory must prove—

- the existence of a physician-patient relationship;
- unilateral severance by the physician without reasonable notice or provision of an adequate medical attendant;
- the necessity of continuing medical attention;
- causal connection between the severance of the relationship and the patient's injuries (proximate cause); and
- resulting damages.

The plaintiff must prove every element to prevail. Where recovery requires a jury finding of several elements, some advocates believe that the opening narrative must set out the specific elements and relate the facts to each to ensure full comprehension by the jury. This approach can detract from the story format. Because juries decide from the schema they create, the story is often more important than a thorough understanding of the legal elements. A compelling story will move the fact finders to find reasons in support of complex legal concepts. The best approach is to concentrate on the story while keeping in mind the legal criteria.

Plaintiff's counsel in the following abandonment case, in the opening statement or closing argument, tells the story of a mother-to-be who seeks out a high-risk obstetrical specialist because she is diabetic. Early ultrasounds indicate the child could be macrosomic (unusually large), necessitating delivery by cesarean section. The saga continues when the mother presents herself in labor at the hospital. The doctor is called. He does not come. After prolonged labor, a resident intervenes and attempts to deliver the child vaginally. A shoulder dystocia results and the baby's shoulders are now wedged in the birth canal. In an effort to free the child, the resident injures the baby's brachial plexus. After the plot is laid out—the story is told—the lawyer winds up by pointing out that all the elements of abandonment were met.

> Dr. McWhorter was Alice's obstetrician. She saw him because of his special expertise in high-risk pregnancies. He knew the baby was large and would have to be delivered by cesarean section. When Alice presented herself to St. David's Hospital, she needed him there. But the defendant didn't show up. A lawyer or judge might use the words

> "unilateral severance without reasonable notice." But most of us would just say the doctor the patient hired didn't show up when the patient needed him.
>
> The defendant doesn't send another highly qualified specialist. He lets the hospital struggle around and find a resident. A doctor in training to be an obstetrician. Someone who is trying to learn what the defendant already knows.
>
> There is no doubt that Alice needed the defendant's help. In the terms of the law, there was a necessity of continuing medical attention. Is there a connection between the defendant's not showing up and what happened? Of course there is. The defendant knew that any attempt at vaginal delivery would injure this child.

Motivation

Crafting a plot also involves considering motivation. As discussed in chapter 5, motive is a part of character. It is also an integral element of plot. What drives the character to act? Fictional storytellers know that identifying the character's motives is paramount. They understand the psychological tolerance that permits audiences to look beyond fault if the character is driven by laudable motives. Audiences do not condemn Brutus in Shakespeare's *Julius Caesar*—even though he is one of the conspirators who kills Caesar—because he is motivated by his love of country. Through most of *The Man Who Shot Liberty Valance*, the moviegoer believes that Ransom Stoddard (played by Jimmy Stewart) killed the despicable bully, Liberty Valance (Lee Marvin). In the end, however, the audience learns that Tom Doniphon (John Wayne) bushwhacked Valance to prevent him from gunning Stoddard down. Doniphon lets Stoddard, a greenhorn lawyer who doesn't know how to handle a gun, take the credit for winning a gunfight so he can become a U.S. senator. In the abstract, the audience would condemn Doniphon; but his laudable motive—helping Stoddard—actually elevates Doniphon's status to that of a noble figure.

The playwright knows the audience will judge characters based on their motives. The characters' motives give the audience a context in which to view the actions and behavior of the characters. Courthouse storytellers often fail to tell a story incorporating the facts that motivated the client. The lawyer examines witnesses, introduces documents, and presents evidence, all to prove who did what when. But jurors, like moviegoers, want to know *why* people did the things they did.

The courtroom is the ideal theater for the storyteller to bring to life powerful plots involving conflict and confrontation. The client suing a large corporation is the underdog. The plaintiff seeking repair for abuse, injury, or wrongdoings caused by corporate mischief is obstructed in her search for justice by superior strength and resources. She shows she is entitled to a jury's verdict by demonstrating perseverance and belief in the fairness of the system. The lawyer lays out the plaintiff's motives, knowing that otherwise the jurors will develop their own motives for the plaintiff.

Allowing jurors to create motives themselves is especially dangerous, because the average citizen may view with suspicion a plaintiff's motives for bringing suit. A study commissioned by the State Bar of Texas revealed that 57 percent of Texans believe that those who file lawsuits have frivolous claims and abuse the system so they can get rich. Only 31 percent felt that most plaintiffs have legitimate claims and are motivated by a desire to right a wrong.[4]

Movies depict characters much like typical plaintiffs who are inspired by legitimate motives. The character Norma Rae, in the movie of the same name, is empowered by her commitment to her family and her desire to improve working conditions for her fellow workers. In *Serpico*, the desire to expose corruption in the New York City Police Department drives Frank Serpico, the police officer played by Al Pacino. Tom Joad, as portrayed by Henry Fonda, struggles for human dignity in *The Grapes of Wrath*. Plaintiff's counsel should not neglect her client's motive in seeking legal redress. It may be to seek the truth, see that the defendant's practices are not continued to the jeopardy of others, or restore pride and self-respect.

Identifying defense motives is equally important. Masters of fiction believe that a story is only as good as its villain, because a strong enemy forces a hero to rise to the challenge. Defense motives do not have to spring from malice. They seldom do. It is difficult in real life to cast defendants as Hans Gruber from *Die Hard* or Gordon Gekko from *Wall Street*. But there are selfish, insensitive people like Miss Millie in *The Color Purple*. Some doctors wrongfully harm patients because they're not committed to the careful practice of medicine. Some corporations benefit financially by developing dangerous drugs and other products while consumers bear the risk of harm. The antagonist's motivation doesn't have to be malicious, but it must be "wrong." The cognitive subplot supports the case theme, and both lead to the conclusion that the defendants are responsible for the plaintiff's harm.

Motivation, whether the plaintiff's or the defendant's, must be consistent with action. Inconsistent behavior can dilute or destroy the motivation the audience has attributed to the character. Misdirection works in plays and movies, but not in trials. The genre of *Psycho* and *Dressed to Kill* is premised on surprise—the facts are not what the audience thinks they are. Lawyers who "misdirect" the trial story do so at their peril. Ignoring unfavorable events, observations, or documents may be disastrous.

Jurors don't just look at what motivates the parties. They are also concerned with what drives the lawyer. The courtroom plot carries through not only what happened to give rise to the suit but also what has happened since. Often the lawyers become part of the plot. Storytellers become part of the cast. Jurors admire dedicated and caring lawyers like Atticus Finch in Harper Lee's novel *To Kill a Mockingbird* and Jake Brigance in John Grisham's *A Time to Kill*.

TESTIMONIAL STORYTELLING

The presentation of evidence is a different type of storytelling. Witnesses narrate events; the attorney expedites the narration and assists witnesses with questions organized and asked in a manner that allows attestants the opportunity to tell who they are, what they know, and how they know it.

Who the Witness Is

The more critical the witness's testimony, the more important it is to develop that part of the story. How the audience views those giving testimony determines credibility. The most compelling testimony comes from people who are able to communicate clearly to the jury who they are and what they believe to be the truth. The principles of character development discussed in chapter 5 apply. A jury wants to know what relationship witnesses have to the litigants, the issues in the case, their childhood, education, parents, children, work experiences, marital situation, employment, hobbies, and other aspects that help them understand the kind of man or woman before them. The jury must come to know and like the witness as a person. Most importantly, they must trust him. This is done by incorporating examples, illustrations, or stories into the development of the witness's character. Background is presented as a story within a story.

What the Witness Knows

Jurors want to hear from the best person in the world who can testify on a given issue. Skilled advocates ask questions that leave no doubt that the witness on the stand is that person. The interrogator prompts answers that demonstrate the witness's familiarity with and knowledge about the matter before him.

Unlike other narrators, trial lawyers must incorporate into the plot facts that comprise legal elements. The examiner may be required to lay a certain legal predicate before eliciting testimony or a fact or opinion. Counsel will need to have complex hypotheticals written out to ensure that the predicate is accurate and contains all elements.

Many lawsuits are a battle of opinions. The qualification and phrasing of questions sufficient to meet legal requirements is beyond the scope of this book. Suffice it to say that counsel must demonstrate that experts in science, medicine, engineering, law, and accounting are in a position by way of qualification, experience, and the information reviewed to express the ultimate opinion.

In personal injury cases, lay witnesses are often called on to express opinions that bear on damages. What kind of person was the decedent? How have the injuries affected the plaintiff? In this instance, counsel should avoid asking "empty" questions like—

> Was she was a good mother?

> Did he love his children?
>
> Is she a dedicated employee?
>
> Was he physically active?

Instead, use a story.

> Tell us some of the things she did for her children. Describe the occasion when she . . .
>
> Did she volunteer for the tough assignments on her job? Tell us about the time when . . .

A forty-year-old computer programmer is injured when an improperly stacked case falls on him while he is shopping at a discount retailer. His shoulder and back injuries still give him pain and limit his activities at the time of trial. The plaintiff calls a friend and neighbor to testify. Counsel asks about the plaintiff's efforts to teach his twelve-year-old son how to throw a curve ball. The lawyer uses this vignette to illustrate commitment to family and that the father was physically robust and active before the injury. The witness's narrative describes the time his neighbor spent in the backyard with his son, the hours of practice until the boy mastered the pitch. Later, the friend tells how when he visits, the claimant is in his easy chair with a heating pad on his shoulder. He doesn't play with his son and seems to be in pain all the time.

Again, the power of the story is what teaches and involves jurors. Many plaintiff's lawyers like to concentrate their plots on the injured party's condition after the signal event. Experience demonstrates that the opposite is more effective. Counsel uses witnesses to emphasize the way the complainant was before the accident. In a death case, the accent is on the family relationship before the death. Stories are best understood when told in a conversational way. The more the jury hears about how happy, normal, filled with hope and dreams the plaintiff or his family was before the incident, the better they appreciate the harm the defendant's negligence sponsored. Stories bring the audience into a person's life. The more the jury climbs into the "before," the better they understand the "after" and the less likely they will be to trivialize or minimize it.

Emotion is a significant factor in structuring witness testimony. Stories bring not only facts; they also bring feelings. Short and simple questions are best. The examiner knows in advance what emotions she wishes the witness to draw from the jury. Then she looks for the anecdote in the witness's repertoire best calculated to appeal to it.

While checklists are helpful, counsel should never use them as a crutch. Rather, the questioner's pretrial interview yields a clear understanding of what the witness will say. The lawyer then uses signposts to present the testimony in an organized and persuasive manner. This makes the questions and evidence sound less rehearsed and more genuine. The witness becomes a believable narrator.

The State Bar of Texas has published numerous practical guides with proposed checklists for various witnesses in assorted types of cases.[5]

How the Witness Knows It

Witnesses may present facts, opinions, or both. A factual narrator explains what she saw, heard, smelled, or felt. A good technique is to exhaust one sense, then go to the next.

Sight: What did you see? Describe its size, color, location.

Sound: What did you hear?

Smell: Can you describe how it smelled? (Pungent, foul, rotten, sweet.)

Touch: How did it feel? (Texture, rough, smooth.)

Taste: Did you taste anything? (Taste is associated with emotion. Fear can produce a metallic taste. Revulsion and panic may cause a gastric reflux. The witness tastes the sweet-sourness of stomach acid.)

An essential part of effective narration by a witness involves what he felt. Lawyers give witnesses the opportunity to bring the audience into the story with questions like—

What do you recall thinking when . . . ?

What was going through your mind when . . . ?

What was your reaction to . . . when . . . ?

Organizing Examinations

Generally, direct examinations can be organized (1) chronologically, (2) topically or by subject matter, (3) by legal issue, or (4) by witness or document. Because life unfolds in chronological order, most narrators tell stories that way. The trial lawyer may use the chronological approach for the critical part of the examination, but keep in mind that the goal is not only to tell, it is to persuade. The questioner determines what comes first and last. Sometimes background comes first, sometimes the witness's key observation or opinion is early in the testimony. The rules of primacy and recency help the lawyer decide how best to organize an examination. The concept of primacy suggests that we recall best what we hear first. Recency teaches that the audience will retain the last idea on the subject they hear.

The principle of primacy is effective, for example, where a foundation is established quickly and then the witness is questioned early on the key issues. Primacy suggests that the plaintiff's case should always open with its strongest witnesses. A strong witness usually offers basic facts necessary to establish the prima facie case and to support the plaintiff's burden of persuasion. The goal is to both start and end on a high note.

Many lawyers spend significant time organizing and developing their questions for direct examination. But most of the impact of a witness's testimony comes from the nonverbal components. The words spoken may be the right ones, but the speaker's physical and vocal cues overshadow the verbal content. These are discussed in chapter 12.

Signposting

A few witnesses have a one-chapter story to tell. For example, an eyewitness to an auto collision or product failure may have only his description of a few seconds of action to offer. A brief, pointed direct examination may be best. But the testimony of some witnesses is more involved. It is a story with several chapters. Counsel needs to "signpost" these. The questioning is sequenced by topics that the questioner lays out at the beginning.

> Doctor Robertson, I want to cover three areas with you. First, I want to visit with you about your qualifications in the field of postoperative fluid management, and second, about your understanding of the standards of good medical practice in treating a postoperative patient demonstrating symptoms of hyponatremia, and finally, your opinions about whether, if the proper standards had been followed in Delores Donovan's case, her death could have been avoided.

Counsel might signpost a contract dispute by dividing the dialogue into topics: negotiation, execution, and breach. A friend of the family might be told that she will be asked first about the deceased's relationship with his wife and children; second, about how the family learned of his death and the family's reaction; and finally, how each of the survivors is handling the loss, how their lives have changed.

A good direct examination is a story told with a series of verbal pictures. That means you've got to organize the direct as a story, not as a series of legal issues. While you must satisfy the legal requirements of your claim or defense, real people never organize their stories around legal principles, so neither should you. It kills the story.

This method—first announcing the topic and then asking simple follow-up questions—keeps everyone on track. And using words of visualization, like "picture," "saw," and "noticed" in your questions, helps the jury become virtual "eyewitnesses" to your facts.

Theme

Each time the underlying story is retold by a witness on direct examination, it is reinforced. New elements or additional facts may be added, but the basic story and theme remain the same. Critical witnesses may also bring a theme to their testimony.

Window washers use eyebolts anchored in the roofs of buildings to drop their scaffolds from. An eyebolt breaks off, causing a worker to fall several floors to his death. The theme for a metallurgical expert testifying that the eyebolt did not meet contract specifications might be—

> What was written and promised wasn't done.

The signature for the coworker who was on the roof might be—

> We had no reason to think it was unsafe.

Or—

> But for the grace of God . . .

The deceased wife's theme might be—

> A good man who did so much for his family.

Themes are the essence of a witness's story distilled to its purest essence. Sometimes it is stated, repeated. Sometimes not. A witness theme is the picture the audience forms in their minds. For more on theme, see chapters 8 and 18.

Story Climax

The narrator does not write the climax of the story; the jury does. Christopher Vogler, an executive in the screenwriters' department at Twentieth Century Fox and consultant at Disney, teaches that "every story needs such a life-or-death moment in which the hero or his goals are in mortal jeopardy."[6] In the trial story, that moment is the jury's verdict. It is that realization that has led me to believe that good plaintiff's lawyers don't want the jury to see them as a John Wayne character. They want the jury to see *themselves* as "the Duke." They want their jury empowered to bring about justice, write a final chapter in a story—a plot—that inspires a better ending than the one facing them.

7

Let the Audience Live the Action

Abigail's back hurts. Off and on for almost a year, she has been feeling that tightness, those stabs of electricity that begin in her lower back and run down to her buttocks. She knows Dr. Flint can make her well, can make the pain go away. On January 27, 2004, Dr. Flint admits Abigail to Snidely Hospital for a routine myelogram that is done the next morning. The procedure seems to go well.

Lying in her hospital bed that afternoon, she is relieved that Dr. Flint spotted her problems on the myelogram that morning. Their visit was brief but reassuring. Back surgery tomorrow will be followed by a few days in the hospital, a week or so of convalescence at home, and then she will be her old self again. Her stomach begins to growl and then churn. The nausea creeps up from her abdomen into her throat, then her mouth, leaving a watery sweet-sour taste of gastric acid. She feels the urge to vomit. The nurse brings her a bedpan just in time. Abigail empties her stomach but continues to heave. She throws up more over the next hour. The nurses say they will call Dr. Flint for orders. She is tired when she hears the rattle of the wheels of the IV rack being brought to her bedside. The nurse inserts the catheter into her right arm at the wrist. Abigail thinks, "They'll give me something now through my veins. Something to make me feel better." Less than an hour later, she throws up again. Then she throws up again. And again. She isn't able to keep anything down.

At 10:00 PM she tells her nurse, "I'm so sick. I've never been this sick in all my life." The nurse's notes tell us Abigail continues to throw up during the night.

The next morning she is still vomiting. Dr. Flint cancels her surgery. When the nurse comes to check on her, Abigail says, "I'm scared." At 7:00 AM Abigail is crying. We know this because the nurse notes it in her record. At 10:00 AM, Abby tells the nurse she doesn't know why she is so sick and that she's never been sick like this before. She feels the churn in her stomach, grabs the bedpan the nurse has left at her side, and wrenches in agony as the greenish contents of her stomach gush into the stainless steel basin. She calls the nurse, who tells her that her doctor has ordered phenobarbital and Valium. But Abigail knows she's not getting better. She feels helpless lying in the high metal hospital bed. The television is off. It represents nothing to her now but meaningless noise. Her agony prohibits any entertainment, any distraction. She is a hostage to the nausea and pain in her gut. She feels her belly under the hospital gown. It seems swollen and distended.

Abigail's face is pale now. She can't see it but she can feel it. We know the pallor is there because the nurse notes it in the records. The cruel artist of misery paints a grimace on the kind and gentle face. Her voice has a whiny tone. She tries to turn and get into a comfortable position. She tries her right side, then her left. No matter. She is anchored by the IV tubing. No position frees her from the pain.

When will the doctor be in? What is wrong with me? Can't they do something? She feels the gurgling in her abdomen and reaches once again for the cold metal dish lying beside her. . . .[1]

Most storytellers follow a simple formula: set the scene and time, introduce the characters, and tell what happened. It is important that the audience should care about the protagonist, but what will make the story interesting is what happens to her. The narrator behind the lectern or the podium has an advantage over the writer of plays and scripts. The storyteller's creative bounds are limitless, because he not only writes the story but acts it out as it is told. Some speakers are considered gifted storytellers because of their ability to make the audience "live" the story.

CONVEYING ACTION

Action is best communicated by understanding that less can be more. When expressing action, a good general rule is: the fewer words, the better. Action is expressed by the concise ordering of subject, verb, and object. Perhaps some rhythm, but little else. The more specific and concrete the language, the more plausible the picture.

> Sometime that afternoon, Mary slipped on the floor of the defendant's store while shopping.

This description of action lacks punch and appeal because it lacks specificity. Contrast it with—

> Shortly after 2:00 PM, Mary slipped on the grease in aisle number three, falling backward and hitting the back of her head.

Some stories told in the courtroom, auditorium, or church involve a great deal of physical action, while others involve little. The lawyer giving an opening statement or closing argument in a commercial litigation case may introduce as his primary scene business negotiations in corporate headquarters. There may be a lot of intrigue but little physical action. But a trial lawyer representing a plaintiff in an automobile collision, oil-field explosion, or surgical mishap must tell a story that makes the action come alive. The audience must have a clear picture of what happened when. The audience "lives" the action when the lawyer uses the basic techniques of good storytelling. Words are important, but so is the way the narrator adapts voice and movement to the story. Persuasively communicating action in a way that the listener lives the event is accomplished in several ways. These are considered in more detail in chapters 11 and 12.

The storyteller decides whose point of view she will use in telling the story. Normally, the point of view is that of the actor—the storyteller's protagonist. A memorable action sequence resounds throughout the actor's perception—what they saw, heard, and felt. Concentrating too much on the action and neglecting the actor's perceptions is a mistake. Action is always reaction. Consider this memorable scene from *The Adventures of Huckleberry Finn,* in which Mark Twain brilliantly describes Huck's reaction to the townspeople's attempts to bring his supposedly drowned body to the surface of the Mississippi River.

> "Stand away!" and the cannon let off such a blast right before me that it made me deef with the noise and pretty near blind with the smoke, and I judged I was gone. If they'd a had some bullets in, I reckon they'd a got the corpse they was after. Well, I see I warn't hurt, thanks to goodness. The boat floated on and went out of sight around the shoulder of the island. I could hear the booming now and then, further and further off, and by and by, after an hour, I didn't hear it no more. The island was three mile long. I judged they had got to the foot, and was giving it up. But they didn't yet a while. They turned around the foot of the island and started up the channel on the Missouri side, under steam, and booming once in a while as they went. I crossed over to that side and watched them. When they got abreast the head of the island they quit shooting and dropped over to the Missouri shore and went home to the town.[2]

Movement and sound connote action. This may seem to be a statement of the obvious, but it is a principle often overlooked by storytellers. Twain opens his scene with a description of sounds, followed by the actor's perception of their meaning.

Some words denote action by the way they sound. Shakespeare admonished that words should be chosen not only for their meaning but by their sound. The sound of the word, in addition to its meaning, may convey specific action. Such words have the quality of onomatopoeia. Many of us read Vachel Lindsay's "The Congo" in high school. It is the classic example of poetic onomatopoeia with its chorus of "Boomlay, boomlay, boomlay, BOOM."[3] Successful courtroom storytellers often use the concept of onomatopoeia.

> As John's car entered the intersection, he heard the *squealing* of brakes and the *screeching* of rubber *grinding* on pavement. The defen-

> dant had run the red light and was in a panic stop. Then came the *boom,* the *thud,* the *crunching* of metal and *tinkling* of broken glass on the pavement. The *whoosh* of the air bag on John's Lexus couldn't stop his head from hitting the window on the driver's side. He heard the *thump* of his skull on the glass. Then there was darkness until he heard the *wailing* of the siren in the ambulance taking him to the hospital.

Because onomatopoeic words are particularly effective in conveying action, the trial lawyer tries to incorporate them when possible.[4]

LIVING THE ACTION

An action sequence depicted almost completely internally, within the actor's mind, is found in Edgar Allan Poe's "The Tell-Tale Heart," in which the narrator is driven to murder and then to a horrible confession because of the unending distraction of sounds within his own head. The climax of the story comes when he can no longer stand the unvoiced accusations of the investigating police officers.

> I paced the floor to and fro with heavy strides, as if excited to fury by the observation of the men—but the noise steadily increased. Oh God! What *could* I do? I foamed—I raved—I swore! I swung the chair upon which I had been sitting, and grated it upon the boards, but the noise arose over all and continually increased. It grew louder —louder—*louder!* And still the men chatted pleasantly, and smiled. Was it possible they heard not? Almighty God!—no, no! They heard!—they suspected!—they *knew!*—they were making a mockery of my horror!—this I thought, and this I think. But any thing was better than this agony! Any thing was more tolerable than this derision! I could bear those hypocritical smiles no longer! I felt that I must scream or die! And now—again!—hark! louder! louder! louder! *louder!*—
>
> "Villains!" I shrieked, "dissemble no more! I admit the deed!—tear up the planks! here, here!—It is the beating of his hideous heart!"[5]

Like Twain, Poe blends the actor's perception—what he is seeing, hearing, and feeling—with a vivid description of action. It is this quality that makes the audience live the event through the eyes of the storyteller.

In crafting the action sequence of the narrative, the storyteller should look for specific images. Jurgen Wolff and Kerry Cox, in *Successful Scriptwriting,* offer the following examples:

> Larry sits down at the dinner table. He looks hungry and takes the first possible opportunity to help himself to the chicken.
>
> Larry sits down at the dinner table. He eyes the food like a vulture, and immediately grabs a drumstick.

Clearly, the second description is more animated and powerful, as opposed to the first, which is bland and lifeless.[6]

Courtroom narrators not only may use the technique of novelists and screenwriters, it is often imperative that they do. Telling the story in the third person does not preempt the storyteller from presenting the client's point of view. It is essential that jurors live the tragedy through the plaintiff's eyes. They must understand that the same thing could have happened to them if they had been where the client was and had done what he or she did.

Consider what a courtroom storyteller can do with action. The lawyer representing the young female student raped in a college dorm tells how she returns to her room, locks her door, and feels a sense of security. She has no idea that the college had allowed a psychologically unstable male student to have access to the master key for the rooms in her dormitory. She is in bed sleeping. A noise awakens her. Peering into the darkness, she sees a figure. The figure comes toward her. The burly hand grabs her arm and presses her down on the bed. She begins to struggle. Then she feels it. The cold sharpness of it. A knife is at her throat. "Be quiet and I won't hurt you. . . ."

Does this trial story involve the audience? Do they live the action? The difference is that the lawyer tells it in the present tense. This technique is explored in more detail in chapter 12.

Use all of these methods in describing action. Create the scene from the actor's point of view. Include a description of the character's perception that leads to the action. Don't neglect the actor's internal reactions during the critical events. Move the story along. Tell it in the present tense. Use your imagination and create a scene that inspires specific images in the listeners' minds. These techniques all bring power and presence to the story.

Testimonial Description

Although lawyers tell the story first during opening statement, the tale told by witnesses is what the fact finders rely on to decide the case. For this reason it is fundamental that counsel's examination sponsor testimony that is an unambiguous, positive, easily understandable description of action and events, the who, what, when, where, and why. As indicated in previous chapters, the questioner elicits testimony of place (where). The witness sets the scene by describing the color, shape, and position of things. The plot follows, the who that did what. The "what" is the action.

Signposting Time

Questions establish the time. Sometimes this represents exact clock time; more commonly, it involves how events relate or correspond. Next, the witness identifies and describes who was present. The men, women, or children involved in the event are introduced by their relationship to each other. Were they strangers involved in an auto collision or business competitors engaged in contract negotiations? What brought them to the place? What did they intend to accomplish? Where were they going? Where had they been?

> *During the time* the parties were negotiating the contract . . .
>
> *Before* Carlos Lopez signed the contract . . .
>
> *After* Carlos Lopez signed the contract . . .
>
> *While* they were leaving the building . . .
>
> *As* Carlos Lopez was getting into his car . . .

Having supplied the elements of when, who, and where, the narrative turns to action. Each question gives a clear reference to location, time, and people. The witness should not have to wonder "when" or "at what point in time" or where you are speaking about, that is, space or location. The query must be in interrogatory form and must direct or point the witness in the precise direction you want him to go or respond. Setting the scene in time, people, and place leaves us with the "what" and "why."

Signposting Action

The core phrase in the interrogatory directs the witness and the audience to a component of action. The interrogator asks about events in relationship to setting, the place and people present. For this reason, it is important to signpost things and people in the setting to each other with terms like—

> Where in relation to . . .
>
> How far was . . . from . . .
>
> How close was . . . to . . .
>
> Which direction was . . . facing . . .

The psychodrama techniques discussed in chapter 4 work well when asking a witness to describe critical events. Counsel encourages the witness to "relive" the events and tell them as though they were happening in the present tense. As discussed in chapter 12, present-tense narratives cause the audience to become involved.

> What does she do?
>
> What do you say?
>
> What do you do?
>
> Then what happens?
>
> Does she seem (happy, sad, upset, and so forth)?
>
> What are you (thinking, feeling, experiencing, and so forth)?

Putting the Witness Center Stage

As discussed in chapter 15, the lawyer is the storyteller during cross-examination. During direct examination, the witness is center stage—the focus—the narrator. Counsel is the friendly facilitator helping the witness tell his story. She shows she is genuinely interested in the testimony and the testifier, is attentive, courteous, and concerned about the witness's comfort.

Counsel assists by asking questions in a way that invokes the proper mood. For example, picking up the pace of an examination may convey an impression that the events described occurred quickly or may create a sense of excitement. Deliberately slowing the pace will signal the jurors that the witness is giving important testimony and that they should pay close attention to these details. At critical points in the testimony, counsel can slow down the questioning and reveal the critical facts in a logical fashion.

Witnesses help themselves to the center stage by naturally and comfortably looking at members of the jury while testifying. They pick out a friendly face and talk to that person. Counsel occasionally looks over to show by her demeanor that she believes the witness and shares his conviction, experience, and feelings.[7]

Whether the lawyer or the witness is narrating, the audience needs to be a part of the action to understand what happened and be moved by it. The words are important, but the nonverbal aspects of communication are even more critical. The best storytellers see and relive the events as they tell the tale. They describe it in the present tense with specific, concrete language. They talk about the actor's perception and reaction. In short, they involve the audience.

8

Choosing a Cognitive Theme

GEORGE GAINER READ *the court's instructions to his fellow jurors slowly and deliberately, taking care with his pronunciation of the legal terms. He began to read the first question: "Was the negligence of any person . . ."*

Hank Bowen, Juror No. 9, interrupted and jump-started deliberations in plaintiff Ray McFarland's case against Paul Porter. "All I know is one thing. I would never have gone up that ladder in the first place."

"But is that really the point?" asked Diane Selby, Juror No. 6. "I mean, the question is who was negligent. Isn't the issue who acted responsibly and who refuses to accept the responsibility for their actions?"

Raymond Brown, Juror No. 3, agreed. "You can't say Ray McFarland wasn't being careful. He was using a ladder that Porter owned. He volunteered to help Porter put it together, and Porter said 'no.' Porter put it together and said it was OK. Ray insisted that Porter set up the ladder so it wouldn't tip over. Then he asked Porter to go up the ladder first. Ray watched him go up the ladder to make sure it was safe. Only then did Ray decide it was safe to go up on the roof."

Juror No. 10, David Rigby, an engineer, pressed the issue. "I can't say that I would have gone up that ladder either, but I don't think you can say that McFarland was careless or that he is responsible for what happened to him when the ladder broke."

The mythical fly-on-the-wall plaintiff's attorney would be smiling at this point. Jurors were now echoing a chorus of the themes and anchors planted during the voir dire examination, watered during opening statement, and cultivated during the examination of witnesses.

The stream of consciousness that now flowed from many voices in the tight chamber resonated a common term: "personal responsibility." It was the hook plaintiff's counsel had set three days earlier. As intended, this phrase captured the essence of the plaintiff's theme, piqued the jurors' curiosity, and compelled them to listen to the evidence.

Barbara Rodriguez, Juror No. 12, parroted the plaintiff's theme. "Isn't this case about who should be responsible when a man doing his job is hurt?" Juror Rigby offered the core question—the key issue they were to address: "Who should be responsible when a man breaks his foot when the ladder he is using comes apart because it is not put together right?

The man who was helping his friend and doing his job or the man who owned the ladder, put it together, and assured his friend it was safe?"

The verdict the jury would return reflected their belief that Ray McFarland had acted responsibly because he had taken care. He had been asked to climb a foldout ladder to inspect the roof of a client's home. He and the homeowner were friends. During the plaintiff's presentation, the hook, central theme, and core questions were all reinforced by the presentation of evidence.

The jury accepted the plaintiff's premise that Ray McFarland had acted responsibly because they believed from the evidence that he had asked the homeowner, Paul Porter, if he was familiar with the ladder before he started assembling it. Paul said he was. Ray asked him if he had used the ladder before. Paul said he had. Ray asked him if the ladder was safe. Paul said it was. Ray asked him if he could help assemble the ladder. Paul said he could do it himself. Ray asked him to stabilize the ladder against a wall. Paul did. Then Ray asked Paul to climb the ladder first to ensure that it was safe and secure. Paul climbed ahead.

Ray had, in the words of the child at the school crossing, stopped, looked, and listened for signs of danger.[1]

Well-told narratives are held together by a theme. A story's theme is the concise idea that an audience gets from the characters and their actions. Speakers and lecturers use vignettes that teach a lesson. Preachers use personal experiences and take stories from the Bible that have an identifiable moral. These speakers have no opposition. No one questions the facts of their narrative or the message it carries. Not so the trial lawyer.

A trial is a competition of stories. The conflicting facts, opinions, and scientific principles are a part of the opposing stories. Trial advocates must first persuade the listeners to adopt a narrative. Then they must empower the jury to act on it.

THEME AND CORE QUESTIONS

Compelling stories develop a central theme and ask a core question. The two go hand in hand. The central theme is what the case is about. The core question is what the jury must decide. The core question does not have to be in interrogatory form; it may be a statement.

> Wasn't the defendant's speeding through the school zone the cause of little Brenda's death.
>
> Because they didn't want to spend an extra $2.50 on their product, Billy McKinney lost an eye.

> The defendants knew the Status Corporation wouldn't buy into their company if they told them the truth about the financial shape the company was in.

Lawyers use cognitive themes to persuade the fact finders to adopt their account over its competition. A cognitive theme is an aspect of the story that can be quickly and interestingly summarized in a line or two. Some argue that a theme for a case is not the words the speaker and audience use to describe it. Rather, the case theme is the unifying image, idea, or concept each person uses to remind himself what the story is all about. The listeners in court will determine what the plaintiff's theme is fairly quickly, and very little can change that determination once it is completed. Every case will have a theme in the mind of each juror, whether counsel offers one or not.

Many historians consider the Battle of Gettysburg the single most significant military engagement in American history. It was in fact the largest battle ever fought in the western hemisphere, and it was here that the outcome of the Civil War conflict was decided. But why Gettysburg? The reasons most historians give illustrate how attempts to excuse folly often turn into myths.

In the summer of 1863, General Robert E. Lee, realizing he must take the war into Yankee territory, moved north into Pennsylvania. The Union forces, the Army of the Potomac, had experienced a revolving door of commanders as President Lincoln searched for an aggressive military leader. In June, General Joe Hooker resigned and Lincoln named General George Gordon Meade commander. The battle officially began on July 1, 1863. A common myth is that Confederate forces were attempting to capture a supply of shoes in the town of Gettysburg. In fact, neither Lee nor General Meade wanted to fight at Gettysburg.

General Lee's original strategy was to concentrate his forces at the Cashtown Gap, an easily defended pass. It was ideally situated to defend against any Federal frontal attack and to maintain Lee's line of communication with Virginia. Lee had ordered his commanders not to force an engagement until he could concentrate his forces. Contrary to these orders, General Harry Heth attacked the Union cavalry just outside of Gettysburg and pursued them into the town. He knew that a decisive victory over some Yankees would make him a hero. Later, when forced to defend his actions, in his written report to General Lee he tried to justify his blunder that he kept going despite Lee's orders to the contrary so he could "get those shoes."

There were no shoes to be had. There was not and had never been a shoe factory in Gettysburg. Confederate General Jubal Early's forces had been in Gettysburg four days earlier and would have lifted any meager stores of shoes held by town merchants.

Historians agree that both sides blundered into battle. In violation of General Lee's orders, Heth committed his forces to a full engagement. Lee then had no alternative but to support him. Yet Heth's note attempting to exculpate himself on the basis that he was after supplies sorely needed by the Confederate forces was picked up in newspaper articles and, later, history books.

Often in a trial we will find a fact, observation, or explanation documented in a medical record, corporate minutes, or logbooks in an effort to excuse or exculpate. We have an expression for these. They are called "CYA" notes. Others then pick up the contrived justification and act on it as if it were fact. The myth of the "shoes in Gettysburg" can be told to illustrate how a false excuse can be spread so that others accept and rely on it.[2]

A powerful story will lead to twelve people attributing basically the same motives and drawing basically the same moral. For example, twelve different people can watch *The Treasure of the Sierra Madre* and draw slightly different conclusions, but all will be in one form or another that "greed can destroy." Interestingly, the theme of that story about three men down on their luck who go up into the mountains of Mexico in search of gold is never spoken. It is not contained in one line of the movie. This fact underscores the suggestion made by some jury consultants that implicit suggestions are always more powerful than explicit ones.

The traditional approach to case theme is that it must be an idea or concept that considers all the evidence and guides the jurors throughout the entire trial. Other disciplines recognize the concept of theme as a means of bringing a specific and distinctive quality, characteristic, or concern to a specific subject or topic. Political strategists, advertisers, and public-relations experts consider a compelling theme to be the very cornerstone of a successful campaign.

In 1988, the Democratic candidate for president, Michael Dukakis, was running ahead of George H.W. Bush in the national polls. The Bush campaign came up with the "revolving door" ad. In sixty seconds, against the backdrop of a revolving door, the Bush campaign strategists told the story of Willie Horton, a black man who had been sent to prison for murder. He was released on a furlough program that allowed him to flee Massachusetts to Maryland, where he raped a white woman after stabbing her male companion. The ad told a simple story. The theme was that Dukakis, the governor of Massachusetts at the time, was weak on crime and willing to let dangerous criminals out of jail. Bush would protect us from the likes of Willie Horton. The theme—the image—stuck. Bush rose in the polls. The Dukakis campaign tried to answer with commercials filled with statistics proving that Dukakis was not soft on crime and that as many criminals had been released from the federal penitentiaries (under Bush's jurisdiction as vice-president) as had been released in Massachusetts. But the Dukakis commercials had no unifying theme. No "picture" was created in the mind of the audience. Bush never lost his lead in the polls after the "revolving door" ad and was elected president.[3]

A theme can take the form of a slogan, label, axiom, or platitude. Themes work because they recognize the psychological principle that people are cognitive conservatives. Obscure dates and facts are made memorable by phrases like "In 1492, Columbus sailed the ocean blue," or "Thirty days hath September, April, June, and November, all the rest have thirty-one . . ." Parallelism and reversal are rhetorical techniques that help us remember; for example, "Ask not what your country can do for you—ask what you can do for your country." Repetition makes Rev. Martin Luther King, Jr.'s, "I Have a Dream" speech vivid. In short, we remember what the speaker gives us reason to remember.

Human beings have a finite ability to process information, so they simplify complex problems by finding the path of least resistance toward comprehension. As Pratkanis and Aranson observe in *Age of Propaganda*, the listener "accept[s] a conclusion or proposition—not for any good reason but because it is accompanied by a simplistic persuasion device."[4]

Theme is critical when the storyteller's goal is to persuade. Most people base decisions on what "feels" right. The average person cannot accept a new proposition unless it is a logical extension of their already-held views. Experienced trial advocates know that most jurors make decisions early in the case and adopt a specific premise for evaluating the facts presented in evidence. The way facts are viewed will depend on the framework of the original premise. Evidence, to be persuasive, must make sense and fit into the framework the listener has adopted. That is why it is critical that trial advocates whose goal is to persuade develop a story theme early and reinforce it throughout the presentation.

The Essence of Theme

The theme or premise must make sense to listeners in terms of their perceptions and attitudes about life. It must be consistent with what they think is right and what they think is wrong. The speaker creates the original premise, which multiplies the opportunity for the desired conclusion. In the courtroom, a good theme—

- is easy to remember;
- is something that the favorable juror can use during deliberations;
- makes sense and is consistent with the juror's concept of fairness and justice;
- is consistent with and supported by the evidence; and
- carries a strong causal implication.

Constructing a strong, compelling case theme can be a long, challenging journey for the trial advocate. The road map is one that leads from ideas to phrases, and the journey courses the terrain of recognized rhetorical devices. The first step is the use of the focus group. Focus group deliberations distill the issues in the case to the simple and memorable facts. These deliberations also identify the basic values that support the plaintiff's theme.

A person's values are usually expressed in terms such as "should," "must," and "ought to," coupled with words like "everyone" and "anyone." They are internal standards that people use to weigh what is proper behavior and what kind of conduct will be looked upon as wrong. For example, a hospital "should be somewhere you go to get well, not to be injured."

A good theme also has a certain rhythm to it. Its memorable quality comes from its rhyme or parallelism. The case theme may be constructed from an alliteration ("the defendant's product was unfit, unfinished, and unguarded"), analogy ("an orthopedic surgeon is like a carpenter—the carpenter measures three times before he cuts"), or a famous proverb or epigram ("a little learning is a dangerous thing").

Adulteration and modification often work well. For example, the proverbial "safety first" is corrupted into "profits first, safety last" in a products liability case. "Err on the side of caution" becomes, for a medical negligence case, "The defendant erred on the side of (speed, convenience, and so forth) but not on the side of caution."

Accordingly, the approach many plaintiff's attorneys take is to develop a theme—a simple statement of a common-sense principle that compels assent early in the opening statement. Virtually any word or phrase may serve as a case theme. A single word can sometimes express the nucleus of a courtroom narrative.[5] Proverbs, clichés, familiar phrases that capture the fiber of an idea may serve this purpose. Thus, "the left hand didn't know what the right hand was doing" may be used in a case involving miscommunication between corporate executives. "One drink too many" underscores the defendant's intoxication as the cause of the wreck.

Sometimes parallelism and the rule of three are used to formulate themes. In a wrongful death case, plaintiff's counsel might suggest that the defendant's negligence produced an event that was needless, senseless, and endless. It was needless in that "Johnny Brown's death could have been avoided by the exercise of simple care and ordinary prudence on the part of the driver of AMC's eighteen-wheeler." It was senseless in that "as a result of the defendant's negligence, the parents have lost their only son." It was endless in that "the parents must now face the many years of life that lie ahead of them without the comfort, aid, and protection that a loving son would have provided them."

Experience teaches that—

- jurors deliberate in themes;
- the case theme is the primary mental organizer that helps jurors remember the facts;
- a good theme enables jurors to look for evidence that "fits" the story and to disregard evidence that does not; and
- themes facilitate evidence comprehension and enable jurors to reach predeliberation verdict decisions.

Using the Theme

The conscious mind is the target of cognitive themes. A theme simplifies and makes memorable the logical conclusion the speaker wants the listener to draw. It reinforces an idea. Advocates use themes for many persuasive purposes. Plaintiff's counsel may choose a case theme to emphasize and make memorable all or part of the story. A case theme may—

- emphasize the defendant's negligence;
- highlight the most incriminating evidence on the defendant's liability;
- compare the defendant's culpability with the plaintiff's innocence;
- create an image of the connection between the defendant's actions and the plaintiff's harm;
- answer the main defense; or
- highlight vicarious liability.

The Defendant's Negligence

The most common case themes in personal injury actions focus on liability. This is understandable because most such trials are won or lost on this issue. Here is a list of the forty-one most common liability themes.

Attentiveness

- Better safe than sorry.
- Be prepared.
- Danger.
- A job worth doing is worth doing right.
- Don't just do something, stand there.
- Skating where the sign clearly said "Thin Ice."
- Hope for the best but plan for the worst.
- Asleep at the helm.

- The red flags were there.
- They never missed an opportunity to miss an opportunity.

Qualifications and Ability

- He bit off more than he could chew.
- He was in over his head and wouldn't admit it.
- Quality is better than quantity.
- A little education is a dangerous thing.
- Experience is the best teacher.
- The greatest ability is dependability.
- Understaffed, overcommitted.

Inadequate Efforts

- A rushed job is a botched job.
- Too little, too late.
- They put profits over people.
- A job well done is worth two half-done.
- The best way to get out of trouble is not to get in it.
- A hasty man is seldom out of trouble.
- A short time is long for the unprepared.
- Actions speak louder than words.
- A stitch in time prevents the crime.
- When the (manufacturer, doctor, hospital) gambles, who puts up the stakes?
- Too busy, too big.

- When in doubt, you must rule it out.

Failure to Follow Rules

- They failed to follow the rules of the road.
- They thought the rules didn't apply to them.
- Not up to spec.
- Be in control of your vehicle at all times.
- Recipe for disaster.
- The long way home may be the surest.
- Cautious rules slow innovation.
- Sell first, ask safety questions later.
- The consequences were obvious.

Failure to Communicate

- The right hand did not know what the left hand was doing.
- They were not on the same page.
- To one who understands, few words are needed.

A central theme may be a simple phrase often repeated that speaks to the underlying wrong. Barbara is a managed-care patient. Her employer provides medical coverage through a freestanding clinic that employs staff physicians. The forty-year-old computer programmer suffers serious complications following elective female surgery. Complications lead to a drawn-out hospitalization and substantial medical expenses. A gravamen of the complaint is that "managed care meant that Barbara never knew her doctors and her doctors never got to know her." The simple theme is reinforced by repetition of a phrase that carries the central issue. The opening narrative describes Barbara's coming to the clinic complaining of pain on sexual intercourse. She sees a gynecologist she does not know and has never met.

> He is a Kelly-Summers Clinic doctor. He is her doctor now.

The story describes how Barbara is referred for an ultrasound test. There is some delay and difficulty in scheduling the diagnostic tests. Three weeks later, a nurse does it. Another gynecologist interprets it.

> She is a Kelly-Summers Clinic doctor. She is Barbara's doctor now.

The gynecologist interprets the ultrasound as demonstrating a benign neoplasm. Barbara calls the clinic for a follow-up visit. She returns five days later and sees a third gynecologist. He does not do a pelvic examination but recommends surgery.

> Dr. Patrick is a Kelly-Summers Clinic doctor. He is Barbara's doctor now.

Almost a month later, the doctor attempts the laparascopic examination, which Barbara understands is to be outpatient surgery. Dr. Patrick has trouble during the procedure and converts to a full-blown laparotomy (opening of the abdomen), removes the patient's appendix, and muddles around in the abdominal cavity.

> Dr. Patrick is the surgeon. He is Barbara's doctor now.

Following surgery, Barbara's temperature spikes up. Diagnostic tests suggest that her bowels are not functioning normally. The gynecologist calls in a surgical consultant and then leaves on vacation. Another clinic doctor sees the patient. His identity cannot be determined from the entry. Now the phrase is rhetorically mutated.

> Is he Barbara's doctor now?

The same day another gynecologist sees Barbara and makes medical orders. The next day, still another gynecologist sees her and writes a medical order that the patient can have clear liquids if it is all right with the surgeon. The surgeon has left on vacation. The narrator describes the medical note made by this gynecologist and asks,

> Is he Barbara's doctor now?

The next day Barbara is discharged from the hospital by still another clinic physician.

> Is he Barbara's doctor now?

Barbara goes home where she languishes for a couple of days and then comes back into the hospital through the emergency room. She is seen by still another clinic physician.

> She is Barbara's doctor now.

The story will go on to tell of surgical consultants who come into the case and operate for an infected bowel. But the point is the story is told in a way that underlines the plaintiff's theme that the patient didn't know her doctors and the doctors didn't know her.

Highlighting Incriminating Evidence

A thirty-six-year-old oil-field worker is crippled and paralyzed when a wire cable fails, causing three hundred pounds of ball and chain to drop onto his head. The corporate defendants had been using the wire cable for several years. A visual inspection of it anytime within the previous thirty days would have revealed the defect. The evidence suggests that no fewer than twenty of the defendant's employees had the opportunity to discover the problem. The case theme:

> Look.

A middle-aged man goes to the emergency room complaining of chest pain. The EKG shows signs of an impending heart attack. The ER physician either does not carefully look over the strip or misinterprets it. The doctor sends the patient home that night. He dies two weeks later from the untreated heart condition. The strongest evidence for the plaintiff is the EKG strip. The case theme:

> It was there to be seen, it was there to be treated, it was there to be cured.

Comparing Culpability and Innocence

A forty-three-year-old school teacher discovers a lump in her breast on self-examination. She consults her gynecologist, who refers her to a surgeon. After taking diagnostic mammograms, the surgeon recommends that the suspicious mass be surgically removed and biopsied. The hospital pathologist misdiagnoses the mass as intraductal carcinoma. The surgeon recommends a mastectomy, which the plaintiff submits to five days later. The mastectomy was unnecessary. The case theme:

> Lois trusted the wrong people to do the right thing.

A forty-year-old woman carrying her fourth pregnancy goes to a Houston hospital in labor. A minimally trained nurse administers Pitocin during the second stage of labor. This results in the rupture of the mother's uterus and brain damage to the child. The admitting obstetrician had not ordered Pitocin. The hospital contends that the nurse's action was appropriate and supported by her clinical judgment. The case theme:

> This is a case about the wrong person doing the wrong thing at the wrong time.

This theme conveys the essence of the plaintiff's contention that a nurse who had been trained in a foreign country and given responsibility for direct patient care administered Pitocin, a dangerous drug, without a doctor's order at a time when it was improper to do so. The theme also implies the causal connection—that the nurse's actions produced the damage to the mother and the child.

Creating an Image of Causation

Some case themes imply results. Many malpractice cases are defended on the issue of legal causation. In those instances, a case theme incorporating a simple concept to underscore the legal element of proximate cause is appropriate. Where the primary issue is cause and effect, the case theme emphasizes the connection between the defendant's conduct and the plaintiff's harm. Thus the theme of "a doctor should presume that a suspicious lump is cancer until it is proven otherwise" carries the causal implication that a thorough examination was not done and a proper approach would have led to the diagnosis and treatment of a curable cancer.

An apartment project maintains a large swimming pool. The shallow end of the pool is only three feet deep. The posted signs warning of the shallow end and its depth are removed, probably by vandals. Management has been aware of the absence of the signs for more than four months when a twelve-year-old boy visiting a school chum goes swimming and dives into the shallow end. He sustains crippling injuries to his neck. The case theme:

> A place looking for an accident.

A thirty-one-year-old asthmatic firefighter breaks his leg while running an obstacle course. He is admitted to the hospital for surgery. During his postoperative course, morphine is prescribed on an as-needed basis. The man dies after eighteen hours of morphine administration. The plaintiffs contend that the death was due to respiratory arrest caused by excessive morphine administration, that the patient was not properly monitored for adverse effects of morphine, and that the resuscitative efforts were untimely. The case theme:

> Too much too soon, too little too late.

A sixty-seven-year-old laborer is admitted to the hospital because of an impending stroke. His doctor prescribes heparin in an effort to prevent further blood clots. A nursing error leads to the patient receiving seven times the dose ordered. This results in cerebral bleeding and neurological damage. The case theme:

> Too much of a good thing.

Answering Defenses

A case theme may concentrate on putting down the defense of comparative negligence.

The plaintiff, a twenty-four-year-old machinist, loses his hand while operating the defendant's high-speed lathe. The defense wants to blame the operator. The lathe came equipped without certain safety devices and warnings for use. On twelve prior occasions, machinists were seriously injured using a lathe identical to the one the plaintiff was operating at the time of his injury. All these incidents were reported to the defendant manufacturer. But the defendant took no remedial actions and did not issue any warnings to those who had purchased the machines. The case theme:

> They knew—he didn't.

Highlighting Vicarious Liability

The purpose of the case theme is to define the critical issue and highlight the plaintiff's most compelling proof as to why he should prevail on that issue. Sometimes the critical issue is not negligence and causation but, rather, vicarious liability.

An eight-year-old girl undergoes heart surgery at a major hospital. The surgery goes well. The heart defect is corrected. After spending time in the recovery room, she is extubated—her breathing tube is removed—and the orderly takes her to her room on the floor. The attending nurse sees dramatic changes in pulse and blood pressure. She calls the code. A young resident with limited experience in intubating children comes. He has difficulty getting the tube back down. The child suffers brain damage. Negligence and causation are clear. The issue that will win or lose the case for the plaintiff is vicarious liability. The hospital claims that the resident was not its employee and stands in the legal position of an independent contractor. The plaintiff says that the affiliation agreement between the medical school and the hospital makes the hospital liable for the resident's actions. In this setting, the plaintiff's theme might be—

> This is a case about a hospital that won't own up to the contracts it makes.

Such a theme focuses on the provisions in the affiliation agreement specifying that the interns and residents at the medical school are under the supervision of the hospital's medical staff.

Many lawyers believe their courtroom narrative should have only one theme. I disagree. Trial stories are like *The Maltese Falcon* or *Citizen Kane*'s "Rosebud." The story introduces the image early, but it is not until we've heard the whole story that the image has meaning to us. The opening statement tells the story of men shaking hands on an agreement; a driver running late for a delivery; a school superintendent ignoring complaints that a teacher was making improper overtures to students. In the end, during closing argument, we learn the moral: honor means we stick to our agreements even if we get a better deal; it is more important to be safe than on time; we must protect our students.

The opening statement focuses on the facts of the case. A cognitive theme is the common thread weaving the facts together. After the jury hears all the evidence, counsel retells the story incorporating the affective theme. This dichotomy is discussed in more detail in chapter 10 and in part 4. Whether the story is the opening statement or closing argument, a good theme is essential for effective storytelling. It helps guide the hand when crafting the story. Theme directs emphasis and compels the narrator to focus on the facts that are most persuasive. At critical junctures, the theme, or some variation of it, is repeated for emphasis. Storytellers who approach their presentations this way are most likely to be seen as powerful and persuasive.

9

Negating the Negatives

HO TRAN GOES BY AMBULANCE to Southwest Memorial Hospital about an hour after the defendant broadsided her at the intersection of Gessner and Highway 59. The emergency room doctor treats her cuts and bruises, gives her a strong muscle relaxant and painkiller, puts her in a neck collar, and sends her home with written instructions to see her family physician. Two days later, she sees Dr. Yan Hoc. He treats her neck injury with pain pills, muscle relaxants, and physical therapy. She doesn't get better, so Dr. Hoc continues to care for Ho for the last two and a half years. Thirty-eight office visits and forty-five trips to the physical therapist, and she is still having problems. Her work as a manicurist requires that she stoop over the hands and feet of other people. It is manual labor that most of us wouldn't want to do. Working head down, arms out, puts a lot of strain on your neck. And so she goes home from work most days with a headache and pain in her neck and shoulders.

Dr. Hoc is one of the medical witnesses you will hear. Dr. Brian Wilson is the other. The defendant's physician, Dr. Wilson, will tell you based on his single examination that Ho is completely recovered, cured, has no disability. Dr. Hoc disagrees. He feels Ho's injury is real and continues to incapacitate and cause pain. Ho has traumatized and hemorrhaged ligaments and tissues in her neck that still give her problems and will probably cause physical torment and pain for the rest of her life. Dr. Hoc, like Ho, is Vietnamese. He has been practicing for only ten years, but he is a hands-on doctor. He is one of those old-time family practitioners who still makes house calls. If there were a test of who knows the most about medical books and medical terminology, the defendant's doctor, Dr. Wilson, would beat Dr. Hoc hands down. But in this case we are talking about an injury that cannot be seen on an X-ray. The only way we can determine whether Ho is disabled, has permanent injury, is whether she is telling the truth. If this were a test between Dr. Hoc and Dr. Wilson on knowing people, I would suggest that Dr. Hoc would win. He knows his patients like a family friend knows you.

Everyone will agree that there are no medical tests that can show the type of injury we will be talking about. The simple issue in this case is whether Ho is telling the truth. Hands-on medical treatment and care and experience—not knowledge of medical books—is the best way to know this.

Dr. Wilson is a fine person, but he just doesn't believe in what we're doing here today.

He certainly has a right not to like lawyers who do the type of work that I do or people like Ho who ask to be repaid for their injuries. But his feelings toward me and lawyers should not affect his judgment about this lady. His feelings against malingering patients shouldn't color his view of honest ones. Unfortunately, the longer doctors are around, and the more specialized they become, the more they get the "God" complex. In cases like this, the doctor can say, "I believe her" or "I don't believe her." Ho is just a manicurist. She is not a member of Dr. Wilson's country club or his yacht club, she doesn't sit in the luxury boxes at ball games and tennis matches or go to the high-priced restaurants. She lives on the wrong side of town. But she is just as honest as someone from the right side of town. She is just as honest as the friend or neighbor you trust and respect whether they are black, brown, white, or oriental.

Dr. Hoc is a young doctor just starting off. He hasn't made it yet, and he still believes that doctors should try to heal. He believes in what his patients tell him. He knows people can be hurting and no diagnostic test in the world will show it in black and white. He knows that sometimes the nerves, ligaments, and muscles have microscopic hemorrhaging that never goes away, never stops giving real and significant pain. He knows a thousand times more about Ho than any doctor who examines her one time for the defense can possibly know.

The underlying theme of this book is that trial lawyers are the best storytellers. Novelists create protagonists with flaws, but writers handle them in such a way that the flaws are accepted. Screenwriters have their characters make mistakes, but the point of the story is that the characters overcome their transgressions. Authors of fiction have no competing story. No adversarial narration. No one poking holes in the plot, challenging character, questioning motive.

The defense is apt to challenge every aspect of the plaintiff's narrative. What happened wasn't the result of a careless misadventure; it was an "honest mistake" or "a matter of judgment." Even if the wrong thing was done, it is not what caused the plaintiff's injury. In any event, the plaintiff is undeserving of justice because of who he is or what he has done. The plaintiff's experts are biased, unqualified, and unfair in their judgment and analysis. In short, there are reasons to doubt the plaintiff's cause, question the merits of the case, and dislike the one seeking compensation.

Warts on the Plaintiff's Story

It is a rare case that doesn't have "warts." Some blemish the defense tries to exploit to show that the plaintiff's narrative is fatally flawed. A wart is any fact or circumstance of the plaintiff's case from which jurors may draw a negative inference. Often plaintiff's lawyers overlook warts because in many instances the negative inference drawn is greater than the objective relevance of the evidence. But as the adage teaches, "Small leaks sink big ships." Many things can blemish the plaintiff's cause in the listeners' minds. They run the gamut from personal appearance to lifestyle or personality traits of witnesses to case-specific facts.

Witnesses

Ethnicity

Studies demonstrate that blacks tend to recover less than three-fourths of the damages that whites recover from the same situation and injury. The criminal conviction rate for blacks is much higher than for whites.[1] If counsel feels that race discrimination may play a role in the jury's verdict, she may want to consider some inoculation during opening statement.

Nationality

Sometimes the plaintiff may have recently immigrated to this country or may not be an American citizen. It may be appropriate for the plaintiff's advocate to remind the jurors during opening statement that the claimant is just like their grandparents or great-grandparents who came to this country looking for a better life.

Sex

Women tend to judge other women more harshly than men judge them. A common perception held by many of both sexes is that women should be expected to earn less than men and, therefore, their losses due to a permanent disability should be less.[2]

Many people do not like to think of such things as color and sex as constituting warts. It is, after all, the most blatant form of prejudice.

In the voir dire examination, counsel should raise the potential bias against the earning capacity of females. Proper questioning may lead to a challenge for cause. Where damages are the principle issue, the attorney may want to consider using peremptory challenges on those not disqualified for cause but who evidence a bias against a female's earning capacity or other economic damages. As part of the opening statement, the plaintiff's lawyer might innoculate with—

> Dena Morrison worked hard at her job for Nabors Drilling Company. In the fifteen years she worked there, she rose from bookkeeper to office manager. She had fifteen years of work life left when the defendant's negligence robbed her of what she had struggled so hard to get—rewards that go with honest labor. Look at her work record and see if you don't agree that she would probably have advanced with her company, gone on up the ladder and enjoyed bonuses, raises, and advancement. You will write the final chapter in Dena's tragedy. You will determine the value of her loss of earning capacity. As you do, you will want to keep in mind one salient, incontrovertible fact: there are no glass ceilings in this courtroom.

Appearance and Presentation

The personal appearance of the plaintiff can have negative impact because of the psychological principles of association and disassociation. If the plaintiff reminds the juror of someone he does not like or respect, he sees the plaintiff in a negative light. If the juror sees similarity in the plaintiff and herself, she may want to disassociate from the plaintiff's actions or tragedy. For example, an obese juror may disassociate with the obese plaintiff where the defense is claiming that the plaintiff contributed to his disability because of the failure to follow doctor's instructions to exercise and lose weight. Jurors who have marked similarity to the plaintiff may disassociate on the grounds that "that could not happen to me." They will be overly critical of the plaintiff's conduct, subconsciously thinking that they would have done something different and thus avoided the tragedy.[3]

Lifestyle

Some lifestyles are so out of the mainstream as to be considered by many aberrant, abnormal, or wrong. Someone who is openly gay may evoke hostile feelings in some conservative communities. Some people have a negative attitude toward artists, freethinkers, musicians, and others they view as "Bohemian." A person's wealth may be a problem. Some will assume that because of the wealth the plaintiff already possesses she doesn't need money damages.

Habits and Behavior

A number of personal habits or behaviors may be problems the plaintiff's counsel must address, including—

- alcoholism or use of alcoholic beverages at the time of the injury
- drug use
- criminal record
- claims history—previous claims for personal injury
- psychiatric problems
- medical problems

Demeanor

The demeanor of a witness may negatively impact the impressions formed in the listener's mind. Among the more common problems with plaintiff demeanor are—

- the whiner

- the exaggerator
- the overemotional
- the arrogant
- the unresponsive

Factual Warts

Plaintiff's counsel is sometimes faced with difficult facts that do not constitute legal defenses but are nonetheless problems. Factual warts can be many things:

- The absence of a demonstrable defect in a product liability action. The offending part may have been lost, destroyed, or tampered with.
- Medical or employment records that contradict the plaintiff's contentions.
- The fact that the plaintiff does not intend to call certain witnesses.
- The fact that the defense has more eyewitnesses or expert witnesses.
- The parties' preexisting relationship. The plaintiff is suing a close friend or a longtime family physician who treated members of the family.
- The parties' relationship after the suit. The plaintiff continued to see the physician after the alleged malpractice occurred, continued to shop at the same store where she fell, and so forth.
- The absence of plaintiffs. Some who could be suing are not.
- The remarriage of the claimant in a wrongful death case.
- The fact that family members or close friends will testify for the defense.
- Plaintiff's experts' fees are substantial.

Facts like these may require an inoculating argument during the opening statement.

Every Story Has Its Negatives

I have never seen or heard of a "perfect" plaintiff's case. Every story has its negatives. Faults of character, inadequacies of documentation, vagaries of facts can all be deficiencies that make the trial less powerful than it would be if we had the ability of the novelist to fictionalize. The sedulous advocate discovers what these problems are, and, if possible, pulls them out of the tapestry of the story that the jury will consider. By motion in limine, negatives may be excluded on the basis of irrelevance or prejudicial effect. Failing in this, trial counsel may use the voir dire examination to ferret out those who would overemphasize or be unduly influenced by these pejoratives.

As a general rule any major wart is best dealt with early in the case. Early disclosure desensitizes the fact finder. The negative can be dealt with in the form of an argument. This fact underscores one of the advantages of constructing the opening statement from a story. An argument can be made within a story, but it is hard to tell a story within the confines of an argument.

Inoculating During Opening Statement

An inoculating argument works during the opening statement the same way medical immunization works. A small dose of a bad thing is given so that the patient (the jury) does not come down with the full-blown disease. Whatever the weakness, problem, or negative issue, the plaintiff should disclose it during opening statement. However, counsel does not dwell on it. She discloses the weakness after other good and favorable points are made.

The plaintiff's advocate profits in gaining trust as she identifies the frailties and imperfections of her client and case. Since the jury will learn about the case deficiencies anyway, counsel might as well admit them early and gain credibility. The following illustrate the concepts of inoculating arguments.

Plaintiff's Criminal Record

The plaintiff, Georgia Barlow, was in a multiple car accident when she was hit from the rear by the defendant and knocked into the car in front. She has a past felony conviction for shoplifting a $5,000 wristwatch. Plaintiff's counsel might inoculate the jury as to the criminal conviction by stating:

> Georgia will be the first to admit that she has not led a model life. She was convicted of shoplifting three years ago and served a year behind bars. She has broken the law in the past and she wants you to know that she regrets her actions but has paid her debt to society. Most of us say that shouldn't have anything to do with this case. But we know the defense will make an issue of it, and even if they didn't, Georgia would want you to know that fact because she wants to be up front with you about everything.

Counsel is showing the jurors that she is playing straight with them and intends to hide nothing.

Weaknesses in Plaintiff's Witnesses

In some cases plaintiff's counsel needs to inoculate jurors against weaknesses in the plaintiff's witnesses. For example—

> We have just one eyewitness in this case. We want you to know that this witness, Tom Foster, is a heavy drinker. He had been drinking at the K-Y Corral that night and was getting into his car when he saw the defendant run the red light and crash into the side of Mary's car. What he saw, he will tell you. We want you to know he is not perfect. He was not a sober man that night. But he saw what he saw.

Contradicting Documentation

Additional facts can sometimes inoculate against bad ones. The plaintiff falls in a hallway just outside his hospital room while nurses are moving him to a different bed. In the plaintiff's premises case, he contends that the nurses were negligent in not assisting him in his debilitated condition. The nursing notes contain a reference that "the patient's fall occurred when he refused assistance in moving to the air mattress." The inoculating argument incorporates a significant fact developed during discovery.

> Sometime after Sidney falls and breaks his hip, Nurse Brannon writes in her nursing notes that Sidney fell because he refused to let the nurses help him move from bed to bed. Most of us put a lot of stock in written records. This is particularly true in a hospital. We want to think that when the records say something happened—the nurse gave a medication, took a blood pressure, changed an IV solution—she did. But Nurse Brannon didn't see Sidney fall. She saw him lying on his side on the floor, groaning. She admits she didn't talk to the nurse who was changing out the beds in Sidney's room. When you hear the defense refer to what the nursing notes say, you will want to remember that this note was written by someone who doesn't recall where she was when Sidney fell, didn't see him fall, and didn't talk to the nurse who was helping Sidney. According to Sid, when Nurse Brannon asked him what happened, he tells her the same thing he will tell you. The nurses never offered to help him move from bed to bed.

Failure to Call Witnesses

The plaintiff may, for various reasons, choose not to call certain witnesses. The witness may be unavailable, may not be able to add anything significant to the plaintiff's case, or may be antagonistic to the victim's cause. The most common situation involves the plaintiff's decision not to call a treating physician. Counsel may want to inoculate during opening statement with—

> The defense may try to make something out of the fact that we do not intend to call Dr. Mason, one of Jane's treating physicians. You know that I am not the only lawyer in this case with subpoena powers. We have made the determination that we do not need Dr. Mason to make our case because we will present other highly competent expert testimony. You may wonder when the defense makes this argument whether they needed Dr. Mason and are just trying to put the matter off on Jane. Treating physicians don't always support injured victims even when their cause is just and their injuries significant. They don't always cooperate with their attorneys. It comes as no surprise to you that some doctors just don't like lawyers. So when the defense suggests that Jane's case is flawed because Dr. Mason didn't appear in her behalf, you may want to remind yourself that if his testimony could have helped the defense, they would have subpoenaed him.

The Costly Expert

Jurors know that the parties and their attorneys pay expert witnesses for their time. But sometimes the plaintiff has an expert whose total professional charges are so significant as to warrant an immunizing argument. This can be particularly true in the product liability, environmental tort, and medical malpractice areas. The reason is obvious. Because the plaintiff's expert spends substantial time reviewing extensive records, reports, diagnostic tests, plant records, governmental documents, and policies and procedures to become familiar with the case, she may end up investing hundreds of hours before the plaintiff calls her to the stand. On the other hand, if the plaintiff calls an expert to testify who has not spent a great deal of time in preparation, the expert becomes vulnerable because of lack of familiarity with the facts of the case. An inoculating argument might be—

> When the defense cross-examines Dr. Rodriguez about the time he has spent preparing to give his opinions in the case, you may want to ask, "Which would we rather have, an expert who simply glanced at the matter and formulated opinions, or an expert who is committed to a thorough, comprehensive, in-depth review of the matter?"

The 20/20 Hindsight Contention

A common line of defense is to argue that the plaintiff's expert's opinions are based on 20/20 hindsight. The defendant says that because the plaintiff's experts have the benefit of looking back on the events, they are not to be believed. Because the plaintiff's experts knew that the course of events was going to lead to death, disability, or some type of injury, they are judging the case after the fact. An inoculating argument might be—

> Dr. Randolph tells us that the defendant's treatment of Cheryl was below the standards of good medical practice and this led to her death. All his opinions resulted from his analysis, review, and consideration of the medical records prepared by the defendants, Dr. Brown and the nurses at General Hospital. Mr. and Mrs. Boudreaux didn't make the records. Certainly little Cheryl didn't write anything in her hospital chart; she could not even sign her own consent form for the surgery since she was not of legal age. It was not until after this tragic event occurred and we obtained the medical records for these parents that they had any idea what was in there. Dr. Randolph's opinions will be based totally on the medical records. The defendants' documentation. Records written solely by them. The fact that we can evaluate these defendants' actions in light of their consequences does not change the fact that their actions constituted a deviation from the accepted standards of good medical practice. If we approached these matters any differently, we would stifle any type of scientific research, learning, or improvement.

Successful plaintiff's counsel is conscious of potential warts—blemishes, defects, distractions in documents in the case, the facts of the case, or witnesses—identifies them, and then inoculates against them in opening statement.

Testimonial Warts

The same concept applies during testimonial storytelling. Counsel brings out the bad during direct examination. The inoculation takes the sting out of cross-examination when the witness can say, "Yes, as I said when plaintiff's counsel was questioning me . . ." When the negatives of the trial story appear early they often lose their impact. When the advocate tells the story the last time, in closing argument, their role in the narrative has become a trivial side road that does not distract the audience from the power of the underlying theme—to do justice.

A plaintiff free of flaws, unimpeachable evidence, events beyond dispute, witnesses beyond debunking is a fantasy no one would offer up even in the world of fiction. Skilled advocates minimize the bad and make the good drive the story.

10

Complete the Circle with a Strong Ending

I HAVE SAVED ONE PART of Mario Bohorquez's story for the end. It is important that we consider this. We need to think hard about it. We need to question.

Mario is in his room at Mercy Memorial Hospital a little after five o'clock. His doctor transferred him from Alamo General because he knew they couldn't care for a patient who had an aneurism. Mario's doctor wanted him watched carefully so that if the aneurism started to bleed, he could step aside from what he was doing and come immediately to the hospital and operate. At 5:35, the defendant's nurse has the lab work that shows a drop in hemoglobin and hematocrit. She takes the vital signs and sees the significant drop in blood pressure. Mario needs a doctor. The defendant's nurse knows that. She writes in the chart that the doctor was called. Mario's doctor says he never got the call. The logs of his answering service document that no call was received from the hospital until three hours later.

Now the hospital says that nothing could be done for Mario. That his bleeding aneurism would be fatal no matter what. Did the nurse call? She says she did, but no one else witnessed it, the doctor says he didn't get it, and his answering service logs document that it wasn't made. She didn't make the call. If calling the doctor at 5:35 wouldn't have made a difference, then why does the defendant hospital need to claim that the call was made?

Mario needed a doctor. He needed one at 6:00 PM, not 9:30 PM. You and this family have heard experts tell us it was the delay that killed Mario. You and this family have heard the hospital's expert say the delay didn't make any difference. What we all want to hear now is the hospital explain why their nurse would fabricate and come up with the fable that she had called when she hadn't. Why invent such a story, why misrepresent the facts, why falsify the records if it didn't make any difference?[1]

How a story begins and how it ends determines how it is told. Storytellers know if you have a strong beginning and ending, the middle takes care of itself. But the whole story fails if the ending fails. Longfellow said, "Great is the art of beginning, but greater the art is of ending."[2]

Psychologists teach that understanding the rules of primacy and recency are essential to persuasion. The rule of primacy relates to the intensity of belief. It teaches that "first impressions count" and people remember and accept what they hear first. Recency relates to the ability to remember. What is said last is most memorable because it is the freshest piece on the plate. Show-business performers call their closing lines "taglines." They are the words the performer uses to conclude the act and finish strong.

WHAT THE CONCLUSION SHOULD DO

Storytellers know the importance of a strong ending. The ending summarizes and ties everything together. If the speaker's goal is to teach, the ending encapsulates the lesson. The pastor or rabbi wants his congregation to leave with a memorable, inspiring moral; the religious lesson of the day is summarized or made simple and clear in the last words delivered from the pulpit.

In the world of novels and screenplays, a good ending—

- resolves the conflicts that the story dramatized;
- satisfies the listener; and
- echoes in the imagination after the last lines are read or spoken.

Writers of fiction strive for endings that pack a punch. They want stories to end with a strong emotional bang. The last words of the story are powerful, resonating phrases that linger in the mind of the reader.

The young boy seeking treasure and adventure in Robert Louis Stevenson's *Treasure Island* joins up with pirates and quests for treasure. The concluding lines summarize what the experience taught the narrator.

> The bar silver and the arms still lie, for all that I know, where Flint buried them; and certainly they shall lie there for me. Oxen and wain-ropes would not bring me back again to that accursed island; and the worst dreams that ever I have are when I hear the surf booming about its coasts, or start upright in bed, with the sharp voice of Captain Flint still ringing in my ears: "Pieces of eight! pieces of eight!"[3]

The Red Badge of Courage by Stephen Crane tells of a young Union soldier's excitement of going into battle. He runs from the enemy at the first engagement but then regains his grit. His romantic view of warfare changes with his experiences. The closing lines show his newfound respect for the tranquility of home.

> The procession of weary soldiers became a bedraggled train, despondent and muttering, marching with churning effort in a trough of liquid brown mud under a low, wretched sky. Yet the youth smiled, for he saw that the world was a world for him, though many discovered it to be made of oaths and walking sticks. He had rid himself of the red sickness of battle. The sultry nightmare was in the past. He had been an animal blistered and sweating in the heat and pain of war. He turned now with a lover's thirst to images of tranquil skies, fresh meadows, cool brooks—an existence of soft and eternal peace.
>
> Over the river a golden ray of sun came through the hosts of leaden rain clouds.[4]

Some authors of fiction use the conclusion to give the story a sense of irony. O. Henry's "Gift of the Magi" is a Christmas tale of two young people living in a small flat, each struggling to give the other a Christmas gift. The wife sells her hair to buy a fob chain for the husband's watch. The husband sells his watch to buy handsome combs for her beautiful hair. Both have sacrificed what the other admired to enhance the pleasure of that which is now gone. In Poe's "The Tell-Tale Heart," a murderer who has chopped up the body confesses to the police at the end because he thinks he can hear the victim's heart beating under the planks of the floor where he buried it. The ending powerfully encapsulates the theme of how a man's guilt can betray him. In tales like these, the unexpected twist at the end brings the story to a powerful conclusion.

Surprise and irony normally don't work well in the courtroom because the trial advocate from the beginning is telegraphing the end he hopes the fact finders will write. Trial lawyers don't write the conclusions to our stories. Juries do. Our narrative must present facts, circumstances, and inferences that lead our audience to a conclusion that represents justice for our clients. Plaintiffs need Capra-like endings. George and Mary Bailey's friends come to their rescue. Pottersville never becomes a reality. The corrupt and powerful cannot bring him down when *Mr. Smith Goes to Washington* because good, ordinary people discover the truth.

The opening statement leaves a perception of what the case is about. Jurors screen the evidence they hear through the perceptions formed early in the case. Witnesses and exhibits enhance the goal of the story. Finally, the tale comes together in summation so that the answer—the verdict—is clear.

Draw the Circle

When crafting a story it is easy to visualize events as a chronological road that runs from point *A* to point *B*. But seeing the story as a straight line can result in a lame trial story that ends weakly. While a narrative usually has an identifiable beginning, middle, and end, power comes to it when the story is viewed as a circle. The beginning ties in and supports the ending, and vice versa. Some talented authors have constructed their stories by writing the ending first. An example is Steven Spielberg's movie *Close Encounters of the Third Kind*. Regardless of whether the writer visualizes the ending or beginning first, the two should be seen as tied together. The completion of the ring of people and events produces a unique dynamism. The most popular story design in novels and movies is the circular or closed form, in which the narrative returns to its starting point. The hero comes full circle back to the location he started from; or the return may be circular in a visual or metaphoric way, replaying an initial image or repeating a line of dialogue or situation from the first scene.[5] Two recent movies illustrate the principle.

In the Academy Award–winner *Saving Private Ryan*, the audience first sees an aging veteran at the Normandy cemetery. Tears come to his eyes as he approaches a grave site with his family. The story then flashes back in time to the D-Day invasion. For half an hour the audience sees the battle on the Normandy beaches in graphic detail. The story then progresses with Captain Miller (Tom Hanks) assigned to "bring back Private Ryan." For the rest of the movie the audience remains curious about which of the soldiers they are following is the survivor in the opening scene. Ultimately we learn that it is Private Ryan himself when the scene is revisited at the movie's conclusion.

Moviegoers saw a similar technique in *Titanic*. Again, the beginning is today—salvage operators are considering ways to raise the *Titanic*. The interest focuses on a necklace that one of the passengers owned and that is said to have incomparable value. The salvage operators seek an elderly female survivor's assistance. The story flashes back to the voyage and her romance aboard the *Titanic*. Through the story the audience learns of the unrequited love the woman has carried since the ship sank. The audience travels through the romance to the ship hitting the iceberg and the panic that led to the loss of so many lives. The final scene fades back to the present, and the elderly woman drops the necklace off the stern of the salvage ship in a romantic gesture.

Speakers appreciate that much of the motivational power of a verbal presentation is a product of the way it ends. Many speeches are remembered for their emotional endings.

On May 12, 1962, General Douglas MacArthur returned to West Point to address the cadets of the academy he had once served as commandant. His memorable speech incorporated as theme the code from the legend on the West Point coat of arms—"Duty, Honor, Country." General MacArthur introduced the theme at the very beginning of his speech and returned to it at its conclusion:

> In my dreams I hear again the crash of guns, the rattle of musketry, the strange, mournful mutter of the battlefield. But in the evening of my memory I come back to West Point. Always there echoes and re-echoes: Duty, Honor, Country.
>
> Today marks my final roll call with you. But I want you to know

> that when I cross the river, my last conscious thoughts will be of the Corps, and the Corps, and the Corps.[6]

On June 26, 1963, more than a million Berliners lined the streets to hear a youthful American president reaffirm our country's commitment to democracy in West Germany. John F. Kennedy's theme was captured in a phrase repeated several times in his short speech, "Let Them Come to Berlin." His conclusion reinforced the theme and took it to a higher emotional plane. The closing line, delivered in German, brought down the house.

> Freedom is indivisible, and when one man is enslaved, all are not free. When all are free, then we can look forward to that day when this city will be joined as one and this country and this great Continent of Europe in a peaceful and hopeful globe. When that day finally comes, as it will, the people of West Berlin can take sober satisfaction in the fact that they were in the front lines for almost two decades.
>
> All free men, wherever they may live, are citizens of Berlin, and, therefore, as a free man, I take pride in the words *Ich bin ein Berliner.*[7]

Houston's Barbara Jordan was a relatively obscure U.S. representative before the Nixon impeachment hearings began. Her persuasive power and eloquence was no secret after she gave her historic speech to the House Judiciary Committee on July 25, 1974. Her theme was her faith in the Constitution. Her conclusion was an appeal to reason, not passion.

> If the impeachment provision in the Constitution of the United States will not reach the offenses charged here, then perhaps that eighteenth-century Constitution should be abandoned to a twentieth-century paper shredder. Has the president committed offenses and planned and directed and acquiesced in a course of conduct which the Constitution will not tolerate? That is the question. We know that. We know the question. We should now forthwith proceed to answer the question. It is reason, and not passion, which must guide our deliberations, guide our debate, and guide our decision.[8]

Finish Strong

We've all heard speeches that seemed to die at the end. We've read books and seen movies where the ending seemed contrived or left us unfulfilled. The beginning and body of the presentation are sacrificed in vain when the ending fails to support and empower the story.

In a trial, the plaintiff's counsel has three distinct opportunities to tell the story:

the opening statement, closing argument, and rebuttal. Add to that a fourth, and it is of signal importance: when lawyers examine and witnesses testify. The concept of bringing power to a conclusion by rounding back to the beginning works in all four narratives. Opening statement tells the audience the story the witnesses will bring them. In a malpractice death case alleging that improper fluid maintenance caused hyponatremia and ultimately death, the plaintiff might begin with the hook, "How often have we heard 'better safe than sorry?'" The circle would be tied at the conclusion of the opening with—

> At the end of this case, I will stand before you and say again, for the final time, that we would not be here today if these defendants had adhered to basic scientific principles, good medical practices. If the defendants had given isotonic solution, IV with salts rather than sugar water following Abigail's myelogram, we wouldn't be here and this family would still be intact, healthy, and happy.
>
> If these defendants had done that, they would have been safe and we wouldn't be hearing how sorry they now are.
>
> If they had given isotonic solution to Abigail, when caution required, we wouldn't be hearing how it was difficult to cure her once she lapsed into her acute state.
>
> Better safe than sorry.
>
> Caution is better than any cure.

The same theme can be used for a strong conclusion to the opening statement in a products case. The defendant manufactured an orthopedic appliance (an intramedullary rod) that failed (cracked) six months after the orthopedist used it to repair a serious fracture of the plaintiff's femur. Plaintiff's counsel introduces the thematic catchphrase much earlier in the opening statement and now repeats it as part of the conclusion:

> Orthogone should have followed the adage "better safe than sorry." If the defendant had only been safe, Bobby wouldn't be here in this courtroom, crippled for life, hearing how sorry the defendant is.

In the course of bringing the audience through the client's side of the controversy, lawyers teach through witnesses in a variety of disciplines from soft to hard science. They advocate with the facts composed of people, places, and events, and reason with logic and rationality. This is the stuff from which advocates build their opening statement and closing argument. Closing argument brings together the bits and pieces from the documents, exhibits, and witnesses. It is an overview of the facts now before the audience. Rebuttal suggests a moral and what the jury should do about the story as they now see it. The trial lawyer inspires by appealing to what is good and great in humanity. The quadripartite trial story—opening statement, presentation of evidence through witnesses, summation, and rebuttal—suggests that each be constructed differently.

Plaintiffs have unique opportunities at the close of the evidence. Because we have the burden of proof, the law gives us the right to open and close. Two arguments, two stories; two beginnings and two endings. While we call it closing argument, structuring the summation around a story can be particularly effective. Because I suggest that the opening of the closing summation should have a cognitive appeal, incorporating the facts, science, and logical left-brain analysis, the theme will be a cognitive one. The close or rebuttal should empower the jury. It is the affective, what some might call emotional, right-brain argument.

The plaintiff should have a good idea what she will argue in opening the summation. The witnesses have laid out the evidence, and the court has charged the jury. Even a small case doesn't rob counsel of the opportunity for an enduring conclusion. Consider how plaintiff's counsel might conclude her summation in an auto wreck case. The defendant broadsides the plaintiff at a residential intersection. The defendant has a posted stop sign, the plaintiff does not. The single working mother with two young children sustains soft-tissue neck and back injuries resulting in medical expenses of $2,200. She loses a month from work over the next year. Her treating physician expects no significant permanent disability.

> After this collision, the defendant walked off, had his car fixed, and was done with his few seconds of carelessness. But Sarah couldn't. She had to get her prescriptions filled, wait in the doctor's office, go to the physical therapist, get up on days when she wondered if she could. She worked in pain and took care of her children when sometimes she wasn't up to it, cleaned the house, did the laundry, cooked meals.
>
> The defense says Sarah's sacrifices to responsibility have little value and ignoring them is of little moment. Do we walk away as the defendant did? Or do we take the hard course and compensate fully the person sitting here who has demonstrated her commitment to the values we all share?

Because the courtroom story is a narrative of facts tied together with a cognitive theme, a strong conclusion closes the hook, complements the headline, suggests the answer. The ending completes the circle. The concluding lines reinforce the "why we are here."

End with a Question

One way for the plaintiff to conclude both the opening statement and opening of summation is to challenge the defense with a question.

Consider the following conclusion to the plaintiff's argument in a products liability case:

> If it wasn't the design department and it wasn't manufacturing that decided not to equip this high chair with the seventy-five-cent safety strap, then who was it?

Ending with a question is an especially effective technique for concluding closing argument because it puts the defense off balance and may mandate that they refocus their summation. If no answer or an implausible answer is given, the plaintiff can use this defense failure as a theme in rebuttal, on either liability or damages.

In a premises case, counsel might ask—

> If three complaints about the bad lighting in the stairwell weren't enough to alert the defendant that someone might fall because of bad lighting, then how many are enough?

Counsel for a plaintiff seriously injured in an auto accident might push for an answer to the question—

> Where is the doctor, where are the medical records that say Susan will ever be able to walk normally?

Caution is the byword when counsel chooses to conclude with a question. It had better be one he is sure the opponent does not have a solid, plausible answer to.

REBUTTAL

Rebuttal is different. The rebuttal or final courtroom story incorporates ethos and pathos. Trial stories put in issue the credibility of the advocate, parties, and witnesses. Final summation summons this credibility in support of counsel's position. Advocates use an ethos appeal when they bring values into the story. Stories that appeal to justice, freedom, faith, and human dignity are in this category. These values are coupled with the human need to do right to those who have been wronged. The concept of pathos recognizes that people are motivated by compassion and sympathy for others.

Creative advocates build great themes and taglines for rebuttal from words, phrases, or arguments defendants use during closing argument. Successful plaintiff's lawyers listen carefully to the defense arguments and remain flexible for the riposte.

The plaintiff is forced to accept a small settlement in a medical malpractice case because her lawyer fails to timely designate a critical expert on a liability issue. She sues her lawyer for malpractice. In closing argument, the defense argues that no lawyer can ever guarantee his client a good result. Plaintiff's counsel begins the rebuttal with "There are no guarantees," and responds to the evidentiary arguments. The conclusion rounds back to the introduction with—

> This family didn't expect the defendant to give them a one-hundred-percent guarantee of results. They did expect that he would give them one-hundred-percent effort, be one-hundred-percent honest, and be one-hundred-percent fair. If he had given one-hundred-percent effort, he would have had the experts he needed on time. If he had been one-hundred-percent honest, he would have told them how he dropped the ball and put them in the position where they had to give away any chance for justice they had by accepting the defendant's meager settlement offer. If he was one-hundred-percent fair, he would own up to it and accept the responsibility for his mistakes. But that is not going to happen if you are only committed to fifty percent of justice. For once, let's give this family one hundred percent of what they deserve.

An affective theme empowers the jury. Justice is the goal, but it can be reached by an appeal through many emotions and human virtues. For example, it may be a call to the jurors to be better people than the defense. In a medical negligence case, the tagline might be:

> She's in your hands now. Please take better care of her than they did.

The close may be an appeal to look for the good in people:

> You write the obituary. You tell us the kind of life this was. Write in the value of love, commitment, and integrity. Add up the worth of a human being who gave all he had to his wife, children, parents, and community.

Courage is a good affective theme:

> Dr. Goodwin could have just looked the other way when he saw this medical misadventure. He did something that isn't popular with his colleagues. He testified that the defendant violated the standards of good medical practice. It was the right thing to do. It was the hard thing to do. Don't let his valor be in vain.

The ending lines for closing argument should inspire the answer to "What are we going to do about it?" The closing argument expands the cognitive theme with the affective components of ethos and pathos. Chapter 18 presents some ideas for formulating an affective theme to appeal to the conscience, soul, and heart of the audience.

PART 3

TELLING THE STORY

IT'S NOT EASY BEING a trial lawyer. If you represent injured plaintiffs, you are bad for business, the reason people lose jobs and the courts are clogged. If you represent criminal defendants, you are someone who gets the guilty off. Since one side wins and the other side loses, half the time our clients are unhappy. People come to us when they are in trouble. They only need us when there is a problem. They have a tale to tell but they don't like the ending. Prospective clients bring us stories that, as presented, teach only that "bad things happen to good people" or that "the innocent are falsely accused." The trial lawyer's job is to take the facts and present a compelling narrative. The facts lead to a moral. The moral spurs a verdict. The verdict justly resolves the conflict and repairs the injustice.

We have the best system in the world for resolving controversies between citizens and citizens and between citizens and government. It is not a perfect system and, like any imperfect thing, is sometimes seen more for its faults than its virtues. Because the system is flawed, people become skeptical. They lose faith. Some clients come to believe that real justice is beyond their reach—that due process is reserved for the dues-paying members of the elite—that maybe, just maybe, they don't deserve it.

When I hear that, I am reminded of a story often told by Dwight Lyman Moody, a prominent nineteenth-century preacher who is considered the father of modern-day evangelism. Moody was the wellspring from which flowed Billy Sunday and ultimately Rev. Billy Graham. He was the innovator of community church services held in tents and of nondenominational community revivals. Moody commonly used real-life anecdotes in his sermons, such as the following experience he had in the state prison of Ohio.

After Moody delivered his sermon, the prison chaplain told him of a memorable incident that had taken place in the very room of Moody's sermon a few years earlier. The commissioners of the prison went to the governor and asked him to pardon five men for good behavior. The governor consented with the understanding that the record was to be kept secret, and at the end of six months the five men highest on the roll would receive a pardon, regardless of who or what they were. At the end of six months, the eleven hundred prisoners were brought into the chapel. The commissioners and the warden stood on the platform. The president of the commission put his hands in his pocket, brought out some papers, and said, "I hold in my hand pardons for five men."

The prison chaplain told Moody he had never witnessed anything like it. Every man was as still as death. Many were deadly pale. The suspense seemed to shrink the large chapel. It seemed as if every heart had ceased to beat. The commissioner went on to tell the men how they had gotten the pardons. The chaplain interrupted him. "Before you make your speech, read out the names."

The commissioner said, "Reuben Johnson will come and get his pardon," as he held it out. No one came forward. The commissioner asked the warden, "Are all the prisoners here?" The warden told him that they were. The commissioner spoke again, this time in a louder voice. "Reuben Johnson will come and get his pardon. It is signed and sealed by the governor. You are a free man." No one moved. The chaplain looked right down to where Reuben was. He was well known; he had been there for nineteen years, and many were looking around to see him spring to his feet. Reuben was looking around to see the fortunate man who had gotten his pardon.

Finally, the chaplain caught his eye and said, "Reuben, you are the man." Reuben turned around and looked behind him to see where the lucky man was. The chaplain said for a second time, "Reuben, you are the man." A second time he looked around, thinking it must be some other Reuben.

The point that Moody makes in this sermon is that sometimes life's messages are so good that some people pass it over their shoulder to the next person. In this true story, the chaplain could see where Reuben was and had to say three times, "Reuben, come and get your pardon." At last the truth began to sink into the old man. He got up and came down the aisle, trembling from head to foot. When he got the pardon and looked at it and went back to his seat, he buried his face in his hands and wept. When the prisoners formed into ranks to go back to their cells, Reuben stepped in line. The chaplain had to call to him, "Reuben, get out of the ranks, you are a free man, you are no longer a prisoner."[1]

I look upon our clients as being prisoners. I see us as the wardens trying to get pardons for the good behavior of those in our custody. The young man who is brain damaged because the manufacturer of industrial steel cable cut corners. The beautiful woman who is mutilated and scarred because her breast biopsy was misinterpreted as malignant. The parents who lost their son because a bar served a patron too many drinks. The young boy hit in the head with a baseball who is tragically brain damaged because of the delay in transferring him from an emergency room to a facility that could surgically alleviate the swelling and damage caused by the epidural hematoma. In the eyes of any objective observer, they are innocent. They did no wrong. Their tragic results can only be explained by decisions others made. They know that strangers or those they trusted visited an injustice on them. They know they have been imprisoned in debilitated bodies or oppressive circumstances that will last a lifetime. They, like Reuben Johnson in Moody's sermon, begin to doubt they are worthy of justice—whether they deserve any relief or pardon.

I say they are. Let's speak for them. Let's do it in a professional and honorable way, giving credit to our profession and maintaining dignity for our system. This is, after all, what being a trial lawyer is about.[2]

A good story makes a point. It teaches or informs. The narrator using a story to entertain may appear boorish if the audience feels the story was told without purpose. The absence of a lesson either expressed or implied is what prompts the listener to ask, "What was the point?" The lesson, the point, the moral, is the storyteller's signature. A speaker should know what he wants from the audience before he says one word.

On some occasions, the goal is only to entertain. A luncheon or after-dinner speaker may view her charge as humoring the audience with interesting stories and anecdotes. Aside from those occasions, most audiences expect to learn something from the speaker. I follow the rule that if the audience is not sitting at a table where they ate, then every story must make a point that is relevant and hopefully interesting to them. The point is, or is part of, the lesson. Of course, anything that happens in a courtroom is aimed at informing, educating, and persuading.

Speakers who seek not only to inform and teach but also to motivate face a tough challenge. Yet this is the test for every courtroom advocate. Trial lawyers not only must teach the facts, science, and accounting, they also must inspire the jury to a just verdict. It is this element of the courtroom story that I term "soul." A strong case for the plaintiff has all the elements of a morality play. The proper presentation of character, plot, and motive leads to a moral requiring the audience's actions.

I tell true stories. As with all trial lawyers, my narratives must be consistent with the facts, logical in their development, and accurate in their portrayal of events. My friends (I have no clients) bring me their reality, which is tragic, painful, poignant, even cruel. These stories as amplified and explained by the documentation of medical treatment, product development, or business intrigue present tales of the worst in humanity—ignorance, laziness, corporate greed, professional indifference, arrogance, deceit—injustice.

These are the stories the trial lawyer must tell. The narrative of the opening statement is confined to the facts that witnesses will present to the audience—the jury. If our courtroom stories ended there, I couldn't tell them. If I were confined to presenting black narratives in the Poe tradition, the depressing crawl through the sewer of humanity of *Pulp Fiction*, the stroll through the corrupt immorality of *Boogie Nights*, I could not do it. Thankfully, this is the paradox of courtroom storytelling: the opening statement and witness testimony are not the whole story. A trial is like one of the old *Columbo* TV episodes. In the opening statement, the listeners see who did what, when, where, how they did it, and why they did it. In the following days they watch the detective (the trial lawyer) work the story backward and solve the mystery. The listeners get this feeling when counsel, like Columbo, asks the witness at the conclusion of the examination, "Just one more thing . . . " At the end, the mystery is solved and the story becomes something different. Values come into play. Whom do we applaud and whom do we condemn? Whom do we admire and respect and whom do we want to punish?

Our legal system gives the audience the opportunity to revise the portrait the evidence paints from the palette of events and the dark hues of real people on the canvas of life. In closing argument the courtroom storyteller calls on his listeners to find the bright colors of virtue—the good in people. I ask my audience to put soul in my story when they write the final chapter. I hand my listeners the brush and palette so they can refine the portrait with the vivid colors of hope, promise, and compassion.

The advocate's clients bring her the story. She further develops character and plot through legal discovery. She assembles all the relevant records, propounds interrogatories, requests for admissions, and motions for production, and takes the oral depositions of lay and expert witnesses. After she completes the discovery phase, she becomes the author of the trial story. But it is the final stage that is most critical for the courtroom storyteller. When she rises to address the jury, the lawyer is the actor—the one who delivers the lines. Successful trial advocates understand the power in this final sequence. The power of the person, telling, and sequence. We consider our audience in judging how the story will be told and use the power of pictures and the power of the story from adverse witnesses, a phase of trial we know as cross-examination. Winning with stories in the courtroom requires that the narrator have more than a good yarn to spin; it demands that the portrait be painted by a master artist—someone who brings power to the story, who inspires and motivates.

11

The Power of the Person

ABOUT 1900, Wilhelm Von Osten purchases a horse in Berlin, Germany. The horse is named Hans. Herr Von Osten begins training his horse to count by tapping his front hoof. He has no idea that Hans will soon become one of the most celebrated horses in history. Hans is a rapid learner and soon progresses from counting to adding, multiplying, dividing, subtracting, and eventually to solving problems involving factors and fractions. Even more startling, when Von Osten exhibits Hans to public audiences, he counts the size of the crowd or the number of people in the audience wearing eyeglasses. Still responding only with taps, Hans can tell time, use a calendar, recall musical pitch, and perform numerous other seemingly fantastic feats.

Von Osten teaches Hans an alphabet that can be coded into hoofbeats. Hans is able to answer virtually any question. Hans, a common horse, seems to have complete comprehension of the German language.

This is a true story. You will find it in the scientific literature of the day.

Without any promotion by Madison Avenue, the word spreads quickly. Hans becomes known throughout the world. He is soon dubbed "Clever Hans." Because of the profound implications for several scientific fields and because some skeptics think a gimmick is involved, an investigating committee is established to decide, once and for all, whether to prohibit Hans's performances on the grounds that the results are contrived. Professors of psychology and physiology, the director of the Berlin Zoological Garden, a director of a circus, veterinarians, and cavalry officers are appointed to the commission. To ensure that the experiment is accurate, Von Osten is required to be absent. There is no change in the apparent intelligence in Hans. The commission announces that no trickery is involved.

A German professor thinks he knows the explanation for this scientific conundrum. He asks for another go at it. A second commission is appointed, which turns out to be the end of Clever Hans. Von Osten is asked to whisper a number into the horse's left ear while another experimenter whispers a number into the horse's right ear. Hans is told to add the two numbers. The answer is one that none of the onlookers, Von Osten, or the experimenter knows. Hans fails the test. Similar tests are performed, which Hans continues to fail. The experimenter, Oskar Pfungst, has discovered that Hans can answer a question only if someone in his visual field knows the answer and is attentive to the situation.

When the inquisitioner gave Hans the question, onlookers who knew the answer would assume an expectant posture, increase their body tension, and bend their heads slightly forward. When Hans reached the correct number of taps, the onlookers would relax, let out a breath, shift their weight, or move their heads. Evidence suggests that Hans could read head movement as slight as one-fifth of a millimeter. Subsequent experiments found that Hans would also cease tapping as a knowledgeable onlooker raised his or her eyebrows or even showed a dilation of the nostrils.[1]

You will find the phenomenon of Clever Hans reported in many of the books on nonverbal communication. The story illustrates that animals can detect human attitude that is reflected in the most obscure and imperceptible physical responses. If animals can read nonverbal communication, can detect our response when the truth appears, why would we presume humans can't? Humans do, and they do it quickly. Early on, jurors form impressions about the lawyers, the clients, and the cause. These impressions can be critical to the outcome.

Great speakers look good. This is not to say that only Hollywood-handsome people or tall, imposing personalities can be inspiring storytellers. Physical size is not the measure of the person. Two of the greatest courtroom tale-tellers I ever heard were at opposite ends of the spectrum. Houston's Percy Foreman was well over six feet tall and a large man by any standard. Louis Nizer didn't stand much over five feet and had a quiet voice and demeanor. Most people did not see them as strikingly handsome. They dressed appropriately, but neither was ever a candidate for *Gentlemen's Quarterly*.

Accomplished speakers have mastered the mechanics of gesture and movement. They bring appropriate demeanor to the setting and make good eye contact with their audience. What separates the gifted and great from the average and mediocre is the elusive quality of charisma.

CHARISMA

What is charisma? John F. Kennedy, Martin Luther King, Jr., and William Jefferson Clinton had it. While both were equally successful militarily, Douglas MacArthur had more of it than Dwight Eisenhower. The middle of the last century was filled with charismatic personalities: Churchill, Roosevelt, Hitler. Great women are remembered because of their strong and dynamic personalities. Houston's Barbara Jordan had it, as did Jacquelyn Kennedy. Regardless of political persuasion, most would admit that Ann Richards possesses a unique persona that inspires support among her followers. Oprah Winfrey's success as a television talk-show host is due in large part to her charismatic personality. Charismatic people inspire others in business, medicine, law, and politics. All successful business leaders and professionals have some degree of what Webster's calls "a personal magic of leadership arousing special popular loyalty or enthusiasm."[2]

Psychologists and political commentators have argued for years about the qualities necessary for a charismatic personality. In the courtroom, charisma is king. A dull, cold, insipid personality is apt to be overwhelmed by the persuasive mystique and magnetism of the charismatic trial lawyer. In the boardroom, business decisions are driven by those who project this mystical quality of leadership. The most successful teachers, realtors, social workers, small-business owners, and entrepreneurs all have some degree of personal chemistry that sets them off from others.

Charismatic speakers project certain qualities and create certain perceptions.

Connection

Public speakers and one-on-one conversationalists connect with others not just by what they say but how they say it. They use eye contact, motions, and emotions to couple with those with whom they are interacting. An essential to connecting with others is remembering and addressing them by name. The University of Houston's Dave Maggard is one of the most admired and respected athletic directors in the country. He astounds alumni groups when he goes through a luncheon crowd of two hundred or more and introduces every man and woman in attendance.

Care for Others

They know their audience, understand their problems, share their aspirations. Average Americans saw President Clinton as one who "shared their pain." A trial lawyer who projects concern not only for his client but for individual jurors creates the image of an empathetic person.

In the business world, supervisors knows about their employees' personal problems because they ask and show concern. Successful salespeople demonstrate a desire to understand the customer's problems before attempting to sell their product. They live by the adage, "The customer comes first." Caring for others is the sine qua non for plaintiff's lawyers. It is what sets us apart from those who defend corporations and powerful professionals. Charismatic personalities are often involved in charitable causes and helping those less fortunate.

Interest in Others

How often have you watched a television interviewer cut off someone in midsentence or follow with a question that indicates he didn't even hear the previous answer? Much of Oprah Winfrey's charismatic quality comes from her being an attentive listener. She conveys interest in what her guests have to say. Trial lawyers create this image during the voir dire examination by letting the venire panelist do most of the talking. With their facial expressions and body movement, they also convey sincere interest in what they are hearing.

Respect for the Lesser

People admire those who are courteous to persons of lesser authority or who occupy a lesser social station. "Yes, sir" and "No, ma'am" are persuasively potent when they come from someone older or more authoritative to someone younger or junior on the social scale.

Use of Simple, Concise, and Direct Language

Charismatic speakers sound like ordinary people. There is no pomp or panoply in their language. (See chapter 12, pages 146–48.)

Use of Metaphors and Analogies

The Reverend Martin Luther King, Jr., often used analogies, similes, and metaphors in his sermons. Charismatic speakers paint clear and vivid pictures of the concepts they are applauding or condemning. (See chapter 12, page 148.)

Self-Confidence and Assurance

The more public speaking one does, the more experience one has standing before an audience and talking to them. Everyone gets more confidence from experience. The person who knows his subject well shouldn't be nervous. By the time the trial lawyer is before the bar with his client, he should know more about the case than anyone else.

Self-Enjoyment

Charismatic speakers are playful and happy even when dealing with a serious topic. Self-deprecating humor helps create this image.

Energy

Some dull people hold political office, others rise in the corporate hierachy. Sometimes they are even successful in the courtroom. But most winning lawyers bring a level of energy to their presentation. Their voices convey their convictions. They never speak in a monotone but rather use inflections, tone, and pauses to bring a dynamic quality to their storytelling. (See chapter 12, pages 156–58.)

Passion

Charismatic speakers have an opinion about the topic on which they speak. They care about it. Their physical, vocal, and verbal content and mannerisms project their emotion, enthusiasm, and conviction.

View of the Broader Scheme of Things

Charismatic speakers project their view of the world as one that would be a better place if their ideals prevailed. They are expansive, inspiring, and uplifting by showing the audience how they can contribute to a better life.

Positive Outlook

People don't like to hear negativity. They want to hear solutions. Even if the trial advocate is dealing with a tragedy, the audience still wants to have a positive outlook that something meaningful can be done about it.

Smiling

Albert Mehrabian was a psychologist who did extensive studies at UCLA in the 1970s, attempting to identify those qualities that make us "like" someone. He postulated that the physical aspects of communication (how we look, stand, gesture, and so forth) are more determinative of whether we will be liked and our ideas accepted than the words we use or how we say them.[3] We like people who smile often. During the height of the Republican inquisition of Bill Clinton, the president never lost the ability to smile even when being vigorously questioned or attacked. Charismatic people have mastered the ability to smile in the face of adversity.

Finally, the charismatic person is a credible source.

Perceptions

Credibility is not so much an objective characteristic as it is a perception on the part of the observer. What matters is what the juror or judge perceives about the believability of an attorney or witness.

Daniel O'Keefe, professor of communication studies at Northwestern University, concludes that the effectiveness of a message depends to a large extent on the audience's perception of the source (speaker). Actuality matters not a whit. The audience's perception is all. The speaker's job is to control and determine the audience's perceptions.[4] O'Keefe suggests that modern scholars have determined that there are seven dimensions of source credibility. He lists them in order of importance.

- *Competence:* The level of knowledge and experience the audience perceives in the speaker. Preparation, body language, appearance, and educational level are important determiners of credibility.

- *Trustworthiness:* The reliability of the speaker. Does the speaker do what she says? Sometimes the title or position of the person can affect perception; for example, used-car salesman versus experienced mechanic.

- *Dynamism:* Aggressiveness, force, energy, loud or soft, rhythm, body language, and so forth. Credible sources eliminate verbal noise such as "and," "ah," "uh," and "you know" from their language.

- *Power:* Much of the perception of power is a result of appearance and whether the speaker can provide rewards and punishment, wealth, and so forth.

- *Goodwill:* The degree to which a speaker has the audience's versus his own best interests in mind.

- *Idealism:* The degree to which the speaker is perceived as having values and qualities that the audience esteems and desires. Rev. Martin Luther King, Jr., is an example of a speaker with a high level of idealism.

- *Similarity:* The degree to which the speaker is perceived as resembling the audience. Senator Lamar Alexander wore a plaid shirt to establish similarity. Fred Thompson rented a pickup truck during his Senate campaign.

Jurors are very sensitive to how counsel treats them, other attorneys, and the judge at trial. They like respectful, polite behavior and tend to devalue the attorney who is rude or hostile. Most jurors are not familiar with the hierarchical system law firms use at trial. Because jurors are new to the trial situation, they are likely to scrutinize the lead counsel's treatment of others on the trial team, particularly when those others are female or minority members. Asking female trial counsel to take on significant clerical or assistant duties ("Get me that file!") or to act as Vanna White with courtroom storyboards can be offensive to some jurors. Not including a minority attorney at sidebars or speaking in a condescending manner will have the same effect.

There can be no doubt about it: we like people who are like ourselves. We want to be with others who are similar to us. We look for it consciously in our friends. We associate with people from the same office, in the same profession, of the same socioeconomic status. We are comfortable with people who are like us and uncomfortable with people with whom we have no similarities. Many lay people start with the presumption that lawyers are not like them. A stereotype in their heads is a man or woman who is self-centered, pompous, domineering, and inconsiderate. Jurors may seize on even the slightest manifestations of insensitivity and stiff, aloof behavior to confirm the rest of the negative stereotype. That is why it is so important that the lawyer come across as a real person, someone the jury would like to know and have as a friend.

Appearance

Jurors form initial impressions of the plaintiff's advocate during the voir dire examination.[5] This image is expanded during opening statement. Appearance plays a significant role in the persuasion process. Defense lawyers do not lightly approach the way they dress and the impression their appearance makes in the courtroom. Victim's advocates should aim for the most neutral look that jurors will find acceptable. For most plaintiff's trial counsel, this does not mean looking like the "Philadelphia lawyer" or the stereotypical polyester ambulance chaser. For example, in most southern, midwestern, and western states, few male plaintiff's lawyers wear suit vests to trial because of the unfavorable subliminal image that this may convey to some jurors.

How the female advocate dresses can be even more critical because some men and women jurors tend to judge them more harshly. The successful woman trial lawyer does not wear the upscale styles of Chanel, Christian Dior, or Givenchy. She wears a classic midscale business suit and avoids the use of too much eye shadow, too much blush, dark lipstick, and other forms of heavy makeup. The female advocate looks for the natural look where her makeup blends with her neck. Hairstyle is particularly important. Successful female trial lawyers wear their hair in a current, classic form, avoiding too much hair spray and an overdone style.

When appearing before a jury, the lawyer should consider the venue of the trial. Rural jurors expect attorneys to be more approachable, down to earth, and informal. It is important that plaintiff's advocates not affect any particular type of appearance. The trial advocate tries to project his true self. Counsel whose approach is low-key and likeable may project the desired image by wearing a conservative sports jacket rather than a suit. To enhance this look, plaintiff's counsel wears more touchable fabrics, such as tweed—even a sweater vest if that is appropriate for the climate.

Some lawyers "pace" their attire. The advocate begins trial in a sports jacket during jury selection and opening statement, moves to a gray suit (power dress) during cross-examination of the defendant's witnesses, and then wears a dark suit during closing argument to convey the somber and serious nature of the undertaking the jury is about to begin.

Appearance affects jurors' perceptions. Does the jury see the plaintiff's advocate as intimidating and cold or as a warm, trustworthy friend? Most successful trial advocates strive for a blend between approachable and credible.

During opening statement, counsel wants to project the image of integrity and professionalism. This image enhances the narrative. Experience teaches that it is difficult to overcome an unfavorable impression that has been formed on the basis of appearance, even with excellent verbal content. For this reason, the plaintiff's champion brings to choice of dress the same discipline used in preparing and presenting the case. Shirts are neat, pressed, and subdued. Shoes are cleaned and shined. A general rule is that the lawyer should strive to "look like a lawyer." But what kind of lawyer? Most successful plaintiff's lawyers convey an image of the down-to-earth professional who is competent, friendly, and sincere.

Adjustments in appearance during trial may convey subtle images to the jury. Loosening the tie during argument suggests informality, vulnerability, and eagerness to engage in the intellectual struggle. Pushing up one's coat sleeves gives the impression of a lawyer hard at work on the critical issues. Likewise, the advocate who stuffs into his coat pocket a sheaf of papers containing his notes may project the image of the approachable, down-to-earth country lawyer. The successful plaintiff's lawyer realizes that his appearance and dress must be used to promote the desired verdict in the same way that gestures and language are used.

Posture, Gestures, and Movement

The moment a lawyer rises and faces jurors, he is telling them about himself. He may shuffle, stride belligerently, move about with jerky motions, or walk in a quiet and purposeful manner to his position in front of the jury box. During the opening statement, the jury senses at once the meaning conveyed by the advocate's physical approach to them. Those who study speech and communication have learned that the audience tends to mirror the speaker's movements. This is true even though the listeners seldom outwardly change their posture. The inner pull is there. The storyteller's audience is always inwardly imitating what they see.

Therefore, counsel's bodily action will do one of three things to those who listen:

- Jurors relax too much or even become drowsy in response to the advocate who uses no action, or almost none.

- Jurors become nervous or irritated with counsel who fidgets and fumbles or constantly meanders back and forth.

- Jurors find it easy to pay attention and listen to a trial lawyer who uses controlled and purposeful action.

Trial lawyers talk to juries with their bodies. Unfortunately, many advocates underestimate the significance and effect of this type of communication. The way counsel stands before a jury tells them whether the lawyer is trying to shrink from them or is indifferent or self-conscious about her case. Inappropriate posture can convey arrogance, anger, or defiance. A solid but comfortable posture can convey that counsel is eager to tell her listeners something important.

Accomplished speakers stand erect when addressing the audience and do not assume a hunchbacked or defensive posture. A trial lawyer who stands with her weight equally distributed looks strong. She is on solid ground. However, this posture, if it is too rigid, can make her look stubborn. It is not a conversational look.

When the speaker stands with more weight on one foot, she is adopting a more relaxed posture. Counsel may look off-balance but conveys a softer, more vulnerable image. For this reason, many trial lawyers assume this posture from time to time, depending on the image they are trying to present. A relaxed posture increases likeability and approachability.

Gestures are made with the whole body. Even the simplest action of the hand or arm, if gracefully done, is supported by the whole body. A novice trial lawyer who gestures with her arms while her body is tense and frozen is unconsciously being as funny as the comedian who does so deliberately. The experienced advocate learns to cultivate her entire bodily action. She supports the slightest movement of her hand by balancing her whole body, moving her head, or coordinating her hips, knees, and ankles. She gives each gesture with abandon, yet with vigor.

Timing of a gesture is particularly important. The stroke of a gesture is timed with the emphasized word or syllable. Emphasizing the statement "This is significant" is never done by spreading the gesture over the entire sentence in one wild, awkward jab. Nor is it done by spreading the gesture over the whole emphasized word. The voice emphasizes only one syllable of the phrase—sig*nifi*cant. The courtroom storyteller coordinates the stroke of the gesture with vocal emphasis on the syllable. He gestures only at the time the emphasized syllable is spoken.

Accomplished storytellers know to avoid gesturing at the beginning and ending of the narrative. Subtle and small movements—a nod, a smile, a movement of the shoulders—are more effective in starting. The plaintiff's narrator withholds vigorous gestures or comments until both she and the audience are in the mood.

Movement may involve myriad aspects ranging from simply smiling at the jury, to deciding how much of the courtroom to use, to determining whether and how to touch the client.

The storyteller has not been born that can give an effective narrative while standing in one spot, rigid and stiff. On the other hand, too much uncontrolled movement is distracting. Counsel who delivers her opening statement by pacing back and forth uncontrollably is like a tiger in a cage. She distracts jurors with her movements and gestures. No good speaker keeps the same posture long. She adds meaning and interest to her words by changing position.

How much should the advocate move? That question depends on three things:

- the trial lawyer's personality;
- what counsel is talking about—whether he is attempting to educate, inform, motivate, elicit feeling; and
- the extent to which counsel is referring to visual aids.

Movement always depends partly on what part of the story the trial lawyer is telling. If counsel is conveying feelings, such as pain and suffering, death, or the lack of ability to enjoy life, he may be relatively quiet and use relatively little movement. But in discussing the liability aspects of an accident, counsel may become animated and, where appropriate, "walk" the jury through what happened. If the plaintiff slipped and fell because of a grease spot on the defendant's floor, the lawyer may walk through the events, even imitating the plaintiff's fall. If the plaintiff was struck in the eye when a high-pressure gauge exploded, counsel may grab her eye in mock pain during that part of the narrative. Examples of bringing the jury into the action can be found in chapters 26 through 30.

Deciding how much to move also requires an appreciation of the principle of controlling space. Most people equate the accumulation of space with status and dominance. The bigger someone's house, the larger the car or office, the more responsibility, power, and authority people perceive that person as having. Status and space correlate in the courtroom as well. Lawyers who are seen as more powerful and confident have greater control and ownership of space in the courtroom.

In projecting confidence, however, counsel avoids invading jurors' territory. This is particularly important during the opening statement, when the plaintiff's lawyer and the jurors are still strangers. For this reason, most successful advocates do not approach within three to four feet of the jury rail during opening statement.

The opening narrative is the plaintiff's opportunity to anchor the case theme. When counsel delivers the cognitive theme, she stands in the same place and delivers it in the same manner. When the scene of the narrative changes, counsel moves to a different point in the courtroom.

Experienced trial lawyers know that it is important to project likeability with their movements and actions. The advocate who smiles with jurors or nods in agreement with them with comments she wants them to support enhances her likeability as a storyteller. Smiling is one of the most important characteristics for projecting likeability.[6] Smiling is considered a highly rewarding behavior. When a trial lawyer smiles, people generally tend to smile with her and like her more.

Demeanor

Emerson said, "What you are speaks so loudly that I cannot hear what you say."[7] The trial lawyer's demeanor says more to the jury about who she is than what she says. Counsel's demeanor, as well as that of her client, must be consistent throughout the trial. The trial lawyer cannot on one hand attempt to project anger or disgust with the defense and on the other convey closeness and comradery during breaks and recesses. The trial lawyer does not need to be "standoffish" to convey respect for the proceedings and the opposition. For example, while opposing counsel is addressing the jury, the plaintiff's lawyer conveys a neutral but attentive behavior. She sits upright in her chair to reflect courtesy and respect for opposing counsel.

The goal of the plaintiff's storyteller is to obtain the trust and respect of the jury. The lawyer's demeanor can have a significant influence on how the jury sees him. Demeanor reflects various attitudes. The trial lawyer shows affection, respect, and empathy for the client. By facial expression and attitude he demonstrates belief in the justness of the cause. And, most importantly, counsel's demeanor evidences the commitment to being in all things truthful and candid.

A Winning Personality

The basic rules for good verbal communication in the courtroom are: avoid legalese, simplify legal and factual concepts, use words and phrases familiar to the jury, and, most importantly, do not be condescending or project arrogance.

Plaintiff's counsel talks to the jurors as she would a friend or neighbor sitting in her kitchen. She is pleasant and erect. For oral presentation to be effective, the trial advocate should present her message through all three channels of communication—verbal, vocal, and physical. Persuasionists use all three channels to project that they are genuine, honest, sincere, and confident.

There is a difference between *being* confident and *portraying* confidence in the courtroom. If the trial lawyer portrays too much confidence, she may cross the invisible line into arrogance. On the other hand, the failure to project confidence in the client and his cause may create the image of someone who expects to lose.

One of the most common stereotypes in our country is that of "winners" and "losers." When people are asked to describe a winner, they say that person has good posture, keeps his shoulders back, holds his head high, maintains direct eye contact, breathes deeply and evenly, uses expansive gestures rather than gestures close to the body, takes large steps when walking, and appropriately controls his space. Winners act as if they know what they are doing even when they do not. Winners also have lower voice tones. Their voices project confidence. They control their voices by using pauses effectively. They never seem to be rushing because of nervous energy or to be talking too slowly. Winners use powerful speech that creates memorable images in the minds of the audience.

Losers, on the other hand, have poor posture, avoid eye contact, angle their heads backward, move slowly or haltingly, appear to be in a confused state, do not speak fluently, and use impotent speech. Powerless or impotent speech includes hedging words such as "like," "kind of," "perhaps," and "maybe," as well as frequent pauses with "ah," "and," and "you know."

Successful plaintiff's advocates project not only confidence but also approachability, friendliness, and competence. Following the opening statement, the jury is convinced not only that the trial advocate believes in his cause and that he will prove his case but also that he is confident and friendly enough to be the kind of person who would be willing to discuss the case in privacy with them after their verdict. In short, the lawyer's demeanor should convey an impression and feeling of comfort and ease.

12

The Power of the Telling

THE STORY IS A MAGIC CARPET that can carry an audience anywhere. A well-told narrative can transport listeners back in time and thousands of miles away. It can entertain, teach, and inspire. The storyteller puts his audience next to characters both real and fictional. Through the narrative, the listeners live what happened, understand and identify with the characters, learn and are inspired by the moral presented. They see the conflict resolved. Sometimes they are left to resolve it themselves.

Many storytellers are known by their genre. Agatha Christie and James Lee Burke are accomplished mystery writers. The stories of Larry McMurtry and Louis L'Amour have western settings and themes. Modern-day scientific and governmental intrigue are the hallmark of Tom Clancy. Stephen King, one of the most prolific writers of all time, pens tales of the supernatural. Because they are masters of storytelling, their fictional works are popular and critically acclaimed. Novelists write great stories. But lawyers, preachers, and speakers must "tell" the story. The storyteller uses his physical appearance, voice, and personality as well as words to give power to the telling.

The way a speaker tells the story may be more important than the tale itself. Two different people can deliver a narrative consisting of essentially the same facts, and the audience will see one as boring and uninspiring while the other captivates and inspires. The difference is the *way* they spin the yarn.

There is a big difference between speaking to an audience and writing for one. Many of the most prominent novelists and screenwriters flop when they speak to a live audience. While they are legends at putting pen to paper, their oral presentations are less than inspiring. By the same token, many of the great speakers of our time have never penned a meaningful story. This is another reason why trial lawyers are the greatest storytellers. They must both craft a persuasive story and tell it in a compelling way.

The courtroom storyteller uses his physical appearance, voice, and personality as well as words to give power to the telling. Great advocates have the elusive quality of charisma, discussed in the preceding chapter. The accomplished narrator uses her magic carpet of the story to set the audience—jurors—down next to the events that are in litigation. With a single point of view, she uses the active voice and present tense to make her listeners live the story. Simple, ordinary words paint clear and vivid pictures of the people, places, and events. Rhetorical devices and neurolinguistics add to the persuasive purchase.

There may be a few "natural" storytellers, but anyone can master the art. Persuasive storytelling combines verbal, vocal, and physical skills to create the desired image in the audience's mind.

VERBAL

Point of View

Point of view simply means who is observing the action and thinking about it or speaking about it at that point in the narrative. There are three basic points of view: omniscient, first person, and limited third person.

In *To Have and Have Not*, Ernest Hemingway does a unique thing: he takes the first-person viewpoint in the first and last chapters of the novel but tells most of the story from the third-person point of view. While unique, such an approach might be disastrous for the courtroom storyteller. Because jurors crave consistency, it is important that from the beginning the narrator adopt one point of view to intensify the unity of the story. Some advocates like to tell the story from the plaintiff's perspective, in the first person. Others feel that the third person, the concept usually employed by novelists and screenwriters, works most effectively in the courtroom. Regardless of which viewpoint plaintiff's counsel chooses, it is imperative that she use the same one throughout the story.

Some legendary books have been written in the first person: *The Adventures of Huckleberry Finn, Moby-Dick, The Catcher in the Rye*. One of the advantages of the first person is the intimacy it establishes: "Look, this happened to me."

In the courtroom the third-person point of view offers many advantages. It lets the storyteller move from scene to scene. The narrator can describe what is happening in the operating room, move to the anxious parents in the hospital waiting room, and then move back to the surgical action.

A third-person point of view allows the storyteller to move into anyone's head to explain his or her motivations.

> Nurse Johnson is busy today. Too many patients that need her, not enough staff. She has complained before. A lot of good it has done; "Just do the best you can," her supervisors have told her. The patient

> in 939B came in at two o'clock. The EMS told her he was in a lot of pain. When she saw Mario Brannon, his breathing was labored. He said the pain in his abdomen was intense—he could hardly bear it. She saw the tears in his eyes and the worry on his wife's face. A quick check of blood pressure: 74 over 50! *The doctor needs to be called,* she thought. Now, as she dials Dr. Vega's number, she hears, "Dorothy, we need help with medication in room 915." The call will have to wait. Not enough time to make it now.

An effective way to question motivation, particularly in opening statement, is to pose rhetorical questions. An example is found in chapter 26:

> Is he daydreaming? Is his mind someplace else? (See page 447.)

The third person enables the listener as "protector."[1]

> Sitting in the cab of the Monroe Trucking Company eighteen-wheeler as their driver comes down I-45 from Dallas toward Houston, don't we want to say to him, "Slow down, you're getting into heavy traffic." As he approaches the 610 Loop, don't we want to say, "Slow down, there is always congestion at this interchange." As he sees the line of cars backed up in his lane, don't we want to yell at him, "Hit your brakes, before it's too late!"

From the third-person point of view, the narrator can bring the audience into the story. Techniques include the simple suggestion found in chapter 28:

> We are standing off to the side at Parkway Hospital. . . . (See page 464.)

Or the embedded question found in chapter 29:

> Can you see Lois? Can you see her in the operating room? (See page 476.)

Or the embedded command in the same chapter:

> Watch it. We can see it. (See page 476.)

Once the narrator brings the listeners into the scene, they stand in the role of "protector."

> "Don't do that. You don't have a doctor's order." . . . Don't we want to say those things to her? Don't we want her to hear us? (See chapter

> 28, page 464.)
>
> "Wait a minute, doctor. From what we've heard, what you ought to know, you don't freeze a lump that small. Haven't you read the Standards of the American Pathology Association?" (See chapter 29, page 476.)

The bystander view expedites shifts in time. The narrator can jump backward or forward. He can describe the grave site of a child with the large oak growing next to it. How the massive tree represents a life that never was. Then the narrator shifts the scene back ten years to the boardroom and the corporation's directors who made the decision not to equip a high chair with a strap to prevent babies who submarined in the chair from strangling to death.

The use of the third person can enhance counsel's casting the victim into the role of the reluctant plaintiff.

> Now Lois is looking for the truth. . . . (See chapter 29, page 481.)
>
> These folks don't want to be here. If Vernon or Ruby or Lisa could stand before you right now, they would tell you there's a thousand places they'd rather be. (See chapter 30, page 490.)

These are just a few of the rhetorical devices that use of the third person brings to storytelling. Regardless of the point of view the narrator chooses, it must remain consistent throughout the telling of the story to achieve maximum persuasive punch.

Jurors' Perspective

A key to courtroom success is the ability to appreciate the juror's perspective. The lawyer who looks at things like the ordinary citizen—or at least appears to look at things that way—brings significant purchase to the persuasive process. Psychological studies demonstrate that it is difficult to separate the message from the messenger.[2] The average person identifies with and appreciates the lawyer who is—

- sincere;
- honest;
- interested in and understands their problems;
- observes the fundamentals of etiquette;
- faces up to the hard, weak points of the story;

- harmonizes the evidence; and
- puts the opposition on the defensive.

Jurors form impressions about the plaintiff, her case, and her counsel from the nonverbal aspects of the opening statement. Psychological research suggests that what the speaker says (verbal content) is less important to the persuasive process than the physical and vocal aspects. The physical aspects of communication represent 55 percent of the components of whether a speaker is "liked." Vocal aspects, how the speaker uses his voice, represent 38 percent.[3] These conclusions confirm that the courtroom storyteller's appearance, posture, movement, gestures, demeanor, and mechanics of speech significantly impact how the audience views the story. The image the jury forms of the trial advocate can either intensify the story or diminish it.

Active Voice

Good writers and speakers stay in the active voice. Active is more direct and vigorous than passive. Stephen King suggests that timid writers look for passive verbs for the same reason timid lovers like passive partners. The passive voice is safe. King believes that "unsure writers also feel the passive voice somehow lends their work authority, perhaps even a quality of majesty."[4] To paraphrase King, if you find instruction manuals and tort treatises majestic, maybe you should use the passive voice. When writers or speakers lapse into the passive voice, their language loses power. Lawyers, scientists, and bureaucrats are so addicted to the passive voice that they must alert themselves against its drowsy, impersonal pomp.

The use of a passive voice puts useless words in a sentence. In the active voice, the actor is the subject of the sentence. In the passive voice, the actor is always the object of the sentence. Thus—

> I will always remember my first trial.

is better than—

> My first trial will always be remembered by me.

The habitual use of the active voice makes for forcible writing and speaking. It is particularly important that the active voice be employed in narratives concerned with action. Consider the following examples, which illustrate the difference between the passive and active voice:

Passive	*Active*
• There were a number of injured people seen lying on the ground at the accident site.	• Bleeding and moaning bodies covered the ground around the railroad intersection.
• When the doctor entered the operating room, alcohol could be smelled on his breath by the nurses.	• The nurses smelled alcohol on Dr. Jones's breath when he came into the operating room.
• The reason he left college was that his injuries impaired his ability to do his studies.	• John's injuries made him quit college.
• It was not long before he was very sorry he had said what he had.	• He soon regretted his words.

The use of the active voice allows the courtroom storyteller to "backload" his sentences. Backloading means that the significant word comes last. Because it comes last, it can be better emphasized. The critical word is emphasized by drawing out the critical syllable.

The diagnosis was *can*cer.

The cable was de*fec*tive.

The defendant was *speed*ing.

The only way to save John's leg was to *am*putate.

When is it appropriate to use passive construction? In two instances: if the person or thing receiving the action is more important than the person or thing doing the action, or if the person or thing doing the action is unknown or unimportant.

A corollary to using the active voice is putting concepts in positive form. Effective storytellers rarely use the word *not* as a means of evasion.

Negative	*Positive*
• Dr. Jones was not very often on time when he saw his patients in the hospital.	• Dr. Jones usually came late to see his patients.
• Dr. Jones did not think that lab studies would help him with his diagnosis.	• Dr. Jones thought lab studies were a waste of time.
• Childcraft did not think that the reports of injuries to children using their toys were significant.	• Childcraft ignored the reports that their toys were injuring children.

These examples show the weakness inherent in the word *not*. As a rule it is better to express even a negative in positive form.

• Not honest	• Dishonest
• Not important	• Trifling
• Did not remember	• Forgot
• Did not pay any attention to	• Ignored
• Did not have much confidence in	• Distrusted

Stephen King has as one of his primary rules for writing, "The adverb is not your friend."[5] He uses as an example, "He closed the door firmly." A better way of saying it would be that the character closed the door or slammed the door. Adverbs are like the passive voice; the writer uses them because he fears he will not be taken seriously. Adverbs clutter the narrative and draw the storyteller into lazy, rather than powerful, language.

Present Tense

Albert Mehrabian, a psychologist who performed extensive studies in the 1970s at UCLA in the field of persuasion, identified what he termed the "immediacy of speech."[6] In essence, the principle is that the more immediate speech is, the more persuasive it becomes. Thus—

John has done good work.

is less persuasive than—

John does good work.

Any historical narrative recounts something that has occurred. For this reason, most speakers present their stories in the past tense. Some communicators and trial lawyers have suggested that the story must always be told in the same tense. Persuasive speakers understand the power that comes from switching quickly into the present tense during the critical part of the action. Making the audience "live" the story as it is happening involves them emotionally and brings them into the story. The speaker evolves the story to the point where he is telling it as though it is happening now. This involves the listeners to the point at which they must ask themselves, "And then what happened?"

Describing past events in the past tense is the way most people converse. Adopting the present tense lets the narrator live the action. This empowers the audience to better "see" the story. Examples of present-tense storytelling are found in chapter 16 and in the opening and closing arguments of chapters 26 through 30.

Simple, Ordinary Words and Phrases

The problem many lawyers have is that they went to law school. They became so accustomed to the legal shorthand learned there that they have forgotten the language everyone else speaks. As a result, many advocates come across as condescending, pedantic, or insincere. The accomplished courtroom storyteller avoids words and phrases such as—

- constitute
- prior to
- implement
- subsequent to
- necessitate
- heretofore
- by reason of
- in lieu of
- at this point in time

Advertisers recognize twenty words as being the most persuasive:[7]

- suddenly
- now
- announcing
- introducing
- improvement
- amazing
- sensational
- remarkable
- revolutionary
- startling
- miracle
- magic
- offer
- quick
- easy
- wanted
- challenge
- compare
- bargain
- hurry

Other words recognized as carrying persuasive punch are—

- you
- discover
- health
- prove
- guarantee
- new
- love
- safety
- results
- save
- money

Good storytellers use simple, ordinary words. They make their stories compelling by connecting with their audience in language everyone can understand.[8] Choose words carefully with these rules in mind:

- simple words are best;
- the fewer the better; and
- look for words that carry powerful images.

We are well advised to remember the advice of Mark Twain:

> Use the right word, not its second cousin. The difference between

> the almost right word and the right word is really a large matter—'tis the difference between the lightning-bug and the lightning. A powerful agent is the right word.[9]

The great orators in our history have unanimously extolled the virtues of precise word selection. Franklin D. Roosevelt, in his famous address to Congress announcing Japan's attack on Pearl Harbor, originally wrote the opening line: "December 7, 1941, a day that will live in world history." Upon reflection, he changed the broad term "world history" to the more precise word "infamy," which connotes not only the historical event but the contemptuous attitude the American public held toward the Japanese sneak attack.

In products and medical malpractice cases, complex scientific concepts may be in issue. Even then, simpler is better. Use the commonly understood lay term rather than the more accurate scientific one. Thus "heart attack" is better than "myocardial infarction" and "the baby was suffocated during labor" is more compelling than "the baby suffered anoxic encephalopathy."

Persuasive, charismatic, powerful speakers use words that create pictures. Picture words can be used as a hook:

> The bigger the load, the faster the road, the better the bottom line. (See chapter 26, page 444.)

An empowering phrase:

> We have the power to stop those people who would splatter the innocent and leave justice as insignificant roadkill in the rush to a better bottom line. (See chapter 28, page 462.)

> But they're not strong enough, big enough, to grab the bottom rung [of the ladder] by themselves. They need a little boost up to that bottom rung and they'll climb the rest of the way themselves. (See chapter 28, pages 469–70.)

Or a theme (what the case is about):

> This was a drive-by diagnosis followed by a rush to surgery followed by a plunge off the cliff into medical oblivion. (See chapter 29, page 483.)

Use of metaphoric picture words enhances the imagery, particularly those stumbling under the weight of sterile science.

> Is this a drive-by diagnosis? Look for the skid marks. They're not there. (See chapter 29, page 479.)

All the storytelling techniques discussed in this chapter help accomplish the plaintiff's goal of involving the jury. Use of the active voice and present tense brings the listener into the narrative.

Rhetorical Techniques

Repetition

The most commonly used rhetorical technique is repetition. You can use repetition to great dramatic effect, particularly when you select a theme or phrase and continue it throughout the argument. For example, in a product liability case you might want to adopt the phrase, "And then, in an instant, he was crippled."

You could explain the details of the design of the product, establishing the imprudent nature by which the product was conceived. You could point out that this design was such that it placed into the stream of commerce a product that was likely to cause harm. "And then, in an instant, he was crippled."

You may want to discuss the sale of the product to the user—and how the product was overpromoted and its benefits overstated. "When the Clark Company purchased this product, to be used by Bob, they did not know that shortly after he used it, he would be crippled."

Go then to a description of what the plaintiff was doing when he was using the product. Explain how he was using it in conformity with his understanding of proper use, as stated in the manufacturer's own directions. "And then, in an instant, he was crippled."

Repetition gives a jury a sense of predictability. It also involves a creative use of language, rhythm, and reassurance.[10]

The use of repetition as a rhetorical technique is particularly effective during the cross-examination of witnesses. An example is found in chapter 15 at pages 208–09.

The echo effect of repetition is achieved through the repetition at the beginning of successive sentences of one word or phrase that repeats the speaker's theme. This may be a declarative statement such as the phrase "I have a dream," which was used eight times consecutively by Martin Luther King, Jr., or it may be in the form of a rhetorical question that reminds the jurors of their power, such as, "What is this child's life worth in our community?"

For centuries, politicians have understood the effectiveness of refrain in the echo effect by repeating phrases at the beginnings of sentences. Consider the following example of repetition by Franklin D. Roosevelt:

> Whoever seeks to set one nationality against another, seeks to degrade all nationalities.
>
> Whoever seeks to set one race against another, seeks to enslave all races.
>
> Whoever seeks to set one religion against another, seeks to destroy all religion.[11]

For an example of using the echo effect, see chapter 30 and the recurring phrase, "He deserved better. . . ."

Embedding

Another technique for involving the audience is the use of embedded questions, comments, and commands.

Embedded Question

> You will wonder how Corbett Pharmaceuticals could have continued to believe Ivexgen was safe when they were receiving so many complaints of adverse reactions.
>
> You will be curious to learn how the hospital justifies the failure of its nurses to observe the changes on this baby's fetal monitor strip showing that the child was suffocating.

Examples of embedded questions are found in chapter 27:

> If you can't trust your friends, who can you trust? (See page 454.)
>
> You will wonder how a friend who hurts a friend can first accept, then deny responsibility. (See page 454.)
>
> What happened? Was it the wrong kind of pin? Did the defendant fail to pound the pin in the whole way? (See page 458.)

Embedded Comment

> Did you notice how much time counsel for the defendant spent during the voir dire examination asking about your feelings toward the people who drive after they've been drinking?

The use of the embedded comment is illustrated in the closing summation in chapter 28:

> We know what happened on June 24, 1992. We don't need experts to tell us. (See page 463.)

Embedded Command

> As we listen to the corporate representatives of this defendant tell us of the complaints the company received about children strangling in their high chairs, we will be thinking of the number of children who

> died needlessly because this company did not act on what it knew.

The courtroom storyteller uses the embedded command to bring her audience into the narrative. An eighteen-year-old freshman is raped in her dorm room by a male sophomore who works as a resident assistant. As part of his duties, the university gave him a security card that allowed access to the female wing. A review of the computerized records shows that the security cards issued to male resident assistants were being overused to gain frequent access to the female floor. The plaintiff also contends that the premises were defective because the dorm room doors did not have peepholes that allowed residents to see into the hallway before opening their doors.

> Malcolm Hall is four stories tall. The first and third floors are male dormitories. The second and fourth are female dorms. The university claims in its literature and promotional materials that their dorms are safe and secure.
>
> Look! You can see it. Some of the male resident assistants employed by the university are often on the girls' floor. They're using the security card the university provided. Bill Black is the worst offender. The records show he accesses the girls' floor regularly. Can you see him? He was with the group of students drinking beer at Charlie's. He knows Ashley came back to the dorm intoxicated. It is around midnight and he uses his security card to get up on the fourth floor. He goes to Ashley's room and knocks on the door. Ashley is still a little tipsy from the three or four beers she had at Charlie's. She can't look out into the hall and see who is knocking on her door. She opens it. We don't want to watch but we have to. Bill charges into the room and pushes Ashley back on the bed. . . .

An example of an embedded command is found in chapter 29, page 476:

> Watch it. We can see it.

Questions and Empowering

Don't answer all the questions in your story. Sometimes, leave questions for the jury to answer. Let the person who listens to the story answer the questions. The listener becomes empowered. Give the jurors the power.

> The judge doesn't have the power, the president of the United States doesn't have the power, I don't have the power. You have the power to answer the questions in this case. We can put before you what happened, but it is up to you to supply the answers.
>
> Why is it that this company in Pennsylvania did not inspect a defective pipe that was going to carry liquid gas? Why is it that they

> skimped on safety, causing the gas in the defective pipe to seep out, ignite, and then burn, blister, and scald the flesh of James Johnson? Why is that?
>
> Could it be that they were so profit-hungry that they just blew off the cost of inspection as a needless irritant to the bottom line? That just because they were too busy building the business they didn't have time to consider the safety of those who might be working around their pipelines? Did they think that no one would ever learn of the other fifteen times when their defective pipes exploded? Did they think if we did learn that, we wouldn't care? I know the answer to these questions and so do you. But you're the only ones who can make the answers mean anything.

The conclusion of the closing summation in chapter 28 exemplifies using personal experience in storytelling to empower the jury (see pages 470–71).

Transferring an Answer

An effective rhetorical device some storytellers use is to transfer a thought, idea, or answer to a member of the audience so that they "own" it. Many speech professors and persuasionists caution speakers to refrain from using their index fingers to point toward a member of the audience. But breaking this well-established rule can be an effective rhetorical device.

The speaker poses the question, "What is the most common cause of highway fatalities in America?"

As the question is posed, the hand is brought upward and the index finger, held chest-high, is moved to emphasize each word. Then, maintaining eye contact, the speaker surveys the audience. He finds a receptive pair of eyes, a knowing smile, a nod of the head. He then points at the person and gives the answer: "Drinking." The hand is then dropped and eye contact is briefly maintained.

There are those who might condemn this technique, but I have found that it works. The listener has been singled out and in almost every situation will want to "claim" the answer.

Neurolinguistics

Persuasive storytellers appeal to all of the audience's senses. They use words that cause the audience not only to see the story but also to smell it, hear it, feel it. Psychologists teach that effective communication with a jury requires the understanding that people primarily communicate in three sensory-based representational systems. People think in sensory terms. They *picture* something in their minds; *say* things to themselves; or *feel* a sense of what is right, good, or appropriate. People tend to prefer and use one representational system more than the others. A person's preferred system helps determine what he pays attention to, what influences him, how he communicates and how he evaluates others' communication.[12]

Courtroom persuasion depends on the advocate's ability to involve all the listener's senses with the narrative and to appeal through each listener's sensory system.

The three representational systems are—

- visual (seeing)
- auditory (hearing)
- kinesthetic (feelings, touch, movement, smell, taste)

A person's language is a good indicator of his representational system. People use words from their system because that is how they understand and relate to the world. Consider the following examples:

> *Visual:* "I have tried to show you this. I have painted a clear picture, but you just don't see the point."
>
> *Auditory:* "I have tried to tell you. I have explained it as clearly as I can, but you just don't hear what I am saying."
>
> *Kinesthetic:* "I have tried to give you a feel for this. I have struggled as hard as I can, but you just don't grasp it."

Effective courtroom storytellers establish rapport by using predicates from all three representational systems in their narrative.

> As you *listen* to the testimony of Dr. Jones, you will see how the pieces begin to *fit together*. After Dr. Jones tells us how the accident happened, the cause will become *as clear as a bell* and you will *appreciate* the injustice that Dorothy has suffered.

The plaintiff tells a trial story incorporating reference to sight:

> We're standing off to the side as Nurse Tarriman goes to the obstetrical supplies and draws out a dose of Pitocin to give Lisa by IV piggyback drip.

What could be seen at the time:

> Stand off to the side and watch as Nurse Tarriman hangs the Pitocin and begins giving it to Lisa through the IV. (See chapter 28, page 464.)
>
> They turn Mark on his back. They pull off the surgical drapes. Mark is blue all over. His face, his shoulders, his upper body, his thighs. (See chapter 30, page 489.)

A good narrative conveys sound, which may be dialogue:

> Toward the end of the surgery, Nurse Cernosek is up under the drapes. Dr. Stuart says, "What's going on? Is there a problem?" Nurse Cernosek says, "I'm not getting air in one lung." (See chapter 30, page 489.)

The persuasive acoustics of the narrative may be an integral part of the action.

> We hear the puff of air going to the air brakes, the screeching of rubber on concrete. . . . In an instant we hear the thud of metal on metal when the eighteen-wheeler hits the red Datsun and knocks it up under a stopped eighteen-wheeler. (See chapter 26, page 447.)

Sound can be effectively communicated by devices other than those actually involved, such as using a metronome to compare heart rate at the beginning of surgery and how far the defendants allowed it to fall before reacting. (See chapter 30, pages 491–92.)

The sense of smell may be a significant aspect of the narration because it is the sense most connected to the subconscious.

> We can smell the burning rubber being peeled off on concrete. (See chapter 26, page 447.)

> They wheel Mark through the wide doors that go to the operating rooms. It's cooler back here and smells of alcohol, disinfectant, iodine, and chloroform. (See chapter 30, page 489.)

The plaintiff's story incorporates the feelings of the characters. It may be a doctor who treated the deceased:

> You might think he, above all others, would be hardened to it. But when you hear him describe what Eric went through you will know that no matter how often you see it, the torture that burn victims go through tears at your heart. (See chapter 26, page 449.)

Or the plaintiff suing someone he thought was his friend:

> It was a handshake deal, and Ray put his trust in the defendant. If you can't trust a friend, who can you trust? (See chapter 27, page 454.)

Rule of Three

One of the most frequently used storytelling techniques is the *rule of three*, sometimes referred to as the triad.[13]

Consider the following well-known examples in which the triad (italicized) achieves rhythmic eloquence:

> We hold these truths to be self-evident, that all men are created equal, that they are endowed by their Creator with certain unalienable Rights, that among these are *Life, Liberty* and *the pursuit of Happiness. . . .*
>
> . . . [W]e mutually pledge to each other *our Lives, our Fortunes* and *our sacred Honor*.[14]

> Never in the field of human conflict was *so much* owed by *so many* to *so few*.[15]

> *With malice toward none; with charity for all; with firmness in the right.* . . .
>
> *[W]e can not dedicate—we can not consecrate—we can not hallow* this ground. . . . and that government *of the people, by the people, for the people*, shall not perish from the earth.[16]

> *"Duty," "Honor," "Country"*—those three hallowed words reverently dictate *what you want to be, what you can be, what you will be*.[17]

The rule of three works well in trial themes.

> A tragedy that was needless, senseless, and endless. (See chapter 26, page 451.)

> The wrong people do the wrong thing at the wrong time. (See chapter 28, page 462.)

> This was a drive-by diagnosis followed by a rush to surgery followed by a plunge off the cliff into medical oblivion. (See chapter 29, page 483.)

Antithesis

The rhetorical device of antithesis is used to balance contrasted ideas so as to highlight both ideas through the parallel arrangement of key phrases.

For example, consider that President John F. Kennedy's speeches were replete with antithesis. The classic example of the use of antithesis was contained in Kennedy's inaugural address, wherein he entreated the American citizenry with the following challenge:

> We observe today not a victory of party but a celebration of freedom—symbolizing an end as well as a beginning—signifying renewal as well as change. . . .
>
> . . . Let us never negotiate out of fear. But let us never fear to negotiate. . . .
>
> And so, my fellow Americans: ask not what your country can do for you—ask what you can do for your country.[18]

Antithesis works in the courtroom:

> We have seen two Thomas Millers in this case.
>
> One an energetic and active father—the other a bedridden paralytic.
>
> One a helpful and loving husband—the other a helpless patient.
>
> One a hardworking provider—the other a financial burden.
>
> One a healthy, happy Thomas Miller before this defendant's tragic mistake; the other, Thomas Miller for the next forty years.

Trial lawyers use this rhetorical device to remind jurors to consider aspects of the case they might overlook:

> In determining the damages in this case, don't look at the death of this child, but look at the life that never will be.

Vocal

The way the courtroom narrator speaks, or what Albert Mehrabian termed the vocal aspects of persuasion, represents 38 percent of the persuasive process.[19] Vocal mechanics involves the manipulation of three basic variables: vocal pitch (highness or lowness), vocal tone (volume), and vocal rate (cadence or rate of speech). Skilled advocates use these variables to achieve maximum effect of the verbal content of their message. The manner in which these variables are orchestrated depends on the nature of the message being conveyed, its content, and the purpose to be achieved.[20]

Vocal Pitch

The pitch—the highness or lowness of a vocal tone—is a good indicator of emotionality. The advocate who appropriately changes pitch levels attracts the jurors' attention, generates interest, and makes her point in a manner the jurors will more likely remember. As a general rule, it is easier to listen to a lower-pitched voice, and for this reason it is worth the advocate's effort to develop this pitch. Emotions (anger, sympathy, solemnity) can also be expressed through changes in pitch. Accomplished narrators use the voice as a behavior indicator of various moods and emotional states. They visualize what they are talking about. As they tell the story, they are seeing it. This type of imaging helps create color and nuance in counsel's voice.

Vocal Tone

Good storytellers use loudness as a vocal cue. They lower their voice at critical junctions in the story to emphasize what they are saying. Otherwise, loudness is related positively to perceived credibility. Storytellers should speak at a level that conveys that they are in control, are confident, and know what they are doing.

The nuance of storytelling is very important. The narrator enlarges the voice to make it forceful and compelling, then softens it to become more intimate and personal. Tone is a vocal characteristic that often betrays insincerity. Speakers who are too loud may seem to be "in the face" of their listeners. Someone who uses exactly the same tone in describing something sad or touching as he does in describing factual data may come across as empty and disingenuous.

Vocal Rate

Communicators have noted that a person who talks faster is generally regarded more favorably by his listeners. Speakers with a faster rate of delivery are seen as more intelligent, knowledgeable, and objective. People tend to talk longer to those they like. Similarly, people are attentive to speakers whose delivery is consistent with the listeners' conception of confidence and reliability. Effective storytellers use a comfortable rate but pause to highlight important points in the story. The pause is a purposeful interval of silence giving the audience time to digest the information or concept they just heard. The controlled, deliberate pause can have a significant effect by jarring the listener's attention.

Proper vocal mechanics are essential to creating the proper mood in the audience. The feeling must be consistent with content. The way the advocate uses her voice must correspond with the particular drama she is trying to create. There can be no contradiction between verbal content and vocal mechanics. If there is, the jury will believe the vocal behavior over the verbal content.

Interestingly, most speakers naturally assume these speech and movement characteristics when they sincerely feel and live that part of the story appropriate to those characteristics.

The courtroom narrator uses inflections, tone of voice, and dramatic pauses to enhance the persuasive impact of the plaintiff's story. The following are some of the moods or feelings that plaintiff's counsel may need to provoke during the opening narrative.

- *Tragedy*

In speaking of tragedy, the narrator slows the vocal rate and lowers the tone. She uses extremes in vocal patterns. She lowers her eyes, slows her body movements and breathing patterns. She employs dramatic pauses.

- *Anger*

The speaker conveying anger talks faster, at a higher pitch, with a louder volume. He makes direct eye contact with his listeners. His gestures are limited to the mid-waist or higher and are firm and definite. The movement quickens and is decisive. The pauses are placed at dramatic points.

- *Factual information*

When delivering factual information, the advocate keeps her eyes level and breathes evenly. She avoids extreme tones and moderates her behavior.

- *Painting a scene*

To paint a scene in the listener's eye, the speaker uses quicker vocal patterns with uplifted eye movement. Gestures are expansive and charts or photographs are used.

PHYSICAL

Eye Contact

The most important physical aspect of communication is eye contact. It is through eye contact that the speaker connects with the audience. The lack of appropriate eye contact reinforces virtually every negative aspect of a lawyer's demeanor.[21]

Some advocates worry too much about what they are saying. While what counsel says is important, it is sometimes more important that she say it right. The lawyer who is concerned too much with what she is saying is apt to be overly dependent on her notes and forget to "talk" to the audience. Following are some of the reasons that lawyers become too bound to their notes.

- *Fear of betraying the author*

Trial advocates differ from most speakers and actors in that they are the authors of the stories they tell. Actors deliver lines from scripts written by others. Many politicians employ speechwriters for their presentations. The trial lawyer stands before his audience as both author and actor. He wrote the narrative and will tell it—deliver the lines. The advocate does not want to betray the author. He wants to be sure the lines are delivered just as he wrote them. But the effective advocate does not harbor this fear and knows that the way he gives the lines is more important to the persuasive process than being sure that he recites the lines verbatim.

- *Leaving something out*

Another explanation of why some lawyers chain themselves to their notes is their fear that they may forget something. She may leave some detail out of the narrative. She may forget some statistic. Notes for the opening statement are helpful, but they should not be extensive. The critical facts of most opening narratives can be written on a couple of index cards or sheets of paper. The lawyer who has lived the case should know the essentials of the story so well she can tell it without leaning on the crutch of a detailed manuscript.

- *Fear of the jury*

Some attorneys are not comfortable looking at their audience. If they read their opening statement or closing argument, they don't have to make eye contact with jurors. This is the poorest excuse for overreliance on notes.

The importance of good eye contact with the jury during opening statement and closing summation cannot be overstated. Great advocates connect with their audiences. A primary way of connecting to the listener is by eye contact. Successful lawyers know they are communicating to twelve audiences, not an audience of twelve people. They address different points or arguments to different members of the jury. This produces a type of roving eye contact. When a new point is made, counsel addresses it to a different listener. Generally, the rule is that eye contact with any one person should not exceed thirty to forty-five seconds; otherwise the listener will feel "invaded."

Anchoring

Anchoring is a well-accepted psychological technique. Anchoring is a technique whereby a word, phrase, or theme is repeated. It is repeated from the same spot, with the same gestures, with the same facial expressions, the same tone of voice, and with the same mannerisms. The late, great Jack Benny had a certain way of folding his arms, putting his hand under his chin, and saying the word, "Well . . ." Pretty soon he was getting laughs without saying the word and then he did not even need to put his hand under his chin. He just used part of the gimmick and the anchor worked.

Courtroom storytellers use the technique of anchoring to emphasize a cognitive theme. The narrator chooses a spot in the courtroom where she will stand each time she states the case theme. She uses that spot or area to anchor the initial presentation of the theme in the voir dire examination. She stands in approximately the same place when presenting it in opening statement. During closing argument, she stands in the same place again, using the same facial expressions, tone of voice, and mannerisms.

Physical anchoring works at the subconscious level. Just about any gesture can be used to physically anchor an idea. The more the gesture mimics the action, the better it works as an anchor. A tug on the earlobe may anchor the idea that critical information was not heard. An index finger to the temple may imply that the defendant didn't read a critical report or document. Using the hand as if it were holding a mock glass and slightly raising it toward the lips may lock in the idea of "one drink too many." Repetition reinforces the anchor. Whether in voir dire examination, opening statement, direct or cross-examination of witnesses, or closing argument, the courtroom storyteller uses the same gesture when she refers to the action or idea.

Anchoring may also be directional. When counsel consistently stands to the left side of the jury box he may question, cross-examine, or examine on the subject of damages. The charts supporting this element are placed on the left, facing the jury box. The right side of the jury box is used for liability. When counsel examines or cross-examines liability experts, he stands to the right of the jury box. Liability exhibits are placed on the right side. This telegraphs what the speaker is about. Subconsciously, the mind says, "Oh, he's moving to the right and we're going to hear more about fault . . ."

Anything that connects the jury to the case involves them. Time lines, charts, or diagrams counsel and a witness created during trial involves the listeners in their creation. A flow chart that incorporates points from each witness involves the audience such that they anticipate what the witness must add to the next column. The power of visual aids—pictures—is discussed in chapter 14.

A good story told well can entertain, educate, and inspire. And these are, after all, the three basic challenges every trial lawyer faces.

13

The Power of the Sequence

"She's dead, too." EMT Stewart didn't need to check for a carotid pulse to confirm his diagnosis. The blue Dodge Ram pickup had crashed into the side of Charlie and Sarah Edwards's Toyota Camry with such force that only a smoldering, mangled mass of metal was left. The passenger side was caved in and seemed welded to the contortion that once was the Dodge truck's grille. The impact drove their car eighty feet out of the intersection. The explosive coupling of metal, glass, and plastic crushed her chest and heart, broke his neck. Both Charlie and Sarah were wearing their seatbelts. It did them little good.

It was two minutes after ten when Sonny Castle ran the red light on Westheimer and broadsided the Edwardses. The Houston Police Department was on the scene ten minutes later. The ambulance pulled up twelve minutes after that. Charlie was pronounced dead at 10:31, Sarah at 10:38. They had on their red polo shirts prominently displaying "The University of Houston." Charlie's U of H baseball cap was found in the street. They were on their way home from a Cougars football game. They were five blocks from home.

The tragedy didn't begin at 10:02. It started about the time Charlie and Sarah were pulling into the parking lot off Scott Street on the west side of Robertson Stadium at a little before 6:00 PM. It was about this time that Sonny drove his pickup into the parking lot of Bubbles Men's Club on Richmond. He had his first drink, a double bourbon and Coke. About fifteen minutes later he had his second while one of the girls performed a table dance. Then a third and a fourth. He staggered on his way to the restroom. His voice was slurred when he asked the bartender for two more doubles "because I don't want to have to wait for service."

Standing off to the side in this dark topless bar, don't we want to say, "Don't serve this man any more whiskey!" Shouldn't we insist that they call him a cab? But more drinks are served, and by the time Sonny leaves Bubbles, his blood alcohol level is four times the legal limit.

We don't have to see Sonny get into his car, do we? We don't have to see Sonny as he turns east on Richmond instead of west, discovers he's going the wrong way, and makes a left on South Rice Avenue over to Westheimer. We don't even need to see him turn onto Westheimer and pick up speed trying to make the green light at Chimney Rock. We already knew this tragedy would happen. More importantly, the people at Bubbles knew it when they served Sonny not one drink too many, but eight drinks too many.

Trial lawyers are the greatest storytellers because they face the greatest challenges. Our stories do not come from the author's limitless imagination but from real-life drama, with the characters and events already in place. Most people are accustomed to hearing stories flow as they happen—in chronological order. Plaintiff's counsel tells her story in the opening statement and then calls or cross-examines witnesses who tell it again. Finally, she retells the story in closing argument. Whether the narrator is advocate or witness, the view of events is sequential, minute by minute, day by day. But trial advocates must do more than simply present a diary. They must construct a compelling courtroom narrative of negligence, indifference, insensitivity, injustice, betrayal, and tragedy. Although the construct comes from real people, real places, and real events, this reality should not hamper the narrator. Rather, the audience's judgment of the events may be influenced by the sequence used.

HOLD SOMETHING BACK

Because the opening statement has such signal importance in the persuasive process, it must be full, complete, and compelling. The trial lawyer is setting the schematic filters jurors will use to sift evidence. But this does not mean that the plaintiff's attorney should disclose every strong piece of the narrative in the opening statement. There are many reasons why she may want to hold some things back for use during the trial. A piece of evidence may play more dramatically when counsel uses it during the examination of a witness. Counsel can then emphasize this critical evidence during closing argument to strengthen the persuasive picture the jurors formed during opening statement. Sometimes the plaintiff may want to hold things back until the defense takes its position. The advocate may want the defendant well out on the limb before she begins sawing.

What can the plaintiff hold back? When should trial counsel hold something back? The answer always takes into account the strategic view of the trial as a whole. Sometimes evidence is so devastatingly incriminating that it best comes to the jury from the witness's mouth. For example, in a sexual harassment case, evidence of a long history of abuse by a supervisor may be so unbelievable in the vacuum of the opening statement that such sordid details are best saved for cross-examination. The same principle applies where the defendant's driver has multiple traffic violations and license suspensions.

Sometimes there is an event that will lose its dramatic appeal if mentioned in opening. A pathologist misdiagnoses a tonsil biopsy. He issues a written report that the slides are "benign." Thirteen months later, the patient, who is still having problems, obtains his slides and has them reviewed by a specialist at a well-known cancer hospital. The specialist makes the correct interpretation of cancer and forwards a written report to the treating physician and the original pathologist. The treating physician goes to the original pathologist's office to discuss the report. The first words out of the pathologist's mouth are "I blew this case." The treating physician's testimony at trial will be a dramatic high point. It will be lessened, if not lost altogether, by mentioning it in opening statement. In this type of situation, will the defense try to solve the strategic problem by including it in its opening statement? Probably not. If the defense does refer to the events in the way they actually happened, it will probably do substantial harm to the "picture" the defense is trying to create with its opening statement.

In every case there will be some tidbit of evidence, some document, some fact that is best reserved for the evidence stage. Counsel then expands and dramatizes the story in closing argument with the benefit of the additional facts. An example of "holding back" is found in chapter 29, page 478. In that case, we held back until closing argument the fact that the operative report showed that it was five minutes from the time the patient was opened until being closed. This suggested that the pathologist had made only the most cursory review of the frozen breast tissue section. It implied an even more sinister explanation—that he had not looked at it at all.

The Self-Fulfilling Plot

"I knew that would happen." Everyone has had the experience of attending a movie or play and, as the forces of the characters and actions came together for the plot's critical conflict, thought, "I knew that was going to happen." The audience's reaction is what the authors wanted. The storyteller put the characters and events so perfectly in place that the audience could predict the critical turn of the story just before it happened. For lack of a better term, I call this the "self-fulfilling plot."

In *Shane*, we know halfway through the film that Shane (Alan Ladd) will be in a gunfight with Jack Wilson (Jack Palance). Twenty minutes into *West Side Story*, the audience knows not only that the Jets will fight the Sharks but also that the romance of Tony (Richard Beymer) and Maria (Natalie Wood) will end tragically. In *Cape Fear*, it is no surprise when Max Cady (Robert De Niro) seeks revenge on his attorney Sam Bowden (Nick Nolte).

People who study and make their living telling stories suggest that the primary purpose of institutions is to insist that problems have solutions and that undesirable outcomes can and should be avoided.[1] This psychological principle works well for the plaintiff's lawyer, whose narrative always contains an identifiable cause and the concept of prevention as an essential element. The plaintiff is at a persuasive advantage if counsel can tell her story in such a way that the jury connects the defendant's actions to the plaintiff's harm before introducing the tragic events. The concept of the self-fulfilling plot is another rationale for introducing the antagonist's (defendant's) character and actions early in the trial story.

An indispensable element of the tort cause of action is legal causation. The jury must believe that it was the defendant's actions that caused the harm. The plaintiff presents a persuasive trial story when the jury sees the ending before they hear it. Using words that signal to the jury that they know what will happen next not only shows an appreciation of juror intelligence but also ties together cause and effect in the audience's subconscious.

Plaintiff's counsel tells her story in a way that allows the jury to understand basic facts, medicine, and science. In the products case, counsel talks about how the corporation came up with a product they knew had some problems. She talks about how the marketing department ignored the problems despite the fact that the corporation was receiving reports of injury to consumers. The plaintiff's lawyer leads up to the point where she says to the jury—

> I don't need to tell you what happened next.

Or—

> You can see this tragedy coming.

Or—

> You don't need an expert to tell you that what the defendant did is going to hurt somebody.

Telling the trial story in the form of a self-fulfilling plot arouses curiosity and makes the narrative more interesting. An example of this sequencing can be found in the telling of Bushell's Case in chapter 16, page 220.

BACKFILLING THE PLOT

Antithetical to the self-fulfilling plot is backfilling the plot. The narrator tells the basics of the story but leaves out critical facts. Having sketched the parameters, the advocate comes back with the critical facts that make a difference in the conclusions the audience draws. When this technique is used, counsel introduces it with, "Did I leave anything out?" or, "But there is more to this story."

Storytellers who use this technique put the bad facts up front. The audience begins to draw the wrong conclusion. Just at the point when the listeners are concluding there should be no defendant culpability, the plaintiff jerks them back toward justice by completing the picture. He fills in the gaps with blocks of compelling evidence.

> Dominic was born March 3, 2000. When his obstetrician delivered him, he was limp, flaccid, and pale. He was barely alive, scoring a 2 out of a possible 10 on the universal APGAR scoring system. The

treating pediatricians transferred him to the ICU. Within a short time, Dominic started seizing. It was obvious he had brain damage. Today, Dominic is almost two, he can't sit without assistance, he can only crawl with the aid of a supporting mechanism, he has a feeding tube in his stomach, he is developing contractions of his hands and feet.

Dominic's mother went into preterm labor at thirty-two weeks and was put on Turbutaline, a drug that stops premature labor. The doctor put her to bed for several weeks. So Dominic's mother did not have a normal prenatal course.

Dominic's mother went into labor at home. Her bag of water broke around 11:30. The father drove her to the hospital, where they admitted her around midnight. Electronic fetal monitoring was begun within a short time. The mother had delivered her first baby vaginally. The obstetrician had used a vacuum extractor to pull the baby out. The first baby was normal and healthy and weighed six pounds, eleven ounces. There was no reason to believe Dominic could not be delivered vaginally.

The initial fetal heart monitor tracing showed normal contractions and normal fetal heart rates from midnight on. The obstetrician arrived at 5:30 AM. At 6:40, the obstetrician told the mother to start pushing.

At 9:25, 9:26, and 9:34, the obstetrician applied the vacuum extractor and pulled on Dominic's head. The third attempt delivered an eight-pound baby boy. A baby that was limp, flaccid, pale, barely alive. How can we blame anybody for this? Isn't this just a story about how bad things happen to good people?

Statistically, we know that 80 percent of children born with cerebral palsy have no identifiable event related to labor and delivery to explain the child's brain damage. Most neurological injuries occur during the prenatal period—in utero. Or the neurological deficit is a result of a defect in hormones, metabolism, or genetics.

Did I leave anything out? Is there more to this story? Maybe a few points. Some important facts to consider. Some missing pieces that give the picture a totally different look. A lot of you know about electronic fetal monitoring. The device obstetricians use looks a lot like the EKG monitors we have all seen applied to us to get a tracing of our heart's electrical activity. The machine measures the mother's contractions and the baby's heart rate. A strip of paper is printed out that shows the frequency and intensity of the mother's uterine contractions and the baby's heart rate. Electronic fetal monitoring is the baby's telephone to the outside world. The way a baby's heart rate reacts to labor tells us whether the baby is doing well or is unduly stressed. It tells us whether the labor is progressing normally or

> whether there is some obstruction that will unduly delay birth and cause the baby to be stressed beyond his physiological abilities.
>
> When a mother pushes or has contractions, the baby's heart rate decreases with the stress of labor. During normal labor, the heart rate returns to its baseline, which for most is around 120 to 130. The electronic fetal monitor will show normal beat-to-beat variability. It shows how the heart beats and then rests.
>
> But when a baby is stressed by some obstruction to labor or compromise of his umbilical cord—his lifeline—he loses beat-to-beat variability. His heart rate will stay down or depressed after the mother's contractions are over. This is what is called early deceleration. If the baby is unduly stressed, his baseline heart rate increases. The baby's heart becomes tachycardic.
>
> Dominic's baseline went from 130 beats per minute at 6:30 to a baseline of 180 beats at 7:30, two hours before he was delivered. Dominic continued to cry out in the only way he could for the next two hours until he had used up all of his reserves and began to suffocate. For two hours, the obstetrician and nurses allowed Dominic to struggle in an effort to come into this world. For two hours, they had clear indications that the mother could not safely deliver this eight-pound child safely through her birth canal. Dominic needed someone to intervene and perform a C-section.
>
> After Dominic was delivered, the pathology results tell us that the umbilical cord was a normal three-vessel cord, of normal length. The placenta was normal. All the genetic testing was normal. No one ever found any other explanation for Dominic's brain damage than that his brain was starved for oxygen for too long during labor. This isn't a case about a child injured in utero before the mother went into labor. This isn't a story about "bad things happening to good people." It is a story about medical neglect of the worst kind. How a baby's cries for help were ignored.

Backfilling the plot is another effective rhetorical device for the courtroom storyteller and is illustrated by how the *Brown v. Board of Education* story unfolds in chapter 16, page 233.

Those who win with stories understand and utilize the narrative magic that attends sequencing. They do not themselves become slaves to the chronology of people, facts, and events. Creative sequencing is one of the hallmarks of the master storyteller.

14

The Power of the Pictures

THOMAS NAST WAS the famous cartoonist whose political cartoons appeared in Harper's Weekly *in the 1870s and 1880s. His greatest campaign was his war against corruption in New York politics. He pilloried the Tammany Hall machine in* Harper's *until "Boss" Tweed writhed. "Stop them damned pictures," Tweed told his henchmen. "I don't care so much what the papers say about me. My constituents can't read. But, damn it, they can see pictures!"*[1]

"Seeing is believing" and "One picture is worth a thousand words" are persuasive truisms expressed in two of the most common and recognizable American proverbs. Said another way, many people follow the axiom, "What I can't see, I never will believe in."[2] While we learn and communicate with all our senses, the eyes are the primary lenses through which most of us absorb and understand information.

I remember the Bible stories the Sunday school teacher taught us in the 1940s before the age of television, computers, and PowerPoint presentations. She used a felt board about the size of a school blackboard. As she told the story, she would put up colored cutouts of the characters, places, and things central to her narrative. This crude but effective presentation helped us follow the stories of Adam and Eve, Noah, Abraham, Moses, Jesus, and the Apostle Paul. The "pictures" that appeared out of her large canvas bag aroused our curiosity and caused us to attend better the lesson she wanted us to learn. The effective storyteller uses pictures, photographs, charts, and whatever her creative mind can conjure up as long as it empowers and doesn't detract from the story.

But some speakers are not storytellers. They don't intend to be. Many professional presentations are dry, sterile lectures. Any visual aid assists this presentation. The lecturer is not attempting to connect to his audience. His goal is not to inspire, motivate, or bring his audience to action. He is teaching. So doctors, accountants, engineers, and scientists fill their presentations with PowerPoint shows, charts, diagrams, and slides. The experienced storyteller knows that too many visuals can kill the narrative. The presentation may affirm that the speaker is prepared and knows his subject, but there is little chance the audience will become truly involved.

When an advocate rises in a courtroom to give an opening statement, his challenge is to involve the jurors in a narrative of people, places, and events that will eventually lead them to resolve the controversy in his client's favor. The jury having heard the evidence, the trial lawyer stands again before his audience challenged to take his story, apply the legal principles contained in the court's charge, and motivate his listeners to construct an ending to the story with a just and fair verdict. Visual aids can assist in meeting this challenge. But if overly or improperly used, visual exhibits can blunt the impact of the story. Jurors must be involved in a narrative to identify with the plaintiff's counsel, empathize with the plaintiff, criticize the defense, and be motivated toward an identifiable end.[3] So the key is balance. Does the visual aid add to the understanding of the story and simplify the issues without detracting from the narrative?

HOW WE LEARN

Social scientists studying how the human brain assimilates data have tried to quantify how the average person gathers information. Their research quantifies the five human senses as follows:[4]

Sight	83%
Hearing	11%
Smell	3.5%
Touch	1.5%
Taste	1%

American society is now considered to be one of "visual learners." From television to computer screens, Americans now learn through visual explanations. "Talking heads" and the spoken word are relegated to PBS. Lawyers need to adapt to a learning age where "seeing is believing."

However, the principle of teaching visually can be undermined by an overreliance on demonstrative exhibits and computer presentations. Jury psychologists such as Eric Oliver warn against using preprepared computer shows that can distance lawyer, client, and, most importantly, story from the jurors. Demonstrative evidence during opening statement or summation should be focused and visceral. Exhibits should always assist the lawyer, rather than the reverse.

Using Visual Aids with Witnesses

Immediacy and dynamics bolster the effect of visual aids. Jurors generally recall and understand lists and charts that are "created" in front of them. Studies have shown that jurors will recollect more aspects of testimony when the witness's verbal content is combined with a summary, whether in words or pictures, that is created on a chart or with a computer in front of the jury while the witness is testifying. This exponential increase in comprehension and recollection is due to the combined sensory inputs of both verbal and visual content. However, when pictures or graphical data are presented as a whole in advance of the verbal explanation and context, the lawyer may actually create a disjunctive focus for the jury. Jurors may focus on the visual and tune out the words when there is too much precreated visual input that is not timed with the verbal content. Therefore, the key is to ensure a contemporaneous presentation to maximize understanding and retention.

Visual aids are not a substitute for live presentation. Because of recent technological advances, including computer-generated presentations, many trial lawyers have gotten carried away and rely on visuals more than story for connecting with the jury and bringing their listeners into the narrative.

Using Visual Aids in Opening Statement and Closing Summation

A few trial judges will not permit the use of visual aids during opening statement. Some even hold that counsel, during closing argument, can use only exhibits the court has admitted in evidence. However, as cases have become more technical and complex, more judges are willing to allow the use of visual aids to illustrate scientific principles, define relationships of events and people, and summarize damages. These exhibits are often necessary to simplify issues and help the jury understand the case. In a case involving a lengthy series of events leading up to the incident, the attorney may use a chart illustrating the chronology of what happened. Where there are significant conflicts in medical or business records or the testimony of lay or expert witnesses, for example, this information may also be incorporated in the storyboard.

Three principles guide the use of visual aids to supplement courtroom storytelling:

- Because some trial judges follow the rule that if the court has not admitted into evidence the visual aid, it cannot be referred to in opening statement. Deal with potential objections without the jury being present before opening statement begins. The same rule applies in closing argument, where charts summarizing conflicts in testimony or damage proof are often used.

- Avoid writing and talking at the same time. Eye contact with the jury is critical for a persuasive presentation. For this reason, visual aids should be prepared before beginning the opening statement or closing argument.

- Carefully consider the opposition's theory. There is nothing more disheartening than presenting a visual aid that helps the defense more than the plaintiff.

WHY VISUALS WORK

Visual exhibits ensure that everyone forms the same "picture." The visual exhibit is passive testimony. It enables the jury to learn on their own. It permits the person seeing it to decide for herself what happened, what it means, what is significant about the facts. When a storyboard is used to outline the chronology of events, counsel should let a few minutes elapse to give the jury time to look at it on their own. The storyboard is put up before beginning the opening statement or closing argument. Let the jury digest its contents before beginning the oral presentation. In this way, the listener feels empowered and in control. As counsel gives her opening statement, she refers to the significant points made. The jury can look at the visual when they want to, or they can look and listen to the advocate. The jury can compare what the lawyer is saying with what they are seeing. The listeners can go back and compare what they heard with what they were thinking about before. It is entirely up to them. Visual exhibits convey that jurors are being treated as mature, responsible adults. They are participating in an educational process. They are learning together.

Today's litigation is document-intensive. Business litigation involves reams of contracts, correspondence, and memoranda. Product liability cases include written standards, design criteria, sales and marketing literature, and in-house correspondence. Medical malpractice cases can entail thousands of pages of hospital and office records. Using a document can be effective if done properly, but pages from books and typed documents have printed letters that are too small, too complicated, and too crowded. The critical language must be emphasized by bringing it out, making it bolder, and putting it in color on either a written board or computer projection.

A demonstrative is not the blowup of the medical records page itself but the graph drawing comparisons from the information written on that page with a national standard or the doctor's previous practice. It may illustrate the difference between what a manufacturer did and what industrial standards require. Voluminous records can be simplified into a time line of significant events. They raise the story to the human level in the visual realm. But normally, as aids, these exhibits do not physically accompany jurors into the deliberation room. Experienced advocates know the power the jury wields over boxes of paper that end up behind the door, unread on the floor, or poorly understood around the table. So the lawyer lays the predicate for the use of aids when the witness testifies that the visuals will assist the jury in understanding the facts or technical aspects of the case. The seasoned trial lawyer looks for ways to get such aids admitted as exhibits. Even if the court sustains a defense objection, the offer demonstrates counsel's effort to get to the fact finders information that is understandable and has been discussed by witnesses.

Presenting a case with pictures, computer animations, illustrations, storyboards, time lines, graphics, and videotape helps tie together the key pieces of evidence. Using television and computers in the courtroom—the media through which most jurors commonly get their information—is a persuasive way to get points across in trial.

Advertisers spend millions of dollars on their thirty-second TV spots before they air them. They do extensive market research to be sure the ad carries the right message. Advertisers and their agencies want to know that they will be getting enough bang for their bucks. The trial lawyer market-researches his visuals with a focus group.

What Visuals Should Accomplish

The best visuals are lean and mean. They have no unnecessary fat. A good visual is something a jury can read and understand within a minute or two. It stands on its own. When people read and listen simultaneously, their concentration is diluted. The audience can't read as fast as the speaker can talk. So, the simpler, the better. When putting a graphic together, cut out fat like *the*, *this*, and *but*.

Visuals are memorable and much easier to recall than words. They remind and reinforce every time they are shown. A failing of many advocates is the overuse of visuals during storytelling. Accomplished trial lawyers do not attempt to give the jury any more information than they can assimilate at a given time. Visual exhibits used in opening statement or closing argument do not contain more information than can be easily incorporated into the story. A visual exhibit may illustrate any of the following:

- major themes
- key issues
- key facts
- conflicts or inconsistencies in testimony
- an illustration of what happened
- an explanation of medical devices, procedures, or concepts
- damages

The use of visual exhibits reinforces the advocate's zeal to make things clear and understandable for the jury. The story becomes a multimedia presentation that maintains the listener's interest. Counsel is projected as an interesting and clear-thinking leader who knows how to get to the heart of the issues.

Whether extensive use of visual aids will enhance the presentation depends on the trial lawyer's level of experience, inherent charisma, and ability to connect with the jury. A diverse selection of visuals in the form of computer presentations, time lines, and charts may amplify the persuasive level of the average trial lawyer. More accomplished champions of the common man use minimal visual aids, preferring to tell the story in a way that allows them to connect personally with the jury.

In planning the use of visuals for the story, counsel focuses on the evidence that she will be presenting. Charts, diagrams, and photographs are part of a comprehensive strategy for illustrating the evidence in the clearest way. Lists of issues, technical illustrations, diagrams, enlarged documents or photos, side-by-side comparisons, and time lines are useful choices for demonstrative exhibits, but any of them could mislead.

VISUAL MISTAKES AND MISSTATEMENTS

It is not the format, size, or shape of an exhibit that determines its suitability for use at trial; it's whether the content—the data on which the exhibit is based—and the message—the clear meaning of the exhibit—are fair and accurate.

For example, "bad" content can include dates and events on a time line that are unverified, exaggerated, or false, or a photograph cropped to hide visible damage. Counsel could convey a misleading message by spacing events on a time line disproportionately (making certain events appear closer together in time than they actually are) or by editing a videotape to show key events out of sequence or to omit them altogether.

In many circumstances, a given exhibit may be on the cusp—technically accurate but potentially misleading. In these situations, the attorney offering the exhibit does so at the risk of a challenge to the exhibit's propriety by opposing counsel or the court. Before offering an exhibit, the attorney should be prepared to defend its accuracy and its relevance.

A spectrum of acceptable exhibits does exist. At one end of the spectrum are exhibits that are strictly informational. They may be well-designed and enhanced with color or legible type, but basically they offer information with little or no spin. In the middle are exhibits that are based on reasonable data but which raise arguments. On the far end are visual aids that are based on false or altered information or that deliberately twist the truth so as to communicate a false message. The best practice is to avoid approaching the misleading boundary.

The story loses power when technology becomes the strategy, not the tool. "I want all my visual evidence to appear on a TV monitor, because we are the TV generation." Due to this simplistic "television generation" reaction, a philosophy emerges that any visual on a TV monitor is a good visual. Expensive mistakes can be created that fail to communicate the intended message.

THEMATIC PRESENTATIONS

The spine of the plaintiff's cause is the case theme. The case theme is the "picture" or phrase that concisely tells what the case is about.[5] Visual exhibits can illustrate points relevant to the theme or even the theme itself. For example, a case theme such as "the defendants took the gamble, but only the patient put up the stakes" may be illustrated by a "choice" chart summarizing the many choices made by the health-care providers as opposed to the few made by the patient. Cases involving nursing errors in administering medications or fluids may be best supported by a case theme of "too much too soon." The visuals would contrast the differences between the correct dose and the amounts given the patient.

Life experience ascribes a meaning to visual data just as it does to words. Graphic images standing for concepts or themes help reinforce the thought conveyed. For example, color has specific connotations for most Americans. Green can convey safety, while red suggests danger. To exemplify that a defendant doctor "ran a medical red light," consider a graphic depiction of a stoplight seen at any intersection. Green represents a safe condition, while red represents the clinical presentation of the plaintiff. Red flags connote a warning to most lay people. Instead of listing risk factors with bullets or numbers, attach a red flag. In this way, a list of "nausea, dyspnea, fatigue, obesity, syncope" is renamed from "Charlotte's Risk Factors for Pulmonary Embolism" to "Ignored Red Flags for Charlotte's Pulmonary Embolism."

Pictures provide connotations and thematic inferences well beyond the simple word. In summarizing trial testimony, a scales tilted to the side with eight persons standing against a single person on the opposite side will graphically convey the preponderance of the evidence better than "eight witnesses versus one." A jug full of 7,300 aspirin tablets can symbolize daily pain more effectively than the numeric formula "ten-year life expectancy x 365 days x 2 a day = 7,300." A key document can be better emphasized when tied contemporaneously to the visual depiction of a smoking gun.

Photographs and Models

Blowups of photographs are especially effective in the courtroom. The photograph may be of an accident scene, vehicles, relevant portions of the premises, postmortem examinations, pathology slides, bodily injuries, or people that include before-and-after shots or pictures of a decedent. An effective visual aid may be an anatomical model or a scale model mockup of a plant, piece of equipment, or premises. Real things that courtroom storytellers can use may be as small as a vial of medicine that is not much bigger than a large pill or the whole chassis of a car alleged to be uncrashworthy. Examples of working photographs into the narrative of opening statement and closing argument are found in chapter 26, page 446; chapter 28, page 464; and chapter 29, page 480.

Charts

Printed charts are the most common visual aid used in telling courtroom stories. They have several advantages. Because they are preprepared, the narrator does not have to do anything while using them other than call the jury's attention to what is illustrated. The speaker who is writing on a board or pad as she is speaking must turn her back to the audience. This disconnects her from the story and her listeners. A preprepared chart can illustrate such things as organizational structure, statistical information, relationship of time and events, the layout of physical premises, and the mechanism of product failure or injury. A chart can simplify the way a product was designed or how it works as well as scientific and medical principles.

Visuals give added impact and clout to what otherwise might be boring statistics. Graphics are to a presentation what spices are to cooking. Use too much, and the dish may be indigestible. Use the right amount, and it adds to the appeal. We call them visual aids because the goal is to "aid." The storyteller is using a chart or storyboard to help the audience better understand the narrative. If the visuals dominate the presentation, the audience's attention is distracted from the speaker and the message.

One of the most effective courtroom tools is the flip chart. As witnesses testify, points are made and lists created. During closing argument, the advocate can reference information on pages of the flip chart. Since most trials involve a number of witnesses, resulting in the creation of many pages, it is wise to tab the pages on the flip chart for quicker and easier reference. The writing should be large, letters no less than three inches tall and made with a dark, thick marker. Since markers can bleed through the paper, it is a good idea to alternate pages with the tabs, leaving every other page blank.

One of the common failings of defense attorneys is their failure to have a cohesive story. Instead, they throw up multiple explanations and "defenses." I never refer to the opposing litigant's arguments as "defenses." Rather, they are "excuses." A chart showing the litany of defenses offered can be a compelling part of the plaintiff's storytelling. An example of how an "excuse chart" can be worked into the plaintiff's narrative is found in chapter 28, page 465.

Electronic Visuals

A modern courtroom is a wonderland of technology. We have electronic visual presenters, overhead projectors, computer projectors, screens, and television monitors. Some judges or their bailiffs have rules about where the equipment must be placed in the courtroom. If the lawyer has any choice in placement, she wants to see that the monitors and screens are large enough and placed so that everyone can see them without any obstruction. Of course, because the jury is the target of the communication, their needs come first.

Laptop or Desktop

The newer laptops have ultrafast processor speeds, advanced video cards, and large random access memory (RAM).

Scanners

A scanner can transfer documents and photographs to an electronic database. Since it can scan documents on site, it is advisable to have one in the courtroom. For example, an opposing expert may bring new documents to court that you want to use in cross-examination, or the expert may say something unexpected. The advocate can use a scanner to hunt down and duplicate a document or article to impeach that testimony and have it ready to project when the witness returns.

Visual Presenters

Electronic visual presenters, such as the Elmo, convey images electronically using a video signal rather than a light shining through a transparency. Visual presenters are best used as a backup display method—when you have an exhibit that has not been scanned into your computer or a physical object that you would like the jury to see up close, such as a cut section of a tire.

There are disadvantages to visual presenters. Having one in court can allow unprepared opposing counsel to use exhibits they have not previously scanned or enlarged. Another drawback is that such presenters can be difficult to focus clearly so that jurors can read a document. Projecting documents from your computer creates sharper images and—when combined with an evidence-presentation software program—makes it easier to highlight or extract and emphasize key portions. If you do use a visual presenter, make sure it has an auto-focus feature so you don't waste time adjusting the visual quality during your witness examination.

Evidence-Presentation Software

An evidence-presentation program, such as Sanction II or TrialDirector, maximizes the efficient and effective use of technology at trial. The available programs are practically interchangeable, but all help you quickly locate and show documents, photographs, and charts to a jury. They allow you to enlarge and annotate exhibits and play video clips easily.

Using these programs you can project a document as scanned, and you can extract and blow up key portions. You can also highlight or underline while questioning a witness about the document, pinpointing the key parts for the jury.

Multimedia Presentations

An organized trial presentation contains photographs, exhibits, and animations that can be put together in a slide show using PowerPoint or a similar program. Using a planned presentation—with an outline and ordered exhibits—can aid direct examination of expert witnesses and persuade the jury. The examination flows smoothly, and you are not left scurrying around the courtroom looking for exhibits.

Yet using a prepared slide show with your expert witness removes spontaneous moments when your expert can leave the witness box and draw on a board or write on a chart. During a slide show the courtroom lights will have to be dimmed, and the jurors' attention will be directed to the screen, not the witness. If you have an expert who is a natural teacher, you may want to cover important points with a preplanned computer presentation but include pauses for the expert to go to the easel and illustrate certain topics.

For closing argument, a slide-show program allows you to seamlessly combine themes, jury instructions, exhibits, animations, key clips of videotaped testimony, and graphics. You can begin preparing this presentation before trial—even using it in pretrial focus groups—then edit as the trial progresses. By the time you are ready to close you will have gone over the presentation several times, making its last appearance a well-crafted, interesting, and forceful argument for the jury.

Computer Graphics and Animation

Other than incidents such as the beating of Rodney King, there is rarely contemporaneous video of an actual event. Animation allows the recreation of past events to be shown in "real time" for the jury. Computer graphics and animation can be used at trial to demonstrate how an accident happened, how an individual was injured, and how a different design of a product would have worked, as well as many other points. You must present these types of demonstrative tools in a manner that allows them to be admitted into evidence.

Video animations must be seen as a multiexpert process. The medical expert, whether obstetrician or cardiovascular surgeon, can work with the animator to explain the medical principles and facts of the case to create the proper inputs to actually show the human body working, both outside and inside. No other medium allows the jury to have a picture of what is occurring inside the body like computer animation. In a case of obstetrical negligence, a cutaway view shows the fetus inside the womb, with the fetal monitor strip superimposed and running in real time at the bottom of the screen. The upper right of the screen depicts a clock and key facts in sequence. As the womb hyperstimulates, both the strip and the animation show the compression on the fetus. Lastly, color is used, as impaired circulation changes healthy placental exchange from red to blue. Thus an animation shows the jury the way uterine hyperstimulation suffocates the baby before she can be timely delivered. The use of this animation in closing argument is found in chapter 28, page 464.

Product defects present a fertile field for computer graphics. An animation can illustrate the complex working of automobiles, airplanes, or heavy equipment. Accident reconstructionists often supervise the preparation of a real-time animation that depicts vehicles, people, and places as the tragedy unfolds. The biomechanics of an injury are better understood when the direction and force of the trauma is animated. In short, any story that involves action may be best told through pictures that move.

When considering whether to introduce computer-generated presentations, you should also consider the type of jury that is likely to be impaneled. Jurors in their thirties may be much more receptive to and appreciative of such exhibits than older jurors.[6]

The expert witnesses and the computer graphics designer who will be creating the exhibit must communicate with each other during preparation. The expert who will sponsor the exhibit at trial must be prepared to testify that the exhibit is a true and accurate depiction. Involving the expert witness in the creation of the exhibit makes it much easier for him to address that issue under examination.

Lengthy hearings on challenges to a computer animation can be costly and time consuming. If you are unable to establish an animation's necessary foundation with the expert, the animation may be barred from evidence. Foundational issues can also allow the expert to be badly damaged on cross-examination.

With computer animations, the other side will probably ask for the input data and program that your expert used, then attempt to change the data to point out faulty assumptions or logic that your expert relied on. It can be particularly damaging to have your expert's carefully prepared animation shown with a few changes or corrections, visually demonstrating that what the expert said happened might not have occurred the way the animation depicted it. It can be very embarrassing—and often devastating to a case—if opposing counsel uses one of your exhibits repeatedly throughout the trial to establish one of their points.

We sometimes fall in love with our exhibits after spending substantial amounts of time and money on them. Test-drive your evidence in front of focus groups or disinterested parties to ensure that it illustrates the point you are trying to make. If your exhibits do not help to prove or clarify a point, don't use them, no matter how much time and money you've spent on them.

Trial Notebooks

I use trial notebooks in every case. A trial notebook contains copies of all the significant written documents and exhibits. A copy is made before trial and submitted to opposing counsel and the court for their approval. But the trial notebook is not passed out to the jury until after the opening statement. Trial advocates know that you never give people something to read while you are talking. The audience will inevitably be reading page ten while you are talking about page three. Having copies of the exhibits and documents assists the jury primarily while witnesses are testifying and referring to a specific record or document.

Storyboards

Jurors need to comprehend "what happened when" to comprehend the story. Blowups or computerized charts can be extremely effective in showing the relationships between people, places, things, and time. For example, multiple parties who may be pointing fingers at one another can be grouped at various points on a storyboard with their pictures. Then, draw different-colored arrows pointing in and among each of the other defendants to show the interrelationships and obvious conflicts ("Everyone's Pointing Fingers; No One Wants to Be Personally Responsible").

Basic storyboards can cue a jury to key themes and significant facts. Video depositions now allow a picture of any deponent to be captured and printed (the lawyer can choose how unflatteringly.) Dates and times can be placed on the storyboard, and the jury can connect them with the faces of the players for specific events. For example, in a failure to diagnose an impending pulmonary embolism, the defendant doctor denies the patient ever suffered shortness of breath. A storyboard may capture the image of the defendant doctor, three chart excerpts from consecutive nursing shifts all recording "SOB" or "shortness of breath," and a red flag image added to connote the warning that was ignored. The demonstrative exhibit summarizes the evidence of shortness of breath while anchoring it to the defendant and visually conveying the plaintiff's theme.

Trial Presentation Shows

TrialDirector, Sanction II, other software specific to trial presentations, and even PowerPoint can incorporate almost any exhibit in the trial, with any type of demonstrative presentation desired, whether it be charts, graphs, X-rays, time lines, storyboards, videotape, or graphics. These programs provide a very professional look to your demonstrative presentation, but it is important to retain flexibility. The pace of the show should be controlled by the presenter, and the information must be shared in a clear and concise way so as not to overwhelm the jury.

There are inventive visual opportunities. For example, a split screen of conflicting video deposition testimony between witnesses can be demonstrated at the same time. A single slide can have two video clips from two deponents, left and right. The title can be as simple as "What did the corporation know?" or "When was the doctor called?" Left nurse testifies "10:00 AM" and freezes, then the right nurse swears "1:30 PM." The conflict leaps from the video screen when the two excerpts are juxtaposed.

Presentation software also allows the lawyer as director to appeal to all senses. The program has self-managing tools to create uniform text. There are templates for consistent colors and images so that the message will not be disturbed. Lastly, the presenter has the ability to show video or play audio files contemporaneous with the text displayed on the slide itself. Thus a medical illustration can be displayed, highlighted, and written on, while an expert testifies by video in the same screen. As long as the principles of demonstrative persuasion are followed, the program is a blank canvas on which the lawyer can work.

Time Lines

The visual depiction of events on a time line may be the single most important demonstrative aid used in many injury cases. Graphically conveying the sequence of events and their temporal relation is imperative for a jury's comprehension of alleged negligence. Time can be a challenging concept to convey. Using persuasive principles, time lines should rely on color, space, and conciseness to emphasize the key issues related to the alleged negligent conduct.

Anatomical Models and Medical Exhibits

The Internet has provided an ever-expanding resource of product and medical information. A Google search of images can find a wealth of free digital files. This now includes medical drawings of basic anatomy and complicated procedures. Of course, a variety of medical atlases provide ready copies of anatomy. In the process of blowing up an anatomical image or artist's rendering, colors can be manipulated to create emphasis simply and economically.

In addition to static anatomy pictures, there are many renditions of medical procedures, including open reductions, laminectomies, and laparascopic procedures. These can be obtained at low or no cost and provide a graphic visual image of the procedure the plaintiff underwent—done the correct way.

There are drawings and schematics of products such as automobiles, medical devices, and industrial equipment. Internet medical and product sites and CD-ROMS inexpensively provide evidence of damages, or even liability, that may not be customized to a case but which demonstrate the issue just the same.

A visual presenter, such as an Elmo or DOAR, can be enhanced with specialized equipment as needed for specific issues in a trial. For example, in a case involving the misdiagnosis of breast cancer, it was necessary for the jury to see and appreciate the different tissue samples a pathologist would view underneath the microscope. A specialized visual presenter, which had a small camera viewing through the eyepiece of a powerful microscope, was able to show to every person in the courtroom exactly what a pathologist would see looking through the microscope. This display of pathology slides, microns thick and the diameter of a green pea, allowed everyone in the courtroom to visualize and get involved in the process of pathology. Experts were able to educate and explain the issues for the jury with live video images of the pathology slides, rather than blowups, so that the jury actually was "seeing" what the pathology experts were explaining. The closing argument in chapter 29 shows how this approach played out.

The same principle applies in products cases involving metallurgical failures. In the industrial environment, microscopic enhancement may illustrate the toxins in the air. The opening statement in chapter 27 incorporated the ladder that was involved in the plaintiff's fall (see page 454).

Videotape

Video demonstrative presentations can include—

- depositions
- day-in-the-life presentations
- eyewitness statements
- video of the accident or incident site
- television news reports
- surgical procedures (for example, arthroscopy, laparoscopy)
- home videos of family events
- hospital videos of dying loved ones
- government tests or file footage
- product failure

A witness can explain videotape contemporaneous with its viewing or after it is shown. Audio may be a touchy evidentiary issue on some videotape demonstrations, but it is generally an additional, and important, sensory input for jurors. Thus the effort to appeal to multiple senses in a familiar format (television) is achieved through the use of videotape.

A video of the plaintiff's loved one before he died of catastrophic injuries caused by the defendant's negligence can pack a big punch. See chapter 30, page 9.

Videotape can also remind jurors of key events or facts better than simple explanations. For example, a two-hour joint video deposition may be offered at trial. That deposition has now become a part of the record and is in evidence. During closing argument, a one-minute excerpt of the key question and answer can refocus the entire offer and remind the jury of the single point that the examiner or cross-examiner made. Using video during argument breaks up the presentation, provides a different sensory input, and reinforces, due to its conciseness and clarity, the videotape offer greater than at any other point during trial. Examples of this technique are found in chapter 29, pages 477–78, and chapter 30, pages 492–93.

Closed-Circuit Television

Closed-circuit video demonstrations can be used to display a victim's injuries. Most states protect the fundamental right of any plaintiff to display and exhibit his injuries to the jury. When available at trial, a closed-circuit demonstration may place some distance between the impact of the demonstration and the witness's insecurities and the jurors' discomfort. For example, in a brain-damaged baby case, a closed-circuit arrangement was set up between the courtroom and judge's chamber. The treating pediatrician performed a basic neurological impairment examination with the child while the demonstration was displayed through closed-circuit TV. The demonstration can be taped for the record on appeal, but the child's privacy was respected and the jury was able to see the doctor's demonstration of impairment, rather than just hear his explanation in words. The doctor took the stand immediately after completing the exam and explained to the jury what they had just seen. Thus a brain-damaged infant was able to "display" his injuries, which were unique to his brain, not his body. (See chapter 28, page 467.)

Rules to Achieve Your Goals

The principles of how average people learn and deliberate suggest certain rules that can be applied to demonstrative presentations. No matter the form of the presentation, the general dos and don'ts will assist the lawyer in creating anything from a PowerPoint slide show to a poster blowup.

The Dos of Persuasive Demonstrations

Keep It Simple

- Use simple pictures or symbols to uniformly convey concepts.
- Use as few words as necessary to present the essence of the thought.
- Create and use recurring labels or titles for slides or blowups to assist in giving context.
- Try to restrict each slide or visual aid to a single thought.

Appeal to All the Senses

- Use effective color combinations for emphasis (for example, black on yellow, white on blue).
- Use color to convey meaning.
- Include auditory cues (let the jury hear a decedent's voice, the sounds of a siren at the accident, the beeping of monitoring machines at a bedside).

- Use aids that can be touched and manipulated (for example, pass around an actual endotracheal tube, indwelling catheter, back brace—let jurors touch things).

Use Effective Means Keyed to the Message

- Use large rear-screen projection TVs or LCD projectors with a good presentation screen to provide the maximum size for any images to be watched.

- If standard TVs are used, assure yourself that there is no glare distracting the viewer.

- Position demonstrations and projection screens for the jury (not so the lawyer can be sure to read along).

- Place blowups as close to the jury as necessary for legibility.

- Place demonstrative aids in position to help your expert teach the jury.

- Place demonstrations to isolate the jury from opposing experts or counsel.

The Don'ts of Persuasive Demonstrations

Overwhelm the Visual Exhibit with Wordiness

- Try to keep text to no more than six words per line.

- Make sure the text is simple and understandable.

- Keep the font size large enough to be legible (sacrifice words before sacrificing size).

Create "Visual Noise"

- Keep graphic design relatively simple.

- Avoid the use of excessive or extreme colors.

- Don't change font styles just because there are many choices.

- Be sure that any overlays or transitions do not clutter or obscure the underlying information.

- It is often better to have multiple charts, graphs, and time lines demonstrating a single parameter rather than have multiple parameters graphed on the same chart, graph, or time line (for example, an anesthesia record graphs systolic and diastolic blood pressure values and heart rate on a single graph, but it is much easier for a jury to comprehend three different graphs showing only the values for (1) systolic blood pressure, (2) diastolic blood pressure, and (3) heart rate).

Use Too Much of a Good Thing

- Trial is live theater; don't let it become a movie. Movies are great, but live theater is a much more powerful experience for the audience.
- Day-in-the-life videos are most effective when used with a live witness, but the audience's connection must still be with the witness on the stand.
- Do not use demonstrative software for the entire summation of a case; rather, use visual slides to emphasize key areas and evidence, but always remember to create personal moments.
- Just because you have an exhibit does not mean you have to use it during trial.
- While it helps, technology will inherently distance the receiver from the emotion of any message. (How do you *feel* about news you receive over the Internet as opposed to news a friend shares by story with you personally?)

Despite all the technology available, lawyers cannot change the facts. Rather, our charge is to present the events and scientific principles in the most persuasive manner. The most persuasive method of communication remains the story.

A good storyteller incorporates compelling themes. She knows to reach out to the personal experiences and universal values that resonate with most citizens. Technology and demonstrative presentations may communicate medical, scientific, or technical concepts. They may aid the understanding of who did what when, and why. But they will not substitute for a dedicated advocate who connects with her listeners with a compelling story and genuine concern for her clients.

15

The Power of the Story from Adverse Witnesses: Cross-Examination Storytelling

IT WAS A HOTLY contested election. The candidates for president represented disparate and conflicting views on the most divisive issue of the day. An issue that incited emotions even more than any issue today. More than the abortion debate. More than prayer in schools. More than flag burning.

No one carried the election. The candidate from Illinois won by a slim plurality and was declared president-elect. His election didn't stop the hatred, the abomination, the distrust harbored by his political opponents. Those charged with his security were so concerned they sneaked him into the nation's capitol in disguise.

He was tall, lanky, awkward, and spoke in a high-pitched voice. When he took the oath of office, many believed he would not finish his term. Many feared he would destroy the nation. Even some of his friends doubted his competence; after all, his image was of a minimally educated, yarn-spinning, backwoods country lawyer.

Four years later his assassination brought jubilation to the hearts of many who opposed his policies. They claimed this man was a disgrace to the office of the presidency and plotted the destruction of the country.

How do you see this man? How do you see the story I've told? Now see this as the direct examination. Is it the whole story? Isn't there something missing, much left out? If we fill in those blanks, do we have a different picture? Wouldn't you love to cross-examine the witness who tried to describe the man that many feel is America's greatest president as a failure, an embarrassment, someone unfit to hold the office of president of the United States?[1]

I use this story to illustrate that if a lawsuit is a competition of stories, then the purpose of cross-examination must be to fill in the blanks, add that which is missing, point out that which is incomplete, in order to present the complete story. The winning story.

Like a novel, a trial has smaller stories that tie into the main narrative. The testimony of an adverse witness adds to the big picture, but the cross-examination may create a smaller story all its own. So the preparation for cross-examination considers first what kind of story the lawyer wants to tell. Once she decides, the advocate becomes the storyteller. This is the key to effective cross-examination.

In previous chapters we've explored testimonial storytelling. The trial advocate is the primary courtroom narrator in the sense that she gives the opening statement and closing summation. Still, facts must come from witnesses. The skilled examiner expedites the telling. But the concept of winning with stories does not end with a consideration of opening statement, closing arguments, and witnesses the plaintiff calls. The same principles and techniques apply to cross-examination.

PREPARATION

A trial is a search for the truth. Cross-examination is our most effective tool for sorting truth from fiction. It is often the dramatic highlight of a legal proceeding. It is the point in a trial where suspense, surprise, and the unexpected intersect.

While cross-examination is part art and part science, the essential prerequisite is preparation. The first rule of cross-examination is *be prepared* and includes—

- knowing the facts;
- identifying the pitfalls;
- investigating the witness's background history and prior testimony;
- organizing the materials; and
- formulating illustrative exhibits.

When preparing for cross-examination, I follow the "story concept." These are the essentials of any witness's narrative:

- Who he is.
- What he knows.
- How he knows it.

Oftentimes, the defense tries to paint a picture that is deceptive. They leave things out. Our job is to see that the story is complete.

Do I Cross-Examine?

Some witnesses represent such barren opportunity to add to the plaintiff's story or impeach the witness that the client's cause is best served by not cross-examining. Often, fact witnesses present a situation where there is no helpful information to be gained and no opportunity to impeach. Bystanders may offer after-the-fact testimony about minor details that do nothing but stress the opponent's theories. Cross-examination often has the potential of the witness merely repeating the information rather than adding anything beneficial to the plaintiff's story.

The rule of thumb is that if the witness does not damage the plaintiff's case, do not cross-examine. Often, a witness will offer peripheral facts that only support that which is immaterial or undisputed.

Cross-examination should be undertaken when the witness provides beneficial testimony for the opponent's case and witness credibility can be undermined. Sometimes a witness will offer testimony that is implausible based on other evidence. In such cases, even if the witness is credible it may not be wise to attempt cross-examination.

When counsel determines not to cross-examine, physical and verbal cues should convey to the audience the reason for the advocate's decision. Disdain, disinterest, sympathy, and acknowledgment can be expressed through voice and body language. A few choice words can convey a significant message:

> Thank you, Your Honor, I do not think the jury needs to hear any more from this witness.
>
> We see no reason to prolong these proceedings with additional questions.

The second rule of cross-examination is *carefully consider the risk-reward potential before deciding to examine adverse witnesses.*

Determining the Style of Cross-Examination

Before initiating cross-examination, counsel must sense what the jury expects. If the jury expresses dislike or distrust for a witness by shaking their heads or showing disinterest, counsel has leave to conduct an aggressive, discrediting cross-examination. But the advocate must use caution and adopt a softer tone if the perception is that the jury wants to protect the witness because of his vulnerability or likeability.

Some lawyers can get away with being disrespectful, contentious, and arrogant.

Although the goal may be to be discredit the witness, we cannot lose sight of the fact that he is a human being. He has taken a solemn oath; whether he has adhered to that oath may be up for discussion. However, truthful witnesses may be discredited in a manner that does not belittle or berate. Tact and respect are admirable qualities in everyone, and quarreling does little to advance the plaintiff's case.

CROSS-EXAMINATION OBJECTIVES

The words "you may cross-examine the witness" present a challenge to every advocate. Too many lawyers attempt cross-examination simply to engage in the process rather than to achieve a particular purpose. Often, such an approach will not be successful. The objectives of cross-examination may range from the simple—emphasizing a beneficial point—to the complex—undermining the foundation of an expert's opinions. Regardless of the desired effect, it is important that counsel define the objectives at the outset to achieve the necessary results.[2]

Potential objectives of cross-examination include the following.

- To redefine the story and add perspectives missing in the direct examination. The story that the witness has told about her qualifications, relationship with the parties, recollection of events, or opinions may not have been the whole story.

- To impeach the witness's credibility, knowledge, or recollection of the story by pointing out inconsistencies or lack of qualifications. In the case of a lay witness, the two primary areas of impeachment are the witness's opportunity to observe or determine and the ability to accurately recall the events described.

- To discredit a witness's honesty or veracity.

- To impeach or examine a witness's qualifications.

- To impeach a witness based on bias, prejudice, or interest.

- To explore a witness's knowledge or the basis of opinions.

- To emphasize weaknesses in the opposition's case.

- To emphasize strengths of your client's case.

- To obtain helpful admissions or concessions from the witness.

- To introduce additional evidence helpful to the jury's understanding of the case. For example, the defense liability expert may present fertile territory for exploring issues and opinions that bear on damages.

- To cause the jury to dislike or mistrust the witness.
- To add drama to the trial.
- To establish trust in counsel or confidence in the facts.
- To make the jury believe that the cross-examining lawyer is closer to the facts than the opposing lawyer.
- To lay a foundation for other evidence and testimony.
- To preview closing argument.

Seldom should a lawyer try to achieve all possible objectives in cross-examination. Few witnesses present this opportunity. Rather, the lawyer adheres to the third rule, which is *select only those areas that present vulnerability.* Which goals the attorney will pursue depend on the witness and the testimony offered.

If the testimony is false, the purpose of cross-examination is to destroy both the witness and the testimony. If the testimony is true in part and false in part, then the purpose must be to destroy only what is false. Skilled trial lawyers know that they must accept what they believe to be true even if it damages the client's case. If the testimony is false only in the sense that it exaggerates or creates a wrong impression, the function of cross-examination is to whittle down the story to its proper size and show its proper relation to other facts.

Jurors pay more attention to cross-examination than to direct examination. Because of this, cross-examination presents a unique opportunity to further the client's cause. It is an integral part of the persuasive process. The ideal cross—because it is controlled and organized—not only accomplishes the goals that have been identified but also maintains the jury's interest.

Cross-examination is viewed by many lawyers as an isolated battle. The skilled advocate knows it is a battle that is relevant to and connects with the whole case. For this reason, counsel needs to know the witness before he begins cross-examination. If the witness is a professional testifier, as many experts are, she will have no difficulty answering hard questions in a convincing manner. Cross-examiners cannot take chances with this kind of witness. Professional witnesses give other opportunities. They are frequently argumentative and dogmatic. They develop a theme and stick to it beyond reason. Frequently, they will not want to give a straight answer to any question that casts suspicions on their opinions. Their answers are never simple or straightforward. They insist on long, explanatory, and argumentative answers to questions. The way to handle this witness is by asking such simple, straightforward questions that the jury can see that the witness is not being fair. The answers result in a successful cross-examination even though counsel obtains no substantial admissions of value.

FORMULATING THE EXAMINATION

Most cross-examinations address a few key points. The effect of adverse storytelling wanes in proportion to the length of the examination. Counsel should not waste time cross-examining on facts or issues that are peripheral. Accomplished advocates follow the principles of primacy and recency and begin and end the cross-examination with winning issues.

One of the basics of a good cross-examination of an expert is to ask simple questions. The subject matter of most experts' testimony is very difficult for the average juror to follow. The trial lawyer quickly loses the jury on complex issues, complicated theories, and scientific and medical principles that are often hard to conceptualize. Perception is the key. The trial lawyer does not want the adverse expert giving explanatory answers. This casts the expert in the role of teacher. Even if the jury cannot follow the concepts, the expert will look authoritative. Thus the fourth rule of cross-examination is *ask simple questions that focus on the story.*

Cross-examination usually follows an organized approach. The competing story is told *A*, to *B*, to *C*, and so forth. However, in the case of experts, some cross-examinations benefit from varying the order of the subject matter addressed. Counsel switches topics quickly and without warning to keep the witness off balance.

BREVITY IS BEST

This leads to the fifth rule of cross-examination: *Brevity should be the goal.* The key is to focus on the story that counsel wants retold during cross-examination and have a clear purpose in mind for the questions asked. The cross-examination should be a logical one. One that can be followed by the jury, will be entertaining to them, and makes points that are structured in such a way that they build on one another and add to the story.

The rule of primacy says that the jury will be most attentive in the first few minutes of cross-examination. Of all the parts of the examination, the jury will likely recall best how it began and the first points that were made.

One approach to cross-examination is to communicate to jurors what subjects will be covered, what will be accomplished during further cross-examination, and what is expected from the jury. Within the first five questions, does the lawyer expect the jury to accept some testimony or reject it all? Under this approach, the first five questions asked must be carefully drafted and posed. They should be short, direct statements with which a reasonable witness must agree. If the witness accepts these initial propositions, further cross-examination may not be necessary.

For example, consider a hypothetical case in which the plaintiff was injured in a car crash. The defense expert is an orthopedist who has conducted an independent medical examination of the plaintiff at the request of the defendant's insurance carrier. The doctor has said in a written report, on the basis of a single examination, that the plaintiff has completely recovered from any injuries and should experience no future disability. The plaintiff's physicians, who have treated the patient over time, will testify about the injuries and future disability.

This scenario presents a significant challenge. One approach would be to use the five-question rule. Under this disciplined system, the lawyer must identify at the outset the goals to be accomplished in cross-examination. Three objectives seem reasonable:

- Impeach the witness's finding of no future disability.
- Compare the foundation of this witness's opinions with that of the treating doctors' opinions. Develop evidence from which the jury can conclude that the treating doctors' opinions are more credible.
- Lay the foundation for closing argument that the verdict should not be based on the defense expert's opinions.

Having identified these goals, the attorney might conduct a five-question cross-examination as follows:

> Q: Doctor, would you agree with the proposition that a physician who is giving medical opinions about an injury or disability suffered by a party to a lawsuit should be objective and not attempt to serve as an advocate for either side?

> Q: Would you agree that, to the extent a medical expert gives opinions that reflect a failure to be objective, those opinions should be discounted?

> Q: Would you agree that the more pertinent information the physician has, the greater the likelihood the resulting medical opinions will be accurate?

> Q: Do you believe that when there is a conflict of medical opinions between physicians of equal qualifications, the opinion of the physician who has had the benefit of greater information is more trustworthy?

> Q: Would you agree that a medical opinion based on a limited, single physical examination and a limited medical history is more likely to be erroneous than one based on a number of

> physical examinations and a detailed medical history from a doctor who has treated the patient over time?

This scenario brings home the numerous advantages of the five-question rule. Depending on the witness's responses, further cross-examination may be abandoned. If the witness gave affirmative responses to all these questions and counsel fears becoming bogged down in unfamiliar or tedious medical terrain or being overwhelmed by the wiles of an experienced defense expert, counsel should refrain from further cross-examination. After five questions the jury is aware of the limitations of the expert's opinions and the superior position of the plaintiff's experts. The lawyer also has obtained answers that support the theme of the closing argument.

LEADING QUESTIONS

The sixth rule of cross-examination cautions advocates to *use leading questions*. Don't ask the witness—tell her. Lawyers who adhere to the principle that a trial is a contest of stories see cross-examination as an opportunity to retell or reemphasize the plaintiff's narrative. Counsel controls the flow of examination by limiting, as much as possible, the breadth of the witness's answers. And leading questions imply that the witness cannot be trusted. Most judges allow witnesses to explain their answers. By the same token, if a witness is extremely evasive, many jurists will eventually require an affirmative or negative response.

Controlling the flow of cross-examination with leading questions requires the examiner to keep the questions as direct and understandable as possible. Experienced cross-examiners avoid compound questions. Rather, a question that is direct and concise forces the witness and jury to focus on a limited, specific issue.

In those few instances where it is necessary to ask a nonleading question, counsel should never begin with "why" or "how." Remember the courtroom scene from the classic movie *The Verdict*, where defense lawyer Edward Concannon (played by James Mason) asks nurse Kaitlin Costello why she kept an original of the patient's admitting form. The question gave the witness an opportunity to devastate both the defendants and their story.

FOCUS ON THE SIGNIFICANT

A good cross-examination adheres to the seventh rule: *focus on major points necessary to solidify or emphasize the plaintiff's story*. Devoting considerable time to peripheral matters will not assist the jury in attending to the primary issues and may detract from the impact of the cross-examination. By the same token, counsel does not rehash points addressed in direct examination beyond those necessary to set the stage for questions in cross-examination. Skilled advocates never try to get a witness to admit he is lying. None of us is Perry Mason; none of us will ever have a witness confess guilt on the witness stand. Counsel uses her knowledge of and familiarity with the facts, documentation, and scientific or business principles to paint the witness into a corner, making sure along the way that all escape routes are closed.

Start Strong

When you put a witness on the stand, you want the witness to be the center of attention. The jurors' focus is on her. When you cross-examine, the witness is irrelevant. You are at center stage, you are the storyteller, you are the credible source. You have a built-in ally to put you at center stage for cross-examination. That ally is curiosity. The psychologist William James taught that a curious audience is an attentive one. Think about cross-examination from the view the jury has. They have just heard an hour or two of direct examination from the defense of a lay or expert witness. They have formed ideas about the witness and his qualifications, what the witness knows, how he knows it, what the witness has proposed as scientific truths, medical literature the witness relied on, his experiences, and, finally, his opinions about the issues presented. Finally, the defense lawyer says, "Your witness."

Your audience's attention turns to you. The jury's first reaction is one of curiosity. How will you handle the witness? Will you be polite and straightforward, or will you be antagonistic and defensive? The jury will form impressions about you, your competence, and the case within the first few minutes of the cross-examination. For a short time they will be curious about what you are going to do. Effective examiners use the eighth rule: take advantage of the listeners' natural curiosity and *start strong*.

There is no certain order I use for cross-examination. I do follow the rule that the beginning should be strong, arouse the jury's curiosity, and give them some idea where I am going with the witness.

Some years ago, my son and I tried an anesthesia wrongful death case. The defense called an anesthesiologist who had some ideas about the case that I thought were weak and had little scientific basis. I began the cross-examination with this question: "Dr. Coveler, what is junk science?"[3]

The doctor's response was that he didn't understand the question. I repeated it. He finally admitted that he had no idea what junk science was. It was an effective beginning for a cross-examination on his theories.

Another example of this principle comes from a case brought by a catastrophically injured child that we tried a few years ago.[4] One of the primary issues in this obstetrical negligence case was legal causation. The child was very depressed following delivery. Brain damage and significant disability were documented. One of the defenses was that the baby's brain damage could not have been the result of anoxia during the delivery because there was no evidence of substantial heart, liver, kidney, or other vital organ damage. The defense called an expert neonatologist from Baylor University in Houston. He had written a number of articles in support of his proposition, which, by the way, was derived from the recognized standards published by the American College of Obstetricians and Gynecologists, Technical Bulletin No.

163, January 1992. The cross-examination began—

QUESTIONS BY MR. PERDUE:

Q: Dr. Speer, would you agree with me, sir, that a predisposition toward a given conclusion may color a person's views toward a medical issue such as is presented in this case?

A: I'm sorry.

Q: A predisposition that a person holds toward a given conclusion may color their views?

A: Yeah, it's possible.

Q: Would you agree with me that predispositions exist in virtually all forms of human behavior, whether it's politics, social, religion, or science?

A: Everybody has opinions for certain.

Q: Everybody has predispositions, don't they?

A: I will agree.

Q: In fact, I'm sure you're aware of this because I know you're a very learned man, but in the social setting, predispositions toward a view of others is what Walter Lippman first wrote about back in 1920 when he referred to the term "stereotype" that we're all familiar with.

BY DEFENSE COUNSEL: I'm going to object, relevance and testimony of counsel.

THE COURT: Overruled.

THE WITNESS: Would you repeat?

MR. PERDUE: Sure.

QUESTIONS BY MR. PERDUE:

Q: Walter Lippman, in 1920, talked about stereotypes being the pictures we all carry in our heads.

A: All right, sir.

Q: That we have certain predispositions, all of us, in science, in politics, in religion. We carry them around with us.

A: All right.

Q: You'd agree with that?

A: Right.

Q: Does that make sense?

A: Stereotypes are stereotypes, yes, sir.

Q: And, would you agree with me that when one's conclusions, one's opinions, are colored and affected by predispositions they hold, one of the results is they tend to arrive at their conclusions quicker?

A: It's possible.

The witness was then asked a series of questions that established that during his career he had seen 120 children with brain damage as significant as the plaintiff's who had similar medical histories. He agreed that—

- brain damage is one of the most significant injuries that a child can experience as a result of obstetrical negligence; and
- obstetrical negligence can cause brain damage.

It was then brought out that he had never testified on behalf of a child who had been brain damaged as a result of obstetrical negligence. That he felt very strongly that hospitals and doctors are wrongly accused of being responsible or negligent in these cases.

The following colloquy then occurred:

QUESTIONS BY MR. PERDUE:

Q: Doctor, would you agree with me that it is your predisposition toward that proposition that colors your views when you go to review these cases that you are asked to consult on for these defendants?

A: Predisposition means a leaning toward a proposition based on thought processes that may or may not be based on fact, and that's why my answer to your statements earlier were global in response. However, it is not a predisposition based on speculation when it's based on facts that are in medical literature, at least in my opinion. You know, it is my predisposition that the sun rises in the east, and the facts substantiate that. So yes, I have a predisposition, but it's based on fact and that is my predisposition here.

Q: What if you have a predisposition that the sun rose in the west?

A: Then I would be wrong, wouldn't I?

Q: Yes. [*long pause*] When you were asked to review this case, the law firm sent you the records of Parkway Hospital, Hermann Hospital, I think several depositions and you reviewed them for about forty-five minutes and formed your opinion; am I correct?

A: In the initial review, yes, sir.

Q: You formed your opinion that you've expressed to this jury in this case in forty-five minutes working, I think you told me when we took your deposition, over your kitchen table at home looking through records?

A: Yes, sir.

Q: You did not look at the fetal heart tracing that was sent to you, and you didn't look at the picture of the ruptured uterus?

A: A picture was not furnished to me, and as a neonatologist, I'm not qualified to comment on fetal monitor strips so I didn't look at them.

Q: And when you reviewed the records, you did not make any notes in the records or on a piece of paper or anything as you were doing your forty-five-minute review?

A: Correct.

Q: You just flipped through them and arrived at your opinions?

A: I went to the relevant documents, some of which have been shown today and formed my opinion.

When an expert testifies, the jury forms a picture of him, his qualifications, how he approaches the case, and the validity of his opinions. This picture is basically the defense witness's story. The story the defense presented of Dr. Speer was of a highly qualified neonatologist who had thoroughly reviewed the medical records, medical literature, and documentation and, using established medical criteria, had arrived at the opinion that the unauthorized and unordered giving of Pitocin by a nurse to a mother in the second stage of labor (whose labor was progressing well) did not cause the child's brain damage. Our story was that the unauthorized Pitocin, even though it was given only for a couple of minutes, had produced tetanic contractions that caused the mother's uterus to rupture, which caused the baby's brain damage.

What we wanted to do by way of cross-examination was to repaint the picture—retell the story of this doctor's involvement in the case. Our story was of a neonatologist who had treated many brain-damaged babies, recognized that obstetrical negligence can produce brain damage, but that in the hundreds of cases he had seen he had not testified for a single patient, that he held the prejudicial attitude that brain damage following birth is not associated with obstetrical negligence, and that because of his innate prejudice he arrived at opinions supporting the defense within a short period of time of reviewing records in a most informal setting—at the kitchen table in his house.

Cross-examination of the expert witness is not handicapped by the same downside potential presented by lay witnesses. Jurors expect the advocate to expose and discredit the testimony of one who is offered as having special knowledge and experience. Few jurors will feel the need to shield the expert from attacks by the lawyer.

Cross-Examination Is a Form of Storytelling

My approach to cross-examination comes from the basic premise that trial is not a scientific debate; rather, it is a contest of stories. Juries form pictures in their heads about all aspects of the case. They form a picture of what happened. That is why the opening statement is so important. That is why we use concepts of theme in our presentations. Our audience forms pictures in their minds about the people, places, and events.

My approach to cross-examination is that I must reshape the story.

The story an expert presents is—

- Who he is (a practicing pediatrician, accident reconstructionist, mechanical engineer).

- What he can know (he has reviewed the medical records, accident report, manufacturing specifications).
- What he knows (he is familiar with the standards of good obstetric practice, the principles of reconstruction).
- What he isn't (he's not a pediatric neurologist, police officer, expert in biomechanics).
- What he can't know (he was not at the delivery, the auto accident, the plant explosion).
- What he doesn't know (the details of the delivery, the accident, the explosion that are not contained in the records).
- His bias or lack of objectivity (relationships with the defendant, the hospital, the medical community, the product manufacturer and whether he is being paid).
- Whether he has made prior inconsistent statements (what the witness has said in depositions, medical, scientific, or technical literature).
- Whether his position is unreasonable (an effective cross-examination pushes the witness to the extremes of his opinion—gets him out on a limb—gets him out on the branches—gets him out on the leaves).

Sometimes an attack on the witness's qualifications is appropriate.

- The witness has little practical and clinical experience in dealing with an issue.
- He has little special training in the area.
- He hasn't participated in any research.
- The research he claims to have participated in or relied on is skewed, inaccurate, shaded.
- He hasn't authored any peer review articles.
- Comparing his experiences with the plaintiff's expert's experiences shows the defense expert is lacking.

In the obstetrical case previously mentioned, a California high-risk obstetrical expert known for his defense work testified. The defense offered him in support of its version of the story that the obstetrical care given was appropriate and within the standards of good medical practice. He buttressed his opinion by saying that he had done extensive research into this question, participated in ongoing studies, and suggested he was one of the most qualified experts in the area. A part of the cross-examination went this way:

QUESTIONS BY MR. PERDUE:

Q: Dr. Phelan, do you maintain a file on this matter you just testified to?

A: Yes.

Q: How many other files similar to this file would be in your office where you maintain these files?

A: I look at about twenty to fifty a year.

Q: What was the address of the office that you do these reports out of?

A: It's Suite 20, 1030 South Arroyo, in Pasadena.

Q: How many stories is in that office building?

A: Two.

Q: And if we did a jury view like they do in some cases in California and went out to that office building and walked in the lobby and looked up on the board for your name, it would say Jeffrey Phelan?

A: That's what it would say.

Q: It wouldn't say M.D., would it?

A: I don't know what it says now. It may not. You're right, we took off the M.D. because we had a robbery and they attacked my office looking for drugs and then they had hit the lab that was next door.

Q: If we walked in the building where you have your office—

A: Right.

Q: —we would walk in and it would say on the building directory, Jeffrey Phelan?

A: Correct.

Q: Second floor?

A: Correct.

Q: Those studies that you have talked to defense counsel about were referenced in your appearance in another case. Those studies are done out of your office; am I correct?

A: Oh, it depends.

Q: The studies that you reference in your testimony in this case and you have used when testifying for the defense in other cases about talking about brain-damaged children, they're not funded by any government agency; am I correct?

A: No, I fund it.

Q: They're not funded by any charitable agency?

A: No, I fund it.

Q: They are not done under the auspices of a protocol at a hospital?

A: No.

Q: You have delivered more opinions in the last five years in support of doctors who were defendants in lawsuits than you have delivered babies; isn't that true?

A: Probably have.

Q: You have delivered more opinions to support a health-care provider's position in a lawsuit than you have delivered babies in the last five years?

A: Oh, I'd agree.

This cross-examination was designed to discredit the witness by completing his story. He was not the impartial scientific researcher the direct examination had painted.

Juries often rely on statistics in making sense of the story. For this reason, it is good to ask these kinds of questions during the discovery deposition:

- How many cases involving . . . have you (treated, operated on, investigated, and so forth)?
- How many of these patients were . . . (use sex, age, underlying medical condition as qualifier)?
- How many accidents involving . . . have you investigated?
- How many of these patients suffered (the injury the plaintiff sustained)?
- Think of all the ways you can quantify the expert's experience in terms relevant to the plaintiff. This often gives a fertile field for cross-examination at trial.

These types of questions often aid in preparing the attack on the expert's work and how he arrived at his opinion.

Impeachment with Prior Deposition Testimony

One way to retell the story and cast doubt on a witness's credibility is by impeaching with prior sworn testimony—usually a deposition transcript. The rules for impeachment by deposition are clear but often ignored or violated. Although I do not like to object, I normally will not allow a lawyer to refer to the deposition without laying the grounds for impeachment. The reasons are that the framing of the question, "Do you remember when your deposition was taken . . ." implies that the witness is testifying to something different when in fact he may not be. For effective impeachment, counsel needs to know and follow the procedural rules. I use the following predicate for impeachment by deposition:[5]

- *Notice that you intend to impeachment.* "Is it your sworn testimony today that you arrived at the hospital a few minutes after 10:00 AM?" (Witness affirms. If not, impeachment cannot continue.) "Have you ever testified differently?"
- *Identification of the time and place.* "Do you recall giving your deposition on March 3, 2005, in the offices of your lawyers, Jones and Beckham, 2002 Main Street, Fifth Floor, Houston, Texas?"

- *Proof that the witness was under oath.* "The court reporter taking your deposition did swear you in before we began questioning you?"

- *There was an opportunity to cross-examine.* "Your lawyers attended the deposition."

- *Proof of the inconsistent statement.* "On that occasion when I asked you what time you arrived at the hospital that morning, what did you say?" (Showing the witness the deposition.) "A few minutes before noon." (Advocates can bring additional drama by having the witness read the prior answer.)

- *A demonstration that the statements are in fact inconsistent.* "There is a big difference between saying you arrived a few minutes after 10:00 AM and saying you arrived shortly before noon."

Introducing Something New During Cross-Examination

Successful cross-examiners bring something new to the witness's story. Something new can take many forms or shapes.

- New facts.

- Additional data or information (something that the witness or expert was not aware of).

- The significance of a fact (something that the witness was aware of but had not attached appropriate significance to).

- Something that the jury was not aware of (a fact known to the expert but not previously known to the jury; this may be something that is discovered upon a review of the expert's file).

Juries love to acquire additional clarification and information during the cross-examination process.

Many are familiar with one of Abraham Lincoln's classic cross-examinations in a criminal case. Lincoln was defending two brothers accused of killing another man in the course of a fight. Each brother knew he had not killed the man but refused to say anything so as not to accuse the other brother. The state's case hinged on the testimony of a purported eyewitness who claimed that he saw the fight and murder. Lincoln's cross-examination of this eyewitness, John Palmer Cass, was immortalized in the 1939 movie *Young Mr. Lincoln.* The following courtroom scene illustrates how the cross-examiner, by introducing something new, discredits the opponent's story and enhances the cross-examiner's credibility. Lincoln calls Cass back to the stand and begins his cross-examination:

Q: Mr. Cass, yesterday you identified Matt Clay as the killer of Scrubb White.

A: Yes, I did.

Q: You're sure of that?

A: Well, sure, I'm sure.

Q: I just wanted to know. You say you were about a hundred yards from the scene of the fight.

A: Just about, yeah.

Q: Are you familiar with the land over there?

A: Yes, sir.

Q: What's the nature of the layout.

A: Well, there's a little clear—

Q: You mean trees?

A: A few.

Q: Where are they?

A: Well, they're between the clearing and the fairgrounds.

Q: And you saw right through the trees?

A: No, sir. I was already through the trees when I saw 'em fighting.

Q: Oh, I see. Um, I suppose the clearing was all lit up by lights from the tar barrels.

A: No, sir.

Q: How'd you see so well?

A: I told you, it was moon bright, Mr. Lincoln.

Q: Moon bright.

A: Yes, sir.

Q: Of course, if it hadn't been moon bright, you couldn't have seen a hundred yards, could you?

A: 'Course not.

Q: But you did see it.

A: I told you I saw it, didn't I?

Q: And, the only reason you're telling us this now is 'cause you feel sorry for one of the defendants.

A: Well, I didn't want to see 'em both get hung.

Q: I don't reckon you'd lie about a thing like that. You can step down.

PROSECUTOR: No further questions, your honor.

Q: Oh, Mr. Cass, I forgot. There's just one other question I want to ask you. Cass, what'd you have against Scrubb White?

A: Well, nothin'.

Q: What'd you kill him for, then?

A: Kill him? I don't know what you're talking about.

Q: Yes, you do. Look at this. Go on, look at it. It's the *Farmer's Almanac*. Go ahead, look at it. Look at page twelve. You see what it says about the moon? The moon was only in its first quarter that night and set at 10:21, forty minutes before the killing took place. So, you see, it couldn't have been moon bright, could it? You lied, didn't you, Cass? And you weren't trying to save these boys' necks, were you? You were trying to save your own, weren't you? Well, come on. Weren't you?[6]

Lincoln continues to cross-examine and discredit the prosecution witness and expose him as a liar about his other testimony until Cass becomes so unnerved he admits to the killing. Both brothers are acquitted.

Here is an example from a case I tried in San Antonio many years ago. The plaintiff was brain damaged because of the emergency room physician's delay in treating a respiratory obstruction.[7]

QUESTIONS BY MR. PERDUE:

Q: Dr. Hills—

A: Yes, sir.

Q: —my name is Jim Perdue, and I've got a few questions for you. As I understand your testimony, your opinions pretty much are bottomed on the fact that Mr. Smith had an anaphylactic reaction to the penicillin; am I correct?

A: Yes, sir.

Q: And so if he didn't have a reaction to the penicillin, you might have to change some opinions.

A: Perhaps.

Q: In your report to defense counsel, you indicate, "Dr. Henderson asked me to look at the records and testify for him. And I looked at the emergency room records. And based on the emergency room records, I don't think he did anything wrong."

A: That's correct.

Q: Now, the emergency room records would consist of this [*indicating*]. Exhibit No. 2, Exhibit No. 3. Isn't that your understanding of what the emergency room records are?

A: Yes, sir.

Q: That's what you looked at?

A: Uh-huh.

Q: You indicated that Evan didn't have any respiratory problems.

A: Yes sir.

Q: Where, on this record, is there an indication of what his respiratory rate was?

A: It isn't on there. But I talked to Dr. Henderson—

Q: Oh—

A: —and he told me—

Q: Oh. You didn't just use the records. We are beginning to get a better picture. Not just the records. You got information from your friend, the defendant, that isn't in the records.

A: Surely; uh-huh.

Q: And, you relied on that.

A: Right.

Q: So, when in your letter you said, "I have reviewed the emergency room records. And, in my opinion, I find no evidence of malpractice on the part of Dr. Henderson," you really should have said, "I reviewed the emergency room records, and I talked to him so he could straighten out any kind of things that weren't clear or just right"; right?

A: I suppose so.

Q: Yeah.

MR. PERDUE: We pass the witness.

BY DEFENSE COUNSEL:

Q: Is the material that you were furnished adequate to support your opinions without necessity of conversation with Dr. Henderson?

A: Yeah, I think so. But I knew—before I saw these, I had already talked to Dr. Henderson, talked to him years ago about this case. So I knew about the case before I saw that.

BY MR. PERDUE:

Q: What you're saying is that you had already told Dr. Henderson you would testify for him before you even saw the records?

A: Yes, sir.

MR. PERDUE:	That's even worse.
BY DEFENSE COUNSEL:	Objection to that sidebar remark.
THE COURT:	Sustained.
BY DEFENSE COUNSEL:	I ask the jury be instructed to disregard it.
THE COURT:	Please disregard the last comment, ladies and gentlemen of the jury.

The Importance of Nonverbal Persuasion

Effective cross-examination is a product of the ninth rule: *perceptions can be more important than substance.*

While many advocates focus on the words (the question), the effective cross-examiner knows that it is the vocal and physical cues that project perceptions vital during cross-examination. The examiner uses the raised inflection when posing questions to witnesses they call. The raised inflection implies that the witness will be giving the essential information. Effective cross-examiners refrain from using the raised inflection except in those instances when they are posing an open-ended question to get a response that they know cannot hurt them.

The trial lawyer assumes control of the courtroom by the power of her voice, the way she sits or stands, and the use of other nonverbal techniques. Standing, when the court allows it, is a more powerful posture than sitting. The lawyer who is standing has more freedom to move about the courtroom, and the erect posture puts her in a more dominant position.

Because the witness is irrelevant, counsel spends little time making eye contact with him except during those intervals when eye contact is a form of intimidation. The lawyer focuses on the jury during the questioning of the adverse witness. This maneuver projects the examiner as the credible storyteller.

Many of the persuasive techniques of storytelling discussed in chapter 12 may be used during cross-examination. Among these are repetition. Counsel asks a question to which she knows the answer or about which she doesn't care what the answer is. She repeats the witness's answer for emphasis and dramatic effect before posing the next question. For example—

> Q: Nurse Ramos, at what time did you last document Mr. Mario Bohorquez's blood pressure?
>
> A: At 2:00 PM.
>
> Q: Two PM. [*pause*] Your last recording of his blood pressure was at two in the afternoon and it was 80 over 55. That is depressed.
>
> A: A little below normal.
>
> Q: When did you last record a heart rate?
>
> A: At the same time.
>
> Q: The last heart rate you observed on Mr. Bohorquez was at two in the afternoon and it was 50. That was below his baseline.
>
> A: Yes.
>
> Q: What about respiratory rate?
>
> A: Same time. Two PM.
>
> Q: You last noted his breathing, his respiratory rate at two in the afternoon. Two PM. And how often were you supposed to observe and record Mr. Bohorquez's vital signs, the blood pressure, pulse, and respirations?
>
> A: Every two hours.
>
> Q: According to Dr. Schulenberg's orders, you were to see the patient, observe them, measure his blood pressure, heart rate, and respirations every two hours. When was Mr. Bohorquez found to be in hypovolemic shock?
>
> A: Around 6:20 PM.
>
> Q: You found Mr. Bohorquez in hypovalemic shock at 6:20 in the evening. You were still on duty?

A: Yes.

Q: He was still your patient?

A: Not my only patient.

Q: But he was still your patient?

A: Yes.

Q: You were the nurse responsible for caring for this patient and advising his doctor of changes in his vital signs. How long had it been since you had last checked Mr. Bohorquez's vital signs before you found him in shock?

A: About four and one half hours.

Q: It had been four and one half hours since you last checked his vital signs?

A: I guess.

Q: Four and one half hours. Not two hours?

A: No.

Q: Not two and one half hours?

A: No.

Q: It had been four and one half hours since you had done a nursing assessment of this patient?

A: Yes.[8]

Perceptions often overcome substance. Good storytellers don't leave significant lines dangling. They don't move on to the next question. They use the persuasive technique of repetition to make the answer memorable—a dramatic point in the story.

KNOW WHEN TO QUIT

A key ingredient in conducting a successful cross-examination is understanding when to quit. Some lawyers become so successful in scoring points that they are driven to continue questioning long after the witness has given up the information that benefits the examiner's position.

There is a big difference in cross-examining the lay person and cross-examining an expert witness. I have seen time and again brilliant and destructive cross-examinations of lay people backfire on the lawyer. If the lawyer looks too "slick," clever, smart, the jury may identify with the lay person and even become protective of him. I tried a case some years ago in Victoria. The wrong drug was given the plaintiff during minor nasal surgery, with the result that he suffered a heart attack on the operating table. The question was primarily one of damages. After the incident, the plaintiff had returned to his old job and was actually making more money at the time of trial than he had before his surgery. The jury awarded us $2 million, the largest malpractice verdict ever recorded in Victoria. The defense lawyer did a masterful job cross-examining the plaintiff. He got him to admit that he was back on his old job, that no one was telling him he had any disability that would cause him to lose his job, that he expected to continue to work there, that he was able to do his work. This was all in an effort to minimize what the plaintiff had said during direct examination—that he had some physical limitations as a result of the heart attack. I remember thinking during the prolonged cross-examination that the defense lawyer was demonstrating his intelligence and skill. But the plaintiff was demonstrating something even more important—honesty. Which leads us to the tenth rule of cross-examination: *know when to quit.*

The truthful witness will bolster the honest parts of the story. The cross-examiner decides what the important concessions are, gets them, and quits. The most difficult witness to cross-examine is the man of integrity who refuses to fudge even slightly. It is best to deal with him precisely and expeditiously.

It is an unfortunate quality of human behavior that many who testify come to the courtroom intent on helping the side that called them rather than being an objective, impartial storyteller. It is this frailty that opens up avenues for adverse storytelling—cross-examination. The cardinal principle is never attack the integrity of an honest witness.

Joseph Sugarman is one of America's top advertising and marketing entrepreneurs, who has built several large businesses. He travels the country inspiring audiences with his insights and secrets of success. His best known quotation is—

> Each time you are honest and conduct yourself with honesty, a suc-

> cess force will drive you toward greater success. Each time you lie, even a little white lie, there are strong forces pushing you toward failure.[9]

Sugarman's philosophy has as much relevance for the courtroom as for the business arena. It applies to witnesses. More significantly, it should govern the conduct of the trial advocate. Which brings us to the final rule of cross-examination: never forget that *honesty and truth are our strongest allies.*

PART 4

OUR VALUES

I AM PROUD TO BE known as a "true believer." Someone who has passionate convictions for the rights of ordinary citizens. Our dogma is that the right to trial by an independent jury is not optional equipment on a democracy. It is indispensable, quintessential equipage that comes from the manufacturer—our founding fathers. We resist the modern-day suggestion that courtrooms should be playpens for the rich. The working class and poor should have unlimited access to justice, and justice ought to be what a jury says it is.

If you talk to any of the great victim's advocates, and it has been my pleasure to know many of our nation's best, you will find that all of them at some time in their lives experienced an epiphany. An event when some essential truth was revealed. Some of us have had several. Here is one of mine.

It is summer in Dallas, Texas, in 1945. My grandmother tells me that a boy about my age has moved into the neighborhood. I ought to go down the street and ask his grandmother if he and I can play together.

Their house is similar to ours. One of those old east Dallas homes built in the early 1920s. Two-story, brick, with a sign out in the yard: "Rooms to Rent." Most of the ladies who live on our block provide for themselves by taking in boarders. This isn't a rich neighborhood even though these old houses have a lot of charm. I ring the doorbell and can hear the chimes sound in the living room. I hear the clicking of a woman's heels on the hardwood floor. A gray-haired lady with a kind face opens the door and I introduce myself. I tell her my grandmother sent me down to meet her grandson so that we could play. She smiles and shows me to a back room where I meet her grandson. He is in a wheelchair, paralyzed from the waist down, a victim of that scourge of the '40s—polio. The boy smiles at me and says, "Would you like to play Monopoly?" I had never played Monopoly and didn't know what the game was. Larry brings out his Monopoly board and we set it up on the floor. I get down on the floor with him and we play all that afternoon.

When I get back to my grandmother later, I tell her that Larry is paralyzed. He isn't a boy I can play with. My grandmother asks me, "Then what have you been doing all afternoon?" I say, "We've been playing Monopoly."

"Did you have a good time?" she asks. I say that I did. My grandmother tells me something that has stuck with me all these years. I didn't know when I met Larry why he was

paralyzed. I don't think I had ever even heard about polio until that day. My grandmother tells me that Larry had been a victim of the disease. A lot of children in those days were. She says, "Jim, we will never know why Larry got polio and you didn't." She admonishes me to remember, "There but for the grace of God go you." I am taught that when we see men coming back from World War II with arms and legs missing that everyone needs to remember, "There but for the grace of God go you." And when we see young children who are paralyzed from polio we should remember, "There but for the grace of God go you."

So that was the lesson I learned from my grandmother that summer in Dallas. We must understand that the plight of the less fortunate and tragically injured are our concern. Justice for them is not a game or a scheme or a racket. The law is about decency. Doing what is right even if it is unpopular.

These are lessons most of us learned one way or another. We can shed tears as we stand around the grave being dug for justice by those who would restrict the rights of citizens to seek civil remedies. We can extend condolences at the crematorium where decency is being burned. Or we can speak out and say it is wrong. I know it's wrong. My grandmother told me so.[1]

John Guinther in *The Jury in America* notes: "There is nothing else quite like them in our society: A group of strangers brought together and required to sit in silence and listen to different versions of a story in which they have no personal interest."[2] Unlike members of the legislative and executive branches of government, they have no purpose, no continuing function, beyond their verdict. Jurors give no reason for their actions and—unlike any other group imaginable—seek nothing for themselves. They are, as Supreme Court Justice William O. Douglas once said, "the one governmental agency that has no ambition."[3]

It is said that in every great trial lawyer lies the soul of a poet. This is just another way of expressing a principle we all know to be true: great advocates have passion for their cause and are committed to the Jeffersonian ideal that every citizen has a fundamental right to present civil grievances to an independent jury.

But lawyers are by nature curious creatures. We want to know not only what the rule is but why we have it and from whence it came. That curiosity provoked me to write *I Remember Atticus: Inspiring Stories Every Trial Lawyer Should Know* (State Bar of Texas, 2004). In it, I identified the stories from legal history that best exemplify the essentials of justice: faith, freedom, equality, courage, and perseverance. I present these stories in this chapter in abbreviated form.

16

The Source of the Trial Lawyer's Values and Beliefs

Faith

ONE OF THE OLDEST court rules is found in rule 267 of the Texas Rules of Civil Procedure. At the beginning of most trials, lawyers "invoke the rule."[1] This rule requires that witnesses be separated and not talk with each other or be in court until they are called to testify. The source of "the rule" is Susanna's story, found in the book bearing her name in the Apocrypha.

The beautiful Susanna is married to Joachim, the town's leading citizen. In those days, judges don't sit in one place; they travel from town to town and usually stay in the home of the most prominent family. Because judges are held to be such men of power, influence, and prestige, it is considered an honor to have them in your home. The two judges in Susanna's story are corrupt, immoral, and lustful. Honor and integrity are not part of their portfolio. After being in Joachim's home a few days, they begin to lust after Susanna. One day, they depart from the house to go their separate ways. Each of them doubles back, hoping to find Susanna bathing in her garden as she does each day at this time. When they come upon each other, they share their perverse ambitions and decide to ambush her. "We will hide in the garden and come upon her and have our way."

When Susanna comes to the garden and dismisses her servants, the judges step from their hiding place, announcing: "You will let each of us have you or we will say we caught you committing adultery." It is a grave alternative, as adultery is a capital offense. "If you call for help, we will make up this story about you." Susanna says she will cry out and tell what the judges tried to do. They scoff at her, telling her that they will back up each other's story against anything she might say. Besides, they are respected, influential judges. Their testimony will carry more weight because, after all, Susanna is a mere woman—what we know today as a homemaker.

Susanna insists, "I'm not going to let you do this," and screams for help. People come. The two men do what they threatened to do and claim they had caught a young man in the act of adultery with Susanna. They tried to capture him, but he was too young and strong; he fought them off and escaped. Susanna is summarily tried, convicted, and sentenced to death. This would be the end of the story were it not for the actions of a man of faith.

Daniel was of royal lineage. Although he was a young man, the palace authorities had selected him to be trained for service in the court of Nebuchadnezzar. Inspired by the Lord, Daniel suggests, "Before we execute Susanna, there's something we should do. Take the judges, separate them, and put them far apart." After sequestering them, Daniel asks the first accuser, "Under what kind of tree did you find Susanna in adultery with this young man?" The judge says it was a mastic tree. They bring in the second judge and ask him, "Under what kind of tree were Susanna and the young man committing adultery?" This judge claims it was a holm tree. They are lying, because the trees are not similar and were in different parts of the garden. In this way, Daniel is able to expose the judges' deceit and conniving and free Susanna.[2]

Many of our modern legal concepts would not exist were it not for the Bible. The book of Exodus contains a body of law that, though handed down thousands of years ago, still sounds in modern tort principles. If a man were to take an ox or a sheep and convert it to his own use, he was required to pay back five head of cattle for the ox and four sheep for the one sheep.[3] If a man grazed his livestock in another's field or vineyard, he was required to make restitution from the best of his own fields or vineyards.[4] One who started a fire and negligently allowed it to spread to another's field was required to make restitution.[5] If a man injured another, and the injured party recovered, then he who injured him was required to pay for the victim's loss of time and should "cause him to be thoroughly healed."[6] If a man injured a woman with child so that she miscarried, the culprit would be punished "according as the woman's husband will lay upon him" and he should pay as the judges determined.[7] If an ox gored a man or a woman, the ox would be killed, but the owner would not be punished. However, if the evidence showed that the ox was dangerous and the owner had failed to restrain it, the owner could be put to death. But he could ransom his life by paying money damages.[8] Exodus further proclaims, "Thou shalt not follow a multitude to do evil"[9] and that every breach of trust would require double restitution.[10]

Our modern civil justice system flows from ancient Judeo-Christian teachings. Our faith in a supreme being and belief that he inspires us to seek justice for those wronged by others compels the trial lawyer's commitment to our clients, our cause, and our legal procedures.

Freedom

In 1999, the New York Times *ran a series of articles on significant events of the last millennium.*[11] *Scholars and authorities in science, entertainment, sports, and politics opined on the most significant event in those areas in the last one thousand years. The legal scholars were asked, "What was the most significant legal case of this millennium?" The answer was Bushell's Case, an appellate decision out of the Court of Common Pleas in England in 1670. From that case flowed the American ideal of and commitment to trial by an independent jury.*[12]

On August 14, 1670, a congregation comes to their church at Gracechurch and Lombard Streets intent on peaceable worship. They find heavy iron chains crisscrossing the doors. In front of the doors stand grim-faced dragoons drawn into a tight rank. The captain of this cadre advises the parishioners that they are prohibited from entering the church by order of King Charles II.

What were they preaching in this church that represented such a threat that the king ordered it closed down? They were Quakers—pacifists. England is beginning its march toward worldwide imperialism. The crown needs young men to fight abroad and extend the borders of the empire. The Quakers' teachings represent a threat to the throne because they discourage young men from serving in the army.

The leader of the Quakers confronts the captain and begs him to stand aside and allow the congregation to worship. When his entreaty is denied, William Penn begins to hold service on the steps of the church. Captain James Cook tries without success to disperse the crowd. In frustration he asks William Mead, who had served in the army with him, to assist. Mead, a Quaker, refuses.

The authorities charge Penn with preaching sedition—treason—and Mead, because he "did abide by it." The criminal trial will require a jury of lay citizens. On Wednesday, August 31, constables arrest people at random off the street. The authorities have little doubt of conviction by those they pull from the streets. English juries know of the tradition of delivering the verdict the crown desires in sensitive cases or risking imprisonment. This is a sensitive case.

The venire is brought to the courthouse, where the court hears excuses, most of which are denied. One of the jury of twelve who is qualified is Edward Bushell. He is a man with a great sense of justice and fairness. A successful sugar merchant, he uses his ships to smuggle Jews out of Europe to escape death at the hands of the Catholic Inquisition.

The prosecution calls three witnesses, who testify that they saw Penn preaching but could not hear what he was saying. The court instructs the jury to retire to the jury room and deliberate its verdict. The men elect Thomas Veer foreman. After short deliberation, Bushell argues for the two young men's innocence, relying on a copy of the Magna Charta he has in his pocket. They deliberate a little over an hour and a half before the bailiff knocks at the door. He tells the twelve that the court is growing impatient with their shallying and "would have you come below at once." Bushell replies that since the jury has no verdict, they cannot come. Eight of the jurors leave the jury room and take their seats in the box. Bushell, Milson, Hammond, and Veer remain. Within a short time the bailiffs are pounding on the door again, demanding that the four follow them down to the Sessions House. One after another the judges shout: "What means this unseemly delay? . . . If the jury does not show respect for this court, you shall all be fined and denied your dinners . . . You will have your noses slit and tongues cut out." Lord Mayor Sir Samuel Starling tells the jurors that they will not be permitted dinner until they have all agreed to a guilty verdict and orders them back to the jury room for another fifteen minutes.

One of the jurors, Will Plumstead, is old, feverish, and sick. He tries for a compromise by proposing that the jury find Penn guilty of speaking on Gracechurch Street. When the jury returns with this verdict, Judge Howell pounces on jury foreman Veer: "Is that all?" Veer replies, "That is all I have in my commission." The judges conclave, and then Howell, staring menacingly at Veer, says, "You had as good said nothing." Veer asks for a pen, ink, and paper. Plumstead asks for some food since they have not eaten in thirteen hours. Starling tells them that only when the jury has delivered a proper verdict will they be fed. The court declares recess until 9:30 that evening.

Back in the jury room, the jurors sign a verdict and wait for the bailiff. At 9:30, they are back in court. Veer announces that the jurors have found Penn guilty of speaking to an assembly on August 14, 1670, and that William Mead is not guilty of anything. The gallery bursts into cheers and roars. "What, will you be led by such a silly fellow as Bushell?" screams Starling. Judge Howell tells them that the court will not accept the verdict. They will be locked up without meat, drink, fire, or tobacco. "We will have a verdict by the help of God, or you will starve for it." The judges leave the bench and the bailiffs begin prodding the jurors with their muskets to get them to move. The gallery shouts its support.

Some of the jurors had prepared for their service by putting sacks of food and flasks of water under their clothes. They share equally what little they have. Even though it is August, the hard wooden floor in the cell is cold and the damp air full of buzzing flies. Without any toilet facilities, they are forced to use a window that opens onto the street below. In these distressful conditions the men loosen their clothes, take off their shoes, and try to sleep. But the conditions under which they suffer invade their persons and clothes. The twelve men brought into the courtroom the next morning cast off an odorous presence so offensive that the clerks cover the judges' bench with a plentiful supply of nosegay, sweet-smelling herbs.

Although Veer is trembling from fatigue and pain, he tells the court again that the only offense they can find Penn guilty of is speaking on Gracechurch Street. The court sends the jury back to deliberate further. They return fifteen minutes later and repeat the same routine. Howell flies into a rage. He screams at Bushell that he will brand him and "keep his eye on him." The court's Recorder comments that maybe England needs an Inquisition like they have in Spain. The jury is told to continue its deliberations. Veer protests, saying that they have agreed on their verdict and can give no other. Other jurors join in the chorus: "We are agreed . . . We are agreed."

The Recorder observes that their verdict is nothing and that if they don't bring in a proper verdict, they will starve for it. The crowd, seeing that Veer appears frail and weak, begins to cheer him on: "Thomas Veer . . . Thomas Veer . . . Long live Thomas Veer. Long live the jury."

After the court has its morning refreshments, they bring the jury into the courtroom. They hope that all of the jurors will convict save Bushell. If they do, the court will accept the less-than-unanimous verdict. But the jury hangs tough and the court adjourns until seven o'clock the following Monday morning.

A platoon of armed bailiffs stands before the jury room. Friends and relatives gather to protest the jury's imprisonment and beg permission to give the prisoners food and water. Women falling to their knees and kissing the soldiers' feet are met with brutal kicks to their faces. Barbara Bailey, the young wife of juror John Bailey, is standing on the fringe of the crowd when her mother-in-law agonizes, "My poor Johnny, my poor boy. He will starve, I know it." Barbara replies, "Trust me, mother Bailey, and he'll not starve. I warrant it."

The Baileys return to the family bakery where they pack a large shopping bag with meats, bread, fruits, and all manner of bakery goods. Barbara fills a jug with water and puts it in a second bag. It is a heavy load for a woman to carry.

Meanwhile, the jurors notice activity on the second floor of an office building across the alley. Because it is the Sabbath, the building is vacant. Several men are busy with some sort of activity. They attract the jurors' attention without revealing themselves to the army patrols below. They hold up jugs and parcels and convey with hand signals the words "night fall." The jurors cannot understand how their friends and allies intend to get the supplies from one building to the next across the expanse of the alley below.

Serendipity brings the two conspiracies together at the same moment. After nightfall, a crowd gathers outside the Old Bailey. They yell insults and throw rocks at the guards, distracting those underneath the jury room window. Through the darkness, a wooden rod comes across from the adjacent building with a crude pulley and instructions on how to use it. Sacks of food and jugs of water follow. At the same time, Barbara Bailey is plying her feminine charm on the guard stationed outside the door. The low-cut blouse reveals a generous cleavage. She lifts her eyebrow, tosses her tresses around her neck, and comes on to her husband's jailer. She plays a game that she is master of against a grossly overmatched opponent. The soldier is so completely seduced that he allows Barbara to slip the key to the door from around his neck. She opens the door and breaks into the room, startling the jurors. "Johnny, it is Barbara with no time but to leave these." Dropping the parcels, she shouts, "Keep your beaks up, lads. All London is with you." She blows a kiss to her young husband and dashes out, struggling to get her dress back on.

The citizen supporters have passed four packages across the slim rail when the soldiers below discover the deception. They fire on the rail, breaking it and causing it to fall into the street below. Its inventors telegraph a fist and thumbs-up victory sign. They disappear as the soldiers storm the building.

The next morning, all eyes in the courtroom are on the jury room doorway. When the jurors step into the courtroom, the crowd gasps. Thomas Veer looks sick and feeble. Onlookers are surprised that he can even walk. When the court calls for the verdict, Veer musters what little strength he has and speaks two words, emphasizing the first: "*Not* guilty." The same verdict is announced on William Mead. The court polls the jury and each takes responsibility for the verdict.

You can see it coming, can't you? The arrogant and powerful will not let this story end here. Courage and commitment to freedom and liberty come at a price. Someone will have to pay for such insolence.

The court refuses to excuse the twelve. Instead, for their "misbehavior, misconduct and going against the evidence, you are each fined forty marks and imprisonment until paid." Bushell argues with the court that the jury has performed its duty in good conscience and has undergone a heavy ordeal. He reminds them that the laws of England require that they be released at once. Says Lord Mayor Starling, "Pay your fines and you shall be discharged. Until you do, you will be taken to Newgate Prison with William Penn and William Mead, there to remain until your fines are paid."

Foreman Veer is now weaving erratically. His eyes are fixed in a glassy stare. His daughter, Harriet, can hold back no longer. She descends to the pit, berating the judges. She opens her handbag and takes out some coins. Others in the audience come up to help her with the fine. She flings the coins on the clerk's desk. Veer speaks feebly, almost inaudibly. "No, daughter, don't pay it. Let me die 'prisoned than yield to them." Veer falls into her arms, whispering, "Not guilty." With his daughter holding him to her breast, he breathes his last and with his final ounce of strength announces again in a muted voice, "Not guilty."

As the Veer processional is exiting, juror Will Plumstead climbs on a stool to get a better view. When the cortege has passed, he shrieks and throws his arms about. His face is a bursting blood red. His wife and friends clamber into the pit, fighting off the interfering bailiffs. They try to take him down but he pushes them aside. He shouts that he is the king, William the Conqueror. His wife fears he has gone mad. With a bone-raking shriek, he shouts, "Not guilty!" and topples to the floor. As they start to carry him away, the Mayor stops them. "He cannot be released until his fine is paid." Plumstead's friends are aghast. They search in their pockets and between them come up with the forty marks. Will Plumstead will die later, long before Edward Bushell and the others' ordeal finds its end. At the urging of Bushell, three others, Bailey, Milson, and Hammond, are committed to play the hand to the end. For their devotion to liberty, they follow Penn and Mead to Newgate Prison, which is next to and connects with the Central Criminal Court of London.

While their families support the courageous stand of the jurors, they fear for them. It is difficult for us to picture a hellhole like Newgate Prison. Run by sadistic jailers, it is an undisguised torture chamber run with more cold-blooded cruelty than we find today in dungeons in the Middle East or Asia.

From the time Edward Bushell tells Judith not to pay his fine, she is determined to pursue his freedom. The Bushells know Sir Richard Newdigate, the former Chief Justice of the Court of Common Pleas. Bushell and the others will need outstanding representation. Sir Richard was an accomplished lawyer and respected judge but is now retired to his estate in Arbury in Warwickshire, one hundred miles to the north.

Judith's sixteen-year-old stepson meets her carriage as it pulls through the gate of their home. She tells Benjamin someone must bear a message to Sir Richard. He insists on undertaking the challenging errand. Still being trained by his father in horsemanship, Benjamin has a small, easy-gaited horse named Mercury. Judith fears his undertaking such an arduous adventure because of his youth and the small horse. He will have to ride all night to reach Arbury by morning. Later, nearing the Newdigate estate, Mercury stumbles and collapses into a crumpled, ugly, twisted heap. Her loyal heart has burst. A young passerby takes Benjamin on the back of his horse and the two reach Sir Richard.

The next morning, Wednesday, September 7, Benjamin, Sir Richard, his secretary and valet, and two coachmen depart by carriage for London. With four changes of horse teams, the coachmen are able to race the carriage steadily at top speed. Once at Newgate, Sir Richard, Benjamin, and the secretary present their demands for an immediate interview with the four jurors. Meeting in the squalid conditions of the prison, the group plans its legal strategy. Sir Richard proposes an ancient writ, rarely used, known as habeas corpus. He further intrigues them by proposing it be filed in the Court of Common Pleas instead of the King's Bench, the court that normally handles criminal cases. Sir Richard knows Sir John Vaughn, the Chief Justice of the court, to be a staunch defender of liberty. On November 9, the court announces its decision and holds that no juror can be imprisoned for his verdict. Sir John Vaughn's words echo today the answer to those who would abolish juries or limit their independence.

> Every man sees that the jury is but a troublesome delay, a great charge, and of no use in determining right and wrong, and therefore trials by them may be better abolished than continued. But this would be the greater mischief to the people.[13]

As soon as he hears the words releasing his father, Benjamin unobtrusively leaves the courtroom. He leaps into the saddle and gallops the six blocks from Westminster to Newgate. Jumping off his horse, he sprints to the visitor's entrance and demands admittance. He flies through the opened gate and up the stairs to his father's ward, where he delivers the good news: "Father, you've won. You'll be free this day!"

When the four men come out, the crowd waiting for them bursts out in cheers and applause. They are gaunt, faces lined by stress and abuse, soiled clothes ill-fitting and smelling. They bear bruises and scars from their beatings. The crowd hoists them on its shoulders to carry them to the carriages. Two jurors have already died in this cause. The six that remain come forward to greet them. Their procession home is delayed by admirers, many throwing coins, which supporters gather from the street and hand to them.

For more than three hundred years now, Bushell's Case has been the touchstone for freedom. The omission of the right to jury trials in civil cases from the United States Constitution caused opposition to its ratification. Thomas Jefferson knew the story of Bushell's Case. He fervently believed that the right to trial by jury was a more fundamental right to a democratic republic than the right to vote. He believed citizen juries were necessary to frustrate the enforcement of unwise legislation and protect ordinary people from powerful interests. Alexander Hamilton and the Federalists distrusted ordinary citizens. They believed that government worked best when left in the hands of well-educated, propertied men. Jeffersonians won the debate, assuring ratification of the Constitution. The Sixth and Seventh Amendments of the Bill of Rights spell out the right to trial by jury.

Free, incorruptible juries do things beyond what representatives dependent on campaign contributions are willing to do. Jurors responsible for these judgments give no reasons for their actions and seek nothing for themselves. The American jury is a unique democratic institution. Citizens are impaneled for one purpose and one purpose only—to determine truth and decide what is fair and just. They exist for only so long as is necessary to accomplish this limited purpose. They expect no reward, and no special recognition comes from their sacrifice. The only thing expected of them is that they will use their best judgment and decide the issue with true impartiality. Who is before them matters not. Rich and poor, black and white, powerful and vulnerable are given equal consideration. Once they have completed their charge, they have no further role or function. And thanks to Bushell's Case, whether their decision is popular with the authorities or the public, they remain free of any personal criticism, contempt, or retribution.

EQUALITY

OUR HISTORY IS benchmarked by times when only a citizen jury stood between the oppression of those in power and vulnerable working men and women. In America, the store of social conscience has little stock at the turn of the twentieth century. Those who advocate against child labor, support a woman's right to vote, seek better working conditions and better pay are castigated and labeled "socialists" or "radicals." The great middle class has yet to emerge—one out of eight Americans lives in poverty. Material wealth is concentrated in the hands of a few who live lives of luxury that ordinary citizens cannot imagine.

It is this setting that makes what a jury in a small mining town in Idaho does on a hot summer day in 1907 all the more notable and remarkable. Twelve ordinary citizens rise up against those who are scarring Lady Liberty's promise of a nation where men can breathe free. These twelve don't concern themselves with whether their verdict is popular, only whether it is right. They turn their backs on the prejudice that a powerful consortium of capital, authority, and influence has provoked against a man dedicated to the cause of those who work the mines of the western states.[14]

The Western Federation of Miners is headquartered in Denver. Charles H. Moyer is the president, and William D. Haywood is the general secretary. Bill Haywood is a giant of a man, powerfully built, with a big head and square jaw. Haywood *is* the Western Federation of Miners. He is to organized labor in the mining country what Churchill is to England during the Battle of Britain, Lincoln to the Union during the Civil War, and the Reverend Martin Luther King, Jr., to the civil rights movement. He is the figurehead, the heart, the soul of the movement for social and economic progress. As such, he becomes the target of all who detest the ideals he represents. The mine owners must bring down Haywood. The opportunity comes just before Christmas 1905.

Frank Steunenberg had been governor of Idaho during widespread labor unrest. He was a printer, carried a union card, and got the union vote. When the strikes came, he declared martial law, and thus the miners view him as one who had received the votes of union members and then deserted them and joined the enemy when they were fighting for their existence. The last Saturday night in December 1905, around six o'clock, a bomb on the gate of his home in Caldwell explodes, shredding his clothes, breaking his limbs, and inflicting mortal wounds. It doesn't take the former governor long to die and even less time for the state of Idaho to begin the investigation.

Within a few days, the authorities arrest a man who calls himself Thomas Hogan. He is later identified as Harry Orchard, a drifter who had worked in the Idaho mines. The evidence incriminating him includes bomb materials found in his room when the sheriff searches it and wet shoes in a trunk that match perfectly the tracks at the scene. And he certainly has motive. Steunenberg's actions in calling out the militia caused Orchard to dispose of his interests in the Hercules Mine, one of the richest in Idaho. The unemployed laborer would have been a multimillionaire if he had been able to hold on to his Hercules stock. Orchard confesses to the crime, but the Pinkertons and their employer, the mine owners, want more than Steunenberg's assassin. They want Haywood, Moyer, and George Pettibone, a prominent member of the union, charged with this capital crime, and they want every branch of government—executive, legislative, and judicial—conspiring for the trio's conviction.

The owners bring in the chief justice of the Idaho Supreme Court. He calls James McParland, the chief of the Pinkerton Detective Agency in Denver, and asks him to take over the investigation. McParland has already reached the conclusion that Orchard acted on behalf of the Western Federation of Miners' "inner circle." With the governor's help, McParland gets Orchard transferred from the Caldwell jail to Boise. The judge who enters the order promises that he will not grant Orchard a writ of habeas corpus. Once in Boise, away from any potential legal interference, McParland is able to coerce the needed confession and fingering of Haywood and the others by promising that if Orchard cooperates, the authorities will be lenient. At the end of the session in the Boise jail on Thursday, February 1, McParland holds in his hands an extraordinary sixty-four-page confession. Orchard not only admits to planting the bomb, he claims Haywood and the others paid him and put him up to it.

The fact that the three men live in Denver and there is no evidence they have ever been in Idaho poses a problem. Overcoming this will require the assistance of the governor of Colorado and the Idaho Supreme Court. The governor arranges for a special train to carry the three men from Colorado to Idaho. Pinkerton detectives arrest Haywood in a rooming house in Denver on Saturday, February 17. Haywood and the others will have no access to a lawyer for three days. By then they are in Idaho.

Edmund F. Richardson, a Denver lawyer on retainer for the union, appears in Idaho's Supreme Court to ask for a writ of habeas corpus the first thing Tuesday morning. The defense stresses the constitutional requirement that only a person "who shall flee from justice" can be extradited to the state "from which he fled." Haywood and the other two union officials are not extraditable, Richardson argues, because they are not fugitives.

On March 12, the Idaho Supreme Court hands down its ruling. Quashing the writs, it remands the prisoners for trial. The defense promptly goes to the U.S. Supreme Court. James Hawley, who argues for the state, has a long talk with Justice Harlan before the oral arguments in the Haywood case are presented. The Court, in an opinion by Justice Harlan, affirms the Idaho court's decision finding nothing unconstitutional in the kidnapping of the three union officials.

The prosecution will try Haywood first. The defense seeks a change of venue from Canyon County on the basis of the strong prejudice that exists there against the labor leaders. With difficulty, the defense obtains the necessary affidavits, and the presiding judge moves the case to Boise and sets it for May 9, 1907.

The mine owners bring in a "dream team." The prosecution cadre is led by James Hawley and William E. Borah. Hawley is active in Idaho politics and has been connected with some of the most important litigation in the state. After the trial he will be elected governor. Borah has, for twenty years, been considered the leading trial lawyer in the state and is elected to the United States Senate just before the trial begins. He is the most popular man in Idaho.

The union's lawyer, Edmund Richardson, needs help. But who can he get? Where can he turn? He needs an accomplished, talented trial lawyer, but most of those are committed to defending corporate interests. Good trial lawyers don't like to lose. Who would be willing to squander his reputation on the dreary prospect of winning an acquittal for someone already scorned in the streets and the press? Richardson makes a call to Chicago to someone who often walked the road less traveled. A man dedicated to the cause of labor who has never feared championing a cause because it is unpopular. A lawyer who has spent most of his professional life speaking out against prejudice, bigotry, and the abuse of power by corporate interests. Clarence Darrow tells Richardson he will take the case.

Over the next several weeks the court summons four different venire panels. Only three men identify themselves as former members of a trade union in the total of 249 summoned. The prosecution strikes them from the panel. The twelve jurors qualified are or have been farmers.

The prosecution calls its chief witness, Harry Orchard. He claims that Moyer and Haywood gave him money to come to Idaho and kill Steunenberg and that George Pettibone was connected with the plot. Orchard admits that he helped blow up a railroad station at the Victor Mine in Colorado where thirty men were killed. He tried to dynamite the mine while the men were at work. He tried to assassinate a member of the Idaho Supreme Court but failed. Later in the direct examination the prosecutor asks, "What is your true name?" The question hangs for a moment in the silent courtroom, the only sound the whir of the wooden fans paddling the muggy air. The witness replies, "Albert E. Horsley."

The defense cross-examination demonstrates that Orchard, who has several aliases, is a womanizer who had run away with another man's wife, deserting his own wife and young daughter, committed bigamy, loses heavily at gambling, often drinks to stupor, and has stolen from employers and friends.

To make a legal case against Haywood, the prosecution needs someone to corroborate Orchard's testimony. It is common for railroad companies and mine owners to buy any witness they need. They approach several but find big holes in any stories that can be concocted. One witness they thought might be credible backs out. Since the prosecution can't corroborate through a fact witness, they try "junk science." They call an alienist. Today we would call him a psychologist. This questionable "expert" testifies he has tested Orchard and concludes that he is in all things truthful.

During the trial, the defense attorneys and their supporters are subjected to constant indignities. Several Socialists are physically assaulted. Merchants brag about having tickets to sell to Haywood's hanging. Haywood's female supporters are spat upon and hissed at. They find notes pushed under their doors telling them to get out of town.

The defense offers evidence painstakingly gathered to show that the Western Federation was the victim of a vast conspiracy by mine owners and the Pinkertons to destroy the union. The presiding judge excludes the evidence. They do manage to call a former clerical employee in the Pinkerton's Denver office who tells of the mine owners' covert operations to drain the union's treasury and provoke dissent and rebellion by the membership.

Haywood takes the stand and flatly denies any connection with Orchard. He testifies that he had no knowledge of Orchard's movements and that Orchard was simply one man of thousands who went on strike with the union. He tells of his suspicions that Orchard had connections with the owners and may have been a plant to destroy the union.

Clarence Darrow has the law and he stresses it. A conspirator's uncorroborated confession is insufficient, standing alone, to warrant conviction. This legal principle is as old as the Bible, which in Deuteronomy 19:15 holds that one witness is not enough to convict. The lawyer from Chicago hammers at the prosecution's failure to call anyone who can support Orchard's questionable testimony.

Darrow is also the master of using the moral of his story to inspire the verdict his client needs. He believes that you must capture men's hearts before you can bring along their minds. His closing argument empowers the jury as he reminds them that Idaho farmers "today would be serfs of Europe, instead of free men" if it had not been for the trade unions of America.

The closing arguments concluded, the judge instructs the jury. When they retire to deliberate, everyone knows the mine owners have their victory. Haywood will hang.

The light in the window of the jury room tells passersby that the twelve farmers are working through the night. Darrow walks around town, unable to sleep. At seven o'clock in the morning, the bailiff notifies the lawyers that the jury has a verdict. At eight o'clock the judge arrives. The lawyers are in their places, the courtroom is packed. People are crowding into the courthouse yard. The foreman hands the verdict to the clerk. The room grows still as death. No one breathes until they hear the words "not guilty." Newspapermen jump up from their seats and hurry off to the telegraph office. It is Sunday, and no one is working. The streets are swarming. Some people are excited, rejoicing. Others are frowning and downcast. The jury's verdict is a shock to the powerful interests that had conspired for Haywood's conviction.

Can you think of any other case from American jurisprudence where an ordinary man faced such a confederation and coalition of powerful interests and prevailed? Equal justice under the law is an ideal that man has struggled with for thousands of years. Twenty-two centuries ago, the Roman dramatist Plautus recognized that "the law for the rich and poor is not the same."[15] In 1756, Voltaire argued that "all men have equal rights to liberty, to their property, and to the protection of the laws."[16] When Thomas Jefferson penned his ideal in the Declaration of Independence, it was far from a reality for many Americans. Almost a century later, Abraham Lincoln reaffirmed the proposition that "all men are created equal."

While we may point to many instances where prejudice and powerful interest have hijacked the paradigm of justice in a courtroom, the Haywood verdict is a shining beacon for those who believe that the ordinary citizen can still find truth there. That there can be equal justice for all.

COURAGE

ALL OF AMERICA is feeling the hard winds of the depression in the spring of 1931. The economic maelstrom's epicenter is the rural South, where privation ignites the fires of intolerance. Many whites blame blacks for the social and economic ills. Poor blacks struggle for survival. Unemployed men of both races hitch rides on trains in Alabama, looking for work.

The Scottsboro Boys[17] are nine black youths who find themselves in the wrong place at the wrong time. They range in age from twelve to nineteen, and some are seriously ill. Partially blind Olen Montgomery gets on the train with his friend, Willie Roberson, who is suffering from a venereal disease and can barely move. Both are seventeen years old. Brothers Roy and Andy Wright, ages twelve and nineteen, and eighteen-year-old Haywood Patterson know each other, boarding at Chattanooga. A fourth Chattanooga native, thirteen-year-old Eugene Williams, joins them. Three others—eighteen-year-old Clarence Norris, nineteen-year-old Charles Weems, and sixteen-year-old Ozie Powell—have never met one another before. They do not know any of the other boys. They are all poor, some are orphans, most have been on their own since they were seven or eight years old. They are broke and on their way to Memphis to look for work. A Southern judge will become challenged by the injustice visited on these boys. His determination to do the right thing exemplifies how courage is an essential of justice.

Two white women, Victoria Price, age twenty-one, and Ruby Bates, eighteen, had spent the night in a hobo jungle near Chattanooga. They get on the train with a friend, Lester Carter, to return home to Huntsville. No one knows how many people were illegally riding the rails that day, March 25, 1931. It may have been as many as ninety white and black boys as well as the two women dressed in dungarees and wearing boys' caps to fit in with the male crowd.

Four white boys cross over the oil tanker where four of the black youths are riding. One of them almost knocks Haywood Patterson off the train. When the train slows coming out of the tunnel underneath Lookout Mountain, two of the white boys jump off, pick up some rocks, and throw them at the blacks, hitting several. Some other black youths join the group from another car and agree to fight back if any of the white boys start throwing rocks again. When the whites resume the stoning, a fistfight follows. The black boys, now outnumbering the whites, throw several of them off the train. Some of the white youths return to Stevenson and complain to the authorities. They in turn place a call to Paint Rock, Alabama, with instructions to pull the black riders off the train. The black youths are met at Paint Rock by a group of armed white men who surround the boxcar with pistols drawn and shotguns showing.

When Haywood Patterson asks, "What's this all about?" the authorities reply that they are charged with assault and attempted murder. A posse takes the nine boys to Scottsboro, the county seat of Jackson County. Shortly after the boys' confinement, a white man comes into the jail with two young white women. He asks the boys whether they know the girls. The boys say, "No, sir." The man, using strong racial epithets, calls the boys liars and charges that they raped the two women.

That evening, a screaming crowd surrounds the jail. Only by a show of force are the sheriff and his deputies able to save the boys from the lynch mob. The next morning, the deputies take the group to Gadsden, Alabama, where on March 31 a grand jury indicts them for rape. The judge schedules their trial for the following week. None of the nine are allowed to talk to a lawyer. When the boys return from Gadsden to Scottsboro, they find the mob has grown and become more belligerent, shouting racial slurs and swearing to kill all the defendants.

Judge A. E. Hawkins, the presiding judge, names Stephen Roddy and Milo Moody as defense counsel. Roddy is unfamiliar with Alabama law. He is drunk when appointed; he is drunk during the trial. The two lawyers meet with their clients for a mere twenty-five minutes before the trial begins.

The prosecution pushes the boys through court by trying them in groups of two or three. The two women tell their stories to the all-male, all-white juries. As the evidence mounts in one case, some of the young men, now known as the Scottsboro Boys, begin accusing each other. The trials last only three days. When the guilty verdict in the first trial is announced, the crowd outside the courthouse roars its approval so loudly that the jury trying the second case hears it. Only Roy Wright is spared the death sentence when the court declares a mistrial because one of the jurors holds out for life imprisonment as requested by the prosecution. The other eleven jurors refuse to accept the prosecution's suggestion and vote to put to death a twelve-year-old boy. The court sentences the defendants after the three juries deliver their verdicts. Never before in American history have eight men been sentenced to death on the same day by the same judge for the same crime.

The International Labor Defense, the legal arm of the American Communist Party, takes over the case and appeals it all the way to the U.S. Supreme Court. In the landmark November 1932 decision of *Powell v. Alabama*, the Court holds that it is an unconstitutional denial of due process to deny a defendant adequate legal representation in a capital case. The Court orders a new trial.

The question of where to retry the boys is no small issue. Feelings against the defendants run high throughout Alabama. Judge James E. Horton had abandoned his successful law practice to run for the bench eleven years earlier. He is popular, well respected, and known to be a man of impeccable integrity. When he is first approached about trying the case, he is hesitant. This is, after all, a high-profile case involving sensitive issues. The white community is outraged at the thought that the black defendants accused of gang-raping two young white women might escape execution. Mobs are threatening lynchings. Newspapers editorialize for conviction. Reluctantly, Judge Horton agrees to hear the case, which is then transferred on a change of venue to Decatur, a small town fifty miles west of Scottsboro. Separate trials having been ordered, the prosecution decides to try Haywood Patterson first. The new trial begins on March 27, 1933.

New York attorney Samuel Leibowitz takes on the case. He prepares the defense meticulously. The defense team hires investigators and brings to court a Lionel model built to scale of the train from which the authorities had pulled the nine youths and the two alleged victims. They will use the model to punch holes in the prosecution's case.

Leibowitz begins by moving that the indictment be thrown out because blacks had been excluded from local jury rolls and were barred from the jury that had initially convicted the youths. Judge Horton concedes the point but denies the motion.

Alabama Attorney General Thomas Knight, Jr., is filled with political ambition. He sees the case and the inherent prejudice against the defendants as an opportunity to further his quest for the statehouse. He will prosecute the case himself. Knight calls as his first witness Victoria Price, who again testifies to the rape. She claims that six of the defendants so brutally attacked and penetrated her that she had scratches on her body and was bleeding after the assault. Leibowitz cross-examines. Price admits that she and Ruby Bates had spent the night before with two men. She also admits to facts suggesting that she is a bootlegger and prostitute.

The prosecution calls a physician who had examined the girls following the rape. He confirms the presence of semen in the girls when he examined them. On cross-examination he concedes that the spermatozoa were immotile—at least twenty-four to forty-eight hours old. The doctor admits that neither Victoria Price nor Ruby Bates were scratched or bleeding and that both appeared calm and composed.

Following the doctor's testimony, the prosecution, in a bench conference with Judge Horton, advises that they do not intend to call the second doctor who participated in the examination. This young physician, recently graduated from medical school, is just beginning his practice in Alabama. The defense does not object. During the recess, the young doctor requests a private conference with Judge Horton and advises him that he found no evidence of rape when he examined the two women and that he was convinced they were lying. Judge Horton tells the doctor, "You've got to testify to that." The doctor not only refuses but tells Judge Horton that if he is put on the stand he will deny the conversation ever took place. He explains that as a young physician in Alabama and with feelings running high against the defendants he cannot afford to sacrifice his medical career by coming forward.

Judge Horton's dilemma is confounding. After hearing the doctor's "confession," how can he continue to preside over the trial? Why would he? Perhaps it is the conviction that nothing wrong occurred. The doctor insisted on the revelation even after being admonished that they should not be talking about the case. If he declares a mistrial on the basis of the ex parte statements, the doctor will deny the conversation. Without corroboration, it will appear as though Horton is trying to duck his responsibilities in a difficult case. More than likely the veteran jurist believes, as have many judges in other cases before and after, that the jury will take care of it. They will do justice with the evidence. After all, Plutarch observed that when men are just, there is no need for courage. Judge Horton presides over the remainder of the trial knowing a critical fact that the jury will never know. It will not be publicly revealed for many years.

Even though he has to issue an instruction during the trial quelling the mob talk of lynching, Judge Horton's hopes of jury rectification grow as the evidence questioning Victoria Price's allegations mounts against her. Leibowitz calls his witnesses: six of the defendants, who deny seeing the girls on the train or attacking them; Lester Carter, one of the two men who were with the women the night before the alleged rape, who tells of his relationship with Ruby Bates and that of Victoria Price and Price's boyfriend Jack Tyler; and a surprise witness—Ruby Bates. Following the second trial, she had written a letter confessing the fraud of the girls' allegations against the defendants. Bates backs up Carter's story and testifies the black youths never raped her or Price. She swears the defendants never touched her and that she and Price never even talked with them. After being pulled off the train, she had been encouraged to fabricate the story by the white boys and Victoria, who told her they had to make up these accusations to avoid being thrown in jail for vagrancy. Upon completing her testimony and leaving the courthouse, the mob on the lawn spits on her and throws eggs that splatter on her clothes and face.

The defense rests, satisfied they have raised reasonable doubt as to the boys' guilt. Privately, Judge Horton is of the same view. The prosecution's closing argument is filled with racial and anti-Semitic invectives. By any standard it is prejudicial and inflammatory, and includes asking the jury: "Is justice going to be bought and sold in Alabama with Jew money from New York?"[18]

On April 9, the all-male, all-white jury finds Haywood Patterson guilty and sentences him to death in the electric chair.

Life's choices are often between doing what is right even when it hurts and doing what is wrong in the name of personal or professional advancement. For Judge Horton, the choices are clear. He is a popular judge who, if he does what is expected of him, will probably advance to the Alabama Supreme Court. He has many reasons to support his abiding of the verdict: the community is solidly behind the conviction, the jury's decision is a popular one, the defense is aligned with the Communist Party, the offense is grave—six black men raping two white women. He gains nothing by setting aside the conviction. The attorney general has promised to retry the case. Setting aside the verdict will only jeopardize Horton's life of service at the bar.

What will this man of integrity, honor, and wisdom do? On the one hand, the road leads to professional ostracism, abuse by the community, the status of a pariah. The other choice is to go along with the mob, be hoisted on their shoulders, proclaimed a champion of law and order, and have his ticket punched for future service on Alabama's highest court. The hard road and the easy road. What is right versus what is expeditious. But men like James Horton never really have a choice.

On June 22, 1933, Judge James Horton grants the defense's motion for new trial on the grounds that Haywood Patterson's conviction is against the weight of the evidence. In his opinion delivered from the bench, he notes that the alleged rape occurred during daylight hours on a clear day on a gondola without a top. The uncorroborated testimony of Victoria Price was that six of the defendants successively had intercourse with her on top of the chert in the gondola in open view of anyone. The train traveled forty miles through the heart of Jackson County, through Fackler, Hollywood, Scottsboro, Larkinsville, Lim Rock, and Woodsville. None of the eight white boys who had been in the gondola testified to the rape. Price claimed that a white boy witnessed the whole scene, yet he never reported it. She claimed she had been hit and scratched during the rape, but the doctor found no blood and no wounds. The semen found in her was consistent with the sex she had had the night before. Judge Horton also notes that Victoria Price's demeanor was questionable. Her testimony was contradictory and evasive, and she refused to answer pertinent questions. He concludes:

> The testimony of the prosecutrix in this case is not only uncorroborated, but it also bears on its face indications of improbability and is contradicted by other evidence, and in addition thereto the evidence greatly preponderates in favor of the defendant. It therefore becomes the duty of the Court under the law to grant the motion made in this case.[19]

There would be more trials, more appeals, another landmark decision. Eventually all of the defendants would be freed, but only after they had spent a total of one hundred thirty years in prison. Attorney General Thomas Knight, Jr., would go on to a successful political career.

The battlefield is not the only place we find bravery. Gallantry isn't limited to the athletic arena. We admire those who are willing to put up their reputations and their well-being for the cause of right. Judge Horton was defeated at the next election. He never again held public office. In the grand tapestry of the Scottsboro Boys cases, his fearless decision probably made no difference in the long run. But it is the action, not the effect, that defines valor. Men and women at the bar or on the bench who take courageous actions in representing their clients or make courageous decisions have names. We call them heroes. Judge James E. Horton was truly a hero of justice—a profile in courage.

Perseverance

EVERY WEEKDAY, school buses carrying laughing children to their studies pass a black minister walking to his school in Clarendon County, South Carolina. They drive by other children who are walking the same muddy roads on their way to school. Black children. The more he sees it, the more it bothers Joseph A. DeLaine. Today he is going to do something about it. His decision will inflict a brutal personal toll but change the fabric of American society forever.[20]

Half the sixty-one black schools in Clarendon County are ramshackle shanties out in the country. The parents are poor farmers and laborers. They don't have the time or the means to get their children to school. So the black children walk to the little schoolhouses. Some have to trudge miles to get there. Reverend DeLaine and farmer James Gibson have had enough. The next day they are at the offices of L. B. McCord, county superintendent of schools. The two law-abiding, taxpaying citizens ask him for one school bus for the black children. McCord tells the two black men that the school district can't give them a bus. It wouldn't be fair to the white citizens who pay most of the taxes. McCord thinks that is the end of the matter. They are just two ordinary Negroes making a foolish request. DeLaine and Gibson aren't strong enough to do anything about it. Poor black people in Clarendon County know to drop things when the authorities oppose them. The gravelly old administrator does not know what persistence and resolve reside in these humble men.

Reverend DeLaine writes the state superintendent of education. The superintendent writes back saying it is a local matter. The reverend writes United States Attorney General Tom Clark. Clark writes back telling him to pursue his request through local officials. The black farmers scrape up enough to buy a secondhand bus to carry their children to school. They ask if the county will pay for the gasoline. The county refuses.

Reluctantly, the black pastor decides to turn to the courts. But he has no legal standing. The plaintiff has to be a taxpayer with children in school. And the complainant has to be brave. Blacks have been killed for less in Clarendon County. Levi Pearson has three children attending the Scott's Branch high school nine miles from his farm, and he had chipped in for the bus that keeps breaking down. So on March 16, 1948, in the United States District Court in Florence County, adjacent to Clarendon on the northeast, Levi Pearson sues the school board alleging his children are being irreparably damaged by the authorities' refusal to provide transportation to school. The suit asks that the board be enjoined "from making a distinction on account of race or color" in providing free bus service for white schoolchildren while denying it to blacks.

The court throws the case out the door in June on the grounds that Pearson has no legal standing. His farm is on the line between School District No. 5, where he pays his property taxes, and School District No. 22, the one his children attend.

The fact that Pearson has lost doesn't keep the authorities from retaliating against the man they know is responsible for the suit. Although J. A. DeLaine has devotedly taught at his little schoolhouse for ten years, the school district fires him. They fire his wife, two of his sisters, and a niece. They tell him it could get a lot worse. Why should he persist? He is a vulnerable black man taking on the white community.

Just to be sure the Negroes get the message, every white-owned store and bank cuts off Levi Pearson's credit at spring planting time. Trying to make it, he cuts down some of his timber to sell for cash. When the man comes to pick it up, he learns what Pearson is up to. He drives off, leaving the wood to rot.

The National Association for the Advancement of Colored People becomes interested in the case in early 1949. Their chief counsel, Thurgood Marshall, takes on their cause. He will file another suit if DeLaine can find twenty black taxpayers whose children attend school in the district. This time, they will ask for more than school buses. They will ask for equal treatment in all aspects of education, including buildings and teachers' salaries.

Word gets out that Reverend DeLaine is pushing the school board. Some angry whites throw bricks through his church's windows. His house burns down while the white fire department watches. But he hangs in and gets the twenty signatures requested by Marshall. It takes him eight months to get them. The plaintiffs' being named in alphabetical order means that the case is styled *Harry Briggs v. R.W. Elliott, the Chairman of the Board of Trustees of School District 22.*

The defense is straightforward. Black children should be educated separately from whites in their own facilities. The black schools are adequate for black students. It is an argument that has withstood judicial scrutiny for almost one hundred years. Separate but equal. In some Southern states, separate editions of textbooks are used for black and white students. Others say that white and black voters cannot enter a polling place in the company of one another, ban interracial athletic contests, and require separate washrooms in factories. Ten states mandate separate waiting rooms for bus and train travelers. Eleven states require black passengers to ride in the backs of buses or streetcars. Parks, playgrounds, and theaters are segregated in eight states. So by custom and precedent segregation flourishes in the South. Why should the courts entertain a complaint from a few black parents living in a rural community in South Carolina?

Is this all of the story? Did I leave anything out? Maybe a few significant facts, some other things to consider.

In Clarendon County, there are thirty school buses for the white children. None for the black students. Each of sixty-one black schools, more than half of them ramshackle, falling-down shanties, accommodates one or two teachers and their charges. The white students attend twelve schools. The total value of the sixty-one black schools attended by 6,531 pupils is officially listed as $194,575. The value of the white schools attended by 2,375 youngsters is put at $673,850. You do the math and you will see that for every dollar the school district spends on a black child, almost ten is spent for a white student. There is marked disparity in teacher pay, too. In Clarendon County, a white teacher earns on average two-thirds more than his black counterpart.

These are some of the facts Marshall has when he appears before United States District Judge J. Waites Waring, a prominent liberal jurist. Waring's astute judicial maneuvering causes Marshall to dismiss the case and refile, asking not for equalization but desegregation. Since the suit raises constitutional issues, a three-judge panel will hear it. The pastor who had only wanted a single school bus, the farmers who upped the stakes to several school buses, are about to be plaintiffs in one of the most significant cases in American legal history. The fat is in the fire.

When the case goes to trial in May 1951, the state's lawyer has an ace up his sleeve. He admits that while there may be significant discrepancies between the black and white schools, the state legislature has just adopted "legislation of a broad and sweeping nature." Collection of the new sales tax to finance the school program will start in just a few weeks, and the defendant trustees have already requested a survey by the director of the new State Educational Finance Commission "so that they may formulate and submit to proper authorities a plan to bring about as speedily as possible equality of buildings, equipment, facilities and other physical aspects of the district."[21]

Marshall doesn't bite. He insists on presenting his case. Evidence suggested about one-fourth of the entire black population in America was functionally illiterate in 1946. The civil rights champion is determined to try his case like a trial lawyer. He uses experts to prove damage. Ken Clark is a Howard University social psychologist who studied the self-image of black children by using dolls resembling white and black babies. Clark's research on children in Philadelphia, Boston, and several cities in Arkansas showed that black children, even by the age of three, had a preference for the white dolls and thought the black dolls were "ugly." Marshall ties Clark's evidence in with other studies demonstrating that blacks are retarded in their mental age due to lack of educational opportunity. Marshall calls as a witness one of the defendants, Clarendon County's superintendent of schools, L. B. McCord. McCord admits to the discrepancy in facilities, defending on the basis that the Lord intended the races to be separate and implying his belief in the inferiority of the Negro.

The trial takes two days. Three weeks later, Judges Parker and Timmerman deny the plaintiffs' plea for an injunction abolishing segregation of the races in the schools of South Carolina. Judge Waring files a twenty-page dissent. The case is on its way to the United States Supreme Court.

Harry Briggs now joins Reverend DeLaine and Levi Pearson as personas non grata in Clarendon County. Briggs is a thirty-four-year-old Navy veteran with five children. For fourteen years he had worked at the Carrigan service station on Main Street. The owner fires him on Christmas Eve. The owners of a Summerton motel fire his wife. The family stays on, trying to farm twenty acres while the legal fight over the schools comes to a boil. During that time, the Summerton bank cuts off their credit. Harry Briggs goes twenty-three miles up the road to Sumter and gets a loan there. When they find out who he is, they call the money in.

Other plaintiffs in the case feel the whip of retribution. Bo Stukes is let go at his garage. Esso fires James Brown from his position as a driver-salesman. The owner of the land that Mrs. Maisie Solomon rents, tosses her off with no notice. She has to move in with another family. John Edward MacDonald, a thirty-one-year-old veteran of Iwo Jima and Okinawa, can't get any financing for a tractor to farm his hundred acres. The gins refuse to handle the plaintiffs' cotton. The funeral home refuses to accept black decedents.

A companion case to *Briggs* is on its way to the Supreme Court from Kansas. It has been forty-eight years since a black tried to enroll his child in a school set aside for whites only in Topeka, Kansas. Oliver Brown is joined by a dozen more black parents in his suit against the school district. *Briggs* gets to the Supreme Court first but is expunged for further hearings before the district court. This leaves the Kansas case of *Brown v. Board of Education.* The Court later brings up *Briggs* as a companion case. The lead decision on school segregation would now be *Brown,* a case that didn't come to the Court from the South. If the justices decide that segregation is unconstitutional, the nation will not see the case as just a Southern issue.

The lawyers first argue the case on December 9, 1952. The defendants are represented by John W. Davis, the most accomplished and admired appellate lawyer in America. Since the Court is divided, they decide to have the segregation cases restored to the docket and reargued in December 1953.

Chief Justice Fred Vinson dies before the segregation cases can be reargued. President Eisenhower names Earl Warren chief justice. Warren and his brethren continue to ponder the segregation cases. The more he thinks about it, the more Warren is convinced that the doctrine of separate-but-equal rests on the concept of the inferiority of the Negro race. Warren decides to spend a few days visiting Civil War monuments in Virginia. His black chauffeur drives him. At the end of the day, the driver pulls into the hotel where the jurist has reservations. Warren assumes that his chauffeur will find someplace to stay other than his expensive hotel. When he comes out the next morning, he finds the chauffeur sleeping in the car. He asks why. The chauffeur explains that there are no hotels in the area that allow blacks. Embarrassed, Warren cuts his tour short.

We know the rest of the story. The unanimous 1954 Supreme Court decision is probably the most important of the twentieth century, if not in the history of the Court.

A few years later, Lyndon Johnson would sign into law civil rights legislation. In 1967, Johnson appointed Thurgood Marshall as the ninety-sixth man to serve on the nation's highest court. He was the first black. And all of this happened because one man was determined to persevere in his search for justice. They could fire him, they could fire his wife, they could fire his family, they could threaten him, let his house burn down, they could stone his church, and they could concoct a scheme to drive him into bankruptcy. It didn't matter what they did. Rev. J. A. DeLaine and the black farmers who joined with him would get justice. They didn't want it for themselves. They wanted it for their children.

The trial lawyer's commitment and dedication to the rule of law comes from three thousand years of enlightenment as humanity has searched for the meaning of justice. Every benchmark in this quest tells a story. A narrative of faith, freedom, equality, courage, and perseverance. The people's advocate who knows these stories and has been inspired by them never waivers in her devotion to our procedures, zealous representation of clients, and resolve to find the truth.

17

Consider Your Audience

HE IS A GOOD, DECENT, hardworking fellow. The family has a respected name. His father and grandfather before him worked in the same business. You would like him if you met him. He is a tall, thin, good-looking man who appears to be in his early forties. His face is leathered and wrinkled by hours in the sun. It is an honest patina acquired from long, hard, manual labor.

But times and fortunes are not good to Mr. Stone. He has some business reverses. His savings are wiped out. All he has is his meager business and the land on which it stands. When the defendant comes to him, the stranger finds a vulnerable and willing ear. The defendant makes a compelling business proposition that will reverse all the misfortune. Mr. Stone can make back all he has lost and more. The stranger doesn't ask for much in return, simply a mortgage on something that this good man owns. There is nothing dishonest or illegal in what is proposed. The terms the defendant demands are severe. But the man is desperate and so he agrees to the proposition.

When I tell you that the defendant lives up to every bit of the bargain that he made with my friend, I am sure you will wonder how a lawsuit comes out of this. But that is what happens. The defendant lives up to his promises and Mr. Stone's business prospers. The defendant's novel business methods, ideas, and practices bring this decent fellow more success and riches than we can imagine. Mr. Stone becomes one of the most prosperous men in this part of the country. When the time of the contract is up, the defendant asks for satisfaction of the bargain. He demands that the plaintiff deliver to him the property that had been promised. But this Mr. Stone does not want to do.

He consults a lawyer, not just someone who is well known in this part of the country. A lawyer known all over this nation. A lawyer who is considered the preeminent trial lawyer of the day. The lawyer says he will take on the case. You might think that with such prominent trial counsel the defendant would back off and be willing to negotiate.

As the trial begins, the defendant scoffs at the plaintiff and tells him that he can have any lawyer he wants; it really doesn't matter, because he, the defendant, claims the right to have the case tried by a jury of his choice.

By now this story should be familiar. It is, of course, Stephen Vincent Benét's "The Devil and Daniel Webster." It illustrates as much as any tale I could tell that which we all know.

The most important part of a trial is jury selection. In the world of romance and fiction, trial lawyers like Daniel Webster are persuasive and win cases even before the most antagonistic and hostile of juries. The twelve jurors brought straight from hell to try Mr. Stone's cause against Mr. Scratch ultimately turn on the Devil. But the real world is not like that. Prejudice, bigotry, and bias are always hungry and forever need feeding. Only by carefully selecting our audience—the jury—can we protect our clients and causes from those who would feast on the victims of negligence who come before the bar seeking justice.[1]

Successful speakers and storytellers know their audience. Your listeners may be friendly and supportive, openly hostile, but hopefully not indifferent. In my forty years of speaking to civic and professional groups, I have addressed many audiences: lawyers and physicians, probusiness and tort reform groups. An audience that does not share your values can be a tough sell. They know they don't like you before you're introduced, have a mind-set that is not going to accept your message, and often wonder how you ever got the courage to show up in the first place. In speaking to a hostile audience, I use humor and stories to diffuse the tension. A speaker who does not appear to be lecturing or arguing with those turned out for the event may be favorably received in even a venomous environment. Storytellers aren't seen as advocates. They are historians and entertainers. We educate to our point of view by engaging with compelling narratives.

The courtroom is different from the lecture hall, auditorium, or dining room in a hotel or restaurant. The trial begins by giving each side an opportunity to "deselect" its audience. Those openly hostile to our case and claim may be struck for cause. Lawyers use their peremptory challenges to strike those not so openly hostile but who prompt us to have some reservations about them.

The State Bar of Texas, Texas Trial Lawyers Association, Texas Association of Defense Counsel, Association of Trial Lawyers of America, and Defense Research Institute, to name a few, have held as many continuing legal education programs dedicated to jury research and jury selection as to any other subtopic in the field of trial advocacy. I have heard a myriad of approaches to voir dire and jury selection, some with which I agreed and some with which I didn't. There are many fine treatises on the subject. My approach to picking a jury is simple: I am looking for the best audience for my story. If the trial is indeed a competition of stories, then I want people on the jury who are apt to like me (the messenger) and my client (the protagonist), who will not identify with a defendant (antagonist), who share our values about what justice requires, and who will accept our contentions (the cause of action) and be motivated to do justice.

Juries decide cases based on the facts before them. The audience, sifting through what it hears about the people, places, and events, uses logic and reasoning to determine what is credible and should be believed and what is questionable and should be discounted. Twelve people assemble a consensus narrative that enables them to resolve the conflict and decide the case. But since justice is a uniquely human enterprise and undertaking, it never occurs in a vacuum devoid of personal experience, individual values, and imperfections of the flesh.

While the trial narrative may inform, educate, and even entertain, to be effective it must do more, because more is required of our audience. At the end of the story, the listeners must act—decide—judge. The most challenging aspect of courtroom storytelling is to inspire the audience to our cause and motivate it to action. This is accomplished by appealing to values and core beliefs. But such an appeal falls flat if our audience does not share our admiration and agree with our condemnation. That is why a part of the jury selection process is to identify those committed to a view of life that is inconsistent with our client's character, story, or cause. These people must be deselected from our audience with our cause and peremptory challenges. To do this, the trial lawyer must believe in the common man and have no misgivings about the absurdity of the myths that are circulated in an effort to promote anticonsumer, probusiness agendas.

Among these myths are the following.

"Corporations Are Overtaxed and Overregulated."

Citizens have argued since the beginning of our Republic about the form and purpose of our democratic institutions. Hamiltonians believed that the affairs of government, society, and the law were beyond the ken of ordinary laymen. They were committed to the view that the levers of power must remain in the hands of educated, propertied white men because only they possessed the wisdom and maturity necessary to secure stable institutions and protect them from the capriciousness of the rabble. Men of wealth, if left to their own devices, would ensure the public good. Hamiltonianism popularized the slogan, "What's good for General Motors is good for America."[2]

Thomas Jefferson believed that government worked best when all citizens had a seat at the table. He was a firm believer in the jury system, insisting that it was more essential to a democracy than the right to vote.[3]

In the mid-twentieth century, corporations paid 35 percent of all federal taxes.[4] Today they pay only 7.4 percent.[5] During the same time period, the share of federal revenues paid by individuals has almost doubled, from 48 percent to 80 percent.[6] Many corporations escape paying any federal income taxes.[7] Noted historian and economist Kevin Phillips, in his book *Wealth and Democracy*, points out that by virtue of legislative exemption corporations avoid paying some $60 billion per year in taxes while at the same time collecting some $75 billion in subsidies.[8] Corporations avoid not only federal but also local taxation. In 1957, corporations paid 45 percent of local property taxes, but by 1987 their share had plummeted to 16 percent.[9] Enron paid no income tax at all during the four years before its failure but collected $382 million in tax refunds.[10] Individual tax rates would be lower if the international corporations were not so effective in avoiding their tax responsibilities but instead paid their fair share.[11] Corporations in the United States have a lower tax rate than in any other industrialized country.[12]

Governmental standards for products are often inadequate, and those that are on the books are ignored[13] because the federal commissions and agencies whose job it is to monitor corporate America are woefully underfunded.[14] The best recent example is the Firestone case. It wasn't the government that caught Firestone making defective tires and then hiding the truth from the public. It was trial lawyers representing consumers.

How do corporations get such favorable tax and regulatory treatment? They buy it.[15] The timber industry spent $8 million in campaign contributions to preserve the logging road subsidy, worth $458 million. Glaxo Wellcome invested $1.2 million in campaign contributions to get a nineteen-month patent extension on Zantac, worth $1 billion. Most folks would love to have that kind of net return on an investment: 83,333 percent. The tobacco industry spent $30 million in contributions for a tax break worth $50 billion, for a return on investment of 167,000 percent. For a paltry $5 million in campaign contributions, the broadcast industry was able to secure free digital television licenses, a giveaway of public property worth $70 billion. That's an incredible 1,400,000 percent return on investment.[16]

Considering all these facts, it is no wonder that historian Arthur Schlesinger, Sr., observed how "America, in an ironical perversion of Lincoln's words at Gettysburg, ha[s] become a government of the corporations, by the corporations and for the corporations."[17]

"Corporations Make Wealth for Everyone."

Plaintiff's advocates use this myth to draw the line between Hamiltonian prodefense jurors and Jeffersonians, who accept more readily the cause of action for personal injuries brought by an individual. Hamiltonians see no vice in the concentration of wealth. Progressive citizens share the concerns voiced by President Franklin Delano Roosevelt in 1938 when he warned, "Among us today a concentration of private power without equal in history is growing. This concentration is seriously impairing the economic effectiveness of private enterprise as a way of providing employment for labor and capital and as a way of assuring a more equitable distribution of income and earnings among the people of the nation as a whole."[18]

For the last decade, the executives of American big business have claimed they deserved their nine- and ten-figure bonuses because they were rewarding shareholders by increasing value in stocks in their companies.[19] Even though corporate executives' salaries rose at a rate hundreds of times the rate that ordinary workers' wages were increasing,[20] they pointed to the greatest bull market ever in American history as the basis for their entitlement.[21] CEO pay jumped 535 percent in the 1990s, but the average worker's pay increase barely kept up with inflation.[22] If average production workers' wages had grown at the same rate as CEOs' pay, their annual earnings in 1999 would have been over $115,000 instead of the roughly $24,000 they made.[23] In a recent survey, the median compensation package of two hundred highly paid, big-company CEOs jumped to $17.6 million in 1999. That's up 111 percent from a similar group of CEOs in 1998.[24]

American prosperity depends on the three legs of the economic stool: capital, management, and labor. All must be strong and growing for the country to be sound. But during the past few decades we have witnessed an unprecedented accumulation of wealth in the hands of the investor class while working Americans have enjoyed little progress.[25] Ironically, during the same time, the tax burden has shifted from the capital and management legs of the stool to the working class.[26]

The bottom 80 percent of the American workforce hasn't seen a pay raise, when you factor in inflation, since the 1970s.[27] The great wealth that was created in the 1980s and 1990s went into the hands of few people. More than 60 percent of the new wealth created went to the top 1 percent of the population; 99 percent went to the top 20 percent.[28] In 1977, the total after-tax income of the bottom 40 percent of American workers was double that of the richest 1 percent. By 1990, the richest 1 percent made more than twice that of the bottom 40 percent.[29] The total net worth of average Americans hasn't budged since 1989, despite the 1990s bull market. The reason: Most families have taken on additional debt that outweighs any stock gains. In 1997, the middle fifth of households had a net worth—assets minus debts—of $56,000, down from $58,000 in 1989, after adjusting for inflation.[30]

The wealth boom of the 1990s didn't raise any ships at the bottom of the ladder. If anything, more people slid into poverty. The poverty rate in 2001 was 11.7 percent, up from 11.3 percent in 2000.[31] This means that 32.9 million Americans live below the poverty line.[32] The real tragedy of these figures is that poverty hits children the hardest. According to the United States Bureau of Labor Statistics and Bureau of the Census, almost twelve million children are living in poverty in this country.[33]

Historian Kevin Phillips has studied the evolution of the American workforce and concludes that we now work longer, for less, than workers in any other industrialized country.[34] Real disposable (after-tax) income for nonsupervisory workers peaked in the late 1960s.[35] In contrast to the financial statements of the *Forbes* 400 and the *Fortune* 500, ordinary families pressed to maintain their purchasing power sent new waves of women into the labor markets. This gave the United States the world's highest ratio of two-income households, with its hidden, de facto tax on time and families. Whereas back in 1960 only 19 percent of married women with children under six had worked, by 1995 fully 64 percent did, exceeding the other industrial nations. Wage earners in the United States collectively began the millennium with less pension and health coverage than the rest of the Industrial West as well as with the least amount of vacation time, shortest maternity leaves, and shortest average notice of termination.[36]

Even as Americans are working harder and making less, multinational corporations are exporting jobs to countries like India, Russia, China, and the Philippines.[37] Experts estimate that 1.3 million manufacturing jobs have moved abroad since 1992—most of them since 2000.[38] The illusion that America, because of her technological supremacy, could withstand the loss of manufacturing jobs to cheaper labor has faded as more and more corporations move their technology support abroad.[39]

People look at Europe, where they still have kings, dukes, and earls, and think that here citizens enjoy an equality of opportunity and prosperity. The truth is we are the most economically stratified country in the world.[40] We are ahead of Ireland, which is number two, and England, which is number six.[41] The disparity of wealth in the United States is the greatest it has been since 1945. The gap between the wealthiest 10 percent and the poorest 10 percent is greater in the U.S. than in any other country except Russia.[42]

"People Are Poor Because of Their Own Actions."

The prodefense Hamiltonian believes corporations are victimized by fraudulent plaintiffs served by the big industry of trial lawyers. The undeserving poor in popular welfare legends easily translates into the undeserving plaintiff.[43]

Almost four out of ten Texans believe that poverty is self-inflicted.[44]

> Jeannie Johnson and Frank Harris were born the same day at the same Houston hospital in 1967. They grew up within five miles of each other. Their fathers both died in 1990. Each had a marriage lasting approximately four years, and each has two young children. Jeannie works in a high school cafeteria and has a second job as a cashier in a drug store. She is up seven days a week at 5:00 AM and picks up her children from the day-care center at 6:00 PM. The family lives in a modest 1,100-square-foot apartment. Jeannie worries about how she will feed and shelter her family, where she would get the money to fix her car if it broke down, provide medical care if her children got sick, survive if she lost her job.
>
> Frank Harris lives in a 10,000-square-foot mansion, plays golf five days a week, gets together with his friends for a night of poker regularly, has been abroad three times this past year, and puts in little time at his office or with his children, who live with their mother. His afternoons are spent drinking at a neighborhood bar or the country club. Frank's only worries are his golf handicap or how much he lost in the last poker game.[45]

The difference between Jeannie and Frank? She is the daughter of underprivileged parents. Frank was born into money. The plaintiff's lawyer rejects the proposition that wealth, not virtue, is the measure of a man. Yet many people count success by the width of the wallet and virtue by the square footage of the office and home. It is said that virtue and riches seldom settle in one man. If nothing else, recent events in the business world demonstrate that the Gordon Gekko character in the movie *Wall Street* preaching that "greed is good" is not far from the truth in some quarters.[46] It is this mentality that puts the honest businessperson at a disadvantage and makes the poor laborer seem less valuable to society. Many people trapped in the pit of poverty scratch hard to get out. Some people living in the lap of luxury do nothing to deserve it. Lawyers have to believe in the value and virtue of ordinary working men and women if they are to be persuasive courtroom storytellers for the wrongfully injured.

Business scandals like Enron remind us that there is a mentality in America commanded by the corporate oligarchy that believes it is moral to take first and most from the weakest and poorest to benefit the wealthy. A century ago, the men who owned the wealth of this country claimed that their riches came from God. George F. Baer, the president of the Reading Railroad and owner of extensive coal-mining interests, said, "God in his Infinite Wisdom has put the control of business into the hands of Christian gentlemen."[47] Ironically, many people now believe that anybody can be rich who wants to be and that it is a matter of choice if a person is poor.[48] There is a close correlation between attitudes about the poor and probusiness feelings.[49] These attitudes are likely to prevent anyone's being moved by a plaintiff's affective theme aimed at holding business or professionals accountable and awarding fair damages.

"Large Personal Injury Awards Are Unjustified and Hurt the Consumer."

The National Safety Council put disabling work injuries at about 20 percent of all accidental injuries in 1998.[50] The Bureau of Labor Statistics reports that there were 5.5 million occupational injuries in 1998, plus another 400,000 occupational illnesses.[51] Based on estimates by the National Safety Council, these workplace injuries and illnesses cost workers approximately $141.6 billion per year.[52] This estimate does not include the suffering and death from cancer contracted in the workplace.[53] The National Safety Council has estimated that between 23 percent and 38 percent of all cancer deaths each year are due to workplace exposure.[54] This translates to roughly 151,000 lives lost annually from exposure to such dangers as radiation and chemical carcinogens on the job, although the number is increasing every year.[55] The total is undoubtedly understated, since diagnosis of cancer often occurs years after initial exposure. For example, the National Cancer Institute estimated that workplace inhalation of asbestos fiber, only one of a number of workplace carcinogens, would be responsible for 67,000 premature cancer deaths per year throughout the next thirty to thirty-five years.[56] The truth is that corporate wrongdoing and mischief cause far more tragedy and harm to working men and women and cost the country many times more than is ever paid out in damage awards.

Each year 98,000 Americans die as a result of medical malpractice.[57] More people die in a given year as a result of medical errors than from motor vehicle accidents, breast cancer, or AIDS.[58] It has been estimated that only 10 percent of the victims of malpractice ever consult a lawyer.[59]

Those who argue that less regulation makes business more efficient and responsible ignore the facts. Every year, consumer products cause 21,700 deaths and 28.6

million injuries, costing us about $200 billion.[60] The amount recovered by injured consumers comes nowhere near the losses due to injuries from defective products. Product liability verdicts and settlements in the United States against all manufacturers in 1993 cost $4.1 billion—less than Americans spend on dog food ($5.1 billion, according to the Pet Food Institute) and less than the annual profits of a single corporation such as Ford Motor Company ($5.3 billion) or Royal Dutch/Shell ($6.2 billion).[61]

> George McKinney was the CEO for Koppel Medications, Inc. He claimed credit for the company's profitability and the success enjoyed from its cholesterol-controlling drug Lexicorin. Koppel put Lexicorin on the market in the United States in 1998. It generated half a billion dollars in sales for the company the first year. Lexicorin and other pharmaceuticals developed by the company produced unparalleled profitability.
>
> In 1999, the company learned that Lexicorin was causing serious liver problems. It ignored the reports, then questioned their scientific validity. The company doctored documentation submitted to the FDA. Finally, in 2001 the company pulled the drug from the market. From the time Koppel learned of the liver problems caused by its drug until its untimely decision to remove it, Koppel realized half a billion dollars in profits.
>
> Ahmed Musarek took Lexicorin for nine months in 2000. During the fall, he experienced loss of appetite and weight, nausea, vomiting, general malaise, and weakness. Later he experienced indigestion and abdominal distention. Small red spidery marks appeared on his face, arms, and upper trunk in early 2001. His doctor took him off Lexicorin. Diagnostic tests confirmed that Ahmed had serious liver damage. His renal specialist attributed the problem to Ahmed's taking Koppel's cholesterol-controlling medication. In August 2001 Ahmed died, leaving a wife and two college-aged daughters. The family filed suit and went to trial. The jury found in their favor and awarded $10 million in damages. The verdict was criticized by the corporate and insurance camarilla as "excessive and unjustified" and an example of why we must reform the civil justice system.
>
> George McKinney resigned as CEO of Koppel in 2002. Koppel paid him salaries, bonuses, and stock options amounting to $200 million during the time that Lexicorin was on the market. Other executives enjoyed equally generous earnings. No one was ever charged, convicted, or fined because of the deaths of patients who took Lexicorin.[62]

Those who complain about the damage awards recovered by individuals as a result of personal injury lawsuits ignore the fact that corporate wrongdoing siphons off national wealth at a rate hardly approached by what is recovered in damage suits. The national cost of these corporate crimes will always be difficult to estimate reliably, for obvious reasons. Criminals, including corporate criminals, prefer to keep their crimes secret. There is no admission in the corporate annual report of discrimination, income tax fraud, bribery, overbilling, off-the-books slush funds, falsification of defense contract charges, money laundering, mail and wire fraud, short-weighing, adulterated and padded shipments, price-fixing, illegal political contributions, bid-rigging, and "creative" accounting.[63]

The cost of corporate crime is difficult to assess because the FBI lacks a congressional mandate to collect the data. However, credible estimates suggest that the total cost of white-collar crime in America in 1997 was $338 billion.[64] The General Accounting Office calculates the annual cost of healthcare fraud at $100 billion.[65] It has been estimated that the Enron executives alone cost employees and shareholders $60 billion by their corporate mischief.[66]

America has a grand and glorious history of the rich and powerful fleecing ordinary citizens of their hard-earned dollars.[67] As columnist Peter Carlson noted in the *Washington Post*, "Stock scamming is the kind of crime that attracts people who are well-bred, well-dressed, well-mannered. Financial crooks tend to be respectable, patriotic folks who demonstrate their patriotism by giving large sums of money to America's hard-working politicians, asking nothing in return except perhaps the teeniest tiniest little amendment to the tax code."[68] Enron is just the latest chapter in our unseemly corporate history:

- During the Civil War, J. P. Morgan sold the government 5,000 rifles for $22 each. The rifles cost him $3.50 and were defective, causing soldiers to shoot their thumbs off. The judge ruled the deal legal.[69]

- In the 1860s, the Union Pacific Railroad Corporation soaked shareholders out of their money while using millions of acres of free land to build the transcontinental railroad.[70]

- The 1920s saw the infamous Ponzi scheme. Charles Ponzi guaranteed investors a 50 percent profit in forty-five days and was able to pay them with money obtained from later investors. The *Boston Post* unmasked his scam and he spent a decade in jail.[71]

- After the stock market crashed in 1929, Congress investigated Wall Street, exposing countless instances of chicanery, skullduggery, and plain old fraud. Liberals called for the creation of a federal agency to regulate and police the market. Robert Whitney, president of the New York Stock Exchange, disagreed, assuring Congress that it could police itself without interference from meddlesome bureaucrats. When Whitney's apple liquor company tanked, he stole $150,000 worth of bonds belonging to the New

York Yacht Club and $667,000 from the Stock Exchange Gratuity Fund, which had been set up to aid the widows and orphans of brokers.[72]

- The equity fund scandal of the 1960s and 1970s lost investors $300 million. Equity Funding sold an investment package that was a combination of mutual funds and life insurance. Customers bought a mutual fund whose dividends paid the premiums on the insurance policy. Equity then sold the insurance policies to reinsurance companies. The funds officials decided they could make more money by creating false insurance policies and pocketing the money. Equity stock rose from $6 to $90 until an Equity employee, dissatisfied with the size of his Christmas bonus, decided to blow the whistle.[73]

Corporations do much that is good. They also hurt innocent people. They proudly claim the good. Nobody accounts for the harm. However measured, the cost is clearly enormous, a serious drain on the national economy and a coerced cost to corporate stakeholders.

"There Has Been a Litigation Explosion of Frivolous Personal Injury Cases."

Some suggest that the difference in values seen in modern-day jurors is but an extension of the Jefferson-Hamilton debate.[74] Those who espouse probusiness, antiplaintiff views are modern-day Hamiltonians. They are the spreaders of stories about the supposed redistributive instincts of civil jurors, even when evidence suggests otherwise. Hamiltonians are convinced that lay jurors (1) despise the rich, (2) have it in for big corporations, (3) love to put their hands in deep pockets and redistribute other people's money, and (4) believe no harm will be done by holding defendants liable since their insurance companies will pick up the tab.[75] The higher the family income and socioeconomic status of the Hamiltonians, the more critical they are of civil litigation.[76] They subscribe to the principle that "hard work means you keep what you get." Civil plaintiffs are attempting to bypass this rule. They are looking for something for nothing and use lawsuits as a lottery for their personal enrichment. People of the Hamiltonian persuasion believe that plaintiff's lawyers are an unsavory lot serving undeserving clients.[77] Broad segments of the American public are Hamiltonians, according to researchers Valerie Hans, Shari Seidman Diamond, and Neil Vidmar.[78] More than 80 percent of jurors believe there are too many frivolous lawsuits. Only about one-third think plaintiffs have legitimate grievances. Probusiness jurors will speculate on the motives of the plaintiff for bringing the suit as much as on the behavior of the defendants. They tend to blame rather than sympathize with personal injury victims.[79]

Proconsumer jurors believe in Jeffersonian ideals and are modern-day populists. They believe that while they would prefer to stay out of politics and off juries, sometimes they are needed to clean up a corrupt system. These people respond to the moral heroism of deserving victims whose water, air, and lungs have been poisoned by corporate giants.[80] Populists want their victims to be pure, hardworking, self-reliant, and reluctant to go to lawyers or enter courtrooms. They want the injuries to be severe, caused by hazards the plaintiff did not even know existed. At the same time, populists are fiercely suspicious of faceless corporations, the arrogance of power, and the lack of individual moral responsibility for the actions of the company.[81]

Just under half of all Texans believe that most lawsuits are filed needlessly and that most people irresponsibly sue over small matters that could be better resolved outside the justice system.[82] Much of the antiplaintiff rhetoric is the result of extensive ad campaigns by insurance companies and big businesses. Some of the negative attitudes toward the civil justice system are the results of political rhetoric. Christopher Cox, a Republican representative from California, claimed during a news interview in February 1995 that there were one hundred million lawsuits filed annually in the United States.[83] This figure was misleading. It has nothing to do with tort law. The National Center for State Courts reports that just under ninety-four million cases were filed in state trial courts in 1992. But fewer than twenty million of these were civil cases. The rest were traffic violations, criminal cases, and juvenile adjudications. Only 9 percent of the civil cases—less than 2 percent of all cases—were tort cases. The largest category in the civil case docket is domestic relations.[84]

According to a study by the RAND Corporation, only 10 percent of people injured in accidents ever use the tort system to seek compensation. Other authoritative studies have found that litigation is actually down overall.[85] People find that it is too expensive, slow, and difficult. Cases that are truly without merit are subject to legal motions to dismiss and summary judgment, and courts may sanction any party or lawyer who files a "groundless" or false pleading.[86]

A primary reason given by proponents of federal product liability legislation is to curb "excessive" products liability litigation and punitive damage awards won by injured consumers.[87] But 47 percent of all punitive damage awards are in business-to-business suits, whereas only 4.4 percent of such awards are assessed in product liability cases.[88] The truth is that businesses sue each other more than individuals sue businesses for injury. Business-to-business lawsuits pose a much greater "burden" on corporations than do product liability suits.[89] Eleven percent of new civil case filings in general jurisdiction state courts are contract cases, typically between businesses. This is more than ten times as many lawsuits as are filed by injured consumers in products liability and medical malpractice actions combined.[90] Almost half of all federal court cases are businesses suing each other.[91]

To some people, whether a lawsuit is frivolous or not depends on who is doing the suing. In 1980, several Texas trial and appellate judges were returning to Houston from a judicial conference. Southwest Airlines tossed them off their flight because it had been overbooked. The judges sued Southwest in federal court because they felt they had been lied to by the airline.[92] They weren't hurt, their reputations weren't sullied. But the "wrong" offended them.

In the late months of 1983, the executives at Pennzoil met with executives of Getty Oil Company to discuss the acquisition of Getty by Pennzoil. Negotiations led to Pennzoil's increasing its tender per share. Before any agreement could be formalized, Pennzoil prematurely issued a press release stating that it was buying Getty for $110 per share. Texaco then met with the Getty stockholders, made them an offer of $125 per share, and signed a formal agreement for the sale. Pennzoil sued Texaco for tortious interference with contract and recovered the largest civil judgment in the history of the State of Texas.[93] Pennzoil didn't lose any money, but they did lose the opportunity to make a lot.

In 1997, the Texas Legislature passed a law holding managed-care companies accountable for harm when they deny or restrict medical treatment to covered patients. The insurance companies opposed the bill, claiming it would lead to a "flood of lawsuits." When the legislation went into effect, the first suit filed was by Aetna in federal court attempting to block enforcement.[94] Aetna hadn't paid out a dime under the new law; they just wanted to be sure they would never have to.

Fox News is known for its conservative, probusiness views. Since its inception, its newscasters and commentators have prattled against "frivolous lawsuits." In the summer of 2003, liberal satirist Al Franken's book *Lies and the Lying Liars Who Tell Them* was published with the subtitle *A Fair and Balanced Look at the Right*. Fox filed suit in federal court in New York asking for an injunction to block the book. U.S. District Judge Denny Chin said Fox's claim was "wholly without merit."[95]

No one calls the lawsuit "frivolous" when large corporations, respected and powerful people, or insurance companies file suit, even if the theory is dubious. In some people's minds, only small, ordinary people who are physically or emotionally injured can have a claim that is, on its face, "without merit."

"Large Damage Verdicts Are Always the Result of Sympathy."

Some believe that corporations and professionals are at a disadvantage in the courtroom because most people will sympathize with the plaintiff.[96] In today's conservative political climate, it is more likely that jurors will identify with the corporate defendant or professional sued for medical misadventure. While it is true that people can identify with the misery and misfortune of others, experience teaches that of all the core values sympathy is the least likely to inspire a plaintiff's verdict.[97] The modern political climate has turned the phrase "kindness by a stranger" into an oxymoron. Juries hold plaintiffs seeking remedy for civil wrong to a high standard. Lawyers representing the injured know that the defense will suggest that the only way the plaintiff can achieve full justice is through an appeal to sympathy. Cases involving catastrophic and tragic injuries present unpleasant facts. Sometimes they are not pretty facts, they're not easy to look at, and they don't go down easy. But they are facts. Plaintiff's advocates bring proof of worry, disgrace, pain, and agony into their courtroom stories not for sympathy but because they are a part of the legal cause of action.

Injured consumers and patients don't go to court looking for sympathy. Sympathy is a form of charity and is demeaning. By the time their cause is determined by a jury, the friends and relatives have called and dropped by, the coworkers have wished them well, the people who truly care have expressed condolences at their loss or disability. By the time the plaintiff gets to court, the well of hurt has run dry. The time for tears is over. Victims don't need sympathy cards or condolences, they don't even want to hear how sorry the defendant is. What the person wronged at the hands of others is looking for in the courtroom is a verdict that is just, fair, and full.

If we are successful in deselecting those who have bought into the anticonsumer, probusiness claptrap, we will have an audience capable of being moved by traditional American values. Successful trial advocates do not view trials as legal arguments or scientific debates. A well-told courtroom story is a morality play. A trial is a competition of stories that presents good versus evil, right versus wrong, the innocent versus the guilty. The people's lawyer's challenge is to tell a tale that trumps any negative view against the rights of hard-working families to petition their neighbors for full justice when they are wronged. The next chapter considers how we may take the fundamental core values that move all of us and use them as a blueprint for justice. How we can make of our client's cause an inspiring story.

18

Inspiring with Your Trial Story

EVEN AS A STRANGER in town you can pick it out. No matter its architectural style—a modern, square building with large bronze windows, classical limestone Renaissance, or a combination of Victorian styles—you know instinctively what it is. Often it is close to other impressive edifices where we worship, teach our children, and run the daily affairs of government, activities critical to a civilized society. But none is more important than the work that goes on in the building dedicated to justice. In these halls, ordinary citizens have their say about the way things ought to be.

Somewhere in this building, in the foyer, the hall, the chambers, there is a depiction of a woman who holds in one hand a sword and in the other a scales. The sword shows she has the power to enforce right, the scales that she weighs carefully before she judges. But the most significant aspect of the Lady of Justice is that she is blindfolded. She cannot see the parties before her. Their color, religion, sex, economic or social position are of no significance to her. While she may be blind to who the parties are, she never ignores what they represent. She rightly rewards courage and penalizes cowardice, prizes honesty and condemns corruption, elevates those who persevere against great odds, recognizes those who are sincere, and punishes those who betray her trust. She is never cruel in her judgments, never worries if her decision will be popular, and looks beyond the letter of the law to what is just, right, and fair. And nothing motivates her more to render a just decision than an inspiring story.

Good stories, narratives that stimulate and arouse, have a strong emotional component. Consider an example of two accounts of the same historical event. It is a day we all know—we studied it in school. The first account is factual, told by a historian.

> *The number of Mexican forces attacking the post was reported as high as 4,000 to 5,000, but only about 1,400 to 1,600 soldiers were used in the investment and the final assault. Santa Anna planned the final assault for March 6.... The Mexican army attacked the Alamo in four columns plus a reserve and a pursuit and security force, starting at 04:00 AM. The attacking columns had to cover 200 to 300 yards of open ground before they could reach the Alamo walls. To prevent any attempted escape by the fleeing Texans or reinforcements from coming in, Santa Anna placed 350*

> *cavalry to patrol the surrounding countryside.*
>
> *. . . The Texans initially pushed back one of the attacking columns. Santa Anna's remaining columns pressed forward and breached the north wall. The Mexicans seized the Alamo by 6:30 that morning, after hand-to-hand combat, killing virtually all of the male defenders.*[1]

That is the account of the last hours of the Battle of the Alamo that is contained in an encyclopedia. Now let's see the same picture painted by a master storyteller, James Michener.

> *By seven that Sunday morning the battle was over, as complete a victory as any general could have hoped for. The Tejas rebellion was crushed almost before it was fairly launched, and Santa Anna, joyous in his triumph, gave one last order: Burn them all. And the pyre was lit. . . .*
>
> *Into an unmarked grave, unhonored and spat upon, were thrown the ashes of the Alamo heroes, but even before the acrid fumes from the fire died away, men in various parts of the world were beginning to utter the name with reverence, and anger, and hope, and determination. "The Alamo!" screamed newspapers throughout America. "The Alamo!" whispered men to their wives as they prepared to leave for greater battles in the future. And in the weeks ahead, when men from all parts of Texas and the United States began to muster to avenge this savagery, they voiced a threat, a blood-oath that would bind them together: "Remember the Alamo!"*
>
> *From the heroism of these ordinary men, from their unmarked grave rose an echo of immortality. By their deaths, the living were morally obligated to finish what they had begun. From their skeletons, burned to ashes, the backbone of a new nation would be formed.*[2]

Which is the more memorable version? Michener's, of course. It is more memorable because it is a story filled with emotional content. The example proves these rules of persuasion:

People remember best information presented in story form.

People are moved best by stories that have a strong emotional component.

If you are a trial lawyer, you have told inspiring stories. Through the opening statement, examinations of witnesses, and closing arguments, you have narrated events that teach lessons in courage, grit, perseverance, honor, decency, and humility. You've also told tales that condemn bigotry, insensitivity, the abuse of power and authority, arrogance, indifference, and brutality. We tell our clients' stories in the hope they will lead our audience to justice. Still, the challenge sometimes seems overwhelming, given today's political climate. For the last quarter century, insurance companies and corporations have propagandized the American public to believe that the problems of the country can be blamed on trial lawyers, that people who sue for personal injuries are just "playing the lottery," that courts and juries keep the country from "heading in the right direction," and that we are awash in frivolous cases that cause people to lose jobs and businesses to fail. I often question whether Atticus Finch, in his defense of Tom Robinson in *To Kill a Mockingbird,* faced more prejudice and bias than trial lawyers representing injured claimants do today.

A trial lawyer's first challenge is to deselect from the venire those who have bought into the myths, lies, and distortions the insurance companies and corporations have spread over the last twenty-five years. People who are free of anticonsumer, probusiness prejudice can be inspired by a trial story involving a wrongfully injured plaintiff seeking fair and just compensation. The trial lawyer's job is to help people up who have been knocked down. But we are not the heroes. Jurors must feel that they are the John Waynes or Clint Eastwoods in our stories.

A psychological principle that guides courtroom storytellers is:

> Man is not a thinking machine, he is a feeling machine that thinks.[3]

Emotional needs drive human beings and explain why they act the way they do. Of all God's creatures, only man can feel and understand the pain and anguish of others. And just as others' happiness enriches our lives, the courage, integrity, and commitment of others inspires.

The moral of a trial story is about empowerment. Inspiring the jury to do something for someone who is weak, vulnerable, and not able to make things right without the jury's help. The trial lawyer's job is to help people up who have been knocked down. But the lawyer's boot camp prepares its recruits poorly for courtroom wars over the hearts and souls of ordinary citizens. Legal education denies emotion. Students are taught the cold logic of inductive reasoning—a thought process essential to law review commentary, legal brief writing, and analysis of appellate court decisions. As Professor Kingsfield of *The Paper Chase* says, "mush" has no place in the lawyer's mental atlas. But inductive analysis is a faulty road map for the courtroom. Ordinary citizens resolve conflicts by deciding first what seems "right" and then making the facts fit their sense of justice. Legal thought offers few signposts to guide the average person's approach of making decisions based on emotion and validating them with logic.

Yet legal education seems committed to the proposition that the fleet that carries the precious cargo of justice is made more roadworthy by draining the crankcase of all human emotion. The inductive reasoning that is the cornerstone of legal analysis condemns as illogical the pull of the heart toward what feels "just, fair, and right." Viktor Frankl in *Man's Search for Meaning* suggests that man's core desire is to matter.[4] Trial lawyers should ask themselves, "What part or aspect of the story can inspire jurors to believe that their verdict is important? How will the verdict make a difference in the world?"

Although the trial lawyer does not have the dramatist's freedom to construct characters and plot from a preconceived theme, this should not paralyze the effort to make the case mean something. The lawyer who represents someone wronged is charged with writing a play that empowers the jury. The jury writes a final act that brings some meaning to the enigmatic riddle, "How can bad things happen to good people?"

The plaintiff's theme is justice, and the only way to get it is by persevering against superior forces. The dramatic parallels are *Rocky, The Longest Yard, Hoosiers,* and *Field of Dreams.* People admire and respect the trial lawyer who is a true champion of his cause. Trial counsel who muddle and ramble through their cases in a disorganized, half-hearted, perfunctory manner put their clients and their causes in grave jeopardy. Successful plaintiff's advocates convey by the way they know their case and present it that they not only have confidence in their client, the case, and the civil justice system, but that they are also willing to fight for them. In the words of the late Senator Richard Russell, "You fight until hell freezes over. Then you fight on the ice."

Chapter 8 discussed choosing a cognitive theme. Theme is a persuasive concept that teaches that some simple phrase, adage, or proverb can hold the facts together in such a way that the audience draws the desired conclusion. This is the cognitive theme of the story. It becomes the jury's frame of reference—the means by which the facts are communicated to and perceived by jurors. The fact finders construct a consensus schema. They agree on the story and decide who did what when.

But trial lawyers need more from the audience. Jurors must be inspired and motivated to return a just verdict. This is accomplished by the affective theme that is the moral of the story—what motivates the listener to action. Cognitive themes appeal to the head. Affective themes appeal to the heart. A cognitive theme anchors the plot; the affective theme inspires jurors to action. The audience does not get the moral until they've heard and understood the whole story.

Good stories teach through the values presented.

Carl Foreman's screenplay of *High Noon* dramatizes the impact of civic irresponsibility on a community. We learn that good people unwilling to stand up against lawlessness run the risk of having a town controlled by criminals. The courage of one man willing to stand up inspires us. The movie *Glory* taught us that valor and patriotism know no color. Larry McMurtry's *Lonesome Dove* brings to life the ideal of keeping your promises, no matter how difficult it may be. In all these instances, the empowering lesson is not felt until we are walking out of the theater or setting down the book. Powerful morals that arouse, energize, and provoke are what directors such as Stanislavsky call the "super-objective."[5]

Every trial presents the potential for an appeal beyond cold facts. Lawyers must spur jurors' imaginations and emotions. A lawyer who brings no more to a story than science will find a jury unmotivated and uninspired. They give nothing because nothing has been asked of them. On the other hand, too much or inappropriate emotional content casts plaintiff's counsel as Vinny Gambini in *My Cousin Vinny* and the client as Harry Hinkle in *The Fortune Cookie.*

In *Verdicts Out of Court,* Clarence Darrow taught that to convince a man of an idea you must first make him want to believe it. The famous New York trial lawyer,

Moe Levine, said that every jury wants to arrive at a verdict it can express with pride. A person's core values drive the emotional component of decision making. Belief in a principle, whether its source is religious or secular, and conviction that the principle will be advanced by the listener's actions are essential to any effort to motivate by story.

The moral of every trial story is protection of the innocent: wrong should not prevail. The whole catalog of human virtues may flavor the combination of facts and law that leads our master chefs to add to the recipe the final ingredient—justice.

During World War I, a French officer was seriously wounded when a German bullet crashed through his skull into his brain. To save his life, the doctors removed part of his frontal lobe. The officer had served as a judge before the war. When the war ended, he went back on the bench. After less than a year he stepped down. His brain injury had left him with all his logical faculties. He could reason and calculate. But he had been robbed of his affective component—compassion, fairness, justice. In resigning his bench the judge said that no one should serve in the justice system who possessed only abilities to reason. To do justice one must possess more. He must bring to his decisions human nature, morality, and ethics, an action that his damaged brain could no longer perform.

This story comes to mind when people criticize lawyers for "injecting emotion" into a trial. Take away human emotion and life is an existence in an arid, lifeless desert. No one could fall in love, no one would stop to help a stranded motorist, no one would be offended when others stole or cheated their neighbors, the churches would be empty, and jury verdicts would be cold, arithmetic calculations without regard to what is decent, fair, or just.

Courtrooms are the scene for many stories that have "soul," a meaningful lesson for lawyers and nonlawyers alike. What a client, lawyer, judge, or juror did taught an inspiring lesson. While all courtroom stories are about justice, they illustrate that its critical ingredient may be other essences of human value.

Successful plaintiff's lawyers understand the values and motivations at play in the average citizen's intrinsic schema. These are, in essence, cause-and-effect statements people apply in their everyday lives. They may also be termed core values.

Core Values That Work for Plaintiffs

The following core values are held by many Americans. Trial lawyers use them as the morals of their stories.[6]

People Should Take Responsibility for Their Actions

People should not blame others for their lack of success, personal problems, or shortcomings. People should be held to written agreements they sign. Corporations should stand behind their products.

Of all the potential themes, the one that currently holds great promise is that of personal responsibility. Plaintiffs can turn this popular defense theme to their own advantage. A cornerstone of many recent political campaigns, this idea has been twisted by the rhetoric into a contorted premise that people should be responsible for any tragedy that befalls them. Victim's advocates can anticipate a defense argument that says, "The plaintiff refuses to accept responsibility and looks to blame anybody else." We serve our client's cause best by admitting at the outset that our client expects to be responsible for his or her actions. Isn't it fair to expect the defendant to do the same?

The premise of accountability motivates jurors, regardless of their political persuasion. It empowers them to protect innocent victims against the abuse of power by corporate profiteers, uncaring professionals, and insensitive managed-care entities. Trial lawyers can mold the personal responsibility theme into a memorable phrase such as, "Mrs. Rodriguez trusted the wrong people to do the right thing." The attorney simplifies the essential facts to what the plaintiff did right and what the defendant did wrong. The causal connection leaps out from the defendant's irresponsible actions and refusal now to be held accountable for the harm done. The cognitive theme incorporates in part the affective value of accountability.

At the end of the case, after the jury has heard all the evidence, the plaintiff injects the affective theme. The plaintiff's affective theme is the moral of the story. While the cognitive theme anchors the plot and synthesizes the facts and science, the affective theme inspires jurors to action. They cannot get the moral until they've heard and understood the whole story. Affective themes of wrongdoers trying to escape accountability work in small as well as large cases.

> It is a cold, clear, crisp evening in Dallas. Margaret Randall is looking forward to a few days off after working the New Year's holiday at the Southwest Airlines check-in counter at Love Field. After she gets on the Central Expressway at Mockingbird, the traffic starts backing up. Margaret applies her brakes and comes to a stop. A second or two later, she hears the squealing of brakes and feels the impact. A Suburban driven by David Warren crashes into the rear of her small Datsun. Margaret goes to the hospital that night in an ambulance. The emergency room doctor diagnoses a cervical strain, puts her in a neck collar, gives her pain medication, and sends her home. She continues to have pain in her neck and shoulder. The family doctor she sees the next day refers her to an orthopedist. The orthopedist sees her for nine months, prescribing physical therapy. Margaret makes fifteen visits to the physical therapist and misses twenty-one days of work. The orthopedist discharges her as having reached maximum medical recovery and approves her return to full duty. She still has problems lifting luggage.
>
> Because the defendant will not accept his responsibility, Margaret files suit. His lawyers answer and deny any liability in their writ-

> ten pleading and answers to written questions. They claim the wreck was all Margaret's fault. When the defendant gives his deposition, his explanation, his justification is that he "just didn't have time to stop." He admits that everyone else did because there were no other wrecks on the freeway. He is not able to point to anything he claims Margaret did wrong.
>
> "We told you during the jury selection and opening statement that if Margaret has any responsibility, she accepts it. All she is looking for is restitution, repayment in the form of reasonable damages.
>
> "There are two kinds of people. Some folks accept responsibility and want to square up and make things right. Others will do anything to avoid being accountable. They bag their limit by taking from those they've abused. They play with our sacred system of civil justice like a child plays with a toy. If they can break it for one person, what does it mean for the rest of us?"

The story the plaintiff tells is that of a defendant carelessly impacting and changing the life of a decent, hard-working citizen and then refusing to be responsible. Justice is not a matter of simple arithmetic, and jurors are not calculators. The culpable compound the offense by arrogantly suggesting, "Let me pay what you're out of pocket and call it square." When someone's carelessness hurts you, sends you to the doctor to wait around until he can see you, makes you drive across town to the physical therapist who is trying to heal your body, imposes on your family who has to deal with your convalescence, and puts your job in jeopardy because you're taking time off, he ought to be willing to do more than bring your bank account back in balance. Instead of accepting responsibility, he puts you through two years of waiting, worrying, and watching him play the system, hoping he can find a judge or juror committed to denying justice to anyone who has a damaged body instead of a damaged business.

Negligence doesn't just lift from the pocketbook, it writes checks against happiness, security, well-being, and contentment. These are human damages as deserving of restitution as economic damages. Perhaps more so. The moral, the affective theme, becomes, "We can set things right for someone who doesn't have the power to do it herself."

Refusal to be accountable resonates loudly when significant injury follows from the mischief of a large corporation. In a products liability case, the moral or affective theme might be that we must all stand up against corporate irresponsibility. Or it might be that we have the power to make manufacturers listen to us, treat us with respect, and be careful with their products. "Business as usual" shouldn't be walking away when you hurt someone. The plaintiff appeals for the responsible exercise of power. The power is the jury's. An affective theme might be, "They wouldn't listen to Robert, but maybe they'll listen to you," or, "These defendants have refused to answer this family's question. Today, you can give them the answer they deserve."

Rules Are Good and Should Be Followed

The rule of law comes from religious principles. If someone breaks the law he ought to be punished. Professions and industry should comply with established standards. An institution's rules and regulations should be followed by its staff. Rule breakers are responsible to those they hurt.

The world was a poor place three thousand years ago. Palaces were hovels, a man was old if he reached his fourth decade, the average person's most valuable possessions were the clothes on his back, and a family was rich if it owned two oxen. In those crude and meager times, man turned to his Creator for guidance about how he should treat others. Our religious lessons had one common theme—the value of the human being. Today we know all too well that some cultures do not share this principle. Our belief that every man, woman, and child is unique and precious is the cornerstone of our civil justice system.

Many people have managed to survive the hurt or tragedy carelessness hammered on them because of their faith. Their belief that there is a just God and that he would not allow injustice to escape the final accounting by the law sustains them. The same principles that measured restitution three millennia ago in bushels of wheat or flocks of sheep still guide us in defining justice. Health, happiness, and life itself, when taken wrongfully, deserve recompense. Unlike the impoverished ancients, we have the unbridled wealth of an affluent society as a reservoir to repair injuries caused by civil wrongdoing.

The only thing that makes people responsible is legal accountability. When citizens and corporations are held to their obligation to act safely, they learn from their mistakes. As children, we learn that if we break the rules, we bear the consequences. So we learn we must behave and follow the rules. Every consumer who buys a product is relying on promises from the manufacturer. Every patient who agrees to treatment has an implied covenant with the healthcare provider. The expectations and obligations are that the rules will be followed. Trust is betrayed when they are not. Trial stories often revolve around the violation of written standards. In the products case, these may be governmental, industrial, or corporate standards. Industrial injuries may be related to a plant's skirting OSHA regulations. The malpractice victim contends that the standards of a medical speciality, hospital, or medical school facility were abused. Violators like to pervert minimal rules in the form of standards into "guidelines," guidelines become suggestions, and crossing the line of good, safe practice is only an honest mistake or a matter of judgment.

The injured victim didn't make the rules. Corporations have significant input into the crafting of governmental and association standards. Members of the medical and nursing staff write protocols and standards for the hospital. When defendants break the rules, they violate the principles they set up for themselves. Surely the defense isn't so callous as to say the rules they made do not apply to them. Surely they don't suggest that mangling their own mandate didn't make any difference. If it didn't make any difference, why did they have the rule? "They didn't make rules that didn't mean anything, and they didn't make rules just so they could be broken."

Sometimes the plaintiff cannot point to a specific written rule or standard that the defendant violated. Often this is because the standards were set too low. If business or medical practices allow and condone perilous imprudence, then maybe they need to be changed. In one form or another, every plaintiff's case is about change. Changing business practices, the way products are designed or marketed, the policies of hospitals, security decisions for premises, the way a doctor practices. Anything less than full justice is a signal that we will tolerate what the defendant is doing. Any discount from decency encourages dangerous practices. Any markdown of restitution is a pat on the back for carelessness.

The plaintiff develops a trial story with the defendant's testimony that he didn't do anything wrong and wouldn't do anything different. The manufacturer's representative admits that they wouldn't change the design of their product or the way it was marketed. The doctor admits that if a similar patient walked in today with the same complaints, she would treat him as she did the plaintiff. Other witnesses and experts describe how careless and dangerous these practices are. The plaintiff's affective theme becomes, "They say they don't intend to change a thing. Maybe after they hear your verdict they'll change their mind."

Hard Work and Perseverance Will Eventually Triumph

The ordinary person who works hard, follows the rules, and obeys the law should be rewarded. For a plaintiff to be seen as deserving of a damage award, jurors must be convinced that she met her responsibilities.

The trial story is about people as much as it is about events. Justice shouldn't depend on character. Everyone, regardless of past trespasses or personality flaws, deserves the full measure of law. Ideally this may be so, but the harsh reality is that people are more likely to help those they like and admire. There is little to revere in whiners, complainers, quitters, liars, or pessimists. But even the cynical have a hard time finding fault with those who represent candor, courage, initiative, dignity, and loyalty. No protagonist is without flaws. The defense will highlight these, but only the most hypocritical look for perfection. The plaintiff's character colors the story. The essence of the person is a part of the affective theme.

A simple rule from the Psalms is that we are to trust in the Lord and do good. The book of Ezekiel teaches that we are to render true judgments between man and man.[7] Many of us follow the teachings of a man who admonished us that we are to act with charity in our hearts and see that men get their due under the law. The Apostle Paul said:

> Be not deceived; God is not mocked: For whatsoever a man soweth, that shall he also reap.[8]

Our faith teaches that we are judged on how we live. We earn our full measure of justice by being good citizens. The plaintiff worked hard for everything she has. She paid her taxes, obeyed the law, cared for her family, contributed to the community, was responsible and committed. Should we not give people like this our full consideration and commitment to what is just and due? Isn't it time we say to people like this that it is time we did something right for them? The affective message is summarized with, "Who would deny justice to someone who has earned it?"

Courage in one form or another can be found in many plaintiffs' stories. We don't have time-share when loved ones are lost. You can't lease out someone else's mother or child or husband. When a child dies, she is gone forever. There is valor to be found in parents who can continue despite their overwhelming grief. Men and women maimed and crippled by the negligence of others continue to look for work even after they've been turned down many times. No matter how hard things get, they are more concerned about their family than themselves. These kinds of people don't talk about family values like the politicians do—they live them.

Perseverance is demanded from anyone seeking civil justice. Not only must plaintiffs deal with their injuries and losses, they must withstand the abuse that is all too commonly heaped on those who call others to account. Being a plaintiff in a lawsuit strips you of privacy, dignity, and contentment. Defendants search employment records, tax returns, medical records. They may point to trivial and remote medical conditions and ailments as an explanation for present problems. Plaintiffs are humiliated by suggestions that they are troublemakers or irresponsible if there is a notation of a problem in years past with a coworker. The human flaws that defendants may trifle with are limitless. Many people are offended when an innocent person is libeled because he has had the temerity to seek redress. In these cases, an affective theme might be, "They don't care who they have to hurt to win."

Then there are the delays. The interminable delays in scheduling depositions, producing documents, and getting to trial. Defense interests know that if they delay long enough they can deny justice. There is no limit of time or treasure to be sacrificed to avoid the final accounting. Only the most determined ever see their neighbors in the jury box. Many people throw in the petition and give up rather than continue to wrestle with powerful interests. They know that even if they win, there will be an appeal. Only those possessed of great perseverance ever see full justice. The trial narrative may lead to a theme: "The defense efforts at detouring this search for justice have failed. Don't let Sally's hard trip be in vain."

Honesty Will Eventually Be Rewarded

The corollary is, of course, Deceit and dishonesty will be punished. Juries award high damages as a way of getting the defendant to acknowledge its responsibilities and correct the problem so it does not happen again.

There are two kinds of greed: trying to get more than you are entitled to and trying to avoid paying all you owe. The mother's milk of avarice is deception. What could be more reprehensible than a negligent defendant who steals a part of a citizen's freedom and then lies and distorts to avoid accountability? It has become all too common for corporations and institutions to destroy or change records, resist producing documents, manufacture critical entries, fabricate and bear false witness in the name of "fair litigation tactics." Many corporations and institutions believe that those who seek to hold them accountable are misguided, corrupted by perverse lawyers, greedy, and loathsome. What they see in others are just reflections of themselves. So anything goes in the name of protecting the corporate vaults from raiding by despicables. One hand washes the other, one lie leads to another, all in the name of "company loyalty."

Should we not demand the highest degree of forthrightness in evidence, aboveboard defenses, and bona fide documents when someone is called to account for the death of a child or parent? The crippling of a wage earner? The hamstringing of a single working mother?

Insurance companies and business interests rant against frivolous lawsuits. Should we not be just as outraged by the frivolous defenses? Many times the defense is nothing more than contrived excuses, alibis, and song-and-dance evasions. Defense counsel offers up a shopping cart cluttered with fish stories, whitewash, and shell games. The thinking is that if they pile the cart high enough, put enough bows on the packages, some gullible jurors will pull out one they like.

Of all the affective themes, the victim's vulnerability enhances this one best. What should we do about corporations that will invent, fabricate, and fictionalize to defeat the claim of an elderly person? How should we respond to those called to account for the injury to a child when they deceive and falsify? Two thousand years ago a man reminded us, "Inasmuch as ye have done it unto one of the least of these my brethren, ye have done it unto me."[9]

Witnesses can sometimes add to the affective theme. The doctor who backs up the patient's contention of malpractice, even though he knows there may be retribution from the local medical community, exemplifies integrity. The coworker willing to risk sanction to verify that machinery was unsafe is courageous. The corporate representative who rather than go along with the cover-up tells the truth, shows valor. The nurse who bucks the will of the hospital and admits to dangerous medical practice is heroic.

Justice Louis Brandeis once said that sunlight is the best disinfectant. Sometimes it is only the voices willing to speak from tightly sealed walls that bring rays of light. In *The Mystery of Courage*, William Ian Miller writes that moral courage differs from physical courage in that it is "lonely courage." It means "making a stand, calling attention to yourself, or running the risk of being singled out in an unpleasant and painful way." Moral courage demands that the person speaking have "the capacity to overcome the fear of shame and humiliation in order to admit one's mistakes, to confess a wrong, to reject evil conformity, to denounce injustice, and also to defy immoral or imprudent orders."[10]

People who speak out and tell the truth even when they may lose that which is dear to them are like the heroes of September 11. They are willing to run in while everyone else is running out. They are characters in a drama where honesty and courage prevail.

Good People Will Come to the Aid of Those Wrongfully Injured and Deserving

Most people agree that the courtroom is an uneven playing field. The side with the most money always has the best chance of winning. Juries composed of ordinary, decent citizens will not be corrupted or intimidated but will see that justice is done.

The right to live free from oppression and be independent of all constraints except those imposed by nature is the essence of the American spirit. Men and women died breaking the chains of British rule. The blood of old and young alike was shed on the battlefields of the Civil War so that people of color could have a seat at the table of liberty. It is not just native soil that has seen sacrifice in the name of freedom. Americans have died all over the world ridding others of tyrants and ideologues whose goal was to enslave people.

Every serious injury represents a loss of freedom. The theft of something valuable is civil larceny. When negligence damages a life, takes away a part of the promise of the human condition, the careless party has damaged and injured something that the plaintiff worked hard to get. When a defendant's negligence causes a permanent disability, the victim finds himself imprisoned in his own body. A coyote will chew its leg off in an effort to get out of a trap. Enslaved people have risked flogging, having a foot cut off, or death in the effort to be free. Wealthy parents have paid fortunes to get their kidnapped child back. Some years ago we spent millions of dollars in an effort to free a young child trapped in a well. Americans will devote vast resources to rescue downed pilots, boaters adrift at sea, and mountain climbers lost in a sudden snowstorm. We do these things because we prize freedom and insist that it is the birthright of every American.

Good, ordinary, innocent people, wrongfully injured, face lopsided mismatches from the beginning. They look across the table at America's prime legal talent representing hospitals, corporations, and professionals who have under their control all the information, research, and documents relating to what happened. The defense stands with legs spread and fists raised, defiant Jimmy Cagneys shouting, "Come and get me copper!"

The American courtroom is the one place where the poor are the equal of the richest corporation. From the beginning, our democratic experiment has searched for the meaning of equality. Today we have laws to ensure equal opportunity for all regardless of race, gender, or religion. These legislative and judicial pronouncements are aimed at protecting our personal rights and individual liberties. Personal rights are just as important as property rights. For some of us they are even more significant. The working man may not have a financial statement that shows assets like a corporation, but what he could earn and what he is to his family are just as valuable as the piece of equipment that can make millions of dollars in profits each year. The homemaker may not earn a wage, but it would take a small fortune to even attempt to replace what she contributes to her family and community. A disabling injury to the single working mother takes a greater toll than it does on the corporate executive, even though his annual income may be many multiples of her modest wages.

We should salute those who are courageous enough to put their cause to a jury. Instead, these brave citizens are often criticized as being greedy, malingering players in an ill-advised justice lottery. Those who do go to verdict have been caned daily for years by the brutality of the injuries the defendant's conduct visited on them. It is bad enough that their injuries are often the result of corporate or professional decisions reflecting the job skills of a Gomer Pyle, but some defendants compound the offense with an Enronesque allegiance to truthful documentation and record keeping. Corporate records are changed and destroyed, and critical witnesses are intimidated. Medical records appear that have had more doctoring performed on them than was given the patient. Once in trial, our clients are subject to daily flogging in the public halls of justice by those who show no remorse for their wrong but who will endorse counterfeit and guileful defenses. They impugn our clients' personal habits and family history, no matter how remote they are to the issues. Each day in court sees a new excuse du jour. They pile on those who are often vulnerable, hurt, and wounded by the defendant's wrong. This picture offends most Americans who believe that decency and fairness should color the courtroom drama. Sometimes the only way this is done is by a jury taking matters into its own hands. Good people will fight for the poor, the powerless, those who can't fight for themselves, if we give them the reasons and rationale to do it.

There will always be those who will say, "It might cost me something if I approve a verdict awarding this plaintiff significant damages for her personal injuries." To them, worry and pain are just a part of life. Bad stuff happens. Get over it. If you're unlucky enough to be in the way of irresponsible, thoughtless drivers, you're on your own. If you are the unfortunate one who is hurt using a defective product, show a little backbone and bear the loss. If you're the one cursed by the tragedy of a medical misadventure, it's just the luck of the draw. All we can say to someone that cynical is that the laws we are committed to enforcing were written for all of us. It is the law our elected representatives put in place. It is the law approved by judges since the birth of our Republic. It is the law that has protected thousands of others and mandated that the repayment be full and adequate. It's not my law or the law of the person seeking redress or the law of the person called to account. It's everyone's law. "We have to look out for each other" echoes this theme.

Simple and Uneducated Working Men and Women Possess a Special Ability to Recognize Truth and Cannot Be Easily Deceived

The average person is apt to assess the merits of a legal dispute in terms of right and wrong. He aims for what is morally correct, rather than what is legally correct. The juror's role is to find truth by ferreting out the motives of the parties and witnesses. He will determine who is being fair and who is trying to distort or deceive.

A party's motive can give rise to an affective theme. Plaintiffs must be motivated in their cause by more than money. Does the widow in a wrongful death action worry about how she will care for and educate her children? Does the fear of how she will provide for herself drive the single woman to sue after she is seriously injured in a car accident? Will the parents of the brain-damaged child continue to care for their son after significant damages are awarded? A part of the plaintiff's affective theme is making the "why" of suing acceptable and honorable.

An acceptable motivation to populist jurors is that the plaintiff is seeking answers, not just money, from those responsible for injuring the public. Plaintiffs are seen as courageous champions for the public. They do not sue for themselves or their children alone; they want to be sure this does not happen to anyone else.

Defendants who callously walk by the plaintiff's problems, stonewall efforts to find the truth, berate the injured, manufacture or destroy evidence, or misrepresent facts may unwillingly be writing the script that leads to outrage. Questionable science, insincere, contrived excuses, and insensitivity to the plaintiff's plight put in issue a defendant's commitment to assist fact finders to discover what is true.

Jurors look not only for the motivation of the parties but also for what drives the lawyer. Emory Buckner was an American trial lawyer who practiced in the 1920s and 1930s. He won a lot of court cases on the proposition that he didn't try to make the jury feel that the client was fortunate to have him as a lawyer. Rather, he wanted the jury to know that he was the lucky one because the client who had such a deserving and just cause had chosen him for representation.

People Help Those Who Help Themselves

The civil justice system is a safety net to catch innocent people wronged by others, who might otherwise be left helpless and destitute. Jurors need to know that if they award adequate damages the victim will continue trying to make the most out of life despite his tragedy.

Carlos Herrera was thirty-two years old, working as a window washer, when defective scaffolding caused him to fall four stories to the pavement below. He survived his broken legs, but the fracture of his spine left him paralyzed from the waist down. It is no appeal to sympathy to remind jurors that a full and adequate award for pain and suffering, loss of earnings, and future medical expenses will not mean that Carlos will have it easy. He still has to face life's challenges in a maimed and crippled body. The affective theme underscores the plaintiff's determination.

> Carlos came to this courtroom looking for a hand up, not a handout. He doesn't expect someone else to push his wheelchair, he just wants to know *he can* always have a good, modern wheelchair. He doesn't

> expect someone to share the worry, the torment and uncertainty, every time he sees a doctor for one of the medical complications that are associated with paraplegics. He does want to be sure *he can* get to and afford the doctor. He doesn't want someone to share the agony and frustration that goes with the physical therapy. But he wants to know that *he can* get all the physical therapy that would benefit him and allow him to realize his full potential. Carlos doesn't expect anyone to help him raise his two young daughters, to help them with their school lessons, see that they are in church regularly, counsel them on all the issues that trouble young girls as they grow up. He just wants the security of knowing *he can* give them the things they will need. He doesn't look for anyone to share the embarrassment and humiliation of disability. He just wants to be *repaid* for what he would have made for the rest of his working life if he had not been robbed of the ability, the rewards, and the dignity of work. He doesn't ask that anyone give him peace of mind because *he'll find* that, if it is possible, the best way *he can*. He doesn't ask that the defendant or you share his pain. *He'll bear* it, but fairness says he should be fully paid for it.
>
> Carlos doesn't expect anyone to climb the ladder for him. He just needs help in getting up high enough so that *he can* grab hold of the first rung. If we do that for him, he'll climb the rest of the way with the help of his family. He'll have some friends to inspire him. The same friends that have helped him this far, his constant companions of determination, courage, resolve, patience, and tenacity.
>
> There's a big difference between living and being alive. Carlos needs your help to live. He will never be alive like the rest of us. Most of you remember *Star Wars*. When Princess Leia faced disaster, she called on a Jedi Knight: "Help me, Obi-Wan Kenobi. You're my only hope." We have Jedi Knights today. They are called jurors. They have the power to rescue and protect. Carlos needs your protection. He deserves your help. All he asks for is justice. As William Penn said, "Anything less than full justice is cruelty."

Some suggest that an affective theme should dramatically capture the essence of the plaintiff's loss or injury. I disagree. In my forty years in court, I have never seen a substantial plaintiff's verdict motivated primarily by sympathy. Jurors find big damages when they are offended and angered by the defense or inspired by what the plaintiff and her witnesses represent. Plaintiff's advocates use symbols, picturesque speech, and tag lines to bring meaning to the plaintiff's loss. "You don't have to wonder why no mirrors are around" captures the essence of disfigurement. "I speak for a man who can no longer speak for himself," or, "Who will be with her when she is lonely?" may animate the damage argument in a death case. Physical pain is made real when jurors are reminded that "it doesn't work eight hours a day. It doesn't check in and out. It works overtime and is always there." A brain-damaged child or adult paraplegic or quadriplegic is "a prisoner in the smallest cell possible, his own body." But in my opinion these are not persuasive, affective themes. The affective theme, like the cognitive, ties everything together. Sympathy is too light a rope to anchor the plaintiff's cause. Why? Because by itself it can never inspire justice on either liability or damages. Everyone has seen tragedy that has no explanation except in the eyes of God. Sympathy can't be the moral, but a strong moral may justify the audience to exercise its human understanding in deciding the issues.

Every case has a soul, a moral, an appeal to the heart with what feels right and inspires dedication to full justice. The visceral tug may come from the story of Susanna, which reminds that justice is an inspired concept. We find truth and do good through independent juries that are the progeny of Edward Bushell and eleven other Englishmen. A century ago, twelve Idaho farmers affirmed in the pages of American legal history that all men, even unpopular ones, are to receive equal treatment at the bar. The courage of judges like James E. Horton, lawyers like Clarence Darrow, and litigants like Joseph A. DeLaine reminds us that courage and perseverance are essential to maintaining the freedoms guaranteed by our system of justice.

The ideals of fair play, looking out for each other, demanding change, the value of family, getting what you deserve, respect for the civil justice system, reverence for personal rights, and just making things right for those powerless to do it for themselves are just a few of the values in the grab bag of affective themes a plaintiff can use to empower the jury.

PART 5

STORIES WITHIN STORIES

THEY ARE GIANTS in American history. One was the son of a Kentucky frontiersman, the second grew up on a dairy farm in North Carolina, and the third was a third-generation Southern Baptist minister. The pioneer's progeny became a lawyer and later, as president, led his country through the bloodiest war this country has ever fought. The son of the dairy farmer became a preacher and filled revival tents around the world. The youngest of the three became the pastor of a Baptist church in Montgomery, Alabama. From there he led the civil rights movement in America. These three men were magnetic personalities. Whether they were visiting informally one on one or speaking to a crowd of thousands, people felt connected.

Abraham Lincoln used tall tales, apocryphal narratives, and humorous anecdotes to persuade and cajole juries and, later, voters on the campaign trail. Rev. Billy Graham and Rev. Martin Luther King, Jr., gave speeches and sermons that inspired and motivated. They seldom preached a sermon that didn't include a story. Sometimes they built their sermons around them.

These men from disparate backgrounds followed different callings and had dissimilar ambitions. Three men who are recognized by many as the greatest speakers in American history. What did they have in common? They were all master storytellers.

Storytelling is an art. It requires skill to relate a series of events to a climax that makes a point. The audience learns from the story. A good storyteller gives others pleasure. He draws people to him, for he has something interesting to say. Self-assured people are masters at working anecdotes into speeches to aid in understanding the lesson.

A speaker can choose from many kinds of stories that make a presentation more interesting: animal tales, myths, fables, biographical stories, legends, folklore, Bible stories, and stories about special days such as Thanksgiving and Christmas. A speechmaker choosing a story considers the audience who will hear it and the literary qualities of the story. He picks a story that interests both him and the audience. Storytelling helps the speaker keep his audience. He may present a narrative that is suspenseful until he reaches the solution of the plot.

Stories within stories are persuasive gimmicks that add punch to the presentation. Some are the products of psychological research, while others are centuries old. Every good storyteller uses them. They are particularly useful in the trial arena.

Stories within stories include—

- labels
- metaphors
- similes and clichés
- analogies
- quotations
- poetry
- anecdotes and humorous stories

These story additions make the speaker interesting and powerful.

19

Labels

THEY CALL US "plaintiff's lawyers," "ambulance chasers," and "tassel-toed trial lawyers." Our clients are labeled as "opportunists," "greedy plaintiffs," and "someone looking to get rich because of their misfortune." The civil justice system is "an ill-advised lottery that costs people jobs." These are the pejorative labels that insurance companies, corporations, big business, and right-wing politicians use to impugn, deprecate, and discredit us, our clients, and the jury system.

We are consumer lawyers, patient advocates, strong voices for those too weak or unable to speak for themselves. Our clients are ordinary citizens who have been wronged and the little man looking for justice. We proudly participate in the greatest system the world has ever seen for finding truth and resolving conflict. We are proud of who we are, who we represent, and the opportunity that our civil justice system gives us to look to ordinary people to tell us what is right, what is wrong, and the way things ought to be. Label us what you will; we are the champions of the underdog and all too often all that stands between unbridled corporate power and greed and personal security, safety, and liberty.

Word association is a psychological phenomenon that storytellers and speakers have employed for centuries. The listener's thoughts and conscious response are directed by the way a thing is described. The narrator uses a label to define an object or event. The audience accepts the speaker's premise because of the way a thing is presented. Cicero recognized this concept in the first century BC. Modern linguists, such as Alfred Korzybski, have confirmed the principle through research. The subconscious stores representations of experiences, real or imagined, and retrieves them in an orderly fashion by word association. Words are representations of the sensory experience, several steps removed from the experience.

Students of persuasion appreciate the importance of power words in giving punch to a story. Pratkanis and Aronson in *Age of Propaganda* observe that the way an object is described and the manner in which a course of action is presented direct the listener's thoughts and channel his cognitive responses about the communication.[1] People tend to act on the names and labels that are given to describe an event or situation. Labels work to achieve the psychological phenomenon of the self-fulfilling prophecy. The mind presumes that people will act and events will occur in a way consistent with the listener's mind-picture formed by the label.

For example, the words used to describe an event affect how people "see" what happened. In one study eyewitnesses were asked to view a film depicting a multiple car accident. After the film some of the subjects were asked, "How fast were the cars going when they smashed into each other?" Other subjects were asked the same question, but the word "smashed" was replaced by the word "hit." Subjects who were asked about smashing cars as opposed to hitting cars estimated that the cars were going a lot faster. They were also more likely to say that there was broken glass at the scene, even though no broken glass appeared in the film.[2] Labels are shortcuts to decisions. The speaker uses care and imagination in selecting words—the labels—that describe critical objects, persons, and places in the story.

Some years ago we tried a case involving a misdiagnosis of cancer. An attractive, divorced schoolteacher submitted to a radical mastectomy following diagnosis of cancer. When the hospital lost her breast tissue and lymph nodes she obtained the original biopsy slides for review by independent pathologists. Multiple reviews resulted in the conclusion that the original frozen slides had been mishandled and misdiagnosed. In scientific terms the case involved an unnecessary mastectomy—removal of the breast. We chose a better label: amputation. The lay term carried a visual jab that the scientific jargon lacked.

The lawyer storyteller is often challenged to simplify complex scientific and medical principles. Labels help. The medical diagnosis for a child brain damaged in labor may be "anoxic encephalopathy" or other complex medical terms. A "suffocated child" or an "oxygen-starved brain" are terms lay people understand. Labels can capture the essence of danger. A defective machine may be a "booby trap," a "time-bomb," or a "bear trap." But caution is the byword. A label seen as too pejorative will not stick no matter how often it is used and repeated. If the label is a good and appropriate one, repetition will glue the description to the object.

Mothers in labor are routinely monitored electronically by a device that measures the heartbeat of the fetus. Changes in the baby's heart rate in relation to its baseline (normal) or following contractions may indicate fetal distress and the need for obstetrical intervention. Prolonged intrauterine stress can produce brain damage in the infant. For this reason, many cases brought on behalf of babies with neurological deficits associated with labor turn on the interpretation of the strip created by the electronic fetal monitor. In the courtroom good advocates label this common hospital appliance as the baby's telephone or an SOS device. This labeling allows the narrator to present a compelling story of nurses or doctors who "did not hear the child crying for help in the only way she could" or defendants who "didn't respond to the baby's SOS call."

Courtroom advocates need labels that work both ways. Labels can be used to either strengthen or denigrate and detract. Following are some common examples.

Courtroom Labels

Common Terminology	*Label*
business strategy	gimmick hook racket
allegation, contention	accusation indictment charge sheet
defense	excuse cop-out cover-up cover story alibi pretext whitewash
expert opinion (good)	sound science scientific fact accepted principle
expert opinion (bad)	theory guess speculation
expert witness (good)	scholar scientist authority
expert witness (bad)	charlatan imposter rogue scientist
damages	repayment payback restitution
culpable action	misadventure blunder blown assignment botched job

Sometimes a synonym alone fails as a label. The alternate conveys no more than the original. Innovative persuaders consider adjectives to empower the label. Vance Packard's *The Hidden Persuaders* references the example of Pontiac automobile ads in the 1950s that promoted by engrafting "big" on the brand name. The "Big Pontiac" spots bemoaned that some people had to pay more for "a smaller shorter car."[3]

Size as a modifier can enhance or degrade. The "Big Mac" and "Jumbo Jack" stress value while "Big Labor" and "Big Brother" suggest corruption and control. Likewise, cost may imply value or lack of substance. Manufacturers of mobile homes hammer on the tab "affordable housing." But a woman would be insulted if she were described as wearing a bargain-basement dress.

Age is a useful adjective. "Old" can imply experience and dependability or used and tired. A new theory suggests it is untested. An old idea is outdated.

Advertisers understand the concept of the modifier as part of the label that implies a result. Maytag is the "dependable appliance"; Sears has "quality workmanship." It is a principle that works in the courtroom.

A young medical student was killed while attempting to assist hospital employees subdue a berserk patient. In the struggle, the group of men crashed against a large louver that covered part of the landing wall in a stairwell. The louver led to a shaft that ran from the basement up to the third floor where the altercation occurred. The architectural blueprints referred to the shaft as a "smoke tower" and "ventilation shaft." It existed as part of the fire prevention system. Few people were even aware that the shaft existed behind the louvers that gave way. We knew the terms "smoke tower" and "ventilation shaft" were rather innocuous. We needed a better label. The word "shaft" implied danger but the adjective "ventilation" detracted from the concept. We chose to call the area a "blind shaft." This label conjured up subliminal images of the danger that was an operative part of our case.

Some trials are lengthy, technical proceedings with numerous experts testifying. Jurors seldom remember their names. Labeling witnesses helps the listener remember them, particularly when the narrator is challenging their qualifications or opinions. An example of this is the closing argument in a case involving pathology misdiagnosis in chapter 29. The defense experts were labeled as "Doctor Anything Goes," "The Wizard of Oz," and "The Wizard of Oz in Reverse" (see pages 481–83).

The storyteller whose goal is to persuade or motivate must create a compelling picture that draws the listener to a conclusion about people or events. Persuasionists appreciate the concept of label and give careful consideration to the way things are described.

20

Metaphors

MENTAL IMAGES ARE magical persuaders. The mystical thing about creating images with words is that each listener paints a picture in his mind that is comfortable to him. Sometimes the image is so powerful it carries a message beyond the words spoken.

Regardless of their politics, most people admired Ronald Reagan for his persuasive talents. His mastery of the psychology of images and messages earned him the title of "the Great Communicator." President Reagan invented the technique, often used by the presidents that followed him, of introducing people sitting in the House Gallery with the First Lady. During his 1985 State of the Union speech, one of the two women he singled out was Clara "Mother" Hale, a black woman and founder of a home for the infants of drug-addicted mothers. As the television cameras fixed on Mrs. Hale's image, the president told of her successes in the inner city of Harlem in getting poor women off the street and off drugs. Americans got the message that—

- *Republicans support minorities;*
- *we do not need federal programs to combat drug addiction;*
- *we are winning the war on drugs.*

None of this was said. It was the message that people created in their own minds. Clara Hale was a visual metaphor for a message that, had it been stated outright, would probably have been questioned.

A form of label is the metaphor. Metaphors make stories interesting. They are the colors that paint the picture on the canvas of words. A metaphor is a figure of speech that uses a word or phrase denoting one kind of object or idea in place of another to suggest a likeness or analogy between them.[1]

Metaphors are more powerful in the courtroom than are analogies or similes. With a metaphor, we do not say something is like something else, but that it *is* that something else. A metaphor may be described as a poetic comparison of two apparently unlike things. What is most powerful about them is that they are less demanding on jurors' brains than are other kinds of comparisons. They paint word pictures that do not require in-depth understanding.

An effective way to organize a presentation is by using the metaphor from a story. Author Stephen King tells of the time when as a small boy he helped his uncle Oren fix a screen window on his parents' house. Oren was a carpenter and had a big three-leveled, handmade toolbox. It had all the tools a carpenter could need and weighed between eighty and 120 pounds. Uncle Oren carried his toolbox to the window. All he needed to fix it was a screwdriver. King asked him why he had brought the entire toolbox if all he needed was the screwdriver. Uncle Oren said he could not know until he got there what tools he might need. "It's best to have your tools with you. If you don't, you're apt to find something you didn't expect and get discouraged."[2]

King uses the metaphor of the toolbox to illustrate how a writer must bring all the tools he has to his writing. He likens the levels of the toolbox to different principles the writer must understand and use to be effective.

A trial lawyer could use this technique in a malpractice case. He could use the toolbox metaphor to show how a doctor needs to have his entire toolbox at the patient's side rather than just a screwdriver. If the physician relied on a physical exam and did not read the results of the diagnostic tests, "He was Mr. Fix-it without a full toolbox." In a case where a diagnostic test was misreported by a radiologist or lab technician, the doctor is the cowboy on a horse that the farrier had left the horseshoes off of.

The story metaphor is an effective organizational technique because it allows the listener to form familiar pictures and apply them to unfamiliar situations.

I love metaphors. They make arguments and stories interesting and memorable. Look at the following paraphrased examples in the illustrative closing summations in part 6:

> The hospital was a casino. (See chapter 28, pages 466–67.)
>
> The defendants left no skid marks following their drive-by diagnosis and rush to surgery. (See chapter 29, pages 476–79.)
>
> Pull the curtain back. There is no wizard back there . . . just some people pulling a bunch of levers to put out a bunch of smoke and colorful images so you can't see the road. (See chapter 29, page 483.)
>
> The nurse anesthetist was asleep at the wheel, the first officer, the anesthesiologist, was having coffee in the coffee bar, and the owners of the ship [the anesthesiology professional associations] were re-

> sponsible for training and supervising them when the ship and its precious cargo [the plaintiffs' decedent] was sailed into the fog of the Bermuda Triangle. (See chapter 30, page 492.)

Metaphors are fun for the storyteller, and the only limitations are imagination and good taste.

Famous Metaphors

Great speakers are known and remembered for their metaphors. The Sermon on the Mount was full of metaphors (italicized):

> Ye are the *salt* of the earth: but if the salt have lost his savour, wherewith shall it be salted? it is thenceforth good for nothing, but to be cast out, and to be trodden under foot of men.[3]
>
> Ye are the *light* of the world. A city that is set on an hill cannot be hid.[4]
>
> Neither do men light a *candle*, and put it under a bushel, but on a candlestick; and it giveth light unto all that are in the house.[5]
>
> The light of the body is the *eye*: if therefore thine eye be single, thy whole body shall be full of light. But if thine eye be evil, thy whole body shall be full of darkness.[6]
>
> Give not that which is holy unto the dogs, neither cast ye your *pearls* before swine, lest they trample them under their feet, and turn again and rend you.[7]
>
> Even so every good tree bringeth forth good *fruit*; but a corrupt tree bringeth forth evil *fruit*. A good tree cannot bring forth evil *fruit*, neither can a corrupt tree bring forth good *fruit*. Every tree that bringeth not forth good *fruit* is hewn down, and cast into the fire. Wherefore by their *fruits* ye shall know them.[8]

On June 16, 1858, in Springfield, Illinois, Abraham Lincoln gave his famous "House Divided" speech. While many people may not know the occasion or content, they remember the metaphor Lincoln used in the first paragraph to build his arguments against the Dred Scott decision and the Kansas-Nebraska Act.

> We are now far into the fifth year since a policy was initiated with the avowed object, and confident promise, of putting an end to slavery agitation. Under the operation of that policy, that agitation has not

> only not ceased, but has constantly augmented. In my opinion, it will not cease until a crisis shall have been reached and passed. "*A house divided against itself cannot stand.*" I believe this government cannot endure permanently half slave and half free. I do not expect the Union to be dissolved—I do not expect *the house to fall*—but I do expect it will cease to be divided. It will become all one thing, or all the other.[9]

William Jennings Bryan, the three-time unsuccessful candidate for the presidency, might well be just a footnote in history if it had not been for the powerful metaphor he used to conclude his speech at the Democratic National Convention in Chicago on July 9, 1896.

> Having behind us the producing masses of this nation and the world, supported by the commercial interests, the laboring interests and the toilers everywhere, we will answer their demand for a gold standard by saying to them: You shall not press down upon the brow of labor this *crown of thorns, you shall not crucify mankind upon a cross of gold.*[10]

Fifty years later, on March 5, 1946, Winston Churchill gave a speech at Westminster College in Fulton, Missouri, which he titled "The Sinews of Peace." While Mr. Churchill used a muscular metaphor to send the message that peace requires strength, it was another metaphor this revered English statesman used that makes the presentation memorable.

> From Stettin in the Baltic to Trieste in the Adriatic, *an iron curtain* has descended across the Continent. Behind that line lie all the capitals of the ancient states of Central and Eastern Europe. Warsaw, Berlin, Prague, Vienna, Budapest, Belgrade, Bucharest and Sofia, all these famous cities and the populations around them lie in what I must call the Soviet sphere, and all are subject in one form or another, not only to Soviet influence but to a very high and, in many cases, increasing measure of control from Moscow.[11]

These great teachers and politicians made their principles memorable by using colorful metaphors to make their point.

Abstract concepts challenge speakers. No one can really reduce to canvas the ideals of justice, honesty, integrity, prudence, tolerance, excellence, or mercy. In the challenge is opportunity. The speaker can use whatever symbol seems best to convey the concept. The power of the metaphor for this purpose is well illustrated by Rev. Martin Luther King, Jr.'s, speech delivered on August 28, 1963, at the steps of the Lincoln Memorial in Washington, D.C.

> In a sense we have come to our nation's capital to *cash a check*. When

the architects of our republic wrote the magnificent words of the Constitution and the Declaration of Independence, they were signing *a promissory note* to which every American was to fall heir. This *note* was a promise that all men would be guaranteed the inalienable rights of life, liberty, and the pursuit of happiness.

It is obvious today that America has defaulted on *this promissory note* insofar as her citizens of color are concerned. Instead of honoring this sacred obligation, America has given the Negro people a *bad check*; a check which has come back marked "*insufficient funds.*" But we refuse to believe that the *bank of justice is bankrupt*. We refuse to believe that there are *insufficient funds* in the great *vaults of opportunity* of this nation. So we have come to *cash this check*—a *check* that will give us upon demand the riches of freedom and the security of justice. We have also come to this hallowed spot to remind America of the fierce urgency of now. This is no time to engage in the luxury of cooling off or to take the *tranquilizing drug* of gradualism. Now is the time to make real the promises of democracy. *Now* is the time to rise from the *dark and desolate valley* of segregation to the *sunlit path* of racial justice. *Now* is the time to open the *doors of opportunity* to all of God's children. Now is the time to lift our nation from the *quicksands* of racial injustice to the *solid rock* of brotherhood.[12]

Concept Metaphors

Metaphors are particularly helpful in defining concepts. James M. Beck authored *The Constitution of the United States: Yesterday, Today—and Tomorrow?* While it is an analysis of the birth of the Constitution, commentators are particularly impressed with his use of metaphors. One of Beck's metaphors reads—

> The Constitution is neither, on the one hand, a *Gibraltar rock*, which wholly resists the ceaseless washing of time or circumstance, nor is it, on the other hand, a *sandy beach*, which is slowly destroyed by the erosion of the *waves*. It is rather to be likened to a *floating dock*, which, while firmly attached to its *moorings*, and not therefore the caprice of the *waves*, yet rises and falls with the *tide* of time and circumstance.[13]

Trial lawyers often deal with abstract concepts. Metaphors make them more understandable. They also make speech more powerful. The following metaphors (some of which combine similes and analogies) illustrate how concepts are transformed into pictures in the courtroom.

Product Liability

The defendant's product was a Wile E. Coyote's trap. Even if you followed directions, it was going to snap back on you.

While the defendants were engraving profits on stone tablets, they were running safety concerns through the shredder.

The defendants treated the reports of adverse effects like junk mail they didn't need to open.

The Taliban treat their women better than this corporation treats its customers.

The fingerprints of bad science, the ballistics of tortured technology, and the DNA of overmarketing can be seen all over this tragedy.

They had jam all over their faces but claimed they didn't touch the jelly jar.

Malpractice

There were a lot of opportunities to treat Gene Harris timely and prevent his heart attack and substantial heart damage. We've seen how medical opportunities are like grapes—they come in clusters. These defendants had a whole vineyard to harvest that ended up dying on the vine.

The medical terrain that the defendants had to cross was not difficult. They had ample directions, their compass course was clear.

The defendants would attempt to make an untidy meal of the scientific principles you have heard and have the patient suffer the indigestion.

Neglect and indifference held high carnival for tragedy this day.

Legal Accountability

God filled up this family's store with hopes and dreams that the defendants' negligence then shoplifted. When the defendants were stopped in the parking lot, their response was that not only do they not feel any obligation to return anything, they also have the right to take from some other family's store sometime down the line.

Damages

The defendants' negligence moved into Robert's brain during those two hours that the hospital delayed in calling Mary's obstetrician. The effect of the defendants' negligence has been living there rent-free ever since. They took out a lifetime lease. Our job is to decide what the rent ought to be.

Permanent, disabling injuries are an invisible trap. Being unable to work, to contribute, to be someone others can depend on puts us under the thumb of an invisible tyrant. His name is Fear and we become the breathing dead. When the negligence of another ensnares us in this trap, we are worse off than the coyote whose foot is caught in steel jaws. The coyote can escape. He just chews his foot off. But the trap of life without hope cannot be seen. It cannot be touched or even understood. This trap has no measurable dimensions. There is no escape. All its captives can do is work harder, try to survive, and learn to live with indignity.

Death-Case Damages

For fifteen years he was her safe harbor. Each night when she crawled into bed beside him she would sigh, "I'm in port now." With him she felt safe. No matter how fierce the storm, Bill was her safe harbor. He was her seawall, the stout dock that she moored alongside to refuel and resupply for her next voyage out into the uncertain and stormy world. Barbara enjoyed her work at Baker Hughes even though it was stressful. Like the sailor who goes to sea, she looked forward to the challenge, the storms, the unpredictable winds, the unforgiving tides. Like most working women today, she had come to accept deadlines, impossible design requirements, and the stress of her world of tool design. But when she was with him the waters were always calm, safe, and secure. Husbands are like that. The home base where everything is familiar, comfortable, and secure.

Warranty/Breach of Contract

The defendants want to disclaim responsibility for the promises they made. They acted like the Wizard of Oz going into the transaction but want to claim they were Forrest Gump when it went bad.

Defenses

The defendants gave care that was half-adequate. Now they offer half-baked excuses, in a half-hearted manner, based on half-truths, in a halfway attempt to have you put a half-Nelson on Lady Justice, and be half-fair with the plaintiffs by offering them half-justice.

Justice

Some say the only place to find truth is in heaven. I cannot be so cynical. We should never approach our responsibilities in such a way that justice can never be the outcome but only the victim. These hallowed halls should never be flashing a "no vacancy" or "sold out" sign.

When we are wronged, we feel lost. The child who loses his mother in a crowd looks for something to grab onto. He looks for a hand to hold, something strong and warm that he can count on to keep him up so that he is not buffeted to the ground by the crowd. When we are victimized by others, when we feel the crowd pushing us down, we reach out like a child grabbing for his mother's hand. When we are wronged our mother is the law and you—the jury—our mother's hand.

People and Place Metaphors

Metaphors are particularly effective in creating quick word pictures that define people and places. Some of the most powerful metaphors come from stories that standing alone are not particularly useful to the speaker as a moral or lesson. For example, Lewis Carroll's *Alice's Adventures in Wonderland* and *Through the Looking-Glass* are tales so obscure, convoluted, and without identifiable moral as to be of little benefit as persuasive stories in themselves. But the characters and places in them represent wonderful metaphors.

To be an effective metaphor the character must be well known and associated with identifiable traits. The most useful metaphors are fictional and will carry a touch of sarcasm or humor when used.

The following is a compendium of classic fictional and historical metaphors.

PEOPLE

Greek Mythology

Stories from ancient Greece contain characters with such readily identifiable characteristics that they work as pure metaphors. Because many people never studied or may have forgotten their Greek mythology, their use sometimes requires a little explanation.

Character	*Metaphor*
Achilles	The hero of Homer's *Iliad.* Achilles' mother dipped him in the river Styx, rendering him invulnerable except in the heel by which she held him. Paris killed Achilles by wounding him with an arrow shot into Achilles' heel. Achilles is a metaphor for a person who *seems invulnerable but has a weak spot.*
Cassandra	Cassandra had the gift of prophecy. She refused Apollo's advances. As punishment, Apollo ordained that no one should ever believe her. A Cassandra is someone who *predicts tragedy but is not believed.*
Midas	The king of Pessinus, capital of Phrygia, to whom Dionysus granted a wish that everything he touched should turn into gold. Midas learned that even his food was not exempt from this influence. Midas is a metaphor for someone who *has great fortune*—"everything they touch turns to gold." He may also be metaphoric of someone whose *fortune brings disaster.*

Narcissus	The young Narcissus saw his reflection in a fountain and fell in love. Narcissus is a metaphor for *someone in love with himself.*
Pandora	She was the first woman endowed with gifts by every god. One of the gifts was a box she was cautioned not to open. Curious, she opened it and out flew all the ills of humanity, leaving behind only hope, which remained. Pandora is the metaphor for someone whose *curiosity unleashes evil.* Pandora's box is full of trouble.

The Bible

Character	*Metaphor*
Cain	Adam and Eve's son who killed his brother, Abel. The mark of Cain is a metaphor for someone who has *killed or injured someone.*
Jeremiah	Various kings ruled Judah during Jeremiah's lifetime (sixth century BC). The kings and the Jewish people believed that the city and the temple had a magical inviolability. The prophet Jeremiah, believing that the people had forsaken God and the Covenant of the Lord by turning to idolatry, prophesied the destruction of Jerusalem by the Babylonians and argued for the surrender of Jerusalem to them. The people, princes, prophets, and priests rejected this defeatist stance. Eventually the city was destroyed by Nebuchadnezzar. Jeremiah is the metaphor for the *apocalyptic prophet.*

The Arabian Nights

The Arabian Nights are a collection of Persian, Arabian, and Indian folk tales handed down through several centuries. One tale involves a sadistic, nasty, well-heeled merchant named Barmecide. His favorite trick was to lure starving beggars to his house and hoodwink them into thinking they were enjoying a feast when, in fact, the feast was only an illusion. The beggars wake up from their Barmecide feast hungrier than ever.

Character	*Metaphor*
Barmecide	A Barmecide feast is a metaphor for *substance that is a deceptive illusion.*

King Arthur's Court

Sir Galahad was the good knight who championed the virtuous and poor. Sir Mordred was the evil knight. Thus when someone is looking for help and is betrayed, he may have thought he had Sir Galahad in his corner only to find it was Sir Mordred instead.

Camelot represents the *best of times* and the *best of people.*

Some works are known essentially for the central characters in the story. While the plot of the story may not be familiar, the fictional people's traits are well known and remembered.

Cinderella

The story of Cinderella, or the Glass Slipper, seems to have originated in China but is also found in children's fairy tales of France, Germany, Norway, Ireland, and Scotland. A gentleman married a second wife who was a most proud and haughty woman. She had two daughters exactly like her. His own daughter was a young girl of unparalleled goodness and sweetness of temper. The stepmother's jealousy caused her to demean and abuse the stepdaughter, Cinderella, while lavishing luxuries on her own children.

The king gave a ball and invited all the lovely ladies of the province. The stepmother saw that the sisters' hair and dress were immaculate. When the stepsisters left for the ball, Cinderella began to cry. Her fairy godmother came to her and said, "Run into the garden and bring me a pumpkin." Cinderella brought back the finest she could find. The fairy godmother struck the pumpkin with her wand and it turned into a fine gilded coach. The fairy godmother turned mice into fine horses, a rat into a coachman, and six lizards into footmen. When she touched Cinderella with her wand her ragged clothes turned into cloth of gold and silver, all beset with jewels. With this done, she gave Cinderella a pair of glass slippers. As Cinderella left for the ball, her fairy godmother told her that she could not stay past midnight and that if she stayed one moment longer, the coach would be a pumpkin again, the horses mice, and her clothes would become the rags she had been wearing.

At the ball, she captured the heart of the king's son. When the clock began to strike midnight, Cinderella hurried away as fast as she could. In her haste, she left behind one of her glass slippers, which the prince picked up.

The prince sent out minions to scour the countryside for the woman of his dreams, telling all that he would marry her whose foot the slipper would fit. When the emissary came to Cinderella's house, the sisters laughed at Cinderella and told the man that he need not try it on Cinderella's foot. But his orders required that he let everyone try and, of course, it fit. Cinderella pulled the other slipper out of her pocket and put it on her other foot. The fairy godmother came and touched her again with her wand, making Cinderella's clothes even richer and more magnificent than those she had worn before.

The young prince married Cinderella and, as in all fairy tales, they lived happily ever after.

Character	*Metaphor*
Cinderella	Cinderella is the metaphor for *someone who prevails against long odds*. The movie *Cinderella Man* is about James J. Braddock, who became heavyweight champion of the world in 1935 when no one thought he could do it. The "Cinderella Team" in sports is the team that rises to great success unexpectedly.
Cinderella's stepsisters	Women who *conspire to put a good, decent woman down.*

Romeo and Juliet

The romance of these two teenagers was made tragic because of the actions of their families.

Characters	*Metaphor*
Montagues and Capulets	Families who *carry ancient grudges.*

Don Juan

Molière's social satire presents one of the most classic character metaphors in *Don Juan*, a notorious philanderer. But a more useful metaphor may be Sganarelle, Don Juan's valet, who knew his master to be the greatest scoundrel on earth.

Character	*Metaphor*
Sganarelle	Someone whose *fear of his master causes him to remain loyal.*

Don Quixote

Miguel de Cervantes's novel, published in 1605, was written to ridicule the books of chivalry that had enjoyed popularity in the sixteenth century. *Don Quixote* has become synonymous for someone who has lost all sense of reality. Alonso Quijano lived in the Spanish province of La Mancha. He became lost in the romances of chivalry and decided to imitate the heroes of the books he read. He changed his name to Don Quixote, donned an old suit of armor, and set out on a bony old nag in search of adventure. His friends tried to cure him of his fancies and burned his library of chivalric romances. Don Quixote believed that his books had been carried off by a wizard. He dedicated his heroic deeds to a peasant wench who was famous for her skill in salting pork. He encountered windmills, which he mistook for monstrous giants. The story is an account of how Don Quixote's friends kept trying to deceive him in an effort to get him to come home.

Character	*Metaphor*
Don Quixote	Someone who *tilts at windmills and pursues an illusion.*

Moby-Dick

Herman Melville's Captain Ahab was master of the whaling ship *Pequod.*

Character	*Metaphor*
Captain Ahab	Someone *obsessed with vengeance.*

Mutiny on the Bounty

We associate Captain Bligh with cruel ruthlessness.

Character	*Metaphor*
Fletcher Christian	A *revolt against the excesses of abusive power.*

Tales of Uncle Remus

Joel Chandler Harris made no claim of having invented the *Uncle Remus* tales. These were in fact stories handed down by slaves. The most familiar *Uncle Remus* story is that of "Brer Rabbit and the Tar Baby." Brer Fox and Brer Bear are metaphors for the wily, evil, and corrupt. Harris noted in his first volume that "it needs no scientific investigation to show why [the Negro] selects as his hero the weakest and most harmless of all animals, and brings him out victorious in contests with the bear, the wolf, and the fox. It is not virtue that triumphs, but helplessness; it is not malice, but mischievousness."[14]

Character	*Metaphor*
Brer Rabbit	Someone who can *triumph* over the more powerful *by using his wits.*

Alice in Wonderland

Lewis Carroll's *Alice's Adventures in Wonderland* is classic children's literature. The characters are known by all and represent metaphoric examples of human traits that are usually not becoming.

Character	*Metaphor*
The White Rabbit	Someone who is *always running late,* in a great hurry.
The March Hare	Someone who *offers something he does not have.*
The Mad Hatter	Someone who asks riddles to which there are *no answers.*
The Queen of Hearts	Someone who is *quick to condemn* ("Off with her head!").
The Cheshire Cat	Someone who is *smiling but doesn't hear* (at least until its ears appear).
The Queen's Croquet Game	*An event without rules.*
The Jurors in the Tarts Trial	People who *cannot remember* anything, including their names. (The Queen of Hearts accuses the Knave of Hearts of stealing some tarts she made).

The King of Hearts	A judge or prosecutor who *tries to make something out of nothing* by declaring to the jury when Alice testifies she knows nothing about the business, "That's very important." He then cross-examines the Knave by saying since he did not sign the letter, he must have meant some mischief or else "you'd have signed your name like an honest man."
The Trial in Wonderland	An obscene judicial procedure where the Queen announces, "*Sentence first—verdict afterwards,*" and Alice denounces the jury as being simply a pack of cards.

Place	*Metaphor*
Wonderland	A place where Alice is *carried farther through a pool of her tears.*

Through the Looking-Glass

Through the Looking-Glass is Carroll's companion tale, which begins with a chess problem. In the first story, Alice fell into Wonderland because she chased a rabbit down a hole. In *Through the Looking-Glass* she fell into a chess game through the mirror in her room. Here everything was backwards as it would be on the other side of a mirror.

Character	*Metaphor*
Alice	A *pawn in a chess game.*
Tweedledum and Tweedledee	Two people who look alike, sound alike, and imitate each other but who are constantly fighting. Everything they say has *two meanings.*
The White Queen	Someone who *promises and never delivers.* The Queen tells Alice that the rule is "jam every

	other day." But the rule is also "jam to-morrow and yesterday—but never jam to-day." This is the effect of living backwards.
Humpty Dumpty	Someone who believes that *words mean whatever he says they mean* since he is the master in that regard.
The Red and White Queens	People who *make all our choices.* They ask impossible riddles and would punish us for wrong answers.
Place	*Metaphor*
The Looking-Glass World	Somewhere where *everything is the opposite.* One must walk in the opposite direction to get from one place to the other. Alice has to run as fast as she can to stay in the same place and twice as fast as she can to get somewhere else.

The Wonderful Land of Oz

L. Frank Baum's classic was first published in 1900 and made into an Academy Award–winning movie in 1939. Of all the children's works discussed here, the characters in Baum's original Oz book are the most familiar.

Character	*Metaphor*
Dorothy	Someone who is innocent and *trying to find her way home.*
Wicked Witch	Someone who *prizes a possession* held by the innocent and pure. The witch seeks Dorothy's ruby slippers (silver slippers in the original book).
The Cowardly Lion	Someone *looking for courage.*

The Tin Man	Someone *looking for* a *heart.*
The Scarecrow	Someone *looking for* a *brain.*
The Wizard of Oz	A charlatan. Someone who pretends to have mystical powers but *deceives with machines* that put out smoke and colorful images.

Place	*Metaphor*
The Yellow Brick Road	A challenging path that leads to the Emerald City where the Wizard resides. *A path to home, hope, or dreams.*
The Emerald City	A magical place where good people and the Wizard live. A place where *dreams can be realized.*

Peter Pan

James M. Barrie's romantic fantasy *Peter Pan* tells the story of a boy who would not grow up. The three principle characters represent identifiable metaphors.

Character	*Metaphor*
Peter Pan	*A person who refuses to grow up.* Peter Pan goes off to live with the fairies so that he will never have to grow up.
Captain Hook	A villain who *preys on children.*
Crocodile	An evil creature who *involuntarily warns of his approach.* The crocodile had swallowed a clock and its ticking warns Hook of its approach.

It is best not to mix metaphors from children's stories. For example, you wouldn't use metaphors from Alice in Wonderland with metaphors from the Wizard of Oz.

Tom Sawyer and Huckleberry Finn

Favorites of young boys are Mark Twain's romantic *Adventures of Tom Sawyer* and its sequel, *The Adventures of Huckleberry Finn*. Tom lived with his Aunt Polly, who loved him dearly. Tom's friend, Huckleberry Finn, was the son of the town drunk. Tom was whipped by the schoolmaster and ordered to sit on the girl's side of the room for associating with Huck. Huck Finn often took advantage of Tom, and it was Huck who convinced Tom to run away from home. Huckleberry Finn swears and smokes, but he has a set of ethics of his own. For example, he could not bear to cheat the three Wilks girls but would not hesitate to steal food when he was hungry.

Character	*Metaphor*
Tom Sawyer	*Respectable, naive.*
Huckleberry Finn	*A user; survives by keen wits and intelligence.*

Gone with the Wind

Margaret Mitchell's *Gone with the Wind*, one of the best-selling novels of all time, is the story of the subjugation of a proud people by war and harsh reconstruction. Mitchell's characters, some strong, some weak, present exemplars of common human traits.

Character	*Metaphor*
Scarlett O'Hara	A southern belle, beautiful, headstrong, willing to *use her wiles for her own personal gain.*
Rhett Butler	*Cynical, materialistic,* forceful, masculine, whose love for Scarlett sponsors his heroic rescue of her. Rhett is hopelessly in love with Scarlett, who loves Ashley Wilkes. Rhett overcomes his love for Scarlett just as she is discovering that she loves Rhett, not Ashley.

Ashley Wilkes	A *weak-willed man* who is an impractical idealist dependent on a stronger will to solve life's problems.

Potemkin Village

Sometimes a metaphor cannot be used without an explanation. You will find that "Potemkin village" has been referenced by several political commentators. It could apply in legal and business settings as a metaphor for something the speaker challenges because it is only illusory. However, some preliminary explanation is required, as many people do not know the story.

Grigori Potemkin was one of Russian Empress Catherine the Great's lovers and ministers. In 1783, Russia had annexed the underdeveloped Crimea, and Potemkin resolved to make it the showplace of Catherine's empire. Potemkin wanted to impress Catherine and the European powers represented at her court. He set about planning a tour of his renovated Crimea. Legend has it that he constructed entire pasteboard villages on the banks of the Dnieper. As the royalty sailed by on riverboats, they viewed the pleasant villages and the peasants, flocks, and herds imported from a thousand other villages to make a show of prosperity. His actions triggered famine in the depopulated hinterlands. Once the procession had passed, he dismantled the village and reconstructed it downstream.

Today, the term "Potemkin village" is a metaphor for something that *appears elaborate and impressive but in actual fact lacks substance.*

Death of a Salesman

Death of a Salesman blends the themes of social and personal tragedy within a dramatic framework. Arthur Miller's play is one of America's best-known stage productions.

Character	*Metaphor*
Willy Loman	A man who accepts at face value the overpublicized ideals of material success. He lives his life through unrealistic dreams. He lives in the past and in the end comes to realize that he has *never been a success and never will be.*
Biff Loman	Could have been a great football star but decides instead to just bum around. *The consummate failure.*

The Picture of Dorian Gray

Oscar Wilde's fantasy tells the story of an artist, Basil Hallward, who painted a portrait of Dorian Gray, a handsome young man. Dorian gave his soul so that the portrait might grow old while he remained forever young. Dorian locked his portrait away. The more mean and cruel things he did, the more the picture changed. Eventually Dorian stabbed the frightful portrait. When the servants found him he was withered and wrinkled, with a knife in his chest. Only by his jewelry did the servants recognize Dorian who, in his desperate attempt to kill his conscience, had killed himself.

Character	*Metaphor*
Dorian Gray	Someone who *hides his corrupt and cruel manner* in his outward appearance.

The Invisible Man

Some people assume that the metaphor for H. G. Wells's Griffin is simply someone who cannot be seen. But the central character in this classic of science fiction robbed his father to fund the experiments that made him invisible so he could terrorize Oxford Street.

Character	*Metaphor*
Griffin	Someone who would *steal from his own family.*

The Time Machine

H. G. Wells's classic science fiction tale finds the protagonist in the future where the human race has been segregated into two groups. The Eloi are peaceful people who exist only to feed the cruel Morlocks. Metaphorically, someone would be an Eloi if he is but *sustenance for the powerful.* The Morlocks of the world *feed on the weak and helpless.*

Character	*Metaphor*
The Eloi	They are *sustenance for the powerful.*
The Morlocks	They *feed on the weak and helpless.*

The Strange Case of Dr. Jekyll and Mr. Hyde

Robert Louis Stevenson's 1886 novel is a psychological allegory.

Character	*Metaphor*
Dr. Jekyll and Mr. Hyde	*Different personalities in the extreme.*

The Grapes of Wrath

John Steinbeck's landmark 1939 novel tells the story of a family's migration from the Oklahoma dust bowl to the California promised land.

Character	*Metaphor*
The Joad Family	They are *lured by capricious promises* of "milk and honey" to a life of poverty and exploitation.

Oliver Twist

Charles Dickens's Fagin was the leader of a den of young thieves in this 1837 novel.

Character	*Metaphor*
Fagin	Someone who would *take advantage of children.*

The Music Man

In this famous broadway musical, later made into an Academy Award–winning movie, Professor Harold Hill, a confidence man, came to town to sell people on the idea they needed a marching band by arousing concern over problems that did not exist.

Character	*Metaphor*
Professor Harold Hill	Someone who sells something to *cure a problem that does not exist.*

Babbitt

Sinclair Lewis's George F. Babbitt, from the 1922 novel *Babbitt,* was a well-to-do realtor in Zenith, a midwestern boom city.

Character	*Metaphor*
George F. Babbitt	Someone who *takes advantage of every person and every opportunity.*

Sherlock Holmes

Sir Arthur Conan Doyle created the English detective Sherlock Holmes in 1887. The character has appeared in scores of stories and numerous movies and television programs. Holmes, the amateur detective, chemist, violin player, boxer, and swordsman (among other talents), is best known for his brilliance in solving crimes. An anecdote explaining Doyle's inspiration for his detective character is found in chapter 25, pages 395–96.

Character	*Metaphor*
Sherlock Holmes	Someone who is *exceptionally intelligent.*

James Bond

James Bond, also known as 007, is the fictional British spy introduced by writer Ian Fleming in 1953.

Character	*Metaphor*
James Bond	Someone who *has great courage.*

Hogan's Heroes

Hogan's Heroes was a hit television series that aired from 1965 until 1971. The basic plot involved the Allied inmates of a German World War II prisoner of war camp conducting espionage and sabotage campaigns under the noses of their guards. John Banner played the role of Sergeant Schultz and made the "I know nothing" line famous.

Character	*Metaphor*
Sergeant Schultz	Someone who lacks intelligence or is unobservant; he "knows nothing."

Star Wars

In 1975, George Lucas conceived and wrote the basic story of Anakin Skywalker's rise, fall, and ultimate redemption. He chose to begin the *Star Wars* movie series with the second trilogy, which focused on the life of Anakin's son, Luke Skywalker.

Character	*Metaphor*
Luke Skywalker	Someone heroic, courageous.

PLACES

Metaphors can be used for places, times, or conditions. In addition to Wonderland, the Looking-Glass World, Oz, the Yellow Brick Road, the Emerald City, Camelot, and the briar patch, discussed above, the following are places in literature, movies, and comic strips that have readily identifiable characteristics.

Tales of Uncle Remus

The briar patch is *a place that seems ominous but is actually a place of safety* to the protagonist because he knows a secret way out.

Brave New World

Human beings are turned out by mass production, and babies are conditioned during childhood for their predestined class in society in Aldous Huxley's *Brave New World*, published in 1932. Science is dominant, art stifled, and religion restrained. Any show of human emotion can end only in tragedy. Huxley's *Brave New World* is the metaphor for a *society driven by technology and devoid of human feeling.*

Utopia

Published in 1516, Sir Thomas More's *Utopia* describes a world free of the problems of the day, all made possible by social reforms. Each family is a part of a group that elects a council that elects a prince who serves for life. Everyone works six hours a day. Because everyone works, society realizes great prosperity. All goods are community owned. In the event of a painful and incurable illness the priests consult with the patient and encourage him to choose death administered painlessly by the authorities. Utopians buy off their enemies and use their wealth to hire foreign mercenaries.

While many consider the word "utopia" descriptive of a place of ideal perfection, in reality More's fictional world is a metaphor for *impractical schemes for social improvement.*

1984

George Orwell's political satire was published in 1949. He depicts the distorted society of Oceania, where *thought control of its citizens is accomplished with the big lie.* Big Brother watches everyone and the party rewrites history as it occurs. All party members must think and feel as Big Brother directs.

Stalag 17

In this German World War II prisoner of war camp, made famous by the 1953 film of the same name, men are imprisoned, brutalized, and constantly *looking for ways to escape.*

Bates Motel

In Alfred Hitchcock's acclaimed 1960 film *Psycho*, the Bates Motel is an ominous place where *mysterious and evil things happen*. People check in but don't check out.

Dogpatch

Created by Al Capp, *Dogpatch* is where most of the *Li'l Abner* comic strip is set, a place *where poor, crude, uneducated people live*.

Pleasantville

In the 1998 movie, *Pleasantville* is a place where *independent thought is discouraged*, books have no content, and people have no feelings. Everything is a matter of routine, habit, and custom. The world is in black and white, and people only gain color when they begin to think for themselves and feel as human beings.

An easy-to-use index to all the foregoing people and place metaphors is found at the end of this chapter.

Misusing Metaphors

While metaphors give spice to speech and make it flavorful, using the wrong one offers up something that the audience may find indigestible and offensive. Which metaphor is appropriate depends on the personality of the speaker, the circumstances of the presentation, and the audience. For example, sarcasm that would be acceptable for a political speech may be seen as mean-spirited in a professional or religious setting. Know your audience and the parameters of good taste. Here are some guidelines I follow when using metaphors.

Don't use real people, living or dead, as metaphors. Regardless of whether the speaker is painting a favorable or unfavorable picture, comparison is dangerous. A hard-working, caring mother victimized by malpractice or injured in an automobile accident may be likened to Dorothy in Oz or Alice in Wonderland but never to Mother Teresa, Florence Nightingale, or Rose Kennedy. A police officer may be described as Inspector Javert of *Les Misérables* but never as Ken Starr or Mark Fuhrman. A doctor whose failure to read a diagnostic test in time to prevent the patient's death may be a Mr. Magoo but never a Dr. Kevorkian.

Don't use fictional or real-life metaphors that are too pejorative. Avoid Adolf Hitler, Judas, the outlaw Jesse James, Jack the Ripper, Benedict Arnold, Dr. Frankenstein, Hans Gruber (the terrorist in *Die Hard*), or Gordon Gekko (the ruthless stockbroker in *Wall Street*).

Don't use clichéd metaphors. Avoid the obvious and overworked Ebenezer Scrooge and Pinocchio. Personal metaphors apply a touch of sarcasm. In the right setting they are appropriate and persuasive. Because a metaphor contains an inherent touch of sarcasm it is not normally used to create a favorable image. In trial, an appropriately chosen metaphor may remind the jury of a witness's failings or shortcomings, which may be particularly helpful in long trials where the jury finds it difficult to remember all the witnesses' names at the end of the testimony.

INDEX TO PEOPLE AND PLACE METAPHORS

PEOPLE—QUALITIES

Children

They *refuse to grow up.*	Peter Pan

Control

They *conspire to put a good, decent woman down.*	Cinderella's stepsisters
They are *quick to condemn.*	The Queen of Hearts
They *try to make something out of nothing.*	The King of Hearts
They want to *make all our choices.*	The Red and White Queens

Courage

They *prevail against long odds.*	Cinderella
They *revolt against the excesses of abusive power.*	Fletcher Christian
Someone who *has great courage.*	James Bond, Luke Skywalker

Deception

They *involuntarily warn of their approach.*	Crocodile
They try to *hide their corrupt and cruel manner* in their outward appearance but find that their deeds betray them in the end.	Dorian Gray

They *offer something they do not have.*	The March Hare
They *promise and never deliver.*	The White Queen
They *sell something to cure a nonexistent problem.*	Professor Harold Hill

Intelligence, Wisdom

Someone who is *exceptionally intelligent.*	Sherlock Holmes
They pretend to have mystical powers and wisdom but *deceive with machines* that put out smoke and colorful images.	The Wizard of Oz
They *survive by keen wits and intelligence and use people.*	Huckleberry Finn
Someone who is *respectable but naive.*	Tom Sawyer
They "know nothing."	Sergeant Schultz
Their *curiosity unleashes evil.*	Pandora
They *triumph by using their wits.*	Brer Rabbit

Prophecy

They *predict tragedy but are not believed.*	Cassandra
They *prophesy doom.*	Jeremiah

Strength

They *seem invulnerable but have a weak spot.*	Achilles

Vanity, Greed

They *love themselves.*	Narcissus

They *prize a possession* held by the innocent and pure.	Wicked Witch
They are willing to *use their wiles for their own personal gain.*	Scarlett O'Hara
A cynical, materialistic individual.	Rhett Butler
The high-powered, agressive salesman who *takes advantage of every person and every opportunity.*	George F. Babbitt
They are *obsessed with vengeance.*	Captain Ahab

Weakness

They *cannot remember* anything including their names.	The Jurors in the Tarts Trial
They are *pawns in a chess game.*	Alice
They are *trying to find their way home.*	Dorothy
They are *looking for courage.*	The Cowardly Lion
They are *looking for a heart.*	The Tin Man
They are *looking for a brain.*	The Scarecrow
A weak-willed man.	Ashley Wilkes
They have *never been a success and never will be.*	Willy Loman
They are *the consummate failure.*	Biff Loman
They are *lured by capricious promises* of "milk and honey" to a life of poverty and exploitation.	The Joad Family

Wickedness

They *prey on children.*	Captain Hook
They have *different personalities in the extreme.*	Dr. Jekyll and Mr. Hyde
They *take advantage of children.*	Fagin
They *have great fortune that brings disaster.*	Midas
They would *steal from their own family* to promote their own sinister ambitions.	Griffin (The Invisible Man)

Actions

Abuse

They are *sustenance for the powerful.*	The Eloi
They *feed on the weak and helpless.*	The Morlocks

Bad

They have *killed or injured someone.*	Cain
They try to *hide their corrupt and cruel manner* in their outward appearance but find that their deeds betray them in the end.	Dorian Gray

Confusing

Two people who look alike, sound alike, and imitate each other but are constantly fighting—everything they say has *two meanings.*	Tweedledum and Tweedledee
They contend that *words mean whatever they say they mean.*	Humpty Dumpty

Someone who asks riddles to which there are *no answers.*	The Mad Hatter
Someone who is *smiling but doesn't hear.*	The Cheshire Cat

Curious

Their *curiosity unleashes evil.*	Pandora

Futile

They *tilt at windmills; pursue an illusion.*	Don Quixote

Loyal

They *remain faithful* and applaud their masters' acts, even though they *really detest them.*	Sganarelle

Promise

They *promise and never deliver.*	The White Queen

Prophesy

They *prophesy doom.*	Jeremiah

Revenge

They *carry ancient grudges.*	Montagues and Capulets

Tardy

They are *always running late,* in a great hurry.	The White Rabbitt

Wealth

They *have great fortune that brings disaster.*	Midas

Winners

They *prevail against long odds.*	Cinderella
They *triumph by using their wits.*	Brer Rabbit
They *revolt against the excesses of abusive power.*	Fletcher Christian

Things

A Barmecide feast is a metaphor for *substance that is a deceptive illusion.*	Barmecide
Something that *appears elaborate and impressive but in actual fact lacks substance.*	Potemkin Village
An event without rules.	The Queen's Croquet Game

Places

An obscene judicial procedure where the Queen announces "*Sentence first—verdict afterward.*"	The Trial in Wonderland
A place where Alice is *carried farther through a pool of her tears.*	Wonderland
Somewhere where *everything is the opposite.*	The Looking-Glass World
A *path to home, hope, or dreams.*	The Yellow Brick Road
A place where *dreams can be realized.*	The Emerald City
The *best of times* and the *best of people.*	Camelot

A *place that seems ominous but is a place of safety* to the protagonist because he knows a secret way out.	The Briar Patch
A *society driven by technology and devoid of human feeling.*	*Brave New World*
Impractical schemes for social improvement.	*Utopia*
Thought control of its citizens is accomplished with the big lie.	Society of Oceania (*1984*)
Men are imprisoned, brutalized, and constantly *looking for ways to escape.*	*Stalag 17*
A place where *mysterious and evil things happen.*	Bates Motel
Al Capp's creation where Li'l Abner and other *poor, crude, uneducated people live.*	Dogpatch
A place where *independent thought is discouraged.*	*Pleasantville*

21

Similes and Clichés

THEY TOLD HER she would be safe there. "Our apartments are a secure and protected environment that will enhance your community living experience." Sheila believed that until the night the unknown assailant broke in and raped her. She knows the truth now. There had been four armed robberies, two muggings, a rape, and ten burglaries in the two years Sheila lived at the Limestone Walls Apartments.

The defendant's complex was like the Bates Motel. Their apartments were about as secure as the Israeli-Palestinian border, their security guards as watchful as Mr. Magoo, and their management behaved like Homer Simpson.

A simile is a figure of speech that compares one thing to another by stating how alike they are. They are introduced by words such as "like," "as," and "than." Similes can make speech colorful. Unfortunately, many speakers looking for word comparisons grab for the nearest cliché. Entertaining speakers create original and colorful similes. The following is a short catalog of colorful similes and metaphors.

SIMILES

Attitude

- They act like everyone else got to lick the red off their candy.
- No more remorse than a fruit fly.
- Tougher than a nickel steak.
- They had a face full of fine and dandy and a heart full of ice water.

- Like the popular boy teasing the wallflower at the dance.
- He thinks the sun comes up just to hear him crow.
- He's all broth and no beans.

Busy

- Busy as a cross-eyed boy at a three-ring circus.
- Busy as a one-armed paperhanger.
- Like a hot dog vendor standing in the middle of a dog pound.

Dangerous

- Like checking in to the Bates Motel.
- Like being on the Unabomber's mailing list.
- As dependable as a Wile E. Coyote trap.
- Like being a third-class passenger on the *Titanic.*
- They gave him the life expectancy of an al-Qaeda recruit on a suicide mission.

Difficult

- Harder than getting Siamese twins into a kayak.
- Like a dog who walks on its hind legs: it's not that it's done well, but that it's done at all.
- As difficult as packing barbed wire in a paper bag.
- As challenging as putting panty hose on a porcupine.
- Hard as sorting bobcats in a burning barn.

Distorted

- Pasted together like a ransom note.
- Like an image seen in a broken mirror.

Documentation

- They acted like their memories were longer than any short pencil.
- Like writing on the wind.
- As accurate as a Russian history book.

Downtrodden

- He was like the first dog kicked and the last dog fed.
- She was like a Taliban wife.

Fast

- Like a dog on a Dreamsicle.
- He can turn off the lights and be in bed before it gets dark.
- Quick as a nun's kiss.

Incompetency

- Like having Enron handle your retirement account.
- Like opening a bottle of bourbon at a Baptist revival.

Intelligence (Superior or Inferior)

- Trying to fool him is like trying to hide sunup from a rooster.
- He's on a different page than the rest of us.
- He acts as though he is overdrawn at the memory bank.
- He acts as though he is half a bubble off of plumb.
- He acts as though he is two tacos short of a Mexican Plate.
- He's got a big hole in his screen door.
- The porch light's on but no one's home.

- Her phone's off the hook.

Negligence

- They planted their crop before they built their fence.
- Like picking the deepest part of the river to cross.
- Like the porch dog that goes to sleep when strangers come up to the house.
- Like trusting your pet rattlesnake not to bite the children.
- They just mailed it in when they needed to show up.
- They skipped that day of class.
- It was like putting it on automatic pilot when you knew you might be flying into a storm.

Pain

- It struck him like a Joan Crawford coat hanger.
- Like being pushed through a window into hell.
- Like a branding iron to the heart.
- Worse than walking around all day with a pebble in your shoe.

Personality

- He's so country he thinks a seven-course meal is possum and a six-pack.
- She's so nervous she has to thread her sewing machine while it's running.

Personal Similarity

- Like being drained from the same crankcase.
- Cut from the same pattern.

Powerless

- As powerless as a minnow in a flash flood.

- Like the runt of the litter at feeding time.
- Like a one-legged man in a field-goal contest.
- When you look around the poker table and can't find the mullet—you are the mullet.

Rare

- As likely to find a turnip in a martini.
- As rare as a dollar cup of coffee in Manhattan.
- As unlikely as a dope dealer declaring bankruptcy after a rock concert.

Slow

- He acted like his motto was "don't do something, just stand there."
- His clothes could go out of style while he was making up his mind.
- As long in coming as Christmas for a four-year-old.

Substance (Lack Of)

- It's like a bumper sticker—the words are catchy but there is little substance.
- It was like Geraldo Rivera opening up the Al Capone vault.

Unreliable

- As reliable as an M-16 in the mud.
- As dependable as an adolescent's promise.

Useless

- Useless as a milk bucket under a bull.
- As useful as a hay baler on a golf course.

Wrongdoer Complaining

- Like an arsonist complaining about the size of the fire department.

THE DEADLY CLICHÉ

Clichés kill stories and speeches. They are crutches that a healthy speaker does not need. Robert Hartwell Fiske's *Thesaurus of Alternatives to Worn-Out Words and Phrases* is an excellent catalog of cliché expressions to be avoided. Along with dead metaphors and similes, speakers should avoid phrases made impotent by overuse.

Cliché Metaphors

- Barking up the wrong tree
- (Go) by the book
- The cream of the crop
- Doesn't know enough to come in out of the rain
- Down the primrose path
- Every Tom, Dick and Harry
- Exercise in futility
- Flash in the pan
- Fresh as a daisy
- From start to finish
- Go off the deep end
- Go to hell in a handbasket
- Hook, line and sinker
- Loaded for bear
- Lock, stock and barrel
- An open book
- Out to lunch

- Put the cart before the horse
- Read between the lines
- Step up to the plate
- The straw that broke the camel's back
- Take a long, hard look (at)
- In two shakes (of a lamb's tail)
- Up a blind alley (a creek, a tree, in the air)

A storyteller who uses a cliché metaphor should, at the least, mutate it. Thus, "he turned over every stone and the ground underneath it" or "he holds all the cards and owns the card factory."

Speakers prove their lack of imagination when they use a cliché simile. These are descriptions so worn out that their use projects the speaker as shallow and unimaginative.

- Gentle as a lamb
- As hard as a rock
- As hard as nails
- As hungry as a bear (horse)
- As light as a feather
- Like clockwork
- As patient as Job
- As plain as day
- Like playing Russian roulette
- Like pulling teeth
- Quick as a cat (a flash, a wink, lightning)
- As right as rain

- Sharp as a razor (tack)
- Like shooting fish in a barrel
- Sober as a judge
- Solid as a rock
- As strong as a horse (lion, ox)

Some phrases are so overworked, redundant, and tired that their use actually drains power from speech. Fiske calls these "dimwitticisms."[1] While witticisms are the work of few words, dimwitticisms represent the toil of many. They disengage the speaker from the audience, distract from the message, and disserve the message. Storytellers avoid them at all costs.

- At this time
- First and foremost
- In spite of the fact that
- It doesn't take a rocket scientist to
- It has been brought to my attention
- It is important to note that
- It is interesting to note that
- It must be mentioned that
- It must be noted that
- It must be pointed out that
- Prioritize
- Pursuant to
- Prior to
- Subsequent to

- There are no words to describe
- When all is said and done

Cliché Axioms as Story Themes

Clichés serve the storyteller in only one way. Cliché axioms or proverbs may be helpful as story themes. However, even these are made more persuasive by mutation. Examples of how this works are presented in chapter 8 on choosing a cognitive theme. Following are some of the common cliché axioms that work for the courtroom storyteller.

- Actions speak louder than words.
- A bad workman always blames his tools.
- Better late than never.
- Better safe than sorry.
- Business as usual.
- Don't change the rules in the middle of the game.
- Don't let the fox guard the henhouse.
- Don't start anything you can't finish.
- Don't tear the wall down unless you are sure why it was put up.
- First of all, do no harm.
- A good beginning is half the battle.
- Haste makes waste.
- I'm from Missouri, you've got to show me.
- A jackass can kick a barn door down, but it takes a carpenter to build one.
- The left hand doesn't know what the right hand is doing.
- Look before you leap.

- A man's word is as good as his bond.
- Never put off until tomorrow what you can do today.
- No man can serve two masters.
- Old habits die hard.
- One man's meat is another man's poison.
- One rotten apple spoils the barrel.
- The operation was a success, but the patient died.
- An ounce of prevention is worth a pound of cure.
- A stitch in time saves nine.
- The straw that broke the camel's back.
- They never missed an opportunity to miss an opportunity.
- Too many cooks spoil the broth.
- Too much too soon, too little too late.
- When in doubt, do nothing.
- In the wrong place at the wrong time.
- You can't judge a book by its cover.
- You get what you pay for.

A novel and catchy simile or metaphor adds spice to speech. Clever phraseology can season the substance. Persuasive speakers choose them carefully and use them wisely.

22

Analogies

MANY TIMES, A PERSON wronged or hurt by another's carelessness doesn't have direct evidence to prove it. She doesn't have an eyewitness to what happened. Sometimes we know someone saw it but didn't come forward or can't be found. Maybe no one saw it happen. When someone is killed, she cannot speak for herself. That is why the law does not require that the plaintiff have direct evidence to prove her case. You can use circumstantial evidence.

We all remember the story of Robinson Crusoe, who was stranded on an island after a shipwreck. For a long time he thought he was alone. Then one day he saw footprints on the beach that he knew were not his. He didn't see the man he would later meet. But he knew he wasn't alone. He used circumstantial evidence to reach that conclusion.

The folks at Mayfield Nursing Home put Hattie Sylvester on a new mattress at 10:00 AM on April 4, 2004. At 11:30, she was found dead in her bed. By the time the family arrived, the nursing home had put her in another room on another bed. Nursing home officials didn't request an autopsy. The family, bereaved and heartbroken, had no reason to ask for one. Weeks later, after Hattie was buried, Nurse Williams called the daughter, Marjorie Phillips, about the suspicious circumstances of her mother's death. The mattress wasn't the right size for the bed. There was a gap between the edge of the mattress and the bed railing. When a nurse found Mrs. Sylvester at 11:30, her head was between the vertical side rails of the bed. She was lying on her right side, the side that her stroke a year earlier had left paralyzed. Her right shoulder was down in the gap between the mattress and the bed rail. There were bruises and discolorations on her neck.

We don't have direct evidence of what killed Hattie, but we have footprints. They tell us what happened that no one saw. Eighty-eight-year-old Hattie rolled over on her paralyzed side after the attendant left her. Her shoulder dropped into the gap left when the defendant's employees carelessly put the wrong-size mattress on Hattie's bed. She got her head between the bed rails and was strangling to death. She couldn't push herself out of harm's way because of her paralyzed arm and shoulder. Just as Robinson Crusoe couldn't see Friday, no one saw the way Hattie died. But the footprints leave us no doubt that is the way it happened. The undisputed facts are like footprints in the sand. We use our common sense and the circumstances to draw a reasonable conclusion.

An analogy by definition is a comparison of resemblances between things that are otherwise unlike.[1] When sociologists explain the functions of society by comparing them to the organs of a human body, they are using an analogy. Analogies are contrasted with metaphors and similes, which are ways of describing something by saying it is like something else. If an employee says her supervisor works her like a slave driver, this is a simile. It is a metaphor to say that the supervisor is a slave driver. Analogies clarify ideas and concepts that would otherwise be difficult to express. When the presentation involves technical and abstract matters, analogies provide a change of pace. They temporarily turn from the unfamiliar to the familiar.

Analogies work well in explaining medical and anatomical principles. The human heart can be compared to a four-chambered pump because that is exactly what it is. The pump analogy is helpful in clarifying the concept of valves, reservoir, and pressure. The dynamics of a closed head injury producing intracranial pressure and swelling that, if unrelieved, cause the brain stem to herniate through the foramen magnum, are dramatized by visualizing the squeezing of an orange until the skin breaks and the pulp and juice squirt out. A malignant tumor is like a fire. It has to be put out quickly.

Blood pressure plays a significant role in diagnosing a number of medical conditions. For example, when a person has internal hemorrhaging, one of the critical parameters the doctors and nurses should be observing is the patient's blood pressure.[2] An appreciation of the significance of clinical hypotension requires an understanding of the basic concept of blood pressure. Counsel may simplify this scientific principle with an analogy.

> We all understand the basic concept of human blood pressure. Human blood is a stream of fairly thick fluid driven by a pump through an elastic rubber garden hose against the partial obstruction of a small nozzle opening. The pump is the heart, the garden hose is the arteries, and the small nozzle openings are the capillaries. Pressure builds up from the piston of the pump to the outlet of the nozzle. The blood pressure monitor is simply a gauge that can be inserted anywhere along the line to measure the pressure. The harder the pump works, the higher the pressure. By the same token, the smaller the nozzle opening at the end of the line, the higher the pressure. Blood pressure is the pressure exerted by the blood on the walls of the arteries. The pressure depends on the action of the pump and the resistance of the capillaries. We all know that if the walls of the arteries are fairly elastic, the artery will expand under the pressure and thus relieve some of the pressure. For this reason, blood pressure depends also on the elasticity of the arteries. Young, healthy arteries are elastic, and this is why blood pressure in young people is lower

> than blood pressure in older people.
>
> The thickness or viscosity of the blood also has an effect on blood pressure. Thicker fluid requires more pushing to get through small openings. While many things can affect a person's blood pressure, most of them develop over time. They do not explain sudden increases or decreases of a person's baseline pressures. But a pronounced smaller volume of blood tends to lower the pressure in the entire system. If you cut the garden hose, water leaks out and you have less pressure in the line. When blood is lost by hemorrhage—bleeding—the blood pressure goes down.

A good analogy has the listeners connecting the points of the analogy with the points under discussion before the speaker even makes the connection. The light goes on and the meaning is clear to the listener. In the courtroom, analogies may be based on personal experience or even some imagined event.

The trial advocate uses analogies with care. The analogy is examined cautiously to be sure it truly applies to the case and creates the right kind of visual image. Analogies clarify issues only if the meaning is clear. An analogy should convey only what is meant and nothing more.

To some, the term "preponderance of the evidence" is hard to conceptualize. I've heard a lot of analogies used by lawyers for illustration. The idea of tilting the scales is a popular one. I normally avoid sports or war metaphors, but it's hard to resist the football analogy to explain this legal concept to a Texas jury.

> Both teams have played hard and the game is over. We've both given our best shots—put on our evidence. As plaintiffs we are the offense. Our burden is to move the ball. We started out on the fifty yard line with both sides being equal. Now the question for you is, "Where is the ball resting on the field?" If you feel the ball is in their end of the field, even by as much as a yard, then we have met our burden. We have proven our case by a preponderance of the evidence. Personally, I don't think it is a close call. Judy's team has been in the end zone several times. The defense's team has tried trick plays and I know some of you wanted to flag them several times. Despite their questionable efforts, they haven't moved the ball. You may disagree on where the ball is now. Some of you may feel it's clearly in the end zone, some of you may feel it's up on the thirty yard line. That is not the question. Preponderance of the evidence only asks if the ball is somewhere in their end of the field.

Analogies are helpful in other areas that involve legal concepts. In the automobile collision case involving little property damage to the plaintiff's car, counsel may be faced with the dilemma of trying to convince the fact finders that the driver could have sustained serious injuries in a minor accident. To deal with this problem the advocate may use the analogy of a loading dock that was backed into by the defendant's eighteen-wheeler. On the dock were stacked some priceless pieces of crystal. The crystal was knocked off the dock, onto the ground, and broken. The lawyer hypothesizes the argument that the trucking company's lawyers would use—that the crystal should not have been on the dock. They would argue that cartons of groceries, like those carried in the defendant's truck, should have been on the dock. The cases of cans and boxes could have been picked up off the ground and sent on their way without any problem. The analogy is between the plaintiff's fragile neck with an existing arthritic condition and the crystals on the loading dock.

A similar analogy that has been used a lot is the "ping-pong ball analogy." Often an injured plaintiff may have some preexisting condition such as osteoarthritis, obesity, or old age. An analogy is made of the poultry farmer on his way to town to sell his goods. The farmer's truck is hit from the rear by another truck and his cartons of eggs fly off the truck and crash to the ground. The farmer loses all of his egg production for that run. No one would question the farmer's suing for damages for what he would have been paid for his eggs. By analogy, the plaintiff's condition with its preexisting problems are likened to the farmer's eggs. Both are easily cracked or broken. On the other hand, a young, healthy person might be likened to someone transporting a crate of ping-pong balls. When his truck is hit the ping-pong balls bounce harmlessly down the highway and may be gathered up and restocked in the cartons. This analogy can be brought home to juries by pointing out that no one would accept a defense argument in the farmer's case to the effect that, "Well, the poultry farmer should have been carrying ping-pong balls instead of eggs."

A product liability case involving the issue to adequately warn may be simplified by comparing it to someone loaning another a car and telling him that the radio doesn't work but neglecting to say that the brakes are low. The duty to warn of danger in a workplace is like a person inviting someone to her home and not warning about a lion in the bathroom. The doctor who doesn't base his diagnostic decisions on appropriate tests is playing Russian roulette with the patient's safety. A doctor who makes a diagnosis while the patient is on antiseizure medication is comparable to the mechanic who adjusts a carburetor without the engine running.

Statistics often require an analogy for explanation. A doctor evaluates a woman and concludes that she has a 10 percent physical disability. It doesn't sound like much, does it? An analogy clarifies and explains what might otherwise be trivialized. A watch with a 10 percent disability will lose two and four-tenths hours a day. A $100 watch that loses this amount of time is not worth $90. A watch that loses two and a half hours a day is not worth anything.

The critical difference that 10 percent can make can be measured in athletic contests. Forty years ago no one ever heard of someone running a mile in less than four minutes. But if anyone could reduce that time by 10 percent, he would run a mile in just over three and a half minutes, a figure that needs no elaboration. There are a hundred golfers on the professional circuit who can shoot the average course in 72 any day. But a 65 is a score of a champion at his best. Take your average professional basketball player who is six feet, seven inches tall. Add 10 percent and you have a star seven feet, three inches tall.

In her award-winning book *Encountering God: A Spiritual Journey from Bozeman to Banaras,* Diana Eck of the Harvard Divinity School explained the world's diversity in these words:

> If our world were a village of a thousand people, who would we be? The World Development Forum tells us that there would be 329 Christians, 174 Muslims, 131 Hindus, 61 Buddhists, 52 Animists, 3 Jews, 34 members of other religions, such as Sikhs, Jains, Zoroastrians, and Baha'is, and 216 would be without any religion. In this village, there would be 564 Asians, 210 Europeans, 86 Africans, 80 South Americans, and 60 North Americans. And in this same village, 60 persons would have half the income, 500 would be hungry, 600 would live in shantytowns, and 700 would be illiterate.[3]

One of the most effective uses of analogies is the explanation of the relationship of time. Noted trial lawyer Don Keenan of Atlanta, Georgia, uses time analogies when he talks about a doctor's delay in attending a patient or performing an emergency C-section. The significance of the passing of a few hours without action may be trivialized in a static setting. But put it in real terms and the doctor's absence comes alive. In the example of a four-hour delay in performing an emergency cesarean section, Keenan points out that he could have left the courthouse, driven to the airport, had a cup of coffee, boarded a plane, enjoyed lunch, and been in Los Angeles sipping a cocktail in the airport in the time it took the doctor to get to the hospital.

Some years ago as part of a trial technique program I argued a hypothetical case involving the failure of a lawyer to properly prepare and prosecute a case on behalf of his clients. I used the following analogy to help the audience appreciate the time involved.

> From March 1994 to May 1995, the defendant handles this case saying he doesn't need an expert in neurology or genetics to link the obstetrician's negligence to Angelita's brain damage. During that time the Astros played 162 games and the Rockets played 93 games on their way to a World Championship. When both teams traveled out of town to play half those games, the defendant sat on the case. Fourteen months passed between the time the defendant took on this family's case until the time the obstetrician's lawyers designated their geneticist. For fourteen months the defendant decided the family didn't need a neurology or genetics expert. You could have heard the evidence in the O. J. Simpson criminal case, the O. J. Simpson civil case, and the Menendez Brothers criminal prosecution and had weeks left over during the time the defendant persisted in his decision, "I don't need to know what the defense for the obstetrician will be, I don't need anything else."

Then Dr. Wilson named his expert, but it was weeks before the defendant-lawyer deposed him. You would think that Dr. Wilson's naming a geneticist would ring a bell, turn the light on, shake the bed. It didn't. The defendant still decided he didn't need a neurologist or genetics expert. He didn't take any steps to get one. After Dr. Gordon was designated, the defendant piled up a lot of letters but little action. Some college students completed an entire summer course and picked up six hours of college credit during the time the defendant was trying to schedule Dr. Gordon's deposition.

After the lawyers for the obstetrician designated the genetics expert, it was weeks again before the defendant named a rebuttal expert for the family. I was looking through the *Houston Chronicle* Travel Section last weekend. You could leave Houston, fly down to Mexico, spend two weeks with an archeologist in the rain forest exploring ancient ruins, fly to Cape Town, South Africa, do a bicycle tour, pedal all the way to Gabon, fly to Geneva, hike the Swiss Alps, leave and get on a cruise ship and tour the Adriatic Islands, fly to Antarctica, cruise aboard a Russian icebreaker, come back home, and have days left in the time from when the defense designated its geneticist and the defendant asked for more time to name Dr. Childs as an expert for the family.

Where unfamiliar legal or scientific concepts are involved, the only way the storyteller can create a persuasive word picture is by using an analogy of something familiar to the audience. The choice of the analogy is critical; it must be one that is not only appropriate but also cannot be turned against the advocate. Many cases because of their complexity demand the use of an analogy. Trial lawyers know that the same principle that applies to case themes applies to analogies: if you don't give the jury a good one, they will come up with their own.

23

Quotations

A FAMOUS *A*MERICAN *known as much for his philosophical comments as for his baseball playing, Yogi Berra said, "You can observe a lot just by watching."*

When the defendant walked out of his front door, down the path in front of his house, and got into his pickup, Johnny and two other boys aged six and seven were playing on the sidewalk with their toys and tricycle. The defendant says he didn't see them, even though they were just a few feet west of his driveway—the passenger side. He didn't see Johnny on his tricycle when he started up his truck. He didn't see Johnny or the other children when he started to back out. He didn't see Johnny behind his truck when he ran over him. He just didn't observe any of these things. Well, as Yogi says, "You can observe a lot just by watching."

Famous quotations, axioms, proverbs, and witticisms are a form of story within a story. They illustrate with things that notable figures believed, common shared values, and novel expressions. Speakers use them because they express a concept pointedly and persuasively. Sources for quotations are plentiful and include *The Oxford Dictionary of Quotations*, Edwards's *New Dictionary of Thoughts*, Evans's *Dictionary of Quotations*, and *Bartlett's Familiar Quotations.*[1]

Many speakers feel that sprinkling a few quotations around is a surefire way of making the speech interesting. Nothing could be further from the truth. Unless the quotation makes the point in a memorable and interesting way, the speaker would do best by not using it. Quotations are good devices that help the listeners remember something. If they don't accomplish that, they distract from the story.

Some ideas, concepts, and lessons recur often in the courtroom. The following is a list of helpful lawyer quotations.

Age

"Antique people ought to be as valuable as antique furniture."

"The one good thing about being in your nineties is that you don't have to worry about peer pressure."—*George Burns, American comedian and actor, on his 99th birthday*

"The trouble is that the young don't know what to do, and the old can't do what they know."

"I'm too young to be old, and I'm too old to be young."—*Jessica Tandy, American actor, in* Fried Green Tomatoes

"With age comes wisdom."—*American proverb*

"To me, old age is always fifteen years older than I am."—*Bernard M. Baruch, American businessman and statesman, in the* New York Times, *June 6, 1984*

"The older we get, the fewer things seem worth waiting in line for."—*Will Rogers, American humorist*

"Some people try to turn back their odometers. Not me, I want people to know 'why' I look this way. I've traveled a long way and some of the roads weren't paved."—*Will Rogers*

Anguish

"Well, every one can master a grief but he that has it."—*William Shakespeare, in* Much Ado About Nothing, *act 3, scene 2*

"Better pain in your heart than shame before men."—*Yiddish proverb*

"Your heart often knows things before your mind does."—*Polly Adler*

"One cannot remove anxiety by arguing it away."—*Paul Tillich, American theologian*

Benjamin Franklin, when asked what condition of man most deserves pity, answered, "A lonesome man on a rainy day who does not know how to read."

Appearance

Abraham Lincoln, on hearing that someone referred to him as being a very common-looking man, replied, "Common-looking people are the best in the world: that is the reason the Lord makes so many of them."

"Looks are nothing—behavior is all."—*American proverb*

"A thing of beauty is a joy forever."—*John Keats, English poet*

"Nothing has such a decisive influence upon a man's course as his personal appearance, and not so much his appearance as his belief in its attractiveness or unattractiveness."—*Leo Tolstoy, Russian novelist*

Attitude (Good)

"I'm just tryin' to get along without shovin' nobody around."—*Tom Joad, in John Steinbeck's* The Grapes of Wrath

"He that is of a merry heart hath a continual feast."—*Proverbs 15:15*

"Hope is the feeling that you will succeed tomorrow in what you failed at today."

"Kindness consists in loving people more than they deserve."—*Joseph Joubert, French essayist and moralist*

"Generosity is giving more than you can, and pride is taking less than you need."—*Kahlil Gibran, American essayist, novelist, and poet*

"Satisfaction is knowing that you left things better than they were when you found them."

"If you want to make enemies, try to change something."—*Woodrow Wilson*

Attitude (Bad)

"Some people think they can't look good unless they're standing on top of someone else."

"The optimist proclaims that we live in the best of all possible worlds; and the pessimist fears this is true."—*James Branch Cabell, American essayist and novelist, in* The Silver Stallion, *1926*

"I'll not listen to reason. . . . Reason always means what someone else has got to say."—*Elizabeth Cleghorn Gaskell, in* Cranford, *1851–53*

"To laugh at men of sense is the privilege of fools."—*Jean de La Bruyère, in* Les Caractères, De la Société, *1688*

"Rudeness is the weak man's imitation of strength."—Eric Hoffer, *American author*

Franklin Delano Roosevelt said that we do not begrudge those men of great wealth; we just expect them not to abuse it.

Babies

"Every baby born into the world is a finer one than the last."—*Charles Dickens, English novelist, in* Nicholas Nickleby

"A baby hires and enslaves you."—*Maltese proverb*

"A baby is God's opinion that life should go on."—*Carl Sandburg, American historian, poet, and novelist*

Bias, Prejudice

"Whose bread I eat, his song I sing."—*old German saying*

"Prejudices are the chains forged by ignorance to keep men apart."—*Marguerite Gardiner, Countess of Blessington*

"No man can see his own prejudices."—*Francis Wright, in* A Few Days in Athens, *1822*

"[W]e must be ever on our guard, lest we erect our prejudices into legal principles."—*Louis D. Brandeis,* New State Ice Co. v. Liebmann, *285 U.S. 262, 311 (1932)*

"No one can eliminate prejudices—just recognize them."—*Edward R. Murrow, American journalist*

"For those who do not think, it is best to at least rearrange their prejudices once in a while."—*Luther Burbank, American horticulturist*

Blame

"The man who always criticizes others for his failures never credits them for his successes."

"It is a poor workman who blames his tools."

"The early bird gets the worm, but the second mouse gets the cheese."—*Steven Wright, American comedian*

Character

"What you are stands over you the while, and thunders so that I cannot hear what you say to the contrary."—*Ralph Waldo Emerson, American essayist and poet*

"I ask you to judge me by the enemies I have made."—*Franklin Delano Roosevelt*

"You are only what you are when no one is looking."

"A man's character reaches town before his person."—*Danish proverb*

Children

"Childhood is that wonderful time when all you have to do to lose weight is take a bath."

"Children are the anchors that hold a mother to life."—*Sophocles, Greek dramatist*

"A child does not know his father's poverty."—*African proverb*

"Who takes the child by the hand takes the mother by the heart."—*Danish proverb*

"There is only one pretty child in the world, and every mother has it."—*Chinese proverb*

"Children are poor men's riches."—*English proverb*

"He who has no children does not know what love is."—*Italian proverb*

Compassion (Those Who Have It)

"Charity is to will and do what is just and right in every transaction."—*Emanuel Swedenborg, in* Heaven and Hell

"Sympathy without relief is like mustard without beef."—*English proverb*

"He has the right to criticize who has the heart to help."—*Abraham Lincoln*

Compassion (Those Who Don't)

"I rather think there is an immense shortage of Christian charity among so-called Christians."—*Harry S Truman*

"Hardening of the heart ages people more quickly than hardening of the arteries."

Confusion

"I can't say I was ever lost, but I was bewildered once for three days."—*Daniel Boone's answer to Chester Harding, an American artist painting a portrait of Boone who was then in his eighties*

"If you don't know where you are going, you will probably end up somewhere else."—*Laurence J. Peter and Raymond Hull, in* The Peter Principle, *1969*

Contentment

"I have all the money I want and he hasn't."—*American Naturalist John Muir's explanation of why he thought he was richer than magnate E. H. Airaman*

"It is astonishing how little one feels poverty when one loves."—*John Bulwer*

"Think contentment the greatest wealth."—*George Shelley*

"Be content with what you have, and not with what you are."

"Content makes poor men rich; discontent makes rich men poor."—*Benjamin Franklin*

Contracts

"The big print giveth, and the fine print taketh away."—*Bishop Fulton J. Sheen, American theologian*

"Don't look for loopholes in the contract, but for a contract in the loopholes."

Conviction

The famous eighteenth-century philosopher David Hume, reportedly an agnostic, was asked why he would attend the services conducted by the famous Scottish preacher John Brown. Hume replied, "Well, I don't believe everything he says, but I like to hear a man who believes what he is saying."

"Conviction is the conscience of the mind."—*Sébastien-Roch Nicolas De Chamfort, French dramatist*

"Some men are just as firmly convinced of what they think as others are of what they know."—*Aristotle, in* Nicomachan Ethics VII

Corporations

"Corporations have no souls, but they can love each other."—*Henry Demarest Lloyd, in* Wealth Against Commonwealth, *1894*

"Anybody can cut prices, but it takes brains to make a better product."—*Alice Hubbard*

"A corporation is an ingenious device for getting individual profit without individual responsibility."

Courage

"There's only one thing more important than background and that's backbone."

"There are heroes and there are legends. Heroes get remembered, but legends never die."

"It was the nation . . . that had the lion's heart. I had the luck to be called upon to give the roar."—*Winston Churchill, celebrating his eightieth birthday in 1954*

"Courage is rightly esteemed the first of human qualities . . . because it . . . guarantees all others."—*Winston Churchill*

"If a man is right he can't be too radical; if he is wrong, he can't be too conservative."—*Josh Billings*

"Cowardice asks the question, 'Is it safe?' Expediency asks the question, 'Is it politic?' Vanity asks the question, 'Is it popular?' But conscience asks the question, 'Is it right?'"—*Rev. Martin Luther King, Jr.*

"Heroes don't just shoot people. They put supper on the table."—*Dabney Coleman, American actor, expanding his son's understanding in* Cloak and Dagger, *1984*

"Keep your fears to yourself but share your courage."—*Robert Louis Stevenson, Scottish novelist*

"Never run from a fight. If you're gonna get hit, it's better to take it in the front than in the back—and it looks better."—*Texas Bix Bender, in* Don't Squat With Yer Spurs On! A Cowboy's Guide to Life, *1992*

Defenses

"Some men make good; others make up good excuses."

"It is better to offer no excuse than a bad one."—*George Washington in a letter to niece Harriett Washington, October 30, 1791*

"The absent are never without fault, nor the present without excuse."—*Benjamin Franklin*

"Failure accepts no alibis. Success needs no explanation."

"No problem is too big to run away from."—*Charles M. Schulz's Charlie Brown, 1981*

"I will defend my opinion to the last drop of my ink."—*Jean-Baptiste Poquelin Molière, French dramatist*

"The weaker the defense, the stronger the language."

Doctors, Medicine

"All doctors who treat accident cases are not obstetricians."

"A doctor is a general practitioner who calls in a specialist to share the blame."

"The physician can bury his mistakes, but the architect can only advise his client to plant vines."—*Frank Lloyd Wright, American architect, in* the New York Times, *October 4, 1953*

"Why was Jesus born in a manger? Because Joseph belonged to an HMO."

"They that are whole need not a physician."—*Luke 5:31*

"Better no doctors at all than three."—*Polish proverb*

"Only a doctor can kill you without punishment."—*Hungarian proverb*

"Heaven defend me from a busy doctor."—*Welsh proverb*

"Let no one suppose that the words doctor and patient can disguise from the parties the fact that they are employer and employee."—*George Bernard Shaw, English dramatist*

Documents (Destruction Of)

"If at first you don't succeed, destroy all evidence that you tried."—*Steven Wright, American comedian*

"Better shred than read."

"What they can't read, can't hurt us."

"Paper doesn't bleed."

Documents (Reliability Of)

"The spoken word flies away but the written word is here to stay."

"Are you going to believe your lying eyes or what I tell you?"

"The palest ink is more reliable than the best of memories."

"No memory is long enough to stack up against a short pencil."

Economics

"If you would know the value of money, go try to borrow some."—*Benjamin Franklin, in* The Way to Wealth, *1757*

"If all economists were laid end to end, they would not reach a conclusion."—*George Bernard Shaw, English dramatist*

"An economist is one who knows more about money than the people who have it."

"Economists are always half right in their forecasts of better or worse conditions; but they are never sure which half it will be."

"If all the economists were laid end to end, they would point in different directions."

Evidence

"The absence of evidence is not evidence of absence."

"Facts do not cease to exist because they are ignored."—*Aldous Huxley, English novelist and poet*

"It ain't so much people's ignorance that bothers me as it is what people know that ain't so."—*Will Rogers, American humorist*

"Three may keep a secret, if two of them are dead."—*Benjamin Franklin, in* Poor Richard's Almanac, *1735*

"Judge a man not by the words of his mother, but from the comments of his neighbors."—*Jewish folk saying, in Leo Rosten,* Treasury of Jewish Quotations, *1972*

"Some circumstantial evidence is very strong, as when you find a trout in the milk."—*Henry David Thoreau, in* Journal, *November 11, 1854*

"Human nature constitutes a part of the evidence in every case."—*Elisha R. Potter, American jurist*

Experience

"Learn by experience—preferably, other people's."

"Those who cannot remember the past are condemned to repeat it."—*George Santayana, Spanish philosopher, in* The Life of Reason, *1905*

"They may forget what you said, but they will never forget how you made them feel."—*Carl W. Buechner*

"Experience keeps a dear school, yet fools will learn in no other."—*Benjamin Franklin, in* Poor Richard's Almanac, *1743*

"Experience is a hard teacher because she gives the test first, the lesson afterwards."—*Vernon Law, "How to Be a Winner,"* in This Week, *August 14, 1960*

"If a man deceives me once, shame on him; if he deceives me twice, shame on me."—*Italian proverb*

"Experience is the name everyone gives to their mistakes."—*Oscar Wilde, English novelist and dramatist, in* Lady Windermere's Fan III

Experts

"An expert is defined as someone who is wrong but for more sophisticated reasons."

"Professionals built the *Titanic*; amateurs the ark."—*Frank Pepper*

"An expert is someone who takes something you already know and makes it sound confusing."

"An expert is someone who always has a good reason for guessing wrong."

"An expert is a man who has stopped thinking—he knows!"—*Frank Lloyd Wright, American architect*

Family

"A family consists of a husband who gets an idea, children who say it cannot be done, and a wife who does it."

"The family is one of nature's masterpieces."—*George Santayana, Spanish philosopher, in* The Life of Reason, *1905*

"In time of test, family is best."—*Burmese proverb*

"As the family goes, so goes the nation and so goes the whole world in which we live."—*Pope John Paul II*

"All happy families resemble one another, but each unhappy family is unhappy in its own way."—*Leo Tolstoy, in* Anna Karenina

"You don't choose your family. They are God's gift to you, as you are to them."—*Bishop Desmond Tutu*

"You can always tell the family man: he's the one with the wallet full of snapshots."

Fathers

"One father is more than a hundred schoolmasters."—*George Herbert, in* Jacula Prudentum, *1651*

"If you live without being a father, you die without being a human being."—*Russian proverb*

Husbands

"Marrying a man is like buying something you've been admiring for a long time in a shop window. You may love it when you get home, but it doesn't always go with everything else in the house."—*Jean Kerr*

"A good husband is merely a good son grown up."

"Without a husband, you are naked."—*African proverb*

"A good husband makes a good wife."—*Robert Burton*

"Some pray to marry the man they love,
    my prayer will somewhat vary;
I humbly pray to Heaven above,
    that I love the man I marry."—*Rose Pastor Stokes*

Indifference

"The greatest tragedy is indifference."—*Red Cross motto*

"The worst sin towards our fellow creatures is not to hate them, but to be indifferent to them: that's the essence of inhumanity."—*George Bernard Shaw, English dramatist, in* The Devil's Disciple, *1901*

Injury

"Everything is funny as long as it is happening to someone else."—*Will Rogers, American humorist, "Warning to Jokers: Lay Off the Prince," in* The Illiterate Digest, *1924*

"It is the insult and not the injury that makes the deeper wounds."—*H. L. Mencken, American critic and commentator, 1924*

"[A] wise and frugal Government, which shall restrain men from injuring one another, shall leave them otherwise free to regulate their own pursuits of industry and improvement, and shall not take from the mouth of labor the bread it has earned. This is the sum of good government."—*Thomas Jefferson, in his first inaugural address, March 4, 1801*

Injustice

"Injustice anywhere is a threat to justice everywhere."—*Rev. Martin Luther King, Jr., in his letter from the Birmingham jail, April 16, 1963*

"Delay in justice is injustice."—*Walter Savage Landor*

"The love of justice in most men is simply the fear of suffering injustice."—*François Duc de la Rochefoucauld, in* Reflections, No. 78, *1665*

Integrity

"This old anvil laughs at many broken hammers. There are men who can't be bought."—*Carl Sandburg, in* The People Will Live On, *1936*

"It is better to deserve honors and not have them than to have them and not to deserve them."—*Mark Twain, American humorist and author*

"Ease and honor are seldom bedfellows."—*English proverb*

"Few men have virtue to withstand the highest bidder."—*George Washington*

"Confidence in another man's virtue is no slight evidence of one's own."—*Michel de Montaigne*

Judgment

"My dog is a good fighter, he's just a terrible judge of dogs."—*Theodore Roosevelt, commenting on his dog, who was forever getting into fights and forever being beaten*

"Don't judge a man by what he stands for but by what he stands up for."

"Everyone complains of his memory, and no one complains of his judgment."—*François Duc de la Rochefoucauld, in* Reflections, No. 89, *1665*

"Good judgment comes from experience, and a lot of that comes from bad judgment." —*Will Rogers, American humorist*

"There are three kinds of men. The ones that learn by reading. The few who learn by observation. The rest of them have to pee on the electric fence and find out for themselves."—*Will Rogers, American humorist*

Jury

"[N]o fact tried by a jury, shall be otherwise reexamined in any Court of the United States, than according to the rules of the common law."—*The Seventh Amendment to the Constitution of the United States*

"There are two things that even God does not know: who a woman will marry and a jury's verdict."

"The American imbues all classes with respect for the thing judged and with the notion of right . . . it teaches men to practice equity; every man learns to judge his neighbor as he would himself be judged."—*Alexis de Tocqueville, French statesman, during his visit to America*

"'Tis better to suffer wrong than do it."—*Thomas Fuller*

"Few men like to serve on a jury except in a beauty contest."

"Most women dislike jury service because it's all listening."

Justice

"Justice is ensured when those who have not been injured are as indignant as those who have been."—*Statement attributed to an unnamed philosopher in ancient Athens struggling to define the concept of justice*

"The only justification for looking down on somebody is if you are going to stop to help them up."

"It is justice, not charity, that is wanting in the world."—*Mary Wollstonecraft Shelley, English novelist*

"Wherever there is a human being there is a chance for justice."

"We may have all come over on different ships, but we're in the same boat now."—*Rev. Martin Luther King, Jr.*

"But what is Freedom? Rightly understood, A universal licence to be good."—*Hartley Coleridge, in* Liberty, *1833*

"The test of our progress is not whether we add more to the abundance of those who have much; it is whether we provide enough for those who have little."—*Franklin Delano Roosevelt*

Labels

"Putting a Picasso on the outhouse door doesn't change the nature of the facilities."

"You can't tell the depth of the well by the handle on the crank."

Laws

"Ye shall have one manner of law, as well for the stranger, as for one of your own country."—*Leviticus 24:22*

"Laws must be justified by something more than the will of the majority. They must rest on the eternal foundation of righteousness."—*Calvin Coolidge, January 7, 1914*

"It is said that even in a primitive society there is medicine, but law comes with civilization."

"The best protection for people on a street is a lot of other people on the street."

"The great can protect themselves, but the poor and humble require the arm and shield of the law."—*Andrew Jackson, in a letter to John Quincy Adams, 1821*

Lawyers

"The minute you read something that you can't understand, you can almost be sure that it was drawn up by a lawyer."—*Will Rogers, American humorist*

"Woe unto you also, ye lawyers! for ye lade men with burdens grievous to be borne, and ye yourselves touch not the burdens with one of your fingers."—*Luke 11:46*

"The first thing we do, let's kill all the lawyers."—*Dick, the butcher in Shakespeare's* Henry VI, Part 2, *act 4, scene 2, describing how criminal conspirators can carry out their plans for anarchy*

"Counsel is like the Statute of Limitations—the more often he is interrupted the longer he runs."

"Plaintiff lawyers take from the rich and give two-thirds to the poor."

"Defense lawyers are social workers for the rich."

"Lawyers earn their bread by the sweat of their browbeating."—*James G. Huneker*

"Well, I don't know as I want a lawyer to tell me what I cannot do. I hire him to tell me how to do what I want to do."—*John Pierpont Morgan, American banker*

"Ninety-nine percent of lawyers give all the rest a bad name."—*Steven Wright, American comedian*

Mankind

"Man is the animal who loves."—*Archibald MacLeish, American poet*

"Conscience is the inner voice that warns us somebody may be looking."—*H. L. Mencken, American critic and commentator, in* A Mencken Chrestomathy, *1949*

"In spite of everything, I still believe that people are really good at heart."—*Anne Frank*

"Man is the only animal that laughs and weeps, for he is the only animal that is struck with the difference between what things are, and what they might have been."—*William Hazlitt, English author*

Mothers

"Mothers oppose war because they realize better than anyone else how long it takes to make a man."

"A mother is a person who, seeing there are only four pieces of pie for five people, promptly announces she never did care for pie."—*Tenneva Jordan*

"The mother's heart is the child's schoolroom."—*Harriet Beecher Stowe, American author*

"The mother of the hero is the first to weep."—*Serbo-Croatian proverb*

"God could not be everywhere and therefore he made mothers."—*Rudyard Kipling, English novelist*

"There was never a great man who had not a great mother."—*Olive Schreiner*

Negligence

"First of all, do no harm."—*The First Rule of Medicine*

"Nearly all men die of their remedies, and not of their illness."—*Jean-Baptiste Poquelin Molière, French dramatist, 1672*

"There is nothing so laden with regret as the sound of the words, too late."

"Don't just do something, stand there."—*Clint Eastwood, American actor and filmmaker*

"For of all sad words of tongue or pen, / The saddest are these: 'It might have been.'"—*John Greenleaf Whittier, in "Maud Muller," 1856*

"Want of care does us more damage than want of knowledge."—*Benjamin Franklin, 1732*

"Eighty percent of success is showing up."—*Woody Allen, American writer and filmmaker, 1982*

Garfield said, "When you find yourself in a hole, the first rule is to quit digging."

"The easiest way to get into trouble is to be right at the wrong time."

"The cautious seldom err."—*Confucius,* The Confucian Analects, *book 4:23*

"Some men always recognize their duty in sufficient time to sidestep it."

Originality

"If you steal from one author, it is plagiarism. If you steal from two authors it is called research. If you copy the works of three or more, you're called a scholar."

"Don't expect anything original from an echo."

"When a work appears to be ahead of its time, it is only the time that is behind the work."—*Jean Cocteau, French poet, dramatist, and filmmaker*

"A thought is often original, though you have uttered it a hundred times."—*Dr. Oliver Wendell Holmes, Sr., American physician, poet, and essayist, in* The Autocrat of the Breakfast Table, *1858*

"The man with a new idea is a crank until the idea succeeds."—*Mark Twain, American humorist and author*

Poor People

"They need a hand; they get the finger."

"They were too poor to paint; and too proud to whitewash."

"The poor are cured by work, the rich by the doctor."—*Polish proverb*

"Poor men's reasons are not heard."—*Thomas Fuller, English clergyman*

"The greatest man in history was the poorest."—*Ralph Waldo Emerson, American poet and philosopher*

"You have no reason to be ashamed of your poverty if you acquired it honestly."

Power

Jay Gould, the famous American railroad magnate, built up his vast empire in the southwestern states. Just before an impending strike, he observed, "I can hire one half of the working class to kill the other half."

"Might never makes right, but it never gives up trying."

"I have always thought that all men should be free; but if any should be slaves, it should be first those who desire it for themselves, and secondly those who desire it for others. Whenever I hear anyone arguing for slavery, I feel a strong impulse to see it tried on him personally."—*Abraham Lincoln, address to Indiana Regiment, March 17, 1865*

"Tolerance is the belief that people who disagree with you have the right to be wrong."

At the height of the civil rights crisis in 1958, the Reverend Billy Graham said in Clinton, Tennessee, "Hot heads and cold hearts never solved anything."

Predictions (Faulty)

"Louis Pasteur's theory of germs is ridiculous fiction."—*Pierre Pachet, professor of physiology at Toulouse, 1872*

"This 'telephone' has too many shortcomings to be seriously considered as a means of communication. The device is inherently of no value to us."—*Western Union internal memo, 1876*

"Heavier-than-air flying machines are impossible."—*Lord Kelvin, president of the Royal Society, 1895*

"Everything that can be invented has been invented."—*Charles H. Duell, director of the U.S. Patent Office, 1899*

"Sensible and responsible women do not want to vote."—*Grover Cleveland, 1901*

"Airplanes are interesting toys but of no military value."—*Marshal Ferdinand Foch, Professor of Strategy, École Supérieure de Guerre, 1912*

"Ruth made a big mistake when he gave up pitching."—*Tris Speaker, 1921*

"There is no likelihood man can ever tap the power of the atom."—*William Millikan,*

Nobel Prize–winner in physics, 1923

"Who the hell wants to hear actors talk?"—*Harry M. Warner, Warner Bros. Pictures film producer, 1927*

"Computers in the future may . . . perhaps only weigh 1.5 tons."—Popular Mechanics, *forecasting the relentless march of science, 1949*

"But what . . . is it good for?"—*Engineer at the Advanced Computing Systems Division of IBM, commenting on the microchip, 1968*

"There is no reason for any individual to have a computer in their home."—*Ken Olson, president, chairman, and founder of Digital Equipment Corp., 1977*

"640k ought to be enough for anybody."—*Bill Gates, founder of Microsoft Corp., 1981*

Religion

"My country is the world, and my religion is to do good."—*Thomas Paine, in* The Rights of Man, *1792*

"Faith is the sister of justice."—*Latin proverb.*

"[T]he best way to know God is to love many things."—*Vincent van Gogh, Post-Impressionist painter*

"Those who have loved God most have loved men least."—*Robert Green Ingersoll, American statesman*

"Many have quarreled about religion that never practiced it."—*Benjamin Franklin*

"Whatever you are, be a good one."—*Abraham Lincoln*

Responsibility

"The buck stops with the guy who signs the checks."—*Rupert Murdoch*

"Our actions are our own; their consequences are not."

"The real man is one who always finds excuses for others, but never excuses himself."—*Henry Ward Beecher, Congregational minister*

"Some people recognize their responsibilities in time to dodge them."

Silence

"In Germany they came first for the Communists, and I didn't speak up because I wasn't a Communist. Then they came for the Jews, and I didn't speak up because I wasn't a Jew. Then they came for the trade unionists, and I didn't speak up because I wasn't a trade unionist. Then they came for the Catholics, and I didn't speak up because I was Protestant. Then they came for me, and by that time no one was left to speak up."—*Attributed to Martin Niemoeller, a German, recalling events in Nazi Germany at the time of his death*

"Silence is the virtue of fools."—*Francis Bacon, English philosopher*

"The cruellest lies are often told in silence."—*Robert Louis Stevenson, Scottish novelist*

"We will have to repent in this generation not merely for the hateful words and actions of the bad people but for the appalling silence of the good people."—*Rev. Martin Luther King, Jr., in his letter from the Birmingham jail, April 16, 1963*

"As long as the world shall last there will be wrongs, and if no man objected and no man rebelled, those wrongs would last forever."—*Clarence Darrow, American lawyer and writer*

"Silence gives consent."—*Oliver Goldsmith, in* The Good-Natured Man II

"I have never been hurt by what I have not said."—*Calvin Coolidge*

Statistics

"Statistics are people with the tears wiped from their eyes."

"Facts are stubborn things, but statistics are more pliable."—*Laurence J. Peter, American educator and writer*

"Statistics are like witnesses: you can always get them to testify for either side."

"He uses statistics as a drunken man uses lampposts—for support rather than illumination."—*Andrew Lang*

"Give a statistician some facts and figures, and he will draw his own confusions."

Success

"Hit the ball over the fence and you can take your time going around the bases." *—John W. Raper*

"Success comes to two kinds of men: those who are always on their toes, and those who are always stepping on the other fellow's."

"The secret of success is seldom well kept."

"Success is simply a matter of luck. Ask any failure."*—Earl Wilson*

"If at first you don't succeed, find out why before you try again."

Trust

"We are inclined to believe those whom we do not know because they have never deceived us."*—Samuel Johnson, English lexicographer and author*

"Trust everybody, but cut the cards."*—Finley Peter Dunne, American humorist*

"It is impossible to go through life without trust: that is to be imprisoned in the worst cell of all, oneself."*—Graham Greene, English novelist*

Truth

"It's no wonder that truth is stranger than fiction. Fiction has to make sense."*—Mark Twain, American humorist and author*

During Harry S Truman's famous whistle-stop campaign in 1948, one of the people in the crowd yelled at him, "Give 'em hell, Harry!" To this the president replied, "I never give them hell. I just tell the truth, and they think it is hell."

"He that speaks truth must have one foot in the stirrup."*—Hindu proverb*

"It takes two to speak the truth—one to speak, and another to hear."*—Henry David Thoreau, American essayist and natural philosopher, in* A Week on the Concord and Merrimack Rivers, *1849*

"Get your facts first, then you can distort them as you please."*—Mark Twain, American humorist and author*

"Every man has a right to be wrong in his opinions. But no man has a right to be wrong in his facts."—*Bernard M. Baruch, American businessman and statesman*

"Ye shall know the truth, and the truth shall make you mad."—*Aldous Huxley, English novelist and poet*

"A lie can travel halfway around the world while the truth is still putting on its shoes."—*Mark Twain, American humorist and author*

"The pursuit of truth shall set you free, even if you never catch up with it."—*Clarence Darrow, American lawyer and writer*

"It is the customary fate of new truths to begin as heresies and to end as superstitions."—*Thomas H. Huxley, English biologist*

Vengeance

"There are two things that God will not share—vengeance and glory."

"The smallest vengeance poisons the soul."—*Yiddish proverb*

Vices

"My mother neglected her vices."—*Mark Twain, American humorist and author, explaining why his mother stayed ill despite the fact she didn't smoke and drink and thus didn't have any habits to break that would make her get better*

"He who hesitates is probably torn between vice and virtue."

"The only vice some men have is their claim of being virtuous."

Witnesses

"You can observe a lot just by watching."—*Yogi Berra, American professional baseball player and manager*

"One eyewitness is better than ten hear sayers."—*Titus Maccius Plautus, Roman dramatist, ca. 254–184* BC

"Witnesses may lie . . . or be mistaken . . . but circumstances cannot lie."—*Richard Maunteney, Irish jurist*

Wives

"The wife is someone who laughs at her husband's jokes, not because they are clever, but because she is."

"If you want to know about a man you can find out an awful lot by looking at who he married."—*Kirk Douglas, American actor*

"A good wife and health are a man's best wealth."—*Benjamin Franklin*

"Where there is no wife, there is no home."—*American proverb*

Women

"Whatever women do they must do twice as well as men to be thought half as good. Luckily, this is not difficult."—*Charlotte Whitton, former mayor of Ottawa*

"A woman is like a tea bag—you cannot tell how strong she is until she gets into hot water."—*Eleanor Roosevelt*

"If you believe that a woman has a mind of her own, you've never served on a jury."

"For every woman who makes a fool out of a man, there is another woman who makes a man out of a fool."

"Just about the time a woman thinks her work is done, she becomes a grandmother."
—*Edward H. Dreschnack*

George Bernard Shaw said, "I often quote myself; it adds spice to the conversation." Maybe he was telling us that original thoughts are best. But when we use another's, in fairness, we should give them credit. For some of the quotations in the foregoing list no source could be found, so we must attribute them to "Anonymous."

An appropriate quotation makes the point the speaker wants to make in a memorable way. It adds to the narrative by underlining an essential concept. Examples of how quotations can fit into a courtroom story are found in the opening statements and closing arguments in chapter 26 (John Milton, page 450) and chapter 30 (the Apostle Paul, page 488; Robert Fulghum, page 490).

24

Poetry

THE DEFENDANT USED a sheet of three-quarter-inch plywood to cover this twelve-foot span on their construction site. It wouldn't break when a man walked across it. But when Lamont Washington comes across it pushing his wheelbarrow with three hundred pounds of bricks, it bends, then cracks. Before he can get across, it breaks in two and Lamont falls fifteen feet. He's lucky the bricks don't land on him or he would have been killed. Still, he breaks a leg, badly injures his back, and strains his right arm. The defendant says that using the plywood was "good enough." At the beginning of this case we told you the question would be, "Was it safe enough?"

I'm reminded of a few words from Edgar Guest, the man they called the people's poet.

> *My son, beware of "good enough,"*
> *It isn't made of sterling stuff;*
> *It's something any man can do,*
> *It marks the many from the few,*
>
> . . . .
>
> *The flaw which may escape the eye*
> *And temporarily get by,*
> *Shall weaken underneath the strain*
> *And wreck the ship or car or train,*
> *For this is true of men and stuff—*
> *Only the best is "good enough."*[1]

A persuasive storyteller sometimes uses a short poem to reach deep into the hearts of his listeners. Sometimes a poem is the only way to express the inexpressible. Poetry has a lot of the elements of music. A good poem is a melodious, rhythmic sentiment expressed in a way that embeds a thought in the minds of the audience.

As a general rule, speakers do not attempt to quote extensive verses, as this will detract from the power of the story. I follow these rules when deciding whether a poem can be used in the courtroom or on the lecture circuit:

- The passage must be short.
- The language and words of the poem must be common, everyday language and not stilted.
- The passage must directly relate to the subject of the speech or the issues in the case.

The following are some of my favorites.

THIRTEEN POEMS THAT MAKE A POINT

Use of Force

Be afraid of no man
No matter what size.
When trouble threatens, call on me,
For I shall equalize.[2]

—*A rhyme used to describe Samuel Colt's invention of his famous "six-shooter."*

It Is Wrong

For of all sad words of tongue or pen,
The saddest are these: "It might have been!"[3]

—*John Greenleaf Whittier, "Maud Muller"*

If, of all words of tongue and pen,
The saddest are, "It might have been,"
More sad are these we daily see:
"It is, but hadn't ought to be."[4]

—*Bret Harte, "Mrs. Judge Jenkins," parodying John Greenleaf Whittier's "Maud Muller"*

Suspicion

As I was walking up the stair
I met a man who wasn't there.
He wasn't there again today.
I wish, I wish he'd stay away.[5]

—Hughes Mearns, "The Man Who Wasn't There"

Doctors, Medicine

Surgeons must be very careful
When they take the knife!
Underneath their fine incisions
Stirs the Culprit—*Life!*[6]

—Emily Dickinson, "Surgeons must be very careful" [J108/F156]

Holding Grudges

He always has something to grumble about,
    Has the man with a chip on his shoulder;
The world to the dogs is going, no doubt,
    To the man with a chip on his shoulder;
The clouds are too dark, the sun is too bright.
    No matter what happens, it is never right;
When peace is prevailing he is spoiling to fight,
    The man with a chip on his shoulder.[7]

—Unknown, "A Chip on His Shoulder"

Anger

Let dogs delight to bark and bite,
    For God hath made them so:
Let bears and lions growl and fight,
    For 'tis their nature, too.
But, children, you should never let
    Such angry passions rise:
Your little hands were never made
    To tear each other's eyes.[8]

—Isaac Watts, "Against Quarreling and Fighting"

Lawyers Can Distort Language

I know you lawyers can with ease
Twist words and meanings as you please;
That language, by your skill made pliant,
Will bend to favour every client;
That 'tis the fee directs the sense,
To make out either side's pretence,
When you peruse the clearest case,
You see it with a double face:
For scepticism's your profession;
You hold there's doubt in all expression.[9]

—*John Gay, "The Dog and the Fox"*

Seeing the Good in People

Wouldn't this old world be better
    If the folks we meet would say—
"I know something good about you!"
    And treat us just that way?

. . . .

Wouldn't life be lots more happy
    If we praised the good we see?
For there's such a lot of goodness
    In the worst of you and me!

Wouldn't it be nice to practise
    That fine way of thinking, too?
You know something good about me,
    I know something good about you?[10]

—*Louis C. Shimon, "I Know Something Good About You"*

A Father's Love

"My son!" What simple, beautiful words!
    "My boy!" What a wonderful phrase!
We're counting the months till you come to us—
    The months, and the weeks, and the days!

"The new little stranger," some babes are called,

But that's not what you're going to be;
With double my virtues and half of my faults,
You can't be a stranger to me!
. . . .
And you shall lie in your mother's arms,
And croon at your mother's breast,
And I shall thank God I am there to shield
The two that I love the best.[11]

—*Captain Cyril Morton Thorne, "To My Unborn Son"*

Sometimes the poet's thoughts are so compelling and powerful the speaker feels that any effort to excerpt or shorten is a form of mutilation. My favorite poet is the American Edgar A. Guest, who died in 1959. His poems were noted for their plain and simple language and inspirational content. The following two poems are extended excerpts from two of Guest's better-known works.

Perseverance

Somebody said that it couldn't be done,
But he with a chuckle replied
That "maybe it couldn't," but he would be one
Who wouldn't say so till he'd tried.
So he buckled right in with the trace of a grin
On his face. If he worried he hid it.
He started to sing as he tackled the thing
That couldn't be done, and he did it.

Somebody scoffed: "Oh, you'll never do that;
At least no one ever has done it";
But he took off his coat and he took off his hat,
And the first thing we knew he'd begun it.
With a lift of his chin and a bit of a grin,
Without any doubting or quiddit,
He started to sing as he tackled the thing
That couldn't be done, and he did it.

There are thousands to tell you it cannot be done,
There are thousands to prophesy failure;
There are thousands to point out to you one by one,
The dangers that wait to assail you.
But just buckle in with a bit of a grin,
Just take off your coat and go to it;

Just start in to sing as you tackle the thing
    That "cannot be done," and you'll do it.[12]

—Edgar A. Guest, "It Couldn't Be Done"

Indifference

We found the car beneath a tree.
"The steering knuckle broke," said he;
"The driver's dead; they say his wife
Will be an invalid for life.
I wonder how the man must feel
Who made that faulty steering wheel."
. . . .
Perhaps the workman never saw
An indication of the flaw;
Or, seeing it, he fancied it
Would not affect his work a bit,
And said: "It's good enough to go—
I'll pass it on. They'll never know."

"It's not exactly to my best
But it may pass the final test;
And should it break, no man can know
It was my hand that made it so.
The thing is faulty, but perhaps
We'll never hear it when it snaps."
. . . .
Perhaps he whistles on his way
Into the factory to-day
And doesn't know the ruin wrought
By just one minute's careless thought.
Yet human life is held at stake
By nearly all that toilers make.[13]

—Edgar A. Guest, "The Broken Wheel"

The following poem is presented in its entirety. It is an excellent example of a poem that tells a story. The lesson is one that ties in with a lot of courtroom stories.

A Legacy for Our Children

An old man, going a lone highway,

Came, at the evening, cold and gray,
To a chasm, vast, and deep, and wide,
Through which was flowing a sullen tide.
The old man crossed in the twilight dim;
The sullen stream had no fears for him;
But he turned, when safe on the other side,
And built a bridge to span the tide.
"Old man," said a fellow pilgrim, near,
"You are wasting strength with building here;
Your journey will end with the ending day;
You never again must pass this way;
You have crossed the chasm, deep and wide—
Why build you the bridge at the eventide?"

The builder lifted his old gray head:
"Good friend, in the path I have come," he said,
"There followeth after me today
A youth, whose feet must pass this way.
This chasm, that has been naught to me,
To that fair-haired youth may a pitfall be.
He, too, must cross in the twilight dim;
Good friend, I am building the bridge for *him*."[14]

—Will Allen Dromgoole, "The Bridge Builder"

This final poem I include because it reminds us that there are mystical forces of good that inspire all of us.

The Wreck on Highway 109

A drunk man in an Oldsmobile
they said had run the light
that caused the six-car pileup
on 109 that night.
When broken bodies lay about
and blood was everywhere,
the sirens screamed out elegies,
for death was in the air.

A mother, trapped inside her car,
was heard above the noise;
her plaintive plea near split the air:

"Oh, God, please spare my boys!"
She fought to loose her pinioned hands;
she struggled to get free,
but mangled metal held her fast
in grim captivity.

Her frightened eyes then focused on
where the back seat once had been,
but all she saw was broken glass
and two children's seats crushed in.
Her twins were nowhere to be seen;
she did not hear them cry,
and then she prayed they'd been thrown free,
"Oh, God, don't let them die!"

Then firemen came and cut her loose,
but when they searched the back,
they found therein no little boys,
but the seat belts were intact.
They thought the woman had gone mad
and was traveling alone,
but when they turned to question her,
they discovered she was gone.

Policemen saw her running wild
and screaming above the noise
in beseeching supplication,
"Please help me find my boys!
They're four years old and wear blue shirts;
their jeans are blue to match."
One cop spoke up, "They're in my car,
and they don't have a scratch.

"They said their daddy put them there
and gave them each a cone,
then told them both to wait for Mom
to come and take them home.
I've searched the area high and low,
but I can't find their dad.
He must have fled the scene, I guess,
and that is very bad."

The mother hugged the twins and said,
while wiping at a tear,

"He could not flee the scene, you see,
for he's been dead a year."
The cop just looked confused and asked,
"Now, how can that be true?"
The boys said, "Mommy, Daddy came
and left a kiss for you.

"He told us not to worry
and that you would be all right,
and then he put us in this car
with the pretty, flashing light.
We wanted him to stay with us,
because we miss him so,
but Mommy, he just hugged us tight
and said he had to go.

"He said someday we'd understand
and told us not to fuss,
and he said to tell you, Mommy,
he's watching over us."
The mother knew without a doubt
that what they spoke was true,
for she recalled their dad's last words,
"I will watch over you."

The firemen's notes could not explain
the twisted, mangled car,
and how the three of them escaped
without a single scar.
But on the cop's report was scribed,
in print so very fine,
An angel walked the beat tonight
on Highway 109.[15]

—*Ruth Gillis*

Poetry used to be a staple commodity for plaintiff's lawyers, preachers, and inspirational speakers. If used appropriately, briefly, and with sincerity, it is still an effective persuasion technique—a story within a story.

25

Anecdotes and Humorous Stories

RAMON SALAZAR NEEDS a doctor. That's all little Ramon needs. This eleven-year-old boy gets to the defendants' emergency room at 11:30, one half-hour after he is hit in the head with a baseball. If a neurosurgeon operates on him anytime during the first six hours after he has been hit, Ramon will have no neurological injury. The bleeding epidural hematoma needs to be drained. If it is timely drained, the brain swelling won't get out of hand. The brain cells won't die.

But there are delays. Ramon lies on a gurney in the hallway of the emergency room for an hour and a half before the ER doctor sees him. It takes the defendants another hour to get a skull X-ray. A half-hour passes before the ER doctor looks at it. Another hour passes before they do the CAT scan. Forty-five minutes before the ER doctor learns the results. They waste eighty minutes calling around to find a neurosurgeon. They wait another forty-five minutes before making the first call to the medical center hospital to arrange for the transfer. After they arrange the transfer, it is two hours and forty minutes before Ramon is in the medical center with the neurosurgeon doing the emergency surgery. The operation to relieve the epidural hematoma doesn't begin until 9:00 PM that night. Nine and one-half hours after he gets to the emergency room. By then, it is too late. Ramon is brain-damaged.

The defense now wants to say, "Well, we saved his life. If we hadn't transferred him he would be dead." When I hear this kind of excuse, I am reminded of John Steinbeck's classic Of Mice and Men. *You remember the story about Lennie Small and his friend, George Milton. Lennie was as strong as an ox but not particularly bright. George took advantage of Lennie because Lennie was slow-witted. He was always playing mean tricks on him. But one day, George quit. The cowboys working the ranch with them asked George, "Why?" George told them that he just couldn't get over what happened when he played his last trick on Lennie. As they were walking by the river, he told Lennie to jump in. Lennie did, even though he couldn't swim. George had to jump in and pull him out. George felt sorry for Lennie after that because Lennie kept telling him how he had saved his life and would be eternally grateful. As George put it, "Poor Lennie wasn't smart enough to realize that I was the one that caused him to be drowning in the first place."[1]*

That's the way it was with Ramon. The little boy came to the hospital with a condition that is treatable by a qualified expert—a neurosurgeon. The hospital knew they didn't have any neurosurgeons on duty. They should have immediately transferred Ramon, but instead they fiddled around so long that by the time they were doing the right thing, brain damage was already occurring.

Speakers use short stories or anecdotes in many ways. A humorous story loosens up an audience. The personal story, one that shares common experiences and values with the audience, may help connect the speaker to his listeners. Religious stories underline the importance of core values. Stories from history make a point with an event or person familiar to the audience. In deciding to use an anecdote or short story, make it—

- short;
- relevant; and
- interesting.

Most anecdotes should take no longer than a minute or two to tell. Occasionally, where the point is critical to the overall story, the speaker uses a longer narrative, omitting the basic elements of scene and character. The essentials of the anecdote are what happened and what lesson the audience should learn.

Don't use an anecdote just because it is an interesting story. Telling an irrelevant joke or funny story may be seen as a gratuitous and unnecessary effort to humor the audience.

Don't get bogged down in irrelevant details. Focus on the essential facts. Give the audience just enough for them to understand the story and learn the lesson.

Finally, the anecdote must be something of interest to the audience. Speakers look awkward and impotent when they tell a story about something everyone knows in a way that everyone has heard before. Familiar events can be used as long as the speaker puts some unique or novel twist into the telling. Original stories—something the audience has not heard before—are best.

I have been compiling stories from various sources for more than forty years. These stories make a point or illustrate a value or creed. They are arbitrarily organized under the following headings:

- Ancient History
- The Bible
- Children's Stories

- Modern History
- Plays, Books, and Folklore
- Personal Experience

Finally, there is a catalog of humorous stories drawn from many sources.[2]

Ancient History

Greek Mythology

The Twelve Labors of Hercules

Hercules was the son of Zeus and Alcmene. He was rendered subject to Eurystheus and compelled to perform all his commands. Eurystheus mandated him a succession of desperate adventures that are called the "Twelve Labors of Hercules."

- *The Nemean Lion*

The first was the fight with the Nemean lion. The Valley of Nemea was infested by a terrible lion. Eurystheus ordered Hercules to bring him the skin of this monster. After using in vain his club and bow and arrow against the lion, Hercules strangled the animal with his hands. He returned carrying the lion's hide on his shoulders. But Eurystheus was so frightened at the sight of the animal's hide and the prodigious strength of Hercules that he ordered him to deliver his future accounts outside the town.

Don't order others to do things you aren't willing to witness.

- *The Hydra*

The second labor was the slaughter of the Lernaean Hydra. This monster ravaged the country around the city of Argos and dwelled in a swamp near the spring of Amymone. The Hydra had nine heads, of which the middle one was immortal. Hercules struck off the heads with his club, but in place of the head knocked off, two grew forth each time. At length, with the assistance of his faithful nephew Iolaus, he burned away the stumps of the heads of the Hydra and buried the ninth or immortal one under a huge rock.

Evil is not easily vanquished.
Trouble keeps coming back until you destroy the source.

- *Atlas and the Apples of the Hesperides*

The most difficult labor of all was getting the golden apples of the Hesperides. Hercules did not know where to find them, for they were apples Hera had received at her wedding from the Goddess of the Earth. After various adventures Hercules arrived at Mount Atlas in Africa. Atlas was one of the Titans who had warred against the Gods, and after they were subdued, Atlas was condemned to bear on his shoulders the weight of the heavens. Hercules wanted Atlas to find the apples and bring them to him. But how could he send Atlas away from his post; who would bear up the heavens while he was gone? Hercules took the burden on his own shoulders and sent Atlas to seek the apples. Atlas returned with them and, though somewhat reluctantly, took his burden upon his shoulders again and let Hercules return with the apples to Eurystheus.

Relief of another's burdens may free them to help you.

- *Antaeus*

A celebrated exploit of Hercules was his victory over Antaeus. Antaeus was the son of Poseidon and Gaia. He was a mighty giant and wrestler, whose strength was invincible as long as he remained in contact with his mother earth. He compelled all strangers who came to his country to wrestle with him on the condition that if he conquered them they would be put to death. Hercules encountered him and, finding that it was to no avail to throw Antaeus, for he always rose with renewed strength from every fall, lifted him up from the earth and held him in the air until he died.

Understanding the source of an opponent's strength is a key to victory.

The Flight of Icarus

Daedalus built a labyrinth for King Minos. Afterwards he lost the favor of the king and was shut up in a tower. He contrived to make his escape from the prison but could not leave the island by sea, as the king kept strict watch on all the vessels and permitted none to sail without being carefully searched. So Daedalus aspired to escape by air. He fabricated wings for himself and his young son, Icarus. He wrought feathers together, beginning with the smallest and adding larger ones, so as to form an increasing surface. The larger ones he secured with thread and the smaller with wax and gave the whole a gentle curvature like the wings of a bird. Daedalus equipped both himself and his son with these wings. When all was prepared for flight, he said, "Icarus, my son, I charge you to keep at a moderate height, for if you fly too low the damp will clog your wings, and if too high the heat will melt them. Keep near me and you will be safe."

During the flight of escape Icarus became exultant in his flying and left the guidance of his father so as to soar upward to reach heaven. The nearness of the blazing sun softened the wax holding the feathers together and they came off. Icarus fell into the sea and died.

Ignoring rules can lead to disaster.

Stories from Ancient Greece

- *Odysseus*

In Homer's *Odyssey,* Circe tells him how to pass safely by the coast of Sirens. The Sirens were sea nymphs who had the power of charming by song all who heard them, so that the unhappy mariners were irresistibly impelled to cast themselves into the sea to their destruction. Odysseus directed his seamen to fill their ears with beeswax so that they could not hear the songs and to bind him to the mast. He told his sailors that they were to keep him tied until they passed the Sirens' island. As they passed the island, the notes of the music were so ravishing and attractive that Odysseus struggled to get loose. He cried out and gave hand signals to his sailors to release him. But they disobeyed his orders and went so far as to tie him tighter. They held their course until the music grew fainter and ceased to be heard. Odysseus then gave his companions the signal to unseal their ears, and they relieved him from his bonds. They sailed safely on in search of their adventure.

Sometimes you have to seal your ears against temptation.
Success requires absolute focus on your goal.

- *Envy*

A Greek story tells of a man who killed himself through envy. His fellow citizens had erected a statue to one of their number who was a celebrated champion in the public games. But this man, a rival of the honored athlete, was so envious that he vowed to destroy the statue. Every night he went out into the darkness and chiseled at its base in an effort to undermine its foundation and make it fall. At last he succeeded. It did fall—on him. He fell victim to his own envy.

What we wish on others we bring on ourselves.

- *Socrates' Examination of Meletus*

The oldest example of an effective cross-examination is found in the trial of Socrates. Socrates was charged with corrupting the youth of Athens. He was tried before a jury said to have numbered about five hundred. Socrates was seventy years old at the time of his trial. He conducted his own defense. During the trial he questioned Meletus, who led the prosecution against him, about the charge that he was guilty of corrupting the young. He asked Meletus, if Socrates had corrupted the youth, who were the people who had improved them? In his reply, Meletus first mentioned the jurors. Socrates led him, step by step, to mention everyone in the entire citizen body. This resulted in the ridiculous conclusion that every Athenian except Socrates had improved the young.

Arrogance condemns itself.

- *An Unnatural Speaker*

Many people excuse their failings as public speakers with the comment, "I'm not a natural-born speaker." Those who feel that way should consider the story of Demosthenes. Today he is considered by many to be the greatest orator who ever lived.

Demosthenes lived in ancient Greece. His father died at an early age and left him to the care of guardians, who neglected his property and left him penniless. This inspired the young man to be a champion of justice and dedicate himself to confronting injustice wherever he found it. Demosthenes determined to be what would be the ancient Greek parallel of the modern plaintiff's lawyer. But in the beginning he was a very ineffectual speaker. He threw his arms about and presented his arguments in an unorganized and confusing fashion. Worse still, he stuttered. Not only did he lose cases, but people laughed at him when he spoke.

One day Demosthenes met an actor who asked him to repeat some verses. After Demosthenes said the lines, the actor gave the speech himself. The young Greek saw what a difference there was in the two ways of saying the lines. He worked on his bad speaking by putting a pebble in his mouth and speaking in such a way that he could be heard. "If the audience can understand me when I have a stone in my mouth, they surely will be able to understand me when there is nothing there."

Demosthenes would walk up hills and run as he talked to master his breathing. He practiced before a mirror so he could see his own gestures. He built an underground room and studied his oratory for months. He took others' speeches, improved them, and then learned them word for word. Through his determination and efforts this man, who had everything against him—bad stammer, awkward gestures, lack of confidence, and difficulty in saying anything extemporaneously—became known as the greatest orator in ancient Greece.

Other historic figures who overcame speech impediments include Aristotle, Isaac Newton, Clara Barton, Lewis Carroll, Charles Darwin, Winston Churchill, and the voice behind the best-remembered villain of moviedom, Darth Vader—James Earl Jones.

Hard work and dedication can make anyone a good speaker.
Cheating someone may inspire him to be committed to justice.

Aesop's Fables

According to the historian Herodotus, Aesop was a slave who lived in Samos in the sixth century BC. His master eventually freed Aesop. His fables were preserved through Babrius, Phaedrus, Planudes Maximus, and La Fontaine's verse translations, and the most modern English translations are those by George Fyler Townsend. Aesop's most famous fables are "The Fox and the Grapes" and "The Tortoise and the Hare." Those two fables are not included among the following examples in the belief that their overuse has pushed them into the "cliché anecdote" category.

- *The Young Crab and His Mother*

Aesop's tale begins with the mother crab asking her son why he walks sideways. The mother instructs her son that he should walk straight forward, with his toes turned out. The little crab obediently asked his mother to show him how to walk. "I want to learn." The mother crab tried and tried to walk straight forward. But she could only walk sideways, like her son. When she tried to turn her toes out, she tripped and fell on her nose.

Do not tell others how to act unless you can
set a good example.

- *The Wolf and the Crane*

A bone stuck crosswise in the throat of the wolf was the problem presented in Aesop's "The Wolf and the Crane." The wolf could not get it out of his throat. He could not eat a thing, which was an awful state of affairs for a wolf. The wolf hurried off to the crane, who he knew with her long neck and bill would be able to reach the bone and pull it out. The wolf promised the crane a handsome reward if she would pull the bone out of his throat. The crane was uneasy about putting her head in a wolf's throat. But she did what the wolf asked her to do. When the wolf felt the bone was gone, he started to walk away. The crane anxiously asked about her reward. The wolf replied indignantly, "Isn't it enough that I let you take your head out of my mouth without snapping it off?"

Expect no reward for serving the wicked.
The powerful believe the weak exist at their mercy—
even when the weak aid the powerful.

- *The Boy Who Cried Wolf*

Tending sheep can be dull work. Without doubt, boredom is what led to the tragic result in this fable. The young shepherd boy grew tired of talking to his dog or playing on his pipe and began to think what he would do if he saw a wolf. His master had told him to call for help from the village. Even though he had not seen anything that even looked like a wolf, he ran toward the village shouting at the top of his voice, "Wolf! Wolf!"

The villagers heard the cry, dropped their work, and ran in great excitement to the pasture. But when they got there they found the boy doubled over with laughter at the trick he had played on them. A few days later he again ran to the village and shouted, "Wolf! Wolf!" Again the villagers ran to help him, only to be laughed at again.

Then one evening as the sun was setting a wolf really did spring from the underbrush and fell upon the sheep. In terror, the boy ran toward the village shouting, "Wolf! Wolf!" But though the villagers heard the cry, they did not run to help him as they had before. "We will not let this young boy fool us again," they said.

The wolf killed a great many of the boy's sheep when the flock was left defenseless. Then the wolf slipped back into the forest unharmed.

Liars are not believed even when they speak the truth.
Too many false alarms kill credibility.

- *The Sheep and the Pig*

A shepherd discovered a fat pig in the meadow where his sheep were pastured. He ran the pig down, and when he picked it up to carry it off the pig began to squeal. The sheep in the pasture were astonished and amused at the pig's behavior. They asked the pig why he squealed like that. They pointed out that the shepherd often caught one of them and carried them off. But they never made a fuss about it. The pig replied that that was all very well since the shepherd was only after their wool. He was squealing because he knew the shepherd wanted his bacon.

It is easy to be brave when there is no danger.
The sheep who gives wool is committed. But the pig
who gives bacon shows real commitment.

- *The Ass, the Fox, and the Lion*

An ass and a fox were good friends. They were constantly in each other's company, helping the other out. One day the pair met a lion. The ass was very frightened, but the fox calmed his fears.

"I will talk to him," the fox said. The fox pulled the lion aside and told him privately that if he would promise not to hurt him he would lead his friend, the ass, into a pit where the lion could feast at his leisure. The lion agreed, and the fox returned to the ass and told him that he had extracted the lion's promise not to hurt them. The fox enticed the ass to go to a good place to hide until the lion was gone. The fox led the ass into a deep pit. But when the lion saw that the ass was his for the taking, he decided to eat the fox and save the ass for later.

Expect no reward for betraying a friend.

- *The Wolf and the Lamb*

A young lamb strayed out from the herd and was drinking on the bank of a stream. A hungry wolf came along hunting for something to eat. Because the lamb looked so helpless and innocent the wolf felt he needed some excuse for taking its life.

"You're paddling in my stream and stirring up the mud," the wolf growled. "You need to be punished for this misbehavior."

The trembling lamb begged the wolf's forgiveness and told him that he couldn't possibly be muddying up the water the wolf was drinking from because the wolf was upstream.

The wolf retorted that the lamb did muddy up his stream, and besides that, the lamb had told lies about him last year. The lamb answered, "How could I have done so? I wasn't born until this year."

"If it wasn't you, it was your brother."

"I have no brother."

The wolf snarled, "Well, it must have been someone in your family. No matter who it was, I do not intend to be talked out of my breakfast."

Without any more ado the wolf grabbed the poor lamb and carried her off into the forest.

One bent on mischief needs no excuse.

- *The Ass and the Lapdog*

This is an Aesop story that demonstrates that currying favor in an inappropriate way may have the opposite result. The lapdog was the favorite of his master. Every day the dog would run to meet the master and leap up to lick his hands and face. The master gave the dog gentle pats, kind words, and choice bits from his plate. The ass, although well fed and contented, felt the master hardly ever took any notice of him. Being jealous, the ass decided to win his master's favor by acting like the dog. One day he left his stable and clattered eagerly into the house. Finding his master seated at the dinner table, he planted his forefeet on his master's knees and rolled out his tongue to lick the master's face, as he had seen the dog do. But his weight upset the chair, and the ass and the man rolled over together in the pile of broken dishes from the table.

The master was alarmed at the strange behavior of the ass and called for help. The servants came and, believing their master was in danger from the clumsy beast, set upon him and drove him with kicks and blows back to the stable. The ass was left to mourn his own foolishness in the solitude of the barn.

Behavior that is appropriate for one may be considered
rude and vulgar by another.
Currying attention by acting the fool gains no favor.
Pretending to be something you are not to gain
favor doesn't change who you really are.

• *The Dog and His Bone*

A butcher threw a dog a bone. The dog was hurrying home with his prize when he crossed a narrow bridge, looked down, and saw himself reflected in the quiet water. The greedy dog thought he saw another dog carrying a bone much bigger than his own. He dropped his bone and sprang at the dog in the river, only to find himself swimming for dear life to reach the shore. When he reached the shore, he realized how stupid he had been because he had lost his prize bone trying to capture the reflection of what he already had.

We may already have what we lust for.

• *The Fox and the Crow*

A fox spied a crow sitting in a tree with a bit of cheese in her beak. The fox decided to goad the crow into giving up the morsel so he could enjoy a breakfast. He trotted up to the foot of the tree and stared up admiringly at the crow. "Good morning, beautiful creature," he said. The crow watched the fox suspiciously. She kept her beak tightly closed on the cheese and did not return his greeting. The fox continued to charm the crow, telling her how beautiful she was and how her feathers shone. "You are such a beautiful bird, you must have a lovely voice. Could you sing just one song, for I know I will hail you as queen of the birds."

The crow, hearing the flattering words, forgot all her suspicion. She wanted very much to be called queen of birds, so she opened her beak wide and uttered her loudest caw. The cheese fell into the fox's open mouth. As the fox walked off he muttered under his breath how vain and stupid the crow must have been to have given up the cheese for such insincere and phony flattery.

Those easily flattered are easily fleeced.

• *Two Travelers and an Ass*

A traveler hired an ass to carry him on a distant journey. The owner of the ass went along to drive the ass and point out the way. The road led across a treeless plain. The sun beat down so intensely that the heat became unbearable. The traveler decided to stop for a rest and, there being no other shade, sat down in the shadow of the ass. Wishing also to rest in the shade cast by the ass, the owner began to quarrel with the traveler, saying he had hired the ass and not the shadow it cast. The two soon came to blows, and while they were fighting the ass ran off.

Better to compromise than quarrel over form.
You can lose your ass fighting over the amenities
associated with the substance.

- *The Miller, His Son, and Their Ass*

Aesop's fable "The Miller, His Son, and Their Ass" was paraphrased by Benjamin Franklin in the *Pennsylvania Gazette* in 1731. A miller and his son were on their way to market with an ass that they hoped to sell. They drove him very slowly, hoping to keep him in good condition for the sale. As they walked along the highway some travelers began to laugh at them and call them foolish for walking when they might as well ride. The miller did not like to be laughed at, so he told his son to climb up and ride. They had gone a little farther when three merchants passed by. "Respect old age, young man. Get down and let the old man ride." Though the miller was not tired, he made the boy get down and climbed up himself to ride, just to please the merchants.

At the next turnstile, they passed some women carrying market baskets. They criticized the miller for riding while making his young son walk. Trying to gain acceptance, the miller told the boy to climb up behind him. They had gone only a short distance when another group of travelers began to criticize them for overloading the ass. "They look more able to carry the poor creature, than he to carry them. They must be on their way to sell the poor thing's hide."

The miller and his son scrambled down and, improvising, they slung the donkey from a pole. When they arrived in town, a crowd of people ran out to get a close look at the strange sight. The ass did not like being carried and, with so many people laughing and shouting at him, he began to kick and bray as they were crossing the bridge into town. The ropes holding the ass gave way and he tumbled into the river and was killed.

If you try to please all, you please none.
We can lose our ass listening to others.

- *The Lion, the Fox, and the Ass*

A lion, a fox, and an ass were hunting in company and caught a mountain goat. The lion asked the ass to divide the spoil. He did this very fairly, giving each an equal share. The lion flew into a rage and with one stroke of his huge paw he added the ass to the slain mountain goat. Then he turned to the fox.

"You divide it," he roared.

The fox wasted no time and quickly piled all the game into one giant heap. From this he took a very small portion for himself, and that being the undesirable bits, such as horns, hoofs, and entrails.

"Who taught you to divide so fairly?" the lion asked. The fox replied that he had learned his lesson from the ass as he carefully edged away.

Learn from the misfortunes of others.
The powerful have their own views of what is a fair distribution.

Rome and Medieval England

- *A Roman Soldier*

In ancient Rome, an old soldier was involved in a lawsuit that seemed likely to go against him. He therefore accosted his former commander, Caesar Augustus, in a public place, asking him to appear in court on his behalf. The Emperor at once selected one of his officers to appear for the man and introduced him to the litigant, but the soldier, rolling back his sleeve to reveal his scars, shouted, "When you were in danger at Actium, I didn't choose a substitute but fought for you in person." Chagrined, Augustus appeared in court on the veteran's behalf.

Loyalty requires a personal appearance.

- *Beowulf and the Dragon*

The idea that old age disqualifies one from accomplishment is dispelled by the legend of Beowulf. Beowulf was in the fiftieth year of his reign when, legend has it, great terror fell upon the land in the form of a monstrous fire-breathing dragon. It flew by night from its den in the rocks, lighting up the night with its blazing breath and burning houses and homesteads, men and cattle, with the flames from its mouth. When the news came to Beowulf that his people were suffering and dying and that no warrior dared risk his life in an effort to deliver the country from this devastation, the aged king took up his shield and sword and went forth to his last fight. He found the dragon's cave and called the dragon out. In the course of the combat Beowulf slew the dragon but suffered a fatal wound. According to his last wishes, his followers gathered wood and piled it on a cliff head. Upon this funeral pyre was laid Beowulf's body, which was consumed to ashes.

You are never too old for the challenge.

- *A Knight's Sword*

A centuries-old English folk story tells of a brave knight who could cut a horseshoe in two with his sword. This greatly impressed his comrades in arms. They often talked about the wonder of their friend's sword—its strength and sharpness. Finally one day, one of the other knights asked to borrow the sword. The knight granted the request. The knight who borrowed the sword tried to cut a horseshoe, but the sword just bounced off it. Then he put the nail from the horseshoe in a vise and struck at it. He could not cut the nail. He returned the sword to the lender, saying that it couldn't be done. The knight took back his sword and by way of demonstration cut the horseshoe in half. He explained that while he was happy to lend his sword, he could not lend his arm.

It is the workman, not the tools, that explains the result.

- *Gossip*

A peasant had a troubled conscience and sought the help of the village elder. The peasant had repeated some slander about a friend, and later he had found that his words were untrue. He asked the elder what he could do to make amends. The man advised, "If you want to make peace with your conscience, you must fill a bag with goose feathers, go to every door in the village, and drop a feather on each porch."

The peasant took a bag, filled it with goose feathers, and did as he had been told. Then he returned and asked, "Is this all I have to do?"

"No, that is not all," was the answer. "There is one thing more. Take your bag and gather up every feather." The peasant left. After a long period he returned, saying, "I could not find all the feathers, for the wind had blown them away."

The village elder retorted, "So it is with gossip. Unkind words are easily dropped, but are difficult to take back again."

The harm done by slander is not easily repaired.

- *The Incredible Marksman*

The following story was told to me many years ago by physician and lawyer Ken Mathis of Pasadena, Texas, now deceased.

Many years ago, in one of Europe's feudal kingdoms, there was a prince who considered himself the greatest marksman in the country. One day he came to a city. Like all the cities of that time, there was a wall constructed around it. The wall was littered with targets that had been painted on it. In the middle of each target was a bullet hole.

The prince sent from his cadre of officers an emissary to the city demanding that they bring before him this great marksman. Out of the city came a young boy with an ancient musket.

"Are you the one who shot all these targets?" the prince asked. The young boy replied that it was indeed he. The prince demanded that the young lad demonstrate his marksmanship.

The young boy took his ancient, rusty musket and carefully loaded and primed it. With great difficulty he raised the heavy weapon and fired at the wall. Then he walked to the point in the wall where the bullet had entered, pulled from his pocket a can of paint and a paintbrush, and began to paint a circled bull's-eye around the bullet hole.

If you can define your goal after you've acted,
you can always claim success.

STORIES FROM THE BIBLE

Old Testament

The Bible is an excellent source for stories that illustrate a concept. Many consider it the inspired Word of God. It is the most popular book ever published. Hundreds of millions read it and follow its dictates. Nine out of ten Americans own a Bible, but fewer than half have ever read it. Nonetheless, it is a source of inspiration that everyone recognizes and accepts.

Frank McCourt has referenced recent statistics that show why stories with a religious component are persuasive.[3]

- 96 percent of Americans believe in God.
- 80 percent of Americans believe in an afterlife.
- 72 percent believe in heaven; 56 percent in hell.
- 79 percent of Americans pray to God and feel that he has helped them to make decisions.
- 33 percent of Americans believe that the Bible is the actual word of God.

While one of William Shakespeare's characters observes in *The Merchant of Venice* that "the devil can cite scripture for his purpose," many business leaders and political figures use biblical passages in their speeches. Avoiding the cliché applies to biblical stories. If the story is a common one, tell it with a novel twist or in a unique way.

- *Adam and Eve*

A man and a woman inhabited a paradise. The Creator of that paradise told them they could enjoy it forever if they obeyed his law: they were not to eat of the tree of knowledge of good and evil. A devious creature, a serpent, came to the woman asking her if she could eat any fruit she pleased. "Yes," she said. "Any fruit except that from the tree of knowledge. If we eat that, we die." The serpent told her that they would not die if they ate of the tree but rather would discover the difference between good and evil and be equal with God.

The woman ate of the forbidden fruit and gave it to her husband. We all know this story from Genesis[4] as the story of the Garden of Eden. But many of us are unaware of the fact that the translation from the original Hebrew, later commented on by Mark Twain in his writings, tells us that when Eve offered the forbidden fruit to

Adam he made a conscious decision before he ate of it. Adam realized that he would rather live outside the Garden with Eve than inside Paradise without her. The story of Creation and the Paradise of the Garden confirms that one of God's greatest miracles was the power of love he gave for a man and a woman to share.

Spousal love is one of God's gifts.

M. Scott Peck in *The Road Less Traveled* offers another interpretation of the story of Adam and Eve. He suggests that the true sin committed by Adam and Eve was that they never approached God to discuss the comments made by the serpent about the tree of knowledge: "They listened to the serpent, but they failed to get God's side of the story before they acted."[5]

Don't make decisions based on half the facts.

- *Abraham's Sacrifice*

When Abraham was one hundred years old God told him to take his son Isaac and offer him as burnt sacrifice. Abraham never questions and does as he is told. As they are leaving for their journey into the wilderness, Isaac asks his father where the sacrificial lamb is. Abraham answers, "God himself will provide the lamb." Abraham binds the boy, lays him on the altar, and holds the knife over him. An angel stops him. Abraham is told that he passed the test—he "fears" God. A ram is substituted for the young boy on the altar.[6] Many of the stories from the Bible can only be described as frightening. This is certainly the case of Abraham's sacrifice. The practice of sacrificing burnt offerings as a measure of faith disappeared thousands of years ago. But the story of Abraham is still told to illustrate that since the beginning of time we believe—

The loss of a child is the greatest sacrifice
a human being can make.

- *Joseph and the Coat of Many Colors*

A man in an ancient land had twelve sons. Of all his sons he loved Joseph the most. He made Joseph a beautiful coat woven in all the brilliant colors of the rainbow. Jacob's other sons were jealous of Joseph because he was so favored. When they saw him in his coat of many colors they hated him even more. Jacob sent Joseph out to check on his flocks. His brothers saw him coming in his multicolored coat and decided that they would throw him into a pit and claim to their father that a wild animal had attacked him. Ruben, the brother with a kind heart, told his brothers that they should not have Joseph's blood on their hands. He counseled that they should just throw Joseph into the pit and leave him to his fate. The brothers agreed—not knowing that secretly Ruben was planning to return later to rescue Joseph.

When Joseph reached his brothers, they attacked him, ripped off his coat, and threw him into the pit. They left him without food or water. While they were sitting down next to the pit eating, a group of Ishmaelites passed on their way to Egypt. One of the brothers suggested they sell Joseph as a slave to the travelers. In this way, they would be rid of the brother they hated without killing him. They sold Joseph for twenty pieces of silver.

The brothers killed a young goat and dipped Joseph's coat in its blood. Jacob was filled with horror when they showed it to him. "This is Joseph's coat! My beloved son must have been killed by some wild beast!" Jacob thought that his beloved Joseph was dead on the basis of the deceptive evidence brought to him by the wicked brothers. It was evidence that was manufactured; it was false, and it led Jacob to the wrong conclusion.[7]

The book of Genesis tells us that Joseph rose up from slavery in Egypt by virtue of his wisdom and dedication. He does kindness to his brothers and is later reunited with his family. But the story of the deception of Joseph's brothers and how manufactured evidence can lead to a wrong conclusion is a classic lesson of the Old Testament.

Manufactured evidence can mislead.

- *Pharaoh's Promises to Moses*

The book of Exodus tells of broken promises that Pharaoh made to Moses to free the people of Israel.[8] Moses pleaded to let his people go. Pharaoh refused to listen. Moses and Aaron touched the waters of the river Nile, causing it to turn to blood. The fish died and rotted. Then frogs in the thousands came hopping out of rivers and streams into people's houses and even into their beds. Pharaoh sent for Moses and told him that if his God would take away the plague he would let the people go. Overnight the frogs died and were gathered up into evil-smelling heaps. But when Pharaoh saw the plague was over, he went back on his word.

Then Aaron struck the sand beneath his feet and millions of grains of sand turned into millions of lice that crawled and seethed over every man, woman, and beast that lived in Egypt. Next came a cloud of flies that crawled into people's mouths and under their eyelids. Again Pharaoh begged Moses to rid him of the plague. He promised to let the Israelites go. When the flies were gone, Pharaoh was gone. He took back his promise.

Next came a disease that killed every horse, camel, oxen, goat, and sheep. Still Pharaoh would not let the children of Israel leave. Moses and Aaron took a handful of ashes from the fire and threw them up into the air. The ashes spread a hideous sickness that broke out in boils, covering the skin of both men and women. Pharaoh still would not move. Then God told Moses to stretch his hand toward the heavens, and instantly there was a clash of thunder and red-hot lightning. A heavy hail fell from the sky, flattening whole fields and smashing open the trunks of trees. Pharaoh summoned Moses and told him that if he would stop the storm, he would let his people go. Even though the hail and thunder stopped, Pharaoh went back on his word.

That same day an east wind began to blow, and with the wind came locusts. They covered the sky until it was black. They covered the land and ate every remaining blade of grass and every fruit hanging from the trees. Pharaoh repented, and God turned the wind and the locusts were blown into the Red Sea. God told Moses to stretch out his hand, and darkness fell upon Egypt and there was no light for three days. Pharaoh sent for Moses and told him that his people could go but they had to leave their flocks behind. Moses replied, "That I may not do." Pharaoh told him that he would keep his people as slaves, and he forbade Moses to ever come in his presence again upon penalty of death.

The Old Testament teaches that nine plagues were visited on Egypt before Pharaoh freed the children of Israel. The tenth plague would come at midnight, when every first-born child throughout the country would die. God told Moses to have his people kill a lamb and daub a doorstep with the blood of the slain animal so that when the Angel of Death passed over he would leave untouched the houses marked with blood. This marks the day of the Passover. As God promised, death was everywhere. From the poor to the richest, the first born both of man and beast drew their last breaths and died. Only then did Pharaoh send for Moses and Aaron and tell them they could take their people and their flocks and herds from Egypt.

Pharaoh broke his promises to Moses and his people. It was only when the cruel calamity of losing his first-born son was visited on him that Pharaoh agreed to keep his promise. Even then, he later changed his mind and set out after Moses, who was able to escape with God's help.

Broken promises carry a heavy price.

- *Shibboleth*

In the book of Judges, Jephthah's men, the Gileadites, held the fort at the river Jordan with words to suffer no Ephraimite to cross over. When challenged with the question, "Art thou an Ephraimite?" the men of Ephraim would answer, "Nay." "Say now, Shibboleth," the Gileadites said. The Ephraimites could not pronounce the word correctly. They pronounced it "Sibboleth." There was no "sh" sound in the Ephraimite dialect. In this way Jephthah's men were able to hold the fort against the Ephraimites.[9] The word "shibboleth" has come to mean a test or formula used to identify adherence to a particular cause or sect. Unfortunately—

There is no shibboleth that people can use today
in judging a person's character.

- *The Choice of David*

What is within us determines who we are. The book of Samuel tells of the challenge to choose a king of Israel.[10] God spoke to Samuel telling him to go to Bethlehem where he would find a man called Jesse. God told Samuel that he had chosen one of the sons of Jesse to be the next king. Samuel met with Jesse and, one by one, seven of Jesse's sons came to the prophet to be blessed. When Samuel saw the men standing before him, tall and handsome, he thought to himself, "Surely, one of these must be the chosen one." But as the brothers came before him in turn, he heard the Lord's voice telling him, "This is not the man. God does not judge the way people do. Do not look at the face but into the heart."

Finally, Samuel turned to Jesse and told him that God had chosen none of the sons. He then asked, "Are all the children here?" Jesse replied that all were but David, the youngest, who was out in the fields looking after the sheep. Samuel asked that David be brought to him.

When David appeared Samuel took the holy oil and anointed David in front of his whole family. We know how great a king David turned out to be. He was courageous, as his victory over Goliath demonstrated. He later had to go into hiding when Saul became jealous and turned against him. But the Good Book teaches that David was chosen because of what was in his heart, not what could be seen from the outside.

Judge people on the basis of what's in their hearts,
not how they look.

- *Solomon's Wisdom*

A lesson we all learned as children teaches the meaning of wisdom.[11] Solomon was David's son, who became king after his father's death. He talked with God, who asked him what he most wanted. Solomon replied that he had no idea how to govern and asked for wisdom. God told Solomon that since he had asked nothing for himself, neither for long life, nor wealth, nor victory over his enemies, he would grant his desire.

Soon afterward two women came before Solomon. They shared a house, and each had recently given birth to a child, but one child had died. Now both mothers were claiming the living baby as theirs.

"It is her baby who died," the first woman insisted. "Do you think I do not know my own child!"

The other mother claimed otherwise. "It is her baby who is dead. While I was sleeping she stole mine from my side."

Solomon asked for his sword so he could cut the baby in two, giving half to each of the women. One of the women declared Solomon wise, saying the baby should be cut in two so that neither of them could have him. But the other mother burst into tears and pleaded with Solomon not to kill her baby. She cried, "I would rather give him away than have him hurt." The woman's words demonstrated to Solomon that she was the true mother. He gave the child to her.

A mother will make any sacrifice to save her child.
Wisdom requires an understanding of human nature.

- *The Conviction of Daniel*

The book of Daniel tells us that Darius the Mede was so impressed by the wisdom of Daniel that he appointed him the most powerful man in the kingdom, after himself.[12] This made the other officials jealous, and they plotted to bring about Daniel's downfall. Finding no fault with him, they decided the only way to bring him down would be to make it appear that Daniel was doing something against the law. The officials requested that Darius issue a ruling that for the next thirty days no one should pray to any god. All prayers had to be addressed to the king himself. Daniel continued to pray to God three times a day before his open window in defiance of the new law. Daniel's enemies, seeing that he continued to pray to God, reported his actions to the king.

The penalty for violating the law was to be thrown to the lions. Even though Daniel was Darius's favorite, he had no alternative but to cast Daniel in the lions' den. The next morning the king hurried to where the lions were penned. Daniel was still alive. He told Darius that the Lord had sent an angel to stand beside him and the lions had left him untouched. Darius gave the order for Daniel's release. Then Darius had all the conspirators arrested and commanded them to be thrown to the lions.

No one should use the law out of envy.

New Testament

The greatest and most inspirational speaker in history used stories to make his point. Some have suggested that Jesus was critical of lawyers. In truth, the criticism that he expressed while dining with the Pharisees was of those who load men down, do not help them, and take away knowledge.[13] Perhaps in this context it would be more appropriate to ask whether any criticism of lawyers contained in the New Testament is more appropriately aimed at those who would deny full justice for those orphaned or crippled by the torts of others.

Among Jesus's teachings were—

- Good men will obey and teach the law.[14]
- Whoever is hostile toward his brother courts judgment.[15]
- Whoever ridicules his brother faces a court sentence.[16]
- If someone sues you, settle out of court before you have to pay a fine.[17]

But Jesus's primary teachings came in the form of stories—parables. Every trial lawyer should know them, as they contain morals that are often relevant to issues in civil litigation. Since they are short and easily told, they can be used in arguments to inspire the jury to understand the lesson counsel hopes his audience will learn.

The Parables of Jesus

The most often used stories from the Bible are those Jesus told to illustrate a point during his teachings. There are more than thirty parables in the Gospels. Some are short, consisting of only a line or two of an extended metaphor. Others are more complex stories such as the parables of the prodigal son and the good Samaritan. Many of Jesus's parables contain very simple moral lessons, while others are more Zen-like and obscure. For example, the parable of the unjust steward has had thirty-seven explanations suggested, and five volumes have been written about it.

The following are those of Jesus's parables most commonly used in sermons, speeches, and courtroom arguments.

- *The Sower*

Wherever Jesus went, large numbers of men and women would follow. One day, Jesus was teaching by the Sea of Galilee. The crowd grew so large that he stepped into a boat on the lake so that people could gather by the water's edge to listen. There he told them the parable of the sower.

A man is sowing seeds for the next year's harvest. As he scatters handfuls of wheat to the right and the left, some of the seeds fall on the beaten path and are quickly eaten by birds. Some of the seeds fall on rocky ground and wither away. Others fall in the midst of thorns and are choked. But some of the seeds cast by the sower fall on good soil and bring forth good crops. In the religious context, the seeds of this parable are the word of God, and the soils are the various ways people respond to Jesus's teaching.[18] In the secular sense this story could illustrate—

Some people make their own opportunities.
The wise person benefits from acts that are lost on others.

- *The Evil Tenants*

Jesus told the parable of the evil tenants to the priests and scribes. A landowner rents out his land to tenants who don't pay and then kill the men sent to collect the rent. The landowner eventually destroys the tenants.[19] The story is used for the proposition that—

In the end, justice will prevail.

- *The Lost Sheep*

A large crowd surrounded Jesus to hear him speak, including tax collectors and lawbreakers closely gathered around him. Jesus was criticized as someone who associated with the immoral, criminal element. To rebut the criticism, he told a story comparing God to a shepherd who has a flock of a hundred sheep. If the shepherd sees that even one sheep is lost, he will leave the other ninety-nine and search the mountainside for his lost sheep. When he finds it, he will return home full of joy. He will rejoice more over the return of the one that had strayed than over the rest of the flock that remains safe in the fold.[20] The religious lesson is that God celebrates when the unrighteous change their ways and return to the flock. In the secular sense this parable is used to illustrate that—

All of us, even the least, has value.

- *The Unjust Steward*

A rich man is about to leave on an extended journey. He entrusts each of his three employees with an amount of talents. To understand this story it is important to recognize that a talent was not a denomination of money but rather represented a measure of weight. It was equal to more than a hundred pounds and represented about three thousand shekels. Thus a talent represented several years' wages. According to the parable, each man is given according to his seniority and ability. To the senior employee the rich man gives five talents; to the second, two talents; and to the most junior employee, one talent.

The senior man takes his five talents and cleverly buys and sells so that before long he had doubled his money. The second servant does the same, returning with twice the sum he had been given. The third—the most junior—digs a hole in the ground and buries his talent.

When their employer returns and asks what they have done with the money, the two most senior return to him multiples of what he had given. But the third gives back to him that which he buried.[21] The lesson is that—

We are charged with doing the best with what we have.
Responsibility is associated with any trust.
A trustee cannot take the easy way out. He must use
his talent and time to see that the thing of value
is not only preserved but enriched by his efforts.

- *The Unforgiving Servant*

Peter came to Jesus and asked him a question. "Lord, how many times should I forgive a man who has done me wrong? Up to seven times?"

Jesus replied, "Not seven times, but seventy times seven. There is no limit to forgiveness." To illustrate the point he told his disciples a story.

There was a king who was good to his servants, often lending them large sums of money. The day when the accounts had to be settled, one man came before him who could not repay the debt. The king threatened to seize all the servant's possessions and sell him, his wife, and children into slavery. The servant begged for mercy. The king was so moved by the man's despair that he canceled the debt and set the man free.

Soon afterward the same man came across a fellow servant who owed him a small amount of money. He took the man by the throat and demanded payment. The fellow servant fell to his knees and begged for mercy. But the servant showed no pity and had the man thrown into prison until he could pay back the debt. The other servants were shocked by what they saw and told their master what had happened. The king summoned the man to come before him. He reminded his servant that when he had asked for mercy it had been given, but that he had failed to show mercy to someone who owed far less than the servant owed his master. The king ordered the man taken off to jail.[22]

To show you deserve mercy, give it to others.

- *The Prodigal Son*

A rich farmer had two sons. The youngest asked his father to share with him the property that was due him. The father agreed, and the young man took his share of money and goods and left home to settle in a far country. There he lived like a prince, gambling and spending his money on rich clothes and jewels. Night after night he entertained crowds of friends with dancing girls and enjoyed the most expensive wines. In time, he spent all his money. The country fell into famine and he grew poor. The young man's friends disappeared and his possessions were sold to pay his debts. Eventually, he was hired by a farmer who sent him into the fields to watch over pigs. He became so hungry that he longed to eat the pods that he fed to the pigs. Finally, in despair, he said to himself, "My father has many servants, all of them well clothed and fed, and here am I, his son, penniless and starving. I will go to him now and beg his forgiveness and see if I may work for him as a servant."

The father saw him coming from a long way off. Overjoyed, he ran to meet his son, threw his arms around his neck, and kissed him. The son told his father that he had done wrong and was not worthy to be called the man's son. But the father called for the best robe to be brought out. He put a ring on his son's hand and gave him new shoes. He killed a fat calf and called a feast.

When the elder brother returned home that evening from working in the fields, he was astonished to hear the sound of music and dancing. He asked, "What is the meaning of this?" The servants told him that his father was holding a feast in the honor of the brother who had returned. The elder brother was furious and refused to enter the house. The father came out to see what was wrong. "Father, how could you treat me like this? I, who have worked hard all these years, have never received anything from you. And yet for your other son, who left home and squandered his inheritance, you kill the fattest calf."

His father told him that he was very dear to him and that everything the father had belonged to him. But since his younger brother was lost and now found they should celebrate his return.[23]

Jesus used this parable to illustrate God's love and forgiveness. The secular lesson might be that—

No matter what mistakes our children make,
we love them just the same.

- *The Good Samaritan*

Only the book of Luke tells the most commonly quoted of Jesus's parables. One day a young lawyer asked Jesus a question, thinking he would trip him up. "What should I do to gain eternal life?"

Jesus replied, "You know the law. What does it tell you?" The young lawyer replied, "You must love God with all your heart, and you must love your neighbor as yourself." Jesus said the man had answered truthfully. The young lawyer persisted. "But who is my neighbor?" In reply, Jesus told the story of a man who was going from Jerusalem to Jericho when thieves beat him, robbed him, and left him for dead. Not long afterward, a priest came by and, seeing the wounded man, crossed over to the other side. Next came a Levite, one of the men who assisted the priests in the temple. He, too, gave a quick look and then passed by on the far side of the road.

The third traveler to approach was a Samaritan. Some historical perspective is necessary to understand this parable. The Samaritans were the enemies of the Jewish people. The animosity that existed between them was much like that which exists in the Middle East today between some of the Arabs and Jews. It was the Samaritan who, seeing the man half-conscious and covered in blood, was filled with pity. Gently, he cleaned the man's wounds with wine and oil before bandaging them with strips of linen. Then he put the stranger on his own donkey and took him to the nearest inn, where he looked after him all night. The following day before leaving, he gave the innkeeper money so the invalid would have whatever he needed. He told the innkeeper if more was spent he would give what was owed the next time he passed.

Jesus then asked the young lawyer, "Now, which of these three men was the true neighbor?" The lawyer replied, "The Samaritan." Jesus reminded the man that he was to behave toward other people as the good Samaritan did.[24]

We should be kind to everyone, not just our friends.

- *Mary's Compassion*

The books of Matthew, Luke, and John tell us that while Jesus was staying at the house of Simon the Pharisee and Martha, Mary, the sister of Martha and Lazarus, came to visit Jesus. She brought an alabaster jar of precious spikenard, and stood at his feet behind, weeping. She began to wash his feet with her tears and wipe them with the hair of her head, and kissed his feet, and anointed them with the ointment. Bible scholars feel Mary was more than likely a very well-known and prosperous prostitute. Still, it was a sign of great immodesty for a Jewish woman to allow her hair to flow over her shoulders in public. Simon, who was himself a leper, was full of self-righteousness. He could not understand how Jesus would allow a person as sinful as Mary to touch him and condemned him for it.

Judas was also offended that anything so expensive should have been used in this way. He believed the ointment should have been sold and the money given to the poor. Jesus's reply was that the poor would always be with them, but they would not always have him. Jesus defended Mary by saying that she was preparing him for the day of his burial and that her kindness would always be remembered.

Mary's actions show that she was not concerned about what people thought of her. She was not impressed with the customs and prohibitions of the day. She acted out of concern and love for Jesus rather than what would be considered popular or acceptable.[25]

If you are acting out of love and compassion,
don't worry about the criticism of others.

- *A Famous Metaphor*

Jesus's most famous teaching by metaphor was a part of his answer to a young, rich ruler who told Jesus how he was dissatisfied with his life. The story is found in the tenth chapter of the Gospel of Mark with other details in the books of Matthew and Luke. The young ruler wanted something he did not have, something he could not find through his present way of living. He was discontented with his whole way of life. While he had accumulated much in worldly possessions, life had not brought any real meaning or satisfaction to him.

When he came running to Jesus, he tried to flatter him by calling him "Good Teacher." Without catching his breath, he asked Jesus what he must do to inherit eternal life.

Jesus reminded him that only God is good. The man sought eternal life on the wrong terms. He was mainly concerned with himself. Jesus asked whether the man had kept the Commandments. The man said that he had. But Jesus suspected that this young man had not gained his riches honestly or by his own efforts. In those days, as in ours, often the rich had gained their wealth by fraud, taking advantage of others. What the man lacked was righteousness. Jesus told him to go and sell whatever he had and give it to the poor. The man refused to do it because, as the Bible tells us, he "had great possessions."

Jesus used humor to drive his point across. He said, "It is easier for a camel to go through the eye of a needle, than for a rich man to enter into the kingdom of God."[26]

Jesus was not teaching that the wealth one accumulates honestly by his efforts in helping others should be condemned. He was teaching that people who trust only in themselves can never find peace or contentment. People's possessions can imprison them in a world of illusions. They are owned by the things they possess. It is only by giving, by being charitable, that we can hope to gain God's favor.

Wealth for the sake of wealth is wrong.

For an example of using one of Jesus's parables in a closing argument, see chapter 29, pages 474–75.

Children's Stories

Parents have taught children values, ethics, and morals through the ages with stories about animals, children, and imaginary places. Children's stories are easily told and bring about an immediate association with the audience, since they appeal to the child in all of us.

- *The Goose and the Rooster*

Here is an old Jewish (Hasidic) tale. It is included under *Children's Stories* because the point is made with farm animals—a common component in narratives told to young people.

A maggid—preacher—decided to settle in a small town. When he met the community's rabbi, he explained his purpose. The rav said that he did not know how the maggid would make a living when the community already paid its rav such a small amount. The maggid told the following parable by way of answer:

> A goose belonged to a thoughtless owner and often suffered from hunger because her master forgot to feed her. One day, the man bought a rooster and placed him in the same coop with the goose. The goose was greatly concerned. "Now I shall surely starve. There are two of us to eat from my small portion."
>
> "Do not worry," retorted the rooster. "I can crow when I feel hungry, and this will be a reminder to our owner. Then we shall both be fed."[27]

Sometimes those we think will take from us actually help us realize more.

- *The Teddy Bear Who Had No Clothes*

Teddy bear stories have long been popular in American children's books. This is one of the most popular. Teddy Thomson was Kayta's teddy bear. When Kayta went to school, Thomson was left to play with the other toys. They began to tease him because he had no clothes. They teased him because he was not like them. The rag doll offered Thomson one of her dresses. Thomson put it on but thought it made him look silly with all the pink frills and ribbons. The clown offered a spare clown suit. Teddy put it on, looked in the mirror, and thought he looked even worse. In desperation Thomson got some of Kayta's finger paints and painted himself. When Kayta came home and saw Thomson, she burst into tears. "What's happened to your beautiful golden fur?" So Kayta washed her teddy bear in soapy water and hung him out to dry.

Kayta scolded her other toys for not accepting Thomson for what he was—a teddy bear. We use this story to teach our children that we need to accept others as they are.

Having the freedom to be ourselves requires
that we be tolerant of others.

- *The Fisherman and His Wife*

This centuries-old fairy tale comes from the Brothers Grimm. A poor fisherman lived with his wife in a hut near the shore. Neither of them cared much for housework, and the place was a disgrace. But the fisherman's wife would grumble, "We live in a place that is so poor it wouldn't matter what we did to fix it up."

One day the fisherman caught a huge carp. To his astonishment, the fish began to speak.

"Please, throw me back into the sea," it said. "I am no use to you, for I am not a fish at all but an enchanted prince."

The fisherman was so amazed he didn't know what to say but threw the fish back as it had asked. When he got home that night and told his wife what had happened, she criticized him and called him a fool. "You should have asked it to grant a wish, not just let it go like that. Go back and ask for a pretty little cottage instead of this miserable hut we live in."

The fisherman did as his wife told him. He called out to the enchanted fish, who immediately came swimming to the surface. The fisherman asked the fish to grant him and his wife a wish. The fish replied that the wish was granted and that when the fisherman returned home he would find a neat little cottage house.

When the fisherman got home to his new house he told his wife that now they wanted for nothing. His wife wasn't so sure. A few weeks later she began to complain that the house was too small. She told her husband to go back and ask the fish for a castle. She reminded her husband that, after all, he had saved the fish's life.

Reluctantly, the fisherman went back to the shore and called to the fish. The fish asked him, "What do you want now?" The fisherman explained his wife's wish. The fish told him to go home and find that his wish had been granted.

When the fisherman arrived home, he found his wife in gorgeous clothes ordering a whole army of servants around a huge castle. "Now our happiness is complete," said the fisherman.

But a few days later his wife was complaining again. She told her husband that she really thought they deserved a kingdom to rule. The fisherman argued, but in the end gave in and, against his better judgment, made his way back to the shore and called the fish. This time when the fish heard what the fisherman had to say, a great storm blew up. The fisherman could hardly stay on his feet in the gusts of wind and spray. But when he went home, he found his wife in a royal palace with a crown on her head and subjects waiting to see her. "Now at last," he said to himself, "she cannot want for anything more."

All was well for a week or two, until the morning when the fisherman's wife woke up with a new idea in her head. "Ruling a few thousand people like this is nothing," she declared. "I want to be ruler of the world!"

He tried to talk his wife out of her unreasonable wish, but she was not to be moved. When he told the fish their most recent wish, thunder rumbled overhead. The fisherman heard the fish tell him to go home and see that his wife had what she deserved. When he arrived home he found his wife back in the poor hut where they had started. The fairy tale tells us that they are still living there to this day.

Demanding too much may result in realizing little.

- *The Elephant and the Mouse*

This fairy tale has versions in many cultures; in Aesop's fables it is the lion and the mouse. A huge gray elephant lived in a jungle, where he was master of the kingdom. One day, while strolling beneath a banana tree, he heard a tiny crying sound. "Oh, please be careful!" he heard it wail. "You're standing heavily on my tail." The elephant looked down in surprise to see a little mouse twitching his nose. The mouse told him that if the elephant would lift his foot and let him go, he would reward him someday. The elephant replied that he did not intend to harm any fellow creatures but did not see how a creature as small as a mouse could ever benefit him.

A few months later the elephant was trapped in a net that had been set by hunters. As he was awaiting his fate, he heard a tiny voice whisper in his ear. "Don't worry, elephant, you have nothing to fear." The mouse from the encounter of months before bit into the net and began to gnaw. In the blink of an eye the elephant was free. The elephant thanked the mouse and went on his way.

Helping others, even the smallest, may bring big rewards.

- *Chicken Little*

A favorite fairy tale of children everywhere is the story of Chicken Little, who became frightened when an acorn fell on his head. He decided that the sky was falling and he must go at once and tell the king. On his way to find the king he met Henny Penny. She asked Chicken Little where he was going. He told her that the sky was falling and that he was going to tell the king. Henny Penny said she would come, too. On their way they met Cocky Locky. Chicken Little repeated his tale and Cocky Locky joined him. Then they met Ducky Lucky. Now the rumor was repeated by three people. Ducky Lucky joined into the procession. Then they met Drakey Lakey. When he heard the rumor repeated by four people, he decided to join in. Then they met Goosey Loosey, who, when told that the sky was falling, decided to join the others to tell the king. Next they met Gander Pander, who also came along. Finally, they met Turkey Lurkey, who, on hearing the rumor now voiced by Chicken Little, Henny Penny, Cocky Locky, Ducky Lucky, Drakey Lakey, Goosey Loosey, and Gander Pander, decided to join in as well.

We all remember what happened next. On their way they met Foxy Loxy, who asked where they were off to that day. All of them repeated the tale and their mission to tell the king. Foxy Loxy convinced them to follow him, as he knew a shortcut. But he didn't take them to the king. He took them to his den in the forest where he, his wife, and his children ate them all.

One who is willing to follow a false rumor is apt to fall victim to those who would use the rumor for their own gain.

- *The Emperor's New Clothes*

Hans Christian Andersen tells the story of two tailors who swindle an emperor and his ministers into believing that their cloth has the strange quality of being invisible to anyone who is a fool or unworthy. Even though no official or citizen can see anything, since the tailors did not weave any cloth, no one wanted to admit that he couldn't see the cloth and be called a fool or unfit. It was only as the emperor was walking naked before all of his people in a parade that a child finally said, "But the emperor has nothing on at all." It took a child to expose the tailors as the swindlers they were.

Sometimes deceit escapes detection simply because no one has the courage to expose it.

- *The Old Man and His Grandson*

Another Brothers Grimm fairy tale is that of "The Old Man and His Grandson," sometimes appearing as "Grandmother's Table." It involves a very old man, whose eyes had become dim and his ears dull of hearing. His hands trembled, and when he sat at the table he could hardly hold the spoon and spilled the broth on the tablecloth or let it run out of his mouth. His son and his son's wife were disgusted at this, so the old grandfather at last had to sit in the corner behind the stove, and they gave him his food in an earthenware bowl, and not even enough of it. And he would look toward the table with his eyes full of tears. Once, too, his trembling hands could not hold the bowl, and it fell to the ground and broke. The young wife scolded him, but he said nothing and only sighed. Then they bought him a wooden bowl for a few pennies, out of which he had to eat.

Once they were sitting at the table when their four-year-old son began to gather together some pieces of wood. "What are you doing there?" asked the father. "I am making a little trough," answered the child, "for you and mother to eat out of when I am big."

The man and his wife looked at each other for a while, and soon began to cry. Then they took the old grandfather back to the table and from then on always let him eat with them, and likewise said nothing if he did spill a little sometimes.[28]

Through the eyes of a child we see ourselves.
Those with a pure heart can teach us how
we are failing others.

Stories from Modern History

A great source for stories that make a point is history. The best historical anecdotes involve a familiar and respected figure. Familiar events told in a unique way with new facts and twists can intrigue an audience and empower a moral. A historical vignette about someone or something unfamiliar to the audience can be an excellent source for a "story within a story." The following stories are offered in chronological sequence.

- *Tobias Hobson*

In the late sixteenth century, Tobias Hobson owned a stable in Cambridge, England. He rented horses to students but required the lessor to take the horse standing nearest the stable door. This stipulation deprived customers of any choice at all. In 1630, the English poet Thomas Ward coined the phrase "Hobson's Choice":

> Where to elect there is but one,
> 'Tis Hobson's choice—take that or none.[29]

Saying we have a choice doesn't necessarily mean we really have one.

- *Jefferson's Commission*

When Thomas Jefferson went as American Minister Plenipotentiary to represent his country in France in 1785, he paid his respects to the French minister for foreign affairs. "You replace Monsieur Franklin?" asked the minister. "I succeed him," was Jefferson's reply. "No one can replace him."[30]

Great men can only be succeeded, not replaced.

- *Jefferson as a Lawyer*

Thomas Jefferson's grandson Jefferson Randolph once asked an old man, who remembered the president as young lawyer, how his grandfather had sounded as a speaker in the courtroom. "Well," said the old man, "it's hard to tell, because he always took the right side."

When you're right, you always sound good.

- *George Washington's Letter*

Following the Battle of Yorktown and the surrender of the British, the American Revolution was at a critical juncture. By 1782, officers in the American Army were on the verge of revolt. They felt that they had made great sacrifices in the war and had been ignored by Congress. General Washington called a meeting at New Windsor, Maryland, a little town northeast of Baltimore. The officers convened in "the Temple," a crude log structure used for meetings and church services.

No one thought Washington would speak. He hoped the officers could work out their grievances. When it became apparent that the officers were talking of revolt and seizing the government, the general decided to address the group. He cut a magnificent figure, standing six feet, three inches tall, and he had inspired his army through the hardships of both war and cold, bitter winters.

Washington had in his coat pocket a letter from one of the members of Congress, entreating the officers not to revolt. He reached into his pocket, pulled it out, and placed it on the lectern. He looked down at the letter and told the men that he could not read it. He took out his spectacles, put them on, and said, "I have grown gray in the service of my country, but I have also grown blind."

He read the letter. It is not known whether anyone paid any attention to the contents. But observers said there was not a dry eye in the house. The officers were so inspired by Washington's humble speech that they did not revolt against the government, and the formation of the new nation was assured.

Sacrifice and commitment inspire.
Those who suffer in a cause lead us to believe in it.

- *A Doctor's Mercy*

More than two hundred years ago a physician in France ran for the legislature, campaigning against cruelty. By today's standards he would be considered a bleeding-heart liberal. The doctor argued that public executions were unnecessarily cruel and akin to torture. The opposition in the legislature confronted him with the obvious argument—what do you suggest as a better way? Our French liberal did his research. He studied the ways of executing people from other countries and ancient times. He discovered that Italians used a very efficient way of carrying out executions, but they reserved it only for those of noble birth. The doctor suggested tests on cadavers. The analysis and test results were reported to the legislature and, in 1791, the doctor's proposal for the guillotine was accepted.

The doctor was Joseph I. Guillotin.

Mercy sometimes takes a cruel form.

- *Benjamin Franklin's Advice on Writing*

After Thomas Jefferson drafted the Declaration of Independence, members of Congress began to suggest changes and alterations. Benjamin Franklin noted Jefferson's distress over the revisions and commented that he had made it his rule to avoid becoming the draftsman of papers to be reviewed by a public body. Franklin told Jefferson the story of an incident from when he had been a journeyman printer. One of his friends was an apprentice hatter. He had served his time and was about to open a shop for himself. His first concern was to have a handsome sign board prepared with proper inscription. He composed it in these words: "John Thompson, Hatter, Makes and Sells Hats for Ready Money." The figure of a hat was appended to the sign. The hatter decided to submit it to his friends for their amendments. The first friend thought the word "hatter" unnecessary because the words "makes hats" showed that he was a hatter. It was struck out. The next observed that the word "makes" might as well be omitted because customers would not care who made the hats. He struck it out. The third said he thought the words "for ready money" were useless as it was not the local custom to sell on credit. He struck these words, and the inscription now stood, "John Thompson Sells Hats." "Sells hats!" said his next friend. "Why, nobody will expect you to give them away. What is the use of that word?" It was struck, and "hats" followed when it was pointed out as redundant with the symbol painted on the board. So his inscription was reduced simply to "John Thompson" with a picture of a hat.[31]

A good message can be conveyed with few words.

- *Andrew Jackson's Mother*

Andrew Jackson had a spartan mother. When he was five years old, she saw him crying one day. "Stop that, Andrew," she ordered. "Don't let me see you cry again! Girls were made to cry; not boys!" "What are boys made for?" asked Andy. "To fight!" she told him. After that, he never cried again.

When Jackson was twelve, a much older boy gave him a severe beating. Andy's uncle wanted to have the young man charged with assault and battery. "No, sir!" exclaimed Jackson's mother. "No son of mine shall ever appear as complaining witness in a case of assault and battery! If he gets hold of a fellow too big for him, let him wait until he grows some."

Fighters don't complain, they just wait until they are bigger.

- *He Voted against Jackson*

A man called on President Jackson to plead the case of a soldier who had lost his leg on a battlefield and needed to retain a small postmastership to support his family. "But I must tell you," the man said frankly, "that he voted against you."

"If he lost a leg fighting for his country," said Jackson, "that is vote enough for me."

Sacrifice is admired even in those who oppose us.

- *A Small Statesman*

The following story is told about David Lloyd George, the famous British prime minister. The chairman of a meeting introduced Lloyd George with the jocular comment: "I had expected to find Mr. Lloyd George a big man in every sense, but you see for yourselves he is quite small in stature."

"In North Wales," replied Lloyd George, "we measure a man from his chin up. You evidently measure from his chin down."[32]

Physical size has nothing to do with success.

- *A Letter from a Parishioner*

Arriving at Plymouth Church one Sunday, the famous minister and author, Rev. Henry Ward Beecher, found in his mail a letter containing just one word: "Fool." During the service that morning, he related the incident to his congregation, adding the remark, "I have known many an instance of a man writing a letter and forgetting to sign his name, but this is the only instance I have ever known of a man signing his name and forgetting to write the letter."[33]

Shallow people make themselves look foolish.

- *A Football Story*

The benchmarks of history are men and women doing something different and unconventional. Many bright stars mark the evolution of science, law, and the arts. They are the actions of iconoclastic individuals who betrayed convention because it just didn't make sense anymore. I'll offer an example that in the grand scheme of things does not seem that important. However, it is an interesting example of the idea that desperate times demand desperate measures. Convention is no bar to imagination.

In 1823, Rugby, a school in England, was playing another school at soccer and losing. The game was about to end. It was the last play of the game and William Ellis, a Rugby student, was determined that Rugby would not lose. Instead of heeling the ball for a kick he grabbed it, tucked it under his arm, ran for the goal, and scored. The other team cried foul. But Ellis's actions got people to thinking. Maybe the game would be more interesting if players were allowed to run with the ball.

When we watch on television the great spectacle of American football with its college and professional teams, huge stadiums, commercial promotions of teams and their insignias, we should realize that this is the result of the desperate action of a young man playing in a game almost two hundred years ago who decided he would do something different rather than lose the game.

Sometimes desperation is the mother of invention.

- *A Bad Decision*

History judges the choices men and women make. Some people's decisions have grave consequences for others. Because of the gravity of the issue and its potential for good or bad, decisions made by the U.S. Supreme Court are supposed to be reasoned, thoughtful, and fair. The judicial branch was envisioned by our founders as the last bastion of liberty and a brake on the excesses of the legislative and executive branches. Many Supreme Court decisions, such as those in *Brown v. Board of Education,* are historic in that they set into motion social changes that add to the majestic fabric of the most powerful nation on earth. But there is one Supreme Court decision that is so notorious in its error that it is often cited as the worst decision any court ever made.

Dred Scott was the slave of John Emerson, an Army doctor. Emerson took Scott to different Army posts in the United States and the western territories. After Emerson's death in 1843, Scott claimed he was free and no longer a slave under the Missouri Compromise after he had spent two years in the free territory of Minnesota. Scott began a series of lawsuits in Missouri in 1847 to gain his freedom. In 1855, the case reached the Supreme Court. The Chief Justice of the Supreme Court was Roger B. Taney. Taney was eighty years old at the time and was Andrew Jackson's appointee to fill the vacancy left by the death of the legendary John Marshall. Taney had freed his own slaves in 1818 but still believed that slavery was necessary.

The Supreme Court vote was along partisan lines. Seven Democratic justices were opposed by two Republican justices. Nine different opinions were issued. But Taney's was the one most cited for its far-reaching consequences.

Taney held that no black man, free or slave, was a U.S. citizen. Since no black man could be a U.S. citizen, he had no right to sue in federal court. Taney then ruled that Congress never had the right to ban slavery in territories because the Constitution protected people from being deprived of life, liberty, or property. According to Taney, slaves, like horses or cattle, were property and could be taken anywhere under U.S. jurisdiction.

While history condemns the *Dred Scott* decision as inherently wrong, it aided the anti-slavery cause. The new Republican Party gained strength when many fence-sitters joined the ranks of those more passionately opposed to slavery. Additionally, the decision widened the division over slavery within the Democratic Party.

Dred Scott and his family were purchased and freed by the abolitionist sons of Scott's first owner after the ruling, and he died the following year.

Sometimes bad decisions can be responsible for good results.

Lincoln Stories

Abraham Lincoln is America's best-known storyteller. He understood the power of the story to disarm antagonists and nudge toward agreement. Most of his stories were short anecdotes spiced with a bit of humor and a dose of psychology designed to get the listener to accept his point of view.

There are a number of books and essays compiling Lincoln stories. The best and most comprehensive is P. M. Zall's *Abe Lincoln Laughing.*

• *The Battlefield Pass*

A curiosity seeker wanted a permit to pass through the lines to visit the field of Bull Run after the first battle in July 1861. President Lincoln replied with the story of a man in Cortlandt County who had raised a hog of such unusual size that strangers went out of their way to see it. One of them met the old gentleman and inquired about the animal. The owner admitted that he had a pretty large critter, but he guessed he would have to charge the curious stranger for the privilege of viewing the porker. The stranger eyed the old man for a minute or two and then pulled out the desired coin and handed it to him. Then he started to go off. "Hold on," said the owner. "Don't you want to see the hog?" "No," said the stranger, "I have seen as big a hog as I want to see!"

The point that President Lincoln made to the curiosity seeker is that by visiting the battlefield he might happen to see a few live Rebels there as well as dead ones.[34]

Misguided curiosity can be dangerous.

• *Bap's Rooster*

General George McClellan was a little man whose vanity and lack of military imagination and aggression were known throughout Washington. He fancied himself a political rival to President Lincoln. After McClellan's fizzle before Richmond, Lincoln remarked to a friend that McClellan reminded him of a rooster that his friend Bap McNabb had. Old Sangamon Town held rooster fights. Bap entered his splendid red rooster. After the crowd arrived, the owners tossed all their chickens into the ring. But no sooner had Bap's rooster discovered what was to be done than he dropped his tail and ran. Bap was disappointed and picked up his rooster and went home, losing his bet. As soon as he got home he tossed his pet down in the yard on his own dung hill and the little fellow stood up and flitted out his feathers and crowed, as brave as a lion. Seeing this caused Bap to say, "Yes, you damn little cuss! You are great on parade, but you are not worth a damn in a fight."[35]

Some people are long on show and short on substance.

• *Joe Wilson's Henhouse*

In January 1862 there was public dissatisfaction with Abraham Lincoln's cabinet. Some people called upon President Lincoln to fire the entire cabinet. Shortly after Simon Cameron resigned as secretary of war, a delegation called on Lincoln to urge the reconstruction of his cabinet. He headed them off with a story about his friend Joe Wilson, who had built a log cabin not far from where Lincoln lived. Joe had put up a poultry shed and in it a lot of young chickens. His henhouse was being raided by skunks. One night Joe was awakened by the cackling and fluttering among his chickens, and he went out to see what was going on. He soon caught sight of half a dozen of the skunks, which were running in and out of the shed. Joe loaded his shotgun and fired into the skunks. Somehow he killed only one, with the rest of them scampering off across the field. In telling the story, Joe would always pause here, and hold his nose. His neighbors then asked Joe, "Why didn't you follow them up, and kill the rest?" Joe replied that it was eleven weeks before he got over killing one. "If you want any more skirmishing in that line you'll have to do it yourself."[36]

It's easy to criticize someone doing the dirty work.

- *Jones's Wife*

In 1862, General J. W. Phelps took Ship Island near New Orleans. One of his first acts was to issue a proclamation freeing the slaves. President Lincoln was indifferent to the act. He considered neither the military victory nor the unilateral proclamation significant. Lincoln used a story to illustrate the point.

"I feel about that a good deal as a man named Jones, who I once knew, did about his wife. He was one of your meek men, and had the reputation of being badly henpecked. One day his wife was seen switching him out of the house. A day or two afterward a friend met him in the street and said: 'Jones, I have always stood up for you, as you know; but I'm not going to do it any longer. Any man who will stand quietly and take a switching from his wife, deserves to be horsewhipped.' Jones winked and patted his friend on the back. 'Don't feel that way. The switching didn't hurt me any, and you have no idea what a power of good it did Sarah Ann.'"[37]

Don't worry about what other people do
that doesn't hurt you.

- *The Lion and the Woodsman*

W. C. Reeves of Virginia wrote President Lincoln advising him that he should surrender the forts and property in the Southern states after the rebellion. Lincoln in his reply to Reeves reminded him of the fable of the lion and the woodsman's daughter. Aesop, said Lincoln, reports that a lion was very much in love with a woodsman's daughter. The fair maid, afraid to say no, referred the lion to her father. The lion applied for the girl. The father replied that his teeth were too long. The lion went to a dentist and had them extracted. Returning, he asked for his bride. The woodsman again refused, telling the lion that his claws were too long. He went back to the dentist and had them pulled. When the lion returned to claim his bride, the woodsman, seeing that the lion was disarmed, beat out his brains.

President Lincoln used the story to illustrate the point that if he gave up all that was asked he left the nation vulnerable to further demands.[38]

Never surrender a source of strength.

- *Sam Brown's Credit*

In 1898, an eighty-eight-year-old man who knew Abraham Lincoln recounted a story the president once told that demonstrated the way he valued things. There was a lawyer, Sam Brown, in Illinois. He could not make a living practicing law so he decided to enter the merchandising business. He ordered a large bill of goods from an eastern firm. The firm at once wired its correspondent in regard to Brown's credit. The correspondent replied that Sam was worth over $100,000 and gave the following itemized statements of his possessions:

"He has a beautiful wife, with black hair and lustrous eyes; I would say she is worth $50,000. He has two children, one a little girl, who is the image of her father, and the other a bright and amiable boy. The girl is worth at least $25,000 and if the boy were mine you could not buy him for $50,000. Besides these objects of value, Mr. Brown has an old table worth 25 cents, an inkstand worth 10 cents and a pocket-knife worth 5 cents. But, over and above all I have named, Sam has, in the corner of his office, a great big rat hole that is worth looking into."[39]

Our family is the most valuable thing we have.

- *A Dog Bite Case*

The following story is a good example of Lincoln's skill in turning the opposition's facts against them. There was a man who by vile words first provoked and then made a bodily attack on another. The latter, in defending himself, gave the other much the worst of the encounter. The aggressor, to get even, had the one who thrashed him tried in circuit court on a charge of assault and battery. When Lincoln defended he told the jury that his client was in the same fix as a man who, in going along the highway with a pitchfork on his shoulder, was attacked by a fierce dog that ran out at him from a farmer's yard. In parrying the brute with the fork, its prongs stuck into the dog and killed him.

"What made you kill my dog?" said the farmer.

"What made him try to bite me?"

"But why did you not go at him with the other end of the pitchfork?"

"Why did he not come after me with his other end?"[40]

Don't demand moderation if you're not willing to give it.

- *Drunk in Church*

President Lincoln, on noting that only one member of his cabinet supported his policies designed to avoid conflict with England, resorted to the following story to illustrate his position. "A fellow out of my state of Illinois happened to stray into church while a revival meeting was in progress. This fellow was not entirely sober, and with that instinct which seems to impel all men in his condition to assume a prominent part in proceedings, he walked up the aisle to the very front pew.

"All noticed him, but he did not care; for awhile he joined audibly in the singing, said 'Amen' at the close of the prayers, but, drowsiness overcoming him, he went to sleep. Before the meeting closed, the pastor asked the usual question—'Who are on the Lord's side?'—and the congregation arose en masse. When he asked, 'Who are on the side of the Devil?' the sleeper was about waking up. He heard a portion of the interrogatory, and, seeing the minister on his feet, arose.

"'I don't exactly understand the question,' he said, 'but I'll stand by you, parson, to the last. But it seems to me,' he added, 'that we're in a hopeless minority.'"[41]

If we don't understand the issue, we end up disagreeing with everyone else.

- *A Greedy Farmer*

On one occasion President Lincoln said that the claim that the Mexican War was not an aggressive one reminded him of the farmer who asserted, "I ain't greedy about land, I only just want what joins mine."[42]

No one admits to greed.

- *The Englishman and the Indian*

Following a lecture delivered by Bishop Matthew Simpson in Wesley Chapel, Washington, D.C., to a large audience, Lincoln told the following story:

"John Bull met with a North American Indian, and in the course of conversation was very anxious to impress him with the greatness of the British Empire. 'The sun,' said Mr. Bull, 'never sets on English dominion. Do you understand how that is?' 'Oh, yes,' said the Indian, 'that is because God is afraid to trust them in the dark.'"[43]

Power bears watching.

- *Lincoln in Louisiana*

Abraham Lincoln often condemned apathy. To illustrate the vice of indifference he told the story of being in New Orleans and seeing a slave stretched out between two ropes with his master lashing him across his back. Some in the crowd urged the whipping on, some stood silently and watched, but most just walked on by. Lincoln's comment was that he could not understand how one human being could beat another, could understand less how people would shout encouragement or watch the beating. But the people that really disturbed him were those who could just go on about their business without being involved at all.[44]

Injustice is never repaired by ignoring it.

- *Lincoln's Gettysburg Address*

Four and one-half months after the pivotal battle at Gettysburg, President Lincoln traveled to the battleground to participate in ceremonies dedicating the cemetery. A renowned orator of the day, Edward Everett, was the featured speaker. His oration that day, November 19, 1865, lasted more than two hours. The president followed him with a speech that was so brief the photographers did not have time to capture Lincoln on film as he gave it. The only known photograph of Lincoln at Gettysburg is one taken three hours earlier. When Lincoln finished, he stepped back from the lectern and is said to have commented to those on the stage, "Well, that went over like a wet blanket, didn't it." Today Lincoln's Gettysburg address is considered by many to be one of the most significant speeches ever given in the English language.

Sometimes we do not realize the significance of our accomplishments until others can give them due consideration.

- *Lincoln in Richmond*

Charles Coffin, a newspaper reporter for the *Boston Journal,* documented what might have been considered a trivial and insignificant event in April 1865. We now know that it was one of those moments in history that served as a benchmark in the changing of laws, customs, and traditions.

Coffin was covering the capture of Richmond by the Union army. He had corresponded with his newspaper from the first Battle of Bull Run four years earlier and through Grant's campaigns in Virginia in 1865. President Lincoln arrived in the fallen Confederate capitol and was unable to find a carriage. So the president with his young son walked to Jefferson Davis's mansion. During the walk the president halted a moment to rest. An old black man removed his hat and bowed. He had tears rolling down his cheeks as he said, "May de good Lord bless you, President Linkum!"

The president removed his own hat and bowed in silence. It was a gesture that marked the end of the customs, laws, and traditions that had evolved from centuries of slavery.

Great moments in history are sometimes marked by seemingly trivial gestures.

Civil War Stories

- *Dr. James Berry*

Sometimes a high price is demanded for personal success. This was certainly true of Dr. James Berry, who rose to be Inspector General of the Army Medical Corps during the nineteenth century. As a young man, Dr. Berry volunteered for hospital work even though he had no experience. It took just eighteen months in the hospital before they declared him competent to serve as an assistant surgeon. Twelve years later he was a Surgeon Major in the U.S. Army.

Dr. Berry's professional career was a stormy one. He was often sent home under arrest for breaches of discipline. His fellow officers chided him for his effeminate ways, and this often provoked confrontation. It was only after Dr. Berry died in London in 1865 that the deception necessary for professional success was discovered. The highest-ranking medical officer in the United States Army was a woman.

A determined person is not deterred by artificial barriers.

- *The Rebel Prisoner*

A Confederate soldier was brought before General Benjamin Butler, a famous figure in the Union army, to take the oath of allegiance at the end of the Civil War. The soldier impudently remarked, "We gave you hell at Chickamauga, General!" The furious Butler warned him that if he did not take the oath immediately he would be shot. With some reluctance the rebel duly took the oath. Then he looked Butler in the eye and said, "General, I suppose I am a good Yankee and citizen of the United States now?" The General replied benignly, "I hope so." "Well, General, the rebels did give us hell at Chickamauga, didn't they?"

Some witnesses will stick to their stories no matter what.

- *Origin of "Taps"*

We have all heard the haunting melody of "Taps." But few know the story behind the song.

In 1862, Union Army Captain Robert Ellicombe held a position near Harrison's Landing, Virginia. The Confederates were on the other side of the narrow battlefield. During the night, Captain Ellicombe heard a severely wounded soldier moaning out on the field. Heedless of the soldier's Union or Confederate status, the captain decided he must recover the wounded man and give him medical attention. Captain Ellicombe crawled below the gunfire to reach the man and pulled him back to his own lines. There he discovered he had actually brought back a Confederate soldier, who was now dead. Lighting a lantern, he was shocked when he saw the face of the soldier: it was his own son. Before the Civil War, the boy had been studying music in the South and, without telling his father, he had enlisted in the Confederate Army.

Heartbroken, Captain Ellicombe asked permission to give his son a full military burial despite his enemy status. The request for a group of Army band members to play a funeral dirge was denied, but out of respect he was given one musician. He chose a bugler and asked him to play a series of musical notes he had found on a piece of paper in his son's pocket. The haunting melody that we now know as "Taps," used at all military funerals, was born.[45]

A father's love of his son who fought with the enemy inspired the tribute we now give to every fallen soldier. We never stop loving our children even when they oppose us.

- *Lee at Gettysburg*

He was his country's most able military leader. Most considered him a master strategist and leader among men. He rose to fame during a foreign war that resulted in his country's capturing its enemy's capital and forcing them into extensive land concessions. When civil war broke out twenty years later, he was the first man chosen by the president to command the nation's armies. He refused because of his loyalty to his home state.

In the bloody conflict that followed, Robert E. Lee demonstrated his military genius time and again. He won battles even when his forces were significantly outnumbered. Many in the North considered him invincible. It was Lee's strategy to take his army north to Pennsylvania. He hoped that one last decisive battle would bring an end to the war. Twists of fate and decisions made by lower-ranking Union officers led up to the historic Battle of Gettysburg on ground unfavorable to the Confederacy. General Longstreet told Lee that he was opposed to the battle plan. Longstreet wanted to withdraw to higher ground and make the Army of the Potomac attack the Army of Northern Virginia. The gray-bearded general disagreed. On the third day of the battle, he ordered the infamous Pickett's Charge. Almost all of General Pickett's division was wiped out attacking the Union in its fortified position behind a stone wall. When the Confederate troops came straggling back, Lee went out to meet them, proclaiming, "It's all my fault. It's all my fault."

Robert E. Lee today is admired not only for his accomplishments on the battlefield but because of the fact that he was always man enough to admit his mistakes.

Good men and women are willing to admit their mistakes.

Singular Individuals

- *Robert Fulton's Invention*

We studied in school the famous American inventors. One of these was Robert Fulton, who conceived and built one of the original steamboats. When Fulton was going to put the *Clermont* out for its first test run, a huge crowd gathered. For some hours the strange craft belched smoke and sparks from its tall, thin stack as engineers attempted to get up the necessary head of steam. The crowd continued to grow. Fulton ordered the crew to cast off the lines, and the boat shook and vibrated violently. Some of the skeptics in the crowd began to shout, "She'll never start! She'll never start!" Finally, the boat pulled itself together and actually started to move up the river. After a few moments of astonished silence, the voices of the scoffers resumed their shouts. "She'll never stop! She'll never stop!"

Pessimists will always find a reason to criticize.

- *Dr. Oliver Wendell Holmes, Sr., Obstetrician*

Advances in obstetrics have come along over strong opposition. Babies were originally delivered at home with midwives. As the medical specialty of obstetrics came into being, deliveries were moved to hospitals. But outbreaks of a mysterious fever began to rage through the hospital obstetrical wards. Within hours of giving birth, previously healthy women came down with infections that rampaged through their bodies. Febrile and delirious, many of them died within days of blood poisoning, their abdomens bursting with pus. Though the symptoms of childbirth fever had been known for centuries, in some hospitals up to 70 percent of women now contracted the disease and up to a quarter of them died.

Hospitals, only recently elevated from warehouses for the destitute sick, became feared. Meanwhile, women who were delivered at home with midwives did not develop childbirth fever. What caused the infections was beyond medical comprehension. It would be decades before French chemist Louis Pasteur would prove that germs, not vapors and humors, caused infectious disease. It would be still longer before a young English surgeon named Joseph Lister would discover putrefying bacteria in septic wounds, thus pioneering the practice of antiseptic surgery. Obstetricians, helpless in the face of so much dying, ventured their own theories—from self-poisoning by vaginal fluids, to a specific disease like smallpox, to the poverty and perceived immorality of many hospital patients, to the foul stench emanating from the body cavities of victims.

Among the first to propose a connection between the epidemics and the new practice of obstetrics was a young American, Dr. Oliver Wendell Holmes. A professor at Dartmouth College, Holmes had studied in Europe and was celebrated for combining learnedness with common sense. Hearing accounts in Boston of women's deaths and the deaths of doctors who had autopsied their patients, he theorized that some doctors were carrying the disease from patient to patient. They picked it up doing postmortem examinations on infected women. Doctors, he suggested, were carrying the lethal material in their examining fingers and instruments. Obstetricians, scandalized, attacked Holmes bitterly. A famous Philadelphia physician denounced his theory as a "vile, demoralizing superstition." Another blamed him for cruelly and needlessly alarming patients.

Holmes's contention was supported by the work of a Hungarian obstetrician, Ignaz Semmelweis. Semmelweis had practiced in the 1840s at the Vienna General Hospital, where there were two obstetrical divisions. One was run by doctors and medical students, the other by midwives. Autopsies were then the supreme instrument of medical education. Doctors and medical students performed several a day, racing back and forth between the morgue and the delivery area without washing their hands. Keeping careful records, Semmelweis noted that the incidence of childbirth fever was ten times higher in the doctor-run division than in the ward run by midwives, who did no autopsies. He showed that by making doctors wash with a chlorinated solution between examinations, he could reduce the cases of childbirth infection in the doctors' division to the level of the midwives' division. The authorities denounced Semmelweis more vehemently than Holmes.

Although the medical establishment castigated Drs. Holmes and Semmelweis, science ultimately accepted their then-novel theories. The introduction of antiseptic technique into obstetrics virtually eliminated the phenomenon of childbirth fever.

Tradition is sometimes an impediment to scientific advancement.
Standard and acceptable medical practice may
not be good and safe medical practice.

- *Inspiration for Invention*

Can you imagine what modern-day life would be like without the telephone? With all of today's conveniences it is difficult to argue that any one of them is more essential to social and commercial life than the telephone. Unlike a lot of scientific developments, its invention was not inspired by the dream of personal profit and wealth. Concern and commitment to others led to the discovery of the electronic transmission of the human voice.

Alexander Graham Bell was a schoolteacher—a speech therapist who worked with deaf children. He became interested in working with deaf children because his mother, also a teacher, was deaf. When Alex and his brother invented their first talking machine, the first word spoken by it was "Mama."

Alexander's wife, Mabel Hubbard, came from a rich family. Mabel was also deaf. One of America's greatest inventors devised an instrument that would let people talk great distances as a result of work he was doing to help deaf people—his students, mother, and wife—people he loved. The irony is that his invention never benefited any of them. But efforts that began as a search to help deaf people communicate led to the modern miracle that we find in businesses and homes throughout the world.

Sometimes caring is the mother of invention.

- *Late to Speak*

They tell a story about Albert Einstein, the physicist, one of the most brilliant men to ever live. As a child, he was late to talk. His parents worried about it. At last, at the supper table one night, he broke his silence to say, "This soup is too hot." His parents were amazed and asked him why he had never said a word before. The young Einstein replied, "Because everything was in order and I never had any reason to complain."

When things are going well, people don't complain.

- *The Discharged Priest*

Many people disagree about whether the words of the Bible should be literally interpreted. Many historians have argued that modern-day Christianity as practiced in most churches is a perversion of Christ's teachings. One man who lived more than a hundred years ago took the words of the Great Teacher to heart. He wanted to be a man of God—a preacher. In 1879, he traveled to a mining town in southern Belgium. A short time after he arrived a mine disaster injured many workers. This young man, who was then only twenty-five, worked night and day trying to rescue and tend to the injured miners.

He would scrap through the slag heaps for chunks of coal that the villagers used to heat their homes. He tended the miners when they were sick. He became the most popular preacher in the village. One day an official from the church visited and found this man living in a hut, dirty and dressed in rags. When the church elder asked him what he had done with his wages he said that he had given it to the miners. The church official criticized the young preacher for living more miserably than his parishioners. The man responded that this was his interpretation of Christ's teaching. The official was offended. He told the young preacher that if other young ministers acted that way they would destroy the church. The cleric dismissed the young preacher.

A few days later the young man saw an old miner walking along carrying an enormous bag of coal. He began to sketch the weary figure before he moved on. His first drawings were very crude and elementary. He was determined to do better. Since he could not preach to these people he could tell the world of their difficult existence and the virtue of these humble people through his paintings. This man, who was condemned for preaching the literal teachings of Christ, went on to become one of the world's greatest artists, Vincent Van Gogh.

There are many ways of expressing your concern
for your fellow man.

- *Approach to Diagnosis*

Dr. Joseph Bell served as the head of the Edinburgh University Medical School in the 1880s. History does not preserve a long footnote for him. He is remembered because of one of his students. He taught medical students the importance of listening to your patients, observing them, and using the information to assist in making a diagnosis and recommending treatment.

Dr. Bell ran an outpatient facility. His students would join him there and be fascinated by the deductions the good doctor made from subtle observations. On one occasion Dr. Bell told his class that the patient was a cobbler—a bootmaker. The surprised patient confirmed his trade. "How did you know?" Dr. Bell replied that the man's trousers were worn at the inside of the knee where the cobbler's lapstone sits.

On another occasion Dr. Bell told a brand-new patient that he was recently discharged from the Army where he had served as a noncommissioned officer in a Highland regiment stationed in Bermuda. The students were amazed. He explained to them that while the man was respectful, he did not remove his hat, which was the custom when entering an orderly room. The patient had an air of authority and was obviously Scottish. His complaint was a rash on his forehead, a disease normally contracted in Bermuda and not common in Scotland.

Dr. Bell was not particularly famous. He was just a good doctor who practiced and taught medical students that the essence of a good diagnostician was listening, observing, and deducing from the available facts. The only reason Dr. Bell is remembered today is that one of his students was Sir Arthur Conan Doyle, the author of the Sherlock Holmes mysteries.

A good diagnosis is the product of careful observation and attentive history taking.

- *Late to a Lecture*

The famous English biologist Thomas Henry Huxley was setting off to give a lecture. He jumped into a cab, crying, "Top speed!" The cabman whipped up his horse and they set off as fast as the horse could go. A thought then dawned on Huxley; sticking his head out of the window, he called to the cabman, "Hey, do you know where I want to go?"

"No, your honor," shouted back the cabman, "but I'm driving as fast as I can!"

If your direction is not clear, you may not get there.

- *A Premature Obituary*

Alfred Nobel was the inventor of dynamite. He became known worldwide as an arms manufacturer and amassed a great fortune. He awoke one morning in 1888 and read his own obituary. His brother's death caused the newspaper in its haste to research the life of Alfred and print it as the obituary. The obituary described Alfred Nobel as the "dynamite king" and the "master of death." Alfred Nobel was greatly disturbed by the thought that this was the way he would be remembered after his death. He was so distraught that he withdrew a large part of his fortune and founded the Nobel Foundation, which annually awards the Nobel Peace Prize to the individual who has contributed most to world peace. He did this because he didn't want to be remembered the way he found himself described in the mistaken obituary.

Our charity during life is what people remember when we are gone.

- *A French Duel*

At a Paris railroad station on the way to one of his numerous duels, Georges Clemenceau, the famous French statesman, surprised his second by asking for a one-way ticket. "Isn't that a little pessimistic?" asked the second. "Not at all," replied Clemenceau. "I always use my opponent's return ticket for the trip back."

The skilled are always confident.

- *"F" for Grammar*

A critic once had the temerity to correct Winston Churchill on the grounds that he should not have ended a sentence with a preposition. Churchill scribbled a note of his own. "This is the sort of English up with which I will not put."

You can look foolish trying to correct a knowledgeable person.

- *A Boy's Lesson*

Two boys got into a fight. One was rich, had nice clothes, lived in a beautiful house, and ate the best food. The other boy was poor, his clothes were ragged, and he had very little to eat. Not surprisingly, the rich boy won the fight easily. The poor boy complained, "If I had good food to eat like you, I could have won." This experience was the turning point in the rich boy's life. He would decide to give his life to helping the poor. He was one of the world's most famous men. His name was Albert Schweitzer. It was this humanitarian—missionary—doctor—writer—who, perhaps more than any other of the twentieth century, instilled a reverence for life and reminded us that all life is sacred.

God's gifts are to be shared, not exploited.

- *This Offense Was Not Frivolous*

A case buried in history and seldom studied today is *Murphy v. Western & A.R.R.* At the height of the Jim Crow laws in the South, a black man purchased a first-class ticket on a two-car train from Georgia to Tennessee. He took a seat in the car that was designated "for ladies and those who escorted them," and remained there without complaint for the early part of the trip. When two white women got on the train, their male companions told him to leave the car. Mr. Murphy refused to move, so the men assaulted him and threw him into the second car. This was the "smoking car," which was often referred to as the "Jim Crow" car. Blacks were the primary occupants, although some whites might sit there. Witnesses testified that the passengers in the ladies' car had no objection to Mr. Murphy staying in his seat. They told the assailants to leave him alone.

Mr. Murphy sought out a lawyer. Today, this would be one of those cases that many people would refer to as "frivolous." You can imagine that a lawyer suing a railroad for damages because a black man had been moved to the back of a train was not too popular in his community. The public was outraged at this lawyer stirring up frivolous litigation. But he pursued the case and recovered damages because the judge recognized that there could be no equality of right when the money of the white man purchased luxurious accommodations among elegant company and the same amount of money purchased for the black man inferior quarters in a smoking car.[46]

Many meritorious causes were viewed as frivolous claims at the time they were brought.

- *A Brave Texas Lawyer*

San Saba, Lampasas, and Llano lie about one hundred miles northwest of Austin, Texas. It's hard to believe how lawless this part of Texas was just over a century and a quarter ago. Cattle rustling was prevalent. The rustlers formed western mobs that would provide each other with protection and alibis when anyone was charged with a crime. Ranchers organized countermobs. As you would expect, the ranchers' "San Saba Mob" was soon taken over by unsavory characters. The trademark of the San Saba Mob was assassination by ambush. Three men would put exactly nine holes into the head and body of each victim.

In the years leading toward the turn of the twentieth century, more than fifty people were murdered in mob killings. Even a contingency of Texas Rangers had been unable to put a stop to the violence. The neighbors of a farmer by the name of Turner found him murdered. Jim and Matt Ford were mob members suspected of the killing. A young lawyer from Plano, W. C. Linden, ran for district attorney on a platform of ending mob violence. He promised a conviction of the Fords.

Two trials resulted in hung juries. Determined to get a conviction, District Attorney Linden while cross-examining Little Jim Ford began to chastise the jury. He noticed that mob leaders were sitting in the courtroom. He told the jury he knew they were too cowardly to convict a man backed by the mob. The judge had warned Linden against making this kind of statement, fearing what would happen. The defense attorneys, too astonished to object, let out a gasp when Linden turned and his coat flew open, exposing a Colt pistol on his hip. The young lawyer said, "Yes, I carry a gun. I carry it for just such occasions as this, and you all know I can use it."

When Linden left the courthouse for his hotel that evening, he was met by Little Jim Ford, who threatened him with a knife. Linden noticed Ford's friends nearby, all wearing coats they had not been wearing in the courtroom. Linden pulled his gun and said, "Why don't you carry out your plot?" One of Ford's relatives spoke up and asked what Linden thought the "plot" was. Linden responded that he knew they had put up Little Jim to start an argument so they could kill him and claim self-defense. He dared the crowd by telling them that because they were so used to murdering men from ambush they wouldn't dare kill a man who was facing them. "Besides, you don't know which one of you I'll kill while you're killing me. I think I can get three of you before you get me. Now you turn around and walk away from here, and I'll shoot the first man that stops or turns around."

Linden went on to his hotel. Later he got the news that the impossible had happened—the jury had brought in a verdict of guilty. Mob violence was ended in the San Saba area.[47]

Sometimes only men of courage can end violence.
At least a show of force may be required to ensure the rule of law.

- *Two Explorers*

In 1886, a man set out on a quest that would obsess him for twenty-three years. Some seven hundred and fifty men had died in the pursuit of this prize. Given the time and the resources available, it was now appearing to many that the challenge was too great—the goal unattainable.

Robert is a civil engineer with a burning desire to secure a place in history. In the 1890s, he hires a black man as a valet. Matthew becomes more than a domestic servant. He joins Robert in his dangerous mission and saves him from death more than once.

The fame that each of these men seeks is to be the first to stand where there is no east and west. To be the first man standing on the North Pole. These two men and their teams launch several unsuccessful expeditions. Robert loses the toes of his feet to frostbite. Several times they almost make it but weather and lack of planning and supplies turn them back.

In 1908, Robert, Matthew, and a team of courageous explorers set out on the sailing ship *Roosevelt* for their Ellesmere Island base camp. In 1909, the two friends are within a few miles of the North Pole. When they go to bed that night, Robert tells his friend that he intends to go alone the next day to the Pole. He does not want to share the honor. Matthew rises early, boards his dogsled, and gets within a short distance of the North Pole and stops. When Robert catches up with him, he asks why he had stopped. Matthew tells him there is plenty of honor to share. They would capture their prize together. The men reach the North Pole at the same time. By any measure, they are the codiscoverers.

Commander Robert E. Peary went on to receive great honor for his accomplishment. He was awarded medals, given dinners and receptions. Articles and books heralded his exploits. On his death in 1920 he was buried in Arlington National Cemetery. His grave site is topped by a huge globe honoring him as the discoverer of the North Pole.

Matthew Henson lived a life of anonymity. His accomplishment was not recognized until 1988, when his body was moved from an obscure cemetery in New York to Arlington. He is now buried near Peary with a plaque acknowledging him as "Co-Discoverer of the North Pole."

Henson never had any animosity toward Peary or was jealous of his acclaim. Both men accomplished the same thing. Henson could have stolen the glory if he had wanted to. But he was content to share it with his friend. Peary was driven by blind ambition and the need for recognition. On the other hand, Henson sought only the personal satisfaction of knowing what he had accomplished up to that time seemed to be an impossible task.

Personal satisfaction is sufficient reward for some while others seek only acclaim.

Jack Dempsey Stories

Jack Dempsey was one of the greatest heavyweight boxing champions of all time. He was also a good storyteller.

- *A Cowboy Offers to Buy a Railroad Ticket*

A story recalled by one of America's most admired prizefighters involved an incident that occurred when he was a young boy. It affected him for the rest of his life. The Dempseys were very poor and moved from town to town in Colorado trying to scratch out some kind of living. There were thirteen children in the family. The father had a hard time keeping a job and the family together. One winter at the turn of the twentieth century, as the family was attempting to make its way across Colorado in search of better opportunities, Mrs. Dempsey got seriously ill. Mr. Dempsey realized that she could not continue in the covered wagon. He decided to take all the family's meager savings and send the mother back to Denver to stay with her sister. Young Jack and his younger brother and sister were put on the train with her. However, the family had enough money to buy only Mrs. Dempsey a ticket.

As they were riding on the train through the snow-crested mountains, the conductor came by, checking tickets. He discovered that Jack did not have a ticket. Jack was almost nine years old. The conductor said he would have to throw Mrs. Dempsey and her children off the train since they had paid for only the adult's fare. Needless to say, Jack was anxious and frightened. He says it was on this occasion that he finally realized just how poor the family was.

A well-dressed cowboy sitting across the aisle told Jack not to worry because he would pay Jack's fare if necessary, but he was sure the conductor was bluffing about throwing them off the train. "Don't you worry about a thing, pardner," said the cowboy. In Jack Dempsey's autobiography, he tells that it was this incident that so inspired him later in life to accomplish something so that he could "pay for as many fares as I wanted."[48]

A kindness remembered is the seed for many acts of charity.

- *The Tonic Salesman*

Jack Dempsey reminisces in his autobiography about a tonic salesman who used to come to the small towns in Colorado where Jack's father was working on a ranch. The hawker would sell his worthless tonic as some kind of elixir, which would revolutionize the lives of those that purchased it. As Jack tells the story, some of the people in the town would fall for this line and some could see through it. Those who did fall for the barker's pitch and bought the stuff would always claim that it did all it was represented to do. It was obvious that their reason in doing this was that they would rather confirm the conman's exaggerated claims than admit that they had been taken.[49]

Some would rather vouch for fraud than be known as fools.

- *The Wheelbarrow*

Leonardo da Vinci, the great inventor and artist, is best known for having painted the *Mona Lisa*. However, few realize that he also invented the wheelbarrow. When Jack Dempsey was visiting Paris, he was taken to see the *Mona Lisa*. He was too embarrassed to admit that he didn't know who the great Leonardo was. An American tourist standing beside Dempsey asked him if he realized that Leonardo not only created the *Mona Lisa* but also invented the wheelbarrow. Jack replied, "You don't say? I'm very well acquainted with the wheelbarrow."[50]

People of modest beginnings are more familiar with practical inventions than artistic creations.

- *From Chicago*

Many years ago, Al Capone owned Chicago. Capone wasn't famous for anything heroic. He was notorious for enmeshing the windy city in everything from bootlegged booze and prostitution to murder. Capone had a lawyer nicknamed "Easy Eddie." Eddie's skill at legal maneuvering kept Big Al out of jail for a long time. To show his appreciation, Capone paid him very well; not only was the money big, but Eddie also got special dividends.

For instance, he and his family occupied a fenced-in mansion with live-in help and all of the conveniences of the day. The estate was so large that it filled an entire Chicago city block. Eddie lived the high life of the Chicago mob and gave little consideration to the atrocity that went on around him.

Eddie did have one soft spot, however. He had a son that he loved dearly. Eddie saw to it that his young son had the best of everything: clothes, cars, and a good education. Nothing was withheld. Price was no object. And despite his involvement with organized crime, Eddie even tried to teach him right from wrong. Eddie wanted his son to be a better man than he was.

Yet with all his wealth and influence, there were two things he couldn't give his son: he couldn't pass on a good name and a good example. One day, Easy Eddie reached a difficult decision. Easy Eddie wanted to rectify wrongs he had done. He decided he would go to the authorities and tell the truth about Al "Scarface" Capone, clean up his tarnished name and offer his son some semblance of integrity. To do this, he would have to testify against the Mob, and he knew that the cost would be great. So he testified.

Within the year, Easy Eddie's life ended in a blaze of gunfire on a lonely Chicago street. But in his eyes, he had given his son the greatest gift he had to offer, at the greatest price he could ever pay.

World War II produced many heroes. One such man was Lieutenant Commander Butch O'Hare. He was a fighter pilot assigned to the aircraft carrier *Lexington* in the South Pacific.

One day his entire squadron was sent on a mission. After he was airborne, he looked at his fuel gauge and realized that someone had forgotten to top off his fuel tank. He would not have enough fuel to complete his mission and get back to his ship. His flight leader told him to return to the carrier.

Reluctantly, he dropped out of formation and headed back to the fleet. As he was returning to the mother ship he saw something that turned his blood cold. A squadron of Japanese aircraft was speeding its way toward the American fleet.

The American fighters were gone on a sortie, and the fleet was all but defenseless. He couldn't reach his squadron and bring them back in time to save the fleet. Nor could he warn the fleet of the approaching danger.

There was only one thing to do. He must somehow divert them from the fleet. Laying aside all thoughts of personal safety, he dove into the formation of Japanese planes. Wing-mounted .50 calibers blazed as he charged in, attacking one surprised enemy plane after another. Butch wove in and out of the now broken formation and fired at as many planes as possible until all his ammunition was finally spent. Undaunted, he continued the assault.

He dove at the planes, trying to clip a wing or tail in hopes of damaging as many enemy planes as possible and rendering them unfit to fly. Finally, the exasperated Japanese squadron took off in another direction. Deeply relieved, Butch O'Hare and his tattered fighter limped back to the carrier. Upon arrival, he reported in and related the event surrounding his return. The film from the gun camera mounted on his plane told the tale. It showed the extent of Butch's daring attempt to protect his fleet. He had in fact destroyed five enemy aircraft.

This took place on February 20, 1942, and for that action Butch became the Navy's first ace of World War II and the first naval aviator to win the Congressional Medal of Honor. A year later, Butch was killed in aerial combat at the age of twenty-nine. His hometown would not allow the memory of this World Ward II hero to fade, and today, O'Hare Airport in Chicago is named in tribute to the courage of this great man. So the next time you find yourself at O'Hare International, give some thought to visiting Butch's memorial displaying his statute and his Medal of Honor. It's located between Terminals 1 and 2.

So what do these two stories have to do with each other?
Butch O'Hare was Easy Eddie's son.[51]

You can't predict what a man or woman may become from the status of the parent.

- *The Truman Doctrine*

Harry S Truman could not stand hypocrisy. When he was in high school he worked at Clinton's Drug Store in Independence, Missouri. While he worked there, he noticed that there was a small closet under the prescription case that contained several bottles of whiskey. On a regular basis, customers would come in for an early morning drink from the closet, paying ten cents an ounce, then carefully depart. The fourteen-year-old Truman saw these leading citizens and "amen-corner-praying churchmen" drink in private and then condemn publicly the vice of alcohol. Truman would later comment: "There were saloons aplenty around the square in Independence, and many leading men in town made no bones about going into them and buying a drink. I learned to think more highly of them than I did of the prescription-counter drinkers."[52]

Hypocrisy and statesmanship are incompatible.

- *Woodrow Wilson on Giving a Speech*

A cabinet member is said to have once praised Wilson for his short speeches and asked him how long it took to prepare them. "It depends," Wilson told him. "If I am to speak ten minutes, I need a week for preparation; if fifteen minutes, three days; if half an hour, two days, if an hour, I am ready now."

The more prepared a speaker is, the briefer the speech.

- *An Anatomy Lesson*

Josef Hyrtl was a nineteenth-century Austrian anatomist who spent most of his life as professor of medicine at the University of Vienna. Reportedly, he was once examining a candidate for the medical degree who seemed more than ordinarily nervous. "What can you tell me about the function of the spleen?" was the first question. The candidate wiped his forehead. "Herr Professor, I did know exactly what it was, I knew it just a minute ago, but now I've forgotten," he stammered.

"Miserable creature," cried Hyrtl. "You're the only man in the world who knows anything about the function of the spleen—and now you've forgotten it!"

Some people try to fake how much they know.

- *The Honest Doctor*

At the turn of the twentieth century, Dr. A. C. Scott bought a mansion in Gainesville, Texas, intending to convert the great house into a hospital. At about this time the Santa Fe Railroad hired Dr. Scott as the company doctor, and this meant he would have to move his practice to Temple. One of the first things Dr. Scott did when he arrived in Temple was buy a horse and buggy. This seemingly innocuous event led to Dr. Scott meeting Mrs. Sterling, a longtime resident of the city. Mrs. Sterling, hearing a rap at her door, opened it to find Dr. Scott's hat crushed, his clothes torn, and his hands scraped and bleeding. Dr. Scott asked Mrs. Sterling whether she had a gun or pistol in the house. Although her husband was away, and she was afraid of firearms, Mrs. Sterling admitted that she had a pistol.

Scott asked to borrow the gun, explaining that he intended to shoot his horse as it had run away and wrecked his buggy. Mrs. Sterling asked Dr. Scott whether that wasn't rather extreme under the circumstances. Dr. Scott told her that the horse was a fine animal, that he had paid $250 for it only the day before. He considered himself badly fooled but would not feel right letting some horse trader sell the animal again and possibly get an innocent person killed. Dr. Scott took the horse to a hackberry grove, shot him, and returned the gun.

The railroad medical practice in the small East Texas town grew into the world famous Scott & White Clinic.[53]

Responsible people don't pass on their problems to others.

- *General Electric Questions a Bill*

Charles Steinmetz was a German electrical engineer who immigrated to America. He became known as the "electrical wizard of Schenectady." History tells us that Steinmetz knew more about electromagnetic phenomena than anyone living at the time. He did most of his work in the early 1900s. Eventually, he was hired by General Electric and worked in their laboratory. Once GE persuaded him to work out some bugs in one of their new generators. After Steinmetz arrived, he walked around the generator humming, looking, and listening. He then asked for a piece of chalk. He climbed the ladder and made a mark. Then he told the engineers to cut the casing open at that point and take out exactly sixteen windings of the stator. The generator then worked perfectly.

Steinmetz sent GE a bill for $1,000. The accountants asked for an itemized statement. Steinmetz complied with the following:

Marking chalk on generator	$ 1.00
Knowing where to make chalk mark	$ 999.00

The bill was promptly paid.[54]

Experience is what gives labor its value.

- *Four Mothers' Boys*

Mothers decide the type of man their sons will become. But many believe if a young boy grows too attached to his mother his manly development will be stifled. The term is "momma's boy." Four well-respected—even revered—Americans' lives serve as compelling testimony against the proposition.

Ted was the type of young man that you might call immature. He never grew up. His mother had a compulsion for order, organization, and cleanliness. Ted shared that compulsion. Up until her death long after Ted's name was emblazoned in American history as a soldier, athlete, and outdoorsman, he still began letters to her with "Darling beloved little motherling."

Woodrow remained close to his mother well into his adulthood. He was known for his scholarship and was in all respects the quiet, introspective gentleman. He claimed that he came to love the best in womanhood through clinging to his mother's apron strings.

Frank couldn't even go off to Harvard University without his mother. For sixty years of Frank's life she ran everything, attending to every detail even long after he was married. Through devastating disease, rise to political prominence, and marriage to a woman she could never bring herself to approve, she continued to assert her dominance.

Harry's mother lived to be ninety-four, and right up to the end he was conducting business from his mother's bedside.

These men's lives all evidence the influence of their mothers. If their mothers had too much influence on them, history will perhaps forgive them because the men were Teddy Roosevelt, Woodrow Wilson, Franklin Delano Roosevelt, and Harry S Truman.

A mother's love makes the man.

- *A Mayor's Confession*

Reportedly, the famous New York mayor Fiorello LaGuardia felt that the New York police were being too hard on young offenders and tried to point out to them the difference between a mischievous prank and true juvenile delinquency. "When I was a boy," he said, "I used to wander around the streets with my friends until we found a horse tied up to a post. We'd unhitch him, ride him around town, then tie him up again."

"Are you trying to tell us," asked one of the policeman, "that the mayor of New York was once a horse thief?"

"No," replied LaGuardia, "I'm telling you that I was once a boy."

Don't judge children too harshly.

- *The Hawthorne Effect*

Research can be misused and misinterpreted. One of the most notable examples is the "Hawthorne effect," a centerpiece of the literature of social psychology in the 1930s and 1940s. The literature reported a study from 1927 to 1932 of factory workers at Western Electric's Hawthorne plant in Illinois. The study showed that regardless of the changes made in working conditions—more breaks, longer breaks, or fewer and shorter ones—productivity increased. Researchers drew many conclusions from this research. Some of the early psychologists suggested that the workers produced more because they saw themselves as special. Since they were participants in an experiment their interrelationships improved. Other academics claimed that the study proved that change itself is good and that anything done produces positive effects. A later study demonstrated that only five workers took part in the original study and two were replaced partway through for gross insubordination and low output. Today, psychologists call the Hawthorne effect a "glorified anecdote."[55]

Using an inadequate base for research may lead to false conclusions.

- *Naval Service*

Charlie Lightoller was a chicken farmer and retiree in England. As a hobby, he enjoyed sailing and owned a medium-size yacht. During the first few months of World War II, the call went out for all available ships to appear and volunteer their services for the transportation of troops. The English Army was trapped at Dunkirk. Charlie Lightoller, the chicken farmer, began the treacherous journey from the English coast to the French coast. On the way over his vessel was attacked by German planes. He had to dodge their shells until a destroyer appeared, which fended off the German attackers. He finally arrived at Dunkirk and began to load soldiers. He stowed them below deck as well above, lying on their stomachs. On the way back, he was again attacked by German aircraft and had to weave his craft through the treacherous waters, dodging enemy bombs. When he arrived back in England, he didn't have the fifty maximum that had been estimated by the Navy. One hundred and thirty-one soldiers got off the vessel.

The interesting thing is that twenty-eight years earlier, Charlie Lightoller had achieved fame as the Second Officer on the *Titanic*.[56]

Failure can inspire courage.

- *The Power of the Mind*

A story is told of a prisoner who volunteered for an experiment during World War II. Doctors were attempting to determine the amount of emotional stress that a soldier might experience on the battlefield. They told the prisoner they were going to withdraw blood from him until he lost consciousness to see how much blood loss he could sustain. Actually, the doctors were not going to withdraw any blood from the prisoner. A large vial was placed in front of him while he was lying on an operating table, and the tubing was connected so that the vial would fill with what appeared to be his blood. As the vessel began to fill, the prisoner's blood pressure rose, his heart rate increased, and, finally, he suffered a heart attack. Not an ounce of his own blood had been taken. These physiological effects resulted from the man's own perceptions rather than what was actually happening to him.

Anguish of mind can produce physiological effects.

- *A Question*

Upon discovering the atrocities that had occurred in the Nazi concentration camps following World War II, many people asked, "Where was God?" One Jewish survivor responded to those inquiries with another question: "You ask me where was God at Auschwitz or Treblinka or Buchenwald? I ask you, where was man?"

Don't blame God for the failures of man.

- *A Young Minister*

The Baptist church had one of the largest congregations in this small town in Alabama. The black congregation was led by its pastor, Rev. Vernon Johns. Johns was appalled at the brutality that was regularly visited upon the black citizens of his town by the police force, which was then all white. One day, some white policemen were brutalizing a black man when another black minister attempted to intervene. The white policemen then attacked the black minister and killed him. Vernon Johns condemned the actions of the police force and spoke out against this inexcusable violence. All that Johns suggested to the congregation was that they not stand by and fail to act but to stand up against brutality. He preached against silence and inactivity. He was one of these heroes who refused to hide.

The deacons of his congregation cautioned him "not to stir up trouble." After one of the most eloquent Johns sermons preached against brutality, violence, and prejudice, the deacons of the church voted unanimously to fire him. They wanted to assure the community that the preacher of their church was not stirring up trouble. After Vernon Johns was fired from the church, the deacons hired a new minister. He was a very young man, only twenty-seven at the time. They picked him because they wanted a minister who would "go along" and not be the source of any trouble in the black community. The name of the young preacher was Rev. Martin Luther King, Jr. Later, he would say, "We will have to repent in this generation not merely for the hateful words and actions of the bad people but for the appalling silence of the good people."[57]

People expected to "go along" sometimes don't.

- *When Yogi Got Lost*

Yogi Berra, driving with his wife to the Baseball Hall of Fame in Cooperstown, New York, realized that they were not only very late but hopelessly lost. When his wife complained, Yogi told her, "That's all right. We're making good time, though."

If you're lost, it doesn't matter how fast you're going.

- *The Space Shuttle Tragedy*

One of the greatest tragedies in American history was the explosion of the space shuttle *Challenger*. The government's investigation turned up the fact that Allan MacDonald, one of the engineers at the launch site, disapproved of the scheduled launch because he felt the temperature was too low to safely fire the propelling rockets, that the cold particularly affected the integrity of the solid rocket booster O-rings. Mr. MacDonald was overruled by a number of other engineers and representatives. His view was a minority one—the expression of an unpopular opinion. We know in retrospect that it was not safe to make the launch that morning. On the occasion in question, MacDonald became the target of verbal criticism and castigation because of his position. But history tells us that he was right.

The unpopular view may be the correct one.

- *The Rescuing Hug*

Kyrie and Brielle Jackson were born October 17, 1995, at the Massachusetts Memorial Hospital in Worcester, Massachusetts. Each of the twins weighed but two pounds at birth. Though Kyrie was putting on a bit of weight in the days following her arrival, Brielle was not doing as well. She cried a great deal, which left her gasping and blue-faced.

Brielle was having a particularly bad day. NICU (Newborn Intensive Care Unit) nurse Gayle Kasparian tried everything to calm her. She had her dad hold her. She wrapped her in a blanket. She suctioned her nose. Nothing worked.

Then she remembered hearing about a procedure done in Europe. She put Brielle in the incubator with her sister Kyrie. Almost immediately, Brielle snuggled up to Kyrie. Her blood-oxygen saturation levels, which had been frighteningly low, soared. She began to breathe more easily. The frantic crying stopped and her normal pinkish color quickly returned. Over the next weeks, her health improved steadily in her new, less lonely quarters.

The children survived their rocky beginning and in time went home with their parents. When last heard from, Brielle and Kyrie were healthy preschoolers.[58]

The love of another can strengthen us.
Innovation can be an essential of good medical care.
The best medicine is the love of others.

Stories from Plays, Books, and Folklore

Many plays, books, and folk tales carry a strong moral. The following is a short catalog of works, some fictional, some adaptations of historical events, that are empowered with a strong theme.

- *The Merchant of Venice*

Most people believe that if it is written, it must be true. When a fact is documented in a record, we give it greater credibility. By the same token, most people give high sanctity to and insist on enforcement of written agreements—contracts. Sometimes the terms of a contract are too harsh. It is the nature of the human spirit to insist on enforcement and performance of agreements, even hard ones, at the same time reserving the option to view cautiously and with suspicion contracts that by their terms are cruel or oppressive.

Antonio was a merchant who lived in a major mercantile city. His friend Bassanio wanted to court a beautiful lady. But the custom of the community required an elaborate and expensive romancing. He asked Antonio to lend him the money so that he might present himself before the fair lady as a suitor of equal worth among his rivals. All of Antonio's ships were at sea. His fortune was tied up in their cargo. As a favor to his friend Antonio borrowed the money from Shylock. Shylock was notorious for lending money under severe terms, and he detested Antonio, because Antonio was a generous man who often lent money without interest. This practice brought down the interest rates that Shylock could charge. As terms for the loan, Shylock insisted that if Antonio failed in his obligation he would be bound to repay with a pound of his own living flesh.

With the help of the wealth borrowed by Antonio, Bassanio was able to win his heart's love, Portia. Then bad times fell upon Antonio. His ships were lost at sea. He was unable to pay the debt. Shylock sued to enforce their written contract calling for a pound of Antonio's flesh. Portia, who was a wealthy woman, offered to pay Shylock several times the value of Antonio's bond, but he refused to accept it. He insisted on specific performance of the contract.

The men appeared in court and Shylock made his case. The court was about to announce its decision. Shylock had taken out his knife and was steadily sharpening it. Suddenly there appeared in court a young lawyer recommended by the most learned lawyer in the community. (Actually, the young lawyer was Portia in disguise, a person who had no legal training but who had been tutored by the learned lawyer.) The lawyer entreated Shylock to take the money that had been offered, which was many times the value of the bond. Again, Shylock refused and insisted on his pound of flesh. Portia then pointed out that while the written contract provided for a pound of flesh, it did not account for the shedding of a single drop of blood. The result was that not only was Shylock unable to extract his pound of flesh but he was also forced to convert to Christianity and forfeit half his wealth.

The lesson of Shakespeare's *The Merchant of Venice* is that documents and agreements are normally respected, but when the result of enforcing them is harsh and cruel, it is human nature that we look at them with a keen eye to the fine print to avoid an injustice.

Look closely at harsh agreements.

- *Preparation*

According to an old legend, a woman went to heaven and looked about the streets for her mansion. She saw many beautiful homes, but hers was not among them. At last, on a small side street, she saw a tiny cottage. She was told it belonged to her. She was indignant, but an angel said, "When you were on Earth you built a beautiful and expensive home, but you sent very little material here for your heavenly home. Here we can only use virtue, charitable deeds, and kindly thoughts as building materials. You failed to send much of it up ahead of you."

We are measured by good deeds, not material possessions.

- *Lonesome Dove*

One of my favorite books is *Lonesome Dove*. Larry McMurtry's story, set in the mid-nineteenth century, portrays a fictional cattle drive from Texas to Montana. Augustus (Gus) McRae and W. F. Call, former Texas Rangers, are lifelong friends. Gus is a romantic figure, who has a way with women and the sense to leave well enough alone. Call is the pragmatist, whose dream is a cattle ranch in Montana.

While riding scout for the herd, Gus is ambushed by Indians and narrowly escapes. He takes an arrow in his leg. He barely makes it to a settlement, where the doctor has to remove his leg. When the doctor tells Gus that he will have to remove the other leg for him to live because of the spread of gangrene, Gus refuses. As Gus lies dying, he asks Captain Call for a promise—to be buried by a little grove of live oaks on the south Guadalupe River. Call thinks his friend is delirious.

"You want me to haul you to *Texas*? We just got to Montana."[59]

The reason Gus wants to be buried there is because he had picnicked with his friend Clara on that spot, long ago.

Call grants McRae's wish and promises to bury him in Texas. The rest of the novel depicts the heroic challenges that Captain Call faces in keeping his promise to his friend.

When Call passes Clara's ranch in Nebraska, she encourages him to bury Gus on her place and get on back to Montana to be with his men and his son. It would have been the easy thing to do, but Call had made his promise. Captain Call carries Gus's body in a buggy three thousand miles through hostile territory and rugged terrain. People along the way come out to see this fool who is carrying his friend back to Texas because he made a promise. Toward the end of his trip, the buggy comes apart crossing a river. He finally runs out of water; the mule that had been pulling the buggy is too weak to continue. Call and his horse, pulling a travois, finally make it to the Guadalupe, where he buries Gus.

A lot of people were inspired by the book. Millions more were moved by the miniseries starring Robert Duvall and Tommy Lee Jones. The story of *Lonesome Dove* reminds us that—

Keeping your word requires commitment and personal sacrifice.

- *Texas*

In James Michener's novel *Texas,* he describes the plight of Emma Larkin. Emma lived in the 1860s on the Texas frontier. Her family was killed by the Comanche, and she was dragged away by the Indians. In those days it was the custom of the Comanche to steal a child or two in the course of their raids and then torture the child by burning off his ears and nose. They did this to Emma.

Even though Emma Larkin and the Comanche chief Matark are fictional, Michener's description is not. These types of incidents did occur and are documented in Texas history. When the chief was asked by a white man why they abused the child so, his reply was simple. "It is our custom."[60] This was the only explanation that was ever offered, and it would seem that the Comanche gave no more thought to what they were doing than simply that—it was their custom.

Cruelty is acceptable if no one objects.

- *The Carpenter*

A story that probably comes from American folklore involves a farmer suffering through the hard years of the Depression. The farmer and his next-door neighbor were both widowers. Their children had moved away and they had only each other to talk to during the day. One day the farmer saw a calf on his neighbor's property that he thought was his. When he confronted his neighbor, the neighbor claimed it as his own.

After that, the two men didn't talk for years.

One day a hobo showed up at the farmer's door asking for something to eat. The farmer didn't have a lot but offered him what he had. The stranger then asked if there wasn't some work around the place he could do to earn his keep. The farmer asked him what he could do, and the hobo told him that before the Depression he had been an expert carpenter. The idea of building a fence to separate his land from his neighbor's had been festering in the farmer's mind for some time. The farmer told of his long-standing feud with his neighbor and said that if the man would build a fence across the creek line that separated his and his neighbor's land, he would bed and board him for a few weeks. He said, "I want a fence so high that I won't ever have to see my neighbor again." The stranger nodded and smiled and said, "I know just what you need. I can build it for you."

The next day, the farmer left to take one of his calves to market. When he got back, to his shock and dismay he saw that his hired man had not built a fence but instead had constructed a bridge across the creek. He was about to chew the carpenter out when he saw his neighbor coming across the bridge leading a cow on a rope behind him. The neighbor held out his hand and told the farmer that he would never have had the courage to build the bridge but admired him for doing so. He handed the farmer the lead for the cow and said, "That calf was probably yours anyway."

The carpenter was standing off to the side, witnessing the conversation. A broad smile stretched across his face. The story goes that he was never again seen by the farmer afterward.

It's better to build bridges than walls.

- *Two Angels*

Two traveling angels stopped to spend the night in the home of a wealthy family. The family was rude and refused to let the angels stay in the mansion's guest room. Instead, the angels were given a small space in the cold basement. As they made their bed on the hard floor, the older angel saw a hole in the wall and repaired it. When the younger angel asked why, the older angel replied, "Things aren't always what they seem."

The next night the pair came to rest at the house of a very poor but very hospitable farmer and his wife. After sharing what little food they had, the couple let the angels sleep in their bed where they could have a good night's rest. When the sun came up the next morning, the angels found the farmer and his wife in tears. Their only cow, whose milk had been their sole income, lay dead in the field. The younger angel was infuriated and asked the older angel, "How could you have let this happen? The first family had everything, yet you helped them. The second family had little but was willing to share everything, and you let the cow die."

"Things aren't always what they seem," the older angel replied. "When we stayed in the basement of the mansion, I noticed there was gold stored in that hole in the wall. Since the owner was so obsessed with greed and unwilling to share his good fortune, I sealed the wall so he couldn't find it.

"Then last night as we slept in the farmer's bed, the angel of death came for his wife. I gave him the cow instead."

Things aren't always what they seem to be.

- *Flowers for Algernon*

The touching book *Flowers for Algernon*, by Daniel Keyes, documents the pain of a mentally retarded person. Some people recognize this story from the movie *Charly*, based on this book. Cliff Robertson plays a man mentally retarded since birth. He worked in a bakery as a janitor. Charly was chosen for a medical experiment to cure his mental handicap. The surgery was a success. Charly not only was cured, he developed a brilliant mind. There was just one complication: the cure was only temporary. After a period of months, Charly would return to a state of retardation. At the end of the story, right before he relapsed into his mental cloud of intellectual deficiency, Charly was the epitome of a man without hope—a man whose anguish was all the greater because he knew what his life could have been. The story was about dreams, ambition, and hope—qualities we all possess but take for granted. Charly teaches us that the destruction of the human mind is a much more severe trauma to any person who has experienced what we call independence. It is only because he has known what he could become that he is devastated by what he has left.

To really hurt a man, take away his hope.

- *Catch-22*

Sometimes life presents no-win situations. This was the premise of Joseph Heller's novel of World War II, *Catch-22* (1961). Yossarian, Heller's protagonist, is determined to avoid being killed. He reasons that the best way to achieve his goal is to be grounded by reason of insanity. But according to *Catch-22*, anyone who wants to get out of combat duty can't really be crazy. *Catch-22* specified that a concern for one's own safety in the face of dangers that were real and immediate was the process of a rational mind. In short, if Yossarian flew the missions he was crazy and didn't have to; but if he didn't want to, he was sane and had to.

Sometimes you are damned if you do and damned if you don't.

- *The Price of Victory*

The legendary American sports writer Grantland Rice was a dedicated college football fan. He believed in the purity of the game and that victories achieved by breaking the rules were meaningless.

> For when the One Great Scorer comes,
> to write against your name—
> He marks—not that you won or lost—
> but how you played the game.[61]

It's not whether you win or lose but how you play the game.

PERSONAL STORIES

Storytellers often use personal experiences for material. They tell of some real-life situation in the first person. Personal stories can be powerful and persuasive, but I have heard many speakers who fail to appreciate that something that happened to them might not be that interesting or instructive to others. Stories that are truly personal to the speaker are best if they relate a moving or memorable experience.

Some lecturers tell third-person anecdotes. I include some examples in this section for illustration. But for the most part, I continue to believe that the best personal stories are descriptions of life that are truly unique and personal to the storyteller. My belief is that if the story is not unique, touching, and compelling of a strong moral, the speaker had best leave out private moments of truth. On the other hand, the personal experience of a third person related by the storyteller may convey a powerful message.

- *Rev. Martin Luther King, Jr.'s Story of Marian Anderson*

On August 27, 1967, at the Mount Pisgah Missionary Baptist Church in Chicago, Illinois, the Reverend Martin Luther King, Jr., told the following story about a famous black American:

There is a magnificent lady by the name Marian Anderson. She started out as a little girl singing in the choir of the Union Baptist Church in Philadelphia, Pennsylvania. And then came that glad day when she made it. And she stood in Carnegie Hall, with the Philharmonic Orchestra in the background in New York, singing with the beauty that is matchless. Then she came to the end of that concert, singing "Ave Maria" as nobody else can sing it. And they called her back and back and back and back again, and she finally ended by singing, "Nobody Knows De Trouble I Seen." And her mother was sitting out in the audience, and she started crying; tears were flowing down her cheeks. And the person next to her said, "Mrs. Anderson, why are you crying? Your daughter is scoring tonight. The critics tomorrow will be lavishing their praise on her."

And Mrs. Anderson looked over with tears still flowing and said, "Im not crying because I'm sad, I'm crying for joy. When Marian was growing up, I worked in a kitchen till my hands were all but parched, my eyebrows all but scalded. I was working there to make it possible for my daughter to get an education. I remember one day Marian came to me and said, 'Mother, I don't want to see you having to work like this.' And I looked down and said, 'Honey, I don't mind it. I'm doing it for you and I expect great things of you.'"

In later years, somebody asked Marian Anderson, "Miss Anderson, what has been the happiest moment of your life? Was it the moment that you had your debut in Carnegie Hall in New York?" She said, "No, that wasn't it." "Well, Miss Anderson, was it the moment that Sibelius of Finland declared that his roof was too low for such a voice?" "No, that wasn't it." "Miss Anderson, was it the moment that Toscanini said that a voice like yours comes only once in a century?" "No, that wasn't it." "What was it then, Miss Anderson?" And she looked up and said quietly, "The happiest moment in my life was the moment that I could say, 'Mother, you can stop working now.'" Marian Anderson realized that she was where she was because somebody helped her to get there.[62]

Great people realize their achievements are due to the help of others.

- *The Generous Customer*

We grew up very poor. I went to work at an early age. When I was fifteen years old, I worked in a grocery store in Angleton, Texas, every day after school until 10:00 PM and all day Saturday. I stocked the shelves, bagged the groceries, and carried them out to the customers' cars. A young man can learn a lot about people in that kind of job. Some of the well-to-do people in that small town would tip generously. Some of the well-to-do people didn't tip at all.

One elderly black man came to the store every Saturday driving an old beat-up truck. His was a big family. It took a lot of groceries to feed that family and this old black man was one of the store's best customers. I don't remember ever carrying out less than five or six bags to that old beat-up pickup truck. As poor as the old man was, he was the best tipper. He would usually give me fifty cents for carrying his groceries to his truck. Fifty cents in those days was a big tip—an hour of wages. I always thought the man should be treated with respect because he was polite, cared for and loved his family, worked hard, and didn't ask anything from anyone.

One day the store manager pulled me aside and said, "Did you address that [a word I wouldn't use] as 'sir'?" I told him that I had. "When he gave me my tip I said, 'Thank you, sir.'" The manager told me I should never address a black man as "mister" or "sir." Well, I must tell you that I would normally do what my boss told me to do. But in this instance, that was one order that went into my mental file 13. Until the last day I worked at that grocery store, that old black man was still "mister" and "sir" to me because of his generosity and what he stood for.

Virtue knows no color.

- *A Stormy Day*

A little girl walked to and from school daily. Though the weather that morning was questionable and clouds were forming, she made her daily trek to the elementary school. As the afternoon progressed, the winds whipped up, along with thunder and lightning.

The mother of the little girl felt concerned that her daughter would be frightened as she walked home from school and she herself feared that the electrical storm might harm her child. Along with the roar of thunder, lightning, like a flaming sword, would cut through the sky. Full of concern, the mother quickly got into her car and drove along the route to her child's school. As she did so, she saw her little girl walking along, but at each flash of lightning, the child would stop, look up, and smile.

Another and another followed quickly and with each flash the little girl would look at the streak of lightning and smile. When the mother drew up beside the child she lowered the window and called to her. "What are you doing? Why do you keep stopping?" The child answered, "I'm trying to look pretty. God keeps taking my picture."

May God bless you today as you face the storms
that come your way.

- *Big Wally's Big Heart*

For years now whenever Christmas pageants are talked about in a certain little town in the Midwest, someone is sure to mention the name of Wallace Purling.

Wally's performance in one annual production of the Nativity play has slipped into the realm of legend. But the old-timers present in the audience that night never tire of recalling exactly what happened.

Wally was nine that year and in the second grade, though he should have been in the fourth. Most people in town knew that he had difficulty in keeping up. He was big and clumsy, slow in movement and mind.

Still, Wally was well liked by the other children in his class, all of whom were smaller than he, though the boys had trouble hiding their irritation when Wally would ask to play ball with them or any game, for that matter, in which winning was important.

Most often they'd find a way to keep him out, but Wally would hang around anyway—not sulking, just hoping. He was always a helpful boy, a willing and smiling one, and the natural protector, paradoxically, of the underdog. Sometimes if the older boys chased the younger ones away, it would always be Wally who'd say, "Can't they stay? They're no bother."

Wally fancied the idea of being a shepherd with a flute in the Christmas pageant that year, but the play's director, Miss Lumbard, assigned him to a more important role. After all, she reasoned, the innkeeper did not have too many lines, and Wally's size would make his refusal of lodging to Joseph more forceful.

And so it happened that the usual large, partisan audience gathered for the town's yearly extravaganza of crooks and creches, of beards, crowns, halos, and a whole stage full of squeaky voices. No one on stage or off was more caught up in the magic of the night than Wallace Purling. They said later that he stood in the wings and watched the performance with such fascination that from time to time Miss Lumbard had to make sure he didn't wander onstage before his cue.

Then the time came when Joseph appeared, slowly, tenderly guiding Mary to the door of the inn. Joseph knocked hard on the wooden door set into the painted backdrop. Wally the inkeeper stood inside, waiting.

"What do you want?" Wally said, swinging the door open with a brusque gesture.

"We seek lodging."

"Seek it elsewhere." Wally looked straight ahead but spoke vigorously. "The inn is filled."

"Sir, we have asked everywhere in vain. We have traveled far and are very weary."

"There is no room in this inn for you." Wally looked properly stern.

"Please, good innkeeper, this is my wife, Mary. She is heavy with child and needs a place to rest. Surely you must have some small corner for her. She is so tired."

Now, for the first time, the innkeeper relaxed his stiff stance and looked down at Mary. With that, there was a long pause, long enough to make the audience a bit tense with embarrassment.

"No! Begone!" the prompter whispered from the wings.

"No!" Wally repeated automatically. "Begone!"

Joseph sadly placed his arm around Mary and Mary laid her head upon her husband's shoulder and the two of them started to move away. The innkeeper did not return inside his inn, however. Wally stood there in the doorway, watching the forlorn couple. His mouth was open, his brow creased with concern, his eyes filling unmistakably with tears.

And suddenly this Christmas pageant became different from all the others.

"Wait, don't go, Joseph," Wally called out. "Bring Mary back." And Wallace Purling's face grew into a bright smile. "You can have my room."

Some people in town thought that the pageant had been ruined. Yet others—many, many others—considered it the most Christmas of all Christmas pageants they had ever seen.[63]

Compassion oftentimes moves people to do things
that don't fit with life's script.

- *My Mother's Suitcase*

Some years ago, my mother took a trip to attend a funeral of a close family member. On her way home, her suitcase was stolen at the airport. The person who stole the suitcase found inside it the following:

- Some old family photographs, one dating back to the early 1900s.
- Some letters from her deceased mother.
- The deed of a small interest in a family farm.
- Two or three modest dresses.
- Her only warm coat.
- Miscellaneous toiletries and underwear.

The person who stole the suitcase and later opened it probably threw it in the nearest garbage can, saying, "Nothing in here but junk." I am sure it was worthless to them.

But the suitcase and things in it were of great value to my mother. The pictures had been given to her by relatives at the funeral. The letters from her mother were the only ones she had. It took us a lot of time and trouble to get proof of the deed, since it had been executed by people no longer living.

If someone were asked to value that suitcase and its contents, what would be fair and reasonable? To the person taking it, it would be "zero." To my mother, thousands of dollars would not repay her. Perhaps thousands of dollars would be too much, but reasonable compensation would be a lot more than the value that was placed on it by the person who stole it, looked at it, and threw it away saying it was "worthless."

The thief may find little value in that
which the owner prizes.

- *A Building Fire*

Some years back, a one-story office building in Houston caught fire. By the time the fire department got there, the building was ablaze. The building covered most of a city block. Crowds gathered at the front and back of the building. The firemen couldn't get in the back of the building. The crowd in back saw the firemen come around, look at the fire, talk to each other, and then go around to the front.

The crowd in the front of the building saw firemen breaking out windows and crawling into the building to save people.

All the people inside the building were saved. But if you asked the people at the back of the building what they thought of the fire department's performance, they would say they were inept, maybe even cowards. The people at the front of the building would say the firemen were all heroes. Both crowds were looking at the same event but from different vantage points.

Judgments depend on one's point of view.

- *A Child's Kite*

Billy Graham tells the story of seeing a small boy who was out flying a kite. It was a fine day for kite flying. The wind was brisk, and large, billowy clouds were blowing across the sky. The kite went up until it was entirely hidden by the clouds.

"What are you doing?" Graham asked the little boy.

"I'm flying a kite," he replied.

"Flying a kite, are you?" Billy said. "How can you be sure? You can't see your kite."

"No," said the boy, "I can't see it, but every little while I feel a tug, so I know for sure that it's there."

It takes just a tug to let you know
what you believe is there.

- *The Children of London*

Billy Graham illustrates the point that children are not so much upset by physical insecurity as they are by emotional upheavals or the lack of love. During World War II, when Britain was being bombed nightly, many British parents sent their children to the countryside, where they could be safe from the bombings. But studies made after the war showed that the children who stayed in London with their parents where, despite the bombings, they could have the security of love and understanding were less disturbed than those who were isolated from home in areas of comparative safety.

No matter how safe the place, it can never be
a substitute for a parent's love.

- *The Broken Toy*

Years ago one of my friends told me the story of the boy who wanted a toy for Christmas. The family was very poor, but somehow his mother bought the toy. The boy played with the toy on Christmas Day, and toward the evening the toy broke. The child got upset and carried on and carried on. Finally, his mother said, "Son, don't get so upset about small things." The boy replied, "Mother, what are small things?"

What is important is a matter of perspective.

- *A Parent's Request*

Many years ago my pastor, Charles Williams, now deceased, told this true story:

A two-year-old girl was diagnosed with a fatal blood disorder. The only treatment was a transfusion. The doctors performed medical tests on the family and found that the most compatible donor was the girl's older brother. The parents sat down the eight-year-old boy and told him that the doctors needed his blood to save his sister's life. They wanted to know whether he would agree to a transfusion.

The boy told his parents he would have to think about it. He went in his room and began arranging his toys. He sat down and studied his walls that were filled with athletic posters. His parents couldn't believe that he would hesitate to agree to the procedure. Finally, he came out of his room and said that he would do it. His bewildered parents asked him why it took him so long to decide. His reply was, "If I give my blood to my sister, then I will die."

The boy obviously didn't understand that the transfusion involved only a small amount of blood and that it would not take his own life. Still, he was willing to make the sacrifice for his sister if it took that to save her.

Love sponsors great sacrifices.

• *A Client's Perspective*

We've all heard the phrase, "No one should have to bury their children." No mother should have to grieve over the one she brought into this world with pain, nurtured from her own body, and attended to every basic need until the child was toilet trained and able to dress himself. No father should have to grieve over a child he nurtured, loved, and educated.

After Hurricane Katrina swept the Gulf Coast on August 29, 2005, I was visiting with a client whose child had died as a result of medical negligence. He recalled watching a television news program where a father, mother, and their children were in a boat fleeing flood waters that had wiped out their home. The father in the boat tearfully said that he had lost everything. My client's thoughts were, "No, sir, you have everything, and it is with you in that boat."

Only those who have lost a child understand the tragedy.

HUMOROUS STORIES

Storytellers use humorous anecdotes in many ways. Sometimes humor is the best introduction for a serious subject. William K. Zinsser said, "What I want is to make people laugh so they'll see things seriously."

W. Somerset Maugham suggested that "humor teaches tolerance." Henry Ward Beecher observed that "men will let you abuse them only if you make them laugh." Finally, Malcolm De Chazal argued, "The man who can make others laugh secures more votes for a measure than the man who forces them to think."

All the following humorous stories can be used to make a serious point.

• *The New Bull*

Three bulls lived on a ranch. One day one of the bulls said to the others, "I hear they are bringing in a new bull."

The oldest bull, who had been there for many years, said, "Well, I hope the new bull doesn't expect to get any of my heifers. I've been here a long time and I have one hundred females I service. I don't intend to let him have one of them."

The next bull, who had been on the ranch a shorter time, said, "Well, I haven't been here as long as you, but I have twenty-five heifers. I hope the new bull doesn't think he is going to get any of mine."

The youngest bull was equally indignant. "You boys know I've been here the shortest time. But I have ten heifers all staked out; I certainly don't intend to give any of them up."

About that time a large eighteen-wheeler pulled up at the gate and dropped the rear ramp. A huge bull came staggering out. The bull was so big that when he walked across the cattle guard the bars bent. The ground shuddered as this monster strode onto the ranch.

The oldest bull took one look at him and said, "Well, on second thought, I really haven't been doing service to all one hundred of my heifers. It would probably be best if he took some of those off my hands."

The second bull said, "Come to think of it, twenty-five heifers is too much for any one bull. He's certainly welcome to some of mine."

The older bulls looked over at the young bull, who was pawing the ground and snorting loudly. "Youngster, you don't intend to take on that monster, do you?" inquired the oldest bull.

"Hell, no," the young bull stammered. "I just want to be sure that he knows I'm a bull."

To be respected you have to stand for something.

- *Aspiring for Acceptance*

An old black man aspired to membership in a very exclusive church. This man was staunchly religious but innocently unaware of the prejudices held against him. The white pastor attempted to put him off with all sorts of evasive excuses. The old black man, instinctively becoming aware of the fact that he was not wanted, finally told the pastor he would sleep on it. Perhaps the Lord would tell him what to do.

Several days later he returned. "Well," asked the pastor, "did the Lord send you a message?"

"Yes, he did," the black man answered. "He told me there wasn't any use. The Lord told me he had been trying to get into your church for ten years and still hasn't made it."

Don't worry if others don't accept you;
they may not be worthy of your company.

- *The Preacher's Attention Getter*

A young minister graduated from seminary. His bishop sent him to his first church. The pastor at this church was quite elderly and obviously very experienced in the ways of preaching and caring for his congregation. The church was always filled for Sunday services. The young preacher asked the old preacher what the secret of his success was. The old preacher told him that you had to be attentive to when the audience began to drift off. As the old preacher explained, it was usually about halfway through the sermon that the women would start to cough, the children would start to fidget, and the men would nod off. It was at that point in the sermon that the preacher had to do something to get the attention of the congregation.

The young preacher saw the principle in action during the old preacher's next sermon. Sure enough, about halfway through the women started coughing, the children started fidgeting, and the men started nodding off. At this point in the sermon, the old preacher said:

"Just last night I was in the arms of a woman who is not my wife."

Everyone, startled by this admission, sat up and began to take notice. The old preacher went on, saying that the night before he had been holding his elderly mother who was quite ill in the hospital.

About a year later, the young preacher finally got his own church. Recalling the lessons of the old preacher, he prepared for his first sermon. Sure enough, about halfway through the sermon he noticed that the women were coughing, the children were fidgeting, and the men were nodding off. He decided to use the old preacher's tactic.

"Just last night I was in the arms of a woman who is not my wife."

Then suddenly, finding that his mind had gone blank and he could not recall the old preacher's punch line, he struggled for composure, and said, "And for the life of me I cannot remember who it was."[64]

Don't try an attention getter you have not mastered.

- *A Deathbed Observation*

A few years ago, an old man lay dying in his bed. He turned to his wife who stood beside the bed and murmured softly, "When I limped home from the final campaign in 1918, you were waiting for me, Rachel. When I was released from Dachau at the end of World War II, you were by my side." Overcome with emotion, the old man stopped to snort loudly into a handkerchief and then continued. "Rachel, when we sold everything to start a business in the New World and it went bust and left us penniless, there you were. And now, here I am breathing my last, and here you still stand by the bedside. Rachel, I'm telling you—you're a jinx."

Devotion isn't always appreciated.

- *A Golf Match*

The prime minister of Israel invited the pope to play a game of golf. Since the pope had no idea how to play, he convened the college of cardinals to ask their advice. "Call David Duval," they suggested, "and let him play in your place. Tell the prime minister you're sick or something."

Honored by His Holiness's request, Duval agreed to represent him on the links. The pope, again on the advice of his staff, appointed him a cardinal to make the arrangements seem more legitimate.

When Duval returned to the Vatican, the pope eagerly asked how he had done. "I came in second," was Duval's reply.

"Second! You mean to tell me the prime minister of Israel beat you? How?"

"No, Your Holiness," said Duval. "Rabbi Woods did."

A suitable substitute doesn't guarantee success.

- *A Burglar Finds Religion*

A burglar broke into a mansion in River Oaks. He was in the dining room going through the cabinets in search of silver and jewelry, when from the darkness he heard a voice say, "Jesus is watching you." The voice startled him and he looked around in the darkness. Seeing no one, he continued in his mischief. He heard the voice again: "Jesus is watching you." He pulled out of his pocket a small flashlight. The light fell on a parrot in a cage in the corner of the dining room. The parrot said, "Jesus is watching you." The robber turned off the light and went about his crime. Finally, the parrot in a very demanding and insistent voice said, "Jesus is watching you!" The burglar shined his light back in the corner and this time he saw lying at the base of the parrot's cage a large black Doberman with fire-red eyes and fangs bared. The parrot then said to the burglar, "Say hello to Jesus."

A show of force is sometimes necessary to ensure responsible action.

- *A Cautious Estimate*

Bob was a tall, thin fellow—six three and no more than 180 pounds. He and two of his best friends, Earl and Terry, flew to Alaska on a hunting expedition. Earl and Terry were not small men. Earl weighed 350 pounds, and Terry was bigger than Earl.

In Anchorage, the pilot of a single-engine four-seat seaplane taxied his aircraft up to the pier for the flight that would take the group into the back country. The plane was old and looked a little rickety. The pilot said to the group, "To calculate my fuel and make proper flight adjustments I need to know how much each of you fellas weigh."

Earl hemmed and hawed a little bit and then said, "I guess I weigh about 230 now."

Terry followed with, "I'm a little heavier, probably about 240."

When the pilot turned to Bob, the thin fellow spoke out without hesitation, "I weigh exactly 575 pounds."[65]

Truth may require making up for the falsehoods of others.

- *A Futile Warning*

A vacationing school teacher was hiking in Montana. She came across a sheer cliff alongside the trail. She commented to the tour guide that this was a dangerous precipice and wondered why they didn't put up a warning sign. The tour guide replied, "Yes, it is dangerous, but they kept a warning sign up for two years and no one fell over, so it was taken down."

Just because someone isn't hurt doesn't mean something isn't dangerous.

- *A Pious Father*

There was once a wealthy man who prided himself on being good and pious. Each day he would lead his family in prayer for all the sick and needy in the world. In particular, he prayed that God might help an aged couple who lived near his estate and who were ill as well as poor.

One morning his son asked him whether he ever stopped to visit the unfortunate couple. The father said he had not. The boy remarked, "Dad, I wish I had your money."

"Why?" the father asked.

"Because," the boy responded, "then I would answer your prayers."

Action, not pious thoughts, is what counts.

- *A Mean Mule*

A farmer was shoeing his mule in his barnyard when a neighbor dropped by. The neighbor asked the farmer if the mule ever kicked him. The farmer replied, "No, he ain't yet, but he frequently kicks the place where I recently was."

Recognizing trouble allows you to avoid it.

- *The Lumberjack*

There was a scrawny, seemingly undernourished old man who entered a restaurant and asked who he needed to see to get a job at the nearby lumberjack camp. The restaurant owner told him that he didn't have to go far, as the supervisor was having lunch in the café. He pointed to a nearby booth.

The job seeker approached the supervisor and exclaimed, "I'm looking for a lumberjack job." The boss politely tried to talk him out of the idea. Surely this weak old man wouldn't be able to fell a tree let alone keep up with the daily quotas. "Give me a few minutes of your time and I'll show you what I can do," suggested the old man.

When the two arrived at a grove needing to be cleared, the slender, persistent old man picked up an axe and proceeded to chop down a huge tree in record time. "That's incredible," the boss said. "Where did you learn to fell trees like that?" "Well," said the old man, "you've heard of the Sahara Forest?" Hesitantly, the boss replied, "Don't you mean the Sahara Desert?" The old man produced a smile and said, "Sure, that's what it's called now."

Never underestimate a determined person's abilities.

- *Trouble at Sea*

This is the transcript of a radio conversation of a U.S. naval ship with Canadian authorities off the coast of Newfoundland in October 1995. It may or may not be authentic.

Radio conversation released by the Chief of Naval Operations, 10/10/95:

Americans:	Please divert your course 15° to the north to avoid a collision.
Canadians:	Recommend you divert *your* course 15° to the south to avoid a collision.
Americans:	This is the captain of a U.S. Navy ship. I say again, divert *your* course.
Canadians:	No. I say again, you divert *your* course.
Americans:	This is the aircraft carrier U.S.S. *Lincoln*, the second largest ship in the United States Atlantic Fleet. We are accompanied by three destroyers, three cruisers, and numerous support vessels. I demand that you change *your* course 15° north, that's one five degrees north, or countermeasures will be undertaken to ensure the safety of this ship.
Canadians:	This is a lighthouse. Your call.

Don't make demands until you have all the facts.

- *A Medical Examination*

A seventy-three-year-old man consulted his physician. The physician, after examination, remarked that the man seemed to be in very good shape for his age.

"How old was your father when he died?" asked the doctor.

"What makes you think my father is dead?" answered the man.

The doctor replied, "How old is your father?"

"My father is 101 years old."

"How old was your grandfather when he died?" asked the physician.

"What makes you think my grandfather is dead?" replied the patient.

The doctor replied, "Well, how old is your grandfather?"

"He's 125 years old and he's getting married next week to a twenty-three-year-old girl."

The doctor in amazement asked, "Why would your 125-year-old grandfather want to marry a twenty-three-year-old girl?"

To which the patient replied, "What makes you think he *wants* to marry her?"

Don't assume too much.

- *A Quick Comeback*

George Bernard Shaw wrote Winston Churchill before the opening of his famous *Pygmalion,* "Am reserving two tickets for you for my premiere. Come and bring a friend—if you have one."

Churchill wrote back, "Impossible to be present for the first performance. Will attend the second—if there is one."

Wit can always turn sarcasm.

- *The Supercomputer*

In the United States, they gathered a group of the world's most renowned scientists. The goal was to build the greatest, most sophisticated and most powerful computer. Technologists were brought from all over the world, including computer experts. This large group of scientists eventually constructed the world's largest and most powerful computer. It was housed in a large building. After the construction was completed, the scientists decided to test the computer with a difficult question. The question was: "Is there a God?"

After a few seconds, the computer spit out the following answer: "There is now."

Technology may someday be the master of us all.

- *A Walk in the Woods*

The following story can be told about two individuals or groups competing.

A plaintiff's lawyer and a defense lawyer went on a hike in the woods. Before they left, they were warned that they should avoid the grizzly bears who were lurking in the woods. The people at the lodge where they were staying told them that the grizzlies were quite savage, had not been fed in some time, and might be provoked to attack. They were told that if they saw a grizzly the first thing they should do would be to climb a tree.

Sure enough, they hadn't been out very long before the lawyers came across a grizzly bear. Unfortunately, there were no trees in sight and nothing to climb. The plaintiff's lawyer sat down and began taking off his hiking boots and pulling track shoes from his knapsack. Seeing this, the defense lawyer asked in amazement, "What do you think you're doing? There is no way we're going to be able to outrun that bear."

To which the plaintiff's lawyer replied, "I don't have to outrun the bear, I just have to outrun you."

Success means you're better than your competition.

- *Caught by a Bear*

A young seminary student took a vacation in Alaska. He was enjoying the salmon fishing on the riverbank when he spied an ugly grizzly. He ran through the woods trying to escape the grizzly but was unable to do so. Just as the grizzly grabbed him and wrapped him in a deathly bear hug, he raised his hands to the heaven and prayed, "Oh Lord, please make this bear a Christian."

Whereupon, to his relief, the bear released him and clasped its paws together in a prayer-like position. To his dismay, he heard the bear say, "Dear Lord, we thank you for this food that we are about to receive."

Don't let gestures mislead you as to intentions.

- *The Lab Rat*

A laboratory rat was talking to another and said, "I've got my scientist so well trained that every time I push the buzzer he brings me a snack."

Control is a matter of perception.

- *A Crowd at the Pearly Gates*

The pope died and went to heaven. Upon his arrival at the Pearly Gates he found a very lengthy line waiting to be processed for admittance. Becoming impatient with the lack of progress, the pope walked down the line and approached St. Peter.

"As you know, St. Peter, I am the pope and spent my entire life on Earth doing God's work. I would like to go on to heaven as I am very curious as to what it will be like."

To which St. Peter replied that the pope would simply have to take his place in line and wait to be processed like everyone else. "Up here in heaven, everyone is treated the same."

The pope returned to the line, which was still moving very slowly. After a while the pope observed a man walk by the line down to St. Peter. The man was dressed in a white medical smock and had a stethoscope in one pocket and a tongue blade in the other. After speaking a few words to St. Peter, the man went right through the Pearly Gates.

The pope could not stand what he felt was an imposition and again approached St. Peter.

"St. Peter, it is obvious what that fellow is and he was allowed to go directly into heaven. I thought you said up here everyone was treated the same."

"Don't worry, that's just God. He sometimes thinks he's a doctor."

Some doctors are overimpressed with their own importance.

- *A Religious Paradox*

What is the difference between heaven and hell? the theologian was asked.

"In heaven," he replied, "the English are the police, the French are the cooks, the Italians are the lovers, the Swiss are the administrators, and the Germans are the mechanics.

"Whereas in hell," the religious savant continued, "the English are the cooks, the French are the administrators, the Italians are the mechanics, the Swiss are the lovers, and the Germans are the police."

Misplacing talent can doom success.

- *Wrong Number*

A couple of fellows were talking about the use of words and how people get them balled up. One of them said, "Let me show you the difference between three similar words—irritation, aggravation, and frustration."

It was about three o'clock in the morning, and he went over to a phone booth and dropped coins in. He picked a number at random out of the book. He dialed the number, and a sleepy voice answered, "Hello?"

He said, "Is Winterbottom there?"

The fellow at the other end said, "What number do you want?"

He said, "555-5353."

"No, you have the wrong number. There's nobody here by that name. Now, do you mind letting me get back to sleep?" And he hung up.

The guy said, "See? That's what you call irritation."

Twenty minutes later he went back to the phone and dialed the same number. The other fellow answered the phone and said, "Hello!"

"Is Winterbottom there?"

The fellow said, "Look, I told you there isn't anybody by that name here at this number. Now, go to sleep, and let me go to sleep, you dumb jerk." And the fellow hung up.

The guy said to his friend, "That's aggravation."

About half an hour later he dialed the same number again. This time the fellow answered the phone and said, "HELLO!"

The guy said, "This is Winterbottom. Have there been any calls for me?" And to his friend he said, "That's frustration."

It's easy to let fools frustrate you.

- *The Compulsory Golf Story*

Two old friends had played golf together every Saturday morning for twenty-five years. One day while they were on the golf course they made an agreement that the first of them to die would try to get in touch with the other from the afterlife to tell the living friend whether or not there were golf courses in heaven. Sure enough, one of the men died, and the other was awakened in his sleep by a voice one night. "George, is that you?" he said.

"Yes, Bill, I am here in heaven. I have some good news and bad news for you."

"What's the good news?"

"The good news is that heaven has some of the finest golf courses I've ever seen—better than any on Earth."

"What's the bad news, then?"

"You have a tee time at ten o'clock in the morning."

Good news sometimes comes with a catch.

- *What a Preacher Knows about Farming*

A young farmer was giving his minister a tour of his farm. The minister was very impressed with the farmer's crops and how well the farmer was doing. "My, look at that corn," said the minister. "Those are the biggest ears of corn I've ever seen—the Lord certainly has worked wonders." The minister then commented on the size of the watermelons that the farmer had growing on his vines. Then, looking at the farmer's tomato crop, he exclaimed, "The Lord certainly can work wonders—look at those tomatoes." Finally, exasperated, the farmer said to the minister, "You should have seen the way this place looked while God was taking care of it."

Good things come from hard work.

- *A Dedicated Missionary*

A young priest was sent to do God's work in a small village in South America. He had been there but a short time when a severe storm hit the village and it began to rain. The waters continued to rise, but the priest remained at his station in his church. Finally, after the waters had risen appreciably, a motorboat came by aiding survivors.

"Climb aboard, Father, we're taking everybody out. The weather forecast is for more rain."

The priest replied that he would not leave, but that he would leave his fate to the Lord—he was doing the Lord's work.

The waters continued to rise and the rain continued. The priest had to move to the second floor of the church. Another boat came by. They called to the priest, "Father, you had better get aboard, the forecast is for more rain. Everyone has evacuated but you. We have brought this boat in with great difficulty just to get you out safely."

To which the priest replied, "No, I'll leave my fate in the Lord's hands, I am doing the Lord's work."

The rains continued and the father found himself hanging from the steeple of the church. The waters were still rising. Overhead appeared a helicopter. With a bullhorn they hollered down to the priest, "Father, we'll drop a rope ladder to you. Grab ahold of it and we'll pull you up."

The priest replied, "No, I'll leave my fate to the Lord, I am doing the Lord's work."

The waters continued to rise and the priest drowned.

Later, he found himself in heaven and was brought before the Almighty.

"God, I know you work in mysterious ways. However, I had dedicated my life to you and trusted in you. I do not understand why with me doing the Lord's work you did not make any effort to save me from the flood."

To which God replied, "What do you mean I didn't try to help you? I sent you two boats and a helicopter."[66]

Don't blame God when you miss opportunities.

- *Wrong Answer?*

Bubba was from a prominent family and was a popular member of the student body at Texas A&M University. He had attended A&M for eight years but had not been able to pass enough courses to graduate. The president and chancellor of the university met and decided that they had to figure out a way for Bubba to get his degree from Texas A&M. Collectively, they decided to give him a simple oral examination consisting of one question. When Bubba successfully answered that question he would receive his degree. At first, they decided they would do this in a little ceremony in the chancellor's office. But word got out to the faculty so, of course, all the faculty wanted to attend. With the faculty and their friends in attendance, the ceremony would have to be held in G. Rollie White Coliseum, the basketball stadium at A&M. But then word got out to the student body. All the students wanted to see Bubba get his degree. It was the same with the alumni. Everyone who had anything to do with Texas A&M wanted to attend the ceremony. They transferred the whole proceedings to Kyle Field. They set up a small podium out in the middle of the stadium. An overflow crowd of A&M faculty, students, and alumni packed the stands. Bubba stood on the podium before the multitude, and the chancellor told him, "Bubba, the question you have to answer to graduate from Texas A&M is this: 'What is six plus one?'" Bubba studied real hard, shuffled his feet on the ground, scratched his head, and finally answered: "I am not sure, but I think it is seven." Whereupon the multitude in the stadium rose to their feet and yelled "Give Bubba another chance!"

Sometimes everyone is wrong.

- *A Hole in One*

A young priest decided he would play hooky from his parish one day and play golf. He went to the nearby golf course and teed off. He hooked his ball into the woods. As the ball was rolling a bird came along, picked it up in its beak and flew toward the green. The bird dropped the ball and the ball rolled into the cup for a hole in one.

An angel watching from above looked up at the Lord and said, "What kind of punishment is that? The priest was playing hooky."

To which the Lord replied, "Yes, but who is he going to tell?"

Little satisfaction comes from an accomplishment that can't be shared.

- *The Tall Truck*

Two truckers in a semi were coming into a small town. They came to a tunnel that bore above it the sign, "Height Limit 11 feet, 6 inches."

The two truckers got out and measured the height of their rig. It was thirteen feet. One trucker looked at the other and said, "Let's chance it, there are no cops around."

Rules can't be avoided by ignoring the facts.

- *A Dog Story*

A traveling salesman was working the county roads. He came upon a farmhouse surrounded by a picket fence. On the porch of the farmhouse sat an old farmer. Inside the fence lay a mean-looking dog. The salesman called over the fence to the farmer, "Does your dog bite?" The farmer answered that his dog didn't bite. The salesman then opened the gate, entered the yard, and approached the farmer to try to interest him in a set of encyclopedias. Suddenly the dog attacked the salesman, biting viciously at his legs. The salesman was able to extricate himself from the dog and get back outside the fence. His trousers torn and his face haggard, he looked back over the gate to the farmer and said, "I thought you told me your dog doesn't bite."

To which the farmer answered, "My dog doesn't bite, but that isn't my dog."

Don't assume facts that are not in the evidence.

- *The Legacy*

Carlson, an elderly miser, lay on his deathbed. He had no friends, so he summoned his doctor, lawyer, and minister to his bedside. "They say you can't take it with you, but I'm going to prove you can," gasped the dying man. "I've got $300,000 in cash under my mattress. It's in three envelopes of $100,000 each. I want each of you to take an envelope now, and just before they shovel the dirt on me, throw the envelopes in."

The three attended the funeral and each threw in his envelope. On the way back from the cemetery, the minister said, "Gentlemen, I want to confess. I needed $30,000 badly for a new church building, so I took that out and threw only $70,000 in the grave."

"I've got to tell the truth, too," said the doctor. "I'm building a hospital and took $50,000 and threw in only $50,000."

"Fellows," said the lawyer, "I'm shocked. Keeping that money was a shameful thing to do. I threw in my personal check for the full amount."

Real honesty is a matter of integrity.
Valueless gestures are never a true tribute.

- *Left Hand—Right Hand*

The telephone operator in a tiny town received a call every single day requesting the exact time. Finally her curiosity got the better of her, and she asked her caller why he did so.

"I have to know the correct time," he explained, "because I have to blow the factory whistle right at noon."

The operator gasped, "Oh, my goodness—I always set my clock by your whistle!"

If nobody checks the facts, we can all be wrong.

- *The Trees Are Still Standing*

An illiterate farmer went into a hardware store and told the clerk that he needed a saw that would cut at least an acre a day. The clerk told him they carried the latest model lightweight power saw that was made, and it would certainly cut an acre a day. The farmer bought the power saw. He returned three days later demanding a refund.

"I thought you said this saw would cut an acre of wood a day. I've been working with it for three days now and I've only cut down three or four trees."

The clerk took the saw, pulled the cord, and started it up. The startled farmer asked, "What's that noise?"

If you don't know what you're doing,
ask questions.

- *They Drink a Lot in East Texas*

In Coldspring, Texas, there was a fellow who was known as the town drunk. One night on his way home from the local tavern he decided to take a shortcut across the graveyard. Unbeknown to him a grave had been dug earlier that day for a funeral that was going to take place the next day. In his sojourn through the graveyard he fell into the grave. He tried for some time to get out. He tried digging handholds and footholds in the walls. He tried jumping up and grabbing at the top of the grave to pull himself out. All these efforts proved unsuccessful. In frustration, he curled up at one end of the grave in the darkness and decided to wait until morning came when someone would come and get him out.

While he was lying there in the shadows, a second fellow came along who was also drunk. He also fell into the grave. The second fellow went through all the steps the first drunk had. He dug footholds and handholds in the side in an effort to climb out. He tried jumping up and grabbing at the top. In frustration, the second fellow stood looking up at the top of the grave, kind of shaking his head, oblivious to the first drunk, whom he had not seen. Finally, after watching the fellow go through all of this, the first drunk said to him, "You'll never get out of here."

Whereupon in one great leap the second drunk jumped out of the grave and ran out of the graveyard.

With strong motivation, we can accomplish miracles.

- *A Letter from Sis*

The McKenzies were thrilled to get a letter from their daughter, who was halfway through her freshman year in college. They were less thrilled as they began reading:

"Dear Mom and Dad:

"Just wanted to fill you in on my plans. I have been going with a really cool guy named Lance for a couple of months now. He doesn't believe in the capitalist system, but he makes enough playing occasional gigs with an acid rock group to help support the two little children from his first marriage. As soon as his divorce comes through we want to get married, but until then I think I'm just going to move into his trailer. It's kind of far from the campus, but I was planning to drop out—maybe I'll go back someday. I need to save some money anyhow, because I think I might be pregnant."

Sweating and white-faced, the McKenzies turned the page:

"Mom and Dad, none of what I have written is true. It hasn't happened, I promise. But it is true that I'm failing computer science and barely pulling a C in Asian studies. And it is true that I'm overdrawn and need $300 more to get through the semester."

"Lots of love from your darling daughter . . . "

It's never as bad as it could be.
If you want bad news accepted, show how bad it could be.

- *Another Dog Story*

A man bought a new retriever and took him out duck hunting. Standing in his blind that morning, he shot at a duck and the duck fell down. The dog skipped right out on the water, tiptoed over, picked up the duck, and brought it back in again. The man looked at the dog and thought, "I couldn't have seen that right."

So he shot again, and another duck fell. The dog just skimmed out over the water, tiptoeing, and came back with the duck. The man thought, "Boy, that's something!"

A friend of his was in a blind nearby, so he went over to him and said, "Joe, come here. I want to show you something." Joe came over and they stood there. More ducks came over, the man shot, and this time two ducks fell in the water. The dog skipped out over the water, picked up the ducks, and tiptoed back in.

The guy looked at Joe and said, "How about that? How about that? Don't you notice anything remarkable about the dog?"

Joe said, "Yes, he can't swim."

The pessimist finds fault in any talent.

- *A Medical Diagnosis*

A team of archeologists from a large university were digging in the Middle East. They came upon the remains of a man who obviously had been dead for three or four thousand years. The elderly archeologist examined the remains and announced to the team that the man had died of a heart attack. The younger members of the team challenged the older professor, indicating that no one could know this without further study. They gathered the body up and shipped it back to the States for extensive testing. After all the medical tests had been accomplished, a telegram was sent back to the archeological team confirming that the man had, in fact, died of a heart attack. When the younger members of the team asked the old professor how he could know that, he replied simply, "Because I found this in his hand," and the professor produced a slip of paper that read, "Ten thousand shekels on Goliath."

Don't ignore the obvious when looking for answers.

- *Rising Healthcare Costs*

A man was standing in his front yard with his dog. Suddenly the dog bolted, ran out into the street, and was run over. The man rushed over, picked up his dog, and took the animal to the vet.

The veterinarian examined the dog for quite some time. Finally, he turned to the man and said, "Sir, I'm sorry, your dog is dead." Upon hearing this the man was devastated and replied, "Oh, Doctor, it can't be! I don't know how I will tell my children. They love this dog so much. Isn't there anything you can do for him? Oh, please, please see if you can do anything for him!"

The vet bent down and picked up a basket. He opened the basket, and a cat jumped out and onto the examining table with the dog. The cat meowed, sniffed the dog, rubbed on him, and meowed again. The cat then jumped back into the basket.

The vet turned to the man and said, "Sir, I'm terribly sorry, but the cat says your dog is dead." The man, overcome with grief, said, "Oh, Doctor, he can't be dead. I just know there's something you can do for him. Please, oh, please try to help my dog. My wife loves this dog more than she loves me!"

Whereupon the veterinarian went out to his pen and brought back a Labrador retriever. The Lab jumped up on the table, barked a few times, sniffed at the man's dog, and barked a few more times. The Lab then jumped off the table and returned to his pen.

The vet turned to the man and said, "Sir, the Lab tells me your dog is dead." After hearing this, the man replied, "Well, OK. I know you did your best. I guess I'll just have to break the news to my family, as hard as it is. What do I owe you?"

The vet told the man, "The bill comes to $650." The man exclaimed, "$650!? How could I possibly owe you that much money for just looking at my dog?" The vet replied, "Sir, I told you your dog was dead and my fee would have been $50. But you insisted on having a CAT scan and Lab tests."[67]

It costs to question a doctor's diagnosis.

- *An Evening on the Town*

A couple was dressed and ready to go out for the evening. They turned on a night-light, turned the answering machine on, covered their pet parakeet, and put the cat in the backyard. They phoned the local cab company and requested a taxi. The taxi arrived and the couple opened the front door to leave their house.

The cat they had put out into the yard scooted back into the house. They didn't want the cat shut in the house because she always tried to eat the bird. The wife went out to the taxi while the husband went back inside to get the cat. The cat ran upstairs, the man in hot pursuit.

Waiting in the cab, the wife didn't want the driver to know the house would be empty for the night. She explained that her husband would be out soon. "He's just going upstairs to say good-bye to my mother."

A few minutes later, the husband got into the cab. "Sorry I took so long," he said, as they drove away. "Stupid bitch was hiding under the bed. Had to poke her with a coat hanger to get her to come out! She tried to take off so I grabbed her by the neck. Then I had to wrap her in a blanket to keep her from scratching me. But it worked. I hauled her fat ass downstairs and threw her out in the backyard!"

The cab driver hit a parked car.

A comment can be misunderstood
if you don't know the context.

- *Self-Made Man*

The youngster stood gazing intently at his father's visitor, a homely man of large proportions. At length the portly one became a bit embarrassed and said, "Well, my boy, what are you looking at me for?"

The boy replied that his daddy had told his mother that the man was a self-made man. The boy wanted to see what he would look like.

"Quite right," said the gratified guest. "I am a self-made man."

"But what did you make yourself like that for?" asked the boy with considerable surprise.

We don't choose how we look.

- *A Highjacker's Whisper*

Roy Burns, a defendant charged with aggravated robbery, pleaded "not guilty" before the jury. He vowed he had been nowhere near the store that was robbed by three men.

The jurors listened intently as a witness on the stand swore under oath that fifteen people were in the store at the time of the robbery.

At that point, Roy leaned over to his attorney and whispered loudly enough for the jurors to hear: "There weren't that many people in the store."

By being such a stickler for accuracy, Roy ensured that justice was meted out. The jury's verdict: ten years hard time.

Accuracy can betray deceit.

- *Oil in Hell*

A speculator in oil leases died and went to heaven, only to find the place so crowded that he could barely find room inside the door. The speculator hit upon a trick that he hoped would relieve the congestion. He produced a scrap of paper and a pencil from his pocket and scribbled a note, "Oil discovered in hell," which he dropped to the floor. Soon the note was picked up and read. The man who read it whispered to a few other persons and slipped away. Those in whom he had confided similarly whispered to others and followed him. There was a regular exodus in the direction of the reported strike. Watching the procession, the man who had started the rumor grew more and more restive. He could stand it no longer. "There may be something in this thing—I guess I'd better look it over," he said, as he joined the stampede.

Greed feeds on itself.

- *The Ships' Log*

Sometimes the way an entry is made, or the fact that one was made at all, can be deceiving. A sailor celebrating a long-awaited ship's leave got very inebriated. When he staggered back up the gangway, the captain sternly entered in the log: "Mate drunk tonight."

When he saw the entry, the mate objected violently. "Captain, the boat was moored. You know I have never been drunk on board before. I have never been drunk on duty. If this stays on the record, I will never get work on another ship."

Stonehearted, the captain refused to modify his entry. "It is the truth and it shall remain on the record."

A few days later, the captain was checking over the log and came across an entry written by the mate: "The captain was sober today." The outraged captain summoned the mate and accused him of creating a false impression. "Anyone reading this will think my sobriety was unusual, that I am usually drunk," he bellowed. "The statement is true," the mate calmly asserted, "and it shall remain in the log."

Even the clearest of documentation is subject to interpretation.

- *Sunday's Lesson*

A minister wound up one morning by previewing his sermon for the following Sunday. "Next week I will be preaching on the subject of liars. In preparation for that lesson I'd like for all of you to read the seventeenth chapter of Mark."

The following Sunday the preacher addressed his congregation. "Would all of you who have prepared for the lesson for today and read the seventeenth chapter of Mark please raise your hands?" Nearly every hand in the hall went up. The preacher said, "You are the very people I want to talk to. There is no seventeenth chapter of Mark!"

Procrastinators will deny that they aren't prepared.

- *Misguided E-Mail*

A man left for a vacation to Jamaica. His wife was on a business trip and was planning to meet him there the next day. When he reached his hotel, the man decided to send his wife a quick e-mail message. Unable to find the scrap of paper on which he had written her address, he did his best to type it in from memory.

Unfortunately, he missed one letter, and his note was directed instead to an elderly preacher's wife whose husband had passed away the day before. When the grieving widow checked her e-mail, she took one look at the monitor, let out a piercing scream, and fainted. Her family rushed into the room and saw this note on the screen:

> Dearest wife, just checked in. Everything prepared for your arrival tomorrow. Your loving husband.
>
> P.S. Sure is hot down here.

Be sure your message is directed to the right audience.

- *Taking Precautions*

An English tale involves a gentleman of means testing the character of applicants for the position of chauffeur. He took them to a narrow road that bordered on a deep precipice.

"How near this dangerous cliff can you drive without fear?" he asked. One said, "A few feet." Another replied, "A few inches." A third man answered, "I should drive as far from it as possible. The place is dangerous and I would avoid it altogether if it were possible."

The third man was engaged because he could be trusted. He was too wise to encounter needless peril.

We want the most cautious people taking care of us.

- *Hiring an Engineer*

Bubba applied for an engineering position at a refinery in Lake Charles, Louisiana. A Yankee applied for the same job. Both applicants having the same qualifications, they were asked to take a test by the manager. Upon completion of the test, both men had missed only one of the questions. The manager went to Bubba and said, "Thank you for your interest, but we've decided to give the Yankee the job." Bubba asked, "And why are you giving him the job? We both got nine questions correct. This being Louisiana, and me being a Southern boy, I should get the job!"

The manager said, "We have made our decision not on the correct answers but rather on the one question that you both missed." Bubba then asked, "And just how would one incorrect answer be better than the other?" The manager replied, "Bubba, it's like this—on question number four the Yankee put down: 'I don't know.' You put down, 'Neither do I.'"

If you cheat on your answers you may not get the job.
You can only succeed if you do the work yourself.

PART 6

COURTROOM STORIES

ARNOLD CAPLAN WAS a fortunate man. His parents' genetic pool had given him not only good looks but also good fortune. He grew up in the monied Turtle Creek neighborhood in North Dallas. Large, well-appointed houses painted a Martha-Stewart tableau inside and out. The wide boulevards ran through thick, plush yards of green velvet. The large Colonial and Victorian homes called out to him as a child the lessons of his parents that rich people are different from the rest of us. Because you know important people, the right doors will be opened. Because you have money, you are entitled to do as you please.

He attended Yale undergraduate as a matter of privilege, law school at the University of Texas as a matter of choice. Not wanting to squander his Highland Park contacts, he accepted John Robertson's offer and became that firm's youngest associate in 1968. It was a small firm then, occupying only a part of the floor in a downtown office building. The tax, estate, and divorce practice was booming in the 1990s. Robertson, Friedman & Elders moved to a prestigious Highland Park address. Ten years later, they had sixty lawyers; fifty-one were white and male. A handful had been together for more than a quarter of a century.

Caplan fit right in. He married a Dallas debutante, and a year later they moved into their home off Forest Lawn. He did all the right things that rich, powerful men do. He joined the Dallas country club, bought tables at the charitable events, served on bar committees. To those who might say he seemed arrogant, disdainful, or contemptuous, he would probably reply that rank has its privileges and the world would be a better place if we left things in the hands of propertied, well educated, white male Christians.

Cindy Baker never knew Caplan's world. She graduated from Woodrow Wilson High School on the east side of Dallas. Working people who did heavy lifting and got their hands dirty put food on the tables of families in her neighborhood. She went to college for a year but dropped out when her father got sick and couldn't help her with the tuition any longer. Her typing and computer skills got her a job at the county. A year later she found a secretarial position with a four-man law firm. She worked there for several years before hiring on at Robertson, Friedman & Elders.

The tall brunette with the soft brown eyes didn't socialize with anyone outside the office. Raising her ten-year-old daughter and eight-year-old son didn't leave her any time for that. What free time she had, she spent at her church. Some might call her straitlaced, but she didn't see herself that way. She was just a thirty-two-year-old woman who believed strongly in her conservative and traditional values. Her ex-husband's infidelity had left her shattered. His lack of financial responsibility for their two children meant she had to work. She loved her job, got along with her coworkers and the firm's clients.

But today was the last straw. No woman should have to endure this abuse.

Managing partner Arthur Glassman's office was at the end of the hall. Cindy asked Mona if she could see Mr. Glassman. A few minutes later, she stepped off the office-grade carpet onto the thick wool pile and into the world of those who have the power to set the rules. Glassman was correcting a legal document as she sat down in the heavy leather chair facing his desk. The words came streaming out as soon as he looked up. "I can't take this anymore." He knew what was coming. He had heard it before.

Arnold Caplan can't keep his hands to himself. If he was as good looking, witty, and clever as he thinks he is, he would be making all the lawyers rich with his divorce practice. Still, he has had some success and is a steady, predictable producer of billable hours. How often had the thought crossed Glassman's mind, "Why doesn't he just go home after his four-martini lunches rather than coming back to the office."

Cindy had been with Robertson, Friedman & Elders for only a couple of months last Christmas. The ladies at the office had all dressed up for the annual holiday event, the secretaries' lunch. A part of the hierarchy of a law firm this large is the lawyers' black-tie dinner at the Dallas Country Club and the secretaries' luncheon the next day at one of the Mockingbird Avenue restaurants. Cindy had a glass of white wine with her salmon salad. She was back at her desk at two-thirty, typing up a property settlement agreement Arnold Caplan had dictated that morning. She didn't notice the unsteadiness of gait or redness in his eyes when he came down the hall and went into his office. Later, when Caplan buzzed her, she thought it strange that he asked her to close the door. "Have I done something wrong?" ran through her mind. He said he just wanted to go over the letter she had typed that morning to opposing counsel. But after handing her the letter, he stood behind her chair and began to caress her neck. Startled, she stood up.

"You're a very sexy lady. Are you as good as you look?"

She didn't know how to handle the situation. She certainly hadn't run into anything like this before. She changed the subject back to the letter. Mr. Caplan said something about how her blouse accentuated her breasts. Cindy left and went back to her desk. Nothing else happened that day. She decided to forget it. He had been drinking at lunch. It wouldn't happen again. But it did. Always in the afternoon, after the martini lunches.

Some time in January, Cindy was in the coffee bar getting a diet soda from the refrigerator and didn't hear him come up behind her. When she turned around, they were face to face. A lot of people can't smell vodka on the breath, but she could.

"Let's slip out and have a drink together."

"Mr. Caplan, you know I can't do that."

"You need to put some fun in your life," he said as he put his finger to his lips and smiled. Cindy couldn't avoid brushing his arm and shoulder as she got by him to go back to her work. This time she complained. That afternoon, she sat down with Arthur Glassman and told him what had happened that day and last December. Glassman said he would talk to Caplan about it.

Things didn't change. They got worse. Caplan called her at home one night, obviously drunk, and asked if he could come over. Another time, he left the office with her. When they got to the lobby, he said he would walk her to her car. Cindy politely declined but Caplan insisted. She had a hard time getting rid of him but excused herself with the truth—she had to get home to her children. In April, her boss was in trial. One of the lawyers working with him told her she would have to stay late to prepare a trial memorandum. She called her friend, Jeannie, and got her to pick up the children at 6:00 PM from the day care. When Caplan got back to the office, he opened up his credenza and made himself a couple of strong vodka and tonics. Around eight-thirty, Cindy finished. As she was putting on her coat to leave, Caplan helped her with it. The fondling of her breast was not accidental.

Again she complained to Glassman. Glassman said he would talk to Caplan about it.

The trial was over in a few days. Caplan asked her what arrangements she had made to work late to type up the trial memorandum. She told him about her friend Jeannie. Caplan wanted her to make some arrangements the next night so they could have "dinner" together. Cindy spoke to the managing partner about it. He promised to "get Arnold straight."

Yesterday she was sitting at her desk when Caplan came in from lunch. He told her the fellows had been talking about what a "good lay" she would be.

Cindy had had all she could take. "Mr. Glassman, I've talked to you about this several times. But nothing changes." Glassman said he was sorry, that Arthur Caplan can sometimes be a real embarrassment to the firm. "You must see that these things stop," Cindy said, wiping her eyes. Glassman assured her that it would not happen again.

Cindy quit that Friday when Caplan staggered in at four o'clock and stopped in front of her desk, leaned over, ran his tongue between his lips, and asked, "Has anyone ever done this for you?" So Cindy made an appointment with Rhonda Ramirez, one of Dallas's top employment lawyers. Twenty months, reams of discovery, and twelve depositions later, the case went to trial.

Labor law can be a briar patch for the aggrieved employee. There are many legal thorns and thistles that can hang up a plaintiff trying to navigate the bramble of federal statutes and regulations to a just result. The same can be said of every action that involves a claim to the person—product liability, medical negligence, industrial injuries.

Jury selection in Cindy's case took almost a day. Picking a jury in an environment clouded with propaganda from insurance companies, corporate interests, and professionals isn't easy. When it came time to give her opening statement, this trial lawyer remembered something she had heard at a State Bar of Texas CLE program. One of the speakers taught that a lawsuit is not a debate over facts and legal concepts. They are important, but a lawsuit is really a competition of stories. So when Rhonda gave her opening statement, she told the story of Arnold Caplan, the kind of man he is, how he got to be that way, and why he would feel that he had the right and power to abuse the Cindys of the world. She told the story of Cindy—her decency, innocence, and vulnerability. She described the humiliation and how what Caplan had done had damaged Cindy's ability to get and keep a job. Through the witnesses she told other parts of the story until all of it, from different perspectives, was before the jury.

After the judge read the legal charge to the jury and called on counsel for closing summa-

tion, Rhonda didn't argue her case—she told a story. Her arguments were draped from the branches of the story. Her story had a theme. It had a moral. It was a compelling narrative of character and plot that cried out for her audience to act and write the final chapter of justice for a hard-working secretary who was sexually harassed by a powerful superior.

Rhonda concluded her narrative of people, places, and events and discussion of the legal concepts in the charge by empowering the jury:

"Work gives us all pride, dignity, and respect. No one, no matter how powerful, has the right to demean, disgrace, and abuse."

26

Illustrative Opening Statement

Truck-Auto Collision Kills Plaintiff's Son

In 1986, the case of *C. Glen Walker and Lynn Walker, Individually and as Surviving Parents of Stephen E. Walker, Deceased v. William Conkle, Poole Truck Lines, Inc. and Williams Bros. Construction Company,* Cause No. 83-346,896, was called to trial in the 133rd District Court of Harris County, Texas. Following the opening statements, it settled for a confidential amount in the low- to mid-seven figures. In an unfortunate but common playing out of this family's tragedy, the parents of Eric Walker divorced about a year after the settlement.

At the time of his death, Eric was twenty years old. He had lived apart from his parents during his junior year in high school. During that time, he developed some major medical problems that resulted in his being hospitalized for several weeks. Some of his treating physicians were of the opinion that the symptoms were consistent with the early onset of multiple sclerosis. Upon his discharge from the hospital, Eric returned home to his parents. He graduated from high school but was never gainfully employed before his fatal accident.

Eric Walker was driving one of the cars involved in a major multivehicle accident that happened on the east side of Houston on June 28, 1983. The five-vehicle collision was in the westbound lanes of Interstate 10. The Texas Department of Highways had initiated a program for major improvements along I-10 East in 1983. The state hired a construction company to widen the freeway and improve exit ramps. Eric Walker's fatal accident occurred in an area where a construction company had undertaken this work.

The city of Baytown is approximately thirty-five miles east of Houston. Between Baytown and Beaumont, Interstate 10 is relatively flat with few elevated overpasses. The area between Baytown and Houston, being more populated, has more exits and more elevated overpasses. The accident occurred west of the Sheldon Road overpass when a truck owned and operated by Poole Truck Lines rear-ended a Datsun pickup and crashed into the side of Eric Walker's car. Another car received minor damage. The defense contended that their driver could not see the traffic just over the crest of the Sheldon Road exit that had backed up due to the construction activity along the freeway. For reasons that were never completely clear, the investigating officer issued no traffic citations following the accident.

After Eric Walker's car was struck it caught on fire, trapping him inside. Passers-by rescued him but only after he had been severely burned. The Life Flight helicopter transported Eric to the John Sealy Burn Institute in Galveston. Despite the doctors' heroic efforts, he died eight days later.

The plaintiff faced more than the usual problems in a wrongful death action involving the loss of an adult child. We had only one true eyewitness to the collision, and her version conflicted with some of the findings made by the investigating officer. In other ways, her testimony was completely consistent with physical facts and photographs of the scene. While the defense contended their driver had acted prudently and that if anybody was at fault it was the construction company, the real battle would be over damages. The defense had evidence that the plaintiff's deceased son had some serious underlying medical condition. The corporate defendant could also fairly contend that the son and the parents were not close since he had left the home and lived apart from his parents while he was in high school. The opening statement would have to inoculate against these defense arguments.

We believed a major component of our recovery would be the conscious pain and suffering Eric suffered before his death. While he survived for only eight days, the evidence of his injuries was graphic. We held back from the jury the gruesome photographs showing the nature and extent of Eric's burn injuries. We chose to stress in opening statement the hours of torment that Eric knew before his death.

THE OPENING STATEMENT

Mr. Jim M. Perdue:

The bigger the load, the faster the road, the better the bottom line.

That was the Poole trucking company's motto. They never said it. They will deny it today. But we know that was their corporate policy. Their drivers lived by it. That's the way they were paid. A bigger load delivered faster meant a fatter paycheck for the driver. The quicker the turnaround, the better the wage. That company policy is why the defendant's driver smashed into four cars going west on I-10 on June 28, 1983. Eric Walker was in one of those cars. His car caught fire. By the time they got Eric out he was burned over 50 percent of his body.

A little over fifteen minutes earlier, Eric was at home at his folks' house in Baytown. His dad had asked him to run a family errand. To this day this father blames himself for his son's death.

May it please the Court, ladies and gentlemen:

At the end of the evidence in this case you will have an opportunity—a rare opportunity—to put a father's and mother's minds at ease. You can tell them that it was irresponsible corporate policy that claimed their son's life and yes, we do understand your loss.

It is about 11:05 AM on June 28, 1983. It is Tuesday. It's a sunny, clear day. It's Houston hot but not unbearable. The men working the highway construction near the Deldale exit are in their shirt sleeves. Their work has closed down one lane of traffic, but there is no problem. Traffic is congested, but the drivers are handling it well.

The defendant's driver, William Conkle, leaves Beaumont in his Poole company truck. It is a big rig, 74,000 pounds, over thirty-seven tons. This eighteen-wheeler is the maximum length allowed by law. He's carrying a big load. The quicker he gets it to Houston, the sooner he can load up and be on the road again. I-10 is a four-lane interstate between Beaumont and Houston. It is open road with few curves. The kind of highway the Poole drivers love. Not a lot of traffic and not a lot of law enforcement.

As the Poole truck approaches the Sheldon Road overpass, it passes other cars. On the other side of the Sheldon Road overpass, the freeway takes a turn to the right. The highway engineers have put a lot of study into designing these freeways. The design assures a minimum safe viewing distance. These highway engineers tell us that the layout of Interstate 10 in this area allows and ensures that drivers can see traffic and congestion in plenty of time to deal with it. Particularly a driver high in the cab of a diesel tractor.

We can only guess how many cars came over the Sheldon Road overpass, slowed down, merged, and safely went by the construction near the Deldale exit. Probably thousands that morning. Eric Walker and the drivers of the cars around him didn't have any problem. They were all going westbound toward Houston. As he approached the congestion Eric slowed his automobile and brought it to a safe, prudent stop.

The defendant's driver knows what kind of rig he is running. He knows it doesn't have the handling characteristics of an automobile. He knows he's getting close to Houston and can expect that traffic will be more dense and congested than it has been out on the open highway between Jefferson County and Harris County. But the driver just keeps on coming. The witnesses to this monstrous crash estimate the Poole driver was going seventy miles an hour as he approached the Sheldon Road overpass. He just keeps on coming. The driver can see the congestion if he just looks. But he just keeps on coming. It is not until he is right on top of the cars that he makes any application of his brakes. The Poole truck crashes into four stopped cars. The first car the defendant's driver hits is a red Datsun operated by Mr. Cowan. The Poole truck knocks the red Datsun up underneath another eighteen-wheeler that was stopped in the right-hand lane. The Poole truck then hits a pickup before it crashes into the side of Eric Walker's car, shoving it down the ramp for the Deldale exit.

We get some idea of how fast the Poole truck was going when it hit Eric's car from the damage done to it [*showing pictures*]. Eric's car was demolished. Worse, it caught on fire with Eric trapped in it.

The Poole trucking company lawyers will stand before you and say that this accident was not their fault. They will say that their driver wasn't speeding. They will point to the posted speed limit on Interstate 10. They will say that seventy miles an hour in a seventy-mile-per-hour posted zone can't be excessive. They will say their driver applied his brakes in a timely and proper manner. They will say their driver was keeping a lookout for the traffic and traffic conditions just like any reasonable driver would do.

There aren't a lot of witnesses to this crash. There are a lot of people who were there who can't tell us anything. Mr. Cowan, the driver of the Datsun that was hit first, has no recollection of the accident. Eric can't give his version. He is never well enough for the investigating officer to interview. He dies before he can give his version. Since the Poole truck was approaching from the rear, some of the people stopped on the freeway do not know how the accident happened. Mrs. Carol Sue Brewer was driving a pickup that was struck a glancing blow by the Poole truck just before it crashed into the side of Eric's car. She is completely impartial. She has no interest in this case one way or the other. She saw what she saw and remembers it well.

I need to apologize in advance for the quality of the videotape of Mrs. Brewer's testimony. We had to take her deposition in Indiana where she now lives. When we put this all together—the photographs taken on the scene shortly after it happened, the location of the vehicles, the marks on the road—Mrs. Brewer's version is consistent with all the known physical facts. Her testimony is consistent with the other witnesses who saw the Poole truck going seventy miles an hour as it came up on the Sheldon Road overpass. Mrs. Brewer saw how the Poole truck continued to race toward this disastrous collision. She saw how the driver never applied his brakes until it was too late. She saw the impact between the Poole truck and the other cars and the resulting devastation.

We are here today to consider a needless, senseless, endless tragedy. The defendant's driver says he doesn't see the congestion ahead as he is coming up the overpass, even though the highway engineers tell us he could have if he had just looked. The Poole driver is now on top of the overpass going seventy miles an hour. There is no question he can see all of the traffic ahead for a mile or more down the freeway. From the top of the overpass to where the cars have slowed and stopped to get by the construction is 250 yards. Seven hundred and fifty feet. But the defendant's driver just keeps on coming. The skid marks the eighteen-wheeler lays down before it hits the red Datsun measure 102 feet. It takes time for the air brakes to catch and lock the wheels. We must also consider the driver's reaction time. But even taking all that into account, five or six seconds pass from the time the defendant's driver crests the Sheldon Road overpass until he becomes aware of the danger and begins to act on it. Five or six seconds doesn't seem long. But the Poole driver is at the top of an overpass and sees traffic backed up ahead of him. For one, two, three, four, five, six seconds he does nothing. Is he daydreaming? Is his mind someplace else? We know he cannot be paying attention and driving carefully, because if he was, he would have begun to apply the truck brakes within a second or two after he crested the overpass.

We hear the puff of air going to the air brakes, the screeching of rubber on concrete. We can smell the burning rubber being peeled off on concrete. In an instant we hear the thud of metal on metal when the eighteen-wheeler hits the red Datsun and knocks it up under a stopped eighteen-wheeler. The Poole truck keeps on coming. Our ears fill with the sound of crashing and twisting metal. We hear the thump, thump as the Poole truck hits the pickup before it crashes into the side of Eric's Toyota [*referring to diagram depicting the impact between the vehicles and their final resting places*].

After all the cars come to rest, after the sounds of this catastrophic collision are gone, we see Eric's car burst into flames. The man driving the eighteen-wheeler that Mr. Walker's Datsun is knocked under grabs a fire extinguisher from his truck. He rushes with other people to Eric's car. He begins putting out the fire. A lady brings a blanket and starts swatting at the lingering flames. Eric is unconscious. Using the blanket, someone is able to open the door on the passenger side. A couple of courageous men crawl in and pull Eric out while flames still fill the air around Eric's car. Black smoke rises from this scene as Eric is wrapped in a blanket and laid on the ground. We can see how badly burned he is. Police officers are arriving and calling for the Life Flight helicopter. As we stand here waiting with Eric for help, can we say anything else but "how needless—how needless?"

Everything that happened that morning could have been avoided if the Poole driver had operated his truck in keeping with what we all understand to be ordinarily safe, careful, and prudent principles. The rules of the road that we require of ourselves and expect of others who use our freeways.

Now, years after Eric's death, these parents find themselves in the courtroom asking that this corporate defendant be held accountable for the death of their son. With what we know about what happened, does it make any sense that this defendant would try to lay the fault for what happened at the feet of others? The papers on file in this cause [*putting hand on top of court's pleading board on the counsel table*] claim that the crash was Eric's fault. The defendant's pleadings contend that other drivers in this pileup were negligent and they caused Eric's death. They claim it was the construction company's fault. They cross-act against the construction company, alleging they should have had additional warnings or signs in place. While Glen and Lynn Walker believe that the only people responsible for their son's death are these defendants, we adopt in our pleadings Poole's contentions only to fully protect the interest of these parents.

None of this makes any sense to these parents. Rather than being accountable for their actions, the defendant corporation and its driver point the finger at everyone else.

If you were to ask Glen and Lynn what their definition of justice is, they would reply, "decency." Just do the honorable, decent thing. But these defendants reply with well-paid experts committed to convincing us that speed is irrelevant, distance is illusory, and irresponsibility can be justified by complex calculations. This makes no sense to these parents. This is a senseless tragedy. But even sadder is the fact that Glen and Lynn's ordeal will never be played out. The catastrophe of June 28th is endless for them.

Eric Walker was born on September 16, 1962. He was a healthy, normal child. His parents, a Baptist minister and a homemaker, live in Baytown. Within a few days of his birth, Eric was living in a modest home but one filled with love. God blessed Eric with a good family. He had two wonderful sisters, one who was older and one younger. While his parents were people of modest means, they provided him with the love, attention, and care that, unfortunately, not all of us get. This was a close family who did everything together. They went to the beach, Astroworld, and ball games. They went on vacations together. Eric loved sports and became active in Little League baseball.

At an early age Eric discovered he shared his father's interest in music. He learned how to play the piano. Eric was in the school band. He enjoyed the youth activities at his father's church. This common interest was shared between him and his father up until that fatal day when Glen sent Eric on the family errand.

All this is not to say that Eric did not have some periods of adjustment in his life. When he was a junior in high school, he lived apart from his mother and father for a while. Like many youngsters that age, Eric became rebellious for a short period of time. His parents didn't press the issue. They realized this was only a passing phase, one their son would outgrow. As fate would have it, Eric did indeed find that his sought-after sense of responsibility was not all that it was cut out to be. Because of the pressures that he placed on himself to be completely financially independent from his parents, he experienced an episode that required medical attention. He was hospitalized and treated for a medical problem that at one time some of the doctors thought might be multiple sclerosis. It turned out not to be. Eric got better. He continued to improve. He had been thinking about joining the Marines. But after he got well he decided that he wanted to be an EMT—an Emergency Medical Technician. He wanted to drive and work in ambulances. He was a young man intent on helping and benefiting others. He came back home and began to pursue his career. He took up again his interest in music. Eric is finally at peace with himself and the world when he leaves to run his father's errand.

The defense says that they are not responsible for what happened. They will point to how the written report of the investigating officer conflicts with some of the eyewitness testimony. The state trooper didn't talk to all the witnesses. With the pandemonium at the scene, he didn't get a lot of information that we have now. A lot of these facts wouldn't have seen the light of day had not these parents insisted and persisted in knowing the true facts of their son's death. We will hear the testimony of witnesses who were there but moved out of the Houston area. Every available witness who can shed any light on what happened has testified under oath. It is crystal clear that this multivehicle crash was the result of the recklessness and carelessness of the Poole driver who was goaded by corporate greed. His irresponsibility was sponsored by a corporate policy that encouraged speed even in places where it couldn't be safe.

When we hear the defense talk about the inconsistencies with the witnesses and the findings of this dedicated state trooper, we need to remember that the most frustrating part of the work of these officers is the fact that when they do their job, when they attempt to charge the lawbreaker, whether he be the felon who steals into your house, or the reckless truck driver, it is juries who let these people go. If we do not enforce our responsibility stringently, find legal responsibility where it exists, find full damages that have been proven, are we not documenting what some of these officers suspect—that since nobody else cares, why should they?

The front of the Poole eighteen-wheeler crashed into the side of Eric's car. The impact knocked Eric unconscious. No one knows how or why, but the gasoline spilled on the ground under Eric's car and caught fire. Eric was trapped for several minutes while flames engulfed his car. He was burned severely over 50 percent of his body. The Life Flight helicopter took him to the John Sealy Burn Institute in Galveston. The burn specialists treated him for 196 hours before he died on July 5, 1983.

Dr. David Hearndon is the chief of staff of the John Sealy Burn Center. He is imminently qualified as a burn specialist. Dr. Hearndon knows all about the problems presented by burn patients and the type of complication that claimed Eric's life. There will be no doubt—there will be no reasonable scientific or medical debate—that Eric Walker died as a result of the injuries he received in that collision. Had the collision not occurred, Eric would have lived a full and complete life. Eric was suffering from no medical disease or infirmities known to medical science that would have in any way shortened his life expectancy or interfered with his enjoyment of life. He had no physical problems that would have prevented him from contributing and progressing and remaining a loving son and a source of love and affection for his parents for the rest of their lives.

We don't want to think about the agony, the suffering, the torment, the torture that Eric experienced during those 196 hours before he died. Dr. Hearndon has seen a lot of burn victims. You might think he, above all others, would be hardened to it. But when you hear him describe what Eric went through you will know that no matter how often you see it, the torture that burn victims go through tears at your heart.

It is easy to consider time as an absolute. It is not. A minute, sixty seconds, can be the blinking of any eye or an eternity. I have been given forty-five minutes for this opening statement. Because I am so dedicated to this search for truth and justice, and concerned that we all understand what happened, I know my allotted time will fly. Before I know it, the judge will be saying, "Time is up, counsel."

People who enjoy golf say that time just seems to fly on the golf course. Whether it is tennis or fishing, if it is something that gives us pleasure, hours seem to become minutes. How many times have you, after visiting over a cup of coffee with a friend, found yourself glancing at your watch, realizing you had something else to do, and remarked "Look at the time—I didn't realize I had been here that long." After a couple of days off over the weekend, we return to our offices on Monday and remark to our coworkers, "Gee, the weekend just flew. It seems like I just left the office a short time ago."

But when we face pain, agony, and tragedy—time stands still. When the dentist tells you that you are going to be an hour in the chair, you think, "Gee, that's a long time." Yet that hour, that treatment, is given with the benefit of modern drugs—Novocaine—and is in most instances painless.

The kind of pain that Eric Walker knew does not pass like a minute on the golf course or a minute visiting with good friends. Minutes of pain become hours, hours of pain become centuries, and days of pain become eternities.

In this case, it is not the hell of the flesh we must understand. It is the hell of the mind. The burning and scarring of the body pales when we consider the burning and scarring of the soul. The blind poet, John Milton, said:

> The mind is its own place, and in itself can make a Heaven of Hell, a Hell of Heaven.

You will understand Eric's torment when you see the photographs doctors took at John Sealy. The photographs show Eric's physical hell, but they can't show the hell that these parents were cast into. You will not see photographs of the minds of Eric and Glen and Lynn.

The people who know this family best, who shared pleasures with them, who consider themselves friends, tell us that this was a close family. They also say that Glen and Lynn have never gotten over Eric's death, and they don't think they ever will.

During the voir dire examination we talked about the elements of damages parents can recover when they lose a son. Glen and Lynn Walker have life expectancies in excess of thirty years. Even though they are in their "middle ages," they know it won't be too long before they are in their twilight years. The time will come when they will be less able to care for themselves and would rely on their children to help around the house, provide maintenance, support, and counsel, and just help with things that get hard to do when you are older. When we say the loss of Eric was endless, the defendants say, "Let's not forget, these parents had two other children." The Walkers' girls are now grown. Eric was their only son. Parents of children know there is a special bond formed between mother and son and father and son. No one would suggest that the loss of a daughter is any less than the loss of a son. But we need to remember than Glen and Lynn lost their only son. This is a special loss recognized in the law. To arrive at reasonable compensation—to repay these parents for their loss—we have to consider the nature of the loss and the time over which that loss will be experienced. When we think of it in those terms, we bring ourselves to some appreciation of what is right for these parents.

It will come as no surprise to any of us that, at the conclusion of this evidence, the defense will say that the dollar amounts ought to be lower. Parents who lose a son or daughter are always in a dilemma as far as the defense is concerned. If the child is young, four, five, or six, the defense is that you and the parents could never know whether this would have been a good son or daughter or not. He or she hadn't lived long enough, hadn't matured, hadn't done enough to form a basis for that opinion. If the son or daughter is thirty years old, established and doing well, then the argument is that the loss is not great. After all, the child had grown, matured, and was no longer living at home with the parents.

When a teenager is killed, we hear that he was rebellious, irresponsible, or had the vices of adolescence. You will hear some of that in this case. As the defense suggests that Eric Walker was not a good, responsible boy, imagine the effect on these parents. This good father and mother have suffered a tragic loss. Now they must deal with this corporate defendant who would trivialize their tragedy. A tragedy that was needless, senseless, and endless.

A couple of evenings ago, I went out to dinner with my family to a nice restaurant. They had the television on at the bar. The Houston Rockets were playing. No one was really watching the television except a couple of ladies sitting at the bar. Everyone else was enjoying their supper. The next time I looked up, the television screen was filled with flame and fire. One scene after another of automobiles crashing into each other and fire spewing out was flashed across the screen. I don't know whether they changed the channel or if this was a commercial. We can only imagine how Glen and Lynn feel when they see something like that come on television.

There are many constant reminders when you lose a son. His room, his pictures, his things. These parents have a peculiar reminder. Every time an eighteen-wheeler speeds by them on the freeway—they are reminded. Every time they see on television conflagration, fire, explosions, cars crashing into each other—they are reminded.

Every time they pass the Sheldon Road overpass—they are reminded.

We see these eighteen-wheelers on our freeways. Some are driven by good, cautious drivers. Others seem committed to corporate policies like Poole's—the bigger the load, the faster the road, the better the bottom line. Sometimes the drivers act like they want the whole freeway. Glen and Lynn Walker would say, "Give them the whole freeway—just let us have our son back."

No one can give these folks what they want, what they need, what they deserve. Since we can't do that, shouldn't we, at the least, give them the full measure of justice. You know, it is only if we do that, that all of us, all of us, can say that corporate irresponsibility has a price. And that price is based not on what would be cruel to these parents but on what would be decent. What would be just.

27

Illustrative Opening Statement
Premises—Unsafe Ladder

In June 1997, Jim M. Perdue, Jr., tried the case of *Raymond McFarland v. Paul Porter and Green Bull, Inc.*, Cause No. 96-021827 in the 152nd District Court of Harris County, Texas. The defendant had a homeowner's policy with Allstate. Pretrial settlement negotiations resulted in Allstate offering $150,000. We rejected the offer.

On June 18, following a week-long trial, the jury delivered its verdict for $583,000 and imposed 80 percent of the comparative fault on the defendant.

Ray McFarland was a sixty-seven-year-old self-employed property damage claims adjuster. Ray's specialty was analyzing damage to rooftops, especially commercial and residential properties. He had climbed ladders and walked roofs for most of his professional life.

A commercial builder for whom Ray had done some work before asked Ray to look at some potential damage at a townhouse property. This visit to the roof was a favor, not a formal job. The builder had a unique ladder that featured opposing joints hinging together three separate four-foot sections. The ladder folds into a very small space. Its unique utility is that it will fit in the trunk of a car. After the ladder was secured and both men had gone up to the roof, Ray McFarland was the first one to come back down. The bottom hinges of the ladder collapsed. Ray fell approximately ten feet, suffering a shattered heel bone and broken dental bridge work.

The focus group identified two primary issues of concern. First, the comparative responsibility a jury might attribute to Ray McFarland could be substantial. He had worked with ladders and climbed roofs as a main part of his profession. He chose to climb up the ladder himself, not as a job but as a favor. He had stood by and watched as the builder erected and secured the ladder. It was important to focus on the defendant's conduct to minimize the plaintiff's comparative fault. Second, the mechanism of the ladder collapse was difficult to explain. The ladder had been assembled and both men had successfully climbed it to the rooftop. The ladder collapsed when Ray, as the first one down, began to descend from the roof. How could the ladder have been secure and held the weight of both men as they went up but collapsed as Ray came back down? Fortunately, the design of the ladder and the testimony of our expert provided an explanation.

Finally, every case needs some juice, or indignation. In this case, the homeowner's insurance company had written a letter to Ray accepting liability for his fall and asking him to send all his medical bills to them for reimbursement. However, as Ray required three operations to rebuild his shattered heel bone and a subsequent revision to a prior hip replacement, the medical bills exceeded $50,000. Suddenly, Allstate changed positions, writing a second letter that suggested Ray was the person at fault and refusing to pay for the medical bills. The subtheme of responsibility was started in opening statement and carried through to closing argument.

THE OPENING STATEMENT

Mr. Jim M. Perdue, Jr.:

Trust. If you can't trust your friends, who can you trust? Ray McFarland trusted his friend, Paul Porter. Paul Porter betrayed that trust on March 16, 1995. That breach of trust changed Ray's life forever.

Ray was doing this defendant a favor when he climbed this ladder [*pointing to ladder in courtroom*]. A ladder the defendant told Ray was safe to use, a ladder the defendant put together; the defendant's ladder. The ladder wasn't safe, it was improperly assembled, it came apart, and Ray fell ten feet. He crushed his heel bone, broke teeth. He has never recovered.

After you hear the evidence in this case, you will wonder how a friend who hurts a friend can first accept, then deny responsibility.

May it please the Court:

The defendant is a contractor that builds roofs for apartment complexes. He is the guy that makes the bids and then contacts subcontractors to do the work. On March 16, 1995, Ray was looking at property damage at an apartment complex when the defendant asked Ray if he would do him a favor. The defendant wanted Ray to come to a rental property he owned, an empty condominium, and see if there was any property damage. It was a handshake deal, and Ray put his trust in the defendant. If you can't trust a friend, who can you trust?

The defendant takes Ray and his daughter Stephanie to his condominium. The defendant owns a ladder that he wants to use to get to the roof. This ladder is an extending ladder that has three joints of four feet. It is a twelve-foot ladder. But the condominium is two stories tall. So Ray, Stephanie, and the defendant go to the second floor of this empty condominium. The defendant brings his ladder. The defendant puts the ladder together so that he and Ray can climb up on the roof. Ray asks the defendant to go up first, and the defendant does. Ray follows the defendant to the roof and does the job as a favor. But as Ray begins to climb down the ladder, after one or two steps the ladder collapses and throws Ray backward. Fortunately, Stephanie stops him from going over the edge of the balcony down even farther to the ground below. But Ray falls, hitting the floor of the balcony. Ray is seriously injured. So hurt and broken that life will never be the same.

After Ray's fall, the medical bills begin to mount. The defense representatives speak with Mr. Porter. They call Ray. They examine the ladder. They accept liability. Liability means legal responsibility. The defendant's representatives write Ray a letter accepting liability—recognizing their responsibility.

Ray's medical bills continue to mount. This was a serious fall that caused Ray's heel bone to explode. The calcaneus bone, or your heel bone, is the most fundamental bone in your foot. When Ray falls to the floor of the balcony his heel bone is crushed. Shattered into so many pieces that the orthopedist, the bone surgeon, can't get enough bone to hold his foot together. The pins the doctor puts in are inadequate and a second surgery is necessary. The orthopedist puts in more pins and cement in a desperate attempt to hold Ray's shattered foot together. Ray has more problems. He is on crutches. He develops serious problems in his hip. He had a hip replacement five years before. It took, and Ray did well. He was doing fine before his fall at the defendant's condo.

But after the fall the stress on the hip becomes too much. The right hip is reoperated. Ray has major dental work because his teeth shattered through the top of his mouth. He woke up in continuous pain. He is limited to walking around on his crutches for no longer than one hundred feet.

The defendant and his representatives accept responsibility until it becomes obvious that Ray's damages are substantial, the injuries permanent. It's a big thing to be responsible until the responsible thing becomes big. All this time Ray is thinking, "If you can't trust your friend, who can you trust?" Now the defendant denies responsibility. "Ray's fall wasn't my fault," he says in pleadings in this Court.

Ray McFarland and his family have always been the type of people who accept responsibility for their actions. At the end of this trial, Ray and I will tell you that if you find him responsible for anything, he accepts that. The defense says in their pleadings on file in this Court, "We deny everything. Prove it."

I am proud to be before you today to represent Ray McFarland, a man I have come to respect. Ray began work in the property damage adjusting field over thirty years ago. Ray is the guy that individual homeowners or apartment complex owners call when they are in a dispute with their property insurance company. When they suffer roofing damage because of a hurricane or a hailstorm or a windstorm, property owners make a claim under their insurance. If the insurance company comes back with an offer to pay for the damage that seems inadequate, the homeowner calls Ray. Ray comes and assesses the damage to the roof and begins to broker for full coverage and replacement value with the insurance company. It has been Ray's job for thirty years to make sure that insurance companies are fair to the people that hold property insurance policies. Ray will tell you that he has been very successful in his job. He was well respected. Ray taught property adjusters and claims adjusters for independent contractors and for insurance companies. Stephanie will tell you that few people could read an insurance policy as well as Ray can and make sure that the property owner who has suffered damage gets their full replacement cost when a hurricane devastates their home or property.

In these cases where medical damages are at issue, it should come as no surprise that Ray's medical history may become an issue. About ten years ago, Ray had some pain in his back. In 1987, Ray had back surgery, but it gave him no relief. The next year, Ray went and saw a different doctor. That doctor diagnosed Ray as never having any real back problems. He said that the back surgery was unnecessary. He diagnosed Ray's problems as caused by his right hip. So Ray had a total hip replacement. Within six months Ray was at full strength, working jobs across Texas, in San Antonio, Houston, and Dallas. He worked jobs in Florida and California. Even working jobs in North Carolina. He climbed ladders and walked pitched roofs. He was active and contributing to his and his daughter's business. He was earning good money.

Ray has not made a dollar since this accident occurred.

Since we've moved from "we want to do the right thing" to "prove it," we have to go back. Back to March 16, 1995. We're at Lyon's Court Apartments. Ray is doing his job. He is here at the Lyons Court Apartments, owned by Harry Reed, because Ray has been doing work for Harry Reed–owned properties for twenty years. A big rain and windstorm hit Houston during the first part of March. Ray goes to look at the roof at the Lyons Court Apartments. The apartment complex provides Ray a ladder. The property manager goes up the ladder and Ray follows. They look at the roof and Ray assesses the damage. Ray climbs back down the ladder and the property manager follows.

At Lyons Court Apartments, Ray runs into the defendant. He has known the defendant for about five years. The defendant is a contractor in the roofing business. He wants to get a bid on the Lyons Court business. But the defendant also has property of his own. He owns eight rental properties here in the Houston area. On one of his rental properties, there is a dispute between the condominium or homeowner's association and the insurance company as to the amount of roof damage due to this same storm. The defendant asks Ray if he would come out and look at the roof of his condominium on Bering Street. He tells Ray this is a favor but that he might be able to get Ray more business through the homeowner's association. It was, without a doubt, a handshake deal. If you can't trust a friend, who can you trust?

So Ray and Stephanie follow the defendant out to his townhouse. These row townhouses look like many you've seen around Houston. Two stories tall [*showing photographs*], brick veneer exterior, balconies on the second floor. It is a bright day, hardly a cloud in the sky. Ray is thinking, "Another good day to be alive and well, and productive."

The defendant shows them into the townhouse and up to the second floor. The defendant gets his ladder. There is no dispute that this is a ladder that the defendant owns. It is a ladder that the defendant has used before.

This is not a normal type of ladder. It is what is called an adjuster's ladder. It fits into the trunk of a car. It comes in three sections that are on hinges that fold out to extend it to its full length. The only person in the group who has ever used this ladder before, that has ever put this ladder together before, that has ever climbed this ladder, is the defendant. The only person that has been to this property before and understood its layout is the defendant. The only person who would benefit from this undertaking is—the defendant.

The way this ladder works is that once it is extended, a steel pin is inserted through holes in the hinges. Once the steel pin is all the way through the layers of aluminum on the ladder, then the hinges cannot move. But recognize that the hinges go in opposite directions [*referring to drawing*]. One hinge will work with gravity and the weight on it when leaned up against the wall. But the other hinge, whether it is the hinge highest or the hinge lowest, depending on which side of the ladder is facing the wall, will always collapse unless the pins are all the way through.

This ladder is not self-locking like an extension ladder. This ladder doesn't have some type of catch that activates on itself and then requires a release. This ladder requires the owner to place this pin through the hinge. The hole for the pin is three-eighths of an inch. And there is supposed to be, on small chains, pins for each hole that are three-eighths of an inch in diameter [*referring to photograph*].

The defendant brings the ladder up to the balcony. He extends it. He begins to put the ladder together. Ray asks the defendant if there is anything he can do, and the defendant responds that he has used the ladder before. Stephanie asks if there is anything she can do, and the defendant responds that he knows what he is doing. Stephanie sees that there are only three pins on the ladder. She asks the defendant where the fourth pin is. And Mr. Porter pulls something out of his pocket and takes a hammer to pound this last, fourth pin through the hole. "Trust me, I know what I am doing," he says as he raises the ladder up from the balcony floor to the roof.

There is no dispute today that there is no fourth pin attached to this ladder today as it sits here in this courtroom. There is no dispute that there was not a fourth pin attached to the ladder the day after this event. The defendant can't explain where the fourth pin is or where it went. It wasn't the one that came with the ladder. The ones that come with the ladder hang by chains like the ones on there now.

The defendant takes this ladder out to the balcony and sets it up against the wall. He tells Ray it's safe. Ray asks the defendant to climb up first. The defendant goes up the ladder to his roof. Ray takes off his boots so that he can be safe and not slip. He follows Mr. Porter up the ladder. Ray and the defendant inspect the roof. Ray will go down first.

Ron Cowick is a professional engineer registered by the State of Texas. Mr. Cowick has worked in petrochemical plants here on the Gulf Coast for most of the past twenty years. He is a person who has managed individuals and investigated accidents. He is also a person who has testified and consulted about product safety. He has focused solely on the technical aspects of the case and the forces that are involved. These pins are tapered at the end. As you can see, they don't come to a solid end but actually have some pointed tip [*demonstrating*]. If they are not all the way through each layer of aluminum, they can work their way back out and be pushed out by pressure on the slanted end of the pins. Mr. Cowick will explain how the forces at the top of the ladder and the weight of Mr. McFarland, who weighs a lot more than the defendant, can work on the pins in this bottom hinge. Mr. Porter testified that he had used WD-40 before on these hinges in an effort to get the ladder extended and get the pins in.

What happened? Was it the wrong kind of pin? Did the defendant fail to pound the pin in the whole way? Ray will never know for sure. We do know this. Sound scientific and engineering principles tell us the ladder will not collapse even with two or three men of Ray's weight if it is properly assembled using the manufacturer's parts. We know the defendant put the ladder together. We know the defendant told Ray it was safe. Ray trusted him. If you can't trust a friend, who can you trust?

As Ray climbs on the ladder to make his way down he puts his foot on the first step. He swings his other foot around and puts his foot on the next rung. As Ray starts down, the ladder hinge collapses. Ray is tossed backward from the roof. Stephanie reaches out desperately and catches Ray before he goes over the edge. She saves Ray from falling even farther. But Ray lands with full force on his left foot. And instantaneously Ray's heel bone explodes. It is crushed by the force of the fall. There is no dispute about the extent of Ray's injuries. They are diagnosed as serious and severe when Ray goes to the emergency room that day. Ray waits in the emergency room at Memorial Southwest for some five hours. The doctors tell him that he has an extremely serious injury, but there is no orthopedic surgeon at the hospital that day. He will have to wait until Monday. One doctor even comments that they might have to cut Ray's foot off. So Ray and Stephanie get in their car and drive home to Halletsville, Texas. That Sunday, Ray calls his orthopedic doctor in Victoria, Dr. John Wright. He explains to Dr. Wright that he thinks he has broken his ankle or foot, and it is extremely swollen. Dr. Wright tells Ray to come in tomorrow.

As soon as Dr. Wright sees Ray's foot, he puts Ray into the hospital and prepares for major surgery. Ever since, Ray's physicians have worked hard to treat this crush injury.

This is a picture of Ray's foot early on, after these first sets of surgeries [*demonstrating*]. As you can see, Ray's foot was demolished.

This is a picture of Ray's foot a month ago [*demonstrating*]. It is still deformed.

Ray won't give up. He wants to walk—to be whole—but he is limited to crutches. He visits a dentist in San Antonio who has to do total bridgework because of the force of Ray's fall. Ray has a lot of physical therapy and home care. Ray has a second foot operation. Ray as he walks on his canes begins to put too much weight on his right hip. The hip replacement that he had, that had been working so well, begins to wear down, and Dr. Wright has to do a revision to the hip replacement so that it doesn't fail. Ray has to take pain pills just so he can move. His shoulders begin to bear all of his weight. And Ray begins to lose his ability not only to do his job but to support his family or enjoy his grandson when they would go fishing or walking in the woods or playing baseball. Things that meant so much to him before March 16, 1995.

Ray has not worked a day since this devastating injury. He hasn't been able to, though he has tried. Stephanie has continued the family business and tried to perform the property adjusting services that Ray used to do. But it's not the same. The business needs Ray's efforts, energies, and expertise. This family has had to pull itself in. Stephanie now lives with Ray and his wife. The McFarlands are a loving and close family. They have struggled to do the right thing. To try to honor their commitments to each other. To accept their responsibilities, to honor their trust. But for Ray, the events that have brought him here are foreign to his family. If you can't trust a friend, who can you trust?

28

Illustrative Closing Summation

Baby Brain Damaged at Birth Due to Obstetrical Nursing Negligence

On September 26, 1995, the jury returned its verdict in the case of *Lisa Lee, Individually, and Next Friend of Alexander Lee, a Minor v. Healthcare Management, Parkway Hospital and Chin H. Lee, M.D.*, Cause No. 93-31897 in the 151st District Court of Harris County, Texas. The plaintiff sued the defendant, Parkway Hospital, and others, alleging negligence on the part of the hospital's nursing staff in administering Pitocin (a uterine stimulant) to the mother during labor without a doctor's order. The plaintiff contended that as a result of the nurse's negligence the mother developed tetanic (strong and unrelenting) contractions, her uterus ruptured, and the minor plaintiff sustained severe and permanent brain damage.

At the time of trial, the minor plaintiff was functioning at the level of a one-year-old. The court submitted damages on behalf of the minor plaintiff for his past and future pain and anguish, past and future physical impairment, past and future physical disfigurement, and future medical, nursing, and custodial care, education, and therapy beyond the age of eighteen.

The court submitted damages on behalf of the mother for the cost of medical, nursing, and custodial care, the therapy required of the minor plaintiff to the age of eighteen, and damage to the familial relationship.

The jury found the defendant hospital negligent and that such negligence was a proximate cause of damages to the adult and minor plaintiff. The judgment entered by the court on the basis of the jury's verdict was for $16 million. The appellate opinion affirming the judgment may be found at *Parkway Hospital, Inc. v. Lee*, 946 S.W.2d 580 (Tex. App.—Houston [14th Dist.] 1997, writ denied).

THE CLOSING SUMMATION

Mr. Jim M. Perdue:

When Lisa Lee went into Parkway Hospital in labor on June 24, 1992, she was filled with the hopes and dreams of a storehouse plentifully supplied by her Creator. She was, like any mother in labor, trusting, responsible, and vulnerable. If the right people do the right thing at the right time, this family's store of treasures remain safe and inviolate. But as you have heard, the wrong people do the wrong thing at the wrong time. A nurse gives Lisa a powerful drug, Pitocin, during her later stages of labor. It is a drug she does not need. It is a drug her doctor has not ordered. It causes her uterus to violently and continually contract—to go into spasms. It rams Alexander's head against an undilated cervix. It hemorrhages his brain and suffocates him. And so the family's store of hopes and dreams are shoplifted by this defendant's negligence. When the defendants are stopped in the parking lot, their response is not only do they not feel any obligation to return anything, they have the right to take from some other family's store sometime down the line.

May it please this honorable Court:

What happened to Lisa and Alexander is nothing less than a nightmare. It is a story filled with the demons and monsters belched forth by medical misadventure. There is no question of continuing and overwhelming medical needs and expenses—they are certain. This is truly a nightmare without end.

But a courtroom is a magical place. I can prove it to you. Ask yourself to think back about a little over five weeks ago when you first showed up in the jury assembly room. You were brought over to the big courtroom we have down on the second floor, and you remember sitting out there in that huge group we started with—the lawyers and the Judge talking to you. If you're like most jurors when your name was called to be on this jury, you were probably surprised, then you had these kind of thoughts: Am I strong enough to serve? Am I smart enough to be able to decide these kinds of issues? Am I patient enough to be fair? Am I courageous, do I have the moral fiber to be just? Have I the ability to live up to the oath that I'm going to take? Up to that point in time you had been told where to go and how to get there and had been marched around in big groups of people and probably—probably felt a little powerless. But a funny thing happens after people are on a jury for a while, after you sit here for a week or two, it starts to dawn on you. As a group of people we have a lot of power. We have a lot of power. It probably started to dawn on you after you started hearing some of the evidence in this case—we have power. We have the power to stop those people who would splatter the innocent and leave justice as insignificant roadkill in the rush to a better bottom line. As you saw that attitude in action, as you witnessed the arrogance of power, maybe you said to yourself, "They've got a little speed bump they've got to get over. A little something to slow them down." A jury.

It began to dawn on you that we have a power to change things. We have the power with our verdict to tell people this is not the way things should be done. We also have some other power. We have the power to protect the innocent. We have the power to do justice. We have the power to change things.

I wonder if when we had been into this case two or three weeks, if you had come in one morning or one afternoon and Judge Garcia had said, "Ladies and gentlemen, you can go home, the parties have settled their case." I wonder if there were any of you that instead of saying, "Well, thank goodness. I can just go back to my life," I wonder if there were any of you who would have said and maybe even come up to me and said, "Jim, why did you do that? Why did you do that? Now we can't answer this. Now we can't by our verdict tell hospitals we don't want our critical healthcare decisions being turned over to poorly trained nurses when we're paying doctors to make those kind of judgments—to make those decisions. We don't want that, and we won't permit it and we don't want corporate executives making decisions in far-away places to better their bottom line, to increase their profitability by holding down their costs." I wonder if there's anyone who would have said, "Jim, you shouldn't have done that. We wanted to answer these questions. We wanted to pass on this. We wanted to send a message."

This is a case about change. It is about change. Parkway needs to change its policies. They say they will not. They come into this courtroom and they say if a lady comes into the hospital tomorrow, they're going to do the same thing to her that they did to Lisa Lee. We say they need to change and the other hospitals in their chain of hospitals that are doing it, they need to change. And change means changing the way they are delivering health care. It doesn't mean we need to change our story. It doesn't mean scripting your defense and coaching your nurses so you can change the facts. It means change what you're doing, not change your story in court when the first and second fall apart.

We know what happened on June 24, 1992. We don't need experts to tell us. The defendant may not like the facts, but they are there for anyone to see. Lisa Lee was forty years old, carrying her fourth pregnancy. At 4:00 AM she began experiencing labor and was driven to the defendant hospital by the father of her child. They got there about 4:30. Lisa was evaluated and put on electronic fetal monitoring. Her labor was followed. The first nurse talked to her obstetrician at 5:30 AM. He didn't authorize or order Pitocin. She didn't need it.

At seven o'clock there was a shift change and Nurse Tarriman came on board. Nurse Tarriman was educated in the Philippines and was working here under a work visa. She was recruited by one of these nursing agencies. She worked in New York for a while until she failed her New York boards. So Coney Island Hospital terminated her.

She took her boards a second time and passed them. Then Parkway in Houston hired her. When Parkway hired her, they didn't verify or check her credentials or references. They brought her right into the hospital, put her on probation for ninety days, and then cut her loose taking care of patients. It was right after the end of her probationary period that Lisa Lee came into the hospital. It is this minimally trained, unsupervised, foreign-educated nurse that the defense says should have the discretion when to use powerful obstetrical drugs.

She was the wrong person at the wrong time.

Then this wrong person does the wrong thing.

We are standing off to the side at Parkway Hospital at 8:30 AM on June 24, 1992. Lisa Lee is in the second stage of labor. Her labor is progressing well. Things are going the way God intended them. Alexander and Lisa's storehouse is full. It is abundant.

Alexander is doing well [*referring to video animation*]. A lot of things tell us that. The fetal heart monitor tracing shows a healthy baby. Alexander has a long cord. The cord is long because a healthy baby pulls on the cord, lengthening it. The cord is planted deep in the uterine wall. It has good vasculature. We know that is the situation because that's what is seen by the pathologist after this delivery.

We're standing off to the side as Nurse Tarriman goes to the obstetrical supplies and draws out a dose of Pitocin to give Lisa by IV piggyback drip. Don't we want to say as we watch her pull out the Pitocin, "Don't do that. You don't have a doctor's order." Don't we want to yell at her and say, "Giving Pitocin to a mother who is in active labor, the second stage of labor, is dangerous!"

Stand off to the side and watch as Nurse Tarriman hangs the Pitocin and begins giving it to Lisa through the IV. Don't we want to shout at her, "Don't do that. It's going to overstimulate this mother's uterus. It can cause it to go into tetanic contractions. It can cause it to rupture and damage the baby." Don't we want to say those things to her? Don't we want her to hear us?

Within a few minutes following administration of the Pitocin Lisa begins experiencing tetanic contractions. These are continuous and unrelenting contractions. Lisa's obstetrician, Dr. Lee, still had not gotten to the hospital. The pain becomes so severe that Lisa screams out. About this time Dr. Lee walks into the labor room. He can see that the electronic monitoring demonstrates Lisa's tetanic contractions. He can see the marked deceleration of Alexander's heart rate.

These tetanic contractions weren't the result of the nurse putting her hand on the TOCO, as the hospital claims. This spasm of the mother's womb was caused by the Pitocin. Standing off to the side, we knew it was going to happen when Nurse Tarriman decided to give the Pitocin without a doctor's order to a woman who was in active labor and progressing well.

They take the fetal heart monitor off. They take Lisa to delivery thirty minutes later. Alexander is born limp and flaccid. His APGAR scores are 2, 2, and 2. Out of a possible 10 points for a healthy baby, he gets just 2 points in the first minute of life, the fifth minute of life, and the tenth minute of life.

The obstetrician then sees that Lisa is bleeding a lot. He checks her and finds that her uterus is ruptured. Dr. Lee removes the ruptured, torn, and shredded uterus [*referring to blowup*]. God didn't do this. Lisa didn't do this. Alexander didn't do this. Lisa's uterus didn't rupture as a result of the delivery of Alexander. The Pitocin caused the tetanic contractions resulting in unrelenting spasms of the mother's womb. And so Lisa has to be castrated. The obstetrician must cut out her female organs to save her life. She almost dies from loss of blood. But the defense says they didn't do anything wrong. They say that Nurse Tarriman had the discretion to give Pitocin. They say the Pitocin didn't cause Alexander's brain damage or the tearing and hemorrhaging of Lisa's uterus.

You are chosen in this case, and if you think back five weeks ago when this case started, the defense has been one of collapsing excuses [*referring to excuse chart*]. As they would throw up one and we'd beat it down, another one would be thrown in its place. I thought I'd just put this up to remind us all what we have seen in this case. These are escape hatches. The defense tried a new one every day. Mr. [the defense attorney] got up on opening statement and said, "Pitocin is not a powerful drug and could not cause the damages sustained by Lisa and Alexander." Remember that, five weeks ago? That's what he told you before you heard any evidence. Then he said, "Pitocin didn't have time to get into her bloodstream." Do you remember that? And we brought the experiment with Dr. DesRosier and set it up so you could see it and you could time it. If we hadn't done that demonstration, they would be arguing right now, "Wait a minute. It didn't get there. It didn't get there." Well, you saw it get there and how it gets into the patient's bloodstream. Then they said, "Well, if it did get into her bloodstream there wasn't enough to cause tetanic contractions." If you don't like that one, "If there were tetanic contractions, they weren't caused by Pitocin." If you don't like that one, "There were no tetanic contractions." [*Referring to listed excuses on chart*].

Remember we had charted what Alexander's heart rate was during Lisa's labor. Everyone said this is a reassuring or good heart rate showing the baby's doing fine, until they give the Pitocin. But do you remember back early in this case they were saying, "Oh, no, Pitocin didn't cause that." And then they say, well—remember Mr. [the defense attorney] earlier in the case asking the doctors, "Well, maybe it was the Stadol that did it." Do you remember that? The Stadol caused him to be depressed. Well, that didn't last long so, well, maybe there wasn't any fetal distress to begin with.

They tried to throw in another excuse during this trial. If Lisa's uterus was—well, maybe it was inherently defective and predisposed to rupture by virtue of her previous D&Cs, it would have ruptured anyway. We heard that. And then we heard, well, maybe she had a placenta abruptio. You don't like that one, maybe she had a placenta previa, which is very different. Then we had, Alexander was suffering from some intrauterine virus. Do you remember that? Some questions to witnesses, maybe it was a virus. They don't know what virus, but it could have been a virus. Then we had the suggestion that maybe Alexander has a genetic defect. Then we had, well, he suffered from some chronic anoxia weeks, months before, and that's why he's brain damaged. Of course, Alexander weighed nine pounds and had no signs of poor development, so that doesn't fit. They've tried every escape hatch they could find to pound on. They are closed by simple, honest truth.

Alexander is brain damaged because the wrong person did the wrong thing at the wrong time.

We get down to the last one, the one that they kind of toss up every now and then. Lisa had an abortion when she was in Korea, and maybe if we toss that in a couple of times, we can prejudice somebody on the jury. And he wants to talk about us getting up and appealing to sympathy. I'll tell you, Lisa Lee doesn't need any of this jury's sympathy, and we've never asked for it. She's not here for sympathy. Lisa gets that from her God and her friends. She is here for justice. Justice under this evidence. Lisa needs that from you.

I'll tell you another thing that may change as a result of your verdict. Maybe we'll change—maybe we can change the way hospitals go about selecting their lawyers and who they pick. Do you remember when Helenbeth Newell was on the witness stand, I said, "When Mr. [previous defense attorney], your previous lawyer, was representing you, did you ever sign any papers, did you ever say anything, was anything ever filed on behalf of the hospital that wasn't true?"

She said, "Absolutely not."

I said, "Since Mr. [the defense attorney]'s been representing, have you ever signed anything that wasn't true?"

She said, "Yeah, he had me sign a false affidavit."

Did they think we would forget that testimony?

When you first came to this courtroom almost two months ago and heard about this case during the jury selection, we asked you, "What kind of care do you expect the hospital to give when a woman in labor comes in to deliver her baby?" We all agreed that we didn't expect perfect care, we know some things are beyond the control of doctors and nurses. But many of you told us at that time that you thought it was fair to expect that the hospital would give the best care they could. You thought hospitals ought to be personally responsible just like everyone else. You told us you didn't think it would be right for corporate owners of a chain of hospitals to take unnecessary risks and gamble with the lives of the patients who trusted them.

I knew then what the evidence was going to be in this case. You know now what I knew then. This whole case is about how far this corporate owner can go with their casino operation. The patients put up the stakes and take the gamble. They make decisions at the corporate level to better their bottom line by cutting back on nursing staff. They stack the deck against the patients when they decide to staff the obstetrical department with minimally trained nurses. Then they give the minimally trained nurses the discretion to administer dangerous drugs. Then they tell us that that's the way they're running their hospital and the way they're going to continue to run their hospital.

If they don't intend to change the way they treat patients, then maybe they ought to change the name of the hospital from Parkway to Hospital Casino. Let patients know that these corporate owners view patients like customers at the roulette wheel and dice table. But the hospital doesn't even want to run a fair game. They want to load the dice in their favor. Let me give you an example.

When our experts testified—Dr. Lucci, Dr. DesRosier, the others—the hospital lawyer kept trying to get them to agree that Alexander Lee's brain damage was in essence mental retardation. They brought out books and articles to support their contention that if a child is mentally retarded then he wasn't brain damaged during his delivery. Our experts all pointed out that mental retardation without motor deficits is not normally the result of a hypoxic injury. They told us that if a child has a hypoxic injury the damage will hit not only the cognitive center or thinking center, it's also going to hit motor function. So mental retardation without motor deficits is not due to an acute anoxic event. That is what they were selling you until we brought Alexander Lee to the courthouse the day that Dr. Yetman testified. Dr. Yetman treated Alexander at Hermann Hospital. He participated in those three months of care when Alexander was clinging to life. Dr. Yetman told you the nature and extent of the brain damage he felt that Alexander had at that time.

We didn't bring Alexander into the courtroom. There are reasons for that decision and I hope you all respect us for it. We brought Alexander into Judge Garcia's chambers and had a closed-circuit television hooked up so that you could see what was going on in that room as it took place. We wanted Dr. Yetman to do a simple examination and evaluation of Alexander that you could see. But when we got to that point: *Objection!* They didn't want you to see Dr. Yetman examine the child in your presence. They didn't want you to see Alexander and learn for yourself what they had done to him.

We brought Dr. Yetman into this courtroom so that you could watch the examination. Why did we want to do that? Why do you think we would do that? Because we wanted you to see. We wanted you to see it, because that way these defendants couldn't get up and say, "Well, Dr. Yetman, you really didn't see that. The child didn't do that. Dr. Yetman, you say he has this problem. He doesn't. You just thought you saw that." [*Playing videotape of examination of Alexander Lee by Dr. Yetman, which was performed during trial in judge's chambers.*]

We wanted you to see the facts—the truth. The hospital didn't want you to see Alexander because it would be apparent that what they had been trying to sell during their examinations of the plaintiff's experts would be seen for the lie it is. Alexander doesn't just have mental retardation, He has spasticity, he has motor damage.

The hospital not only gambled with the lives of Lisa and Alexander while they were under their care, they gambled in this courtroom. They put all their chips on the table in what we know now was an arrogant bluff in the belief that they could convince you that Alexander's brain damage was due to something other than Nurse Tarriman giving Pitocin during the latter stages of labor without a doctor's order when Lisa didn't need it. But when it came time for Alexander to turn his cards over and call their bluff, they want to declare themselves the winner without letting you see Alexander's hand. So when you approach caring for your patients that way, when you approach the question of who is responsible for Alexander's brain damage that way, it's not surprising that when we get down to the end they want you to now gamble with Alexander's future. There's no other way to put it. That's what they expect of you now.

Let's go back to that labor room on June 24th just before the nurse decides to give Lisa Lee the Pitocin. But this time she doesn't do the wrong thing. She does what any responsible nurse would do. She lets the labor progress. There are no problems with it. Why do we have to do anything? Why choose to give a dangerous drug that will hyperstimulate the uterus? [*Using chart of milestones for normal person.*]

Lisa's labor continues to progress, the obstetrician arrives, and a healthy, normal boy is delivered.

Alexander will be a normal baby. When he is about three or four months old his mother will see and hear that which will fill her heart with happiness for the rest of her life. Alexander voluntarily will smile and then he will laugh. For the next eighteen or more years, her home will be filled with the laughter of her son.

He will start sitting when he is about six or seven months old.

Somewhere around nine or ten months he will figure out that pushing off with his knees gives him just the boost he needs to get mobile.

He will learn to go from a crawling position into a sitting position.

When he is one, he will be a competent crawler.

It won't be long until he starts walking.

He will begin to speak.

The first word he will say will fill his mother's heart. "Mama."

At two he will start putting words together.

At two and a half he will begin his potty training.

At three he will learn how to ride a tricycle and begin showing a drive for independence. He will want to do things on his own and sleep in his own bed.

At four he is learning his ABCs.

At five he is in preschool.

At six he begins the first grade.

His mother will start to find his pockets filled with marbles, bubble gum, dead insects, and who knows what else.

He learns to read. Even before he starts school, he is showing his curiosity, asking his mother questions like:

"Why is the sky blue?"

"Where do babies come from?"

Every year in elementary school he learns more. He will learn math, history, and grammar. By the time he finishes elementary school, he is reading, doing multiplication and division, and graphing sentences into nouns, verbs, adjectives, and adverbs.

Middle school is always tough, particularly on boys. He may even get into a few fights, but he'll learn how to defend himself. He'll start noticing girls. He'll be like most boys, shy and intimidated by them. But by the time he's in high school, he'll be asking them out on a date. He'll learn how to drive a car. He'll get his driver's license. He'll go to his junior and senior proms. His mother will be so proud when she sees him dressed up for the first time in a tuxedo.

Lisa knows the importance of education and will encourage him to go to college. He may go to a school here in the city such as the University of Houston. So many working-class youngsters do. Or he may go off to school. He'll get his college degree. He will be a better wage earner with a college degree. We are able to project within reasonable certainty the kind of money he will make. He will get married. He will have his own family. But even with his own family he will continue to help his mother. As she ages he will always be there for her. When she can no longer care for herself, he may take her in with his family or help her find an assisted-care residence. He will be with Lisa when she dies. He will probably speak at her funeral. The last thoughts Lisa will have will be of the wonderful son she raised and how proud she is of all the things he accomplished.

But this is just a fantasy, isn't it? It is what could have been—what should have been. If we could go back to that day and tell the nurse not to give the Pitocin, that would be real magic wouldn't it? Everyone in this courtroom wishes we had it, but we don't. But the magic we have here is far from meaningless.

You've heard the testimony from the doctors that say Alexander has a normal life expectancy. You've heard from the life planners that Alexander is going to need care for the rest of his life. He will never be independent. You've heard from the economist what it's going to take in present-day dollars to see that Alexander gets the care he needs for the next seventy years of his life. I know the figures are mind-boggling [*referring to economic projection chart*].

You have the reports and you've seen the evidence. You've seen the line items for physical therapy, speech therapy, and medications. You've seen the line items and you've seen the photographs of the wheelchairs, vans, special bathing and toilet facilities, and other devices needed to improve both his physical condition and his living situation. The defendant won't bring any witness in here to say that maybe Alexander ought to do with a used wheelchair that costs a little less, or maybe he ought to try to make out with an undertrained nurse instead of one that is qualified. They won't do that. They want you to do that for them. They want you to take the last turn for Alexander on their crooked wheel. When someone says to you that these figures are too much, ask them what do you suggest Alexander does without? If there's something that you all agree Alexander shouldn't have, cross it off. It's entirely up to you. Just cross off the items you agree he should not get. Reduce the total down here at the bottom by the cost of that item. That way Alexander gets what you think he should have and doesn't get anything you think he shouldn't have.

When you read the Court's charge, I hope someone will take the time to count up the number of times the word "evidence" is used in there. It's the most-used word you will find. The reason that the Court uses that word so much is to remind you that your verdict should be based on the proof, the facts you've heard.

These defendants didn't bring you a bit of evidence on the issue of damages. We brought you the evaluations, we brought you the projections of the life-care plan, we brought you the calculations of the economist. The defendants' negligence moved into Alexander's brain during those forty-five minutes after Lisa was given Pitocin without a doctor's order. The effect of the defendants' negligence has been living there rent-free ever since. They took out a lifetime lease. Our job is to decide what the rent ought to be.

We bring you the life-care plan. Why do you think everyone calls it that? All of those figures represent what it takes to give Alexander life. These figures measure just the cost, not the agony. Just the price, not the uncertainty. The fee, not the fear. These numbers are what are necessary to care for, give him life. Give him the ability to get better. Give him the boost to the bottom rung of the ladder. Alexander and Lisa don't look for you or anyone else to climb the ladder for them. But they're not strong enough, big enough, to grab the bottom rung by themselves. They need a little boost up to that bottom rung and they'll climb the rest of the way themselves.

Isn't it interesting that the hospital that injured this mother and baby because they didn't play by the rules, didn't do what they should have in being careful with their patients, now look to you to help them out by doing exactly what they did—not follow the rules. Don't base your verdict only on the evidence you've heard. Do something else. The hospital is hoping that there will be someone on this jury who's going to say that maybe Alexander doesn't need all the things that the doctors, the healthcare planners, and the economists say. Let Alexander get by some other way. Maybe they can use that wheelchair a little longer, maybe Alexander won't need all that physical therapy, maybe they can go stand in line in the dark wards of the charity hospital to get the medical attention they need. They want you to make that last desperate gamble on behalf of Hospital Casino.

I'm not ashamed to ask for the money we've asked for in this case. I'm not embarrassed to stand before you on behalf of this family and tell you this is what it will take—this is what is fair. But I know that I don't have the power to bring justice to this family.

You've heard experts on medicine, rehabilitation, life care, and economic projections. You heard no experts on what is a fair price for Alexander's human suffering. There are no experts on that. Only you know what is it is like to know you should be holding a healthy child but holding instead one who will depend on you for the rest of your life. Someone who, when you are gone, will be struggling in the darkness of loneliness. That is why you are here. You are the experts on this child's worst losses and what they will be as he gets older.

When I was a young boy growing up in Galena Park, I'm not ashamed to say I grew up doggone poor. My mother was a secretary. I wanted to learn to play the trumpet. I don't know how she got up the money, but she got me a used trumpet. I couldn't play the trumpet. Literally, I couldn't. They say I'm tone deaf. I couldn't play the trumpet so I gave it up. That's one of the reasons I love music so much. I love listening to other people make beautiful, melodious, wonderful music. I admire it so much because I can't do it.

I got a little older, I wanted to go to college. I didn't have the money. I said I'm going to become an All-American football player. I'm going to college on a football scholarship. I played football as hard as I could in high school, but I was too short, too slow. I didn't make it. But I guess that's why you'll find me every weekend out at the University of Houston watching those football games because I really admire those people who can do that. I ended up working my way through school at a smelter out on Market Street.

Then I decided I wanted to be a trial lawyer. I wanted to be a trial lawyer and stand up for people. I want to represent the weak. I want to represent one against many. I want to bring justice to those who cannot bring it to themselves. I want to find injustice and strike it down. Do you know what I discovered? Thirty years I've been at it, and I've discovered it's just like the trumpet. It's just like playing football. I can't do it. I can't do it. I have to look to you to do it. You have to do it. I don't have the power.

When Lisa went into Parkway Hospital she expected—she expected that they would be careful with her. When Lisa went in to give birth to Alexander on June 24th, what she expected was for people to be careful with her and her son. I pray to God that all of you, once you get back in there, will be more careful with them than these defendants were. You have the power to do that. Don't squander the magic of this place and this time. Be careful with Lisa and Alexander. They are in your hands.

29

Illustrative Closing Summation

Pathology Mistake Leaves Woman Disfigured

On June 20, 1996, closing arguments were given in the case of *Lois M. Bush v. Don C. Quast, M.D., M. Sidney Anderson, M.D., Woman's Hospital of Texas, Inc. and Anderson Pathology Associates, P.A.*, Cause No. 94-26249 in the 165th District Court in Harris County, Texas. The jury found in favor of the plaintiff against the defendants and awarded $3.5 million in damages.

Lois Bush was a divorced mother of two who taught elementary school in the Clear Lake School District. In 1993, at the age of forty-two, Lois discovered a lump in her left breast on self-examination. She conferred with her gynecologist, who was not particularly concerned but felt that the mass should be surgically biopsied. He referred her to Dr. Quast, a specialist in breast surgery. She presented to Woman's Hospital of Texas on August 13, 1993, where three lumps were removed from her left breast and sent to pathology for frozen-section analysis. Dr. Anderson orally reported to Dr. Quast during the surgery that one of the lesions was malignant. A written report containing the diagnosis of "intraductal carcinoma in situ" was forwarded to Dr. Quast a few days later.

After she woke from anesthesia, Dr. Quast advised Mrs. Bush of the pathology diagnosis and recommended a radial mastectomy with a lymph node dissection. Five days later, on August 18, 1993, Dr. Quast performed the mastectomy.

A few days following the surgery, Dr. Quast told Lois by telephone that the hospital had lost the breast and underarm tissue before any pathology examination could be performed. He recommended an extensive course of chemotherapy and radiation.

Before consenting to the radical procedures her surgeon recommended, Lois consulted her brother, a physician practicing in San Antonio. He suggested that the original frozen-section slides be examined by other pathologists, all of whom confirmed that they were unable to diagnose cancer.

Lois Bush sued the defendants, Drs. Quast and Anderson, claiming that her mastectomy had been unnecessary as breast cancer could not be diagnosed from the biopsy. The hospital argued that the loss of the breast tissue was not a proximate cause of any damages sustained.

Following her mastectomy, Lois underwent four reconstructive surgeries because of various complications. Since these procedures were done during vacation periods, they caused little lost time from Lois's duties as a schoolteacher. One of the plaintiff's challenges was the fact that the "hard" damages consisted of approximately $70,000 in medical expenses. There was evidence of future medical complications, which could require additional treatments and surgeries.

The trial was a war of experts and medical literature. The defense relied on two studies published in national journals that they contended demonstrated that pathologists often disagree over interpretation of breast tissue slides. Thus, they argued that the fact that other pathologists might disagree with Dr. Anderson's diagnosis did not establish that he acted negligently.

THE CLOSING SUMMATION

Mr. Jim M. Perdue:

"Lois, you have cancer. We have to operate right away." Those were chilling words you heard on the afternoon of August 13, 1993. You heard them from men you trusted. It was a devastating diagnosis you got from your surgeon, from your gynecologist of fifteen years, and from a man you never met, the hospital pathologist who had made that diagnosis. And you've learned over the past three years that you trusted the wrong people to do the right thing. You didn't ask for any guarantees. All you wanted was that they would live up to their professional responsibilities, that they would do their best; and now for six weeks, you have heard these doctors and this hospital come with their laundry list of excuses to try and explain away the devastation, the disfigurement, the torment that you have experienced and will experience for the rest of your life. And we've all learned, we've all learned that some people in this case didn't grow up the way we did.

May it please this honorable Court, ladies and gentlemen:

You've probably figured out by now that the hard bark on me comes honestly. I grew up out here east of town on the ship channel in Galena Park. I grew up the way a lot of you grew up. Our country club was the icehouse my daddy hung out in. Our social circle was the church that my mother made sure that my brother and I went to every Sunday, Sunday school, church. We learned some great lessons there from the greatest teacher, a man who lived thousands of years ago and taught in parables.

One of the parables that he used to teach his lessons that most of us try to live by was the parable of the talents. A rich man is going on a long journey. He has three fellows working for him. He gives each of them talents according to their abilities. Now the biblical scholars tell us that a talent wasn't a measure of money. It was actually a measure of weight, but it equaled about three thousand shekels, and it represented several years of wages for most people. And so for the oldest, the most senior guy, he gave him five talents. The next junior employee, he gave two talents. The one with least seniority, he gave one talent. He left on his journey. They were fellows that he trusted, and so he entrusted great value to them. When he came back, he learned that the fellow who was most senior, to whom he had given five talents, had worked to preserve and enhance value. He had taken his effort and his time, and he had multiplied those talents. He turned them back over to his master. The second fellow had done the same. He took them, and he worked. And he spent his effort and his time and turned double the talents back over to the employer. But the third fellow, the junior fellow that was only given one talent, that great teacher taught us that he went and buried it in the ground. Because, you see, he didn't want to spend any time. He didn't want to make the effort. And so when the rich man came back from the journey and the junior servant dug the talent out and he handed him the one talent back, the rich man was angry because he'd let him down. He just sat on what he had. He didn't live up to the trust.

I was a junior in high school, and they were building a ballpark—a Little League ballpark—and one of the fellows in the Kiwanis there knew that we weren't very well off. We were poor. I'd had a little art in school, and the Kiwanis man said, "I'd like to get you to paint some signs, some advertising signs for the companies around the neighborhood to put up in the ballpark."

And he gave me twenty dollars. A lot of money back in 1956. He gave me twenty dollars so I could go buy plywood and the paint. I got with my younger brother and we painted those boards. The fellow came and got them and put them up on the ball field. I remember the day we went out and looked at that ball field, and they had all these signs done by these professional painters, who knew what they were doing, who took their time. Our signs, gosh, I was embarrassed. They weren't any good, not up to snuff.

Alongside the signs that were done right by people who knew what they were doing were our crude, amateurish signs. So when they guy came to pay me, I said, "I can't take your money. I didn't do the job."

Because that's the way we were raised. And I remember I worked in the grocery store after school for about three weeks to save up twenty dollars so I could pay him back the twenty dollars he had given me for the boards and paint. Because, you see, that's the way we were brought up. You and you and you and me, that's the way we were brought up. If you let somebody down, you made up to it and did what you could to make it right.

Lois's case is about to be over in a short time. After you deliver your verdict in this case, you'll be permitted to do something you haven't been permitted to do so far, and that is talk to people about the case. When you leave after delivering your verdict, you know as well as I do, your friends, your neighbors, your relatives, your coworkers, are going to ask, "Well, what was that case about? What was that case about?"

Some of you may say, "Well, that case was about some doctors who made a mistake and they came in with all kinds of excuses and they just didn't want to own up to the mistake they made."

But I'll bet that there's going to be one or two of you who will say, "No, that was a case about a drive-by diagnosis followed by a rush to surgery followed by a plunge off the cliff into medical oblivion. That's what that case was about."

In the summer of 1993, Lois Bush discovers a lump on her breast on self-examination. She does the responsible thing. She goes to her gynecologist, who does some diagnostic studies, who says, "I don't think it's anything to worry about, but just to be cautious, I want to send you over to a specialist, a breast specialist, a surgeon."

Lois sees Dr. Quast for this lump on her breast. Dr. Quast says, "Well, let's do the cautious thing: let's do a surgical procedure. Let's cut into your breast and cut the lump out and take a look at it under the microscope."

Lois agrees. She's a responsible person. She wants to do her best for herself. And so, on August 13, Lois is in the Woman's Hospital of Texas. She's in surgery.

Let's go stand off to the side in the operating room. Can you see Lois? Can you see her in the operating room? She's lying on the operating table as Dr. Quast cuts into her breast and removes three lumps. Watch it. We can see it. This is a medical disaster in the making. This is going to be a drive-by diagnosis followed by a rush to surgery followed by a plunge off the cliff into medical oblivion. There are no skid marks in the road here. Look for them in the evidence because you will not find them.

Dr. Quast cuts three lumps out of Lois's breast. He hands them to the technician to take down to the pathology department. You've heard the evidence. When they arrive at the pathology department, Dr. Anderson takes the lumps and looks at them. He peels one lump out, which is seven millimeters in size [*demonstrating with playdough the size of the lump*]. He says, "This is the lump that looks suspicious. This is the one that looks suspicious. Let's freeze it."

Standing off to the side down in the pathology department, don't we want to yell at him, "Wait a minute, doctor. From what we've heard, what you ought to know, you don't freeze a lump that small. Haven't you read the standards of the American Pathology Association? Haven't you read those standards? A lump that small you don't freeze, and the reason you don't freeze all of it is you won't have enough left to do the permanent section. Freezing can create artifact."

As so, as we see him hand it to the technician and say, "Freeze it," don't we want to holler at him, "Wait. Wait. Slow down. Not so fast. Think about the standards. Think about what you're doing."

But they take it, and they freeze it. They freeze all of it. Dr. Anderson puts the slide under his microscope. He looks at the frozen section, the little slice you've seen on the glass slide. He makes a diagnosis of cancer. He says he sees cancer on the slide.

You've heard six weeks of complex testimony. You have had an amazing experience in this courtroom. You have actually gone into the pathology lab. We have brought you microscopes. We have put up on television screens what the slides look like to the doctors looking in the microscope, and you have seen what different pathology looks like. You have heard experts talk about the size of cells, the shape of cells, the cluster of cells; and you've heard that over the years we have adopted standards. Standards. Standards that tell us when a growth, a lump, a mass, some tissue is intraductal carcinoma, which is what Dr. Anderson diagnosed, and when it is atypical hyperplasia, which is what a lot of women forty, fifty years old have. Standards that tell us cancer, not cancer. And you've heard one of the premier authorities in the country tell us about the criteria for diagnosing cancer and the criteria that Dr. Anderson used.

Can we play that short excerpt?

[*Videotape excerpt played.*]

QUESTIONS BY JIM M. PERDUE, SR.:

Q: Now, Doctor, back on the issues in the case, you have now seen Dr. Anderson's description of the slide upon which he based his diagnosis of intraductal carcinoma. Am I correct?

A: Yes.

Q: And what is your understanding of the criteria he is using in 1993 for the making of a diagnosis of intraductal carcinoma?

A: Well, he is using some criteria that—for the diagnosis of carcinoma in situ—that are not the criteria for carcinoma in situ and, indeed, are the criteria for ordinary hyperplasia.

[*Videotape concluded.*]

Can you imagine that? Dr. Anderson is using the criteria to diagnose cancer that are the criteria for ordinary hyperplasia. He's diagnosing cancer in women who don't have it.

Now the defense in this case is based on the premise—the dangerous and seductive premise—that you ought to decide what is good medical care on the basis of what will get by, the dangerous and seductive premise that you ought to be bottom-fishing for what gets by for good and accepted medical care. The defense comes in, and they make a big chart. You heard that testimony. And they make a chart from the medical literature, the pathology literature, which they put up and they say, "Look here, even your own experts have disagreed. There's a study in the medical literature that shows they sent these test samples out to all these pathologists, and they couldn't agree on these difficult slides. Therefore, breast pathology is really just kind of like modern art. It's all in the eye of the beholder. After all, look here. Your own experts, the most renowned people in the country, couldn't agree on these slides. It's reported in the medical literature. Dr. Anderson's not out of date. He's not a medical anachronism.

This is really tough stuff. It's just in the eye of the beholder."

But those tests that they talked about, those studies that were in the medical literature, you remember what Dr. Fechner said about those.

Let's see the next excerpt, please.

[*Videotape excerpt played.*]

QUESTIONS BY JIM M. PERDUE, SR.:

Q: Those examples, the slides that you got, was it your understanding that those were easy or difficult cases?

A: Oh, these were difficult cases, no question.

Q: Mrs. Bush's slides, is it, to you, an easy or difficult case?

A: This is an easy case.

[*Videotape concluded.*]

We're talking about an easy case here. We're not talking about those difficult cases that they tried to challenge the experts with. We're talking about something that we have now had six pathologists look at under the microscope. They have all said that it is either ordinary hyperplasia or artifact, which was caused when they froze it all.

How could Dr. Anderson be so out of bounds? Is he just a medical anachronism who didn't keep up? Well—ignorance—I don't think anybody would find much comfort if we thought that Lois's tragedy was caused by medical ignorance.

But there is another explanation. It's one that is so sinister and cruel that I know that when it occurred to you, you didn't want to consider it.

About three weeks ago, you recall we offered in evidence—and it was in your notebooks that each of you had—we offered in evidence the records of the operation. Dr. Quast tells us that he removed the three lumps. He gave them to a technician. He waited until Dr. Anderson came up to the operating room and said that she had cancer, and then they closed her up. Dr. Quast, if you'll recall, told us he would never have closed her until he had gotten the diagnosis. We know he had the diagnosis before he closed her up. We offered the records in evidence, and I know that some of you picked up on this. We didn't make a big issue of it at the time. Frankly, I thought I would give the defendants the rest of the case to answer it. But we've heard nothing from them, nothing, zero. There is a note in the record, incision time 10:30, closure time 10:35. Five minutes. Five minutes to remove the lumps, take them down three floors, walk what has been estimated to be about twenty yards, take the tissues, look at them, decide which one looks suspicious, decide to freeze it, freeze it, put it under the microscope, make the diagnosis, walk back up to the OR, and give the report to the surgeon.

Standing off to the side, as we see Dr. Anderson now in the laboratory, don't we want to holler at him, "Wait. Wait a minute. Take your time. Really look at it. Look at it. No, doctor, look at it. Look at it. Really look at it. Look at it. You're making a life-and-death decision on this woman. You're going to tell her she has cancer or doesn't. Look at it. Really look at it, doctor."

Is this a drive-by diagnosis? Look for the skid marks. They're not there.

Lois is told she has cancer. She wakes up from surgery. Dr. Quast and her gynecologist are at her bedside. They say, "Lois, you have cancer. We have to operate right away."

This is a Friday. Dr. Quast says, "We have to have your answer by Tuesday."

He doesn't even have the permanent sections back yet, and he's already telling her she has to have a mastectomy. Is that a rush to surgery? Is it a rush to surgery? Look for the skid marks. You won't find them.

And so the breast and lymph nodes are removed the following Wednesday, and then there is the ultimate insult, the ultimate tragedy. After her breast is removed and her lymph nodes are removed, they're taken and put in the room that you heard about. Lois and two other patients' tissues are sitting on the counter. An untrained orderly comes in. We're off to the side. We see the orderly come in. There's the box of tissues there. The orderly picks up the tissues, and he says, "These go to the incinerator."

Don't we want to yell, "Wait. Wait. What's the rush? Don't take those to the incinerator. Those go to the lab for further diagnostic studies. Those are this woman's breast. They're her lymph tissues. They need to be looked at so that they can tell her, 'There's no cancer in the breast. There's no cancer in the lymph nodes.'"

But he picks up the box and carries it to the incinerator. Lois doesn't know any of this. She doesn't know anything. She was lying on the table unconscious, vulnerable when the surgery was done. She was lying vulnerable, unconscious when the biopsy was done. And so, two days later, when she's at home and they call her and tell her, "Mrs. Bush, we lost the breast tissues. We lost the lymph nodes. We can't tell you how bad your cancer has spread. So we think, out of an abundance of caution, you need to have chemotherapy and radiation," and who knows what else.

To this drive-by diagnosis followed by a rush to surgery followed by a plunge off the cliff into medical oblivion, the defendant offers a head game. They say, "Look, there's really no good and bad medicine. There's really no safe and dangerous medical practice. After all, medicine is a matter of judgment. It's all a matter of judgment. It's just judgment."

They want to take the worst concoction of lawyers, pour it into a contaminated beaker of medicine, and then swirl it around and say it's just all dirty shades of gray. It's just all dirty shades of gray.

Lois comes home. She's in bandages. She's got tubes running out of her. She's in pain. She doesn't know what to do. She's searching for answers. She believes she has cancer. She fears she has cancer. She knows she has cancer. Lois doesn't have the resources to fight the system. She's a schoolteacher. She doesn't have the reserves to demand a repair of this injustice. She has no lobby. She has no hushed corner in the Capitol to go to to tilt the field in her favor, to bring forces to bear. All she has is what she will gather now in her search for the truth.

During the next years as she searches for the truth, you will see Lois transformed from this—and you saw the pictures some time back in the case that we introduced. Lois and her daughter had gone to a modeling competition in New York City just a few weeks before this happened. She was a gorgeous woman. And she was transformed from that to these photographs that you've seen.

When we tried this case, you'll recall we had these photographs. Lois introduced them. All of them were in little folders. We passed them to each of you. You opened them up in a very private way and closed them down and passed them to the next juror. When all those photographs were seen by you, we put them in this envelope. They haven't been seen by anybody else but you. We tried to respect Lois's privacy. I hope some of you will appreciate that. When it comes time in your deliberations where you feel they are appropriate to your considerations, they will be there.

Lois develops a neuroma, a neuroma that you've heard that is so painful that she cannot wear a blouse, she cannot wear a bra. She is in constant torment, constant pain. She ends up having multiple surgeries in an effort to correct that. Dr. Quast's lawyer says, "Well, what makes anybody think that our surgery caused the neuroma?"

You heard from Dr. Withers. He had in his records very clearly, "Neuroma post mastectomy." And he testified to that. He testified to that.

Now I feel compelled to address one issue in this case that I know is going to come up. Somebody on this jury during deliberations may ask or may say, "Well, that would never happen to me. What happened to Lois couldn't happen to me, it couldn't happen to my wife, it couldn't happen to my mother. We would have done something different." Because I know there's a psychological phenomenon that makes you think that. Psychologically, you must think that. Psychologically, you must believe that. "It couldn't happen to me, it couldn't happen to my wife or my mother. We would have done something different. We would have gotten a second opinion."

But, you see, Lois got a second opinion. When Dr. Quast came in and was standing at her bedside and he said, "Lois, you have cancer," her gynecologist of fifteen years was standing right next to her. And he said, "Lois, you have cancer. We have to operate right away."

And then Lois called her brother who is a doctor in San Antonio and said, "They say I've got cancer. I need a mastectomy. What should I do?"

And what did he say? "Follow your doctor's advice."

So Lois got a second and a third opinion. When Dr. Quast was on the stand, I asked him, "Doctor, are you contending that this lady did not get a second or third opinion?" He said, "Oh, no. I have to admit from the evidence I've heard, she got a second and a third opinion."

Lois would believe that she did. So when someone says, "We would have done something different, we would have gotten a second opinion," remind them of the evidence. Remind them of the defendant's own testimony.

So Lois, with the help of her brother in San Antonio, begins what you have heard is a difficult and awkward step. Her brother contacts a pathologist in San Antonio and writes the hospital for the slides. Bear in mind, what she wanted to look at those slides for or have somebody to look at them, they'd lost the breast tissue, they'd lost the lymph nodes, and she said, "Well, let's get the slides and see if we can make out from the slides how bad the cancer is. Maybe we can learn something. Maybe I'll only have to have the chemotherapy and not the radiation, or maybe not so much radiation, or maybe a different kind of chemotherapy. I need some help. I need to know what the truth is."

And so they get the slides so that Lois won't have to blindly submit to the chemotherapy and radiation. They get the slides. Lois starts looking for the truth. Because she's looking for the truth, she becomes the accused.

During the voir dire examination, Dr. Quast's lawyers got up and asked you on voir dire examination, "How many of you know all the problems with silicone breast implants?" We got a lot of hands. And he asked you a bunch of questions about silicone breast implants with his doctor sitting right there knowing that Lois never had silicone breast implants. She had saline. But that's the way you twist things, see, and turn someone who is looking for the truth into the accused.

When Lois was looking for the truth, the first fellow that looked at the slides was Dr. Allred in San Antonio. He said she didn't have cancer. Lois took them to the doctors at M. D. Anderson. They said either it's not cancer or you can't tell from the artifact that's in there from the freezing. Lois took them to Dr. Lechago at Methodist. He says, "I can't diagnose cancer. There's no cancer there."

Lois, in her search for the truth, is looking at four of a kind. That's the hand she's been dealt. Four of a kind is her truth. She comes to us, and we did what I would do for any of you. I said, "Well, let's get the slides, and let's have them looked at by the preeminent authorities in the country, Dr. Page and Dr. Fechner." These are the guys who did all the studies. These are the guys who have participated in all the research. These are the guys who have written the books. These are the guys who have written the standards. Dr. David Lee Page at Vanderbilt and Dr. Fechner at Virginia looked at the slides. They say there's no cancer. Now Lois is looking for the truth. She's got four of a kind and two aces, in her search for the truth.

We know what the truth is. We know what the truth is. This business about these things being confusing—you can call it atypical hyperplasia, you can call it fibrosis and intraductal hyperplasia, you can call it intraductal epithelial proliferation, you can call it epithelial proliferation hyperplasia. You can call it any of those things, but you can't call it cancer. You can call it any of those things, but it's not cancer.

The defense, in order to support their excuses, calls three experts. The first fellow you heard was Dr. Anything Goes. He comes in, and he testifies that they did everything right. He's a surgeon. I asked him in cross-examination, "Doctor, can you give me some examples of medical negligence?"

He said, "Oh yeah, I can give you some examples." He said, "If you operated on the wrong patient." He said, "If you got up and left the operating room and walked out, that would be malpractice."

I said, "Well, doctor, let me ask you this: what if a doctor cut the common bile duct during a gallbladder, would that be negligence?"

He said, "I don't know. Maybe so, maybe not."

Dr. Anything Goes, he's from that brotherhood, you see, who believes that a courthouse call is more important than any code they ever get in a hospital.

The next fellow they call is the Wizard of Oz. He's the guy who comes down from Illinois and claims to be an expert in everything. He's written books. I wrote down some of them. He's written books on microwaving. He's written books on pediatrics. He claims to be an expert in obstetrics. He claims to be an expert in water dynamics. He's an expert in everything. He's the Wizard of Oz. And he comes down, and he says, "Lois, why are you complaining? You can never get cancer in that breast now."

By his theory, if a woman finds a suspicious lump, what she ought to do is go have a double mastectomy and uncork the champagne. This is the way he wants medicine practiced. The Wizard of Oz.

The third expert you heard is a fellow I call the Wizard of Oz in Reverse. He went all the way to Kansas to testify on behalf of a pathologist up there. He works with these defendants all the time. They hire him all the time. He testifies for them in asbestos cases. He's an expert in pathology, but he's really not an expert in breast pathology, by his own admission. His specialty is more in the field of male organs, prostate.

He comes in and tells us, "I'm a pathologist. I've looked at the slides. There's cancer there." We asked him, "Well, how long have you worked on this case to get ready to testify today against Lois?" He's the Wizard of Oz in reverse. He wants to keep her in Oz. Just like the Wizard of Oz who testified before him felt like there wasn't any reason Dorothy couldn't click her heels and just go back. You know, Lois ought to be able to click her heels and just get out of there somehow.

The Wizard of Oz in Reverse wants to be sure she never gets out. "No, Lois, you have cancer." He spent forty hours preparing to testify in this case. Forty hours.

You know what galled me in this case? It may have galled some of y'all. You've heard all these people testify either by deposition or in person, people who were helping Lois try to determine what she should do by way of treatment, world-renowned experts. Every witness we called, every one of them, you heard the defense lawyers, one of the first questions they asked, "Well, what are you charging to testify, doctor? How much are you paid for an hour of your professional time?" Every one of our experts was asked those questions. And then they bring in three people to testify that when they walked in the courtroom, they could not have picked Lois Bush out of any woman in this audience because they didn't know who she was. They had never seen her. This guy spends forty hours to testify. Do you realize how long Dr. Anderson would have to work to put in that much effort looking at breast slides? He says that the time he spent looking at Lois's slide was typical for him. He claims he spent five minutes looking at that slide. Do you realize he'd have to look at 480 slides to equal the time that the Wizard of Oz in Reverse spent getting ready to testify against Lois?

When I asked Dr. Anderson, "How many breast slides do you look at each year?" He said, "Well, a little under a hundred." Do you realize Dr. Anderson would have to work five years, five years to have as much time looking at breast slides as their one expert spent getting ready to try and keep Lois in the nightmare of Oz that they put her in?

Well, those were the witnesses you heard from the defense. I suggest what we ought to do is pull the curtain back. Just pull it back. There is no wizard. There is no wizard back there. There's just some people pulling a bunch of levers to put out a bunch of smoke and colorful images so that you can't see the road. Because they know if you look at the road, you'll see there are no skid marks leading up to this medical disaster. This was a drive-by diagnosis followed by a rush to surgery followed by a plunge off the cliff into medical oblivion.

The hospital says they're not responsible for anything. Their attitude about this case is there's nothing wrong with Lois that wouldn't be fixed with a lifetime supply of Wonderbras. You think I'm kidding. When they lost the tissue, they wrote Lois a letter. It's in evidence. You've seen it. And they apologized for losing the tissue and said, "We're going to make an adjustment on your bill for losing the tissue."

I had the lady from the hospital on the stand, and I said, "Well, these adjustments y'all make, what is that like?"

And she said, "Well, you know, we make adjustments like when a patient complains of a bad meal."

I said, "So this is the kind of adjustment y'all make when somebody gets a bad meal in a hospital?"

She said, "Well, no, but sort of."

Well, since the hospital talked about meals, it's an appropriate topic. Let me talk about that a little bit. You know, meals—and you can look at me and tell they're pretty important—but meals are a part of life. Meals also are something we need so we don't have to endure the pain of hunger. And to nourish ourselves. You'll leave the courtroom today, and some of you will go out to eat, some of you will probably go to the grocery store over the weekend. You go to the grocery store, buy food for yourself, it's a hundred dollars. It is when I go. You go out to a cafeteria, you're going to spend ten, fifteen dollars. If you go get a good meal, you'll spend thirty, forty, fifty dollars easy. Well, we all eat our meal and, you know, we don't think much about it when we do. We pay that out just a few dollars at a time. We don't think about it. We have to eat, and we pay for our meals. A few dollars at a time. We don't think about it. But, you know, justice doesn't work that way. Justice, you've got to put the figure down all at once. You've got to write it in all at one time. So when it comes to the damages, we've only got $70,000 in medical. Lois didn't miss much time from work because she would always use her vacation time, her schoolteacher vacation time and her days off. She doesn't have a lot of lost wages. But for the disfigurement and humiliation that she has experienced, for the injustice that she's experienced, we have asked for $3 million. And when it comes time to consider that figure, I'd hope some of you would think, "Well, let's start by figuring out what it would cost if we were to say to Lois, 'Lois, we're going to give you the price of a real good meal three times a day for the rest of your life.'"

You'd be surprised what that adds up to. It's a start. A good meal three times a day for the rest of your life [*referring to chart with calculations*].

Ladies and gentlemen, that is not my calculation. It's the hospital's. They're the ones who said, "You just kind of adjust like you do for a bad meal."

Well, I know that there's going to be somebody on the jury that when we get to that point, they're going to say, "Well, Mr. Perdue, that's too much money for a verdict in this case. We're not down here to make people rich."

And I hope if you hear that in the jury room, one of you will reply and say, "No, we're not down here to make people undeserving millionaires. That isn't our job. But our job isn't to accept the unjustifiable and let go people who are irresponsible." The idea of civil damages is not just to compensate. It is to encourage—no, it is to compel—that we act responsibly, and you compel accountability. You make people responsible by awarding full damages for the injustice that they do.

So what is this case about? What will you say it's about when you go home after your verdict or go back to work? Some of you will say it's a drive-by diagnosis followed by a rush to surgery followed by a plunge off the cliff into medical oblivion, but I'm going to bet you there's going to be one or two of you who are going to say, "No, that was a case about courage. That was a case about courage." I saw an awful lot of courage in that courtroom. I saw a woman who came after three years of embarrassment and humiliation, after four operations of scarring and disfigurement, a woman who is a single schoolteacher, who has raised her children by herself, who has been independent, who went to work days when she didn't feel like it, when she was drained and fatigued and battered and still went to work. I saw a woman tell us about her most humiliating experiences and never shed a tear. I saw a woman who had the most personal photographs passed to us that we looked at, and she never shed a tear because all the tears were gone. The well had run dry a long time ago. I saw a woman who would do things for her children and worry about her children when most people would have been worried about themselves. I saw a woman who suffered a final humiliation in this courtroom when two weeks ago you heard one of the defense lawyers stand up in trial and say, "Your Honor, we want to request an independent medical examination of Lois Bush by our doctor."

We let them have it. Lois went to their doctor. She disrobed. She showed herself, she bared her body, she showed her scars, she bared her soul to this doctor who they hired. You haven't seen him yet, have you? They didn't call him. And so, ladies and gentlemen, the law says that you are entitled to infer. Since they hired him, since he's their doctor, you're entitled to infer that what he would say supports Lois, supports her.

You've seen a lot of courage in this courtroom. You saw Dr. Lechago out at Methodist Hospital and Baylor College of Medicine come down and testify. That's hard cheese. Listen, that's hard cheese. Baylor and Methodist are right out there by Texas Woman's. They're real close. And here they had the Wizard of Oz in Reverse who is on the staff at Baylor and Methodist, was testifying for them, but Dr. Lechago said, "I don't care. I'm going to testify to the truth."

It took a lot of courage to do that. It took a lot of courage. Well, what will you say the case is about when the evidence is over? Will you say it's a case about courage?

You know, it takes courage to do the right thing these days. Finding against doctors and hospitals isn't popular. Finding significant damages isn't popular. It takes courage. It takes courage. So I hope that this will be a case about courage, the courage of Lois, the courage of Dr. Lechago, the courage of this jury.

Three years ago, two doctors stood at the bedside of Lois and said, "Lois, you have cancer. We have to operate right away."

Today, you're standing at Lois's side in a courtroom. "Lois, you don't have cancer, but you have a heck of an injustice—and we're going to fix that right away."

Thank you very much.

30

Illustrative Closing Summation

Anesthesia Misadventure Kills Husband

Lisa and Mark Alexander had been married but three years when anesthesia misadventure claimed Mark's life. The case of *Lisa Jones Alexander, Individually and as Natural Representative of the Estate of Mark G. Alexander, Deceased, and James Alexander, Individually and Ruby Alexander, Individually v. TOPS Specialty Hospital, Ltd. d/b/a Columbia TOPS Surgical Specialty Hospital, Texas Outpatient Surgicare Center, Inc. d/b/a Texas Outpatient Surgicare Center, Columbia/HCA of Houston, Inc., Columbia Hospital Corporation of Houston, LaVerta Jane Crowder, M.D., Constance Cernosek, Carl J. Battaglia, M.D., P.A., Tommy A. Polk, M.D., P.A., Red Oak Anesthesia Associates, Outpatient Anesthesiology, TOPS Anesthesia,* Cause No. 98-05567, was tried in the 190th District Court of Harris County, Texas, in October and November 1999.

Mark arrested on the operating table at TOPS, a local outpatient facility, during routine arthroscopic surgery. Plaintiffs contended the CRNA (Certified Registered Nurse Anesthetist) left in charge of giving the patient his general anesthesia made numerous mistakes that caused Mark to be inadequately oxygenated. This led to his heart stopping. The defense claimed the arrest was explained by microscopic defects in the conduction tissues of the patient's heart.

On November 1, 1999, the jury returned its verdict against the defendants and awarded the surviving wife and parents $4 million in damages. During the trial, the hospital and CRNA settled. After the verdict, Dr. Crowder settled. The professional association of Dr. Battaglia and Dr. Polk appealed. The court of appeals affirmed *Battaglia v. Alexander,* 93 S.W.3d 132 (Tex. App.—Houston [14th Dist.] 2002). On review, the Supreme Court of Texas affirmed in part and reversed in part, 177 S.W.3d 893 (Tex. 2005).

THE CLOSING SUMMATION

Mr. Jim. M. Perdue:

"Mr. Alexander, my name is Dr. Crowder. I will be giving you your anesthesia today."

It wasn't until after Mark arrested on the operating table, lay in a coma for two weeks, and died, that Mark's widow and parents sought out a lawyer and the lawyer started asking questions that this family learned the fable, the fiction, the foible in Dr. Crowder's words. She doesn't put down the breathing tube that was improperly positioned. Dr. Crowder doesn't put down the esophageal stethoscope that is improperly driven into Mark's lung. She is there when the nurse anesthetist, Cernosek, does it. But she doesn't do it. She leaves OR 6 and only goes back for a few minutes to make adjustments when Nurse Cernosek can't get an alarm on the monitor turned off. Then she leaves again and is gone for almost an hour. She isn't in the operating room when Mark arrests and lies on the operating table for at least ten minutes with no heartbeat before anyone does anything about it. When they stop this routine outpatient procedure on Mark's shoulder and turn him over on his back, he is blue from lack of oxygen. His heart has stopped.

Dr. Crowder didn't give Mark his anesthesia. This family came to know that what would have been routine and safe in the hands of professionals became tragic and catastrophic in the hands of strangers.

Nurse Cernosek was asleep at the helm while the ship was sailing into a storm. Dr. Crowder was the first officer who was down in the coffee bar relaxing when she should have been on the bridge. Dr. Battaglia and Dr. Polk were the captains and the owners of this ship. They hired Dr. Crowder and Nurse Cernosek and were supposed to train and supervise them.

May it please the Court, ladies and gentlemen:

You know, justice doesn't come cheap, and it doesn't come easy. You have to work to get it and you have to deserve it. Defense counsel said several things during his closing argument, but one of them I really have to take exception to is when he told you that in looking at these issues it really wasn't important to consider the kind of man Mark Alexander was.

The Apostle Paul writes in Galatians, "God is not mocked: for whatsoever a man soweth, that shall he also reap." In Paul's other letters, he tells us that God rewards us on the basis of our works.

How much can you learn about a man in three weeks? More than many of us thought we could. We know Mark Alexander. The man who would catch a sparrow, make a waitress laugh, help the stranger whose car broke down on the side of the road, lend a helping hand to coworkers when they couldn't find the answer in the books or the manuals. The big man who stood six feet four but was never so tall he couldn't reach down to pick up the small child or the one whom age had made frail or weakened.

You have two doctors who get an exclusive contract with one of these drive-through surgery centers. We hear how they operate. Day surgery. They give seven thousand anesthesias a year. They charged seven thousand patients for giving them anesthesia in 1997. They don't give the patients the anesthesia. They turn it over to the CRNAs. But they charge seven thousand patients a year for anesthesia.

Nurse Cernosek works there off and on for seventeen years part-time. And during that time, they say there's no indication she ever does anything that would indicate that there's anything wrong with her abilities. We've seen her testify. She was unfamiliar with the equipment. She didn't know whether the alarms on the monitors were on or off. She doesn't know the basics of anesthesia.

Mark and Lisa go to TOPS. Mark will have surgery on his shoulder. Day surgery. He will be operated on and Lisa will be driving him home about noon and he'll be back at work on Monday. They meet Dr. Crowder. Dr. Crowder says, "I'm your anesthesiologist. I'll be giving you your anesthesia today." But she knows, she knows that they will take Mark back behind the operating room doors and she won't put the tube down. She won't be there for the anesthesia. Nurse Cernosek will. A stranger, someone Mark never met. A man like Mark deserves better than that. The way he lived his life, he deserved better than that.

They wheel Mark through the wide doors that go to the operating rooms. It's cooler back here and smells of alcohol, disinfectant, iodine, and chloroform. They take Mark to OR 6. Nurse Cernosek puts down the tube. The defense says nobody knows how deep the tube is. There's all kinds of factors here. We know that you put down the tube, you put the patient on the side, you raise their arm—all this can cause the tube to displace—to go deeper. But Nurse Cernosek does all of that. A stranger intubates Mark. Mark deserved better than that.

After they get Mark on his side, they run the esophageal stethoscope, which is supposed to be down about this far; think about that—in the esophagus, just down where you can measure the temperature. And she runs it—Nurse Cernosek runs it all the way down into his lung. We know that, we all saw the X-ray. Mark Alexander deserved better than that.

Toward the end of the surgery, Nurse Cernosek is up under the drapes. Dr. Stuart says, "What's going on. Is there a problem?"

Nurse Cernosek says, "I'm not getting air in one lung." She's up under the drapes. Dr. Stuart stops operating. They turn Mark on his back. They pull off the surgical drapes. Mark is blue all over. His face, his shoulders, his upper body, his thighs. Dr. Crowder comes back to the operating room. Dr. Battaglia comes in the operating room. They give him heart-starting drugs, they electroshock his heart, they get his heart started again, but Mark is brain damaged. They transfer him across the street to Houston Northwest Hospital. Then they tell the technicians and nurses in the operating room, "Don't talk to anyone about what went on here."

This family deserved better than that.

Mark dies two weeks later in Methodist Hospital. The family hires us to find out what happened. "Do whatever you need to get at the truth."

The defense starts coming up with their theories. And one of them is Mark Alexander had a bad heart—a diseased heart. You've heard the evidence. This is what they did. After the original autopsy is done, the EKGs before and after the surgery are all normal, no one suggests he has any heart problems. The original autopsies don't. No indication of any heart problems.

They go get a court order. They cut into Mark's heart and get sixty slides. They don't find what they need; and so they go back and they cut in 260 more times to—in the words of their expert, if we just keep looking, maybe we'll come up with something.

This family deserves better than that. This family deserves better than that. And most of all, most of all, this family deserves the truth.

Some of you have read Robert Fulghum's book, *All I Really Need to Know I Learned in Kindergarten*. Fulghum makes the point that the basic lessons we all need to know and remember about how to get along with each other are things we learned in the sandbox and Sunday school and kindergarten. One of his basic rules is, "When you hurt somebody, say you're sorry."

These folks don't want to be here. If Vernon or Ruby or Lisa could stand before you right now, they would tell you there's a thousand places they'd rather be. They'd rather be up at Marble Falls working on that old truck with Mark. They'd rather be out sitting around the picnic table with the family. There's a thousand places they'd rather be. There's a thousand places in the last two years they'd rather be. They didn't want to be at Houston Northwest Hospital hoping for the best. They didn't want to be at Methodist Hospital living there for two weeks knowing that the worst was inevitable. There's a thousand places they'd rather be now. But they're in this courtroom, the last place they want to be.

Justice being imperfect as it is, you know what they want? You know what they would say that they would like to have? They'd like to tell you we want specific performance. That's what we want. We want specific performance as the law permits, open the back of that courtroom door and let Mark walk through it.

They'd say we want some injunctive relief. We want the Court to enjoin these people and tell them, you will tell people when nurses are going to give anesthesia. You will introduce them. There won't be anesthesia by strangers anymore at TOPS. Patients will know who's giving anesthesia.

And you will be careful and you will evaluate people and you will train them and you will turn the alarms on. You will turn the alarms on the anesthesia monitors at TOPS because they help warn when patients are in trouble. It's a safety feature. The defense still has no explanation for why the alarms didn't go off when Mark's heart stopped. But I know why and so do you. Dr. Crowder turned them off when Nurse Cernosek called her back because she didn't understand the equipment.

You know, when—when they wheel our loved ones back behind those doors, we've all—if we haven't had this experience, most of us probably will—we expect the people, the anesthesiologists, to be vigilant, to be careful, to be watchful. If something goes wrong, we expect them to attend to it. And we expect to know who's back there, who is responsible for us.

They wheel Mark back. And when they do, they don't have just Mark Alexander on that gurney, they have this family's hopes and dreams. They wheel him into a Bermuda Triangle—a Bermuda Triangle. Think about it. All those hopes, all those dreams disappear into a black hole.

When they turn Mark over, he's blue. He's blue. They don't dispute that. He's blue. The defense says, well, the CPR was done timely. Well, isn't it interesting that of all the people that were there during the surgery, none participated in the resuscitation? Of all those that were there at the time of the arrest, not a single one of them can say they helped in the resuscitation. Resuscitation is all done by people who were—had to come in. More strangers. Mark Alexander deserved better than that.

You would think with a medical catastrophe like this that a thousand ships would have been launched to figure out what happened. But they were operating in that operating room using the same equipment, the same monitors, the same anesthesia equipment an hour later.

Something like this happens to you and you have to start digging hard. How did this ship get lost out there in the fog? What can we get to help us tell how and where the ship was lost, because the defendants are going to say, gee, unless you can show us the exact longitude and the exact latitude where that ship is lost, we have no responsibility. You've heard that. Show us exactly the minute, the degree, the instant.

And so you heard, with some difficulty, we got the memory strip. We got what they had pulled out of the machine and put in Dr. Battaglia's drawer. We didn't have it for a long time, but we got it.

The defense wants to debate this family over the difference in the time on the clock in the anesthesia monitor and the clock on the wall in the operating room. Everyone agrees they do not correspond. There is a time difference between the two clocks. The defense wants to say that that difference was ten to thirteen minutes. They need to say that because if it was a ten-minute difference, then resuscitation efforts began timely. On the other hand, if there was an eighteen- or twenty-minute difference, then Mark lay on the operating table without a heartbeat for ten minutes and no one did anything about it. Nurse Cernosek was asleep at the helm.

We know it was a twenty-minute difference because the first blood pressure they obtained after resuscitation was eighty-eight over sixty-two. That's an unusual blood pressure. We don't find it anywhere else in these records.

And if you line that up, eighty-eight over sixty-two, and say, well, they could not write it down until it showed up on the monitor, you will see it lines up exactly like this. There's not any ten- or thirteen-minute difference like the defense experts claimed. It's more like a twenty-minute difference between the memory tape and the anesthesia records [*using "slide rule" exhibit prepared to compare memory strip with anesthesia and code records*].

Now, what you will find when you line it up is Mark was lost in that Bermuda Triangle. It's true. That's the blood pressure he went in with. This is his heart rate.

That's the signals he was sending out that he was healthy [*referring to metronome beats consistent with beginning heart rate*].

This is when he started sending out an SOS. This is what the SOS signals sounded like that are on the tape [*metronome used to illustrate heart rate*]. Those are the SOS signals. You heard the experts. Of course, Nurse Cernosek says, unless it gets below forty, below forty, she does not worry. There is no problem.

But if somebody back in the jury room says, well, maybe that's not necessary. Maybe the kind of care that Dr. Kirby and Dr. Sheinbaum and Dr. Fromm told us about is a little high. Maybe we ought to settle. Maybe we ought to bottom-fish like the defense said and get down there on the bottom and pick out what gets by. Ask them to play this minute and a half of tape that was done at Methodist Hospital [*video showing Mark Alexander in coma and on life support*]. Ask them to look at that one more time. When somebody starts saying, well, a lesser degree of medical care will get by, consider what that lesser-degree standard of anesthesia care leaves in its wake. This family deserved better than that.

Now, we hear that, well, after all, Nurse Cernosek got a check from TOPS and, therefore, we're not responsible for her. You heard the testimony from Becky Lee. It was by video and I know it was about a week ago about the control these men, Dr. Battaglia and Dr. Polk, exercise over the CRNAs.

Some of you on this jury are old enough to remember Harry Truman. He had a sign on his desk that said, "The buck stops here." Because President Truman was the kind of man that always accepted responsibility. He wouldn't duck it. I think Dr. Battaglia and Dr. Polk must have a sign on their desk that says, "The buck comes here. But not the responsibility." That's their position in this case.

I want to talk to you about percentage of negligence because you're going to have to decide and write some percentages down and there's going to be somebody that says, well, if Nurse Cernosek was at fault then we ought to put most of the percentage on her.

Let me suggest this to you: when they sailed that ship into that Bermuda Triangle into that fog and lost it, they had somebody at the helm. It was Nurse Cernosek. She was asleep at that helm. But if we entrust a precious cargo to somebody and they sail off into a fog, do we blame the lowly helmsman at the wheel? Is that the person we really blame?

Or do we blame the owners of the company who said they'd take good care of our cargo? Or do we blame the captain who's supposed to train the helmsman? Do we blame the first officer who was on the bridge and said, well, I'll just go down and have a cup of coffee for an hour while we sail into the fog?

Don't be misled. Don't get off on what the defense hopes that you will do in this case. The defense brings you a truckload, a literal truckload, of junk science based on guesses and speculation and selective disregard of the facts and accept everything Nurse Cernosek said and ignore everything else anybody in the operating room saw.

They do these cuts. And here's the interesting thing: they cut into Mark's heart some four hundred times. And I'll be honest with you, they could have cut a thousand times, they could have cut two thousand times, and they would have never found what was in his heart that really counted because they can't see it. They'll never be able to see it.

But they cut into his heart. They get a court order, and they cut into it. They get another court order. They cut into it. Because you see, they want Jack Titus, who is the renowned cardiology pathologist, to look at these slides and come in and say, well, we didn't suffocate him. He had a bad heart.

But Dr. Titus wouldn't go along with him.

[*Videotape excerpt played.*]

> Q: You indicated that the microscopic changes you saw in the left bundle branch were a definite abnormality, and that if that were the extent of the fibrosis, you would not expect the patient to have a complete heart block or even a complete left bundle block on an electrocardiograph study.
>
> A: That is correct. That's what I said. I said repeatedly, I did not find complete interruption in the left bundles, and I only found a minor of the right to look at, so I can't comment on that, but just based upon my microscopic findings, as I've said several times this afternoon, and I opined that this patient should not have had complete heart block whether he did not.
>
> Q: The heart can have significant tissue abnormalities that can be seen on autopsies with a microscope and yet not be severe enough to cause the pump to stop working, that is a true statement?
>
> A: Yeah, that could be.
>
> Q: Well, let's take, if I suffocated, if you knew by history that somebody put a plastic bag over my head and suffocated me, you would not attribute my death to microscopic changes, would you?
>
> A: No, I would not.

[*Videotape concluded.*]

Let's take this load of junk science the defendants' hired experts dumped into this courtroom and do the right thing by it. Let's take the molded idea that it was the surgeon's Epinephrine wash that explains why Mark was blue. Let's take the soured idea that Dr. Stuart caused a vagal response by tugging on the suture and that caused Mark's arrest. Let's take the rancid idea of microscopic changes in the heart, and let's put them all in a big bag. And let's carry them off somewhere far away from that hallowed ground that Mark is buried in, the junk science graveyard, and let's dump them out there and give this family what they deserve.

How many times have you heard this statement: someone will have to get hurt before somebody does something about this. How many times have you heard that? Or, why doesn't somebody do something about that?

There are always those who excuse misadventures that claim lives, saying, "Money can't bring Mark Alexander back so what good will money damages do?"

This is your opportunity to say something about the kind of medical care we expect. We hold people accountable. We hold people accountable so they will act responsibly.

You know, if Mark was making a million dollars a year, laying off people to boost up company profits, we would not question that he was a valuable person. If he was making a million dollars a year with some kind of questionable business practice and abusing people, we wouldn't question this family's right to substantial damages.

The courtroom is a magical place. There is no other place like an American courtroom. It is the one place where the ordinary citizen can stand up and say, "These are my values. This is the way things ought to be."

People like Lisa, Vernon, Ruby, and each of you don't have access to the high-priced lawyers and lobbyists who meet in the dark halls in Austin and Washington. The only place we have to be truly heard is in a courtroom.

A lot of people think that in many ways our country has gotten off on the wrong track. We place a greater premium on wealth than we do integrity. We measure people by the assets in their balance sheet rather than the good they wrote in the Book of Life. The businessman who always tells the truth about his product, always shoots straight, doesn't hide anything by what he says or doesn't say is unlikely today to be much of a success. But if he puffs, distorts, and beguiles, he can be successful.

It's a funny thing the way we look at people. The schoolteacher, dedicated to students—maybe she's worth a little less because she doesn't earn as much. Mark was earning $55,000 a year. But you've heard well, you know, the loss can't be great. Not to those who measure a man's heart by the width of his wallet.

But you know, for most of us, what gives us our pride is our family, isn't it? Isn't it our family that we take pride in? There are no human appraisers.

And I'm never ashamed—never be ashamed to ask for the kind of money we've asked for in this case. The parents, now in their seventies, deserve the half million dollars each we've asked for. This widow deserves the three-and-a-half million dollars in damages to repay for her loss. Parents like Vernon and Ruby planted the seeds of mercy, hope, love, and charity in Mark. Lisa planted the seeds of fidelity, commitment, and compassion. What was this family's treasure worth? All we can ask is that for once someone gives Mark and his family what they truly deserve.

Notes

Notes to Chapter 1

1. The allegory regarding Truth and Story has been told in various forms. For example, "Truth, naked and cold, had been turned away from every door in the village. Her nakedness frightened people. When Parable found her, she was huddled in a corner, shivering and hungry. Taking pity on her, Parable gathered her up and took her home. There she dressed Truth in story, warmed her and sent her out again. Clothed in story, Truth knocked again at the villagers' doors and was readily welcomed into the people's houses. They invited her to eat at their table and warm herself by their fire."—Jewish teaching story. *See* http://www.bahai.no/samfunn/utvikling/skoler/maxwell/insight. Regardless, various storytellers contend for the proposition that people reject truth when it is "naked and cold" but embrace it when clothed in a story. "Present the truth 'naked and cold' and people will probably reject it. Clothed in story, people will embrace it. That is the power of storytelling, contends author Simmons." *See* http://www.cultureconnects.com/news.

2. *The National Era,* a weekly abolitionist newspaper, published a wider range of material that, unlike the *National Anti-Slavery Standard,* was not exclusively dedicated to the slavery issue. The *Era* was a mixture of anecdotes, poems, letters, short stories, bulletins, notations, and transcripts collected and written by persons within the United States and foreign countries. The editor of the paper was interested in publishing literary ideas as well as developments and changes taking place during this period of history. With transportation and communication between the major cities and ports still undeveloped, the *National Era* provided the reader with additional news in the form of excerpts and editorials from papers such as the *Liberty Bell, New York Tribune, Philadelphia Inquirer, Cincinnati Gazette, Boston Courier* and *London Daily Times*. Historians and students of letters both find this newspaper useful for its historical documentation and literary content. *See* www.liu.edu/cwis/cwp/library/historic.htm.

Notes to Chapter 2

1. Clarence Darrow, *Little Louis Epstine, in* Verdicts Out of Court 383–92 (1989).

2. Anthony R. Pratkanis & Elliot Aronson, Age of Propaganda: The Everyday Use and Abuse of Persuasion 129–30 (1992).

3. Ray Allen Billington, *Foreword* to Abe Lincoln Laughing: Humorous Anecdotes from Original Sources by and about Abraham Lincoln ix, ix–x (P.M. Zall ed., Univ. Tenn. Press 1995). This particular Lincoln story, while apt, may be apocryphal. "The story of the railroad bridge trial, plausible though it may be, cannot be authenticated as ever told by Lincoln." *Id.* at x.

4. Rodney Jew, *Tell It to the Jury: The Role of Story Telling in Litigation,* News from the Mental Edge, Spring 2003, at 4, 7, 10, 12.

Notes to Part 2

1. Rodney Jew, *Tell It to the Jury: The Role of Story Telling in Litigation*, News from the Mental Edge, Spring 2003, at 12, 16, 22–23.

Notes to Chapter 3

1. The introduction is adapted from the opening statement given in Newsome v. Johnson, No. 79-42525 (133rd Dist. Ct., Harris County, Tex., Feb. 1982).

2. Barnaby Conrad is the author of twenty-one books, including the best-seller *Matador* and the highly acclaimed *Time Is All We Have*. He and his wife Mary founded the Santa Barbara Writer's Conference, which meets annually for one week to educate and inform aspiring writers of fiction. Of the importance of the story's beginning, Conrad says, "The beginning writer, or at least the unknown writer, cannot afford the luxury of a leisurely start. I believe the first page—maybe even the first paragraph—of a story or novel should introduce conflict or hint strongly of conflict to come." Barnaby Conrad, The Complete Guide to Writing Fiction 17 (1990). Conrad illustrates the principle with an example particularly appropriate to the courtroom advocate: "Which story, for example, would you be most interested in reading? One that began like this: 'Their annual picnic was always a peaceful, joyous outing where everyone got along.' Or: 'Usually their annual picnic had been a peaceful, joyous outing where everyone got along. And, at first, that's the way it was this July 4, 1990." *Id.* at 18. Conrad suggests that writers should collect their favorite beginnings and offers the following examples from classic literature: "Elmer Gantry was drunk." (Sinclair Lewis, *Elmer Gantry*) "Tom!" (Mark Twain, *The Adventures of Tom Sawyer*) "It is a truth universally acknowledged that a single man in possession of a good fortune must be in want of a wife." (Jane Austen, *Pride and Prejudice*) "Now at last the slowly gathered, long-pent-up fury of the storm broke upon us." (Winston Churchill, *Their Finest Hour*) "I had this story from one who had no business to tell it to me, or to any other." (Edgar Rice Burroughs, *Tarzan of the Apes*) *Id.* at 22–23.

3. The Declaration of Independence (U.S. 1776).

4. Abraham Lincoln, The Gettysburg Address, delivered at Gettysburg, Pa., Nov. 19, 1863.

5. Daniel Webster, The Seventh of March Speech, delivered to the U.S. Senate, Mar. 7, 1850.

6. Charles Dickens, A Tale of Two Cities 1 (Courage Books 1986) (1859).

7. Edgar Allan Poe, *The Raven*, *in* Complete Stories and Poems 754 (Doubleday 1966) (1845).

8. Robert Louis Stevenson, Treasure Island 1 (Charles Scribner's Sons 1911) (1883).

9. O. Henry, *The Gift of the Magi*, *in* The Best Short Stories of O. Henry 1 (Modern Library 1994) (1906).

10. James Joyce, *The Boarding House*, *in* Dubliners 56 (Penguin Books 1993) (1914).

11. Gone with the Wind 1st title card (Selznick Int'l Pictures/Metro-Goldwyn-Mayer 1939).

12. Donald Alan Schlitz, Jr., *The Gambler* (1977).

13. The story of Jimmy Jackson, given here as recalled by the author, has been told by Prof. Bill

English of Baylor University at numerous academic conferences.

14. Christopher Vogler, The Writer's Journey: Mythic Structure for Writers 81, 90 (2d ed. 1998).

15. Jim M. Perdue, *The Difference Between "Good Enough" and "Safe Enough,"* Trial, Mar. 1996, at 45.

16. *Id.*

17. Wolfgang Mieder, The Prentice-Hall Encyclopedia of World Proverbs: A Treasury of Wit and Wisdom Through the Ages 255 (1986).

Notes to Chapter 4

1. The introduction is adapted from speeches given by the author in 1996 to various bar associations and civic groups in support of the proposed HMO liability law.

2. The principles and presuppositions of NLP are sometimes described as epistemology. NLP claims to study the way people take in information, how they describe it to themselves with their senses, fill it with their beliefs and values, and act on the result. *Neuro-linguistic Programming*, http://en.wikipedia.org/wiki/Neuro-linguistic_programming. NLP was begun in the mid-1970s by a linguist and a mathematician who had strong interests in successful people, psychology, language, and computer programming. NLP has been applied to fields such as sales, therapy, communication, education, coaching, sports, management, business, occult practices, and spiritual development. It is difficult to define NLP because those who started it and those involved in it use such vague and ambiguous language that NLP means different things to different people. A part of NLP deals with teaching how to read "body language" and determine the listener's reaction, such as whether he is accepting or rejecting propositions. A part of the NLP thesis is the identification of a person's Primary Representational System (PRS). It is suggested that a therapist would have better rapport with a client if they had matching PRSs. However, none of this is supported by the scientific literature. *Neuro-linguistic Programming (NLP)*, http://skepdic.com/neurolin.html.

The author was first exposed to the psychological concepts of NLP in the 1980s while teaching at an advanced trial program sponsored by the American Trial Lawyers Association at Harvard. Later, while working with the trial advocacy program at the University of Houston, Professors Richard H. Lucas and K. Byron McCoy brought the concept into their classrooms and to the trial bar in their book *The Winning Edge: Effective Communication and Persuasion Techniques for Lawyers*. NLP postulates that all knowledge comes through our senses. Everything we know, think about, or believe originates from something we see, hear, feel/touch/do, smell, or taste. When we think, we think in sensory terms: we *picture* something in our minds; *say* things to ourselves; or have a *felt* sense of what is right, good, or appropriate. People primarily think and communicate in three sensory-based representational systems: visual (seeing), auditory (hearing), and kinesthetic (feelings, touch, movement, smell, taste). Richard H. Lucas & K. Byron McCoy, The Winning Edge: Effective Communication and Persuasion Techniques for Lawyers 6–8 (1993). Despite the reservations in the scientific community, many trial lawyers subscribe to the theory that communication and persuasion are enhanced when a presentation appeals to all three elements of the PRS. This is accomplished by using the "code words" that trigger each of the representational systems. For example, the trial lawyer summing up her case might say: "We've *painted a clear picture* that everyone can *see* regarding the defendant's culpability. The witnesses have *told* you about the defendant's product defect that caused this woman's injury. They have *explained* it clearly. We all *heard* what they *said*. You *know* that this defendant was reckless in its design. You have *sensed* it and *felt* it from the beginning when you *heard* this tragic story."

3. Johann Wolfgang von Goethe is the first person to have popularized the word "gestalt." In 1810, he published his *Theory of Colors*. Being fascinated by the colors generated from a prism, he conducted his own investigation to challenge some of the phenomena of color suggested by Sir Isaac Newton. Goethe attempted a wide-ranging explanation of color, both in art, such as painting, and in the psychological domain. Among his observations were: rooms in which red strongly dominates seem warm at first sight, making one excited and comfortable. They increase our readiness for sensory consumption. But too much red makes us restless and nervous. Blue produces in us the feeling of distance, depth, coolness, and quiet. Yellow is the lightest of all colors. It works easily, cheers and stimulates us. Goethe noted: "One can notice this warming effect, if man looks at a landscape through a yellow glass, particularly in dull winter's days, most lively. The eye is pleased, the heart extended, and immediate warmth seems to soothe us." Dark green relaxes and calms us. Orange is formed as a concentration and condensation of the yellow. In orange, the energy of the yellow grows, the color becomes more powerful, and it arouses a feeling of warmth and bliss. According to Goethe, passive colors are blue, lilac, and violet. They evoke tender but uneasy and sad feelings. *See Color-Psychology II, Emotional Effect of the Colors*, http://people.freenet.de/cosmobehn/colour2.html. See also Neil Ribe & Friedrich Steinle, *Exploratory Experimentation: Goethe, Land, and Color Theory*, PHYSICS TODAY, July 2002, http://www.aip.org/pt/vol-55/iss-7/p43.html.

More contemporary studies of the psychology of colors have shown that children develop different color preferences as they age, and that some color preferences are inborn rather than culturally conditioned. Newborn babies have a distinct preference for geometric patterns in black and white. As they age, they start to show positive reactions to other shades, with yellow and red usually achieving the highest and earliest recognition rates. After adolescence, men and women vary in their preferences. S. J. Warner conducted a survey of male and female color preferences in the middle of the twentieth century. In his research, women preferred pastel colors, pale and subdued midtones, warm rather than cool, and deep shades. Men preferred brilliant-hued tints, light full colors, cool rather than warm, and gray shades. In our mainly western-influenced culture, we rate red, orange, yellow, and brown as warm colors, and blue, green, gray, and purple as cool colors. Lynne Green, *A Rainbow of Emotions*, VOYAGER ONLINE, Oct. 2003, http://www.voyageronline.com.au/news/0310scifacts.cfm.

Psychologists have accepted Goethe's analysis of primary colors but have extended it by examining shades and tints.

Red: Red is associated with energy, war, danger, determination, passion, desire, and love.

- Light red represents joy, sexuality, passion, sensitivity, and love.
- Pink signifies romance, love, and friendship. It denotes feminine qualities.
- Dark red is associated with vigor, willpower, rage, anger, leadership, courage, and wrath.
- Brown suggests stability and denotes masculine qualities.
- Reddish-brown is associated with harvest and fall.

Orange: Orange represents enthusiasm, fascination, happiness, determination, attraction, success, encouragement, and stimulation.

- Dark gold can mean deceit and distrust.
- Red-orange corresponds to desire, sexual passion, pleasure, and domination.
- Gold evokes the feeling of prestige and symbolizes high quality.

Yellow: Yellow is associated with joy, happiness, and intellect. Yellow, when placed against black, is a combination often used to issue a warning.

Green: Green has great healing power. It is the most restful color for the human eye. Advertisers use green to indicate safety when advertising drugs and medical products.

- Dark green is associated with ambition, greed, and jealousy.
- Yellow-green can indicate sickness, cowardice, discord, and jealousy.

Blue: Blue is associated with trust, loyalty, wisdom, confidence, intelligence, faith, truth, and heaven. Blue is a masculine color and is associated with depth, expertise, and stability.

Purple: Purple combines the stability of blue and the energy of red. It symbolizes power, nobility, luxury, and ambition.

White: White is associated with light, goodness, innocence, purity, and virginity.

Black: Black is associated with power, elegance, formality, death, evil, and mystery. *Color Meaning,* http://www.color-wheel-pro.com/color-meaning.html.

4. Stephen Crane, The Red Badge of Courage 1 (Dover Publications 1990) (1895).

5. Ambrose Bierce, *An Occurrence at Owl Creek Bridge, in* Civil War Stories 33 (Dover Publications 1994) (1891).

6. Stephen King, On Writing: A Memoir of the Craft 175 (2000).

7. Mark Twain, *The Man That Corrupted Hadleyburg, in* The Complete Short Stories of Mark Twain 349–50 (Doubleday 1957) (1900).

8. James Joyce, *The Dead, in* Dubliners 175 (Penguin Books 1993) (1914).

9. James Joyce, Ulysses 355 (Vintage Books 1961) (1922).

10. Smell and memory are closely linked; smell evokes memories. *See Role of smell,* http://www.cf.ac.uk/biosi/staff/jacob/teaching/sensory/olfact1.html; *see also* http://www.artsymbolism.com/1.html. Linda Buck, an assistant professor in the Department of Neurobiology at Harvard Medical School, and Allan Hirsch, an American neurologist who specializes in the treatment of people who lose their sense of smell or taste, are two of the most prominent researchers in the field of nostalgic smells. Dr. Buck postulates that the stimulus to the olfactory system travels to both the limbic system and cortex. The limbic system is the primitive part of the brain that includes areas that control emotions, memory, and behavior. In comparison, the cortex is the outer part of the brain that has to do with conscious thought. Many wonder how certain smells are able to trigger memories of events taking place several years in the past considering that sensory neurons in the epithelium survive for only about sixty days. Dr. Buck suggests the answer is that "memories survive because the axons of neurons that express the same receptor always go to the same place." Maya Pines, *The Memory of Smells,* http://www.hhmi.org/senses/d140.html. The memories are stored in the hippocampus, and through relational memory, certain smells trigger memories. Thus, despite our belief that sight and hearing are the two most important senses to our survival, from an evolutionary perspective, smell is one of the most important senses. The primitive role of smell explains why smells trigger memory more than does seeing or hearing. Shigeyuki Ito, *Smell and Memory,* http://serendip.brynmawr.edu/bb/neuro/neuro00/web2/Ito.html. Dr. Hirsch believes that details evoked by nostalgic smells are not as important as the emotions they recall. Our minds reshape these memories, sending them through a rose-tinted filter that redefines them as "good times." Experiences that may have seemed bad at the time can be reconstructed in our minds to seem better than they were, because they represent periods in our life that are now gone forever. *Nostalgic Smells,* http://www.bbc.co.uk/science/humanbody/mind/articles/intelligenceandmemory/nostalgic_smells.

11. Robert B. Hirschhorn, Lisa Blue, & Macy Jaggers, *Inside the Juror's Mind,* GP/Solo Law Trends & News, Aug. 2005, http://www.abanet.org/genpractice/newsletter/lawtrends/0508/litigation/jurorsmind.html; *see also* Dana K. Cole, *Psychodrama and the Training of Trial Lawyers: Finding the Story,* http://www.aals.org/profdev/newideas/cole.pdf.

12. Tobin v. SmithKline Beecham Pharmaceuticals, 164 F. Supp. 2d 1278 (D. Wyo. 2001). Plaintiff's counsel were noted trial lawyers Jim Fitzgerald of Cheyenne, Wyoming, and Andy Vickery of Houston, Texas.

Notes to Chapter 5

1. The introduction is adapted from a speech given to the Eighth Annual Texas Trial Lawyers Medical Malpractice Conference, Houston, Texas (Sept. 18, 1997). The community college where Prim Gupta worked provided medical care to its employees through a managed-care facility. As part of his annual physical exam, the clinic obtained a chest X-ray that was misdiagnosed as normal. There were early signs of lung cancer. Prim's cancer went undiagnosed and untreated for approximately a year and a half. By the time it was diagnosed, it was too late. The clinic claimed it could not be responsible because, under Texas law, it could not "practice medicine." Texas law did not permit a patient to sue his managed-care provider. The lawsuit was a protracted one; a lot of discovery, doctors deposed, pleadings amended. The fact that the case was not just about money became more evident as Prim realized he was near death. Prim's goals were in some respects modest and in other ways substantial. He wanted to be sure that any settlement gave him the satisfaction of knowing that his children would have ample funds for their college education, would have a secure financial future, and that his wife would be financially independent for the rest of her life. There was one other thing. Prim wanted to make one final trip to his homeland, India.

2. Rodney Jew, *Tell It to the Jury: The Role of Story Telling in Litigation*, NEWS FROM THE MENTAL EDGE, Spring 2003, at 17.

3. HERMAN MELVILLE, MOBY-DICK 23 (Charles Feidelson, Jr., ed., Bobbs-Merrill 1964) (1851).

4. CHARLES DICKENS, HARD TIMES 2 (Bantam Books 1981) (1854).

5. JOHN GRISHAM, THE CLIENT 21–22 (1993).

6. Jew, *supra* note 2, at 19, 22.

7. BARNABY CONRAD, THE COMPLETE GUIDE TO WRITING FICTION 47 (1990).

8. CHRISTOPHER VOGLER, THE WRITER'S JOURNEY: MYTHIC STRUCTURE FOR WRITERS 38 (2d ed. 1998).

9. *Id.* at 39, 42.

10. *See* A. Cheree Carlson, *The Role of Character in Public Moral Argument: Henry Ward Beecher and the Brooklyn Scandal*, 77 Q.J. SPEECH 38, 38–52 (1991).

11. FREDRIC G. LEVIN, EFFECTIVE OPENING STATEMENTS: THE ATTORNEY'S MASTER KEY TO COURTROOM VICTORY 704 (1983).

12. VOGLER, *supra* note 7, at 105.

Notes to Chapter 6

1. The introduction is adapted from a speech given to the 1999 Medical Malpractice Conference, "The Art of Storytelling in Trial," Texas Tech and St. Mary's University Schools of Law, San Antonio, Texas (Apr. 8, 1999). *See* LOUIS NIZER, CATSPAW (1992).

2. MARK TWAIN, FOLLOWING THE EQUATOR ch. 15 (1897).

3. Psychologists and jury consultants emphasize the concept of hindsight bias. This concept

teaches that people tend to overestimate the likelihood of an event's occurring when they know the outcome. Baruch Fischhoff, *Hindsight ≠ Foresight: The Effect of Outcome Knowledge on Judgment Under Uncertainty,* 1 J. Experimental Psychol.: Hum. Perception & Performance 288, 292 (1975).

4. Public Strategies, Inc., *Juror Attitudes and Biases: Detecting Land Mines in the Legal Battleground of Voir Dire, in* State Bar of Tex. Prof. Dev. Program, Advanced Medical, Malpractice, Pharmaceutical & Medical Device Litigation Course B, B-9 (1997).

5. For a searchable database of helpful articles, see the TexasBarCLE Web site at http://www.TexasBarCLE.com/CLE/home.asp.

6. Christopher Vogler, The Writer's Journey: Mythic Structure for Writers 22 (2d ed. 1998).

Notes to Chapter 7

1. The introduction is adapted from an opening statement presentation for a mock trial at the 1995 Products Liability Institute, University of Texas at Austin, Austin, Texas (Nov. 3, 1995).

2. Mark Twain, The Adventures of Huckleberry Finn 37 (Barnes & Noble 1996) (1884).

3. Vachel Lindsay, *The Congo, in* The Congo and Other Poems (1914).

4. For a useful list of onomatopoeic words, see http://www.worsleyschool.net/socialarts/onomato/poeiaentries.html.

5. Edgar Allan Poe, *The Tell-Tale Heart, in* Complete Stories and Poems 124 (Doubleday 1966) (1843).

6. Jurgen Wolff & Kerry Cox, Successful Scriptwriting 99–100 (1988).

7. Some ideas on the direct examination of witnesses come from materials authored by Frank Costilla, an outstanding trial lawyer in Brownsville, Texas.

Notes to Chapter 8

1. Jim M. Perdue, Sr., & Jim M. Perdue, Jr., *Trial Themes: Winning Jurors' Minds and Hearts,* Trial, Apr. 1998, at 34–42.

2. *See generally* James M. McPherson, Hallowed Ground: A Walk at Gettysburg (2003); *Heth, Shoes, Spies, and Lee's Grand Strategy,* http://www.gdg.org/Research/Authored%20Items/dtheth.html.

3. Anthony R. Pratkanis & Elliot Aronson, Age of Propaganda: The Everyday Use and Abuse of Persuasion 28–29 (1992).

4. *Id.* at 31.

5. Examples of one-word themes are "priorities," "danger," "speed," and "trust." The case theme "look" comes from Robert Fulghum's *All I Really Need to Know I Learned in Kindergarten.* Many are familiar

with Fulghum's books, which give simple rules that help people be successful in their relationships with others. His point is that all he needs to know about how to live, what to do, and how to be, he learned in kindergarten. "Wisdom was not at the top of the graduate-school mountain, but there in the sandpile at Sunday School." Among the things he learned are: "Play fair. . . . Say you're sorry when you hurt somebody. . . . [W]atch out for traffic, hold hands, and stick together. . . . And then remember the Dick-and-Jane books and the first word you learned—the biggest word of all—LOOK." ROBERT FULGHUM, ALL I REALLY NEED TO KNOW I LEARNED IN KINDERGARTEN: UNCOMMON THOUGHTS ON COMMON THINGS 6–7 (1993).

Notes to Chapter 9

1. Martha Chamallas, *The Architecture of Bias: Deep Structures in Tort Law*, 146 U. PA. L. REV. 463, 464–66 (1998). "[I]n the realm of torts a higher value is placed upon the lives of white men and . . . injuries suffered by this group are worth more than injuries suffered by other less privileged groups in society." *Id.* at 465. For example, "in cases involving white defendants, awards for African-Americans in state and federal jury trials totaled only 74% as much as awards for white plaintiffs for the same injury." *Id.* at 466 n.13. *See also* Georgia v. McCollum, 505 U.S. 42, 68 (1992) (O'Connor, J., dissenting), arguing that "[i]t is by now clear that conscious or unconscious racism can affect the way white jurors perceive minority defendants and the facts presented at their trials, perhaps determining the verdict of guilt or innocence." *See also* Sheri Lynn Johnson, *Black Innocence and the White Jury*, 83 MICH. L. REV. 1611, 1621 (1985), reporting studies ranging from the 1960s to the late 1970s in which the conviction rates varied from as little as 3.9% more for blacks in a large northeastern metropolitan area to as much as 70% more for blacks in bench trials conducted by two white judges. However, in the studies with larger samples, the conviction rates were less varied. *But see* Clay S. Conrad, *Scapegoating the Jury*, 7 CORNELL J.L. & PUB. POL'Y 7, 39 (1997), arguing that judges are more likely to return a racist verdict than juries and that the 3.9% disparity referenced in Johnson's study is "small enough that if a portion of that disparity is attributable to sources other than bias, it rapidly loses significance." *Id.* at n.227.

2. Sex also plays a role in the damages issue. In fact, courts are often guided by sex-based tables when forecasting the loss of future earnings. *See* Martha Chamallas, *The Architecture of Bias: Deep Structures in Tort Law*, 146 U. PA. L. REV. 463, 482 (1998). "Because of wage discrimination and occupational segregation, predictions of future earnings for women . . . are considerably lower than for . . . men, even when controlled for such factors as educational attainment. Thus, the projected lifetime earnings . . . of a female college graduate have been estimated to be only 65% of those of a similarly situated male college graduate." *Id.* at 482. Chamallas offers the case of boy and girl twins, equally injured in a car accident. By current standards, the boy would be entitled to a considerably higher recovery solely because of his sex. *Id.*

3. When deselecting the jury from the venire panel, counsel is wise to identify those people of low self-esteem. People who are underemployed in terms of education and intelligence may channel their frustration by blaming others for their plight. Those with low self-esteem tend to be less tolerant than those whose self-esteem is high. Low-self-esteem people may refuse to look favorably on someone because of their race or sex, seeing in them the cause of their underachievement. The warts of sex, race, religion, and lifestyle may be magnified when a jury is composed in part of people who have not made much of their lives and tend to explain or justify their failures by blaming a racial minority, people of the opposite sex, or homosexuals.

Notes to Chapter 10

1. The introduction is adapted from the author's closing statement in In re Estate of Mario

Bohorquez, No. 310,024-410 (Prob. Ct. at Law No. 2, Harris County, Tex., Feb. 2001).

2. Henry Wadsworth Longfellow, *Elegiac Verse*, *in* In the Harbor (1882).

3. Robert Louis Stevenson, Treasure Island 273 (Charles Scribner's Sons 1911) (1883).

4. Stephen Crane, The Red Badge of Courage 99–100 (Dover Publications 1990) (1895).

5. Christopher Vogler, The Writer's Journey: Mythic Structure for Writers 223 (2d ed. 1998).

6. Gen. Douglas MacArthur, Farewell Speech, delivered to the Corps of Cadets at West Point, New York, May 12, 1962.

7. John F. Kennedy, Remarks in the Rudolph Wilde Platz, delivered in West Berlin, West Germany, June 26, 1963.

8. Barbara Jordan, Opening Statement to the House Judiciary Committee, Proceedings on the Impeachment of Richard Nixon, delivered to the U.S. House of Representatives, July 25, 1974.

Notes to Part 3

1. Dwight Lyman Moody, *Reuben Johnson's Pardon*, *in* Moody's Anecdotes 45–47 (1898).

2. The Dwight Lyman Moody story in the introduction was included in a speech given to the Louisiana Trial Lawyers Association, New Orleans, Louisiana (Dec.13, 1996).

Notes to Chapter 11

1. *See Clever Hans Phenomenon*, http://skepdic.com/cleverhans.html.

2. Merriam-Webster's Collegiate Dictionary 208 (11th ed. 2003).

3. *See generally* Albert Mehrabian, Nonverbal Communication (1972). Others have questioned Mehrabian's theories; *see, e.g.*, C.E. Johnson, *The Myth of "Nonverbal Dominance,"* http://www.borg.com/~rparkany/CDA/NonverbalDominanceMyth.html.

4. Http://web.utk.edu/~gwynne/source_factors.html. *See generally* Daniel O'Keefe, Persuasion: Theory and Research (1990).

5. The sections on appearance, movement, demeanor, and voice are adapted from Jim M. Perdue, Who Will Speak for the Victim? A Practical Treatise on Plaintiff's Jury Argument 49–73 (1989).

6. B.L. Stern, *When You're Smiling . . . You May Be Saying More Than You Realize*, Vogue, Jan. 1984, at 113.

7. "What you are speaks so loudly that I cannot hear what you say" is a slight mutation of Ralph Waldo Emerson's quotation, "Don't *say* things. What you *are* stands over you the while, and thunders so that I cannot hear what you say to the contrary." Ralph Waldo Emerson, 8 The Complete Works of Ralph Waldo Emerson: Letters and Social Aims 96 (AMS Press 1979) (1883).

Notes to Chapter 12

1. In the eyes of the public, the most important role of the trial lawyer is acting as a protector of basic rights. *See* Gary A. Hengstler, *Vox Populi: The Public Perception of Lawyers: ABA Poll*, 79 A.B.A. J. 60 (1993). Esteemed trial lawyer and past Association of Trial Lawyers of America president Mark Mandell suggests the protector theme as a strong persuasive motivator. "Any argument we make to a jury must stress that the plaintiff needed and deserved protection by the defendant, wasn't provided that protection, and, as a direct result, was harmed." Mark Mandell, *Overcoming Juror Bias: Is There an Answer?*, TRIAL, July 2000, at 28–29.

2. LAWRENCE J. SMITH & LORETTA A. MALANDRO, COURTROOM COMMUNICATION STRATEGIES 273–307 (1985). *See also* ANTHONY R. PRATKANIS & ELLIOT ARONSON, AGE OF PROPAGANDA: THE EVERYDAY USE AND ABUSE OF PERSUASION 85–111 (1992). Harris Polls document that there has been a dramatic decline in the public attitude toward lawyers. In 1977, almost 75% of respondents believed the legal profession had either very great or considerable prestige. Twenty years later, things had changed dramatically. A near majority (47%) of respondents in April 1997 ranked the legal profession as having either some or hardly any prestige at all. *See* Amy E. Black & Stanley Rothman, *Shall We Kill All the Lawyers First: Insider and Outsider Views of the Legal Profession*, 21 HARV. J.L. & PUB. POL'Y 835, 850 (1998). In the early 1990s, the American Bar Association commissioned a public opinion poll from the Peter D. Hart Research Organization. *See* Hengstler, *supra* note 1. The A.B.A. poll indicated that overall respondents gave lawyers a 40% favorability rating while 34% of respondents gave them an unfavorable rating. In 1999 the A.B.A. published results of a follow-up poll from M/A/R/C Research. It revealed that while 30% of respondents were extremely or very confident in the U.S. justice system, only 14% were extremely or very confident in lawyers. American Bar Association, *Perceptions of the U.S. Justice System* (1999), *available at* http://www.abanet.org/media/perception/perception.html. In 1998 the Texas Office of Court Administration and the State Bar of Texas began a comprehensive study of public trust and confidence in the Texas courts and legal profession. A random sample of 1,215 Texas adults responded during the summer of 1998. This survey documented that just 40% rated attorneys as "very" or "somewhat" honest and ethical. Joseph Shields & Cynthia L. Spanhel, *Public Trust and Confidence in the Texas Courts and Legal Profession*, 62 TEX. B.J. 289, 290 (1999). Of additional interest to the trial lawyer is the fact that socioeconomic status plays a significant role in how a person perceives lawyers. *See* Hengstler, *supra* note 1, stating that African-Americans, Hispanics, the poor, and women have a better opinion of lawyers than do college-educated white males with above-average salaries. Apparently, lawyers remain the hope of the downtrodden. "When asked which from a list of six responsibilities are the most important roles for lawyers to play, 52% chose 'a protector of basic rights,' and 37% selected 'a prosecutor of wrongdoers.'" The public (and therefore juries) expect lawyers to protect them from those who would trample their rights, whether in a civil or criminal context. Perhaps that is the most important attribute the lawyer can convey.

3. *See generally* ALBERT MEHRABIAN, NONVERBAL COMMUNICATION (1972). Mehrabian attempts to quantify the persuasive process into components and from them determine "likeability."

4. STEPHEN KING, ON WRITING: A MEMOIR OF THE CRAFT 123 (2000).

5. *Id.* at 124–25.

6. MEHRABIAN, *supra* note 3.

7. David Ogilvy, *Most Persuasive Words Used in Advertising*, at http://urbandreams.ousd.k12.ca.us/lessonplans/consumerism/worksheet08.pdf.

8. Sports columnist Blackie Sherrod suggests that the principle of "Keep It Simple, Stupid" is

the most reliable advice politicians and media people can heed. He illustrates the principle with the parable of the old ship's captain: For forty years, the skipper was widely respected, a solemn and silent man who seldom made a bad decision. But his crew noticed a peculiar habit. Every morning on rising, he went to a safe in the wall of his cabin and spun the combination. He would remove a slip of paper and study it carefully, nod his head, replace the paper, and lock the safe. Every morning. One day the old captain retired, and his executive officer, elevated to his post, rushed to his cabin and opened the safe. He took the paper and read it carefully: Port—left. Starboard—right. Blackie Sherrod, *In Defense of Simplicity*, DALLAS MORNING NEWS, Apr. 18, 1996, at A27.

9. Mark Twain's advice is a grouping of three separate quotations on the subject. MARK TWAIN, *Fenimore Cooper's Literary Offenses*, *in* HOW TO TELL A STORY (1897); GEORGE BAINTON, THE ART OF AUTHORSHIP 87–88 (1890); MARK TWAIN, *William Dean Howells*, *in* WHAT IS MAN AND OTHER ESSAYS (2004).

10. JIM M. PERDUE, WHO WILL SPEAK FOR THE VICTIM? A PRACTICAL TREATISE ON PLAINTIFF'S JURY ARGUMENT 14 (1989).

11. Franklin Delano Roosevelt, Campaign Address, Brooklyn, New York (Nov. 1, 1940), *in* 9 THE PUBLIC PAPERS AND ADDRESSES OF FRANKLIN D. ROOSEVELT at 537 (1941).

12. RICHARD H. LUCAS & K. BYRON MCCOY, THE WINNING EDGE: EFFECTIVE COMMUNICATION AND PERSUASION TECHNIQUES FOR LAWYERS 7 (1993).

13. PERDUE, *supra* note 10, at 6.

14. THE DECLARATION OF INDEPENDENCE (U.S. 1776).

15. Winston Churchill, Address to the House of Commons, Aug. 20, 1940.

16. Abraham Lincoln, The Gettysburg Address, delivered at Gettysburg, Pa., Nov. 19, 1863.

17. Gen. Douglas MacArthur, Farewell Speech, delivered to the Corps of Cadets at West Point, N.Y., May 12, 1962.

18. John F. Kennedy, Inaugural Address, Jan. 20, 1961.

19. MEHRABIAN, *supra* note 3.

20. PERDUE, *supra* note 10, at 69–73.

21. PERDUE, *supra* note 10, at 60.

Notes to Chapter 13

1. MICHAEL ROEMER, TELLING STORIES: POSTMODERNISM AND THE INVALIDATION OF TRADITIONAL NARRATIVE 48 (1995).

Notes to Chapter 14

1. *Boss Tweed*, http://en.wikipedia.org/wiki/Boss_Tweed.

2. Jonathan Belcher, 7 THE BELCHER PAPERS 410 (Mass. Hist. Soc'y 1894) (1732); Fred R. Barnard, PRINTERS' INK, Dec. 8, 1921, at 96; Samuel John Stone, *in* FAMILIAR QUOTATIONS BY JOHN BARTLETT 703 (13th ed. 1955); GREGORY Y. TITELMAN, RANDOM HOUSE DICTIONARY OF POPULAR PROVERBS AND SAYINGS 265, 297 (1966).

3. Portions of this chapter are adapted from Jim M. Perdue, Jr., *The Art of Demonstrative Evidence*, TRIAL, May 2005, at 46–51.

4. DONALD E. VINSON, JURY PERSUASION: PSYCHOLOGICAL STRATEGIES AND TRIAL TECHNIQUES 184 (1993).

5. ATLA's LITIGATING TORT CASES § 37:24 (Roxanne Barton Conlin & Gregory S. Cusimano eds., 2003).

6. Rodney Jew, *Tell It to the Jury: The Role of Story Telling in Litigation*, NEWS FROM THE MENTAL EDGE, Spring 2003, at 12.

Notes to Chapter 15

1. The introduction is adapted from a speech given to the 2003 Medical Malpractice Conference, Texas Tech and St. Mary's University Schools of Law, San Antonio, Texas (Nov. 6, 2003).

2. Portions of this chapter are adapted from Jim M. Perdue, *The Five-Question Rule: Cross-Examination Simplified*, TRIAL, Oct. 1993, at 40–43.

3. Alexander v. TOPS Specialty Hospital, No. 98-05567 (190th Dist. Ct., Harris County, Tex., Nov. 1, 1999).

4. Lee v. Healthcare Management, No. 93-31897 (151st Dist. Ct., Harris County, Tex., Sept. 26, 1995).

5. *See* TEX. R. EVID. 613(a), 801e; Downen v. Texas Gulf Shrimp Co., 846 S.W.2d 506, 512 (Tex. App.—Corpus Christi 1993, writ denied). Not all the predicates listed in this chapter are legally required, but while not technically necessary their inclusion strengthens the impeachment.

6. YOUNG MR. LINCOLN (Twentieth Century Fox 1939).

7. Smith v. Baptist Memorial Hospital System, No. 81-CI8427 (166th Dist. Ct., Bexar County, Tex., June 5, 1989).

8. In re Estate of Mario Bohorquez, No. 310,024-410 (Prob. Ct. at Law No. 2, Harris County, Tex., Feb. 2001).

9. *Joseph Sugarman Quotes*, http://www.brainyquote.com/quotes/authors/j/joseph_sugarman.html.

Notes to Part 4

1. The introduction is adapted from a speech given to the Houston Trial Lawyers Association, Houston, Texas (May 20, 2005).

2. John Guinther, The Jury in America and The Civil Juror: A Research Project Sponsored by the Roscoe Pound Foundation xiii (1988).

3. William O. Douglas, We the Judges: Studies in American and Indian Constitutional Law from Marshall to Mukherjea 389 (1956).

Notes to Chapter 16

1. *See* Tex. R. Civ. P. 267.

2. *Book of Susanna* (Apocrypha).

3. *Exodus* 22:1 (King James).

4. *Exodus* 22:5.

5. *Exodus* 22:6.

6. *Exodus* 21:18–19.

7. *Exodus* 21:22–25.

8. *Exodus* 21:28–32.

9. *Exodus* 23:2.

10. *Exodus* 22:4.

11. Scott Turow, *Order in the Court*, N.Y. Times Mag., Apr. 18, 1999, at 109.

12. *See* Godfrey D. Lehman, The Ordeal of Edward Bushell (1988).

13. *Id.* at 250.

14. *See* J. Anthony Lukas, Big Trouble (1997); Clarence Darrow, The Story of My Life (1932).

15. Titus Maccius Plautus, Cistellaria (ca. 200 BC).

16. Voltaire, Essay on Manners (1756).

17. *See* Gerald Horne, Powell v. Alabama: The Scottsboro Boys and American Justice (1997).

18. *Famous American Trials, "The Scottsboro Boys" Trials 1931–1937*, http://www.law.umkc.edu/faculty/projects/FTrials/scottsboro/scottsb.htm.

19. *Judge Horton Orders a New Trial in the Case of Haywood Patterson, June 22, 1933*, http://www.law.umkc.edu/faculty/projects/FTrials/scottsboro/SB_hor33.html.

20. *See* Richard Kluger, Simple Justice: The History of *Brown v. Board of Education* and Black America's Struggle for Equality (1975).

21. *Id.* at 348.

Notes to Chapter 17

1. The introduction is adapted from a speech delivered at the Texas Trial Lawyers Association seminar "Winning in Trial: Persuasive Techniques for the Plaintiff—From Focus Group to Voir Dire" (June 21, 2002).

2. Jeffrey Abramson, *The Jury and Popular Culture*, 50 DEPAUL L. REV. 497 (2000), *reprinted in* 36 INT'L SOC'Y BARRISTERS Q. 4, 482 (2002).

3. Despite diligent research efforts, the author has been unable to find an occasion when Jefferson specifically declared that he considered the right to trial by jury more essential to a democratic republic than the right to vote. However, it is generally accepted that this was Jefferson's view. JOHN GUINTHER, THE JURY IN AMERICA AND THE CIVIL JUROR: A RESEARCH PROJECT SPONSORED BY THE ROSCOE POUND FOUNDATION (Facts On File Publications 1988). Guinther cites an article in the *Irish Student Law Review*: "Jefferson also expressed the view that the right to a trial by jury was 'more precious to the maintenance of democracy than even the right to vote.'" Gearoid Carey, *Jury Nullification—Democracy and Rationality*, 7 I.S.L.R. 1, 13 (1999). *See also* Gertner, *Is the Jury Worth Saving?*, 75 B.U. L. REV. 923, 924 (1995). In a letter to the Abbé Arnoux, July 19, 1789, in 15 THE PAPERS OF THOMAS JEFFERSON 282 (Julian Boyd ed., 1958), Jefferson said, "[W]ere I called upon to decide whether the people had best be omitted in the Legislature or Judiciary department, I would say it is better to leave them out of the Legislature." "I consider [trial by jury] as the only anchor ever yet imagined by man, by which a government can be held to the principles of its constitution." Letter from Thomas Jefferson to Thomas Paine (1789), 15 *id.*, at 269.

4. Ben H. Bagdikian, *A Secret in the News: The Country's Permanent Poor* (Apr. 3, 2001), *at* http://www.inequality.org/bagdikian2.html.

5. The corporate share of government tax revenue is already at its lowest level since the Great Depression, with the exception of the anomalous year of 1983. Corporations contribute just 7.4% of the federal government's total tax revenue. *Corporate Tax Breaks*, *at* http://www.fairtaxesforall.org/action/corporate. At a time when the federal budget is sinking into needless deficit and states are shutting down schools and slashing healthcare benefits, large corporations are making a mockery of the notion they should be paying their fair share of taxes. And it's not just tax shelters. Corporations also creatively exploit a massive array of special credits, exemptions, and loopholes that are all perfectly legitimate even if they are terrible public policy. The result of all this tax avoidance is that in 2003 corporate revenues represented only 7.4% of federal tax receipts, the second-lowest level on record, according to the Congressional Budget Office. Sixty years ago, corporations paid half of the U.S. tax bill. Corporate income tax revenues, meanwhile, fell from $207 billion in 2000 to $132 billion in 2003, according to CBO estimates. Lee Drutman, *Avoidance Issues* (Oct. 2003), *at* http://www.tompaine.com/feature2.cfm/ID/9252.

6. *Id.*

7. Although the statutory corporate income tax rate is 35%, few companies pay anything close to that. In 1998, the top 250 companies paid an effective tax rate of just 20.1%. That's down from 22.9% in 1996 and 26.5% in 1988, according to Robert McIntyre of the Institute on Taxation and Economic Policy and Citizens for Tax Justice. And between 1996 and 1998, 41 of those 250 companies paid less than zero federal income taxes in at least one year, earning a whopping $3.2 billion in treasury rebates between them despite combined profits of $25.8 billion. Drutman, *supra* note 5; Institute on Taxation and Economic Policy, *Study Finds Resurgence in Corporate Tax Avoidance* (Oct. 19, 2000), *at*

http://www.ctj.org/itep/corp00pr.htm.

8. Kevin Phillips, Wealth and Democracy: A Political History of the American Rich 149 (2002).

9. *Id.* at 150.

10. Julie Mason, Tom Fowler & Patty Reinert, *The Fall of Enron: Enron's History of Ducking Taxes Probed by Panel*, Hous. Chron., Feb. 16, 2002, at A21; Roma Khanna, *Enron's Tax Records Lead Experts to Call For Change in Laws*, Hous. Chron., Jan. 18, 2002, at A21.

11. *Global Outfits Avoid Paying Billions in Taxes, Study Says*, Hous. Chron., Dec. 10, 2001, § Bus., at 4. If Congress had done nothing since 1977 to alter the U.S. tax code, passed no new legislation at all, nine out of ten American families would be paying less. That is, a smaller share of their incomes would be devoted to federal taxes. Yet, paradoxically, the government would be collecting more revenue each year—almost $70 billion more—if none of those tax bills had been enacted. How to explain this? Where did all that money go? Roughly speaking, it went to corporations and to the one in ten families at the top of the income ladder. Their taxes were cut by spectacular dimensions. The tax burden on the richest 1% of the population fell cumulatively by a staggering 36%, compared to what they would have owed under the 1977 tax code. As politicians from both parties congratulated themselves on delivering one tax cut after another, families in the very middle of the income ladder experienced a 7% increase in their federal tax burden. William Greider, Who Will Tell the People? The Betrayal of American Democracy 80 (1993).

12. *Global Outfits Avoid Paying Billions in Taxes, Study Says*, *supra* note 11. According to figures compiled from several sources including the United Nations, the U.S. ranks eleventh in percentage of federal revenues derived from individual income taxes but only seventieth in that derived from corporate income taxes. *Are We Still Number One?*, Parade Mag., Apr. 13, 1997, at 4.

13. In construction, nobody worries about OSHA anymore. They don't take it seriously. The average construction worker has a life expectancy ten to twelve years less than average. In Indiana, the average construction worker dies at sixty—before he even collects Social Security. The bottom line is the working man and woman in this country come in last. The regulators at EPA and OSHA never talk to the working man or the small businessman. They're dealing with big corporations and trade associations and labor unions. In construction, for instance, the serious injury rate was actually higher in 1988 than in 1970, when OSHA was created. Greider, *supra* note 11, at 121.

14. Hundreds of examples can be offered to illustrate that governmental regulations are lax and the agencies charged with protecting consumers are underfunded. Let's consider just one. One in ten Americans has some type of synthetic body part implant. Kit R. Roane, *Replacement Parts: How the FDA Allows Faulty, and Sometimes Dangerous, Medical Devices Onto the Market*, U.S. News & World Rep., July 29, 2002, at 54. The Food and Drug Administration is responsible for determining the safety and efficacy of medical devices and implants. The FDA division charged with device safety, the Center for Devices and Radiological Health, has long complained that its annual funding—about $177 million—fails to keep up with its exploding workload. *Id.* at 56. In addition to reviewing some 17,000 device submissions per year and inspecting more than 15,000 manufacturers, the division must also inspect more than 29,000 mammogram facilities, radiological health firms, and clinical trial investigators. The result is that between 1995 and 2000 the number of inspections of medical device firms in the U.S. dropped by nearly half—from 3,600 to a little over 1,800. *Id.* In 1999, FDA inspectors examined only 575 of the 15,000 clinical sites. When the FDA does inspect manufacturers and lab sites, it finds violations in one out of every seven or eight cases. *Id.* Common violations include failure to assure that a device is being made correctly and failing to submit data about deaths and injuries. *Id.* Under pressure from Congress and the Bush administration, the FDA instituted industry-friendly

measures that compromise safety. One policy requires inspectors to notify managers in advance of inspections. *Id.* The new rules exempt companies from submitting adverse-event reports after the device has been recalled or repaired, and the agency is considering allowing manufacturers with good records to inspect their own facilities. *Id.* Since 1977, the number of manufacturers of medical devices has risen from just over 9,000 to more than 13,000. *Id.* at 54–55. Of the 80,000 medical devices on the market today, 98% were approved through a streamlined process that requires data to show only that the product is similar to one already in use. *Id.* at 54. Additionally, the FDA has a policy of allowing companies to collect most clinical data after a device is marketed. This has the effect of allowing product manufacturers to experiment on people. *Id.* at 56. Unlike automobile recalls, device recalls are mostly voluntary. Doctors and hospitals are not required to report device failures to the FDA. Manufacturers must report failures, but they don't have to make their tracking system public. As a result, many patients are never advised they have defective implants and medical devices in them. *Id.* at 60. The lack of enforcement of the meager FDA regulations has been devastating to consumer-patients. The July 22, 2002, issue of *U.S. News & World Report* cataloged the disastrous consequences of defective heart stents, gastric Lap-bands, hip implants, heart valves, defibrillators, lens implants, pacemakers, and jaw implants on innocent consumers. Barb Drexler was an attractive, hard-working nurse. She never worried about her health; she was active and played softball once a week. In 1977, she bit into an apple. Her jaw locked. A doctor treated her unsuccessfully for a few years and then suggested a jaw joint implant. The doctor chose a Proplast-Teflon joint manufactured by Houston-based Vitek, Inc. The doctors implanted these teflon joints in an estimated 26,000 patients, mostly young women diagnosed with TMJ. Many of these devices began to shatter and erode following implantation, creating tumors that ate through bone and flesh to the brain. In 1999, in an unusual move, the FDA banned the devices and advised surgeons to remove all the implants that had failed. But the federal agency failed to notify the thousands of victims of the recall. One victim was implanted with the device after it was pulled from the market. Normally, it is up to the manufacturer to alert medical institutions about recalls. But Vitek went bankrupt in 1990. Today, Barb Drexler is horribly disfigured. Her once lovely face is a twisted tangle of scars. Her deeply recessed chin is limp and boneless. A morphine pump implanted in her stomach controls the pulses of pain that convulse her face. She has tried to commit suicide because of the pain. In a futile effort to repair the damage inflicted by the device, she has endured thirty surgeries. At fifty-three, she can no longer work, eats only soft food, walks with a cane, and is blind in one eye. Can you imagine the reaction of the Barb Drexlers to the suggestion that corporations like Vitek are overregulated?

15. For a brief moment in the early 1970s the reformers held the field, but they were swept away as soon as the monied interests figured out the new language of politics and learned to play by the new rules. In 1970, only a handful of the *Fortune* 500 companies had public-affairs offices in Washington. Ten years later, more than 80% did. In the same period, not coincidentally, business political-action committees displaced labor as the largest source of campaign money. In 1974, labor unions accounted for half of the PAC money; by 1980, they accounted for less than one-fourth. Public-interest groups, according to a Senate study, were stretched so thin that they were absent at more than half of the formal proceedings on regulatory issues and, when they appeared, were typically outnumbered ten to one by industry interests. On some important matters, industry would invest fifty to one hundred times more resources than the public-interest advocates could muster. GREIDER, *supra* note 11, at 48, 50.

16. PHILLIPS, *supra* note 8, at 326.

17. PHILLIPS, *supra* note 8, at xvi.

18. Dan Mahony, *Wealth & Power: Assets or Addictions?*, *at* http://www.danmahony.com/wp_quotes.htm.

19. John Roth, CEO of Nortel, made $10 million while the stock declined 90% and 30,000 people

were laid off; Rich McGinn, CEO of Lucent, made $12 million while the stock fell 68%; Rick Thoman, CEO of Xerox, made over $5 million while the stock lost 89% of its value and the company cut 5,200 jobs; Donald LaVigne, Executive Vice-President of eMachines, made $10 million while his company's stock lost 96% of its value. David Raymond, *CEO Bandits*, Forbes.ASAP, Mar. 25, 2002, at 33.

20. The average pay, after taxes, for chief executives at the largest U.S. corporations was 12 times greater than the average wage of factory workers in 1960. Today, CEOs make 135 times the wages of companies' regular employees. Mark Shields, *Pay the Workers*, Wash. Post, Aug. 13, 1995, *available at* http://www.house.gov/sabo/shields.htm. But the 1990s broke all records. The ratio of the pay of corporate CEOs to the hourly wages of production workers soared from 93 times that of workers in 1988 to 419 in 1999. While wages for ordinary workers barely kept up with inflation, the average compensation among the top executives of the largest corporations vaulted 481% between 1990 and 1998, to an average of $10.6 million. Corporate profits, by contrast, rose only 108%. Phillips, *supra* note 8, at 153.

21. Not only has CEO compensation risen, but insider trading to the detriment of shareholders and employees has been rampant. Tyco CEO Dennis Kozlowski and his chief financial officer sold more than $500 million in Tyco stock while publicly declaring that they rarely sold their shares. Global Crossing's Gary Winnick cashed in some $735 million worth of stock before the company crashed. John Rigas's family borrowed $1.8 billion from Adelphia. Ken Lay of Enron unloaded more than $100 million of Enron stock in the three years before Enron filed for bankruptcy. Daniel Eisenberg, *Dennis the Menace*, Time Mag., June 17, 2002.

22. Institute for Policy Studies & United for a Fair Economy, *CEO/Worker Pay Gap: The Neglected Campaign Issue* (Aug. 30, 2000), *available at* http://www.ufenet.org/press/2000/exec_excess_2000_pr.html. Since 1973, however, wages in real terms, discounted for inflation, have been stagnant or declining. Factory workers in Italy now earn more per hour than U.S. workers. The rewards changed most dramatically in the 1980s—at the very time government was cutting tax burdens for the well-to-do. During the last decade, the top 1% of American families grossly increased their share of total U.S. income—from 8% or 9% to more than 14%. Greider, *supra* note 11, at 86.

23. Institute for Policy Studies & United for a Fair Economy, *supra* note 22.

24. Gary Strauss, *The Billionaires Club: New Economy Rockets CEO Pay into the Stratosphere*, USA Today, Apr. 5, 2000, at B3, *available at* http://www.usatoday.com/life/cyber/tech/cth683.htm. The gap between CEOs' pay and that of lower-level workers has yawned in recent years. J.P. Morgan, the financier, is credited with suggesting that executives earn no more than 20 times the pay of low-level workers. How quaint: A 2000 study by Towers Perrin showed that chiefs at big domestic companies earned 531 times what their hourly employees did, on average. Gretchen Morgenson, *Explaining (or Not) Why the Boss Is Paid So Much*, N.Y. Times, Jan. 25, 2004, at 3-1.

25. *See infra* notes 27 and 28.

26. The 400 wealthiest taxpayers accounted for more than 1% of all the income in the U.S. in 2000, more than double their share just eight years earlier, according to new data from the Internal Revenue Service. But their tax burden plummeted over the same period. The average income of the 400 wealthiest taxpayers was almost $174 million in 2000. This is nearly quadruple the $46.8 million average in 1992. The minimum income to qualify for the list was $86.8 million in 2000, more than triple the $24.4 million income required in 1992. The top 400 reported 1.1% of all income earned in 2000, up from 0.5% in 1992. In 2000, the top 400 paid 22.3% of their income in federal income tax, down from 26.4% in 1992. The rate actually paid by the top 400 in 2000 was about the same as that paid by a single person making $123,000 or a married couple with two children earning $226,000,

according to Citizens for Tax Justice. *400 Richest Getting 1% of Income*, HOUS. CHRON., June 26, 2003, § Bus., at 1.

27. John W. Lee, *Critique of Current Congressional Capital Gains Contentions*, 15 VA. TAX REV. 1 (1995). The American male worker with a high school diploma saw his real income drop by 30% between 1973 and 1993. Shields, *supra* note 20. Ordinary families gained amid the late-1990s boom, but even in 1999, analysts found that the average real after-tax income of the middle 60% of the population was lower than in 1977—an extraordinary contrast with the huge gains of the top 1%. PHILLIPS, *supra* note 8, at 111.

28. Between 1979 and 1989, the portion of the nation's wealth held by the top 1% nearly doubled, from 22% to 39%. By the mid-1990s, some economists estimated that the top 1% had captured 70% of all earnings growth since the mid-1970s. PHILLIPS, *supra* note 8, at xiii.

29. Shields, *supra* note 20.

30. PHILLIPS, *supra* note 8, at 47 (citing New York University economist Edward N. Wolfe, 1998).

31. U.S. Census Bureau, *Poverty in the United States: 2001* (Oct. 2, 2002), *at* http://www.census.gov/prod/2002pubs/p60-219.pdf.

32. *Id.*

33. *Id.*

34. During the decades after 1945, when the unionized percentage of the workforce peaked and workers on the production line at Ford or General Electric lived better than European bank managers, the average annual hours worked by Americans were below those of the Japanese and many Europeans. In 1980, Americans still worked fewer hours than the Japanese, but put in more time on the job than the British, French, and Germans. Between 1990 and 1995, the average annual hours worked in the U.S. finally passed those of workaholic Japan, leading the International Labor Organization to report in 1999 that Americans toiled the longest hours in the industrialized world. PHILLIPS, *supra* note 8, at 162.

35. PHILLIPS, *supra* note 8, at xviii.

36. PHILLIPS, *supra* note 8, at 113.

37. John C. McCarthy, 3.3 *Million US Service Jobs To Go Offshore* (Nov. 11, 2002), *at* http://www.forrester.com/ER/Research/Brief/Excerpt/0,1317,15900,00. html.

38. Barbara Hagenbaugh, *U.S. Manufacturing Jobs Fading Away Fast*, USA TODAY, Dec. 13, 2002, *available at* http://www.cdfa.net/cdfa/press.nsf/pages/571.

39. It is difficult to get an estimate of the number of tech jobs that corporations such as Oracle, Microsoft, Dell Computer, and others have now outsourced to countries such as India. However, it certainly is in the tens of thousands and may be in the hundreds of thousands. Rachel Konrad, *More Tech Jobs Going Overseas* (July 14, 2003), ARIZ. REPUBLIC ONLINE PRINT ED., *at* http://www.azcentral.com/arizonarepublic/business/articles/0714techjobs13.html; *Tech Jobs Leave U.S. for India, Russia* (July 14, 2003), CNN.com/Technology, *at* http://www.cnn.com/ 2003/tech/biztech/07/14/moves.offshore.ap/index.html.

40. In the percentage of poverty among those over 65, the U.S., Australia, and Britain lead. For child

poverty, the U.S. ranks first. In the percentage of those finishing high school, the U.S. ranks lowest. Taking all factors into account that measure inequality, the U.S. ranks first, with Ireland second, Australia fourth, and Britain sixth. PHILLIPS, *supra* note 8, at 345–46.

41. *Unequal Income Distribution in the United States, at* http:// home.rochester.rr.com/jerryfisher/income.htm; http://www.abcnews.go.com/sections/us/DailyNews/incomes000118.html; http://www.infoplease.com/ipa/A0780376.html (last visited Mar. 13, 2002).

42. *Id.*

43. Abramson, *supra* note 2, at 504.

44. Public Strategies, Inc., *Juror Attitudes and Biases, in* STATE BAR OF TEX. PROF. DEV. PROGRAM, ADVANCED MEDICAL, MALPRACTICE, PHARMACEUTICAL & MEDICAL DEVICE LITIGATION COURSE B, B-9 (1997).

45. These are not real people, but they are metaphors for real people the author has known.

46. Churches and religious groups are not beyond the greed appeal. In the 1990s, the Baptist Foundation of Arizona and two related corporations sold more than 11,000 investors $483 million in investment products. Investors were told they would be paid greater interest than most banks. In fact, the BFA was staying afloat by getting money from new investors to meet its financial obligations. The investors sued and the BFA and its subsidiaries filed for Chapter 11 bankruptcy protection. The accounting firm Arthur Andersen agreed to pay $217 million to settle the claims against it. In March 2002, Anderson backed out of its agreement, citing its insurance carrier's inability to pay claims. Jonathan Weil & Divon Spurgeon, *Arthur Andersen Insurers Rendered Insolvent,* WALL ST. J., Apr. 1, 2002, at C1.

47. J. ANTHONY LUKAS, BIG TROUBLE 320 (1997).

48. Public Strategies, Inc., *supra* note 44, at B-9.

49. Public Strategies, Inc., *supra* note 44, at B-17.

50. Stephen D. Sugarman, *A Century of Change in Personal Injury Law,* 88 CAL. L. REV. 2403 (2000)

51. *Id.*

52. *Id.*

53. *Id.*

54. *Id.*

55. *Id.*

56. *Id.*

57. COMMITTEE ON QUALITY OF HEALTH CARE IN AMERICA, INSTITUTE OF MEDICINE, TO ERR IS HUMAN: BUILDING A SAFER HEALTH SYSTEM 15 (Linda T. Kohn et al. eds., 2000) (citing American Hospital Association, Hospital Statistics, Chicago, 1999); Eric J. Thomas et al., *Costs of Medical Injuries in Utah and Colorado,* 36 INQUIRY 255, 255–64 (1999).

58. Medical malpractice is far worse than most people realize or the media generally report. According to a study published in 1990 by the Harvard Medical Practice Study Group and conducted at Harvard's School of Public Health, one of the most comprehensive and objective studies of medical malpractice ever performed, more than 98,000 patients in hospitals located in New York State suffered "adverse events," injuries from medical care rather than disease, in one year, 1984. The study found that 27% of these adverse events were the result of medical negligence—failure by health practitioners to meet reasonable standards of care. Such negligence resulted in 6,895 patient deaths in the state's hospitals that year. Projecting its figures nationwide, the study's authors estimated in subsequent testimony that approximately 80,000 people die from medical negligence each year, with another 150,000 to 300,000 injured. And those figures represent deaths only in hospitals; they do not include deaths caused by malpractice in clinics or physicians' offices, which have not yet been analyzed. Eighty thousand hospital deaths from medical negligence amount to more annual deaths than are caused by automobile accidents (43,000), homicides (23,730), suicides (32,400), or AIDS (41,930). RALPH NADER & WESLEY J. SMITH, NO CONTEST: CORPORATE LAWYERS AND THE PERVERSION OF JUSTICE IN AMERICA 291 (1996).

59. *Id.* at 265.

60. JAMES CARVILLE, WE'RE RIGHT, THEY'RE WRONG: A HANDBOOK FOR SPIRITED PROGRESSIVES 146 (citing People Helper, *Cutbacks to CPSC Threaten Us All*, TIMES-PICAYUNE (New Orleans), Apr. 28, 1995).

61. NADER & SMITH, *supra* note 58, at 278–79.

62. This story is a metaphor for many true-life situations including asbestos, cigarettes, defectively designed automobile and truck gas tanks, dangerous tires, and hazardous medications that have taken the lives of millions of Americans while corporate executives hid the truth and avoided any personal accountability.

63. NADER & SMITH, *supra* note 58, at 265.

64. Lee Drutman, *Corporate Crime Acts Like a Thief in the Night*, L.A. TIMES, Nov. 4, 2003, *available at* http://www.commondreams.org/views.

65. *Id.*

66. *Id.*

67. Peter Carlson, *High and Mighty Crooked: Enron Is Merely the Latest Chapter in the History of American Scams*, WASH. POST, Feb. 10, 2002, at F1.

68. *Id.*

69. *Id.*

70. *Id.*

71. *Id.*

72. *Id.*

73. *Id.*

74. Abramson, *supra* note 2, at 482–506.

75. Abramson, *supra* note 2, at 497.

76. Abramson, *supra* note 2, at 498.

77. Abramson, *supra* note 2, at 499.

78. Valerie P. Hans, *Attitudes Toward the Civil Jury: A Crisis of Confidence, in* VERDICT: ASSESSING THE CIVIL JURY SYSTEM 248, 257–61 (Robert E. Litan ed., 1993); Shari Seidman Diamond, *What Jurors Think: Expectation and Reactions of Citizens Who Serve as Jurors, in Id.* at 282, 299–399.

79. Neil Vidmar, *The Performance of the American Civil Jury: An Empirical Perspective,* 40 ARIZ. L. REV. 849, 866–70 (1998).

80. Abramson, *supra* note 2, at 483.

81. Abramson, *supra* note 2, at 490.

82. Public Strategies, Inc., *supra* note 44, at B-15.

83. NADER & SMITH, *supra* note 58, at 264.

84. NADER & SMITH, *supra* note 58, at 264.

85. NADER & SMITH, *supra* note 58, at 265.

86. *See* TEX. R. CIV. P. 13.

87. Letter from Joan Claybrook, President, Public Citizen, to United States Senators Concerning Pending Product Liability Legislation (June 24, 1998), *at* http://www.citizen.org/congress/civjus/prod_liability/general/articles.cfm? ID=5345.

88. *Id.*

89. Milo Geyelin, *Suits by Firms Exceed Those by Individuals,* WALL ST. J., Dec. 3, 1993, at B1.

90. Claybrook, *supra* note 87.

91. Geyelin, *supra* note 89.

92. Jane P. Schoemaker, *Wherein an Airline Blows It and Bumps 20 Judges,* PHILA. INQUIRER, May 5, 1981, at A5.

93. Texaco, Inc. v. Pennzoil, Co., 729 S.W.2d 768 (Tex. App.—Houston [1st Dist.] 1987, writ ref'd n.r.e.).

94. Renae Merle & Pamela Yip, *Judge Backs the Right to Sue HMOs but Independent Review Process Endangered,* HOUS. CHRON., Sept. 19, 1998, § Bus., at 1.

95. *Judge Denies Fox's Slogan Suit,* HOUS. CHRON., Aug. 23, 2003, at A2.

96. NADER & SMITH, *supra* note 58, at 266, 276.

97. DECISION BY TRIAL: A COLLECTION OF ARTICLES ON JURIES, JURY RESEARCH AND JUROR ATTITUDES 137 (Phillip K. Anthony & Allan H. Colman eds., 2002).

Notes to Chapter 18

1. *Battle of the Alamo*, http://en.wikipedia.org/wiki/Battle_of_the_Alamo.

2. JAMES MICHENER, TEXAS 385 (1985).

3. *See* JOSEPH LEDOUX, THE EMOTIONAL BRAIN: THE MYSTERIOUS UNDERPINNINGS OF EMOTIONAL LIFE (1996), *as reviewed in* SCI. AM., June 1997, at 140.

4. *See* VIKTOR FRANKL, MAN'S SEARCH FOR MEANING (1963).

5. *Konstantin Stanislavsky*, http://en.wikipedia.org/wiki/Konstantin_Stanislavsky.

6. Surveys and pollings of public opinion have been conducted under the auspices of various associations and organizations to identify attitudes at play in the trial of personal injury cases. One of the more recent of these was conducted by Public Strategies, Inc., for the State Bar of Texas, February 23–28, 1996. STATE BAR OF TEX. PROF. DEV. PROGRAM, ADVANCED MEDICAL, MALPRACTICE, PHARMACEUTICAL & MEDICAL DEVICE LITIGATION COURSE B (1997). *See also* Gary A. Hengstler, *Vox Populi: The Public Perception of Lawyers: ABA Poll*, 79 A.B.A. J. 60 (1993).

7. *Ezekiel* 18:8 (King James).

8. *Galatians* 6:7.

9. *Matthew* 25:40.

10. WILLIAM IAN MILLER, THE MYSTERY OF COURAGE 254, 255 (2000).

Notes to Chapter 19

1. ANTHONY R. PRATKANIS & ELLIOT ARONSON, AGE OF PROPAGANDA: THE EVERYDAY USE AND ABUSE OF PERSUASION 43–49 (1992).

2. *Id.* at 63–64.

3. VANCE PACKARD, THE HIDDEN PERSUADERS 129 (1957).

Notes to Chapter 20

1. MERRIAM-WEBSTER'S COLLEGIATE DICTIONARY 780 (11th ed. 2003).

2. STEPHEN KING, ON WRITING: A MEMOIR OF THE CRAFT 112–14 (2000).

3. *Matthew* 5:13 (King James).

4. *Matthew* 5:14.

5. *Matthew* 5:15.

6. *Matthew* 6:22–23; *Luke* 11:34.

7. *Matthew* 7:6.

8. *Matthew* 7:17–20.

9. Abraham Lincoln, Speech at Republican State Convention, delivered at Springfield, Ill., June 16, 1858.

10. William Jennings Bryan, Speech at Democratic National Convention, delivered at Chicago, Ill., July 9, 1896.

11. Winston Churchill, Speech at Westminster College, delivered at Fulton, Mo., March 5, 1946.

12. Martin Luther King, Jr., *I Have a Dream, in* Martin Luther King: The Peaceful Warrior 111–12 (Ed Clayton ed., 1968).

13. James M. Beck, The Constitution of the United States: Yesterday, Today—and Tomorrow? 202 (1924).

14. Joel Chandler Harris, Uncle Remus: His Songs and His Sayings 9 (1881).

Notes to Chapter 21

1. Robert Hartwell Fiske, Thesaurus of Alternatives to Worn-Out Words and Phrases xvii (1994).

Notes to Chapter 22

1. Merriam-Webster's Collegiate Dictionary 44 (11th ed. 2003).

2. In addition to the patient's blood pressure, diagnostic laboratory tests are helpful. A drop in hemoglobin or hematocrit may signal internal hemorrhaging.

3. Diana Eck, Encountering God: A Spiritual Journey from Bozeman to Banaras 202 (1993), as quoted by W. Eugene March, "A Biblical Case for Religious Diversity—Can Love Become a Heresy?", address delivered at the Annual Convention of the International Society of Barristers, Ritz-Carlton Golf Resort, Naples, Fla., March 4, 2004, and reprinted in 39 Int'l Soc'y Barristers Q. 455 (2004).

Notes to Chapter 23

1. Elizabeth Knowles, ed., The Oxford Dictionary of Quotations (6th ed. 2004); Tyrone Edwards, comp., The New Dictionary of Thoughts: A Cyclopedia of Quotations (rev. & enlrg'd ed. 1961); Bergen Evans, Dictionary of Quotations (1988); John Bartlett, Bartlett's Familiar Quotations (17th ed. 2002).

Notes to Chapter 24

1. EDGAR A. GUEST, *Good Enough*, *in* COLLECTED VERSE OF EDGAR A. GUEST 465–66 (1934).

2. ANON., *Gun Quotable*, http://www.wildbillsconcealment.com/gun_quotes.htm (supposed to have been engraved on the stocks of an Arizona lawman's Colt SAA).

3. JOHN GREENLEAF WHITTIER, *Maud Muller*, http://en.wikiquote.org/wiki/John_Greenleaf_Whittier (1856).

4. BRET HARTE, *Mrs. Judge Jenkins*, http://en.wikiquote.org/wiki/John_Greenleaf_Whittier (1902).

5. HUGHES MEARNS, *The Man Who Wasn't There*, http://en.wikipedia.org/wiki/Hughes_Mearns (1910).

6. EMILY DICKINSON, *Surgeons must be very careful* [J108/F156], *in* THE COMPLETE POEMS OF EMILY DICKINSON 52 (1960).

7. ANON., *A Chip on His Shoulder*, *in* THE BEST LOVED POEMS OF THE AMERICAN PEOPLE 646 (H. Felleman comp. 1936).

8. ISAAC WATTS, *Against Quarreling and Fighting*, *in* DIVINE AND MORAL SONGS FOR CHILDREN, http://www.cgmusic.com/workshop/watts/againstquarl.htm (1715).

9. JOHN GAY, *The Dog and the Fox*, *in* FABLES pt. 2, no. 1, http://www.kalliope.org/digt.pl?longdid=gay2005052960&printer=1 (1727).

10. LOUIS C. SHIMON, *I Know Something Good About You*, *in* THE BEST LOVED POEMS OF THE AMERICAN PEOPLE 116 (H. Felleman comp. 1936).

11. CAPT. CYRIL MORTON THORNE, *To My Unborn Son*, *in* THE BEST LOVED POEMS OF THE AMERICAN PEOPLE 24 (H. Felleman comp. 1936).

12. EDGAR A. GUEST, *It Couldn't Be Done*, *in* COLLECTED VERSE OF EDGAR A. GUEST 285 (1934).

13. EDGAR A. GUEST, *The Broken Wheel*, *supra* note 12, at 418–19.

14. WILL ALLEN DROMGOOLE, *The Bridge Builder*, http://www.angelfire.com/hi/JeNNa/bridge2.html.

15. RUTH GILLIS, *The Wreck on Highway 109*, http://home.att.net/~ruthgill/variety/the_wreck_on_highway_109.htm.

Notes to Chapter 25

1. JOHN STEINBECK, OF MICE AND MEN 72-73 (1937).

2. Sources for the anecdotes and stories included in chapter 25 are numerous and varied; the author has compiled most of this material over the course of more than forty years. Stories from mythology, ancient and medieval history, Aesop's fables, and many of the children's stories are too familiar and

general to require reference. Other stories in this chapter are adapted or reprinted from their sources and used with permission. The author, editor, and publisher have made every effort to identify the sources of those stories that have not been referenced and regret any inadvertent omission of proper credit to the original authors and publishers.

3. Frank McCourt, *When You Think of God What Do You See?*, LIFE, Dec. 1998, at 63–64.

4. *Genesis* 2–3 (King James).

5. M. SCOTT PECK, THE ROAD LESS TRAVELED 272 (1978).

6. *Genesis* 22:1–18.

7. *Genesis* 37:3–33.

8. *Exodus* 7–11.

9. *Judges* 12:5–6.

10. 1 *Samuel* 16:1–13.

11. 1 *Kings* 3:16–27.

12. *Daniel* 6:1–24.

13. *Matthew* 23:13–36.

14. *Matthew* 5:19.

15. *Matthew* 5:22.

16. *Id.*

17. *Matthew* 5:25.

18. *Matthew* 13:1–8.

19. *Luke* 20:9–16.

20. *Luke* 15:1–7.

21. *Matthew* 25:14–26.

22. *Matthew* 18:21–34.

23. *Luke* 15:11–32.

24. *Luke* 10:25–37.

25. *Matthew* 26:6–13; *Luke* 7:36–39; *John* 12:1–7. The author has combined two separate events Jesus experienced—one anointing occurring in the beginning of his ministry and the other on the eve of his crucifixion.

26. *Mark* 10:17–25.

27. *The Goose and the Rooster*, http://www.hasidicstories.com/Stories/Later_Rebbes/goose.html.

28. BROTHERS GRIMM, *The Old Man and His Grandson*, *in* GRIMM'S FAIRY TALES (Edgar Taylor & Marian Edwardes trans., 1823), http://www.gutenberg.org/etext/2591.

29. THOMAS WARD, ENGLAND'S REFORMATION: A POEM IN FOUR CANTOS, Canto 4, 373 (1630).

30. THE LITTLE, BROWN BOOK OF ANECDOTES 306 (Clifton Fadiman gen. ed., 1985).

31. *Hat Lesson*, http://anecdotage.com/index.php?aid=13942.

32. 2500 ANECDOTES FOR ALL OCCASIONS 139 (Edmund Fuller ed., 1980).

33. *Id.* at 263.

34. ABE LINCOLN LAUGHING: HUMOROUS ANECDOTES FROM ORIGINAL SOURCES BY AND ABOUT ABRAHAM LINCOLN 48 (P.M. Zall ed., 1995).

35. *Id.* at 56.

36. *Id.* at 66–67.

37. *Id.* at 70.

38. *Id.* at 77–78.

39. *Id.* at 116.

40. *Id.* at 118–19.

41. *Id.* at 126.

42. *Id.* at 144.

43. *Id.* at 154.

44. This widely known Lincoln anecdote was related to the author by Bill Allen of Houston, Tex. (deceased).

45. *See* Michael Graves, *Taps*, http://www.tsgraves.com/relics/taps.htm.

46. *See* Murphy v. Western & A.R.R., 23 F. 637 (E.D. Tenn. 1885). The jury awarded the plaintiff $217 in damages against the railroad.

47. Adapted from Robert Lewis Dabney, Jr., *The Rule of Law vs. Mr. Colt*, THE HOUSTON LAWYER, Jan.-Feb. 1999, at 13–14.

48. JACK DEMPSEY WITH BARBARA PIATTELLI DEMPSEY, DEMPSEY 9–10 (1977).

49. *Id.* at 15.

50. *Id.* at 149.

51. *Butch and Eddie O'Hare: The War Hero Whose Father Was a Partner with Gangster Al Capone,* http://www.truthorfiction.com/rumors/b/butchandeddie.htm.

52. Harry S Truman, 1 Memoirs 122 (1955).

53. *See* William Warren Sterling, Trails and Trials of a Texas Ranger 7–8 (1968).

54. *Charles Proteus Steinmetz,* http://en.wikipedia.org/wiki/Charles_Steinmetz.

55. *See* Donald Clark, *Hawthorne Effect,* http://pespmc1.vub.ac.be/ASC/HAWTHO_EFFEC.html.

56. *See Titanic's Officers,* http://my.execpc.com/~reva/tioff.htm.

57. Martin Luther King, Jr., Letter from the Birmingham Jail (Apr. 16, 1963).

58. *Rescuing Hug,* www.planetdeb.net/spirit/rescue.htm.

59. Larry McMurtry, Lonesome Dove 876 (1986).

60. James Michener, Texas 686 (1985).

61. John Bartlett, Familiar Quotations 961 (16th ed. 1992).

62. Martin Luther King, Jr., *Why Jesus Called a Man a Fool,* Sermon Delivered at Mount Pisgah Missionary Baptist Church, Chicago, Ill. (Aug. 27, 1967).

63. Dina Donohue, *Trouble at the Inn,* Guideposts, Dec. 1966, at 46.

64. As told by state senator David Sibley of Waco, Tex.

65. As told by attorney Don Keenan of Atlanta, Ga.

66. As told by Ken Mathis, M.D., of Pasadena, Tex. (deceased).

67. As told by Ann Richards, former governor of Texas.

Bibliography

The Apocrypha. *Book of Susanna.*

Bartlett, John. *Bartlett's Familiar Quotations.* 17th ed. Boston: Little Brown & Co., 2002.

Beck, James M. *The Constitution of the United States: Yesterday, Today—and Tomorrow?* New York: George H. Doran Co., 1924.

Bierce, Ambrose. *Civil War Stories.* New York: Dover Publications, 1994.

Brothers Grimm. *Grimm's Fairy Tales.* Translated by Edgar Taylor and Marian Edwardes, 1823. Project Gutenberg, http://www.gutenberg.org/etext/2591.

Conrad, Barnaby. *The Complete Guide to Writing Fiction.* Cincinnati: Writer's Digest Books, 1990.

Crane, Steven. *The Red Badge of Courage.* New York: Dover Publications, 1990.

Dabney, Robert Lewis, Jr. "The Rule of Law vs. Mr. Colt." *The Houston Lawyer* 36, no. 4 (1999): 10–15

Darrow, Clarence. *The Story of My Life.* New York: Charles Scribner's Sons, 1932.

______. *Verdicts Out of Court.* Edited with an introduction by Arthur and Lila Weinberg. Chicago: Ivan R. Dee, 1989.

Dempsey, Jack, with Barbara Piattelli Dempsey. *Dempsey.* New York: Harper & Row, 1977.

Dickens, Charles. *Hard Times.* New York: Bantam Books, 1981.

______. *A Tale of Two Cities.* Philadelphia: Running Press, 1986.

Dickinson, Emily. *The Complete Poems of Emily Dickinson.* Edited by Thomas H. Johnson. Cambridge, MA: The Belknap Press of Harvard Univ. Press, 1983.

Donadio, Stephen, Joan Smith, Susan Mesner, and Rebecca Davison, eds. *The New York Public Library Book of Twentieth-Century American Quotations.* New York: Warner Books, 1992.

Donohue, Dina. "Trouble at the Inn." *Guideposts,* Dec. 1966, 46.

Douglas, William O. *We the Judges: Studies in American and Indian Constitutional Law from Marshall to Mukherjea.* New York: Doubleday, 1956.

Eck, Diana. *Encountering God: A Spiritual Journey from Bozeman to Banaras.* Boston: Beacon Press, 1993.

Edwards, Tyrone, comp. *The New Dictionary of Thoughts: A Cyclopedia of Quotations.* Rev. ed. New York: Standard Book Co., 1961.

Evans, Bergen. *Dictionary of Quotations.* New York: Random House, 1988.

Fadiman, Clifton, gen. ed. *The Little, Brown Book of Anecdotes.* Boston: Little, Brown & Co., 1985.

Felleman, Hazel, comp. *The Best Loved Poems of the American People.* New York: Doubleday, 1936.

Fiske, Robert Hartwell. *Thesaurus of Alternatives to Worn-Out Words and Phrases.* Cincinnati: Writer's Digest Books, 1994.

Frankl, Viktor. *Man's Search for Meaning.* New York: Washington Square Press, 1963.

Fulghum, Robert. *All I Really Need to Know I Learned in Kindergarten: Uncommon Thoughts on Common Things.* New York: Ballantine Books, 1993.

Fuller, Edmund, ed. *2500 Anecdotes for All Occasions.* New York: Avenel Books, 1980.

Goethe, Johann Wolfgang von. *Theory of Colors.* Cambridge, MA: MIT Press, 1976.

Greider, William. *Who Will Tell the People? The Betrayal of American Democracy.* New York: Simon & Schuster, 1993.

Grisham, John. *The Client.* New York: Doubleday, 1993.

Guest, Edgar A. *Collected Verse of Edgar A. Guest.* Chicago: The Reilly & Lee Co. (now Contemporary Books), 1934.

Guinther, John. *The Jury in America and The Civil Juror: A Research Project Sponsored by the Roscoe Pound Foundation.* New York: Facts On File Publications, 1988.

Harris, Joel Chandler. *Uncle Remus: His Songs and His Sayings.* New York: D. Appleton & Co., 1881.

Henry, O. *The Best Short Stories of O. Henry.* New York: Modern Library, 1994.

Horne, Gerald. *Powell v. Alabama: The Scottsboro Boys and American Justice.* New York: Franklin Watts, 1997.

Jew, Rodney. "Tell It to the Jury: The Role of Story Telling in Litigation." *News from the Mental Edge* 9, no. 1 (Spring 2003): 1–26.

Joyce, James. *Dubliners.* New York: Penguin Books, 1993.

_______. *Ulysses.* New York: Vintage Books, 1961.

King, Martin Luther, Jr. *Martin Luther King: The Peaceful Warrior.* Edited by Ed Clayton. New York: Pocket Books, 1968.

King, Stephen. *On Writing: A Memoir of the Craft.* New York: Scribner, 2000.

Kluger, Richard. *Simple Justice: The History of Brown v. Board of Education and Black America's Struggle for Equality.* New York: Vintage Books, 1977.

Knowles, Elizabeth. *The Oxford Dictionary of Quotations.* 6th ed. Oxford: Oxford Univ. Press, 2004.

Lehman, Godfrey D. *The Ordeal of Edward Bushell.* Sacramento: Lexicon Publishing, 1988.

Levin, Fredric G. *Effective Opening Statements: The Attorney's Master Key to Courtroom Victory.* Englewood Cliffs, NJ: Prentice-Hall, 1983.

Lucas, Richard H., and K. Byron McCoy. *The Winning Edge: Effective Communication and Persuasion Techniques for Lawyers.* New York: John Wiley & Sons, 1993.

Lukas, J. Anthony. *Big Trouble.* New York: Simon & Schuster, 1997.

McCourt, Frank. "When You Think of God What Do You See?" *Life,* Dec. 1998, 63–64.

McLynn, Frank. *Famous Trials: Cases That Made History.* Pleasantville, NY: Readers Digest Association, 1995.

McMurtry, Larry. *Lonesome Dove.* New York: Simon & Schuster, 1985.

Mehrabian, Albert. *Nonverbal Communication.* Chicago: Aldine-Atherton, 1972.
Melville, Herman. *Moby-Dick.* Indianapolis: Bobbs-Merrill Co., 1964.
Michener, James. *Texas.* New York: Random House, 1985.
Mieder, Wolfgang. *The Prentice-Hall Encyclopedia of World Proverbs: A Treasury of Wit and Wisdom Through the Ages.* Englewood Cliffs, NJ: Prentice-Hall, 1986.
Miller, William Ian. *The Mystery of Courage.* Cambridge, MA: Harvard Univ. Press, 2000.
Moody, Dwight Lyman. *Moody's Anecdotes.* Chicago: Fleming H. Revell Co., 1898.
Nader, Ralph, and Wesley J. Smith. *No Contest: Corporate Lawyers and the Perversion of Justice in America.* New York: Random House, 1996.
Nizer, Louis. *Catspaw.* New York: Donald I. Fine, 1992.
O'Keefe, Daniel. *Persuasion: Theory and Research.* Thousand Oaks, CA: Sage Publications, 1990.
Packard, Vance. *The Hidden Persuaders.* New York: David McKay Co., 1957.
Peck, M. Scott. *The Road Less Traveled.* New York: Simon & Schuster, 1978.
Perdue, Jim M. "The Difference Between 'Good Enough' and 'Safe Enough.'" *Trial* 32, no. 3 (1996): 45–47.
_______. "The Five-Question Rule: Cross-Examination Simplified." *Trial* 29, no. 10 (1993): 40–43.
_______. *Who Will Speak for the Victim? A Practical Treatise on Plaintiff's Jury Argument.* Austin: State Bar of Texas, 1989.
Perdue, Jim M., Sr., and Jim M. Perdue, Jr. "Trial Themes: Winning Jurors' Minds and Hearts." *Trial* 34, no. 4 (1998): 34–42.
Perdue, Jim M., Jr. "The Art of Demonstrative Evidence." *Trial* 41, no. 5 (2005): 46–51.
Poe, Edgar Allan. *Complete Stories and Poems.* New York: Doubleday, 1966.
Phillips, Kevin. *Wealth and Democracy: A Political History of the American Rich.* New York: Broadway Books, 2002.
Pratkanis, Anthony R., and Elliot Aronson. *Age of Propaganda: The Everyday Use and Abuse of Persuasion.* New York: W. H. Freeman & Co., 1992.
Robbins, Sarah, ed. *Law: A Treasury of Art and Literature.* Westport, CT: Hugh Lauter Levin Associates, Inc., Beaux Arts Editions, 1990.
Roemer, Michael. *Telling Stories: Postmodernism and the Invalidation of Traditional Narrative.* Lanham, MD: Rowman & Littlefield, 1995.
Steinbeck, John. *Of Mice and Men.* New York: Modern Library, 1937.
Sterling, William Warren. *Trails and Trials of a Texas Ranger.* Norman, OK: Univ. of Oklahoma Press, 1968.
Stevenson, Robert Louis. *Treasure Island.* New York: Charles Scribner's Sons, 1911.
Titelman, Gregory Y. *Random House Dictionary of Popular Proverbs and Sayings.* New York: Random House, 1966.
Truman, Harry S. *Memoirs.* Vol. 1, *Year of Decisions.* New York: Doubleday, 1955.
Turow, Scott. "Order in the Court." *New York Times Magazine,* April 18, 1999, 109.
Twain, Mark. *The Adventures of Huckleberry Finn.* New York: Barnes & Noble Books, 1996.

______. *The Complete Short Stories of Mark Twain.* New York: Doubleday, 1957.

Vinson, Donald E. *Jury Persuasion: Psychological Strategies and Trial Techniques.* Englewood Cliffs, NJ: Prentice-Hall, 1993.

Vogler, Christopher. *The Writer's Journey: Mythic Structure for Writers.* 2d ed. Studio City, CA: Michael Wiese Prods., 1998.

Wolff, Jurgen, and Kerry Cox. *Successful Scriptwriting.* Cincinnati: Writer's Digest Books, 1988.

Zall, P. M., ed. *Abe Lincoln Laughing: Humorous Anecdotes from Original Sources by and about Abraham Lincoln.* Knoxville: Univ. of Tennessee Press, 1995.

Story Morals Index

Name and Title Index

C

Q

R

S

Y

Z

Subject Index

Q

T